Documentary Series

Yearbooks

Concise Series

Dictionary of Literary Biography • Volume Seventy-one

American Literary Critics and Scholars, 1880-1900

Edited by
John W. Rathbun
California State University, Los Angeles
and
Monica M. Grecu
University of Nevada at Reno

A Bruccoli Clark Layman Book
Gale Research Company • Book Tower • Detroit, Michigan 48226

Advisory Board for
DICTIONARY OF LITERARY BIOGRAPHY

Manufactured by Edwards Brothers, Inc.
Ann Arbor, Michigan
Printed in the United States of America

Library of Congress Cataloging-in-Publication Data

American literary critics and scholars, 1880-1900/edited by
    John W. Rathbun and Monica M. Grecu.
        p. cm.—(Dictionary of literary biography; v. 71)
    "A Bruccoli Clark Layman book."
    Includes index.
    ISBN 0-8103-1749-4
    1. Criticism—United States—History—19th century.
2. American literature—19th century—History and criticism—Theory, etc. 3. Criticism—United States—Bio-
bibliography. 4. Critics—United States—Biography—Dictionaries. 5. Literary historians—United States—Biography—Dictionaries. I. Rathbun, John Wilbert, 1924-   . II.
Grecu, Monica M. III. Series.
PS74.A46   1988
810'.9—dc19   88-10879
                                                            CIP

For Pauline A. Rathbun and Cornelia Grecu-Arghir

Contents

Plan of the Series

. . . Almost the most prodigious asset of a country, and perhaps its most precious possession, is its native literary product—when that product is fine and noble and enduring.

Mark Twain*

The advisory board, the editors, and the publisher of the *Dictionary of Literary Biography* are joined in endorsing Mark Twain's declaration. The literature of a nation provides an inexhaustible resource of permanent worth. We intend to make literature and its creators better understood and more accessible to students and the reading public, while satisfying the standards of teachers and scholars.

To meet these requirements, *literary biography* has been construed in terms of the author's achievement. The most important thing about a writer is his writing. Accordingly, the entries in *DLB* are career biographies, tracing the development of the author's canon and the evolution of his reputation.

The purpose of *DLB* is not only to provide reliable information in a convenient format but also to place the figures in the larger perspective of literary history and to offer appraisals of their accomplishments by qualified scholars.

The publication plan for *DLB* resulted from two years of preparation. The project was proposed to Bruccoli Clark by Frederick G. Ruffner, president of the Gale Research Company, in November 1975. After specimen entries were prepared and typeset, an advisory board was formed to refine the entry format and develop the series rationale. In meetings held during 1976, the publisher, series editors, and advisory board approved the scheme for a comprehensive biographical dictionary of persons who contributed to North American literature. Editorial work on the first volume began in January 1977, and it was published in 1978. In order to make *DLB* more than a reference tool and to compile volumes that individually have claim to status as literary history, it was decided to organize volumes by topic, period, or genre. Each of these freestanding volumes provides a biographical-bibliographical guide and overview for a particular area of literature. We are convinced that this organization—as opposed to a single alphabet method—constitutes a valuable innovation in the presentation of reference material. The volume plan necessarily requires many decisions for the placement and treatment of authors who might properly be included in two or three volumes. In some instances a major figure will be included in separate volumes, but with different entries emphasizing the aspect of his career appropriate to each volume. Ernest Hemingway, for example, is represented in *American Writers in Paris, 1920-1939* by an entry focusing on his expatriate apprenticeship; he is also in *American Novelists, 1910-1945* with an entry surveying his entire career. Each volume includes a cumulative index of subject authors and articles. Comprehensive indexes to the entire series are planned.

With volume ten in 1982 it was decided to enlarge the scope of *DLB*. By the end of 1986 twenty-one volumes treating British literature had been published, and volumes for Commonwealth and Modern European literature were in progress. The series has been further augmented by the *DLB Yearbooks* (since 1981) which update published entries and add new entries to keep the *DLB* current with contemporary activity. There have also been *DLB Documentary Series* volumes which provide biographical and critical source materials for figures whose work is judged to have particular interest for students. One of these companion volumes is entirely devoted to Tennessee Williams.

We define literature as the *intellectual commerce of a nation:* not merely as belles lettres but as that ample and complex process by which ideas are generated, shaped, and transmitted. *DLB* entries are not limited to "creative writers" but extend to other figures who in their time and in their way influenced the mind of a people. Thus the series encompasses historians, journalists, publishers, and screenwriters. By this means readers of *DLB* may be aided to perceive litera-

---

*From an unpublished section of Mark Twain's autobiography, copyright © by the Mark Twain Company.

ture not as cult scripture in the keeping of intellectual high priests but firmly positioned at the center of a nation's life.

DLB includes the major writers appropriate to each volume and those standing in the ranks immediately behind them. Scholarly and critical counsel has been sought in deciding which minor figures to include and how full their entries should be. Wherever possible, useful references are made to figures who do not warrant separate entries.

Each *DLB* volume has a volume editor responsible for planning the volume, selecting the figures for inclusion, and assigning the entries. Volume editors are also responsible for preparing, where appropriate, appendices surveying the major periodicals and literary and intellectual movements for their volumes, as well as lists of further readings. Work on the series as a whole is coordinated at the Bruccoli Clark Layman editorial center in Columbia, South Carolina, where the editorial staff is responsible for accuracy of the published volumes.

One feature that distinguishes *DLB* is the illustration policy–its concern with the iconography of literature. Just as an author is influenced by his surroundings, so is the reader's understanding of the author enhanced by a knowledge of his environment. Therefore *DLB* volumes include not only drawings, paintings, and photographs of authors, often depicting them at various stages in their careers, but also illustrations of their families and places where they lived. Title pages are regularly reproduced in facsimile along with dust jackets for modern authors. The dust jackets are a special feature of *DLB* because they often document better than anything else the way in which an author's work was perceived in its own time. Specimens of the writers' manuscripts are included when feasible.

Samuel Johnson rightly decreed that "The chief glory of every people arises from its authors." The purpose of the *Dictionary of Literary Biography* is to compile literary history in the surest way available to us–by accurate and comprehensive treatment of the lives and work of those who contributed to it.

The *DLB* Advisory Board

Foreword

This volume of the *Dictionary of Literary Biography* concludes a three-volume survey of nineteenth-century American literary critics and scholars. Previous volumes covered the years 1800-1850 and 1850-1880. Brief biographical information is provided, but the chief objective is to assess the importance of the contributions of individual critics and scholars who first formulated and applied their theories within the period 1880-1900 by concentrating on their principal publications, critical theories, and practical criticism. Many critics and scholars continued to be productive into the twentieth century; in such cases the essays canvass the whole of their work rather than arbitrarily stopping at the century's end.

During these fin de siècle years the social milieu was strained by controversy: western economic depression, labor ferment, populist and socialist unrest, the panic of 1893, for example. But such troubles do not seem to have affected much the professional work of critics and scholars—William Dean Howells and Vida Scudder being two of the exceptions. Yet they were very much a part of and responsive to a milieu that we can call "modern" America. It would persist to the early 1950s, when the United States would again go through another profound cultural change. The electric streetcar encouraged urban expansion, while such innovations as iron buildings, elevators, indoor plumbing, and central heating promoted greater urban concentration. In 1880 one-third of the population lived in cities or immediately adjacent to them. By century's end this was true of virtually one-half the population. In their ethnic and racial diversity, cultural influence, and economically strategic locations, cities exercised an authority and took on a character that psychologically and financially dominated the society. The cause of letters benefited.

Several other factors favored letters. "Adolescence" was identified as an intermediate stage between childhood and adulthood. In a day when labor was abundant, this conception served to delay people's entry into the work force, while on the positive side it led to greater literacy as high schools increased tenfold. Scholars especially became involved in meeting the demand for secondary school textbooks. In higher education the Morrill Act of 1862 had led to the founding of "land-grant" colleges and universities that greatly extended opportunities for a college education. The expansion of higher education, together with a general movement for more "elective" courses, had a number of consequences. Graduate education burgeoned, so that by 1900 more than fifty-six hundred students were enrolled in graduate programs. Academicians could teach courses more directly related to their scholarly interests. And teaching and research faculties cultivated a higher sense of professionalism.

Of the thirty-six critics and scholars covered in the entries, more than one-half are academicians whose views, in a general sense, reflect the evolutionary psychology and sociology of the English philosopher Herbert Spencer and the historicism of the French philosopher and critic Hippolyte Taine. Preoccupation with an existent or emerging American national character, so typical of earlier historical practice, seldom surfaces as a point at issue, nor are there many efforts to vindicate a historical approach to the study of literature. What one detects instead is a confident professionalism that simply assumes literary works are best understood when situated in historical settings.

Americanist scholars generally had a twin aim: to establish and at the same time to open up the American literary canon. Their approach was frequently interdisciplinary insofar as they tended to install writers in various "schools" as defined by literary theory, intellectual history, and social conditions. Through such means Fred Lewis Pattee, for example, asserted the autonomy of American literature and expanded the canon to include western, post-Civil War, and local-color writers. The work of Pattee and many others, as Kermit Vanderbilt points out in *American Literature and the Academy* (1986), would finally culminate in the four-volume *Cambridge History of American Literature* (1917-1921), edited by William Peterfield Trent, John Erskine, Stuart P. Sherman, and Carl Van Doren, an influential history whose list of writers was not substantially altered until the revisionism of the 1970s sought to open up the canon to accommodate more minority and women writers.

Scholars were also active in publishing recensions of literary texts and in advancing the reputations of contemporary English and Continental writers. The kind of work represented by Francis James Child's endeavor to establish Geoffrey Chaucer's metrical system was practiced by others as well, though not always with the same degree of success. Thomas Lounsbury critically collated textual variations in an effort to establish the most plausible reading text of Chaucer's work; Katharine Lee Bates labored similarly in the field of Elizabethan drama; and Basil Gildersleeve tilled the field of classical studies. This generation of scholars tended to range rather more widely than their successors. Lounsbury, for example, also published studies of James Fenimore Cooper, while Bates edited editions of nineteenth-century writers such as Samuel Taylor Coleridge, John Keats, and Alfred Tennyson. Of scholars who called the attention of the reading public to new English and Continental writers, Hjalmar Hjorth Boyesen and Kuno Francke were especially effective in promoting Scandinavians (especially Henrik Ibsen) and the case for German letters respectively. Others belatedly took up the cause of Honoré de Balzac, while Leo Tolstoy, Anthony Trollope, William Makepeace Thackeray, Matthew Arnold, continental dramatists, and other contemporary writers were subjects for articles and monographs.

There was an important cross tie between critical idealism and scholarly historicism. Of the fifteen entries given over to critical idealism, fully nine are drawn from academic ranks: Henry A. Beers, Hamilton Wright Mabie, Brander Matthews, Bliss Perry, William Peterfield Trent, Henry Van Dyke, Barrett Wendell, William Cleaver Wilkinson, and George Woodberry. (Other critical idealists are Thomas Bailey Aldrich, James Lane Allen, George Willis Cooke, F. Marion Crawford, James Herbert Morse, and Maurice Thompson.) Critical idealism, despite the basically ahistorical views of such progenitors as Coleridge and Ralph Waldo Emerson, had always encouraged inquiry into origins. But what most interested its exponents was the way that historicism, aesthetic concerns, and an interest in the moral impact of literature could be combined. On the aesthetic level the instincts of critical idealists were often good, even while their actual discernment of excellence was sometimes weak, the latter a defect frequently charged against them. Still, they knew that words needed to be nicely suited to intentions and that the best rhythms are gained when writers attend on their inner rather than outer ear. Their most important principle was imagination, which they invoked with varying degrees of success. The recognition that a work was "imaginative" led them to examine how selection made for internal consistency and a sort of fine tuning that swelled the work beyond its ostensible subject. At this point the work had entered the realm of the "moral."

Almost all critics, regardless of the critical schools to which they adhered, acknowledged that attention had to be given to the moral dimension in literature. The critical idealists simply stressed it more than others, which had a lot to do with both an American tradition of dwelling on the moral implications of literary works and with the romantic origins of critical idealism. Few critical idealists insisted on a limited system of prescriptive behavior in literature as sometimes counseled in antebellum criticism, but sometimes they were too nerveless in their propriety, conventionality, and moderation–faults found, for example, in the criticism of James Herbert Morse and Hamilton Wright Mabie. In these cases moral sensibility is simply thin. On the other hand, the humanistic socialism of George Willis Cooke or Vida Scudder and the Arnoldian humanism of William Crary Brownell helped them to see that insight and not prescription, moral discernment and not ethical principle, and exploration of psychological motivation and not enjoined behavior traditionally serve the purposes of literature. Such considerations could have their social implications, but at bottom they testified to the view that the moral element in literature is imaginatively encountered in the experience of individuals who come into conflict with others and with circumstance and who succeed or fail in resolving that conflict.

Critical idealists like James Russell Lowell and Edmund Clarence Stedman were sturdy perceptive reasoners on how criticism should deal with the moral, but for some, attention to the moral proved more an obstacle than a measure of the range of literature. Here, the example of the realists becomes pertinent. Morse might complain that a "mania for facts" was characteristic of realism, but that reductive view is not sustained in realist practice or criticism. Henry James was always cool to what he called "photographic realism." And Howells, very active in this period, repeatedly stressed the old ideas of probability of plot and of psychological motivation, and his own well-crafted novels illustrated what he meant. Both James and Howells were interested in the subtle, slight variations that occur, often painfully, in human relations, so that the moral element becomes something to be discovered rather than demonstrated—a position that Cooke and Brownell could appreciate.

While editors such as Stedman and Charles Eliot Norton opened the pages of their magazines to realist writers, on the theoretical level they thought realism too meager in both range and intellectual depth. Critical idealists were especially good on the nature and tradition of poetry and often perceptive in their comments on contemporary poets. Unfortunately, there were not very many good poets around. Realists were not particularly successful when it came to poetry. Howells's poetry is often as attenuated as anything by Bayard Taylor, and James's few forays into the criticism of poetry were disastrous, as when he so lamentably failed to gauge the work of Charles Baudelaire.

Realists were inclined toward the novel as a literary form and seem to have better sensed its appeal to a middle-class reading public. Idealists tended to favor the fictitiously embellished narratives we know as romances, and with the rise of Waverleyism in the 1890s (named after Sir Walter Scott's hugely successful first novel, published in 1814) many thought that the romance had been vindicated from the realists' charges. Indeed, it was to become a staple in popular literature. As advocates of the novel and opponents of the romance, realists worked to perfect the form. Mark Twain said instructive things about how to achieve clarity and rhythm on the level of the sentence and about the usefulness of such conventions as seemingly improvisational meanderings in enhancing storytelling. In both his criticism and literary practice James championed the adaptation of various poetic conventions to fiction: most notably modes of narrative transmission, point of view, and tone; and throughout his career Howells defended attention to the commonplace, the use of ordinary and even low-life characters, and a willingness to use standard and even nonstandard native language. Howells's points, strictly speaking, have more to do with literary than aesthetic theory, but they did extend the range of taste.

Alongside these critical schools aestheticism functioned as a cult of beauty and good taste. A relatively small movement, its numbers could be enlarged by the inclusion of Stedman and James, men who had a vital interest in the expressionistic capacity of literature for growth and development. Ambrose Bierce, James Gibbons Huneker, and Percival Pollard were essentially journalists, though Huneker did better work than that label might suggest. Stylistic exuberance and bohemianism are characteristic of their work, so that one is attracted to their animated, brisk styles even while recognizing the occasional misfirings. While they acknowledged the humanistic content of literary works, they were primarily concerned with calling attention to newly emergent writers, whom they vaguely designated avant-garde. Their response to these writers was of an impressionistic kind: short on sustained analysis, long on enthusiasm and the recording of personal perceptions. The philosophy of Friedrich Nietzsche confirmed their iconoclastic reactions and the value of intense emotion in art and life, while their literary enthusiasms for such widely different writers as Baudelaire, George Bernard Shaw, Isben, August Strindberg, and Gerhard Hauptmann testify to an eclecticism characteristic of their taste.

Lewis E. Gates and George Santayana represent more philosophical commitments to aesthetic inquiry. Gates, a Harvard professor, did not write enough to have much impact on his contemporaries. The biographical orientation of Charles-Augustin Sainte-Beuve and Taine's historicism were influences in his development, as was the impressionism of Walter Pater and Anatole France. These approaches were combined into a coherent theory that anticipates the critical explication and reader-response modes of analysis so popular today.

Santayana is an outstanding specialist in aesthetic philosophy, and a perceptive practitioner of applied criticism when he chose to be. Very much a loner, he neither identified with a school nor worked to establish one. Classical in taste, devoted to the "life of reason," sensitive in both style and thought as they flow from intellectual experience, committed to restoring the ancient bond between reasoned passion and exalted inspiration, averse to romanticism and realism, indeed to virtually all literary orientations from the Renaissance on, Santayana in a series of articles and books blocked out a system of aesthetic theory designed to stem or at any rate explain the decline of art. To Santayana art was a public resource, and criticism existed to "inquire how significant the poet's expressions are for humanity or for whatever public he addresses."

Any period that included the sustained and insightful work of James or Santayana would be accorded its measure of respect. But this period has other matter to hold our attention. Many of these critics, while they often overstated their cases, had a sophistication and balance and a range of reference that continue to set an example. The preoccupation of realists with delineating "what is," as opposed to the idealist concern with "what does it all mean," is not an issue to be embalmed in the specifics of historical time and place. Eugène Ionesco, for example, has recently dismissed realism as "merely a literary school, much more false than the world of the imagination." The touchstone for adverse judgment, or for that matter praise, is still often phrased in terms of whether a literary work succeeds in evoking or fails to correspond to our sense of what is "true." Again, the various schools of criticism— idealism, realism, aestheticism, and historicism— often cross-fertilized one another. Each school had its favored stable of writers, the overall result of which was to broaden the accepted canon. The schools were also supported by editor-critics who helped to popularize critical positions and who published favorite writers. Eight of the entries in this work are addressed to men who played such roles: William Crary Brownell, George Parsons Lathrop, Walter Hines Page, Harry Thurston Peck, Bliss Perry, Horace Elisha Scudder, Maurice Thompson, and William Peterfield Trent. The number can be expanded when we remember that Howells, Charles Eliot Norton, Arthur George Sedgwick, and Richard Watson Gilder (subjects in the second volume) continued to be active in this respect throughout these twenty years. It is also worthwhile remembering that the origins of such critical movements as American Studies, the New Humanism, the New Criticism, and Marxist criticism are to be located in this period.

—John W. Rathbun and Monica M. Grecu

Acknowledgments

This book was produced by Bruccoli Clark Layman, Inc. Karen L. Rood is senior editor for the *Dictionary of Literary Biography* series. J. M. Brook was the in-house editor.

Production coordinator is Kimberly Casey. Art supervisor is Cheryl Crombie. Copyediting supervisor is Joan M. Prince. Typesetting supervisor is Kathleen M. Flanagan. Laura Ingram and Michael D. Senecal are editorial associates. The production staff includes Rowena Betts, Charles D. Brower, Joseph Matthew Bruccoli, Patricia Coate, Mary Colborn, Mary S. Dye, Sarah A. Estes, Cynthia Hallman, Judith K. Ingle, Maria Ling, Warren McInnis, Kathy S. Merlette, Sheri Neal, Joycelyn R. Smith, and Virginia Smith. Jean W. Ross is permissions editor. Joseph Caldwell, photography editor, and Penney Haughton did photographic copy work for the volume.

Walter W. Ross and Rhonda Marshall did the library research with the assistance of the staff at the Thomas Cooper Library of the University of South Carolina: Daniel Boice, Cathy Eckman, Gary Geer, Cathie Gottlieb, David L. Haggard, Jens Holley, Dennis Isbell, Jackie Kinder, Marcia Martin, Jean Rhyne, Beverly Steele, Ellen Tillett, Carol Tobin, and Virginia Weathers.

Dictionary of Literary Biography • Volume Seventy-one

American Literary Critics and Scholars, 1880-1900

Dictionary of Literary Biography

Thomas Bailey Aldrich

(11 November 1836-19 March 1907)

Kenneth M. Price
Texas A&M University

See also the Aldrich entry in *DLB 42, American Writers for Children Before 1900.*

BOOKS: *The Bells: A Collection of Chimes* (New York: J. C. Derby/Boston: Phillips, Sampson/Cincinnati: H. W. Derby, 1855);

Daisy's Necklace: And What Came of It. (A Literary Episode.) (New York: Derby & Jackson/H. W. Derby, 1857);

The Course of True Love Never Did Run Smooth (New York: Rudd & Carleton, 1858);

The Ballad of Babie Bell and Other Poems (New York: Rudd & Carleton, 1859);

Pampinea and Other Poems (New York: Rudd & Carleton, 1861);

Out of His Head, A Romance (New York: Carleton, 1862);

Poems (New York: Carleton, 1863; London: Low, 1863);

The Poems of Thomas Bailey Aldrich (Boston: Ticknor & Fields, 1865);

The Story of a Bad Boy (Boston: Fields, Osgood, 1870);

Marjorie Daw and Other People (Boston: Osgood, 1873; London: Routledge, 1873); enlarged as *Marjorie Daw and Other Tales* (Leipzig: Tauchnitz, 1879); enlarged edition republished as *Marjorie Daw and Other Stories* (Boston: Houghton, Mifflin, 1885);

Cloth of Gold and Other Poems (Boston: Osgood, 1874; London: Routledge, 1874);

Prudence Palfrey: A Novel (Boston: Osgood, 1874; London: Routledge, 1874);

Flower and Thorn: Later Poems (Boston: Osgood, 1877; London: Routledge, 1877);

A Midnight Fantasy, and the Little Violinist (Boston: Osgood, 1877);

The Queen of Sheba (London: Routledge, 1877; Boston: Osgood, 1877);

The Stillwater Tragedy (Boston: Houghton, Mifflin, 1880; London: Sampson Low, 1880);

XXXVI Lyrics and XII Sonnets Selected from Cloth of Gold and Flower and Thorn (Boston: Houghton, Mifflin, 1881);

Friar Jerome's Beautiful Book . . . Selected from Cloth of Gold and Flower and Thorn (Boston: Houghton, Mifflin, 1881);

The Poems of Thomas Bailey Aldrich (Boston: Houghton, Mifflin, 1882; London: Sampson Low, 1882);

From Ponkapog to Pesth (Boston: Houghton, Mifflin, 1883);

Mercedes, and Later Lyrics (Boston: Houghton, Mifflin, 1884); revised in part as *Mercedes, a Drama in Two Acts* (Boston & New York: Houghton, Mifflin, 1894);

The Poems of Thomas Bailey Aldrich (Boston: Houghton, Mifflin, 1885);

The Second Son, by Aldrich and M. O. W. Oliphant (Boston & New York: Houghton, Mifflin, 1888);

Wyndham Towers (Boston & New York: Houghton, Mifflin, 1890);

The Sisters' Tragedy with Other Poems, Lyrical and Dramatic (Boston & New York: Houghton, Mifflin, 1891);

Thomas Bailey Aldrich

An Old Town by the Sea (Boston & New York: Houghton, Mifflin, 1893);

Two Bites at a Cherry with Other Tales (Edinburgh: Douglas, 1893; Boston & New York: Houghton, Mifflin, 1894);

Unguarded Gates and Other Poems (Boston & New York: Houghton, Mifflin, 1895);

Later Lyrics (Boston & New York: Houghton, Mifflin, 1896; London: John Lane, 1896);

Judith and Holofernes. A Poem (Boston & New York: Houghton, Mifflin, 1896);

The Poems of Thomas Bailey Aldrich (Boston & New York: Houghton, Mifflin, 1897);

A Sea Turn and Other Matters (Boston & New York: Houghton, Mifflin, 1902; Edinburgh: Douglas, 1902);

Ponkapog Papers (Boston & New York: Houghton, Mifflin, 1904);

Judith of Bethulîa. A Tragedy (Boston & New York: Houghton, Mifflin, 1904);

A Book of Songs and Sonnets Selected from the Poems of Thomas Bailey Aldrich (Boston & New York: Houghton, Mifflin, 1906);

The Poems of Thomas Bailey Aldrich (Boston & New York: Houghton, Mifflin, 1907).

Editions: *The Writings of Thomas Bailey Aldrich,* 8 volumes (Boston & New York: Houghton, Mifflin, 1897); enlarged as *The Writings of Thomas Bailey Aldrich,* Ponkapog Edition, 9 volumes (Boston & New York: Houghton, Mifflin, 1907).

Thomas Bailey Aldrich established his reputation in 1865 when his poetry was enshrined by Ticknor and Fields in the distinguished Blue and Gold series, one of the highest honors an American poet could then receive. Only twenty-nine years old, Aldrich thus joined company with Henry Wadsworth Longfellow, James Russell Lowell, William Cullen Bryant, and John Greenleaf Whittier. Throughout the Gilded Age Aldrich represented continuity with an older New England past. Fittingly, his best work of fiction, the juvenile classic *The Story of a Bad Boy* (1870), is a nostalgic look at his New England boyhood. In his mature years Aldrich defended and exemplified the literary values of the genteel tradition—decorum, sincerity, refinement—in his role as editor of the prestigious *Atlantic Monthly* from February 1881 to March 1890.

Soon after Aldrich was born on 11 November 1836 in Portsmouth, New Hampshire, his family traveled extensively on business until settling first in New York for three years and then finally in New Orleans. Unfortunately, the family was soon to fall on hard times. As Aldrich remarked in his largely autobiographical *The Story of a Bad Boy,* his father, Elias Aldrich, "invested his money so securely in the banking business that he was never able to get more than half of it out again." In 1849 Aldrich returned to Portsmouth for schooling while his father and mother, Sarah

An 1846 daguerreotype of Aldrich

Abba Bailey Aldrich, remained in New Orleans. His father died of cholera when the boy was twelve. As a teenager Aldrich lived with his grandfather, Thomas Darling Bailey. Grandfather Bailey–the model for Grandfather Nutter in *The Story of a Bad Boy*–was a conservative middle-class New Englander who observed the Sabbath with unquestioning faith: "He used to read a big Bible covered with rough green baize, and believed every word he read, even the typographical errors."

In 1852 Aldrich left Portsmouth for New York City to work in the counting room of his Uncle Charles Frost's commission house. Aldrich had already developed a keen interest in poetry,

and, at the age of nineteen, he published *The Bells: A Collection of Chimes* (1855). Soon afterward Aldrich wrote the "Ballad of Babie Bell" for the *Journal of Commerce*. A popular and critical success, this poem was reprinted by newspapers throughout the country and earned Aldrich praise from leading New York literary figures, including Fitz-Greene Halleck and Nathaniel Parker Willis. The reputation that followed "Ballad of Babie Bell" gave Aldrich the confidence to leave the counting room and to pursue a literary career. In the decade from 1855 to 1865 he progressed from junior literary critic of the *Evening Mirror* to subeditor of the *Home Journal* to associate editor of the *Saturday Press* to managing editor of *Illustrated News* to editor of *Every Saturday*. The position with *Every Saturday*, held from 1865 to 1874, provided Aldrich the financial means to marry Lilian Woodman in 1865 and necessitated a move from New York to Boston. This move suited the temperament and literary tastes of one who regarded himself as not strictly a Bostonian but certainly "Boston-plated."

Aldrich's editing of *Every Saturday* provides little information about his critical principles because his duties were mainly to cull interesting items from foreign periodicals and occasionally to write a brief editorial. A glance at his fiction and poetry can, however, reveal those aspects of his literary theory that are implicit in his literary practice. Aldrich's poems tend to be brief, light, and impersonal. Using established forms, he wrote carefully polished pieces of society verse, striking the middle range of emotions. In fiction Aldrich wanted above all to give pleasure. His stories rarely deal with ideological issues, social problems, or psychological complexities. Aldrich's honest treatment of boyhood in *The Story of a Bad Boy* earned him praise from William Dean Howells and influenced Mark Twain. Yet Aldrich did not regard himself as a realist. Indeed, he quite purposefully omitted the vulgar detail that he associated with realism: for example, after carefully foreshadowing a climactic fight between the protagonist Tom Bailey and a bully, he refused to describe it. Aldrich's other famous work of fiction, "Marjorie Daw" (*Marjorie Daw and Other People*, 1873), also draws attention to a lack of realism through the use of a surprise ending. In this story Edward Delaney, concerned about his friend John Fleming's recovery from a broken leg, writes Fleming a series of letters about a lovely young woman he has seen swinging in a hammock across the way. Thoughts of Marjorie

A ferrotype of Aldrich, circa 1854

pull the invalid out of despair, but when Fleming attempts to meet her at the end of the story he learns that there never was a Marjorie Daw.

A busy, respected, and financially secure writer, Aldrich accepted the editorship of the *Atlantic Monthly* in 1881 because he understood that there was hardly a more influential position in American letters. Like *Harper's Monthly* and *Scribner's Monthly*, the *Atlantic* was careful and serious in tone, generally holding itself aloof from contemporary matters, and wary of offending the tastes of its upper-middle-class readers. Aldrich was a prudent editor who refused to accept material dealing with controversial political and economic issues of the day. His literary judgment was similarly cautious.

In evaluating fiction for the *Atlantic* Aldrich displayed deep reservations about literary realism, once even including realism in his "list of subjects not to be touched." It is clear, however, that he objected only to the harsher forms of realism, especially to writers influenced by Gustave Flaubert and Emile Zola, both of whom he found to

be "malarious." Aldrich thought that too many realists endorsed the tedious, the mundane, the disagreeable, and the homely. Thus, it is not surprising that Aldrich consistently rejected Hamlin Garland's stories which stressed the bleakness of farm life. He admired instead the softer tones of Sarah Orne Jewett and accepted more short stories from her than from any other contributor. No doubt, Aldrich's greatest achievement as an editor was in securing for the *Atlantic* serialization rights for Henry James's *The Portrait of a Lady* (1881), *The Princess Casamassima* (1886), *The Aspern Papers* (1888), *The Tragic Muse* (1890), and a dramatization of *Daisy Miller* (1878).

In evaluating poetry Aldrich developed a reputation for his selectivity; at one time, to encourage an improvement in the quality of submissions, he determined to print only four poems a year. Despite these efforts few of the poems printed by Aldrich can be said to have lasting value. He accepted more poems from Edith Thomas than from any other contributor. As Donald Tuttle remarks, she became the representative *Atlantic* poet "with her numerous classical allusions, nature poems, and echoes of Keats, Milton, Shakespeare, and others, all neatly parceled out in quatrains, sonnets, Miltonic tetrameters, or other conventional or clearly defined verse forms." The other major contributor was Edward Sill, also a traditional poet. Unfortunately, Aldrich failed to see that poetry in the Gilded Age needed to be revitalized, either through the creation of new forms or the resuscitation of the old. A letter written in 1896 to Frank D. Sherman reveals the disdain Aldrich felt toward those attempting to break new ground in verse: "It is plain that the poetry in demand today must be strong, and picturesque, and slangish, with a dash of obscenity. Henceforth the Muse shall wear a cabbage, and not a rose on her bosom."

It may be just as well that Walt Whitman and Emily Dickinson submitted nothing to Aldrich's *Atlantic*. Aldrich had no sympathy with Whitman's verse, concluding that he had ignored the traditions and conventions of English poetry, that his manner was "hollow affectation." (Aldrich's negative assessments of Whitman may have resulted partly from Whitman's remark about Aldrich's first book of poems, *The Bells:* "Yes Tom, I like your *tinkles:* I like them very well.") Aldrich, in turn, believed *Leaves of Grass* (1855) would survive only if kept in a "glass case or a quart of spirits in an anatomical museum." Al-

Aldrich about the time his collected poems appeared in the distinguished Ticknor and Fields Blue and Gold series

drich was convinced that twentieth-century readers would rate the poetry of Henry Howard Brownell above that of Whitman.

Position and prestige never insure good judgment. In fact, Aldrich could be even more mistaken than he was about Whitman. After he stepped down as editor, he wrote an essay for the January 1892 *Atlantic Monthly* entitled "*In Re Emily Dickinson.*" A few sentences reveal the limitations of a wit confronting a genius: "The English critic who said of Miss Emily Dickinson that she might have become a fifth-rate poet 'if she had only mastered the rudiments of grammar and gone into metrical training for about fifteen years,'—the rather candid English critic who said this somewhat overstated his case. He had, however, a fairly good case. If Miss Dickinson had undergone the austere curriculum indicated, she would, I am sure, have become an admirable lyric poet of the second magnitude." Aldrich then proceeded to correct Dickinson's "I taste a liquor never brewed" by regularizing her rhymes.

Aldrich was far more perceptive as a critic when he felt sympathy with an author, as in his appreciative study of the poet Robert Herrick which first appeared in the *Century* in 1900. He praised Herrick's fancy, wit, and "faultlessness of form" and judged that the "brevity of his poems . . . would place him among the minor singers," while "his workmanship places him among the masters." Herrick's songs of "cleanly wantonness" troubled Aldrich, who saw in them "coarseness," but Aldrich concluded that the age rather than the man was to blame. Aldrich also defended Herrick from charges that he lacked originality: "It has wittily been remarked that only mediocrity is ever wholly original. Impressionability is one of the conditions of the creative faculty. . . . What the poet reads, sees, and feels, goes into his blood, and becomes an ingredient of his originality. The color of his thought instinctively blends itself with the color of its affinities. A writer's style, if it have distinction, is the outcome of a hundred styles." Throughout the essay on Herrick it is clear that Aldrich is offering a defense of his own poetic creed, of his own attempt to be brilliant within a narrow range, of his own desire to create a distinctive style without making a break with tradition.

Aldrich and other genteel writers like him were at the center of American culture in the Gilded Age. (When the *Harvard Crimson* polled its readers in 1884 concerning who should make up an American Academy, Aldrich received the second highest number of votes, ranking well above James, Howells, Twain, and Whitman.) Since Aldrich's time there has been a major shift in literary taste, and accordingly, after an initial flurry of scholarship following his death, there has been little subsequent interest in Aldrich's career. One feels certain that Aldrich will never regain the reputation he held during his lifetime. Yet to ignore Aldrich is to be blind to what the educated public endorsed in the late nineteenth century. Aldrich, perhaps more than any other writer, represented for the Gilded Age all that was delightful, polished, cultured, and accomplished.

Biographies:
Ferris Greenslet, *The Life of Thomas Bailey Aldrich* (Boston: Houghton Mifflin, 1908);
Mrs. Thomas Bailey Aldrich, *Crowding Memories* (Boston: Houghton Mifflin, 1920);

Aldrich's Atlantic Monthly *office. He was editor of the magazine from February 1881 to March 1890.*

Charles R. Mangam, "A Critical Biography of Thomas Bailey Aldrich," Ph.D. dissertation, Cornell University, 1950.

References:

Evelyn Geller, "Tom Sawyer, Tom Bailey, and the Bad-Boy Genre," *Wilson Library Bulletin,* 51 (November 1976): 245-250;

M. A. DeWolfe Howe, *The Atlantic Monthly and its Makers* (Boston: Atlantic Monthly Press, 1919);

Paul Elmer More, *Shelburne Essays, Seventh Series* (New York: Putnam's, 1910), pp. 138-152;

Charles E. Samuels, *Thomas Bailey Aldrich* (New York: Twayne, 1965);

John Tomsich, *A Genteel Endeavor: American Culture and Politics in the Gilded Age* (Stanford: Stanford University Press, 1971);

Donald Tuttle, "Thomas Bailey Aldrich's Editorship of *The Atlantic Monthly:* A Chapter in the Belles-Lettres Tradition," Ph.D. dissertation, Western Reserve University, 1939.

Papers:

Thomas Bailey Aldrich's papers are widely scattered, but five libraries have particularly strong holdings. Columbia University has a rich collection of letters and the Huntington, Boston Public, Yale University, and Cornell University libraries own a combination of letters, manuscripts, and miscellaneous documents.

James Lane Allen

(21 December 1849-18 February 1925)

Michael Kreyling
Vanderbilt University

BOOKS: *Flute and Violin and Other Kentucky Tales and Romances* (New York: Harper, 1891; Edinburgh: Douglas, 1892);

The Blue-Grass Region of Kentucky and Other Kentucky Articles (New York: Harper, 1892; London: Macmillan, 1900);

John Gray. A Kentucky Tale of the Olden Time (Philadelphia: Lippincott, 1893);

A Kentucky Cardinal: A Story (New York: Harper, 1895);

Aftermath: Part Second of "A Kentucky Cardinal" (New York: Harper, 1896);

A Kentucky Cardinal, and Aftermath (London: Osgood, McIlvaine, 1896);

Summer in Arcady: A Tale of Nature (New York & London: Macmillan, 1896);

The Choir Invisible (New York & London: Macmillan, 1897);

The Reign of Law: A Tale of the Kentucky Hemp Fields (New York & London: Macmillan, 1900);

The Mettle of the Pasture (New York & London: Macmillan, 1903);

The Bride of the Mistletoe (New York & London: Macmillan, 1909);

The Doctor's Christmas Eve (New York: Macmillan, 1910; London: Macmillan, 1911);

The Heroine in Bronze; or, A Portrait of a Girl: A Pastoral of the City (New York & London: Macmillan, 1912);

The Sword of Youth (New York: Century, 1915; London: Macmillan, 1915);

A Cathedral Singer (New York: Century, 1916; London: Macmillan, 1916);

The Kentucky Warbler (Garden City: Doubleday, Page, 1918; London: Nash, 1920);

The Emblems of Fidelity: A Comedy in Letters (Garden City: Doubleday, Page, 1919; London: Nash, 1919);

The Alabaster Box (New York & London: Harper & Brothers, 1923);

The Landmark (New York: Macmillan, 1925).

PERIODICAL PUBLICATIONS: "The First Page of *The Portrait of a Lady,*" *Critic*, 3 (27 January 1883): 27-28;

"Henry James and Alphonse Daudet," *Critic*, 3 (11 August 1883): 327;

"Night Shadows in Poe's Poetry," *Continent*, 5 (23 January 1884): 102-104;

"Keats and His Critics," *Critic*, 4 (23 February 1884): 85;

"Henry James on American Traits," *Continent*, 5 (19 March 1884): 361-363;

"Pepys' Appetite," *Critic*, 4 (31 May 1884): 253;

"A Word about Heine," *Critic*, 5 (26 July 1884): 37-38;

"Balzac and the Literary Circles of His Time," *Manhattan Magazine* (4 September 1884): 308-319;

"Local Color," *Critic*, 8 (9 January 1886): 13-14;

"Realism and Romance," *New York Evening Post*, 31 July 1886; republished in *The Heritage of American Literature*, volume 2, edited by L. N. Richardson, G. H. Orians, and H. R. Brown (Boston: Ginn, 1951): 283-286;

"Should Critics Be Gentlemen?," *Critic*, 10 (15 January 1887): 25;

"Taylor's *Origin of the Aryans*," anonymous, *Critic*, 17 (6 September 1890): 115;

"On Novelties in Pathos," *Critic*, 19 (31 October 1891): 233-234;

"Two Principles in Recent American Fiction," *Atlantic Monthly*, 80 (October 1897): 433-441.

James Lane Allen, best known for such idealistic and romantic novels as *A Kentucky Cardinal* (1895) and *The Choir Invisible* (1897), spent his writing apprenticeship in literary criticism. Once his career as short-story writer and novelist was launched with the publication of his first book, *Flute and Violin and Other Kentucky Tales and Romances* (1891), he seldom glanced back to the published essay. He let his fiction express his critical viewpoint.

Allen's brief career as a practicing critic took place almost exclusively in the 1880s, the decade of the romance-realism wars. He enlisted under the fair banner of literary taste, tradition, and idealism, and he pointed his genteel lance at the realists—most notably William Dean Howells and Henry James. His heroes among authors were the undisputed greats of the past, the ancient Greeks and William Shakespeare; his sole example of a contemporary star was Rudyard Kipling. Allen's relatively few critical essays quite clearly mark him as a genteel literary critic of a scholarly and idealistic cast of mind. He carried the banner of idealism and taste shyly but consistently into the twentieth century, suffering the cuts of sneering reviewers and the loneliness of having outlived his vogue.

James Lane Allen was born on a farm outside Lexington, Kentucky, on 21 December 1849, the seventh and last child of Richard Allen, of Virginia gentry stock who had migrated to Kentucky, and Helen Foster Allen, the daughter of a Mississippi planter. Allen's mother had the reputation of religious and social seriousness beyond her years, and she took Allen, considerably younger than his six siblings, into her special care. He was, for instance, tutored at home on his mother's argument that the four-and-one-half mile trip to the preparatory school of Kentucky University was too far for a youngster to go alone. Allen did not enroll in that school until he was sixteen. Three years later in 1868 Allen enrolled in Kentucky University (now Transylvania College). The curriculum at Kentucky University, then affiliated with the Church of Christ, was weighted in favor of that sect's theology. Allen avoided the ministerial side of the college; he concentrated his course work in Latin and Greek literature and language and in eighteenth- and nineteenth-century English literature. One biographer, Grant C. Knight, has felt constrained to point out, however, that the young Allen steadily refused to read Henry Fielding's *Tom Jones*. A tone of literary and personal seriousness is evident in Allen quite early.

After graduation in 1872 from Kentucky University, at which Allen delivered the salutatory address in Latin, the young scholar taught at a boys' school in Missouri (en route to which he was robbed by the James brothers) and was later named to a professorship of Latin literature and language at Bethany College in West Virginia, a church-related institution similar to Kentucky University. After some unspecified difficulties, allegedly having to do with the college's promotion of religion over literature and perhaps an unhappy affair of the heart, Allen left Bethany College and returned to Kentucky University, where he entered the Master of Arts program. He was also, at this time, attracted to mathematics, considered enrolling in the doctoral program in literature at Johns Hopkins University, and toyed with the idea of traveling to Germany to study "comparative philology." Practical and familial concerns nixed these plans.

James Lane Allen, then, belongs among American literary critics of his generation whose academic background stamped their critical judgments. He had molded his critical principles upon models in the prose of the eighteenth century, particularly of Joseph Addison and Sir Richard Steele, the romantic lyrics of John Keats and Percy Bysshe Shelley, and the didactic morality and sentiment of Charles Dickens. Among American writers he admired Washington Irving for his cultivated style and Nathaniel Hawthorne for his serious moral tone. His study of science and mathematics contributed to a desire for, perhaps a firm belief in, objectivity in critical judgment and rigidity in standards: there would be good or bad literature as there were correct and incorrect solutions to mathematical problems.

Allen's first published criticism was "The First Page of *The Portrait of a Lady*" (*Critic*, 27 January 1883). Allen examines the first page of James's novel as if it were a scientific hypothesis. He finds, for example, in James's description of the lawn party, shadows that should not have been there given the hour and the season. Allen's penchant for the exactness of science pushes forward in his criticism of James for failing to meet his part of the obligation to the reader "to take his language for what it is and not for what can be made of it . . . " Literature must aspire to the precision of science.

In the August 1883 *Critic* Allen once again chastised James in a review of the latter's essay on Alphonse Daudet, which had appeared in the June 1882 *Atlantic Monthly*. Allen objected to James's five-part division of the essay since he, Allen, saw no coherent beginning, middle, and end in it. If it was, Allen notes, Daudet's habit "not to take things in order," it should not have been James's either. Furthermore, Allen finds James's definition of the novel–"a representation of life"–"vague and virtually useless." He even finds the Jamesian mannerism "as we say" to be irritating. Allen prefers Charles Dudley Warner's position that the novel is nothing if it does not entertain and uplift.

Perhaps more constructive is Allen's essay "Local Color" (*Critic*, 9 January 1886). Allen had by this time published local color stories of his own and had taken the measure of the growing vogue in such fiction, especially from southern writers such as George Washington Cable and Charles Egbert Craddock (Mary N. Murfree). Like the schoolmaster he had been, Allen finds and then promulgates systematic rules for local color in fiction. The "colors" must be true to the region the author aims to depict. In this vein Allen lauds Henry Wadsworth Longfellow as the originator of local color and demotes Howells (the old antagonist) to the level of Cable, Craddock, and Constance Fenimore Woolson as a local colorist. The next rule is that the local colorist must use his palette to guide reader perception to a more ideal truth; gratuitous or uncontrolled atmosphere is useless. The description the local colorist supplies must be a means, not an end. For information on local flora and fauna one can read a naturalist. The true local-color writer

Allen, circa 1890

must be more than a "mere novelist," more than an artist and novelist combined: he must be a scientist who comprehends "the significance of the natural pictorial environment of humanity in its manifold effects upon humanity, and he must make this knowledge available for literary presentation." This is the language of the idealistic, didactic literary priesthood of the Genteel Tradition, of Warner, Josiah Holland, and Richard Watson Gilder. Allen aspired to the order.

Allen's most important critical statements are two essays over ten years apart: "Realism and Romance" (*New York Evening Post*, 31 July 1886), the summation of his thoughts on the prevailing literary debate of the 1880s, and "Two Principles in Recent American Fiction" (*Atlantic Monthly*, October 1897), his schematic fitting of American literature into the Arnoldian tradition of the "best" in the history of Western literary expression.

In "Realism and Romance" Allen expresses great glee at a dispute among realists caused, he surmises, by pronouncements in "The Editor's Study," William Dean Howells's column in the *Atlantic Monthly*. What can the reading public expect, Allen scolds, from an unruly group who acknowledges no authority in literature or any-

Photograph of Allen used as the frontispiece for the 1899 Biographical Edition of Flute and Violin and Other Tales

that romantic character and incident, and adventure, and history, all are interesting, and such is the soul of man that they always will be interesting, until the great Note-Book is opened and we find ourselves—romance and all—analyzed on its pages by the master hand of the Great Realist." Howells and his disciples, who believe romance is childish or weak-minded or worse, will find themselves overwhelmingly rebuked by "human nature." Romance, as Allen sees it, is the marrow of human nature, and the race will never cast it away.

Allen was quite correct in his prediction, as even so proximate a period as the next decade was to show. Of course, romances such as those of F. Marion Crawford and George Barr McCutcheon continued to be bought and read by a large public, and old "local colorists" such as Cable and Hamlin Garland tried to capture a piece of the romance market. Yet the critical tide still ran against them. Not only realism, but naturalism as well, continued to occupy the cutting edge of critical opinion.

Allen's essay "Two Principles in Recent American Fiction" can be seen as his attempt to reconcile the two competing movements in an historical-archetypal process, and at the same time to preserve romance as a necessary element in American literature. Allen's theory is one of vast phases in the history of Western literature; American writing is a little interval on the arc. According to Allen, from about the close of the Civil War to the date of his essay, a principle he chooses to call the Feminine Principle had unilaterally governed American literature. There are three fundamental attributes to the Feminine Principle: Refinement, Delicacy, Grace. With a certain schematic neatness that probably pleased the mathematical side of Allen's mind, he could find three subordinate traits as well: Smallness, Rarity, Tact. The Feminine Principle produced " a literature that held itself fast, and . . . held us fast, to those primary standards of good taste, good thought, and good breeding which we can not more afford to do without in our novels than we can afford to do without them in our lives." Allen, unfortunately, supplies no actual examples of literature generated from the Feminine Principle.

The American national experience of the 1870s and 1880s taught that many things "truly American" were left out by the Feminine Principle. A sort of dialectic then occurred in a short span of literary history. The opposites of the six

thing else? Realism, Allen goes on to argue, is fundamentally unstable as a literary compound; having abolished standards and ideals and turned to "life," it can hope for no more than confusion and disputation.

Turning to a related topic, the condescension of Northern critics to Southern writers by way of the assumption that all things Southern are "oddities" and terminally romantic, Allen voices some literary chauvinism. He warns Northern editors and critics who seem to have made synonyms of the words "Southern" and "odd" that such writers as Cable and Craddock will survive the negative commentary while Howells and his ilk will be read by a continually dwindling number.

The coda to this essay must stand as Allen's fullest homage to romance as a literary and moral influence. Regardless of what the realists preach, Allen avers, "the world in general will go on its old way and believe that the romantic motive *is* interesting; that romance is interesting;

traits began to assert themselves; archetypally the Masculine Principle emerged to counter the Feminine: for Delicacy, Strength; for Refinement, Virility; for Grace, Massiveness. On the secondary level a corresponding shift also occurred. Smallness was offset by Largeness; Rarity by Obviousness; Tact by Primary or Instinctive Action. And so realism, the original irritant, is subsumed under a much vaster process than mere observation of the current event. One must go to the totality of Western literature to appreciate the scope of the dialectical movement. Allen sees equilibrium in classical Greek writing and once again in the works of Shakespeare. Only at these two nodes in the history of Western literature do the Masculine and Feminine Principles achieve a balance and harmony. There is no cause for immediate despair, for Allen sees a third node taking shape. This one is to be ushered in by the likes of Rudyard Kipling, whose poem "Recessional" epitomizes for Allen the balancing of the Masculine and the Feminine Principles.

After "Two Principles in Recent American Fiction" Allen made no major critical statements. His fiction began to reflect his reading of such influential authors as Charles Darwin and Friedrich Nietzche, but he does not himself develop or enunciate a critical theory based on this reading.

James Lane Allen, as a critic, is an adherent of the Genteel Tradition in American literature. For him the primary purpose of a work of literature is to hold up ideals of thought and behavior for the edification of an audience to whom the writer is responsible. On this point Allen and Howells might have agreed; on the content of the message to be delivered they would have differed. Mere facts, Allen felt and argued, are not to be left inert; the moral purpose in their existence and configuration is the author's subject matter. The critic hastens to these absolutes, focuses attention on them, recommends them to the public. In Allen's criticism one comes across absolutes (Tact, Virility, Refinement) but little practical criticism. Allen made himself an antagonist to the realists on this issue: realists presented too much fact unleavened by the moral, ideal absolute. They had betrayed the author's solemn obligation to teach the great lessons of the race.

Allen's critical stature is now diminished and antique. His habit of schematically dividing and subdividing, of setting absolute "rules" for the writing and evaluating of literature is a strategy now almost universally avoided, although the example of such works as Northrop Frye's *Anatomy of Criticism* (1957) indicates that the impulse is still active. Nothing so comprehensive as an "anatomy" was within Allen's grasp. He fought small, contained skirmishes with unwieldy weapons: Masculine and Feminine Principles, the figure of "The Gentleman in Literature." Allen's positions were overrun early, his own critical body of work—modest as it is—left uncollected and largely forgotten.

References:

William K. Bottorff, *James Lane Allen* (New York: Twayne, 1964);

Grant C. Knight, *James Lane Allen and the Genteel Tradition* (Chapel Hill: University of North Carolina Press, 1935);

Fred L. Pattee, *A History of American Literature Since 1870* (New York: Century, 1915).

Papers:

Significant collections of James Lane Allen's correspondence and manuscripts can be found in the following repositories: Duke University Library, Special Collections; Filson Club, Louisville, Kentucky; Kentucky Historical Society, Old State House, Frankfort, Kentucky; and the University of Kentucky Library, Lexington, Kentucky.

Katharine Lee Bates

(12 August 1859-28 March 1929)

Paula M. Uruburu
Hofstra University

BOOKS: *The College Beautiful, and Other Poems* (Cambridge, Mass.: Houghton, 1887);

Rose and Thorn (Boston & Chicago: Congregational Sunday-School and Publishing Society, 1889);

Hermit Island (Boston: Lothrop, 1890);

Sunshine, and Other Verses for Children (Boston: Printed by the Wellesley Alumnæ, 1890);

The English Religious Drama (New York & London: Macmillan, 1893);

American Literature (New York: Chautauqua Press, 1897; London: Macmillan, 1897);

Spanish Highways and Byways (New York & London: Macmillan, 1900);

From Gretna Green to Land's End: A Literary Journey in England, photographs by Katharine Coman (New York: Crowell, 1907; London: Grant Richards, 1908);

America the Beautiful, and Other Poems (New York: Crowell, 1911);

In Sunny Spain with Pilarica and Rafael (New York: Dutton, 1913);

Fairy Gold (New York: Dutton, 1916);

The Retinue, and Other Poems (New York: Dutton, 1918);

Sigurd Our Golden Collie, and Other Comrades of the Road (New York: Dutton, 1919; London: Dent, 1921);

Yellow Clover, A Book of Remembrance (New York: Dutton, 1922);

Little Robin Stay-Behind, and Other Plays in Verse for Children (New York: Woman's Press, 1923);

The Pilgrim Ship (New York: Woman's Press, 1926);

America the Dream (New York: Crowell, 1930);

An Autobiography, in Brief, of Katharine Lee Bates (N.p.: Privately printed, 1930);

Selected Poems of Katharine Lee Bates, edited by Marion Pelton Guild (Boston & New York: Houghton Mifflin, 1930).

OTHER: *The Wedding-Day Book,* edited by Bates (Boston: Lothrop, 1882);

Katharine Lee Bates

Coleridge's Ancient Mariner, edited by Bates (Boston & New York: Leach, Shewell & Sanborn, 1889);

Ballad Book, edited by Bates (Boston & New York: Leach, Shewell & Sanborn, 1890);

Shakespeare's Comedy of The Merchant of Venice, edited by Bates (Boston & New York: Leach, Shewell & Sanborn, 1894);

Shakespeare's Comedy of A Midsummer Night's Dream, edited by Bates (Boston & New York: Leach, Shewell & Sanborn, 1895);

Shakespeare's Comedy of As You Like It, edited by Bates (Boston & New York: Leach, Shewell & Sanborn, 1896);

Browning Studies: Bibliography, compiled by Bates (Boston: Robinson, 1896);

The Chap-Book, edited by Bates (Chicago: Stone, 1896);

English Drama: A Working Basis, compiled by Bates and Lydia Boker Godfrey (Boston: Robinson, 1896); enlarged as *Shakespeare: Selective Bibliography and Biographical Notes,* compiled by Bates and Lilla Weed (Wellesley, Mass.: Wellesley College, 1913);

Keats's The Eve of St. Agnes, and Other Poems, edited by Bates (New York & Boston: Silver, Burdett, 1902);

The Works of Nathaniel Hawthorne, 14 volumes, edited, with an introduction, by Bates (New York: Crowell, 1902);

Hamilton Wright Mabie, *Norse Stories Retold From the Eddas,* edited by Bates (Chicago: Rand, McNally, 1902);

English History Told by English Poets, compiled by Bates and Katharine Coman (New York & London: Macmillan, 1902);

The Poems of Alice and Phoebe Cary, edited by Bates (New York: Crowell, 1903);

The King of the Golden River; or, the Black Brothers: A Legend of Stíria, by John Ruskin, edited by Bates, illustrated by John C. Johansen (Chicago & London: Rand, McNally, 1903);

Tennyson's The Princess, edited by Bates (New York & Cincinnati: American Book Co., 1904);

Tennyson's Gareth and Lynette, Lancelot and Elaine, The Passing of Arthur, edited by Bates (Boston & Chicago: Sibley, 1905);

Nathaniel Hawthorne, *Our Old Home: A Series of English Sketches,* introduction by Bates (New York: Crowell, 1906);

Romantic Legends of Spain, by Gustavo Adolfo Becquer, translated by Bates and Cornelia Frances Bates (New York: Crowell, 1909);

The New Irish Drama, compiled and edited by Bates (Chicago: Drama League of America, 1911);

Chaucer's Canterbury Pilgrims, Retold by Katharine Lee Bates, illustrated by Angus MacDonall, color plates by Milo Winter (Chicago & New York: Rand, McNally, 1914);

Helen Sanborn, *Anne of Britanny,* introduction by Bates (Boston: Lothrop, Lee & Shepard, 1917);

Thomas Heywood, *A Woman Killed with Kindness, and The Faire Maide of the West,* edited by

Bates in 1876, the year she entered Wellesley College

Bates (Boston: Heath, 1917);

Once Upon a Time; A Book of Old-Time Fairy Tales, edited by Bates, illustrated by Margaret Evans Price (Chicago & New York: Rand, McNally, 1921);

Tom Thumb and Other Old-Time Fairy Tales, edited by Bates, illustrated by Price (Chicago & New York: Rand, McNally, 1926);

Helen Corke, *The World's Family,* introduction by Bates (New York: Oxford University Press, 1930).

The academic community of women scholars that flourished at Wellesley College during the period from 1895 to 1920 included among its distinguished professoriate Katharine Lee Bates—scholar, poet, educator, editor, and administrator. Though best known today as the author of "America the Beautiful," in over forty years at Wellesley Bates established herself as a leading figure in the women's intellectual movement of the

Bates, in her academic robe, with her dog Hamlet

sion as set to the music of Samuel Ward's "Materna" has been included in numerous anthologies of patriotic prose and poetry). Completely absorbed in her work at Wellesley, Bates found the time to join a number of scholarly organizations such as the National Institute of Social Sciences, the American Academy of Political and Social Sciences, the Shakespeare Association of America, and Phi Beta Kappa while pursuing her own love of poetry by contributing a number of individual poems to periodicals like the *Christian Century, Contemporary Verse, Lippincott's,* and the *Delineator.* It was through her efforts that some of the most influential poets of the century, including William Butler Yeats, Vachel Lindsay, and Robert Frost, found their way to the Wellesley campus during her years as chairperson of the English department. After years of dedication as an innovative educator and thorough scholar Bates was made professor emeritus in 1925, the year she retired to pursue her own creative writing, which had been somewhat neglected out of a sense of duty and conscience to her beloved

Wellesley. Hampered by weariness and illness, she died in 1929 of heart disease.

While she felt poetry to be her true vocation Bates found her creative impulses consistently relegated by academic necessities to those brief moments in her life when she was not, according to her biographer Dorothy Burgess, involved as a "reluctant captive" in editing numerous volumes of English classics, teaching, giving guest lectures, and generally participating in those aspects of college life which were an extension of her academic activities. A scholar who specialized in Shakespeare and Elizabethan drama, she received wide recognition among academicians for her critical editions of such writers as Samuel Taylor Coleridge, John Keats, John Ruskin, and Alfred Tennyson. The work which established her reputation as a scholar was *The English Religious Drama* (1893), a volume created out of notes from her years at Oxford (and organized in 1893 into a series of lectures delivered in the Summer School of Colorado Springs). This book, which describes, enumerates, and analyzes the dramatic values of Latin passion plays, saint plays, and miracle plays, also clarifies the indebtedness of Shakespeare and his contemporaries to the earlier dramatists. Praising the "dramatic range and noble spirit" of these plays, which others, like James Russell Lowell, deplored as being "dull beyond what is permitted even by the most hardened charity," Bates presented her research in a lively manner and made a normally tedious subject interesting and picturesque. Several scholarly critics, however, failed to find new research in the book.

Her goal as scholar and educator, expressed in both her seminars and in the prefaces to her numerous editions, such as *Ballad Book* (1890), was to "awaken in the student a genuine love and enthusiasm for the higher forms of prose, and more especially for poetry." She told one class attending her "English Drama Through Shakespeare" seminar (which met at her home) that in order to develop one's critical abilities, one must be able to glean an understanding and appreciation from the actual art of the writer and from what we can gather of his life.

Her attention already divided between her love of English classics and her own poetry, Bates turned to the area of American literature, where she is best known for her contribution to a fourteen-volume edition of Nathaniel Hawthorne's works (1902), which entailed a separate introduction for each volume, and for her study entitled *American Literature* (1897), a chronological survey of America's literary progress from the colonial era (including Cotton Mather and Jonathan Edwards) to the national era (including Hawthorne, Edgar Allan Poe, and Henry James). Written primarily as a textbook based on lectures Bates had given on American literature, the book is nonetheless valuable for its attempt to legitimize American literature. Bates asserts that her aim as scholar and critic is to show that American literature is an outgrowth of American life, reflecting a unique national character and point of view which is modified by both local and regional concerns. As she states in the preface, "Our literature, which is in one aspect a branch of the noble parent literature of England, is rightly viewed, also, as the individual expression of an independent nation. Its significance to us, whose history it embodies, naturally outranks its absolute value among the older literature."

Like most of Bates's critical writing, *American Literature* reflects her exactness and thoroughness as well as her genteel personality and education. She often emphasizes personal anecdotes and biographical details of the writers' lives in place of producing straightforward criticism of their literary merit. Understandably, her assessment of who should be considered an important part of the American literary canon differs greatly, in some instances, from those considered by today's critics as essential to the canon. For example, she devotes almost an entire chapter to Henry Wadsworth Longfellow and others in his tradition, of which she considered herself a part through her own poetry, but she classifies Emily Dickinson, that "elfish recluse in her father's house," as one of the minor New England poets along with Lucy Larcom, Nora Perry, and Susan Coolidge. Yet the fact that she even knew of Dickinson's work (the first volume of Dickinson's poetry came out in 1890) reveals Bates's awareness of the literary scene.

While she had a growing reputation as a woman of letters, Bates also developed a reputation abroad; she was, in fact, well known for her two widely read travel books, the results of her sabbatical trips to Europe, Scandinavia, Palestine, and Egypt (*Spanish Highways and Byways*, 1900, and *From Gretna Green to Land's End: A Literary Journey in England*, 1907).

A person of romantic temperament, a "loving despot" as a professor and administrator, known for her sense of humor and her distaste for the drudgery of pedantry, Bates proved to be

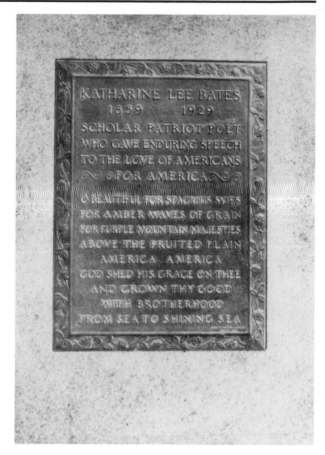

Memorial tablet, designed by John Francis Parimino, which was placed in Boston's Fenway soon after Bates's death in March 1929

one of the driving forces behind the community of scholars at Wellesley who were united not only by sex but by class, family relationships, geographic origins, and social ideals. She said of college teaching, "I don't believe in education much, only when it works by evolution, not by dogmatism." An integral part of Wellesley's social and intellectual milieu, which included such important women scholars of the time as Mary Calkins, Vida Dutton Scudder, and her lifelong friend Katharine Coman, Bates helped to foster that community and establish a faculty "more strengthened by union," which grew as it called "into action the power that already is."

Bates continued to work throughout her career on various editions and books of poetry, completing in 1917 the book which she considered her most scholarly achievement, an edition for the Belles Lettres series of Thomas Heywood's *A Woman Killed with Kindness, and The Faire Maide of the West* (begun years earlier during her study at Oxford). An example of Bates's careful and thorough scholarship, this work established her as an accepted Heywood authority. The work has been acknowledged by critics as a valuable study because of its excellent biography and bibliography, which Bates compiled by going over a considerable amount of material in various diaries, dramatic companies' records, and items in parish and probate registries.

Though today the "mellow scholarship" of outstanding academic women of the nineteenth century is relatively unknown, the period during which Bates lived and wrote is one notable for its progressive dedication to the principle of higher education for women in America. Bates, at the forefront of this movement in many ways, established her place in the cohesive unit forged at Wellesley. By believing that "the mind sins that suffers itself to think timidly and obscurely," she set an example for those who would follow her. Even today her legacy lives on in her hometown of Falmouth, Massachusetts, where a dedicated group has founded a fund to raise money for a statue of Bates. By those who knew her she was called "a poet in her scholarship . . . a poet in her teaching . . . a poet in her friendship."

Biographies:
Eva Phillips Boyd, "Katharine Lee Bates, Poet-Teacher," *English Journal,* 20 (June 1931): 455-462;

Dorothy Burgess, *Dream and Deed: The Story of Katharine Lee Bates* (Norman: University of Oklahoma Press, 1952).

References:
Florence Converse, "The Story of Wellesley (1915)," *Wellesley Magazine* (June-October 1925);

Converse, "Wellesley College: A Chronicle of the Years 1875-1938," *Wellesley Magazine* (June Supplement 1929): 98+;

Caroline Hazard, "Tribute to Katharine Lee Bates," *Wellesley Alumnae Magazine,* 12 (June 1929): 15;

Patricia A. Palmieri, "Here Was Fellowship: A Social Portrait of Academic Women at Wellesley College, 1895-1920," *History of Education Quarterly,* 23 (Summer 1983): 195-214;

Palmieri, "In Adamless Eden: A Social Portrait of the Academic Community at Wellesley College 1875-1920," Ph.D. dissertation, Harvard University, 1981.

Papers:
The Katharine Lee Bates papers, including letters and an 1896 diary, are deposited in the Wellesley College Archives.

Henry A. Beers

(2 July 1847-7 September 1926)

Philip B. Eppard
State University of New York at Albany

BOOKS: *Odds and Ends: Verses Humorous, Occasional, and Miscellaneous* (Boston: Houghton, Osgood, 1878);

Nathaniel Parker Willis (Boston & New York: Houghton, Mifflin, 1885);

The Thankless Muse (Boston & New York: Houghton, Mifflin, 1885);

An Outline Sketch of English Literature (New York: Chautauqua Press, 1886); republished as *From Chaucer to Tennyson: English Literature in Eight Chapters, with Selections from Thirty Authors* (New York: Chautauqua Press, 1890);

An Outline Sketch of American Literature (New York: Chautauqua Press, 1887); republished as *Initial Studies in American Letters* (New York: Chautauqua Press, 1891); republished as *Studies in American Letters* (Philadelphia: Jacobs, 1895); republished as *A Short History of American Literature* (London: Unwin, 1906);

A Suburban Pastoral, and Other Tales (New York: Holt, 1894);

The Ways of Yale in the Consulship of Plancus (New York: Holt, 1895; enlarged, 1903; enlarged again, 1910);

Brief History of English and American Literature (New York: Eaton & Mains/Cincinnati: Curts & Jennings, 1897);

A History of English Romanticism in the Eighteenth Century (New York: Holt, 1899; London: Paul, Trench, Trübner, 1899);

A History of English Romanticism in the Nineteenth Century (New York: Holt, 1901; London: Paul, Trench, Trübner, 1902);

Points at Issue and Some Other Points (New York & London: Macmillan, 1904);

Milton's Tercentenary: An Address Delivered Before the Modern Language Club at Yale University on Milton's Three Hundredth Birthday (New Haven: Yale University Press, 1910);

The Two Twilights (Boston: Badger, 1917);

Four Americans: Roosevelt, Hawthorne, Emerson, Whitman (New Haven: Published for the Yale Review by Yale University Press, 1919);

Henry A. Beers

The Connecticut Wits, and Other Essays (New Haven: Yale University Press, 1920);

Poems (New Haven: Yale University Press, 1921);

Bumblebee (New Preston, Conn.: Bernhardt Wall, 1925).

OTHER: *A Century of American Literature 1776-1876*, edited by Beers (New York: Holt, 1878);

"Split Zephyr," in *Stories by American Authors* (New York: Scribners, 1884), VIII: pp. 48-101;

John Ruskin, *Readings from Ruskin: Italy,* introduction by Beers (Boston: Chautauqua Press, 1885);

Prose Writings of Nathaniel Parker Willis, selected by Beers (New York: Scribners, 1885);

"Hartford in Literature," in *The Memorial History of Hartford County Connecticut 1633-1884,* 2 volumes, edited by J. Hammond Trumbull (Boston: Osgood, 1886), I: pp. 155-174;

Selections from the Prose Writings of Samuel Taylor Coleridge, edited, with an introduction and notes, by Beers (New York: Holt, 1893);

James Fenimore Cooper, Jr., *Afterglow,* edited, with a foreword, by Beers (New Haven: Yale University Press, 1918).

PERIODICAL PUBLICATIONS: "Nathaniel Hawthorne," *Yale Literary Magazine,* 33 (November 1867): 46-55;

"King Victor and King Charles," *Chautauquan,* 11 (May 1890): 148-151;

" 'Crusty Christopher' (John Wilson)" *Century,* 45 (January 1893): 361-362.

One of the most representative of the genteel academic critics of the late nineteenth century was Henry Augustin Beers, who taught English literature at Yale for over forty years. Beers was a versatile writer of fiction, poetry, and essays as well as the author of several popular introductory surveys of English and American literature and a detailed two-volume history of English romanticism. His intimate knowledge of all kinds of literature was legendary among Yale students, to whom he often seemed a shy and retiring figure. His chief contribution was as a popularizer, but a popularizer who wrote with a thorough knowledge and love of his material.

Beers was from a Connecticut family which traced its origins in America back to the seventeenth century. He was very much rooted in the soil of Connecticut. Henry S. Canby, who was one of Beers's students at the turn of the century, wrote of him, "I do not suppose that in twenty years he made as many journeys even of a day, to New York and Boston." Ironically, this Connecticut-bound writer was born in Buffalo, New York, during a visit to that city by his parents, George Webster Beers and Elizabeth Victoria Clerc Beers. He grew up in Hartford, graduated from the Hartford High School in 1864, and entered Yale the following year. At Yale he wrote verse and sketches for the *Yale Literary Magazine* and absorbed the undergraduate life of New Haven so well that he later transferred it into print in a series of sketches published as *The Ways of Yale in the Consulship of Plancus* (1895). After graduating in 1869 Beers studied law in New York City and was admitted to the bar in 1870. The following year, however, he abandoned the practice of law and returned to Yale as a tutor in English. Beers was married in Covington, Kentucky, on 7 July 1873 to Mary Florence Heaton, sister of his Yale classmate Edward Heaton. They had eight children. He remained at Yale the rest of his life, serving as tutor (1871-1874), assistant professor of English literature (1875-1880), professor (1880-1916), and professor emeritus (1916-1926). Early in his teaching career Beers played an important part in redirecting the English curriculum at Yale away from an exclusive focus upon grammar to a more historically based study of literature itself.

Beers's first and last books were volumes of poetry, a fact indicative of his commitment to belles lettres rather than to literary scholarship. In *An Outline Sketch of American Literature* (1887) Beers wrote, "The professors of literature in our colleges are usually persons who have made no additions to literature, and the professors of rhetoric seem ordinarily to have been selected to teach students how to write, for the reason that they themselves have never written any thing that any one has ever read." Beers wrote things that people *did* read. One of his short stories, "Split Zephyr," was included in the important multivolume anthology *Stories by American Authors* (1884).

Beers's first important contribution to literary scholarship was a biography of Nathaniel Parker Willis for Houghton, Mifflin's American Men of Letters series. Published in 1885, the book is one of Beers's most substantial works. In it he reconstructed the life of a poet and essayist who was once regarded in the forefront of American literature but who had slipped dramatically in critical esteem well before his death in 1867. Beers's study of Willis is marked by careful scholarship, an assiduous use of original source material, judicious critical judgments, and a bright, opinionated style. He did not hesitate, for example, to offer this assessment of Willis's novel *Paul Fane* (1857): "It was, in effect, a poor novel; and–what was unusual with Willis, even at his thinnest–it was dull." On the other hand he found many of Willis's sketches and stories "exceedingly clever" and suggested that only the passion for reading the latest publications kept readers of light fiction

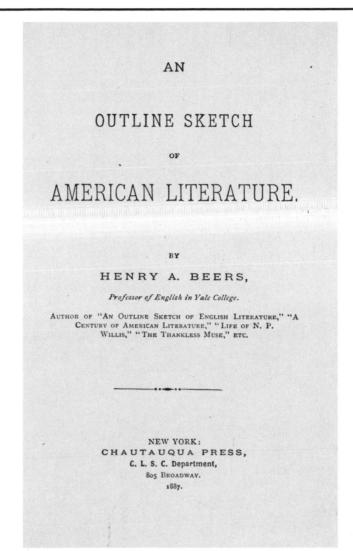

AN

OUTLINE SKETCH

OF

AMERICAN LITERATURE.

BY

HENRY A. BEERS,

Professor of English in Yale College.

AUTHOR OF "AN OUTLINE SKETCH OF ENGLISH LITERATURE," "A
CENTURY OF AMERICAN LITERATURE," "LIFE OF N. P.
WILLIS," "THE THANKLESS MUSE," ETC.

NEW YORK:
CHAUTAUQUA PRESS,
C. L. S. C. Department,
805 Broadway.
1887.

Title page for Beers's popular survey of American literature, written for the use of the Chautauqua Literary and Scientific Circle

away from Willis. He also praised Willis's style and lamented the vogue that regarded style as "increasingly unimportant" and would reduce fiction to something akin to a social science report. Although the flood of scholarship on American literature in the twentieth century has brought new studies of Willis, Beers's pioneering biography is still of value, particularly for its use of original source material, some of which has since been lost.

Although Beers was an academic, he was clearly not interested in making the study of literature merely an academic exercise. Proof of this can be seen in his popular histories of English and American literature which were produced for the Chautauqua Literary and Scientific Circle. The popularity of these volumes, which went through several editions and changes in title dur-

ing the two decades following their first publication in 1886 and 1887, suggests that Beers's version of literary history had a tremendous impact on the middle-class audience which flocked to the Chautauqua's educational programs and in the schools and academies which may have adopted them as textbooks. Such books as these are rather more important as cultural artifacts than as works of lasting critical value. Still it may be said that, particularly in the presentation of American literature as a distinct field of inquiry, Beers's popular histories made a real contribution. Although the books can be termed "popular" histories, they are neither written in a style appealing to the lowest common denominator, nor are they merely a dry-as-dust compilation of names, dates, and book titles. Francis Parsons, a student of Beers's at Yale, found in these introductory volumes a "vividness of statement and portrayal of character coupled with a wise conciseness which seemed to generate a kind of electric sparkle." Clearly it was the hand of Beers the poet and short-story writer which shaped these introductory histories.

Beers's reputation as a literary scholar ultimately came to rest on his two volumes on romanticism, *A History of English Romanticism in the Eighteenth Century* (1899) and *A History of English Romanticism in the Nineteenth Century* (1901). These were, in essence, lectures delivered to his Yale classes reworked for publication. According to Canby they were works which sprang not from Beers's heart but more from the desire to meet the pressing demands of what was considered academic scholarship. They give evidence of his wide knowledge of European as well as English literature. They also exhibit the influence of H. A. Taine on literary history, as Beers attempted to find historical and social distinction in the manifestations of romanticism in different countries. The books were popular enough to run through numerous printings, but they were received with some controversy.

Beers rather boldly took a conservative position in defining his subject. The first chapter of the volume on the eighteenth century treated the definition of romanticism, which Beers chose to consider solely in its older sense as "the reproduction in modern art or literature of the life and thought of the middle ages." Such a stance seemed perhaps less peculiar when Beers was identifying romanticism's eighteenth-century roots. But in the nineteenth-century volume, which treated the full flowering of English romanticism, Beers's definition seemed too narrow to some readers. Edward E. Hale, Jr., in a review in the *Dial,* charged that by separating medievalism from other forms of romanticism, Beers "makes it impossible to get the true understanding of either." He also charged, somewhat justly, that Beers "knows that romanticism is something more than medievalism, for he often uses the word in the broader sense." Beers's critics could not really fault his scholarship itself, within his chosen limits of definition. His narrow definition has made his work of less value to later students who conceive of romanticism in the broader sense. As a survey of the medieval impulse in literature it can still be read with pleasure and profit, for, as Henry Barrett Hinckley said in a review of the eighteenth-century volume in the *Bookman* (June 1899), Beers "is admirably free from that dulness of the specialist which prevents so much excellent scholarship from appealing to the people."

All of Beers's writings are marked by a readable, almost conversational style. Some of his most enjoyable writing is found in his three volumes of essays. His subjects range widely over English and American literature, from William Shakespeare and John Milton to Theodore Roosevelt and James Whitcomb Riley. In *Points at Issue and Some Other Points* (1904) Beers devoted two essays to questions surrounding the role of literature in collegiate education. Both highlight the tension Beers saw between literature and literary scholarship. In "College Entrance Requirements in English" he questioned the utility of making the reading of certain literary works a prerequisite for the reading of certain other literary works. He detected objections to the teaching of literature in those scholars who regarded it as unscientific, "a matter of taste and not of knowledge, and therefore not properly teachable." In "Literature and the Colleges" he posed the question of why most of the leading American men of letters before the Civil War were college graduates while most of the new writers after the war were not. Beers saw part of the reason in the fact that the colleges had been deprived of the educational monopoly they once enjoyed. A deeper reason, however, lay in the relationship between scholarship and creativity. "The truth is that a college as such, *i.e.* as a body of teachers and investigators, is never directly stimulative of creative work on the part of its scholars. . . . The literary gift is the result of nature acted on by life. Scholarship, on the other hand, deals with books rather than life, is retrospective, critical, analytic." Beers went on to attack the academic critics who condescended to contemporary writers. He argued that creative artists should be welcomed to the ranks of teachers of literature, asking, "Who can speak of art with more authority than the artist?"

Four Americans (1919), in addition to remarks on Theodore Roosevelt and Nathaniel Hawthorne, includes an essay on Ralph Waldo Emerson, "A Pilgrim in Concord," which is really a delightful reminiscence of Beers's experiences in the summer of 1879 attending Bronson Alcott's School of Philosophy. The same book also contains "A Wordlet about Whitman." Since Whitman avoided the conventions of poetry, Beers was less inclined to give him high praise as a *poet,* and he cast barbs at the Whitman cult. "The Whitmanites deify him. They speak of him

Beers and his Yale colleague William Lyon Phelps in 1915

constantly as a seer, a man of exalted intellect. I do not believe that he was a great thinker, but only a great feeler." A counterpoint to Beers's piece on Whitman is his tribute to James Whitcomb Riley in *The Connecticut Wits, and Other Essays* (1920). Beers argued that Riley, not Whitman, was the true poet of the people, because the people read and loved his verse. "We do not thrill to Walt Whitman's paeans to democracy in the abstract; but we vibrate to every touch on the chord of family affections, of early friendship, and of the dear old homely things that our childhood knew." The instinct behind such a point of view is one that holds that literature should appeal to all the senses and not be an intellectual exercise.

Beers was a fixture at Yale for over four decades. Canby writes that "his bent frame, his worn clothes, his shy and inward air as he shuffled from his classroom toward the library, were like a survival of a more pinched and austere age." He came to be regarded by some of his younger colleagues and students as something of a frustrated, defeated figure. His true calling was poetry. William Lyon Phelps said of Beers, "Had he had any ambition he would have been one of the best known of contemporary creative writers." Either a lack of ambition or an abundance of financial obligations to a large family kept him at Yale, where he seemed to be increasingly an anachronism in a scholarly world dominated by a rigorous Germanic idea of research. Phelps recalled that Beers "never professed to be a research scholar in the approved Germanic style; but in reality he was one of the most profound and accurate scholars on the Faculty." In a moving tribute Canby explained how Beers put his knowledge of literature at the service of the humanities rather than mere academic pedantry: "He had not acquired knowledge as a tool but because his mind desired it. Where his colleagues knew about literature, he knew literature itself, and more about it that was relevant than the most erudite. His mind was encyclopedic, but it was a commentary not a reference book. Other scholars knew what idyll of Theocritus was a source for 'Lycidas,' he could tell why Milton read it and what he had done with his reading. The college knew, or thought it knew, why literature should be taught, and what should be taught of it. Beers was himself an example of that rebirth in literature which gives margins to the imagination. No one knowing him could doubt the efficacy of the humanities."

A wide range of specialized studies has made Beers's landmark books on romanticism less valuable. His essays are nearly as forgotten as his short stories and verse. But it is the element of personal enthusiasm for the literary imagination which Canby noted in Beers that enables readers still to read his work, particularly the essays, with profit and enjoyment.

References:

Leonard Bacon, *Semi-Centennial: Some of the Life and Part of the Opinions of Leonard Bacon* (New York & London: Harper, 1939), pp. 37-39;

Henry S. Canby, *Alma Mater: The Gothic Age of the American College* (New York: Farrar & Rinehart, 1936), pp. 173-181;

Wilbur Cross, *Connecticut Yankee: An Autobiography* (New Haven: Yale University Press, 1943), pp. 74-76, 143-146;

Obituary Record of Yale Graduates, 1926-1927, no. 86 (1927): 35-37;

Francis Parsons, *Six Men of Yale* (New Haven: Yale University Press, 1939): pp. 125-145;

William Lyon Phelps, *Autobiography with Letters* (New York, London & Toronto: Oxford University Press, 1939), pp. 289-291;

George Wilson Pierson, *Yale College: An Educational History 1871-1921* (New Haven: Yale University Press, 1952), pp. 282-284.

Papers:

There is a small collection of Henry A. Beers's manuscripts and correspondence at the Beinecke Rare Book and Manuscript Library, Yale University.

Ambrose Bierce

(24 June 1842-11 January 1914)

M. E. Grenander
State University of New York at Albany

See also the Bierce entries in *DLB 11, American Humorists, 1800-1950; DLB 12, American Realists and Naturalists,* and *DLB 23, American Newspaper Journalists, 1873-1900.*

BOOKS: *The Fiend's Delight*, as Dod Grile (London: John Camden Hotten, 1873; New York: A. L. Luyster, 1873);

Nuggets and Dust Panned Out in California, as Dod Grile (London: Chatto & Windus, 1873);

Cobwebs from an Empty Skull, as Dod Grile (London & New York: Routledge, 1874);

The Dance of Death, by Bierce and Thomas A. Harcourt, as William Herman (San Francisco: Privately printed, 1877; corrected and enlarged edition, San Francisco: Henry Keller, 1877);

Tales of Soldiers and Civilians (San Francisco: E. L. G. Steele, [1892]); published simultaneously as *In the Midst of Life* (London: Chatto & Windus, 1892; revised and enlarged edition, New York & London: Putnam's, 1898);

Black Beetles in Amber (San Francisco & New York: Western Authors Publishing, 1892);

Can Such Things Be? (New York: Cassell, 1893; London: Cape, 1926);

Fantastic Fables (New York & London: Putnam's, 1899);

Shapes of Clay (San Francisco: W. E. Wood, 1903);

The Cynic's Word Book (New York: Doubleday, Page, 1906); enlarged as *The Devil's Dictionary*, volume 7 of *The Collected Works of Ambrose Bierce* (New York & Washington: Neale, 1911);

A Son of the Gods and A Horseman in the Sky (San Francisco: Elder, 1907);

The Shadow on the Dial and Other Essays, edited by S. O. Howes (San Francisco: A. M. Robertson, 1909); revised and republished as *Antepenultimata*, volume 11 of *The Collected Works of Ambrose Bierce* (New York & Washington: Neale, 1912);

Write It Right (New York & Washington: Neale, 1909);

Ambrose Bierce (courtesy of the Alderman Library, University of Virginia)

The Collected Works of Ambrose Bierce, 12 volumes (New York & Washington: Neale, 1909-1912)—1) *Ashes of the Beacon, The Land Beyond the Blow, For the Ahkoond, John Smith, Liberator, Bits of Autobiography;* 2) *In the Midst of Life;* 3) *Can Such Things Be?, The Ways of Ghosts, Soldier-Folk, Some Haunted Houses;* 4) *Shapes of Clay, Some Antemortem Epitaphs, The Scrap Heap;* 5) *Black Beetles in Amber, The Mummery, On Stone;* 6) *The Monk and the Hangman's Daughter, Fantastic Fables, Aesopus Emendatus, Old Saws with New Teeth, Fables in Rhyme;* 7) *The Devil's Dictionary;* 8) *Negligible Tales, The Parenticide Club, The Fourth Estate,*

The Ocean Wave, "On with the Dance!," Epi-
grams; 9) *Tangential Views;* 10) *The Opiniona-*
tor, The Reviewer, The Controversialist, The Tim-
orous Reporter, The March Hare; 11) *Ante-*
penultimata; 12) *In Motley, Kings of Beasts, Two*
Administrations, Miscellaneous;

Battlefields and Ghosts, edited by Hartley E. Jackson and James D. Hart (Palo Alto, Cal.: Harvest Press, 1931);

Selections from Prattle by Ambrose Bierce, edited by
Carroll D. Hall (San Francisco: Book Club
of California, 1936);

Enlarged Devil's Dictionary, edited by Ernest J. Hopkins (Garden City: Doubleday, 1967);

The Ambrose Bierce Satanic Reader, edited by Hopkins (Garden City: Doubleday, 1968);

Ambrose Bierce–Skepticism and Dissent: Selected Jour-
nalism from 1898-1901, edited by Lawrence
I. Berkove (Ann Arbor, Mich.: Delmas,
1980).

OTHER: *Mark Twain's Library of Humor,* contains
contributions by Bierce (New York: Webster,
1888);

Richard Voss, *The Monk and the Hangman's Daugh-*
ter, translated by Gustav Adolf Danziger, revised by Bierce (Chicago: Schulte, 1892).

Bierce, circa 1870 (courtesy of the Bancroft Library,
University of California, Berkeley)

Within the last two decades Ambrose Bierce
has begun to attract the scholarly attention his
work deserves. For example, Brigid Brophy remarked in 1973 that those who were ignorant of
literary history were hailing postmodern writers
for their startling innovations, unaware of the
fact that Bierce had done–and done better–the
same kind of thing a century ago. Brophy's
aperçu holds not only for Bierce's fiction but for
his methodological works as well. Thus the distinction between criticism and literary theory which
is so marked a feature of the contemporary intellectual scene is one that Bierce had already
made. Since he eschewed the former to concentrate on the latter at a time when it had not yet become a flourishing industry, his writings on that
subject attracted little attention in his own day.
Now, however, it is time to recognize the sound
theoretical basis on which Bierce's short stories
are discussed by such modern writers as Carlos
Fuentes, Brophy, Jorge Luis Borges, Julio
Cortázar, and Ryunosuke Akutagawa.

Ambrose Gwinnett Bierce was born to Marcus Aurelius and Laura Sherwood Bierce in
Meigs County, Ohio, in 1842, but his family soon
moved to northern Indiana. His limited formal

schooling included a brief stint at the Kentucky
Military Institute, but it was his four years as a
Union soldier in the Civil War that constituted
his real education. An abolitionist even while he
was still in high school, he enlisted in 1861 as a private in the Ninth Indiana Infantry Regiment. His
promotion was rapid. By the time he was demobi-
lized in 1865 as a staff topographical officer–
after seeing frontline service in some of the most
famous battles of the war, including Shiloh,
Stones River, Chickamauga, and Kennesaw Mountain–he had achieved the rank of first lieutenant
(he was brevetted to major in 1867).

He considered and rejected professional
service in the army, then settled in San Francisco
to begin a journalistic career. By 1868 he had become an editor for the *San Francisco News Letter*
and California Advertiser, and by 1871 he was contributing his "Grizzly Papers" and other items to
Bret Harte's *Overland Monthly.* On 25 December
1871 he married Mary Ellen (Mollie) Day, and
the two went off to England for three years, from
1872 to 1875, where their first two children, Day
and Leigh, were born. Bierce immediately em-

barked on a successful journalistic career in London, writing for both *Fun* and *Figaro*. Under the pseudonym "Dod Grile" he also published his first three books in England, all of which were gleanings from his periodical writings: *The Fiend's Delight* (1873), *Nuggets and Dust Panned Out in California* (1873), and *Cobwebs from an Empty Skull* (1874). Mollie, whose life abroad was a good deal lonelier than her husband's, sailed for home with their two young sons in April 1875 for what was planned as a visit. She was pregnant, but Bierce, unaware of her condition, eagerly anticipated her return. When he learned that a third child was expected, however, he, too, left England. He arrived in San Francisco in early October, and the Bierces' only daughter, Helen, was born late that month.

Faced with the problem of earning a living, Bierce got a job in the United States Mint. But in 1877 he became associate editor of the *Argonaut;* and in the same year he and a friend, Thomas A. Harcourt, writing under the name "William Herman," published a hoax purporting to be an attack on the waltz, *The Dance of Death*. These activities were not very remunerative, however, and, in an effort to establish a sounder financial footing for his family, Bierce served a brief stint as manager of an ill-starred gold-mining company in the Dakota Territory. When this venture collapsed, he returned to San Francisco and became editor of the *Wasp*.

His personal life during the next few years was marked by tragedy. In 1888 he and Mollie separated, apparently because he had discovered some indiscreet letters an admirer had sent her. The next year an even heavier blow fell. Sixteen-year-old Day was killed, along with his rival, in a gun duel over a girl. In 1901 the second son, Leigh, a New York newspaperman, died of pneumonia; and in 1905 Ambrose and Mollie Bierce were finally divorced, after seventeen years of separation.

But Bierce's literary career had taken a dramatic leap forward in 1887 when he accepted a very inviting offer from the young William Randolph Hearst to join the staff of the powerful and respected *San Francisco Examiner*. From 1895 to 1898 he wrote several articles opposing Hearst's position on the Spanish-American problem. But he joined forces with his employer when Hearst sent him to Washington, D.C., in 1896 to head a lobby opposing congressional passage of Collis Huntington's funding bill for the Central and Southern Pacific railroads. The bill

was defeated, largely through Bierce's efforts, and he returned to San Francisco in 1896. His connection with Hearst, in one capacity or another, continued until 1909, when he resigned to devote full time to preparing his collected works.

He had continued to produce a stream of books composed of selections from his journalism. These included his famous short stories, which appeared eventually as *In the Midst of Life* (1892) and *Can Such Things Be?* (1893), as well as satirical verse, *Black Beetles in Amber* (1892) and *Shapes of Clay* (1903). *Fantastic Fables* appeared in 1899 and *The Shadow on the Dial*, a volume of essays edited by S. O. Howes, in 1909. *The Cynic's Word Book*, a collection of acerbic definitions, came out in 1906; it was revised and published under the title by which it is now known, *The Devil's Dictionary*, in *The Collected Works of Ambrose Bierce* (1909-1912). He also published a small volume on stylistics that is still valuable, *Write It Right*, which first appeared in 1909 and which has been republished many times. One of the most controversial of the volumes with which Bierce's name is associated was not really by him at all: *The Monk and the Hangman's Daughter* (1892), originally a short novel by Richard Voss, *Der Mönch von Berchtesgaden* (1891). A young German-Jewish dentist, Dr. Gustav Adolf Danziger (who later changed his name to Adolphe de Castro), made a rough translation of it which he brought to Bierce for improvement. Bierce rewrote the story from Danziger's manuscript; and, after appearing serially in 1891 in the *San Francisco Examiner*, it came out in book form in 1892. The only changes from Voss's original, however, were unimportant deletions and additions, plus an ironic conclusion. In 1902 Danziger signed over all his rights in the book to Bierce, who included it in his *Collected Works*, with a note indicating that credit really belonged to Voss.

No single volume of Bierce's writings was devoted to literary theory. But he wrote a number of essays on the subject which later appeared in *The Collected Works*, primarily in volume 10; and he implemented his ideas in his relations with other writers. On the West Coast, even before his association with Hearst, he had become a literary panjandrum who was eagerly sought out by young authors of middling talent: Charles Warren Stoddard, Gertrude Atherton, Herman Scheffauer, and George Sterling, among others. He was a born pedagogue and expended much time and energy in helping aspiring writers whom he deemed worthy of assistance. One of

4   THE WASP.

The Wasp

VOLUME XVI.   WHOLE NUMBER, 495.

SATURDAY, · · · · JANUARY 23, 1886.

PUBLISHED EVERY SATURDAY AT 53¾ CALIFORNIA ST. BY
THE WASP PUBLISHING CO.

TERMS TO SUBSCRIBERS :

One copy, one year, or 52 numbers · · · · $5 00
One copy, six months, or 26 numbers · · · · 2 50
One copy for thirteen weeks · · · · · · 1 25

Postage free to all parts of the United States, Canada
and British Columbia. To all other countries one dollar
per year extra. The country trade supplied by the San
Francisco News Company. All Postmasters are authorized
to take subscriptions for the WASP, payable invariably in
advance.

[Entered at the Postoffice at San Francisco for transmission
at second class rates.]

*No questionable advertisements will be inserted in this
journal on any terms.*

Mark Twain has been a funny man in his day,
and though the humor that once set thousands in a
roar has vanished with the poverty which Mark
joked away, a fond public is still unwilling to
believe that the jester is no more. We are sorry
for Mark the Jester and our grief is mingled with
disgust for those who will not let the ashes of the
dead clown be but persist in stirring them up in the
vain hope of evolving a latent spark. Foremost
among those desecrators of the tomb of Mark the
Jester is Mark the Money-worm. Aided and abetted
by the minions of the Associated Press, Mr. Samuel
Clemens takes his spade and dark lantern, hies him
to the burying ground and rattles the skeleton of
poor Mark Twain. His last atrocious desecration
was committed at the Typotheta dinner in New York
one evening of this week. Here is what the Associated Press conspirators say of the infamy :

At the Typotheta dinner last night Mark Twain made a
long and humorous speech, of which the following is
a sample : "The chairman's historical reminiscences about
Guttenberg and Caxton have cast me into the reminiscent
mood. For I also in a small way am an antiquity. I was
acquainted with the printer of the olden time. I swept
out his office for him and carried his papers about for him.
The carrier was then an object of interest to all the dogs
in the town. If I had saved up all the bites I ever received
I could keep M. Pasteur busy for a year."

"Of which the following is a sample." The irony
of those rascals cannot be repressed. They tele-
graph this mournful specimen over three thousand
miles as a sample. They should rather have called
it an epitaph, an indisputable proof
that Samuel Clemens, Esquire, of Hartford, Connecticut, was masquerading in the motley of Mark
Twain, a humorist erst of the Pacific Coast, who
departed this life some years back, and that S.
Clemens, Esq., was making a mighty poor fist of the
business.

Frank Pixley is recognized as a bright-witted man
who writes unusually well and who has a happy
knack of clothing his somewhat eccentric ideas in
pleasant language. Like most men of his order
of genius Mr. Pixley is not averse to notoriety, of
that respectable sort of course which has its origin
in the fact of doing odd things. Therefore when
Mr. Pixley says one thing in his paper one week
and makes a contradictory assertion the next, the
public having been instructed by this remarkable
person himself that he is deficient in sincerity, contents itself with admiring Mr. Pixley's versatility.
Therefore when last week Mr. Pixley denounced
Dr. O'Donnell and republished the crank coroner's
most incendiary sentences, Mr. Pixley's readers

remembered that the very doctrine that gentleman
so vigorously denounced was published in the
Argonaut at so much a line, making that journal a
supplement as it were to the sand-lot and imploring
its readers to get their bombs ready and blow the
Chinese to atoms. It is not fair therefore to cast
stones at the incendiary goose which dropped so
many golden eggs into Mr. Pixley's till. It is
ingratitude of the darkest stripe to assail O'Donnell
for sentiments which Mr. Pixley set before his
thousands of readers for their conversion to dyna-
mite doctrine.

When William Redmond, M. P., talked about
the Russians stabling their horses in the House of
Commons unless Parnell's demands were acceded to
he was committing himself to bosh and no doubt
got rapped over the knuckles by his leader for the
offense. The Home Rulers are entitled to the fullest
sympathy for the gallant struggle they have made
against big odds, but Mr. Redmond's nonsense is of
that character which disgusts those who wish his
party well. Not the least difficult part of Parnell's
management must be the repression of excitable
young orators of Redmond's stripe, who, to be
slangy, must shoot their mouths off when they get
before an audience or burst.

A soldier at the Presidio has confessed that he
painted two hundred pictures in 1885, of which all
were sold with the exception of five or six. This
must be melancholy reading for the professionals
who have not an artilleryman's pay to depend upon
and who must knock down paint and canvas to the
highest bidder or bar their doors against the land-
lord and dye their beards to escape the scrutiny of
the grocer and butcher. The way of the artist is
hard in this city and how so many hang on to such
a profitless profession is an evidence of the fascination that art possesses for its votaries. Yet house-
building goes on, but the people who make homes
for themselves confine their art-longings for the
most part to chromos and engravings. And for the
most part they show their taste and good sense.
For this State can boast of some of the vilest daubers
who ever mixed colors, men who would be better
and more properly employed whitewashing fences
than libeling unprotected nature on canvas. We
have a few good painters, but even those few have
to resort to art-auctions to struggle along. And
nothing is so demoralizing to the artist as the
auction. He begins we will say in January to paint
for an auction in April. His motto is quantity not
quality. He knows that his pictures must be up to
a certain standard, but that certain standard is
usually a low one. There is no time for fine finish,
no time to correct errors or heighten effects. He
trusts to the glib auctioneer to fill in the blanks and
work upon the art-ignorance of the average picture-
buyer. This military artist states that he has
received $400 for his two hundred pictures during
the year. This at the rate of $2 per painting is an
acknowledgment of the modesty of the painter.
And without knowing anything about his work we
venture the opinion they were probably quite as
good as those the auctioneer knocks down for $10 and
$20 (exclusive of frame) at those much-advertised
sales.

The Signal Service people are happy no matter
how the granger and the rest of the world may
growl. When the red flag went up on the Merchants' Exchange Tuesday the old mariners sneered
and protested as they have often done before that
the storm-prophets were away out of their reckoning
this time. But when Wednesday's gale set in and
the rain poured and signs came clattering down and
branches of trees were wrenched off and ships
plunged and tugged at their moorings and umbrellas
were twisted inside out and town and harbor were

ravaged by the fierce blast, the Signal Service men
laughed and knew that for once they had earned
their salaries.

"An autopsy was made yesterday on the body of
William Lewis, who was stabbed New Year's night
by Frank Fabre." "Matthew T. Eddy, who was
shot in the abdomen last Sunday night, died last
evening from the effects of the wound." "David P.
Mish was killed last night by Dr. McDonald.'
These are extracts from one of Wednesday's morning
papers. Can we complain if the Eastern journals
point to San Francisco as a city noticeable for the
frequency of its shooting and stabbing affrays? We
are building new houses, making handsome improve-
ments everywhere, establishing universities, pro-
gressing in almost every channel but this single and
most important one of law and order. In the early
days when the Vigilance Committee took upon itself
to purify the town and give the murderer short
shrift, the laxity of the laws was the apology for its
existence. Crimes of violence are now more prevalent than in those times even with our increase of
population considered. It is no use concealing the
unpleasant truth. This city is in a bad way in this
regard. The man who ponders upon a bloody
reprisal for a real or imaginary wrong knows that
his chances of escape from punishment are as ten to
one against his conviction. Meanwhile Christian
associations, bands of holiness, churches and religious organizations of all kinds flourish. We are
working up a grand superficial piety, but not strong
enough to hide the smoke of the murderer's pistol
or the blood-stains on the assassin's knife.

At this, the close of the third week of the year,
we call attention in all due modesty to the improved
appearance of the *Wasp*, pictorially and typograph-
ically. In changing the form of our pages from two
to three columns we also introduced a new dress of
type which gives a clearer and better impression
than the old and is more attractive to the eye of the
reader. To our cartoons we have added two colors,
making five in all, and no cartoon paper on the
continent employs more, while nearly all of those
west of New York are satisfied with three. Those
five colors give an artistic value and finish to
our pictures, apart from their topical interest.
Our cartoon on the silver question has made the
biggest hit of any picture ever presented by the
Wasp. Though issued two weeks ago we are in
constant receipt of demands for the edition in which
it appeared, an evidence of its popularity in delineating the true significance of this important question.
Our representatives in Washington were each furnished with a copy and expressed themselves highly
gratified with the cartoon and congratulated the
Wasp upon having made a stronger presentation
of the case than any of those illustrated journals who
attempted it. In view of these things we may be
excused for referring to the promise made at the
opening of the year, as a promise fulfilled.

The reporter seeking a sensation will brook no
obstacle. If he is instructed to see the man who
shot his wife, and interview him, and he finds that
there is no murdered wife to grow pathetic over, or
no low-browed, villainous-looking murderer to de-
nounce, he feels like a falcon cheated of his sparrow,
and would incite the swindler to slaughter his wife
if he dared. A few days ago the *Chronicle* insisted
that a little boy in Oakland had been clubbed to
death by his playmate, the doctors certificate to the
contrary. To please the reporter the coroner ex-
humed the body, and the autopsians found the child
had died from natural causes. The question now is
has the coroner won the *Chronicle's* favor by com-
plying with its sensational demands, or will that
journal hate the official because the boy's skull was
unfractured.

Pages from the San Francisco newspaper featuring Bierce's column "Prattle"

PRATTLE.

An old hen named Kate Sanborn has laid a literary egg entitled, *The Vanity and Insanity of Genius*, and all the cockerel "critics" of the country are cackling in its praise. I have not read the thing—God forbid!—but a critical capon all over bejoyed of the performance says, in a local newspaper, that he has "gathered a mass of anecdotes in regard to famous men of all ages, to bear out her theory that there is a very narrow line between genius and insanity"—which gives me all the knowledge of the matter that I want. Her theory indeed! as if it had not been the conviction of every living value dullard from Adam to Job—a conviction so rooted in their bones, so nourished by their envy and bearing such fruit of comfort to their peasant souls that it has served them in place of a religion. When was it not true that he by blockheads was accounted mad who spoke after a fashion that themselves could not understand, challenged the reports of their eyeless observation or disputed the things they thought their thoughts, parroted from one another through centuries of unexamining acceptance?

These paunchpates digestionless have for generations been quoting in their support the assurance of a famous poet that "great wits to madness nearly are allied"—or as we should say to-day, "great abilities" or "talents." Did he mean what they think? Naturally no, for he had himself greater wits than any man living. He was affirming the thinness of the division between reason and unreason, and he put it as strongly as he could, as if he had said—as doubtless he would have said had his meter permitted: "*Even* great wits to madness nearly are allied." How much closer, then, the kinship of little wits. Suppose I write:

Man's works are leveled to the plain at last,
Strong towers, crumbling, fall before the blast—

Must Sir Blockhead take me to mean that strong towers are alone unstable, and feeble ones exempt from decay? May I be buried face downward if I am not fatigued of all fools!

Mad, quoth'a! The only man who is not altogether mad is he who is not altogether destitute of genius. What *is* genius? A thousand definitions have been made. I shall attempt none, yet I think I can help all but the blockheads to an understanding of the matter. In the first place, I believe it to be in some degree a very common faculty. There are few, I fancy, but have been at times conscious of having solved a problem, struck out a bright thought or hit upon a felicitous expression, by some lightning process altogether unlike those customary methods whose deliberate action enables us to trace and record their steps—a process which takes the mind to its mark with as straight and incomprehensible a certainty as the flight of a homing pigeon. In most of us this is a rare phenomenon; in many it never occurs. Many experience but do not mark. But the man to whom this straight and sure process is habitual; in whom it is the natural and customary mental mode; who gets to his conclusions without the help of premises; who, like a master of the rifle, hits his mark without sighting; who is right automatically, he knows not how,—him we call, distinctively, a genius, particularly if his gift display itself in those things which arrest attention and address our sympathies, as art, literature and war.

There are those who deny that there is such a thing as genius, as there are men born blind who, under the same circumstances, would deny that there is such a thing as color. There is genius; it is not a debatable question, for though he who

affirms may know, he who denies cannot be shown. It is no "faculty divine" but a perfectly natural intellectual method or process, though not subject to analysis. By means of it, its possessor may know things without having learned them. It may not be true that Homer instructed the brickmakers how to make bricks, nor the cobbler how to mend sandals. Possibly Lord Brougham did not teach the brewers a trick worth knowing in making beer, but the currency of such anecdotes in all ages attest a truth that is obvious and all literature is full of its illustrations. How did Dickens know the horrors of solitary confinement—not that it is horrible; that we all know; but exactly in what way, succession and order certain emotional feelings assail the sufferer. His description of this kind of torture has been verified by hundreds who have endured it. Yet it is known that he did not derive it from the poor wretch by whose fate it was suggested, nor from anything but his "inner consciousness." How came it that Hugo, a civilian who had never seen a battle, related the story of Waterloo as never battle-story was related before. No soldier can read it with an even pulse; the spirit of battle is in every line; and that is not true of any other prose description of any other battle. Where are the countless other annalists of the gigantic struggle? what has become of their work? Consumed utterly in the conflagration of Hugo's genius. And at this day, in this distant land, there is exhibited to enthusiastic hundreds of thousands a panorama of the fight at Waterloo, where you will see nothing but was painted from Hugo's imagination and hear nothing but the words in which he set down his vision. I confess the pronunciation of most of the proper names is not Hugo's.

I am persuaded that in genius only is perfect mental health. In sickness we are conscious of our condition; the well man thinks not how well he is—counts not his pulse-beats, notes not the action of his lungs, nor by dyspepsia is forced to think of digestion. All his organs perform their offices unthought on. But for sickness, there had been no physiology; but for mental disability, no logic. The mind conscious of its own methods is making a record of symptoms. "I have a liver," says the poor devil yellowing all over with jaundice. "Man has a mind," says the philosopher; and so keen is the preacher's consciousness of this pestering possession that he considers it the sole verity of his existence and expects to endure it forever—as a dyspeptic might affirm the immortality of the stomach, whereas the man of sane digestion would not know he had a stomach unless told. When you can trace the workings of your mind it is because it is working badly. The supple joints of the healthy reason do not squeak. The carrier pigeon takes note of mountain headland and river is lost.

"Well, genius is vain and conceited, anyhow," saith Blocktop. May I never live to be a doddering and imbecile old man if this be not stupidity divine! It was vanity, was it, Gutbrains, when Shakespeare began one of his immortal sonnets:

Not marble, not the gilded monuments
Of princes shall outlive this powerful rhyme.

It would have been vanity in a blockhead; it would conceitedly have introduced a feeble and ephemeral rhyme. It was conceit, was it, Smirkface—the superb unconcern with which Heine answered one of your kind who had assailed him in a newspaper: "I am to be tried in the assizes of literature. I know who I am." It would have been conceit in *you*, Slushwump.

A man brags of his ancestors without offense and bedaubs all his belongings, to the very collar of his

dog, with the visible assertion of his illustrious descent. Your host at dinner is warm in praise of his own wine, and you think it a mighty pretty weakness. I'll be roasted whole if I know why a man having genius should not speak of it! Out with it, Brother Pixley, out with it. *End of the discourse on Genius.*

By careless omission of the words "at Bull Run," last week, my statement that Generals Beauregard and Johnston both "claimed the chief command" was a trifle indefinite, but I trust the *Wasp* has not a reader who did not supply the missing words from his own knowledge and reading. To be ignorant of anything about the civil war—not to know accurately how any considerable event occurred, *both ways*—would be ignorance indeed in these days when every old soldier is in his anecdotage. This business of being an old soldier is overdone: its growth threatens to swallow up every other industry in the country. That is not the worst of it. It will not do to say that the old soldiers fought better than they talk, for most of them talk pretty well, and many didn't fight; but it is certain that the fighting did a deal more good than the talking. These battle yarns, indeed, are nursing a bably war, which now lies mouthing its fat knuckles and marking time with its pinky feet, in a cradle of young imaginations, but in another decade it will be striding through the land in seven-league boots, chewing soap. Every generation must have its war; that is a law of nature; but if the younkers who are now tucking out their mental skins with the gingery comestible supplied by old soldiers do not kick up a shindy compared with which the late war was a season of religious tranquility you may have my share of the national debt.

O Young Men's Christian Association,
  I'd really like to be told—
If the question meets your approbation—
  At what age a young man grows old.

For twenty years I have watched your members—
  Well stricken in years at first—
Bending beneath successive Decembers,
  Like Struldbrugs old and accurst.

Ponce de Leon in Florida's wildwood
  Searched for the Fountain of Youth;
Do you think that you in second childhood
  Have found it, in very truth!

And tell me, pray, another thing, never
  Clearly by me understood:
To wit—at what time of life, if ever,
  Young Christians begin to be good.

We shall at last have a newspaper in San Francisco that is worth reading: a local contemporary has promised us something from the pen of a lady who, the editor assures us, is "a star that pulsates in the heaven of the soul, now exploring the abysmal depths, now soaring in the empyrean of space, urged by the restless fires of feeling and impulse." That's all very well, neighbor; she may pulsate undisturbed in the heaven of your soul, and explore your abysmal depths—which, I take it, is to do pretty much the same thing; but let me catch sight of her soaring in the empyrean of this paper and I'll fill her so full of shot that she'll never dare to swim a creek. If I don't I'm a goat.

My good friends, please don't say, any more, that Clerk McCarthy "got up and dusted." If you *will* use slang, use it with some relevancy to the facts. Our embezzlers all go across the water to Honolulu now. Mr. McCarthy got up and spattered.

It seems to be the prevailing opinion that if Germany holds on to the Samoan Islands an acorn should be planted at once to produce the keel of a first-class man-of-war.

AMBROSE BIERCE LITERARY DISSECTOR
The terror of aspiring bards of the wild and woolly West.

Caricature of Bierce which appeared in the Wasp *in the early 1890s*

the most poignant of these episodes involved his care in tutoring a deprived young deaf woman of eager ambition but no great ability, Lily Walsh, who died before she was able to achieve much in response to his friendly encouragement.

He was particularly interested in the work of promising poets. Of these, Sterling was undoubtedly closest to him personally; yet late in life Bierce also did what he could to further the career of one whose fame would eventually far overshadow Sterling's: Ezra Pound. Although Bierce never met the poet, Pound's father sent him some manuscripts written by his talented son, including "Ballad of the Goodly Fere." Bierce realized that any modern ballad must of necessity be an imitation of what was once for primitive people a natural form, but he was much impressed by Pound's poem. His letters to friends in 1910 praising the ballad and his attempts to get it published in the United States before it was withdrawn reveal him to have been one of the earliest of those who recognized Pound's genius.

As Bierce's fame grew, however, the authors who approached him, including H. L. Mencken, were motivated more by admiration for his own writing than by a desire to get help with theirs. Among these critics were Brander Matthews, Hamlin Garland, William Dean Howells, and, especially, Percival Pollard. But their interest in his work was not always reciprocated, for reasons which become clear in the light of literary history.

Bierce lived and wrote during the period when realism, with its emphasis on the sublunary events of everyday life, was at its height. Howells—who considered Bierce one of the six leading men of letters in America—was the foremost avatar of this movement. Bierce, however, detested realism. Some of his arguments against it were soon to be taken up by the naturalists. He believed that Howells and his followers tried to make the usual happenings in the lives of usual people the basis of probability in their fiction even though admittedly they dealt with not what actually happened but what might happen. On the other hand, they did not go so far as to address the strange and the unusual, for fictional purposes, even when they found it in fact. Thus their "realism" was an extremely circumscribed one. They based their fiction on "life," then equated life not with the whole range of human experience but with a narrow and prosaic segment of it: the ordered and routine phases in the existence of persons who normally led ordered and routine lives. The bizarre and the exotic were rigidly excluded. Bierce frequently pointed out that many strange happenings occurred which were not utilized by the writers who supposedly were basing their fiction on fact. He cited, for example, the case of an ingenious suicide which actually occurred at a San Francisco wharf, but which would have been rejected by the realists as violently improbable ("The Short Story"). Although his arguments on this score would have been welcomed by writers such as Frank Norris and Theodore Dreiser, Bierce was not a naturalist. Nor, despite his admiration for Edgar Allan Poe and Nathaniel Hawthorne, was he a romantic. Rather, he belonged to a movement more or less contemporaneous with realism and naturalism which literary historians have only recently begun to analyze: impressionism, whose tenets he shared with Henry James and Anton Chekhov. It must be confessed, however, that he himself mistakenly equated James with Howells, without seeming to have read much of James's work. There is no indication that he was familiar with Chekhov at all. Consequently the traits he shared with them must be attributed to a common reaction to their zeitgeist rather than to a cross-fertilization of ideas.

Impressionism, as interpreted by Bierce, rested on epistemological foundations directly contravening those of both the realists and even the naturalists. Instead of representing a stable, objective reality—however broadly it was conceived—the impressionists believed that any external object or event could be known only through the awareness of a perceiver. Since different perceivers might have different perceptions, the external world—what Thomas Carlyle and Ralph Waldo Emerson called the "NOT ME"—would appear different to different people.

Moreover, not only external objects and events, but the very forms through which intelligence operates—space and time—were also in a constant state of flux and varied with the interpreter. Consequently a period of time which

passed very quickly for one person could stretch out enormously for another. Bierce presented this idea theoretically in "The Chair of Little Ease," where he noted that an "unnatural exaltation of the senses" might commute a moment "into unthinkable cycles of time." The slowing up of subjective time might also be accompanied by the expansion or contraction of space, depending upon the perceptions of an observer. In Bierce's famous story "An Occurrence at Owl Creek Bridge," which first appeared in the *San Francisco Examiner* on 13 July, 1890, these theoretical ideas bore their remarkable fruit. Still another impressionistic tenet Bierce used repeatedly was what today is called the "epiphany," or the sudden flash of insight by which an individual reorients the gestalt of his surroundings and perceives both his situation and his own character with a profundity which may have shattering psychological consequences.

Perhaps the most complex of Bierce's theories was his attitude toward determinism, which must be distinguished from that of the naturalists. Although writers such as Norris and Dreiser believed in determinism—as did Bierce—their interpretation was simplistic, since in their hands it meant simply that men and women were uncontrollably buffeted by the dictates of their heredity (primarily their instincts) and their environment. Bierce, however, combined determinism with a belief in the ability of the individual to direct the course of his own affairs. Although Jonathan Edwards in 1754 had proved how this might be so in his monumental *Freedom of the Will*, his major contribution to the history of ideas has been neglected. Both his views and Bierce's anticipate those of the Nobel Prize-winning psychobiologist Roger Sperry, who in *Science and Moral Priority* (1983) demonstrated on scientific grounds not only the irrefutable arguments for determinism but also its necessary compatibility with self-determination. On this issue, therefore, as on many others, modern analytical tools have been required in order to appreciate Bierce's position. Consequently the scholar must note not only Bierce's affirmation, in his story "One of the Missing," of that eternally "wondrous mosaic" which constitutes the harmonious pattern of a great design, but also his endorsement of the moral self-determination by which an individual's character directs the way he thinks and feels, makes crucial choices, and acts at decisive points in his life. This complex amalgam underlies Bierce's criticism of Leo Tolstoy's *War and Peace*

Bierce (right) and San Francisco poet Herman Scheffauer (courtesy of Oscar Lewis)

(1864-1869). According to Bierce, Tolstoy "sees everything, but he has not freed his mind from the captivating absurdity, so dominant in the last generation, that human events occur without human agency, individual will counting for no more in the ordering of affairs than does a floating chip in determining the course of the river" ("The Kreutzer Sonata," 1890).

One other aspect of his literary theory that was not in conformity with the dominant trends of Bierce's time was his preference for wit over humor. A contemporary of Mark Twain (Samuel Clemens), one of America's greatest humorists, Bierce approached nonserious literature from a perspective in radical contrast to that of Twain. Stating his conception of the difference between wit and humor, he indicated that "humor is tolerant, tender; its ridicule caresses. Wit stabs, begs pardon–and turns the weapon in the wound. Humor is a sweet wine, wit a dry." We laugh at humor; wit makes us wince. It is "not altogether true, and therefore not altogether dull, with just enough of audacity to startle and just enough of paradox to charm, profoundly wise, as bleak as steel" ("Wit and Humor," 1903). Bierce himself regarded Twain as the leading exponent of humor. Since Twain clearly failed to understand the very different tradition in which Bierce was writing, it is not surprising that he failed to appreciate Bierce's early *Nuggets and Dust*, characterizing it

in a letter which has recently come to light as paying too high a price for every laugh with "five blushes, ten shudders and a vomit."

Although it is easy to find practitioners of American humor, those who prefer wit constitute a much smaller group. Indeed, the only other practitioners who come to mind are Benjamin Franklin (in his bagatelles), H. L. Mencken (a friend and admirer of Bierce's), and Thomas Szasz, the contemporary psychiatric philosopher who was born in Hungary and who acknowledges his debt to Bierce in the preface to *The Second Sin* (1973). Some of the best examples of wit ever penned are found in Bierce's own work: his epigrams, his fables, and most notably his famous *Devil's Dictionary*. When he looked to other writers for examples, however, he had to roam far afield, turning to François Rabelais and François La Rochefoucauld.

Given his nonconformity with the dominant trends of his time, it is not surprising that Bierce took a dim view of what he called "literary criticism," by which he meant the frequently ephemeral judgments of more or less professional book reviewers who represented the establishment attitudes of the day. For Bierce, their criticism had five chief faults: lack of critical standards; the tendency to praise out of all proportion to their intrinsic worth the writings of contemporaries; the proclivity toward evaluating an author's work in the light of his personal life; the propensity to read a moral purpose into literature; and the disposition to consider certain types of writing as the exclusive possession of their most familiar and most eminent exponents.

A clever illustration of Bierce's attitude toward "literary criticism" which at the same time embodies his theories of wit can be found in his fable "A Faulty Performance":

> A pet Opossum belonging to a Great Critic stole his favorite kitten and was about to kill and eat it when she saw him approaching, and fearing detection she concealed it in her pouch.
>
> "Well, my pretty one," said the Great Critic, with condescension, "what new charms and graces have you to-day?"
>
> Before she could reply the kitten set up a diligent and persistent mewing. When at last the music had ceased the Opossum said:
>
> "I've been dabbling a little in mimicry and ventriloquism; I thought it would please you, sir."
>
> "The desire to please is ever pleasing," the Great Critic answered, not without a touch of professional dignity, "but you have much to learn about the mewing of kittens."

Nevertheless, although he derided literary critics and did not consider himself one of their number, Bierce did develop a consistent and cohesive body of literary theory, which he applied in his own work and which he called "the art of literature." Books were merely its result. And he was concerned over the fact that the English language had only one word, *literature*, to cover both the art and the product—the process of writing and the things written. He believed that "the art of literature" was based on universal principles, used by the great masters of the past, including the great critics, which the writer might learn by studying their works and which he could himself then apply to advantage. Bierce defended the empiric basis of the theories he upheld; they were not a priori rules but organic principles which could be derived from an analytical study of recognized masterpieces.

He viewed art as the most significant of all human activities. There was a fundamental unity among its various branches. Despite this unity, however, the arts existed in a hierarchy, with literature the most eminent and the most difficult. Among the literary arts he awarded the palm to poetry (he did not consider himself a poet, despite his considerable production of verse). Next below poetry he ranked the short story. Then

came the romance, as exemplified by the writings of Hawthorne, Victor Hugo, and Sir Walter Scott. At the bottom of his hierarchy was the novel, whose exemplar was William Dean Howells. It would be difficult to exaggerate the disdain with which Bierce regarded the novel, but it must be remembered that he equated it with realism. An extended work of narrative prose fiction not bound by the strictures of realism he called—following Hawthorne—the romance. Although he wrote none himself, the romance was a form he admired, repeatedly pointing out its distinguishing features and noting that "in form [it] so resembles the novel that many otherwise worthy persons are but dimly aware of the essential distinction" ("The Novel").

Certain features of Bierce's theories on the art of literature can be traced to his impressionistic orientation. His emphasis on the primacy of the perceiving mind led him to value literary imagination over strict fidelity to external reality. As he said in *The Devil's Dictionary*, "the first three essentials of the literary art are imagination, imagination, and imagination." Dreams, Bierce believed, were a useful literary property since, as he said in "Visions of the Night," they were a valuable adjunct to imagination. The fact that Bierce believed imagination played a greater role in poetry than in narrative prose fiction was the criterion that led him to place poetry at the top of his literary hierarchy. The short story, since it does not "cloy attention, confuse with overlaid impressions and efface its own effect" ("The Short Story"), was ranked above long narratives. But of the latter, the romance, which possessed both permanency and universality, was far superior to the novel, since "nothing that can be known, or thought, or felt, or dreamed, but is available [to the romanticist] if he can manage it" ("The Novel").

Bierce's emphasis on the importance of the imagination—"that supreme and almost sufficient literary endowment"—did not exhaust his interest in the writer, however. He felt that the author should not only be mentally and morally superior to the rest of humankind but should enrich his experience with suffering and sorrow. And finally the writer should attain skill in the technical aspects of literary craftsmanship. Consequently hard work was a necessary ingredient of artistic success. Above all else the writer must be a master of language. Bierce declared, in a statement which presages the contemporary concern with the importance of language on the part of such writers as Szasz and Michel Foucault, that "the fight against faulty diction is a fight against insurgent barbarism–a fight for high thinking and right living–for art, science, power–in a word, civilization." He then added: "We think in words; we can not think without them. Shallowness or obscurity of speech means shallowness or obscurity of thought" ("The Matter of Manner").

In 1899 Bierce left San Francisco for the East, where he lived in Washington, D.C., until 1913. In October of that year, having completed his collected works and wound up his personal affairs, he left the capital for what he clearly intended to be a rendezvous with death. At age seventy-one his thoughts were turning with increasing nostalgia to the battle scenes of his youth where he had fought, he wrote in a letter, in a "Dream-land," a "Realm of Adventure, inhabited by [beckoning] memories." Consequently he decided to attach himself as a military observer to the revolutionary forces of Pancho Villa, who was leading a popular insurrection in Mexico against a reactionary government. After a leisurely tour of his old Civil War battlefields Bierce made his way to El Paso, Texas, where he crossed the border to Juarez on his way to join Villa's guerrillas. His last letter, dated 26 December, was from Chihuahua. In it he stated that he intended to go to Ojinaga the next day. Despite the numerous fanciful accounts of what happened thereafter–the most recent being Carlos Fuentes's novel *The Old Gringo* (1985)–the present consensus of scholars is that, although the evidence is circumstantial, Ambrose Bierce was almost certainly killed in the battle of Ojinaga on 11 January 1914.

Letters:

The Letters of Ambrose Bierce, edited by Bertha Clark Pope (San Francisco: Book Club of California, 1922);

M. E. Grenander, "Seven Ambrose Bierce Letters," *Yale University Library Gazette*, 32 (July 1957): 12-18;

Grenander, "Ambrose Bierce and Charles Warren Stoddard: Some Unpublished Correspondence," *Huntington Library Quarterly*, 23 (May 1960): 261-292;

J. V. Ridgely, "Ambrose Bierce to H. L. Mencken," *Book Club of California Quarterly News Letter*, 26 (Fall 1961): 27-33.

Bibliographies:

Vincent Starrett, *Ambrose Bierce, A Bibliography*

(Philadelphia: Centaur Book Shop, 1929);

Joseph Gaer, ed., *Ambrose Gwinett* [sic] *Bierce, Bibliography and Biographical Data* (N.p., 1935);

M. E. Grenander, "Au Coeur de la vie: a French Translation of Ambrose Bierce," *Boston University Studies in English*, 1 (Winter 1955-1956): 237-241;

Grenander, "Ambrose Bierce, John Camden Hotten, *The Fiend's Delight*, and *Nuggets and Dust*," *Huntington Library Quarterly*, 28 (August 1965): 353-371;

Paul Fatout, "Ambrose Bierce (1842-1914)," *American Literary Realism, 1870-1910*, 1 (Fall 1967): 13-19;

Grenander, "Ambrose Bierce and *In the Midst of Life*," *Book Collector*, 20 (Autumn 1971): 321-331;

Grenander, "Ambrose Bierce and *Cobwebs from an Empty Skull*: A Note on BAL 1100 and 1107," *Papers of the Bibliographical Society of America*, 79 (Third Quarter 1975): 403-406.

Biographies:

Carey McWilliams, *Ambrose Bierce, A Biography* (New York: A. & C. Boni, 1929);

Paul Fatout, *Ambrose Bierce, the Devil's Lexicographer* (Norman: University of Oklahoma Press, 1951);

Fatout, *Ambrose Bierce and the Black Hills* (Norman: University of Oklahoma Press, 1956);

Richard O'Connor, *Ambrose Bierce, A Biography* (Boston: Little, Brown, 1967).

References:

Howard W. Bahr, "Ambrose Bierce and Realism," *Southern Quarterly*, 1 (July 1963): 309-331;

Lawrence I. Berkove, "Arms and the Man: Ambrose Bierce's Response to War," *Michigan Academician*, 1 (Winter 1969): 21-30;

Brigid Brophy, "A Literary History," in her *The Adventures of God in His Search for the Black Girl* (London: Macmillan, 1973; Boston: Little, Brown, 1974);

Cathy N. Davidson, *The Experimental Fictions of Ambrose Bierce: Structuring the Ineffable* (Lincoln: University of Nebraska Press, 1984);

Davidson, ed., *Critical Essays on Ambrose Bierce* (Boston: G. K. Hall, 1982);

Paul Fatout, "Ambrose Bierce, Civil War Topographer," *American Literature*, 26 (November 1954): 391-400;

Fatout, "Ambrose Bierce Writes about War," *Book*

Club of California Quarterly News Letter, 16 (Fall 1951): 75-79;

Wilson Follett, "Ambrose Bierce—An Analysis of the Perverse Wit that Shaped His Work," *Bookman*, 68 (November 1928): 284-289;

M. E. Grenander, *Ambrose Bierce* (New York: Twayne, 1971);

Grenander, "Ambrose Bierce Describes Swinburne," *Courier*, 14 (Fall 1977): 22-26;

Grenander, "Bierce's Turn of the Screw: Tales of Ironical Terror," *Western Humanities Review*, 11 (Summer 1957): 257-263;

Grenander, "California's Albion: Mark Twain, Ambrose Bierce, Tom Hood, John Camden Hotten, and Andrew Chatto," *Papers of the Bibliographical Society of America*, 72 (Fourth Quarter 1978): 455-475;

Grenander, " 'Five Blushes, Ten Shudders and a Vomit': Mark Twain on Ambrose Bierce's *Nuggets and Dust*," *American Literary Realism*, 17 (Autumn 1984): 169-179;

Grenander, "H. L. Mencken to Ambrose Bierce," *Book Club of California Quarterly Newsletter*, 22 (Winter 1956): 5-10;

Grenander, "A London Letter of Joaquin Miller to Ambrose Bierce," *Yale University Library Gazette*, 46 (October 1971): 109-116;

Carroll D. Hall, *Bierce and the Poe Hoax* (San Francisco: Book Club of California, 1934);

F. J. Logan, "The Wry Seriousness of 'Owl Creek Bridge,' " *American Literary Realism*, 10 (Spring 1977): 101-113;

Fred H. Marcus, "Film and Fiction: 'An Occurrence at Owl Creek Bridge,' " *California English Journal*, 7 (1971): 14-23;

Jay Martin, "Ambrose Bierce," in *The Comic Imagination in American Literature*, edited by Louis D. Rubin, Jr. (New Brunswick: Rutgers University Press, 1973), pp. 195-205;

Robert C. McLean, "The Deaths in Ambrose Bierce's 'Halpin Frayser,' " *Papers on Language and Literature*, 10 (Fall 1974): 394-402;

Carey McWilliams, Introduction to *The Devil's Dictionary* (New York: Sagamore Press, 1957), pp. v-xii;

H. L. Mencken, "Ambrose Bierce," in his *Prejudices, Sixth Series* (New York: Knopf, 1927), pp. 259-265;

Mencken, *A Book of Prefaces* (New York: Knopf, 1917);

Frank Monaghan, "Ambrose Bierce and the Authorship of *The Monk and the Hangman's Daughter*," *American Literature*, 2 (January 1931): 337-349;

Matthew C. O'Brien, "Ambrose Bierce and the Civil War: 1865," *American Literature*, 48 (November 1976): 377-381;

James W. Palmer, "From Owl Creek to *La Rivière du hibou*: The Film Adaptation of Bierce's 'An Occurrence at Owl Creek Bridge,' " *Southern Humanities Review*, 11 (Fall 1977): 363-371;

Lois Rather, *Bittersweet: Ambrose Bierce & Women* (Oakland, Cal.: Rather Press, 1975);

Eric Solomon, "The Bitterness of Battle: Ambrose Bierce's War Fiction," *Midwest Quarterly*, 5 (January 1964): 147-165;

William Bysshe Stein, "Bierce's 'The Death of Halpin Frayser': The Poetics of Gothic Consciousness," *ESQ: Emerson Society Quarterly*, 18 (Second Quarter 1972): 115-122;

Franklin Walker, *San Francisco's Literary Frontier* (New York: Knopf, 1939);

David R. Weimer, "Ambrose Bierce and the Art of War," in *Essays in Literary History*, edited by Rudolf Kirk and C. F. Main (New York: Russell & Russell, 1965);

Napier Wilt, "Ambrose Bierce and the Civil War," *American Literature*, 1 (November 1929): 260-285.

Papers:

The most important holdings of Ambrose Bierce's papers are in the Bancroft Library of the University of California, Berkeley; the Clifton Waller Barrett Collection at the University of Virginia; the University of Cincinnati; the Huntington Library in San Marino, California; the Berg Collection of the New York Public Library; the Division of Special Collections at Stanford University; the George Arents Research Library at Syracuse University; and the Beinecke Library of Yale University.

Hjalmar Hjorth Boyesen

(23 September 1848-4 October 1895)

Marc L. Ratner
California State University, Hayward

See also the Boyesen entry in *DLB 12, American Realists and Naturalists.*

BOOKS: *Gunnar: A Tale of Norse Life* (Boston: Osgood, 1874);

A Norseman's Pilgrimage (New York: Sheldon, 1875);

Tales from Two Hemispheres (Boston: Osgood, 1877);

Goethe and Schiller: Their Lives and Works (New York: Scribners, 1879);

Falconberg (New York: Scribners, 1879);

Ilka on the Hill-Top and Other Stories (New York: Scribners, 1881);

Queen Titania (New York: Scribners, 1881);

Idyls of Norway and Other Poems (New York: Scribners, 1882);

A Daughter of the Philistines (Boston: Roberts, 1883; London: Douglas, 1883);

The Story of Norway (New York & London: Putnam's, 1886; London: Low, 1886);

The Modern Vikings: Stories of Life and Sport in the Norseland (New York: Scribners, 1887; London: Low, 1887);

Vagabond Tales (Boston: Lothrop, 1889);

The Light of Her Countenance (New York: Appleton, 1889);

Against Heavy Odds: A Tale of Norse Heroism (New York: Scribners, 1890; London: Low, 1890);

The Mammon of Unrighteousness (New York: Lovell, 1891);

Essays on German Literature (New York: Scribners, 1892; London: Unwin, 1892);

Boyhood in Norway: Stories of Boy-Life in the Land of the Midnight Sun (New York: Scribners, 1892); republished as *The Battle of the Rafts: Boyhood in Norway* (London: Nelson, 1893);

The Golden Calf: A Novel (Meadville, Pa.: Flood & Vincent, 1892);

Social Strugglers: A Novel (New York: Scribners, 1893);

A Commentary on the Writings of Henrik Ibsen (New York & London: Macmillan, 1894; London: Heinemann, 1894);

Hjalmar Hjorth Boyesen

Literary and Social Silhouettes (New York: Harper, 1894);

Norseland Tales (New York: Scribners, 1894; London: Nelson, 1895);

Essays on Scandinavian Literature (New York: Scribners, 1895; London: Nutt, 1895).

PERIODICAL PUBLICATIONS: "Bjornson's Dramas," *North American Review*, 116 (January 1873): 109-138;

"Ibsen's Keiser og Galilaer," *Atlantic Monthly*, 34 (September 1874): 368-370;

"Tourgenieff," *Century*, 14 (June 1877): 200-207;

"Two Visits to Victor Hugo," *Century*, 19 (December 1879): 184-193;

"Bjornstjerne Bjornson," *Century*, 20 (July 1880): 336-345;

"A New Norwegian Novelist: Alexander Kielland," *Critic*, 2 (17 June 1882): 159-160;

"Social Problems in Norwegian Novels," *Critic*, 7 (19 September 1885): 133-134;

"On Howells' Work," *Cosmopolitan*, 12·(February 1892): 502-503;

"Ibsen's Treatment of Self-Illusion," *Dial*, 15 (16 September 1893): 137-140;

"On Tolstoi's Impersonal Novel," *Cosmopolitan*, 17 (August 1894): 506-507;

"The Evolution of the Heroine," *Lippincott's*, 54 (September 1894): 425-428;

"Two Humorists," *Cosmopolitan*, 18 (January 1895): 378-379;

"Great Realists and Empty Story-Tellers," *Forum*, 18 (February 1895): 724-731.

Considered by some critics as mainly an ardent advocate of the realistic approach to literature, Hjalmar Hjorth Boyesen's role as a scholar and critic of European literature is also significant. Boyesen was in many respects an anomaly among writers generally designated as realists in nineteenth-century American literature. He was a novelist whose first work in fiction derived from his Norwegian background and whose later work was in the stream of American realism; he was a poet whose verse was an expression of his evolutionary beliefs; and, overall, he was best known as a critic who directed American literary taste and interest to the great European realists.

Central to Boyesen's outlook as well as to his introspection was the fact that he was an emigrant from Norway. He was never totally at home in America and sometimes even saw himself as a transitional person never completely at home anywhere. In one sense he overcame his sense of separateness through the freer social structure of America, and except for a year spent in Chicago he was never deeply associated with Norse-American life. But his intellectual interests and connections with Norway, the rest of Scandinavia, and Europe generally deepened as his career continued. He became the pioneer critic and advocate of Henrik Ibsen and other Scandinavian writers in the United States, and he maintained a deep intellectual commitment toward Norwegian culture.

Boyesen was born in Fredriksvern in southern Norway on 23 September 1848 to Capt. and Mrs. Sarolf Boyesen. Probably because of his Swedenborgian beliefs, Captain Boyesen left the army in 1854 and spent a year in America, returning because of family pressure. It may be that his experience influenced his son, Hjalmar, who in 1869 left his home to join the millions of immigrants who came to the Unites States in the latter half of the nineteenth century.

After a year's stay in Urbana, Ohio, as a teacher, Boyesen went to Chicago to become editor of *Fremad* (1870-1871), a Norwegian newspaper in Chicago. Discontinued with the Midwest and the closed Norse community, which was dominated by the rigid Norse Lutheran Synod, Boyesen went east and in 1871 met William Dean Howells. Through Howells's connections Boyesen began a lifelong academic career as a professor of German, first at Cornell (1873-1880) and then later at Columbia University (1880-1895). Howells, then editor of the *Atlantic Monthly*, serialized Boyesen's first novel *Gunnar: A Tale of Norse Life* (1874), and the magazine's subsequent publication of Boyesen's short stories, criticism, and poetry started him on the career of which he had dreamed. In June 1878 Boyesen married Lillie Keen, who was from a wealthy Philadelphia family, and the couple honeymooned in Europe.

Boyesen brought with him a cultural and intellectual outlook markedly different from that of many of his American contemporaries who were promulgators of the realist approach to fiction. Though he shared aesthetic and social views with Howells and others, he also carried with him the seeds of European intellectual idealism, a theoretical, critical, and political viewpoint sometimes at variance with his American confreres.

The problem facing the intellectual immigrant is a recurring theme in Boyesen's work. Certainly the personal experience of adjustment to what he felt was the mediocrity and "barren, materialistic life on this side of the ocean," particularly in Ohio, his first home, was more or less solved for him by his escape to the literary and academic circles of the East. But many of his better short stories, such as "The Man Who Lost His Name" (1876), "Liberty's Victim" (1889), and "Harvest of Tares" (1893), as well as the novel, *Falconberg* (1879), reveal some of the difficulties and disappointments faced by many educated immigrants coming to America in the nineteenth century. His sense of being rootless in the United States and his feeling of separation from his past are described vividly in his essay "My Lost Self,"

(*Literary and Social Silhouettes,* 1894). Returning to Norway after twenty-three years he found that a "somnambulistic confusion of identity haunted me; I saw myself as I appeared to my lost self [his Norwegian self] and I viewed myself [as an American] with sentiments of mingled contempt and pity." In the mirror image of this view his American self saw his Norwegian self as a "simple-minded, patriotic little Cockney." This divided self lies at the center of Boyesen's consciousness of his expectations and hopes, personal and national, for American life, as well as his subsequent disillusion with the Gilded Age.

Despite Boyesen's musings about his "lost self," he ultimately shared, in his late thirties and forties, the best of both worlds through his criticism, scholarship, and teaching. His close associations with Howells and the American literary establishment and his extensive correspondence and interviews with Scandinavian and other European writers established an important role for Boyesen as an advocate of the new writers in Europe and as a liaison between them and the realists in the United States.

Though his earliest critical work, *Goethe and Schiller: Their Lives and Works* (1879), was not well received by the critics, Boyesen's discussions and analyses of the two parts of *Faust* are quite valuable in the light of his social and political views. Boyesen was a solid believer in the idea of social progress. In particular, for example, he viewed Faust's change in attitude in the second part of Goethe's play as a development from an individual to a social consciousness. This point of view about Faust's growth matches Boyesen's own changing critical attitudes; his earlier attachment to romanticism shifted to the scientific and social viewpoint popular in the late nineteenth century. Boyesen correlated this shift with a new function for the novel, whose purpose, he felt, was to clarify and encourage changes in human society. He wrote in *Literary and Social Silhouettes,* "The novel, as soon as it sets itself so serious an aim, is no longer an irresponsible play of fancy, however brilliant, but acquires an historical importance in relation to the age to which it belongs. The Germans are never weary of emphasizing what they call the cultural and historical meaning of novels, and it represents to me the final test by which a novelist is to be judged."

Such a quotation explains Boyesen's view that William Makepeace Thackeray was a realist, while Charles Dickens, with his "romantic sentimental view of life," was not; and it further clari-

Boyesen as a young man (courtesy of Columbia University Libraries)

fies his admiration for American writers like Howells, Hamlin Garland, Ed Howe, George Washington Cable, Harold Frederic, and Mark Twain. In writing about *Pudd'nhead Wilson* in 1895, Boyesen wrote, "the Missouri village . . . is so vividly realized in its minutest details; and the people, in all their fatuous prejudice and stolidity, are so credible and authentic, so steeped in the local atmosphere, that the illusion becomes perfect, and we swallow the melodrama without a qualm" ("Two Humorists"). Boyesen's accurate praise for Twain's novel is offset by his criticism of Henry James for being alienated from the national identity. Though such criticism clearly misses the point relative to many of James's perceptions of American characteristics, it does demonstrate Boyesen's critical view that the novel should have a political and social content.

Drawn as he was to novels which dealt with political and socioeconomic issues, Boyesen's critical and scholarly work has not always been appreciated as it should be. When he is remembered, it is probably because of an essay collected in *Literary and Social Silhouettes* entitled "The American Novelist and His Public." Here he attacks the "silence in American fiction of all the vital things in life." American writers, Boyesen argued, are obliged to repress their best work because "of that inexorable force called public taste," embodied in editors behind whom sits "the young American girl. She is the Iron Madonna who strangles in her fond embrace the American novelists. . . ." When, says Boyesen, "we read a novel like *Anna Karenina,* we appreciate, perhaps, the difference between a literature addressed to girls and a literature intended for men and women." In this essay Boyesen makes his strongest case for a reevaluation of literary tastes and critical judgments by citing the best American fiction, represented by Howells and the *Atlantic Monthly,* and comparing it to the rich and productive literatures of France, Germany, and Scandinavia. The best American writers, he believed, emulated those writers of Europe who were unafraid to deal with social and political subjects in their fiction. It is in this belief that Boyesen went even beyond Howells in his advocacy of realism.

In fact, it was Boyesen's role as a declaimer of the realists' credo, "the affirmation of our faith," as Howells put it when describing Boyesen's contribution, that was his major role. Boyesen thought of fiction as having a definite social and political purpose, and he practiced his preachings in his novels *The Mammon of Unrighteousness* (1891), *The Golden Calf* (1892), and *Social Strugglers* (1893).

In his major critical and scholarly works and in his abundance of literary articles (over seventy-five between 1871 and 1895), Boyesen reasserted the strong influence of Bjørnstjerne Bjørnson and Henrik Ibsen. In much of their work these writers emphasize social and political issues, a fact which appealed to Boyesen's views of literature and its value. *Essays on German Literature* (1892), *A Commentary on the Writings of Henrik Ibsen* (1894), and *Essays on Scandinavian Literature* (1895) are still valuable studies of the work of various authors, although they were written at a time when these writers were just being accepted by a wider public. These books, along with Boyesen's many articles and *Literary and Social Silhouettes,* are his contribution to literary criticism. Their value lies in the comparative perceptions which Boyesen had of European and American culture.

Boyesen's second full-length venture into critical scholarship was his *Essays on German Literature,* comprised in part of articles written in the 1870s and 1880s. Boyesen's complaint about German fiction was similar to his annoyance with American fiction; the literature did not keep up

with political events. However, when Boyesen began discussing German drama he was more positive. He believed that the new spirit of science and social awareness were the most powerful and progressive ideas in Europe, and he realized that the dramatic work of Gerhardt Hauptmann at the end of the nineteenth century was not an accident but the result of the realistic theater of Heinrich von Kleist, Franz Grillparzer, and others. In his most complete statement of this development, his essay "The Drama of Revolt" (1895), Boyesen linked German realistic and social drama with Emile Zola's "Naturalism on the Stage" and with Ibsen's *Ghosts* and *A Doll's House.* It was Boyesen's view that Ibsen's influence on George Bernard Shaw, August Strindberg, and other playwrights would bring greater energy and awareness to the stage. While praising the positive effects of the new European dramatists, Boyesen bemoaned the sad state of American theater criticism, characterizing its practitioners as "narrow visioned antediluvians [whose] ideas would provide amusement for the critics in Berlin." He bitterly remarked that American critics followed the tastes of London, for "in spite of our pretence of independence [we] have always in literary matters followed the lead of England." However, later, in a kinder mood, he supposed that since the English had been slowly accepting Ibsen, American critics might ultimately do the same.

Essays on Scandinavian Literature and *A Commentary on the Writings of Henrik Ibsen* received excellent reviews both for their educational value and their critical judgments. Boyesen's perceptive comments are often clearer and more accurate than those of Shaw, who, in his *Quintessence of Ibsenism* (1891), overemphasized Ibsen's role as a playwright absorbed in social issues and in changing society. Boyesen, however, saw Ibsen's true direction. He realized that, influenced as he was by Søren Kierkegaard, Ibsen was absorbed in the development of the individual personality and in the greater problem of human existence. Social problems were secondary. In fact this view of Ibsen became a sticking point for Boyesen in his commentaries. For although he greatly admired Ibsen's dramatic structure and realistic characterization, Boyesen could never fully agree with Ibsen's lesser emphasis on the social struggle. But for Ibsen's power as a dramatist, his honesty, and his ability to raise valid social issues, Boyesen had only the highest praise.

Boyesen made several trips to Europe that were primarily literary pilgrimages. His plan was

Page from Boyesen's lecture notes (courtesy of Columbia University Libraries) to meet as many authors and literary celebrities as he could. The reason was twofold: he was personally interested in writers, especially advocates of realism in fiction, and he planned to use the interviews with these artists as material for magazine articles. Often described as "An International Boswell" because of his "baiting" technique with interviewees, Boyesen mingled with the Paris literary set and had an informal acquaintance with its writers.

His interviews with Victor Hugo, Alphonse Daudet, and Ivan Turgenev (already a popular writer in the United States) were published in American magazines and were part of Boyesen's efforts to promote among American readers European writers who had a bent toward realism. His correspondence provides plentiful evidence of his work as a liaison between European and American writers and writing, and his exchanges with George Brandes, the important Danish critic, Howells, Twain, Bjørnson, Alexander Kielland, Turgenev, and many others underscore Boyesen's value as a critic who was aware of, and involved in, the literary activity of his time and world. Boyesen's contributions to the advancement and public acceptance of realistic and naturalistic views of fiction and his dedication to the value of fiction as a means of understanding and changing society remained strong until the time of his death at forty-seven from edema of the lungs on 4 October 1895.

Behind most of Boyesen's ideas, both social and literary, lay his belief in Spencerian evolutionary progress. His views of political change in theory and practice in America were clearly governed by the Spencerian view of the new complex industrial society which would replace the outworn institutions of the past.

Among his other interests was his belief in the new role of women in society and in the need for education on all levels to prepare society for the new and better world of the twentieth century. Literature was to contribute to this education by dealing with social issues. Boyesen was also anxious to see the growth of a corps of critical experts to deal with the growing specialization of the times, experts whose range of literary sensitivity would cover foreign as well as American authors and who would be able to compare literature on a world, rather than on a national, basis. He associated the rise of realistic fiction with the growth of American letters, stating that "it is because the American novel has chosen to

abandon the 'spirit of romance' . . . and devoted itself to . . . studying and chronicling our own social conditions, that it is today commanding the attention of the whole civilized world." Like Hippolyte Taine, the French critic, Boyesen believed that literature "is the autobiography of the race," and he wanted an American literature that would stand on its own feet.

Through his fiction and criticism Boyesen attempted to exemplify and explain the role of literature in society. He repeatedly emphasized social values over those of the romantic individual, who, he felt, often impeded rather than furthered the progress of mankind. He saw in realism a great educative force which would make man aware of his place in history as defined by evolutionary processes.

References:

Lars Ahnebrink, *Beginnings of Naturalism in American Fiction* (Upsala, Sweden: University of Upsala, 1950);

Robert Fredrickson, *Hjalmar Hjorth Boyesen* (Boston: Twayne, 1980);

Clarence Glasrud, "Boyesen and the Norwegian Immigration," *Norwegian-American Studies and Records*, 19 (1956): 15-45;

Glasrud, *Hjalmar Hjorth Boyesen* (Northfield, Minn.: Norwegian-American Historical Association, 1963);

Laurence M. Larson, "Hjalmar Hjorth Boyesen," in his *The Changing West and Other Essays* (Northfield, Minn.: Norwegian-American Historical Association, 1937);

Marc Ratner, "Georg Brandes and Hjalmar Hjorth Boyesen," *Scandinavian Studies*, 33 (November 1961): 218-230;

Ratner, "Howells and Boyesen: Two Views of Realism," *New England Quarterly*, 35 (September 1962): 376-390;

Ratner, "The Iron Madonna: H. H. Boyesen's American Girl," *Jahrbuch für Amerikastudien*, 9 (1964): 166-172;

Per Seyersted, *Hjalmar Hjorth Boyesen* (Oslo: Solum/ Atlantic Highlands, N.J.: Humanities Press, 1984);

George Leroy White, Jr., "H. H. Boyesen: A Note on Immigration," *American Literature*, 13 (January 1942): 363-371.

Papers:

Hjalmar Hjorth Boyesen's papers are in the Butler Library at Columbia University.

W. C. Brownell

(30 August 1851-22 July 1928)

Thomas R. Nevin
John Carroll University

BOOKS: *French Traits: An Essay in Comparative Criticism* (New York: Scribners, 1889);
French Art: Classic and Contemporary Painting and Sculpture (New York: Scribners, 1892; London: Constable, 1902; enlarged edition, New York: Scribners, 1905);
Newport (New York: Scribners, 1896);
Victorian Prose Masters: Thackeray, Carlyle, George Eliot, Matthew Arnold, Ruskin, George Meredith (New York: Scribners, 1901);
American Prose Masters: Cooper, Hawthorne, Emerson, Poe, Lowell, Henry James (New York: Scribners, 1909; London: Smith, Elder, 1910);
Criticism (New York: Scribners, 1914);
Standards (New York: Scribners, 1917);
The Genius of Style (New York & London: Scribners, 1924);
Democratic Distinction in America (New York & London: Scribners, 1927);
William Crary Brownell: An Anthology of His Writings Together with Biographical Notes and Impressions of the Later Years, edited by Gertrude Hall Brownell (New York & London: Scribners, 1933).

OTHER: "King at the Century," in *Century Association: Clarence King* (New York, 1904), pp. 211-225;
"The Academy and the Language," in *American Academy of Arts and Letters: Addresses on Language Problems* (New York: Scribners, 1925).

William Crary Brownell had the misfortune of living for over a generation into the twentieth century, well beyond the late-Victorian milieu in which his critical temper worked with synthetic ease and assurance. Increasingly anachronistic as a man of letters, his gentlemanly gaze was for the most part backward, and selectively so, for the subjects of his criticism were all established, if not canonical, names in Anglo-American literature; of these, only Henry James was his contemporary. Yet Brownell is indisputably an important American exponent of criticism that provides a rounded estimate of a writer's art. He took for his central, guiding principle the significance of personality as it determines literary expression. This is merely to remark Brownell's indebtedness to French critic Charles-Augustin Sainte-Beuve, who had made the study of an author's works an expedition into the remotest recesses of his character. Further, Brownell believed that literature must contribute something of moral value to society, and thus he reflects the influence of Matthew Arnold, who established literary criticism as an indispensable arbiter of culture.

Brownell was born in New York City on 30 August 1851 to Isaac Wilbour and Lucia Brown Brownell. Pedigreed on both sides of his family with a respectable New England ancestry, he received privileged schooling from his earliest years and proved a precocious reader. The store of biblical allusions in his writings was built up by his youthful fascination with Old Testament stories, a familiarity which undoubtedly contributed to the moralizing strain that would later make its not-so-furtive way through his criticism. On the eve of the Civil War, when he was not yet ten, he was set in the ways of his upbringing as a staunch Democrat and abolitionist. He carried a moderate, sensible, and unreflected progressivism with him through his adult life that accounts for his enthusiastic acceptance of the complacent nostrums which until World War I hallowed an age of scientific and technological advances.

At nineteen Brownell was graduated from Amherst College and went to work as a reporter for the *New York World*. His superior talents led to his appointment as city editor within two years. He moved to the *Nation* in 1879. In January of 1878 he married Virginia Shields Swinburne, of Newport Brahmin stock. The couple went abroad in 1881, and within the following decade Brownell established himself securely as a man of letters.

Three years spent mostly in Paris provided him the material for his first book, *French Traits: An Essay in Comparative Criticism,* comprised of topical sketches on Parisian culture. Thirty-nine years after its publication in 1889 Edith Wharton would praise the book's precision and exposition of a national character. More than returning a compliment to Alexis de Tocqueville and in an obvious debt to Ralph Waldo Emerson's *English Traits* (1856), *French Traits* occupies an ancillary place in Brownell's literary criticism, which from the first entailed the Arnoldian assumption that society and letters are inextricably bound and mutually determinant. Throughout, the book analyzes French life in a somewhat arbitrary succession of contrasts to American life, chiefly to instruct Brownell's countrymen in the value of dedicated intellectual pursuit of truth.

One may wonder to what extent Gallic intellectuality as he characterized it mirrored Brownell's own perspective, for the habits of mind which he celebrates, notably poise, clarity, self-assurance, and a genius for measure that eschews confusion and uncertainty, are hallmarks of his own literary expression. Or perhaps these synthetic elements conditioned Brownell's maturity, for he clearly reflects in all his subsequent writing the French devotion to impersonal standards and to that most allusive phenomenon, style. Whatever the case, *French Traits* reflects a cosmopolitanism still assumed in Brownell's day to be indispensable to the gentleman-scholar.

Not long after returning to America in 1884 Brownell joined the *Philadelphia Press*. In 1888 he moved to the publishing firm of Charles Scribner's Sons and remained there as editor and literary adviser until his death. In the same year he became a member of New York's Century Association, a group of highly influential cultural arbiters. In and around that circle he furthered acquaintance with prominent writers and painters. *French Art: Classic and Contemporary Painting and Sculpture,* appearing in 1892 as a companion to his first book, reveals Brownell's breadth of critical view at the same time that it indicates one of his chief limitations: beyond securely reputable subjects, his judgments do not hold up well. He could praise obscurities like Jean-Louis-Ernest Meissonier and ignore Georges Seurat and Henri Toulouse-Lautrec. True, he lauds Auguste Rodin, a source of scandal, but Rodin was a friend. His praise of Edouard Manet, however, shows that Brownell could mature with reflection, for that same artist had won in *French Traits* only the offhanded concession that he would likely arrive one day at the Louvre.

The first of Brownell's studies in literary personality appeared in 1901. His selection of *Victorian Prose Masters: Thackeray, Carlyle, George Eliot, Matthew Arnold, Ruskin, George Meredith* will inevitably seem arbitrary today, especially as reputations have fluctuated over the four generations since Brownell wrote. George Meredith and John Ruskin, for instance, have not continued to enjoy high standing. Charles Dickens is a conspicuous omission, as is Anthony Trollope; one may be pleased to find George Eliot in the company. To draw up a list of one's own, however, is to cavil, as Brownell's intent is not to justify the standing of the writers selected but to assess their personalities in their works and to award merit or demerit according to a priori critical standards.

These standards emerge from context but can be briefly summarized here. A disciplined direction of thought, feeling, and expression toward a lofty, impersonal ideal and a corresponding freedom from the vagaries and excesses of a subjective temperament provide

Brownell with a neoclassical bias. Of the need for the primacy of reason over emotion and constraint over caprice he never entertains a doubt, for the pursuit of beauty in art as of truth in criticism requires an elevated purpose. Such disinterested aspiration sounds in itself opaque, but if Brownell can be charged with a predisposition to the platonic, he is gentlemanly about it and scrupulously avoids capitalizing what he assumes to be the good, the beautiful, and the true. He remains free of the academic dogmas one might associate with his neohumanistic contemporaries. At the same time he shows a consistent and pronounced hostility to the impressionism of *l'art pour l'art* which influenced his own and subsequent generations. Mere aestheticism, whether in art or in criticism, can claim no moral purpose; to celebrate beauty in disregard of truth is to betray both for the sensationalistic escape from reality. Brownell rescues his own aesthetic ideal from any hint of escapism by making literary criticism answerable not only to rational criteria but to the society which they must serve. Conversely, it is only through criticism, he maintains in his essay on Matthew Arnold, that the intellectual life of an age can be crystallized and cogently communicated. One might add that it is only through the concrete test cases afforded by the study of a literary personality that Brownell's abstract notions become articulate and impose their value. *Victorian Prose Masters* and its companion study, *American Prose Masters: Cooper, Hawthorne, Emerson, Poe, Lowell, Henry James* (1909), while rendering transparent the influence of Sainte-Beuve's technique, remain in their own right the best examples of Brownell's critical principles at work. It is likely that if Brownell survives as more than a passing figure in the history of modern criticism, it will be due chiefly to these two works.

His essay on Arnold occupies a compelling position because it so frequently seems to speak of Brownell himself, and this not merely at the inevitable points of approbation but also at points where Arnold's deficiencies are frankly set forth. Perhaps chief among the former is what Brownell characterizes as Arnold's lofty pursuit of reason as itself an ideal: concentrating on a subject with the disinterestedness requisite to genuine moral endeavor. He did not, that is, allow personality to obtrude. Brownell took such practice as a lesson and learned it well. No less impressively Arnold invoked doctrine but not the pedantry of a system. His ideas "held with elastic firmness but not developped [*sic*] into any set of

procrustean principles." No statement could better reflect Brownell's own consistent eschewal of academicism and his no-less-consistent fealty to the soundness of reason. He even went so far as to allow that criticism necessarily lacks beauty in having to dwell upon truth. Arnold had shown that the business of criticism is to teach by example. Yet, as Brownell indicates, Arnold's treatment of the Bible as literature accorded with the Victorian separation of faith from dogma. This separation Brownell in his unyielding rationalism hails as merit when in fact it exposed the acute spiritual crisis which beset the age. One wonders how Brownell might have estimated the works of John Henry Newman.

Brownell regards Arnold the poet apologetically. His claim that Arnold was so preoccupied with applying principles of poetic composition that he failed to write emotionally charged, thoughtful poetry simply reflects the strictness of Brownell's own dichotomy between criticism and art as discrete provinces of truth and beauty. Brownell's claim that in Arnold "reason a little overbalances his imagination" begs the question of how a dividing line can be drawn. Indeed, it exposes the tenuousness of such terms taken as absolutes, not to mention the arbitrariness of determining a ratio between them.

If the case of Arnold so suggestively articulates Brownell's own critical strengths and limits, that of Thomas Carlyle does so by the rigorous negations he calls forth. In no one among the English prose masters do the foibles of personality, of subjective temperament work so destructively. Brownell's commendations of Carlyle, for example, for the work on Oliver Cromwell, are incidental, thereby setting in relief what he finds objectionable. "Discipline in thought, feeling and expression is the one thing he conspicuously neglected." Complementing this fault is the intensity of his emotions. Brownell does not contest emotion itself, nor even its intensity–the stuff of art lying on it–but he requires its channeling into inspiration. The price paid for failure to constrain feeling is that one becomes its prey.

Brownell's criticism takes on a kind of clinical acuity as he makes Carlyle into a spectrum of excesses. Without the ennobling curbs of classical standards the writer risks self-disfigurement: being careless of perfection amounts to being insensitive to beauty, indifferent to anything beyond caprice. This caveat, revealing Brownell's genteel impatience with such severe infringements of stylistic propriety as Carlyle afforded,

Photograph of Brownell that appeared in The National Cyclopædia of American Biography

needs to be set against the substantial contemporary influence of literary impressionism (though greater in England and France than in America) to which Brownell was undoubtedly directing it; the cult which encouraged writing as an apotheosis of individuality could not have found a more egregious source for inspiration than Carlyle.

Brownell's censure extends beyond the apparent concerns of literary criticism to include Carlyle's antidemocratic biases and his contempt for the advances of science. Being out of harmony with the scientific spirit condemned Carlyle to anachronism, a most grievous offense to Brownell's progressivism. No matter that Johann Wolfgang von Goethe himself had prescribed for the sake of sanity and equipoise that an artist should lean not with but against the prevailing tendencies of his age.

Despite their marked differences Ruskin fares almost as badly as Carlyle, and because of the same faults: a quixotic subjectivism pitched to evangelical fervor and a corresponding surrender to emotion. Brownell further charges Ruskin with a sentimental didacticism that imposes

rather than argues ideas. Proselytism for art, risking vulgarity, made no more sense to Brownell than an economics based upon the Gospels rather than upon Adam Smith.

Given Ruskin's prophetic distrust of industrialism and Carlyle's scorn of the "cash nexus" predominant in human relations, one might wonder whether Brownell's rationalism was held too consistently to be reasonable, or at least discerning.

Brownell himself came increasingly to decry what he perceived to be the disintegration of literary convention. His *Standards* (1917) allied him most closely with the academic humanists in their scorn of contemporary vulgarities in literary and popular taste, but Brownell never came to share totally their fear of democratic culture. He had the true patrician's ease before the plebeian masses.

His awareness of democratic vistas remained limited, almost parochial in one sense. A New Yorker, he was free from the Bostonian prejudice known as sectionalism; yet only two of his American literary portraits derive other than from New England, and one of them, James Fenimore Cooper, might by proximity be reckoned within that regional scope. Edgar Allan Poe cannot, and it is he who sustains Brownell's heaviest attacks in *American Prose Masters*. Again, one wonders how Brownell would have dealt with the midwesterners Samuel Clemens and William Dean Howells, both of whom he knew personally.

Poe the literary critic emerges as a kind of American Carlyle, his temper too polemicized to be truly critical, his judgments transparently self-indulgent. Brownell does award him the merit of avoiding the extremes of the dogmatic and the impressionistic; Poe's conventions are his own, and he owes no allegiance to past or present tastes. Brownell's impatience with him is that of a father attempting to direct the energies of an unruly boy. Poe's telltale infraction was that he never grew up, never matured to a standard above and beyond himself. What is at work here is not merely Brownell's pique at a recalcitrant adolescence, as it were, but a tilting against the lofty esteem Poe enjoyed in France, thanks to Charles Baudelaire and the *symbolistes*. Brownell seems to want to make clear that in the case of this celebrated failure the neglect should be charged not to American society but to the errancy of the writer himself.

The essay on Emerson is vivified by Brownell's recollection of hearing him lecture. Since youth the impression of personality had lasted

George Willis Cooke

(23 April 1848-30 April 1923)

Robert E. Burkholder

Pennsylvania State University, University Park

BOOKS: *Ralph Waldo Emerson: His Life, Writings, and Philosophy* (Boston: Osgood, 1881; London: Sampson, Low, Marston, Searle & Rivington, 1882);

George Eliot: A Critical Study of Her Life, Writings, and Philosophy (Boston: Osgood, 1883; London: Sampson, Low, Marston, Searle & Rivington, 1883);

Poets and Problems (Boston: Ticknor, 1886);

A History of the Clapboard Trees or Third Parish, Dedham, Mass. now the Unitarian Parish, West Dedham, 1736-1886 (Boston: Ellis, 1887);

A Guide-Book to the Poetic and Dramatic Works of Robert Browning (Boston & New York: Houghton, Mifflin, 1891);

John Sullivan Dwight, Brook-Farmer, Editor, and Critic of Music: A Biography (Boston: Small, Maynard, 1898);

Unitarianism in America: A History of Its Origin and Development (Boston: American Unitarian Association, 1902);

An Historical and Biographical Introduction to Accompany the Dial (Cleveland: Rowfant Club, 1902); republished as *Memorabilia of the Transcendentalists in New England* (Hartford: Transcendental Books, 1973);

Origin and Early History of the First Parish, Sharon, Massachusetts. A Sermon Preached on the Occasion of the 150th Anniversary of the Formation of the Church, July 6, 1890 (Boston: Hight, 1903);

The Social Evolution of Religion (Boston: Stratford, 1920).

OTHER: "Emerson's View of Nationality," in *The Genius and Character of Emerson,* edited by F. B. Sanborn (Boston: Osgood, 1885), pp. 310-338;

"Thomas Wentworth Higginson," in *Authors at Home,* edited by J. L. and J. B. Gilder (New York: Cassell, 1889), pp. 119-162;

Early Letters of George Wm. Curtis to John S. Dwight; Brook Farm and Concord, edited by Cooke (New York & London: Harper, 1898);

The Poetic and Dramatic Works of Robert Browning, edited by Cooke (Boston & New York: Houghton, Mifflin, 1899);

The Poets of Transcendentalism: An Anthology, edited, with an introductory essay and biographical notes, by Cooke (Boston & New York: Houghton, Mifflin, 1903);

A Bibliography of James Russell Lowell, edited by Cooke (Boston & New York: Houghton, Mifflin, 1906);

Theodore Parker, *The American Scholar,* edited, with notes, by Cooke (Boston: American Unitarian Association, 1907);

Parker, *The World of Matter and the Spirit of Man: Latest Discourses of Religion,* edited, with notes, by Cooke (Boston: American Unitarian Association, 1907);

A Bibliography of Ralph Waldo Emerson, edited by Cooke (Boston & New York: Houghton Mifflin, 1908);

Parker, *The Transient and Permanent in Christianity,* edited, with notes, by Cooke (Boston: American Unitarian Association, 1908);

"George Ripley," in *Heralds of the Liberal Faith,* edited by Samuel A. Eliot, volume 3 (Boston: American Unitarian Association, 1910), pp. 330-335.

PERIODICAL PUBLICATIONS: "The *Dial* and Corrigenda," *Journal of Speculative Philosophy,* 19 (July 1885): 322-323;

"The *Dial:* An Historical and Biographical Introduction, with a List of the Contributors," *Journal of Speculative Philosophy,* 19 (July 1885): 225-265;

"Dr. Holmes at Fourscore," *New-England Magazine,* new series 1 (October 1889): 115-123;

"Poetic Limitations of Sordello," *Poet-Lore,* 4 (December 1892): 612-616;

"Browning's Interpretation of Romantic Love as Compared with that of Plato, Dante, and Petrarch," *Poet-Lore,* 6 (May 1894): 225-238;

"Institutional Church," *New-England Magazine,* new series 14 (August 1896): 645-660;

George Willis Cooke

"Harriet Beecher Stowe," *New-England Magazine,* new series 15 (September 1896): 3-18;

"Brook Farm," *New-England Magazine,* new series 17 (December 1897): 391-407;

"The Emerson Centennial," *New-England Magazine,* new series 28 (May 1903): 255-264;

"Emerson and Transcendentalism," *New-England Magazine,* new series 28 (May 1903): 264-280;

"Women in the Progress of Civilization," *Chautauquan,* 56 (September 1909): 19-14; (October 1909): 180-202; (November 1909): 322-341; 57 (December 1909): 19-48; (January 1910): 181-205; (February 1910): 342-362; 58 (March 1910): 19-39; (April 1910): 166-183; (May 1910): 310-332;

"Revolutionary Tendencies in Modern Literature," *Unity,* 87-88; (19 May 1921): 185-186; (26 May 1921): 205-206; (2 June 1921): 215-216; (9 June 1921): 234-235; (16 June 1921): 251-253; (23 June 1921): 266-268; (30 June 1921): 279-281; (7 July 1921): 297-299; (21 July 1921): 313-314; (4 August 1921): 329-331; 88 (1 September 1921): 10-13; (15 September 1921): 25-27; (29 September 1921): 42-44; (6 October 1921): 57-59; (3 November 1921): 120-122;

"Forecasting the Future of Mankind," *Unity* 88 (6 July 1922): 295-301.

George Willis Cooke was a Unitarian minister, scholar, and critic, best known for his studies of American transcendentalism. In a larger sense, however, he is noted for explicating the humanistic and social concerns that he identified as the essence of the transcendental movement for a late-nineteenth-century audience. He also used his understanding of those concerns as a critical perspective from which to view various nineteenth-century English authors and even the history of religion. Significantly, Cooke felt it necessary in his *An Historical and Biographical Introduction to Accompany the Dial* (1902) to deny that he was himself a transcendentalist because he felt himself more scientifically enlightened than members of that group, and yet the idealism and essential humanity that he associated with Ralph Waldo Emerson and his circle are consistently the highest criteria he employed in judging the effectiveness of a literary work.

Cooke began his career as a scholar rather late in life, and there is little suggestion of what he was to become in the facts of his early years. He was born on a farm in Comstock, Michigan, to Hiram and Susan Earl Cooke. Until he was nineteen he worked on his father's farm and received what education he could from the district school. In 1867 he began college preparatory courses at Olivet College, in Olivet, Michigan. Founded by a group from Oberlin, Ohio, Olivet College was noted for its liberalism and was the first institution in the United States to accept male and female students of all races, which it did from its founding. It was perhaps at Olivet College that Cooke committed himself to the causes of liberalism that he would champion throughout his life because from there he moved to the Liberal Institute in Jefferson, Wisconsin, where he spent two years. Finally he attended the Meadville Theological School in Meadville, Pennsylvania, for fifteen months, and on 20 June 1872 he was ordained a Unitarian minister. During that same year he married Lucy Nash of Rochester, Wisconsin, by whom he had two daughters, Florence and Marian, who survived him.

With his ordination Cooke acquired a platform for his ideas about liberal religion and social reform. He preached in Sheboygan and Sharon, Wisconsin, in Grand Haven, Michigan, and in Indianapolis. In his first parish he began publishing a small newspaper, the *Liberal Worker,* which ultimately led to Cooke's part in founding and editing *Unity,* a journal of liberal religion published in Chicago beginning in March 1878. In 1880 Cooke, who had already begun to establish a reputation in liberal religious circles, moved to Concord, Massachusetts, where he formed an acquaintance with the aging Emerson. Within six months of his move east Cooke was settled as the permanent pastor of the West Church, Dedham, Massachusetts, where he apparently continued work on a study of Emerson that he had begun while living in Concord. In 1891 Cooke moved to Lexington, Massachusetts, and became pastor of the church founded by and named for Charles Follen, the church where Emerson often preached in the 1830s. In the late 1890s he was minister at the Unitarian Church in Dublin, New Hampshire. In 1922 he held the combined Congregational and Unitarian pastorates at Francestown, New Hampshire, but between 1899 and 1922 he held no settled pastorate and devoted himself almost exclusively to writing and speaking about his favorite liberal causes. He gave courses at the Rand School of Social Science in New York, the New England Institute for the Promotion of Learning, and the Boston School of Social Science, and he devoted some time to the cause of woman's rights, leaving a manuscript on "Women in the Progress of Civilization" uncompleted at his death. This work, the product of twenty years' thought, was the basis of thirteen articles on women in history published in the *Chautauquan* from September 1909 through May 1910.

While Cooke was politically independent, he did describe himself as a socialist, and he often lectured on behalf of the Socialist party. It should be noted, however, that Cooke was not a revolutionary or anarchist, but one who found in the notion of socialism the political possibility for the humanism that he valued so much in literature and religion. In fact, he dubbed his own approach to socialism "collectivism," which his friend J. T. Sunderland characterized as recognition that capitalism is an unjust and oppressive system that favors only a few, and that the by-products of capitalism—militarism and imperialism—are serious menaces not only to this country but to the whole world. Needless to say, political views such as Cooke's were not popular in the late decades of the nineteenth century or the early decades of the twentieth, and Cooke's dogged refusal to surrender his principles testifies to his courage and supplies a possible reason for his not having been invited to address Unitarian gatherings such as the Ministers' Institutes or the Berry Street conferences. His politics are as well a probable cause for his never having received an honorary degree.

Cooke was, however, extremely proud of his membership in the American Association for the Advancement of Science. He was also honored by the Free Religious Association in Boston on his seventieth birthday by a group of notable speakers that included Edward Waldo Emerson, an occasion that Cooke used to underscore his essential optimism about the future of mankind, even on the eve of World War I.

After the death of his first wife Cooke married Mary Lydia Leggett of Revere, Massachusetts, who was herself a Unitarian minister and the first female graduate of the Harvard Divinity School. The wedding took place on 23 April 1923, and only a week later Cooke died unexpectedly. Funeral services were held at Kings Chapel in Boston. In his eulogistic essay on Cooke, J. T. Sunderland eloquently expresses the appropriateness of the site of Cooke's funeral: "It was fitting that he who far above others was the Historian of the Unitarian movement in America, should be buried from that most historic of our Unitarian church edifices."

Cooke's first book-length publication, *Ralph Waldo Emerson: His Life, Writings, and Philosophy* (1881), is a work that suggests the shape and direction of Cooke's later career as a literary critic and scholar. In his preface Cooke states that the volume is intended as "an introduction to the study of the writings" of Emerson and that he will not attempt to measure Emerson's thought through comparisons with other philosophies. Cooke says that he has attempted neither to make it apparent when he disagrees with Emerson nor to push those ideas with which he does agree. Instead, he claims to write "as a disciple" who is willing to allow "Mr. Emerson to speak for himself as often as possible," because "in this way alone can full justice be done the subject." Despite his denial that he is writing as a critic, it is important to note that in all of his criticism Cooke did have an identifiable and consistent critical approach. While that approach may not have been overtly judgmental, it did express a point of view that seems to have been based on his Unitarian ministry and essential humanism, his respect for Emerson's thought, and his knowledge of transcendental critical ideas, notably those of Margaret Fuller.

Nothing is clearer when reading Cooke than the similarity between his approach to literary criticism and that advocated by Fuller, who, in "A Short Essay on Critics," states that the true critic is one who serves as a mediator between the poet and the reader by perceiving the divine in the work of the artist and by bringing those divine ideas "down" to the rest of humanity "by the analytic process." Cooke as critic dealt almost exclusively with authors with whom he sympathized, with writers in whose works he could recognize divinity. Like Fuller he saw his role as literary critic as somewhat analogous to that of Moses, bringing inspired ideas down from a literary Mt. Sinai to a tribe that might not be able to understand or appreciate those ideas without his aid. The ultimate effect of such an approach is to create a sense of deep sympathy between the artist and the critic, another of Fuller's requirements for the best sort of literary criticism. However, in practical terms, Cooke's sympathy with his subjects often obscures signs of his own personality and point of view.

Cooke's presence is discernible in *Ralph Waldo Emerson: His Life, Writings, and Philosophy* if one cares to look deeply enough. For instance, his appreciation of Emerson's thought causes him to de-emphasize the darkness of such essays as "Experience" and "Fate" and to focus on his sunnier side. In considering "The Man and The Life" Cooke stresses such things as Emerson's hospitality, loyalty, and guileless character, and he concludes the chapter by calling him "a Puritan, with all that is harsh, repulsive, and uncomfortable in Puritanism removed." "Uncomfortable" is an important word here, for it hints at how Cooke ultimately viewed Emerson and his ideas: they were comfortable for him. Cooke makes it clear why such was the case by demonstrating repeatedly his appreciation for Emerson's idealistic humanism, lauding his long philosophical poems, for example, because they deal with the "dark problems of life which concern every soul, and the solutions which form the eras of human thought." Therefore, Cooke believed, he proved Emerson to be "a true interpreter of human motives." The Emerson who explained cosmic mysteries in terms of a man-centered universe most appealed to Cooke as reader, disciple, and minister, and it is that Emerson who emerges from Cooke's literary study of him. Above all, *Ralph Waldo Emerson: His Life, Writings, and Philosophy* is, as a reviewer for the 10 November 1881 *Free Religious Index* contended, both thorough and enlightened because of Cooke's access to Emerson's papers and his mastery of available scholarship and criticism, and this is true, as the reviewer reminds us, even though he "writes *con amore*." But it was Oliver Wendell Holmes who, in a letter to Cooke, perhaps best summarized the value of Cooke's work on Emerson by claiming that "Hereafter no man can pretend to write about Mr. Emerson without having recourse to what you have written—the result of long and patient labor and a genuine enthusiasm for the subject—an enthusiasm made safe by a sound and critical judgment."

Ralph Waldo Emerson: His Life, Writings, and Philosophy was the first product of a study of New England transcendentalism that would occupy Cooke much of the rest of his life and would result in his becoming the best living authority on the transcendental movement. Cooke next shifted his focus from the central figure of the movement to its principal periodical: the *Dial.* In July 1885 he published in the *Journal of Speculative Philosophy* "The *Dial:* An Historical and Biographical Introduction," which was later expanded to serve as an introduction to a complete reprinting of the *Dial* by the Rowfant Club in 1902 and retitled *An Historical and Biographical In-*

troduction to Accompany the Dial. This work remained the standard history of that important periodical into the 1970s. It is still important because Cooke's arguments about the origins and nature of New England transcendentalism prefigure much of what came after him. First, Cooke argued that transcendentalism was indigenous to New England and that it did not originate in the writings of German idealists. In anticipation of Perry Miller and many others, Cooke recognized "a direct line of descent" of transcendental thinking "from Edwards, through Hopkins and Channing, to Emerson. Each of these men was largely influenced by his predecessor, not as to the whole of his theological system, but in the one direction of the growth of idealism." Second, Cooke argued that transcendentalism was not merely a religious and philosophical movement but "more truly moral and practical, aiming at social reforms and the enlargement of education."

In the late 1880s Cooke, whose book on Emerson had been met with welcoming reviews in 1881, turned once again to New England transcendentalism, and between 1898 and 1903 he published a series of works, all of which grew out of his research into the origin and development of Unitarianism in America and his interest in Brook Farm, the *Dial,* and the poetry of transcendentalism.

At the request of Ednah Dow Cheney, the social reformer and biographer of Louisa May Alcott, Cooke undertook a biography of John Sullivan Dwight, which was published in 1898 as *John Sullivan Dwight, Brook-Farmer, Editor, and Critic of Music: A Biography.* In his preface to that work Cooke states that he attempted "to understand the circumstances amidst which Dwight was placed, and to rightly interpret his social and intellectual environment." To that end Cooke drew frequently upon Dwight's correspondence and based many of his observations on personal interviews with Dwight's friends and associates. The attention to detail in this work and Cooke's obvious interest in Dwight are not revelations to those familiar with Cooke's other writings. What does seem curious, at least in a work by Cooke, is the severity of the criticism aimed at Dwight. Among other things, Cooke points out that as a young man Dwight lacked assertiveness, but in his later life, with the relative success of *Dwight's Journal of Music,* he became an autocrat of musical taste in Boston, intellectually crippled by an excessive sense of loyalty to composers he learned to love as a young man and by his lack of technical knowl-edge of music. These handicaps, Cooke asserts, petrified Dwight's taste and destroyed his value as a critic.

Such uncharacteristic criticism is somewhat offset by Cooke's apparent respect for Dwight's idealism and his willingness to credit Dwight with single-handedly establishing a climate for the growth of interest in music in Boston. For example, in his chapter dealing with Dwight's contributions to Brook Farm, Cooke argues that his subject was no transcendental picnicker or utopian dilettante, but rather a true seeker of the ideal who continued to support causes espoused by the community long after Brook Farm had failed. And as for Dwight's contributions to Boston's musical scene, Cooke contends that "A biography of John S. Dwight, on a comprehensive plan, would be a history of music in Boston from 1840-1890." Ultimately, though, Cooke's portrait of Dwight is one of an idealist stranded in a material world that made him uncomfortable, a man of finely wrought sensibilities and a great gift for friendship, but one who could not make a living and who had difficulty in realizing his ideals.

As a result of his research into Dwight's life, Cooke compiled, edited, and published *Early Letters of George Wm. Curtis to John S. Dwight; Brook Farm and Concord* (1898). These letters, linked by Cooke's own commentary, are still valuable for the glimpses they provide of daily life at the utopian community founded by the transcendentalists.

Cooke's other contributions to the history and criticism of transcendentalism are the fruits of his labor as an editor and bibliographer. In 1903 Cooke edited and published *The Poets of Transcendentalism: An Anthology,* a work motivated by his desire to resurrect lost or forgotten transcendental poetry from inaccessible periodicals, and surprising because of some of the poets he chose to include, notably Julia Ward Howe, Helen Hunt Jackson, James Russell Lowell, and E. R. Sill. One of the volume's strengths is the inclusion of many poets whose work is still not readily available, including George Shepard Burleigh, William Henry Furness, Ellen Hooper, Caroline Sturgis, and John Weiss. It is also valuable because in his preface Cooke tries to refine further his ideas about the nature of New England transcendentalism and to offer a definition of transcendental poetry. He expands the point he had made in "The *Dial:* An Historical and Biographical Introduction" that despite the influence of Thomas Carlyle, Samuel Taylor Coleridge, and others, transcendentalism was indigenous to America, and he argues that "it is more just to our poets to claim that transcendentalism was native to America than to assert of it that it came from abroad." To Cooke the movement is best explained as "democracy in contact with Puritanism," and he continues to insist that it was a movement of social reform by emphasizing its humanistic roots: "Transcendentalism was a movement of inquiry, revolt against conventionality, and assertion of the worth and dignity of man. It declared that religion is natural to man, that he may trust his own instincts, that individual freedom is essential to a large and wise living, and that spiritual insight is a direct revelation from God." Finally, while he found the poetry of transcendentalism to be flawed by its philosophical intent, obscurity, and technical imperfections, he constructed a definition of it that is still valid today. According to Cooke, transcendental poetry is essentially individualistic and is based on the doctrine of direct personal inspiration; it is hopeful in tone and always optimistic because of the transcendentalists' belief in man's progressive development; it is ascetic and inwardly directed; it is oracular because of the poet's special relationship with the Oversoul; and it expresses a confidence in immortality. To Cooke, who by this time in his life was more comfortable with scientific explanations of religion, transcendentalism still held a deep attraction because of its idealism and humanism.

Nevertheless, Cooke wrote very little else about transcendentalism. His final contributions to the study of the American Renaissance were two bibliographies, *A Bibliography of James Russell Lowell* (1906) and *A Bibliography of Ralph Waldo Emerson* (1908). Both of these compilations list works by and about Cooke's subjects and, because of their thoroughness and accuracy, both remained standard works for more than half a century.

Cooke's second area of interest was contemporary English literature, but as in his studies of American transcendentalism he dealt exclusively with those authors he could exploit to make a point about the value of humanism. His 1883 work, *George Eliot: A Critical Study of Her Life, Writings, and Philosophy,* focuses on Eliot's disillusionment with conventional religion and her use of a humanistic morality in its place. Because of her skepticism Cooke finds that the most serious defect of Eliot's work "is a want of the ideal element," and yet he is able to find much of value

in Eliot's interest in what he calls "the human side of religion": "George Eliot's religion is without God, without immortality, without a transcendent spiritual aim and duty. It consists in a humble submission to the invariable laws of the universe, a profound love of humanity, a glorification of feeling and affection, and a renunciation of personal and selfish desires for an altruistic devotion to the good of the race."

In *Poets and Problems* (1886) Cooke used similar standards to judge the work of Alfred Tennyson, John Ruskin, and Robert Browning. His reservation about Tennyson is that his poetry is more an expression of sentiment than intellect that results in his longer poems being less effective than his short lyrics; Ruskin, on the other hand, is a poet whose work demonstrates "Whatever is best and whatever is weakest in the art revival" of Victorian England. In other words Cooke believed that Ruskin's poetry suffers from an emphasis on form over subject, and he found Ruskin's greatest poetry in his criticism. Browning is the poet Cooke most admires because he is more idealistic than Tennyson or Ruskin. In fact Cooke claims that Browning is the "last of the men directly affected by the incoming of German idealism," and, not surprisingly, he argues that Browning is the inheritor of the tradition of Carlyle and Emerson as writers of "books of the soul." He writes: "These men were alike in this, that they were prophets more than artists. With one accord they counted it unworthy that life should have no higher than the artist's aim. They spoke because of what they had to say, and not for the sake of the manner of saying." In short, Browning, like Carlyle and Emerson, fulfills the theory that Cooke delineates in the volume's opening essay, "The Poet as Teacher," a theory that owes a great deal to the influence of American and European romanticism as well as Cooke's own sense of vocation as a Unitarian minister. For Cooke, then, "The poet is the true teacher of men, for he inspires and exalts them, and opens them to a knowledge of their real being." "The Poet as Teacher" remains perhaps the fullest theoretical expression of how Cooke would judge literary art by his own humanistic standards.

Just as Cooke's study of Emerson resulted in his publishing works to widen the potential audience for Emerson's work, his interest in Browning resulted in two such projects: *A Guide-Book to the Poetic and Dramatic Works of Robert Browning* (1891), a dictionarylike compilation of notes and explanations to accompany Browning's works, and Cooke's own edition of *The Poetic and Dramatic Works of Robert Browning* (1899).

Cooke's third principal area of interest as a writer and scholar merges his concern with such disciplines as literature, psychology, and sociology with his vocation as a Unitarian minister and, in a significant way, reveals the importance of both religion and humanism to an understanding of Cooke's perspective as a literary critic and scholar. Cooke wrote and published several histories of parishes with which he was affiliated, including *A History of the Clapboard Trees or Third Parish, Dedham, Mass. now the Unitarian Parish, West Dedham, 1736-1886* (1887) and *Origin and Early History of the First Parish, Sharon, Massachusetts* (1903). Both of these slight works are dwarfed by Cooke's *Unitarianism in America: A History of Its Origin and Development* (1902), which he intended as a complement to existing treatments of the history of American Unitarianism by emphasizing its "practical side . . . its organizations, charities, philanthropies, and reforms." This work, like much of Cooke's literary criticism, aims to demonstrate that Unitarianism is essentially a humanistic religion that is at the core of American life and culture. His chapters on Unitarian influence in law, letters, reform, philanthropy, education, and science suggest that his chief purpose is to validate Unitarianism as perhaps the most important influence, both historically and presently, in American life, an argument supported by his claim that such important non-Unitarians as Benjamin Franklin, Abraham Lincoln, John Marshall, and John Greenleaf Whittier were really Unitarians in spirit because they "accepted its principles of individual freedom, the rational interpretation of religion, and the necessity of bringing religious beliefs into harmony with modern science and philosophy." It is undeniable that in the last two decades of his life Cooke strove to find a way to perpetuate religion as a social force in American life, and *Unitarianism in America* prefigures his strongest argument for just that.

In many ways Cooke's final book serves as the ultimate delineation of his views as scholar and critic of literature. *The Social Evolution of Religion* (1920), while not literary criticism, demonstrates the breadth of Cooke's interest and knowledge as well as the humanism and essential optimism that lie at the heart of his beliefs. The humanism is apparent in the book's title, for, unlike William James, Cooke saw religion as a healthy, man-centered activity that arises out of the social needs of mankind. Even in writing a book that is

basically a negative response to an existing situation, he deemphasizes negative criticism and stresses the evolutionary quality of religious development, which presupposes that even in its present dire circumstances, religion contains within it the capability of ascending to the next, more enlightened, level on the evolutionary ladder.

In much of his literary criticism Cooke was motivated by a sincere appreciation for his subject, and in *The Social Evolution of Religion* he appears to have been partially motivated by his interest in Sir James Fraser's *The Golden Bough* (1890), but in this work he is also expressing his commitment to the healthy growth of religion in American culture, something to which he had been dedicated from the outset of his career as a minister. To that end this study is also a response to the influential views of William James. Cooke believed James's psychological explanation of religion in *The Varieties of Religious Experience* (1902) to be wrongheaded, and he complains that James's focus on individual religious experiences is a perversion: "He [James] ignores entirely the historical phases of religion, . . . he feels no concern as to its evolution, . . . [and] he does not connect it with culture and civilization." Cooke thought that James, in concentrating on "abnormal and pathological types of religious devotees," did no service to the future of religion. "It is not from the abnormal and pathological individuals, who see visions, and enter into worlds not known to ordinary man and woman," Cooke argues, "that we are to gain the rational, sane, and vigorously moral development [of religion] the future demands." To Cooke any "radically individualistic" approach to belief is unsound because "religion is always a phase of mass thought and action."

What Cooke offers in place of James's approach is a radically social interpretation that locates the origin of belief in "a group mind or collective soul," and he argues that "the gods of the Navaho, as of the Greeks, were intimately and essentially reflections of the collective life of these peoples, projected into the earth or into the heavens in the form of divine beings they worshipped in ritual, and interpreted in myth." To prove his point Cooke examines the evolutionary stages of religion–communal and tribal, feudal, national, and international–and he concludes that his survey shows that religion is to a large degree an organic growth, human in origin, whose evolution is determined by social and intellectual phases of the progress of culture: "No religion in its origin can go beyond the stage of civilization in which it arises, and no one of them has yet brought to man truths he could not himself discover by other means than those of inspiration and revelation."

Cooke's survey concludes with two chapters that anticipate the new religion that must come if religion is to survive in the world. In his explanation of the highest stage of his evolutionary scale, "Universal Religion," Cooke describes the demands that will be placed on organized religions in the twentieth century, and he suggests that religion must recognize its social origins and functions, work harder to ameliorate human conditions, seek a unity of purpose, accept science and scientific methods, and ultimately become more rational, tolerant, humane, and sympathetic. Finally, in a chapter on "Religion as Cosmic and Human Motive," Cooke argues for the validity of belief in the new "forward-looking, progressive," human-oriented religion that he calls "universal religion": "Because man has been a savage is no reason why he should reject his childhood as the path which has led to his manhood. Because he has believed in magic is no reason why he should reject what is progressive and humanitarian."

These complementary themes of progressive thought and action and humanism are woven throughout Cooke's career. They are the concerns that help explain and give meaning to his life and his devotion to his ministerial calling. Taken as themes for his writing about literature, philosophy, and religion, these concerns help us to understand how Cooke carried on the traditions of transcendental humanism and idealism into an age that generally dismissed such idealism as moonshine.

Reference:

J. T. Sunderland, "George Willis Cooke: An Appreciation," *Unity,* 89 (14 June 1923): 249-254.

Papers:
Most of George Willis Cooke's papers were presumably dispersed or destroyed after his death. A few of his letters may be found in the following collections: the Jabez Thomas Sunderland papers at the Bentley Historical Library, University of Michigan; the Samuel Arthur Jones papers in the Rare Book and Manuscript Collection at the University of Michigan Library; and the Sarah Margaret Fuller Ossoli papers at the Boston Public Library.

F. Marion Crawford

(2 August 1854-9 April 1909)

John Pilkington, Jr.
University of Mississippi

BOOKS: *Mr. Isaacs: A Tale of Modern India* (London: Macmillan, 1882; New York: Macmillan, 1882);

Doctor Claudius: A True Story (London: Macmillan, 1883; New York: Macmillan, 1883);

To Leeward (2 volumes, London: Chapman & Hall, 1883; 1 volume, Boston: Houghton, Mifflin, 1884; revised edition, New York & London: Macmillan, 1893);

A Roman Singer (Boston & New York: Houghton, Mifflin, 1884; London: Macmillan, 1884; revised edition, New York & London: Macmillan, 1893);

An American Politician (London: Chapman & Hall, 1884; Boston & New York: Houghton, Mifflin, 1885);

Zoroaster (2 volumes, London: Macmillan, 1885; 1 volume, London & New York: Macmillan, 1885);

A Tale of a Lonely Parish (2 volumes, London: Macmillan, 1886; 1 volume, London & New York: Macmillan, 1886);

Saracinesca (3 volumes, Edinburgh & London: Blackwood, 1887; 1 volume, New York: Macmillan, 1887);

Marzio's Crucifix, 2 volumes (London & New York: Macmillan, 1887);

Paul Patoff, 3 volumes (London & New York: Macmillan, 1887);

With the Immortals, 2 volumes (London & New York: Macmillan, 1888);

Greifenstein, 3 volumes (London & New York: Macmillan, 1889);

Sant' Ilario, 3 volumes (London & New York, 1889);

A Cigarette-Maker's Romance, 2 volumes (London & New York: Macmillan, 1890);

Khaled: A Tale of Arabia, 2 volumes (London & New York, 1891);

The Witch of Prague, 3 volumes (London & New York: Macmillan, 1891); republished as *The Witch of Prague: A Fantastic Tale,* 1 volume (London & New York: Macmillan, 1891);

F. Marion Crawford

The Three Fates, 3 volumes (London & New York: Macmillan, 1892);

Don Orsino (New York & London: Macmillan, 1892);

The Children of the King: A Tale of Southern Italy, 2 volumes (London & New York: Macmillan, 1892);

The Novel: What It Is (New York & London: Macmillan, 1893);

Pietro Ghisleri (New York & London: Macmillan, 1893);

Marion Darche: A Story Without Comment (New York & London: Macmillan, 1893);

Katherine Lauderdale, 2 volumes (New York & London: Macmillan, 1894);

The Upper Berth (London: Unwin, 1894; New York: Putnam's, 1894);

Love in Idleness: A Tale of Bar Harbour (New York & London: Macmillan, 1894);

The Ralstons, 2 volumes (New York & London: Macmillan, 1895);

Constantinople (New York: Scribners, 1895);

Casa Braccio, 2 volumes (New York & London, 1895);

Adam Johnstone's Son (New York & London: Macmillan, 1896);

Taquisara, 2 volumes (New York & London: Macmillan, 1896);

A Rose of Yesterday (New York & London: Macmillan, 1897);

Corleone: A Tale of Sicily, 2 volumes (New York & London: Macmillan, 1897);

Ave Roma Immortalis: Studies from the Chronicles of Rome, 2 volumes (New York & London: Macmillan, 1898; revised, 1902);

Via Crucis: A Romance of the Second Crusade (New York & London: Macmillan, 1899);

The Rulers of the South: Sicily, Calabria, Malta, 2 volumes (New York & London: Macmillan, 1900); republished as *Southern Italy and Sicily and the Rulers of the South* (London: Macmillan, 1905; New York: Macmillan, 1905);

In the Palace of the King: A Love Story of Old Madrid (New York & London: Macmillan, 1900);

Marietta: A Maid of Venice (New York & London: Macmillan, 1901);

Francesca da Rimini: A Play in Four Acts (New York & London: Macmillan, 1902);

Cecilia: A Story of Modern Rome (New York & London: Macmillan, 1902);

Man Overboard! (New York & London: Macmillan, 1903);

The Heart of Rome: A Tale of the 'Lost Water' (New York & London: Macmillan, 1903);

Whosoever Shall Offend (New York & London: Macmillan, 1904);

Soprano: A Portrait (London & New York: Macmillan, 1905); republished as *Fair Margaret: A Portrait* (New York & London: Macmillan, 1905);

Salve Venetia: Gleanings from Venetian History, 2 volumes (New York & London: Macmillan, 1905); republished as *Gleanings from Venetian History*, 2 volumes (London & New York: Macmillan, 1905); republished as *Venice, the Place and the People* (New York: Macmillan, 1909);

A Lady of Rome (New York & London: Macmillan, 1906);

Arethusa (New York & London: Macmillan, 1907);

The Little City of Hope: A Christmas Story (London: Macmillan, 1907; New York: Macmillan, 1907);

The Primadonna: A Sequel to 'Soprano' (London: Macmillan, 1908); republished as *The Primadonna: A Sequel to "Fair Margaret"* (New York: Macmillan, 1908);

The Diva's Ruby: A Sequel to 'Soprano' and 'Fair Margaret' (London: Macmillan, 1908); republished as *The Diva's Ruby: A Sequel to "Primadonna" and "Fair Margaret"* (New York: Macmillan, 1908);

The White Sister (London: Macmillan, 1909; New York: Macmillan, 1909);

Stradella: An Old Italian Love Tale (London: Macmillan, 1909; New York: Macmillan, 1909);

The Undesirable Governess (London: Macmillan, 1910; New York: Macmillan, 1910);

Uncanny Tales (London: Unwin, 1911); republished as *Wandering Ghosts* (New York: Macmillan, 1911);

The White Sister: Romantic Drama in Three Acts, by Crawford and Walter Hackett (New York: Dramatists Play Service, 1937).

PERIODICAL PUBLICATIONS: "False Taste in Art," *North American Review*, 135 (July 1882): 89-98;

"What Is a Novel?," *Forum*, 14 (January 1893): 591-599;

"Emotional Tension and the Modern Novel," *Forum*, 14 (February 1893): 735-742;

"Coasting by Sorrento and Amalfi," *Century Magazine*, 48, new series 26 (July 1894): 325-336;

"A Kaleidoscope of Rome," *Century Magazine*, 51, new series 29 (January 1896): 322-340;

"Pope Leo XIII. and His Household," *Century Magazine*, 51, new series 29 (February 1896): 590-603;

"St. Peter's," *Century Magazine*, 52, new series 30 (July 1896): 323-339;

"The Greatest Disaster of History: First Paper," *Outlook*, 91 (27 March 1909): 673-690.

The verdict of literary historians and academic critics upon the fiction writers of the years between 1883 and 1909–the period when Francis Marion Crawford was writing novels–has long since been rendered in favor of William Dean Howells, Mark Twain, and Henry James. That judgment is not likely to be reversed, but anyone concerned with the novel in America should realize that the American and British public of this

Crawford at the time he wrote his most important critical work, The Novel: What It Is

period overwhelmingly preferred the work of Crawford to that of those "masters." The popularity of his forty-four novels, each a best-seller in its day, and three collected editions of his works published during his lifetime provide irrefutable evidence of their appeal to readers of novels. In addition to his fame as a novelist American readers applauded Crawford as a lecturer, playwright, critic, and historian. As a professional man of letters he was a glamorous figure, often called the Prince of Sorrento.

Crawford's own romantic life contained the sources of most of his novels. Born on 2 August 1854 at Bagni di Lucca, Italy, the son of Thomas Crawford, the American sculptor, and Louisa Cutler Ward, sister of Julia Ward Howe, Crawford's education included schooling in Rome, New Hampshire, Cambridge, Karlsruhe, and Heidelberg. In 1879 he went to Allahabad, India, to edit the *Indian Herald;* but a year later he came to the United States to seek literary employment with the help of his uncle Samuel Ward, the celebrated gourmet and lobbyist. In 1882 the Macmil-

lan Company published Crawford's first novel, *Mr. Isaacs: A Tale of Modern India,* thereby beginning an association that would last until his death. Shortly afterward he returned to Italy to reside in Sorrento, where, after his marriage to Elizabeth Berdan in Constantinople in 1884, he purchased a villa overlooking the Bay of Naples and the island of Capri. His life henceforth was primarily devoted to his work, but in 1892 he returned to the United States for the first of many visits. At this time he renewed his friendship with Isabella Stewart Gardner, a wealthy Bostonian socialite and art collector whom he had known ten years earlier, and purchased a yacht that he would sail across the Atlantic. Virtually every year he came back to New York to write in a penthouse above the Macmillan Company offices. In Sorrento he lived a luxurious life, and in his last years he turned to writing the history of Venice, Sicily, and Rome, the last left incomplete at his death on 9 April 1909. In his own day he was acclaimed as the leading man of letters in America. Admired for his personal charm, his cosmopolitanism, and his learning, he was a celebrity and the constant source of feature articles in newspapers and literary periodicals. His popular reputation far surpassed that of Howells and James. When Crawford spoke about literary matters he enjoyed a wide audience of not only his readers but also his peers.

During the decade of the 1890s American writers were very much alert to the differing literary principles underlying the production of fiction. Actually the debate had begun in the 1880s when such novelists as Howells, James, and Crawford began to crystallize their writing practices into literary doctrine. Howells, for example, had moved steadily away from the romances of his early years toward realism. In *The Rise of Silas Lapham* (1885) he had explicated his ideas in fictional form while advocating realism in a series of essays in the "Editor's Study," his regular column in the *Atlantic Monthly.* As early as 1879, in *Hawthorne,* James had indicated the direction of his thinking, and in 1884 he published *The Art of Fiction.* Crawford had advanced his theories fictionally in such novels as *A Tale of a Lonely Parish* (1886), *Paul Patoff* (1887), and *With the Immortals* (1888).

These "preliminary" statements of position reached a crescendo in the 1890s. In May 1891, partly as a good business venture, Howells pieced together not very expertly some of his essays into book form. His *Criticism and Fiction* became a mani-

Crawford in his study in New York City

festo of realism and a rebuke to romanticism that seemed to invite reply. James's "The Real Thing" (1892; collected in *The Real Thing and Other Tales,* 1893) may have been written with Howells's volume in mind. Crawford entered the critical debate with *The Novel: What It Is* (1893). Others were to follow. In 1894 Hamlin Garland, in *Crumbling Idols,* offered *veritism* as a variation (and improvement) upon Howells's realism. Henry Blake Fuller's "Howells or James" (1895) distinguished sharply between the theories of the two writers. As the decade wore on Frank Norris published a number of essays in defense of his mingling naturalism with romanticism. The best of them would include "Zola as a Romantic Writer" (1896), "The True Reward of the Novelist" (1901), "The Mechanics of Fiction" (1901), "The Novel with a Purpose" (1902), and "The Responsibilities of a Novelist" (1903).

Although Crawford's critical theories found expression in novels and in two lengthy articles, "What Is a Novel?" and "Emotional Tension and the Modern Novel," published in *Forum* in successive issues, January and February 1893, his major pronouncement appeared in April of that year

with the publication of *The Novel: What It Is.* In defining the novel he began with a candid statement of the economic aspect of novel writing. The fact is, wrote Crawford, that novelists join with publishers to make money from the production of fiction. Together they exist to supply an economic demand. Thus, essentially, the novel is "a marketable commodity," even as it is an artistic, intellectual luxury. With this basic premise Howells and James, along with many other writers, would have agreed.

Howells and Crawford, however, sharply disagreed over Crawford's next point. Crawford believed that "the first object of the novel is to amuse and interest the reader." He had already stated this conviction in *Paul Patoff* through his fictional representative, who declares that he writes "for the sole purpose of amusing you [the reader]," then repeated and elaborated on the point in *The Three Fates* (1892). Although these statements affirm his commitment to the literature of entertainment, they oversimplify his position. He thought the novel should not be merely a "piece of good fun" but instead should be written to amuse from an intellectual standpoint.

Crawford's villa in Sorrento, Italy

As a corollary to his position Crawford argued that the novel should not be designed to instruct the reader. When written to instruct, the novel became a "purpose-novel" and an "intellectual moral lesson" rather than an "intellectual artistic luxury." Indeed, the purpose-novel was really a fraud, since the reader buys a novel for entertainment and instead receives instruction. A novel, he admitted, written to amuse might also improve the reader: "What we call a novel may educate the taste and cultivate the intelligence; . . . it may purify the heart and fortify the mind; . . . it may stand for scores of years . . . as the exposition of all that is noble, heroic, honest, and true in the life of woman or man; but it has no right to tell us what its writer thinks about the relations of labour and capital . . . any more than it has a right to take for its theme . . . temperance, vivisection, or the 'Ideal Man' of Confucius. Les-sons, lectures, discussions, sermons, and didactics generally belong to institutions set apart for especial purposes." The purpose-novel, concluded Crawford, is "an ambush" for an unsuspecting reader. Howells's doctrine of realism led inevitably to the purpose-novel of contemporary issues; and Crawford would have no difficulty in assigning Howells's *A Hazard of New Fortunes* (1889), *The World of Chance* (1893), and *A Traveler from Altruria* (1894) to the category of purpose-novels.

Crawford tried to clarify his position regarding the moral content of fiction. He was certain that "in art of all kinds the moral lesson is a mistake." He felt it was one thing "to exhibit an ideal worthy to be imitated, though inimitable in all its perfection, . . . to make man brave without arrogance, woman pure without prudishness, love enduring yet earthly, not angelic, friendship sincere but not ridiculous." But he added, "it is quite another matter to write a 'guide to morality' or a 'hand-book for practical sinners' and call either one a novel, no matter how much fiction it may contain."

From his own work Crawford could have cited his Saracinesca trilogy–*Saracinesca* (1887), *Sant' Ilario* (1889), and *Don Orsino* (1892). In them Corona and Giovanni Saracinesca had been depicted as individuals whom readers "might really like to resemble, acting in scenes in which they themselves would like to take a part." Thus, they appear as ideal figures, although the novels cannot be said to have been written to inculcate a moral lesson. This distinction between the presentation of the ideal and the teaching of moral lessons Crawford felt was basic to his critical theories.

Much of the debate between Howells and Crawford was actually a reflection of the premises of the Genteel Tradition. In general Howells's practice moved away from the ideals of the Genteel Tradition. As Howells's work became more and more realistic, he departed from the concept of ideality in literature, although he retained much of the tradition's insistence upon the ethical nobility of art. Since Crawford essentially wrote within the tradition, his opposition to realism is not surprising. Both men might agree (and James also) that although Emile Zola could write explicitly about sexual matters in fiction, in America, where the novel was addressed often to young girls, the novelist was restricted. Yet Crawford saw that these matters, if they were to be addressed at all, would be addressed under the aegis of realism. As the realistic method was applied to novels written according to the philosophical premises of naturalism, the truth of Crawford's judgment became evident.

Crawford, moreover, saw realism as "generally a photograph, not a picture–a catalogue, not a description." Not only did it lead to coarseness, but also to ordinary, commonplace incidents that were simply boring to readers. In *Paul Patoff* Crawford told his readers that "the world is not yet turned into a farmyard" and noted that not everybody finds "the beauty of nature in a horsepond." Ordinary events hardly make good fiction. "True stories," wrote Crawford, "very rarely have a conclusion at all, and the necessity for a conclusion is the first thing felt by the born novelist." In criticizing realism he was not arguing against all realism in fiction; on the contrary, he insisted that a novel must be based in reality, but that reality must be heightened, even trans-

formed, by the artist. "Art," wrote Crawford, "if it is 'to create and foster agreeable illusions,' . . . should represent the real, but in such a way as to make it seem more agreeable and interesting than it actually is." The comment is reminiscent of James's insistence upon the "air of reality" rather than reality itself.

Crawford had little regard for the realist's insistence upon authentic description. "Generally speaking, I venture to say that anything which fixes the date of the novel not intended to be historical is a mistake, from a literary point of view. It is not wise to describe the cut of the hero's coat, nor the draping of the heroine's gown, the shape of her hat, nor the colour of his tie. Ten years hence somebody may buy the book and turn up his nose at 'those times.' " For similar reasons Crawford was not in favor of illustrations in fiction. He could also have added that novels employing contemporary social and political issues could be as dated as the heroine's gown.

Crawford always maintained that the general aim of the novelist should be to present the ideal through the delineation of character and incident based in reality. The goal was not to transcribe reality but to provide an illusion of reality. The novel was, in fact, analogous to the play. Indeed, the relationship between the theater and the novel was so close that Crawford described the novel as "a pocket-stage." The most important point, however, in his theory of the novel is that the novelist must write of the verities of human experience, that is, the human heart. "The foundation of good fiction and good poetry seems to be ethic rather than aesthetic. Everything in either which appeals to the . . . aesthetic side, may ultimately perish as a mere matter of fashion; but that which speaks to man as man, independently of his fashions, his habits, and his tastes, must live and find a hearing with humanity so long as humanity is human. The right understanding of men and women leads to the right relations of men and women, and in this way . . . a novel may do good." In his stress upon fiction that dealt with the relations of men and women over novels devoted to social and political causes, Crawford was much closer to James than to Howells.

With the publication of *The Novel: What It Is*, Crawford became the acknowledged leader of the romantic school of fiction, often called the literature of entertainment. No one before or since has argued so forcibly its principles and justification. He provided the critical basis, the literary re-

Crawford's funeral procession in Sorrento, 12 April 1909

spectability, of much of the fiction that was popular in the decades of the 1880s and 1890s. Howells's insistence upon truth to the motives and principles that shape the lives of actual men and women and upon the choice of ordinary, everyday subjects fitted well into tastes of authors who wrote from the premises of philosophic naturalism. Although most novelists of the late 1890s and the first half of the twentieth century now studied in university courses have in the main followed the Howells tradition, there has also been and continues to be an immense body of novels called "popular" or "romantic" that owes much to Crawford's practice and principles.

References:

Mrs. Winthrop Chanler, *Roman Spring: Memoirs* (Boston: Little, Brown, 1934);

Vittoria Colonna, Duchess of Sermoneta, *Things Past* (New York: Appleton, 1929);

Frederic Taber Cooper, "Francis Marion Crawford—An Estimate," *Bookman*, 29 (May 1909): 283-292;

Maud Howe Elliott, *My Cousin: F. Martin Crawford* (New York: Macmillan, 1934);

Mary Crawford [Mrs. Hugh] Fraser, "Notes of a Romantic Life: The Italian Days of Francis Marion Crawford, and the Intimate Side of His Character," *Collier's*, 45 (23 April 1910): 22-24;

John Charles Moran, *An F. Marion Crawford Companion* (Westport, Conn.: Greenwood Press, 1981);

Moran, "F. Marion Crawford's 'An American Politician': Some BAL Addenda," *Papers of the Bibliographical Society of America*, 69 (1975): 267-272;

Moran, "Recent Interest in F. Marion Crawford—A Bibliographical Account," *Romantist*, no. 1 (1977): 53-56;

Moran, *Seeking Refuge in Torre San Nicola: An Introduction to F. Marion Crawford* (Nashville, Tenn.: F. Marion Crawford Memorial Society, 1980);

Ouida [Louise de la Ramée], "The Italian Novels

of Marion Crawford," *Nineteenth Century,* 24 (November 1897): 719-733;

John Pilkington, Jr., "A Crawford Bibliography," *University of Mississippi Studies in English,* 2 (1961): 29-39;

Pilkington, "F. Marion Crawford: Italy in Fiction," *American Quarterly,* 6 (Spring 1954): 59-65;

Pilkington, "F. Marion Crawford's Lecture Tour, 1897-1898," *University of Mississippi Studies in English,* 1 (1960): 66-85;

Pilkington, *Francis Marion Crawford* (New York: Twayne, 1964);

Pilkington, "The Genesis of *Mr. Isaacs,*" *University of Mississippi Studies in English,* 2 (1961): 29-39;

Arthur Hobson Quinn, *American Fiction: An Historical and Critical Survey* (New York & London: Appleton Century, 1936);

Hugh Walpole, "The Stories of Francis Marion Crawford," *Yale Review,* 12 (July 1923): 673-691.

Papers:

The Houghton Library of Harvard University is the largest single repository of Crawford material; the collection includes letters, manuscripts, and other documents relating to Crawford. Additional important material may be found in the Isabella Stewart Gardner Museum, Boston, Massachusetts; the New York Public Library; the Library of Congress; Yale University; Princeton University; and the University of Pennsylvania.

Kuno Francke

(27 September 1855-25 June 1930)

Thomas Haeussler
University of California, Los Angeles

BOOKS: *Zur Geschichte der lateinischen Schulpoesie des XII. und XIII. Jahrhunderts* (Munich: Literarisch-artistische Anstalt [Th. Reidel], 1879);

De Hymni in Cererem Homerici Compositione, Dictione, Aetate (Kiel: Schmidt & Klaunig, 1881);

Social Forces in German Literature, A Study in the History of Civilization (New York: Holt, 1896); enlarged as *A History of German Literature as Determined by Social Forces* (New York: Holt, 1901);

Glimpses of Modern German Culture (New York: Dodd, Mead, 1898);

Deutsche Cultur in den Vereinigten Staaten und das Germanische Museum der Harvard-Universität (Berlin: Gebrüder Paetel, 1902);

German Ideals of To-day, and Other Essays on German Culture (Boston & New York: Houghton, Mifflin, 1907);

Die Kulturwerte der deutschen Literatur in ihrer geschichtlichen Entwicklung, 3 volumes (Berlin: Weidmannsche Buchhandlung, 1910-1928);

A German-American's Confession of Faith (New York: Huebsch, 1915);

The German Spirit (New York: Holt, 1916);

Personality in German Literature before Luther (Cambridge: Harvard University Press, 1916);

Deutsches Schicksal, Tagebuchblätter eines Ausgewanderten (Dresden: Pierson, 1923);

German After-war Problems (Cambridge: Harvard University Press, 1927);

Deutsche Arbeit in Amerika, Erinnerungen von Kuno Francke (Leipzig: Meiner, 1930).

OTHER: *Libelli de Lite Imperatorum et Pontificum Saeculi XI. et XII.*, 3 volumes, volumes 1 and 2 edited by Francke (Hannover: impensis bibliopolii Hahniani, 1891-1892);

The German Classics of the Nineteenth and Twentieth Centuries; Masterpieces of German Literature translated into English, edited by Francke and

Kuno Francke

William Guild Howard (Albany, N.Y.: Lyon, 1913-1914).

Kuno Francke was commonly regarded as the leading Germanist in America for the more than three decades he served as Professor of the History of German Culture at Harvard University. His achievement as a pedagogue, literary historian, cultural critic, and public advocate for German values and ideals was substantial, and he contributed to the fundamental reorientation of the then somewhat limited native tradition in *Germanistik* associated with such names as Karl Follen, George Bancroft, Henry Wadsworth Long-

Francke about the time he became an instructor in German at Harvard University

fellow, and Frederick Hedge. He introduced to his university the broad interdisciplinary method of the *Geisteswissenschaften* (Human Sciences), arguing in particular that the competent consideration of German literature and art necessarily depended upon the larger context of German national history. Francke's publications and public addresses on German literary, philosophical, and social themes provided an English-speaking audience with a comprehensive, expertly informed, and conceptually provocative treatment of German cultural evolution from the Teutonic migrations of the fifth century through the modern age. His intellectual perspective, nowhere better represented than in the acclaimed *Social Forces in German Literature* (1896), was that of the distinguished German historical tradition which—beginning with Johann Joachim Winckelmann and Johann Gottfried Herder and extending through G. W. F. Hegel, Georg Gottfried Gervinus, Gustav Freytag, Jacob Burckhardt, and Karl Lamprecht—was characterized by its efforts to integrate historical and aesthetic experience into a coherent pattern of culturally illuminating symbols and concepts.

Born on 27 September 1855 in Kiel, Schleswig-Holstein, then a crown property of Denmark, Kuno Francke was the son of Judge August Wilhelm and Katherine Marie Jensen Francke. He was "raised in an environment of thrift, unrelenting industry, obedience to duty and conscience, and respect to the higher life." Initially educated in the gymnasium and university of his native Kiel, he ultimately undertook a student's tour of the universities of Berlin, Jena, and Munich, studying with such notables as Friedrich Paulsen, Rudolf Eucken, Heinrich von Brunn, and Wilhelm von Giesebrecht. It was Brunn who persuaded the young Francke to abandon his dramaturgical ambitions in light of what had revealed itself to be a striking aptitude for literary history. Giesebrecht subsequently directed him toward the study of medieval literature and society; supervised his dissertation, *Zur Geschichte der lateinischen Schulpoesie des XII. und XIII. Jahrhunderts* (On the History of Latin School Poetry in the Twelfth and Thirteenth Centuries, 1879); and sponsored his successful application for the König Ludwig stipend for medieval study, which, in 1879, facilitated six months of research in Italian libraries and archives. Upon returning to Germany Francke accepted a teaching position at the Kiel gymnasium, where he remained from 1880 to 1882, and published *De Hymni in Cererem Homerici Compositione, Dictione, Aetate* (On the Homeric Hymns to Ceres, Their Composition, Style, and Period, 1881). His reputation as a young scholar of promise now established, he was invited by the noted medievalist Georg Waitz to become an assistant editor for the famous scholarly series Monumenta Germaniae Historica (Historical Documents of Germany). His contributions to that enterprise during his brief tenure would appear in the initial two volumes of *Libelli de Lite Imperatorum et Pontificum Saeculi XI. et XII.* (Treatises on the Conflict between Emperors and Pontiffs in the Eleventh and Twelfth Centuries, 1891-1892).

Not yet thirty, Francke was thus already a respected scholar when, in 1884, a call arrived from Harvard University offering him an instructorship in German. His name had been advanced by the Harvard ecclesiastical historian Ephraim Emerton and was strongly supported by Paulsen, a noted German philosopher. The latter, having been approached by Harvard President Charles W. Eliot, affirmed, as he later recalled in his *Autobiography* (1938), that "if a faithful representative of the German spirit was desired at Harvard, a representative, that is to say, of the spirit of the older Germany, the Germany of Goethe's time, it would be impossible to find a more genuine incarnation of that type than in Kuno Francke." Francke doubtless fulfilled Paulsen's expectation as he undertook an advocacy of German cultural values which was, as he stated in the preface to *German Ideals of To-day* (1907), "frankly propagandistic" and bore more than a touch of the missionary's zeal (his autobiography, significantly enough, would be entitled *Deutsche Arbeit in Amerika* [German Work in America, 1930]). Presented with an audience which evinced "not only a profound ignorance of the German tradition, but also an instinctive temperamental New England dislike for the far-flung vistas of German thought" (Arthur Davison Ficke, "The Recollections of Kuno Francke," *Harvard Graduates Magazine*, 9 June 1930), he nevertheless succeeded in making his subject of interest. His university lectures and public addresses were judged by his contemporaries to be "more than effective and impressive. He had a kindling quality. Tho far from pretentious or theatrical–indeed by temperament modest–he had yet an oratorial bent. . . . He was welcome and admired as a public lecturer." Several generations of students (among them the art critic Bernard Berenson) and the general public were thereby enlightened with regard to German cultural history, and favorably inclined toward its study.

His abiding devotion to his own native culture did not encumber Francke in assimilating to his new national circumstance. On hearing President Eliot enjoin the incoming Harvard class of 1884-1885 to "Look out and not in, forward and not backwards, up and not down," he was pleasantly reminded of eighteenth-century Europe prior to its disruption by political turmoil, national rivalry, and unhealthy intellectual romanticism. Contemporary America impressed him as comparable to that estimable age and seemed extraordinarily tranquil, well balanced, and potent in comparison with the now-troubled continent. The unaffected individualism, enlightened social conscience, and pragmatic idealism of such men as Eliot and William James inspired in Francke an ever-deepening appreciation for his adopted country. His marriage in 1889 to Katherine Gilbert, with whom he would have three children, and his assumption in 1891 of American citizenship, firmly established not only his residence but his sense of national identification.

Francke had been at Harvard little more than a decade when, in 1896, he published his masterwork, *Social Forces in German Literature*, subsequently expanded under the title *A History of German Literature as Determined by Social Forces* (1901) and further enlarged, as well as partially reformulated, in the three-volume German edition, *Die Kulturwerte der deutschen Literatur in ihrer geschichtlichen Entwicklung* (The Cultural Values of German Literature in Their Historical Evolution, 1910, 1923, 1928). Hermann Grimm, then the preeminent German literary critic, in reviewing *Social Forces in German Literature,* described it as an important extension of the tradition in cultural and literary historiography inaugurated earlier in the century by Friedrich Christoph Schlosser and Gervinus and applauded Francke's determination, unique among his contemporaries, to write as a "student of civilization" rather than as a mere philologist or literary analyst ("Eine neue deutsche Literaturgeschichte," *Deutsche Rundschau,* July-September 1897). For while there was no dearth of works treating German literature from a linguistic or literary perspective, there was a decided need for a work which provided a coherent account of the dynamic and dialectically profound interrelation of German cultural production and sociopolitical experience.

Social Forces in German Literature addressed itself to such need and provided a scholarly, theoretically informed survey of German literary and social history, beginning with the Teutonic contributions to the establishment of "modern" Europe, extending through the periods of Reformation and Enlightenment, and culminating with the unification of the German states in the latter nineteenth century. Its author tended, however, to subordinate questions of a purely literary nature to those of larger historical significance, and texts of dubious artistic merit, yet representative of a prevailing intellectual problematic, were often invoked in his historiographic ruminations. A contemporary American reviewer was thus justified in asserting that, while immensely learned and of monumental ambition, the work was excessively governed by its "plan" (*Harvard Graduates Magazine,* 1896-1897). That plan, described by Francke in his foreword as positing a fundamental dialectic within German culture between the desire for individual freedom and self-fulfillment and the desire for participation in community, determined the analysis of those periods in German history (notably the High Middle Ages, the Reformation, the 1813 war of liberation, the failed revolution of 1848) in which profound intellectual achievement and agitation prepared opportunities for potential synthesis yet failed repeatedly to inspire the strong collective will or enlightened public opinion needed both to balance the German personality and achieve a unified German nation. It was not until the unification of Hohenzollern Germany in 1870-1871 appeared to integrate the German cultural legacy with political praxis, that *Social Forces in German Literature* was provided with its appropriately Hegelian conclusion.

The question concerning the dialectical relation within German culture of principles of individuation and collectivity received further definition and elaboration in Francke's essays and public addresses at the turn of the century. That body of work, collected in *Glimpses of Modern German Culture* (1898) and *German Ideals of To-day*, while generally characterized by an abundant enthusiasm for the burgeoning authority and world influence of Hohenzollern Germany, also revealed Francke's lingering fear that the pattern of the German past might yet reestablish itself. Germany remained "the classic land of moral contrasts," one in which there presided as ever a potentially destructive tension between personal conviction and traditional creeds, idealistic aspirations and materialist impulses, autocratic institutions and democratic ideals. The emergence of such contemporary intellectual perspectives as Friedrich Nietzsche's philosophy of the will to power could not help but appear ominous for Germany's otherwise promising future. On at least one occasion, that of the centennial address, "Emerson and German Personality" (1903; collected in *German Ideals of To-day*), Francke's response, representative perhaps of an increasingly American cast of mind, was to suggest that Germany embrace the example of a Ralph Waldo Emerson, whose intellectual moderation and harmoniousness might "restore to Germany the idealism of her own thinkers in a purified, saner, and more truly human form." The advent of a "new era of German Idealism" would thus be announced by the call: "less Nietzsche and more Emerson; and a new intellectual bond between America and Germany will have been established."

Francke's personal contribution to that intellectual bond was never greater than in the years preceding World War I. In conjunction with Hermann Grimm, designated representatives of Wilhelm II, and a moderate number of interested German-American patrons, he established in Cambridge, in 1903, the Germanic Museum (since renamed the Busch-Reisinger Museum), in which were gathered fine reproductions of German works of art and industry dating from the Carolingian age through his own day, as well as a library of ten thousand volumes on German history and civilization. Francke, having been appointed curator in 1902, delivered over the next fifteen years a series of lectures on a wide variety of German cultural topics, intended, as always, to further provide his American audience with "a systematic and comprehensive study of German artistic and spiritual achievements" ("The Germanic Museum," in *The Development of Harvard University since the Inauguration of President Eliot, 1869-1929*, edited by Samuel Eliot Morison, 1930). That same interest led him, in 1912, to assume the editorial responsibilities for an ambitious, multivolume anthology entitled *The German Classics of the Nineteenth and Twentieth Centuries* (1913-1914), an enterprise then without precedent in its efforts to provide, whenever possible, translations of German texts in their entirety and to represent the various, yet interrelated, endeavors of German literature, philosophy, history, social science, and other humanistic disciplines.

The German classics series ended abruptly in 1915, following the Lusitania incident, having been criticized in anti-German quarters as "fiendish propaganda." As German-American relations worsened, Francke attempted, in a series of journalistic essays later collected in *A German-American's Confession of Faith* (1915) and *The German Spirit* (1916), to elicit American understanding for the German position while discouraging German sympathizers from engaging in anti-British agitation, thus incurring for himself the enmity of both sides. Finding himself a figure of increasing controversy and engaged in an intense self-examination regarding his "intellectual bigamy," he requested, in 1916, that he be granted leave from his university post. The following year, 1917, was marked, ironically, both by his election to the presidency of the Modern Language Association, a testament to his professional stature and personal reputation, and by his formal resignation, following American entry into the war, from his Harvard professorship. He retained only his position as curator of the Germanic Museum, and when it closed in November 1917 due to a "coal shortage" he retired to his summer home in Gilbertsville, New York.

The American critical reception of Kuno Francke has tended to concentrate on that aspect of his work which, for lack of a better term, might be called idealistic nationalism. And while such characterization is appropriate to *Social Forces in German Literature,* it fails to do justice to the intellectual reassessment and reorientation which, born of a profound personal crisis during World War I, is readily discernible in Francke's late work. For beginning with the Lowell lectures of 1915 (collected as *Personality in German Literature before Luther,* 1916), and then again in the second volume of *Die Kulturwerte der deutschen Literatur in ihrer geschichtlichen Entwicklung,* he returned to familiar historical periods and concepts, reengaging them in accordance with a newly tragic perspective on German historical development. Ulrich von Hutten's famous phrase, *Miseram oportet esse Germaniam necessario,* inspired the reflection: "Was Hutten right when he said that it was the fate of Germany to be unhappy? If he was—and it would almost seem so—then it must be said that the tragedy of Germany history is most intimately allied with German greatness." And whereas Francke once desired the emergence within Germany of a strong national will, he sought in *Weltbürgertum in der deutschen Literatur von Herder bis Nietzsche* (Cosmopolitanism in German Literature from Herder to Nietzsche, 1928), the third volume of *Die Kulturwerte,* to emphasize the cosmopolitan tendencies which, beginning with Herder's *Humanitätsidee* (humanistic ethos), culminated in Nietzsche's now exemplary supranationalism. Francke's analysis of German cultural history, begun fifty years before, was thus yet evolving at the time of his death (25 June 1930), and a projected fourth volume of *Die Kulturwerte,* "Der Nationalismus in der deutschen Literatur" (Nationalism in German Literature), lay half-finished on his desk. That latter scholarly permutation and projection finally shall have to be acknowledged and taken into account if Francke, as he largely deserves, is to be recognized as having been not only among the most significant and influential literary historians of his day, but a cultural analyst of increasingly enhanced conceptual comprehension and, not least, uncommon intellectual integrity.

References:

Charles W. Haxthausen, " 'Deutsche Arbeit in Amerika': Zur Geschichte des Busch-Reisinger Museums," *Deutsche Kunst des 20. Jahrhunderts aus dem Busch-Reisinger Museum* (Frankfurt: Städtische Galerie, 1983);

Phyllis Keller, *States of Belonging: German-American Intellectuals and the First World War* (Cambridge, Mass. & London: Harvard University Press, 1979);

Samuel Eliot Morison, ed., *The Development of Harvard University since the Inauguration of President Eliot, 1869-1929* (Cambridge, Mass.: Harvard University Press, 1930);

Richard Spuler, *"Germanistik" in America: The Reception of German Classicism, 1870-1905* (Stuttgart: Akademischer Verlag Hans-Dieter Heinz, 1982).

Papers:

The papers of Kuno Francke, which consist of articles, correspondence (1915-1917), and notes dating from 1890 to 1930, are collected in the Harvard University Archives.

Hamlin Garland

(14 September 1860-5 March 1940)

Charles L. P. Silet
Iowa State University

See also the Garland entry in *DLB 12, American Realists and Naturalists.*

BOOKS. *Under the Wheel: A Modern Play in Six Scenes* (Boston: Barta, 1890);

Main-Travelled Roads: Six Mississippi Valley Stories (Boston: Arena, 1891; London: Unwin, 1892; enlarged edition, New York & London: Macmillan, 1899; enlarged again, New York & London: Harper, 1922; enlarged again, New York & London: Harper, 1930);

A New Declaration of Rights (N.p., 1891?);

Jason Edwards, an Average Man (Boston: Arena, 1892);

A Member of the Third House (Chicago: Schulte, 1892);

A Little Norsk; or Ol' Pap's Flaxen (New York: Appleton, 1892; London: Unwin, 1892);

A Spoil of Office: A Story of the Modern West (Boston: Arena, 1892; revised edition, New York: Appleton, 1897);

Prairie Songs: Being Chants Rhymed and Unrhymed of the Level Lands of the Great West (Cambridge, Mass. & Chicago: Stone & Kimball, 1893);

Prairie Folks (Chicago: Schulte, 1893; London: Sampson Low, 1893; enlarged edition, New York & London: Macmillan, 1899);

Crumbling Idols: Twelve Essays on Art Dealing Chiefly with Literature, Painting, and the Drama (Chicago & Cambridge, Mass.: Stone & Kimball, 1894);

Impressions on Impressionism: Being a Discussion of the American Art Exhibition at the Art Institute, Chicago, by A Critical Triumvirate, by Garland, Charles Francis Browne, and Lorado Taft (Chicago: Central Art Association, 1894);

Five Hoosier Painters: Being a Discussion of the Holiday Exhibit of the Indianapolis Group, in Chicago, by The Critical Triumvirate, by Garland, Browne, and Taft (Chicago: Central Art Association, 1894);

Rose of Dutcher's Coolly (Chicago: Stone & Kimball, 1895; London: Beeman, 1896; re-

*Courtesy of the Hamlin Garland Papers,
University of Southern California Library*

vised edition, New York & London: Macmillan, 1899);

Wayside Courtships (New York: Appleton, 1897; London: Beeman, 1898);

Ulysses S. Grant: His Life and Character (New York: Doubleday & McClure, 1898);

The Spirit of Sweetwater (Philadelphia: Curtis/New York: Doubleday & McClure, 1898; London: Service & Paton, 1898); revised and enlarged as *Witch's Gold* (New York: Doubleday, Page, 1906);

Boy Life on the Prairie (New York & London: Macmillan, 1899; revised edition, New York: Macmillan, 1908);

The Trail of the Goldseekers: A Record of Travel in Prose and Verse (New York & London: Macmillan, 1899);

The Eagle's Heart (New York: Appleton, 1900; London: Heinemann, 1900);

Her Mountain Lover (New York: Century, 1901; London: Dollar Library, 1901);

The Captain of the Gray-Horse Troop (New York & London: Harper, 1902; London: Grant Richards, 1902);

Hesper (New York & London: Harper, 1903);

The Light of the Star (New York & London: Harper, 1904);

The Tyranny of the Dark (New York & London: Harper, 1905);

The Long Trail: A Story of the Northwest Wilderness (New York & London: Macmillan, 1907);

Money Magic (New York & London: Harper, 1907);

The Shadow World (New York & London: Harper, 1908);

The Moccasin Ranch (New York & London: Harper, 1909);

Cavanagh, Forest Ranger (New York & London: Harper, 1910);

Other Main-Travelled Roads (New York & London: Harper, 1910);

Victor Ollnee's Discipline (New York & London: Harper, 1911);

The Forester's Daughter (New York & London: Harper, 1914);

They of the High Trails (New York & London: Harper, 1916);

A Son of the Middle Border (New York: Macmillan, 1917; London: John Lane, 1921);

A Daughter of the Middle Border (New York: Macmillan, 1921);

The Book of the American Indian (New York & London: Harper, 1923);

Trail-Makers of the Middle Border (New York: Macmillan, 1926; London: John Lane, 1926);

Prairie Song and Western Story (Boston & New York: Allyn & Bacon, 1928);

Back-Trailers from the Middle Border (New York: Macmillan, 1928);

Roadside Meetings (New York: Macmillan, 1930; London: John Lane, 1931);

Companions on the Trail (New York: Macmillan, 1931);

My Friendly Contemporaries: A Literary Log (New York: Macmillan, 1932);

Afternoon Neighbors (New York: Macmillan, 1934);

Forty Years of Psychic Research (New York: Macmillan, 1936);

The Mystery of the Buried Crosses: A Narrative of Psychic Exploration (New York: Dutton, 1939);

Hamlin Garland's Diaries, edited by Donald Pizer (San Marino, Cal.: Huntington Library, 1968);

Hamlin Garland's Observations on the American Indian, 1895-1905, edited by Lonnie E. Underhill and Daniel F. Littlefield (Tucson: University of Arizona Press, 1976).

PERIODICAL PUBLICATIONS: "Bret Harte's New Book," *Boston Evening Transcript*, 3 February 1887, p. 6;

"Zury, 'The Meanest Man in Spring County,' " *Boston Evening Transcript*, 16 May 1887, p. 3;

"Carlyle as a Poet," *Boston Evening Transcript*, 2 August 1887, p. 5;

"April Hopes," *Boston Evening Transcript*, 1 March 1888, p. 6;

"Professor Garland's Western Trip," *Boston Standard*, 23 June 1888, p. 3;

"American Novels," *Literary News*, 9 (August 1888): 236-237;

"A Man's Story," *Boston Evening Transcript*, 7 November 1888, p. 6;

"The Greek Play," *Boston Evening Transcript*, 1 May 1889, p. 2;

"Whitman at Seventy. How the Good Gray Poet Looks and Talks," *New York Herald*, 30 June 1889, p. 7;

"Herbert Spenser on Property," *Standard*, 12 October 1889, p. 6;

"Mr. Howells's Latest Novels," *New England Magazine*, new series 2 (May 1890): 243-250;

"Ibsen as a Dramatist," *Arena*, 2 (June 1890): 72-82;

"Mr. and Mrs. Herne," *Arena*, 4 (October 1891): 543-560;

"Wallace's 'Natural Selection,' " *Arena*, 4 (November 1891): xxv-xxviii;

"Mr. George's Work on Free Trade," *Arena*, 4 (November 1891): xlii-xliii;

"Mr. Howells's Plans," *Boston Evening Transcript*, 1 January 1892, p. 6;

"The West in Literature," *Arena*, 6 (November 1892): 669-676;

"The Future of Fiction," *Arena*, 7 (April 1893): 513-524;

"Literary Emancipation of the West," *Forum*, 16 (October 1893): 156-166;

Photograph inscribed by Garland (courtesy of the Garland Collection, Doheny Library, University of Southern California)

"The Land Question, and Its Relation to Art and Literature," *Arena*, 9 (January 1894): 165-175;

"Productive Conditions of American Literature," *Forum*, 17 (August 1894): 690-698.

In spite of his long and productive career Hamlin Garland is a neglected literary figure. With the exception of his early collection of short stories, *Main-Travelled Roads* (1891), and his autobiographical *A Son of the Middle Border* (1917), most of his works have little or no contemporary audience, nor is he studied much in the academy, long ago having been eclipsed by other "realists" of the late nineteenth century or buried among the romantic sentimentalists of the Far West. However, Garland was at one time an influential literary critic and social thinker, and he was the chief spokesman for regionalism in American literature as well as an advocate of literary and artistic impressionism.

Garland was born to Richard H. and Isabelle McClintock Garland on a farm near New Salem, Wisconsin, on 14 September 1860. The place of his birth and the various farms and small towns in which he resided for the early years of his life were all situated in the Middle Border, that nebulous land between the truly settled and cultivated East and the freedom of the open West which Garland was later most celebrated for writing about. Except for a brief period when he was fifteen and resided in town, Garland spent his youth living the boredom and hardship of prairie farm life. In the fall of 1876 he enrolled in Cedar Valley Seminary in South Dakota, attending classes half of each academic year until he graduated in 1881. At the seminary Garland discovered John Milton, William Shakespeare, Nathaniel Hawthorne, and Victor Hugo, and as he read he developed an ambition to excel at oratory. After his graduation in June he headed east, the first of several trips he made in quest of culture and art, and for the next two years he wandered throughout the Middle Border and held a variety of odd jobs. In the spring of 1883 he joined his family in the Dakota Territory to stake a claim for himself, one which he had no intention of ever farming but one which he could sell for some capital to finance another trip, this time to Boston, the mecca of nineteenth-century culture.

It is difficult to exaggerate the importance of Garland's second trip east. Armed with a zealousness for learning bred of his deprived youth, he set himself the task of self-education with the goal of succeeding as an orator and lecturer on matters of cultural and literary significance. Dedicated with an embarrassing earnestness, Garland arrived in Boston with $135 in his pocket, some useless letters of introduction, and the ideas of Hippolyte Taine and Henry George. Taine's *The History of English Literature* (1865) and George's *Progress and Poverty* (1879) had been Garland's reading during the long winter of 1883-1884. These works expanded Garland's predisposition to rationalism and his curiosity about contemporary thought which the reading of Robert Ingersoll's lectures out of a Chicago newspaper had already awakened. Under Ingersoll's influence most of the superstitious faith of Garland's boyhood vanished. When he read *The History of English Literature* he was immediately drawn to Taine's scientific conception of literature which further freed him from the superstitions of his past. *Progress and Poverty* did the same for his belief in perfection of the American economic and political systems. The work of George provided the young Garland with a satisfactory explanation for the injustice and squalor of the frontier he had witnessed firsthand. As Donald Pizer has pointed out, Garland's cast of mind assumed two basic premises: that the past was dead and the future was bright with material and intellectual progress and that complicated social and intellectual processes could be understood if one had the right formula or key.

Garland's idealization of Boston was modified by the circumstances of his economic conditions, which reduced him to living in a dingy room on Boylston Place near the public library. He was at first barred from withdrawing books until in a moment of desperation he visited Edward Everett Hale, one of the trustees, and persuaded Hale to help him procure a library card. Practically the only extravagance Garland could afford that first bleak winter in Boston was an occasional cheap seat at the theater, especially for the Shakespeare plays staged by Edwin Booth. Garland began attending the Boston School of Oratory, and through an acquaintanceship with its principal, Moses True Brown, he was offered the opportunity to deliver a series of three lectures on Hugo, Booth, and modern German and American novels. Because of these lectures he met Charles Hurd, the literary editor of the *Boston Evening Transcript*, who eventually employed Garland to write book reviews, thereby providing him with his first opportunities in print.

Garland's initial months in Boston, however poverty-stricken, were a time of impressive intellectual growth. At the Boston Public Library, his "Harvard College" as he would later call it, Garland read widely and followed his own interests. His acquaintanceship with evolutionary critics like Taine eventually led him to discover Herbert Spencer, who provided him with a scientific approach which organized his native ideas into a clear system. Spencer had extrapolated from Charles Darwin's ideas on biological evolution a similar but social set of ideas which to the nineteenth-century mind, particularly Garland's, provided an adequate and much needed explanation of the rapid change experienced in modern life. Spencer's law of progress provided the key which Garland was searching for, the one simple organizing principle which would reveal the basic harmony of the universe and the progress that was leading humankind toward perfection. The marvel of Spencer's Synthetic Philosophy was its flexibility; it could be all things to all persons. Garland adapted Spencerianism in two ways, to explain the growing complexity of the novel and to relate growth with progress. According to Donald Pizer, both these ideas were employed in his early lecture on contemporary German and American novels. He applied Spencer's notions of social progress, which began in simple homogeneity and evolved into increasingly complex but integrated heterogeneity, to the evolution of forms of art, the novel in particular, which progressed from the plain and particular and isolated into forms interdependent and complex. He found American novels inferior to German fiction because the German novels contained emotional and psychological depths yet to be reached by American fiction. The only type of American prose which approached what Taine had described as the "sentiments," and Spencer would have called heterogeneity, were the local colorists like Bret Harte and Joaquin Miller, writers who absorbed the feeling of their locales. The lectures Garland delivered so soon after he arrived in Boston forced him to solidify his critical ideas and provided the impetus for his greatest contribution to nineteenth-century literary thought, the defense of local color as the basis for a new American literature, one more responsive to the strains of native life than American writing of the past.

Quickly becoming a part of the literary and intellectual life of the city, Garland prepared a second set of lectures, this time focused solely on American literature. During the fall of 1886, in preparation for this series, he drafted an essay, "The Evolution of American Thought," which in Pizer's estimation became the cornerstone for Garland's subsequent literary ideas even though it re-

CRUMBLING IDOLS

TWELVE ESSAYS ON ART
DEALING CHIEFLY WITH
LITERATURE, PAINTING AND THE
DRAMA BY HAMLIN GARLAND

CHICAGO AND CAMBRIDGE
PUBLISHED BY STONE AND
KIMBALL IN THE YEAR
MDCCCXCIV

Title page for Garland's collection of critical essays in defense of local-color writing and impressionistic art

mained unpublished. Revised early in 1887 after Garland's general ideas had once again been influenced by further reading of evolutionary and literary critics, the essay outlined the history of American literature. From the time of the Puritans and the foundation of a native culture, American society had experienced increasing heterogeneity which resulted in the greater need for a national literature and in the conditions to produce a national literary culture. Following Spencer's ideas Garland speculated that, with in-

creasing specialization in the expanding and modernizing world, there was a place for art denied it before, and that art could now perform the valuable social function of elaborating the national diversity and promoting an awareness of the increased heterogeneity implied by the democratic form of American society. The lesson Garland drew from his deductions was that the only real task of modern American letters was to reflect the truths of contemporary life. American literature must be grounded in the present and

Garland in the Klondike, spring 1898

deal with the lives and thoughts and aspirations of the common democratic mass. To write of a former time or of foreign cultures was to beat against a stream of progress and evolutionary thought. This critical system allowed Garland to distinguish which modern writers best fulfilled his criteria, and those were Walt Whitman and the local colorists. The local colorists became the writers most in the vanguard of contemporary artistic thought, thought sanctioned by scientific paradigms and historical observation.

As Garland's argument tightened he came to understand the inevitability of the local colorists' domination of American literature. Since American society had not progressed haphazardly and since literature grew out of social conditions, literature, too, must be governed by a law of development. Because America was so large and diverse in population as well as geography, only by examining it piecemeal could the truths of the American experience be told honestly from one section to another. Only through local-color writing could the real heterogeneity of the American experience be chronicled coherently. Unlike many of the other local colorists, Garland

arrived at his defense not out of a personal predilection but through a process of deduction based on what he felt was irrefutable natural law as spelled out by Spencer. This certainty allowed Garland not only to practice local-color writing himself but also permitted him to become a militant advocate of the genre, attacking all writing which stood in the way of progress, democracy, and a national literature. The publication of *Crumbling Idols* (1894) marked the culmination of Garland's campaign in defense of local color. It also marked the end point of Garland as a literary thinker. He became locked into an intellectual time frame which would become outmoded and would ultimately leave Garland stranded aesthetically in the nineteenth century, unable to move either intellectually or artistically into the modern world.

Although fairly well established, Garland's ideas received another major influence when he read the impressionism of the French critic Eugène Véron as set forth in his *Aesthetics* (1879). Garland's annotations to his copy show that this book influenced him more than anything else he read during the formative period of his life.

Garland's wife, Zulime Taft Garland, and their two children,
Constance Hamlin and Mary Isabel

Adopting a quasi-scientific stance, Véron argued that of the three approaches open to art—imitation of past forms, realistic portrayal of the present times, and individual impressions of the artist—the last was the only true source since it incorporated the personality of the artist. Véron's ideas impressed Garland insofar as they supported his own beliefs that art must reflect change as filtered through the personality of the artist, the highest product of the evolutionary process. This view allowed Garland to stress the importance of individual responses to environment and account for variation within the local-color movement. As Pizer has remarked, Véron's emphasis on personality freed Garland from the dogmatism of insisting that all local-color writing contain uniform characteristics by allowing for variations in mood, material, and approach within literary form.

Garland's new critical system required a revision of his judgments about American writers, especially such local colorists as William Dean Howells, E. W. Howe, and Joseph Kirkland. His newly found position within the literary community also placed him in a prominent position to review new fiction and thereby exert an influence on current literary taste. Garland also began to correspond with such figures as Howells. In both his reviews and correspondence Garland took up the struggle for local color, a battle he waged more or less for the remainder of his life.

During the summer of 1887 Garland returned to the Middle Border to collect materials for his own local-color stories. The trip had immediate and far-reaching effects on Garland's fiction and helped to provide the foundation upon which his fame as a writer largely rests. However, what was of greater importance for his critical thinking was his rediscovery of Henry George's *Progress and Poverty*. George's single tax on land ownership was designed to break the monopoly on land-holding which he felt was the primary cause of economic and social inequality. With Garland's experience of rural poverty in the Middle Border, it was no wonder that he responded to the "Single Tax" idea. Although Garland first read George during his sojourn in the Dakotas in the winter of 1884, it was the application of the evolutionary ideas of Spencer which convinced Garland to espouse George's cause of the single tax. To him the single tax was not only a way of simplifying taxation of landowners and workers, but a way to redress an imbalance caused by man which was thwarting the natural, social process leading to progress. The single-tax programs were coupled with his evolutionary literary ideas in the Middle Border stories that Garland began to write upon his return to Boston in the fall of 1887 and which culminated in *Main-Travelled Roads* (1891). He put into practice the literary discoveries revealed to him by three years of hard study in the East. The fiction which he produced over the next six or seven years established his reputation but also revealed a division in his approach to his material which would have repercussions in his later career. Even in the beginning as a chronicler of the region and in the midst of his most radical period of literary and social thinking, Garland revealed a sentimental side to his view of the Middle Border, one which later would overwhelm his reformist impulses, eventually taking over entirely the tone of his fiction and later autobiographical writings.

Although Garland's efforts on behalf of local colorists increased as did his devotion to the single-tax problem, during the period from 1888-1890 he spent expanding amounts of his professional time in the production and marketing of his own stories, plays, and novels. He turned increasingly toward the more genteel and more literarily acceptable outlets such as *Harper's Weekly, Atlantic Monthly,* and most importantly the *Century.* As a result of appearing in these more conservative magazines Garland's writings underwent subtle but noticeable change, and, although he continued to contribute to B. O. Flower's *Arena,* his radical period was growing to a close.

Garland's life from 1889 until 1891, when he began traveling on behalf of the Populist party, was devoted to a period of dramatic reform as he tried unsuccessfully to redirect the American theater into socially progressive avenues. But like Henry James and other writers of fiction before him, fame and riches on the stage eluded Garland. In spite of his relative failure in drama, his literary reputation was rising, so much so that a Chicago newspaper would declare him the foremost writer of fiction for the year 1892. But his progressive novels and social plays were relatively unsuccessful with the public, and Garland, back in Boston at the beginning of 1893, decided to drop social and political causes from his fiction. He made a second momentous decision at the same time to move to Chicago.

His change of location was motivated in part because the influence of Boston as a literary capital was waning and in part because Chicago had a reputation as a dynamic city of movers and shakers. Prompted by the mediocre reviews received by his own literary efforts and still carrying on his zeal for local color, Garland hoped to use Chicago as a point from which he could "reform" American letters to his way of thinking. Western writers, he perceived, could provide a spearhead of new material if they would divorce themselves from European influences and also from false American ones as well. The conflict between romanticism and realism in American fiction came to a head during the Columbian Exposition through a series of highly publicized debates between Garland and Mary Hartwell Catherwood. Catherwood (1847-1902), an author of historical romance set primarily in the Middle West, felt that Garland's realism was doing irreparable harm to the self-esteem of the region. The

Garland in 1903 (photograph by A. S. Dudley)

debate stumbled throughout the summer and into the fall of 1893 with Garland's "Literary Emancipation of the West," published in the *Forum* in October, being the most celebrated of the documents to come out of the fray. Basically a rehash of his earlier ideas on the evolution of American writing and society, the essay achieved notoriety because of the debate and the prominence of the fair. This final phase of Garland's career as a radical critic culminated with the publication of a series of essays in *Crumbling Idols,* issued by the Chicago firm of Stone and Kimball in May of 1894.

Perhaps the most important effect of *Crumbling Idols,* besides a summation of Garland's aesthetic ideals, was the publication of his defense of impressionism, an approach he called veritism. Unlike the realism of Howells, veritism substituted the individual's subjective reaction to facts for the simple reporting of facts. It eliminated many of the unpleasant aspects of realism since veritism allowed the artist to mute or deflect the unpleasantness of life through the aesthetic filter of artistic vision. Although often compared to

Garland's home in Chicago, where he lived from 1893 to 1916

The one lasting effect of *Crumbling Idols* resides in Garland's defense of impressionism in art, a defense which was among the first to be published in English. Because the tenets of impressionism were supposedly founded on scientific accuracy, especially in the use of lighting and color in the visual arts, and because impressionism also relied heavily on the individual vision in artistic creation, Garland was able to embrace its cause as part of his search for signs of progress in the arts. However, in spite of his real contribution to the aesthetics of impressionism, the thrust of Garland's critical thinking found expression in the soft approach he used toward local color in creating an increasingly sentimental and romantic depiction of the Rocky Mountains. Never very far from such sentiment even in his earlier work and now released from the constraints of realism, Garland gave over to the romance of the mountains, a tactic which insured him a wide readership and increasing wealth but also cost him a significant place in the history of American literature.

For the balance of his career Garland confined his activities to creating a series of increasingly popular romances and finally to writing his serial autobiographical reminiscences, the first of which, *A Son of the Middle Border,* helped to secure his election to the American Academy of Arts and Letters. The second, *A Daughter of the Middle Border* (1921), provided him with the Pulitzer Prize for 1921. Garland left Chicago in 1916 and moved to New York where he led a life dedicated to official literary activities, and in 1930 he left New York for California, where he joined his wife, Zulime Taft Garland, whom he had married on 18 November 1899, and their two children, Mary Isabel and Constance Hamlin. He remained in California for the rest of his life.

Howells's *Criticism and Fiction* (1891), Garland's *Crumbling Idols* approached its subject from a different direction. Howells advocated the more objective and scientific view of art and fiction; Garland, on the other hand, tended to a softer or more subjective notion of the truth of art. In some ways Garland anticipated the modernist tendency toward the subjective, but unfortunately he did not pursue his ideas far enough to make *Crumbling Idols* the truly revolutionary book it might have been. Also, the book's poor reception confirmed Garland's already stated desire to abandon his critical enterprises and devote himself solely to literary projects. With the publication of *Crumbling Idols* Garland's career as literary and social critic came to an abrupt end. He devoted the rest of his life to the writing of books primarily designed to make him money and a literary reputation within the genteel world of letters. Garland's active and influential critical career spanned only ten years.

Garland has been charged with pandering to the popular taste of his time in order to achieve fame and fortune. It can be argued that Garland was incredibly sensitive to public sentiment, and his Rocky Mountain romances merely fed the appetite of a reading public growing weary or afraid of relevant social novels. His autobiographical reminiscences also met a demand for the depiction of simpler times prompted by uneasiness with rapid social and economic changes which occurred following World War I. It is important to note, however, that even the more brutal and "realistic" fiction of the decade from 1884 to 1894 contains a nostalgic note which borders on the sentimental. The dreams which led the

Garland and grandchildren

young Garland from the hardships of life of the Middle Border to the intellectually exciting years in Boston also impelled him toward public and critical acceptance. When he found that his harder-edged critical ideas were not received well by the genteel world of the literary community he modified his ideas, finally abandoning them altogether. He desperately wanted to be included in the pantheon of American letters, and in order to accomplish that he tempered his aesthetic system to emphasize the more pleasant aspects of American life which accorded more comfortably with the general public's notions of literature. Eventually Garland came to feel more comfortable writing works which generated not critical and popular scorn but acceptance and reward. Never really a part of the eastern literary es-

tablishment, he returned to the values and ideas he received as a youth. The hardships of the Middle Border softened with time through a haze of nostalgia, eventually to be memorialized in sentiment in his backward-looking old age.

Unfortunately, what is now remembered about Garland is primarily the sentimental volumes of his declining years, even though *Main-Travelled Roads* in its various editions is read more often. What is missing from the portrait of Garland as a man of letters is the radical period of his youth, a period in which he did make a considerable contribution to aesthetic debates of the late nineteenth century. For a few short years Garland was the most important spokesperson for local-color writing in America. His popularization of the ideas of Spencer and his defense of the theories of George were substantial and impressive. His essays on the importance of impressionism were advanced and prescient. Unfortunately, Garland did not change with the times and his early passions, once truly revolutionary, by his old age became commonplace. The paradox of Garland, as one critic has noted, was that he was an evolutionary with a closed mind. As the times and as literature progressed, he did not, and by standing still he became antique and quaint. Unable to adapt himself to his own principles, he was doomed to live out his life becoming increasingly distanced from the modern and new in American literature.

Bibliographies:

Lloyd A. Arvidson, "A Bibliography of the Published Writings of Hamlin Garland," M.A. thesis, University of Southern California, 1952;

Arvidson, *Hamlin Garland: Centennial Tributes and a Checklist of the Hamlin Garland Papers in the University of Southern California Library*, Bulletin no. 9 (Los Angeles: University of Southern California Library, 1962);

Jackson R. Bryer and Eugene Harding, *Hamlin Garland and the Critics, An Annotated Bibliography* (Troy, N.Y.: Whitston, 1973);

Charles L. P. Silet, *Henry Blake Fuller and Hamlin Garland: A Reference Guide* (Boston: G. K. Hall, 1977).

Biography:

Jean Holloway, *Hamlin Garland, A Biography* (Austin: University of Texas Press, 1960).

References:

Lars Ahnebrink, *The Beginnings of Naturalism in American Fiction* (Uppsala, Sweden: University of Uppsala, 1950), pp. 63-89;

John Chamberlin, *Farewell to Reform: Being a History of the Rise, Life and Decay of the Progres-*

sive Mind in America (New York: Liveright, 1932), pp. 95-102;

Bernard L. Duffy, "Hamlin Garland's 'Decline' from Realism," *American Literature*, 25 (March 1953): 69-74;

Joseph B. McCullough, *Hamlin Garland* (Boston: G. K. Hall, 1978);

H. Wayne Morgan, *American Writers in Rebellion: From Mark Twain to Dreiser* (New York: Hill & Wang, 1965), pp. 76-103;

James Nagel, *Critical Essays on Hamlin Garland* (Boston: G. K. Hall, 1984);

Vernon Louis Parrington, *The Beginnings of Critical Realism in America, 1860-1920* (New York: Harcourt, Brace, 1930), pp. 288-300;

Donald Pizer, *Hamlin Garland's Early Work and Career* (Berkeley: University of California Press, 1960);

John W. Rathbun and Harry H. Clark, *American Literary Criticism, 1860-1905* (Boston: G. K. Hall, 1979), pp. 136-142;

Lewis O. Saum, "Hamlin Garland and Reform," *South Dakota Review*, 10 (Winter 1972): 36-62;

Charles L. P. Silet, Robert E. Welch, and Richard Boudreau, *The Critical Reception of Hamlin Garland: 1891-1978* (Troy, N. Y.: Whitston, 1985);

Walter F. Taylor, *The Economic Novel in America* (Chapel Hill: University of North Carolina Press, 1942), pp. 148-183;

Charles C. Walcutt, *American Literary Naturalism: A Divided Stream* (Minneapolis: University of Minnesota Press, 1956), pp. 45-65.

Papers:

The University of Southern California holds the largest collection of Garland papers, letters, diaries, and memorabilia. The Huntington Library, San Marino, California, possesses Garland's forty-three annual diaries.

Lewis E. Gates
(23 March 1860-1 October 1924)

John S. Coolidge
University of California, Berkeley

BOOKS: *Three Studies in Literature* (New York & London: Macmillan, 1899);
Studies and Appreciations (New York & London: Macmillan, 1900).

OTHER: *Selections from the Essays of Francis Jeffrey*, edited, with notes and an introduction, by Gates (Boston: Ginn, 1894);
Selections from the Prose Writings of John Henry, Cardinal Newman, edited, with notes and an introduction, by Gates (New York: Holt, 1895);
Selections from the Prose Writings of Matthew Arnold, edited, with notes and an introduction, by Gates (New York: Holt, 1898);
Introduction to *The Booklover's Library*, no. 22 (Philadelphia: The Booklover's Library, 1901).

PERIODICAL PUBLICATIONS: "Mrs. Oliphant's English Literature," *Nation*, 56 (March 1893): 351-352;
"Mr. Meredith and His Aminta," *Chap-Book*, 2 (November 1894): 13-24;
"*De Quincey and his Friends*, by James Hogg," *Nation*, 62 (June 1896): 442;
"Mr. Meredith in a New Guise," *Chap-Book*, 7 (November 1897): 443-444;
"*The Masque of Judgment*, by W. V. Moody," *Nation*, 72 (March 1901): 259-260;
"Professor Wendell's 'Literary History of America,'" *Critic*, 38 (April 1901): 341-344;
"*Herod, A Tragedy*, by Stephen Phillips," *Nation*, 72 (April 1901): 343-344;
"Professor Harper's Essays and Mr. Collins's Ephemera Critica," *Critic*, 29 (July 1901): 21-25;
"Recent Verse," *Nation*, 73 (August 1901): 152-155;
"Professor Saintsbury's History of Criticism," *Critic*, 29 (September 1901): 207-212.

Lewis Edwards Gates was born 23 March 1860 in Warsaw, New York. His father, Seth Merrill Gates, a prominent lawyer and politician, served two terms in Congress, where he was an

Lewis E. Gates (photograph by Pach Brothers)

outspoken abolitionist; it is said that a southern planter once put a price of five hundred dollars on his head. Fanny Parsons Gates, Lewis's mother, was a great-granddaughter of Jonathan Edwards, a connection commemorated both in his middle name and in that of his brother, Merrill Edwards Gates, who served as president of Rutgers and then of Amherst. Lewis graduated from Harvard in 1884 and was subsequently an instructor in forensics there for three years. From 1887 to 1890 he studied in Germany, England, and France, then returned to Harvard as an instructor in English. In 1896 he was promoted to an assistant professorship in English, and the following year he became an assistant professor of comparative literature.

At the turn of the century Gates was an emerging figure in American intellectual life, addressing a general literary public in essays and reviews appearing in the *Critic*, the *Chap-Book*, the

Nation, and the *Atlantic Monthly*, and in the introductions he wrote for collections of the prose writings of Francis Jeffrey, John Henry Newman, and Matthew Arnold. These introductions were collected (and the one on Jeffrey rewritten and expanded) to form Gates's first book, *Three Studies in Literature* (1899). Notwithstanding its occasional origin and modest title, this was a very considerable achievement, three skillfully wrought *portraits littéraires*, compendious and seemingly definitive assessments of their subjects' lifeworks. His other book, *Studies and Appreciations* (1900), also consisted for the most part of previously published essays, but together constituted a coherent view of nineteenth-century literature and an exposition of critical principles. Gates possessed an extraordinary conversance, not only with English and American literature, but with modern Continental literature and thought as well, and a style of distinctive cogency and grace. "His criticism," a reviewer observed, "is free from any taint of preciosity, yet the neat turning of many of his phrases would imply deliberate polishing were they not so apt as to appear inevitable."

In 1902 Gates apparently suffered a nervous collapse. *The Twenty-Fifth Anniversary Report (Report VII) of the Secretary of the Class of 1884 of Harvard College* states that he resigned his position at Harvard in June of that year, "his health having been seriously impaired by his excessive devotion to his studies and his work as instructor and professor." An article in the *Critic* the following February, discussing Gates as one of a number of academic figures also known as men of letters, gives no express indication of his departure from Harvard, but the remarks which conclude its treatment of him may be a veiled allusion to his catastrophe: "Mr. Gates is said to live a good deal alone–more with his books than with his fellows. His essays rather tend to substantiate this. He enjoys looking backward at men whose work is finished, and turns less to immediate contemporary life for his comparisons and allusions."

The Harvard class report goes on to say, "He travelled in Europe and continued his studies in Italy, Germany, and England until the autumn of 1904, when his health not permitting the resumption of university work, he took up his residence in Washington, D.C., where his brother, Merrill E. Gates, formerly president of Amherst College, now resides." After his brother's death in 1922 Gates lived in Albany, New York, until his own death two years later at the age of sixty-four. The obituary in the 2 October

1924 *Boston Evening Transcript* says that he "died suddenly in his home." Both the obituary and the Harvard class report mention that he was descended from Jonathan Edwards.

Gates is remembered as the mentor of Frank Norris, whose first novel *McTeague* (1899) is dedicated to him, and as the chief American apologist for the impressionist school of criticism, which is associated especially with Walter Pater. These seemingly disparate associations represent two aspects of a single, coherent literary program based on the conception of nineteenth-century cultural history which Gates sets forth in *Studies and Appreciations*.

For Gates "the era of modern life" can be dated indifferently from the French Revolution or William Wordsworth's preface to *Lyrical Ballads* (1798). The two events are practically interchangeable, the former having been essentially a cultural trauma–a "shock" which "went crisping over the nerves of the nations of Europe, stirring all men to novel thoughts and new moods, and startled them into fresh ways of envisaging life"–while the latter was in reality "the manifesto of a revolutionary movement." The modern era is a "new dispensation" in the spiritual history of mankind, and Wordsworth is its prophet. His preface "specifies or suggests nearly all the aspects of the complete renovation of literature which the new age was to accomplish, and nearly all the varieties of new spiritual experience which the men of the new dispensation were to win and interpret."

This "revolutionary movement" was first of all a revitalization of the human sensorium: "The senses became alert and thrillingly sensitive"; and "the human spirit won many new aptitudes and new powers and acquired a new range of sensitiveness to a myriad hitherto unperceived shades of beauty and feeling." Thus it was very far from endangering the moral and social codes that had prevailed in English life, traditional relations to the state, or the fixed gradations of the English social order. On the contrary, "Wordsworth's regenerating influence" imparted "a new virtue" to conservative sentiments, reinforcing them "by masses of delicate and tender and ennobling emotion." The objective facts of social life were not so much altered as "transfigured" or–one of Gates's favorite words–"redeemed."

In this way the new sensibility could be powerfully conducive to social cohesion and all those "sweet and tender relationships and affections that make human life endurable." But in fact its tendency proved to be the opposite. In their eager preoccupation with hitherto unsuspected possibilities for the individual psyche, the Romantics tended to solipsism. "They lived inside their own individual heads, in the circle of their own eccentric personalities." Gates displays an unaccustomed vehemence as he expatiates on the radical individualism whereby "Romanticism bid fair to lead to social disintegration."

Recognizing this tendency, the poets of the post-Romantic period made a concerted effort to compensate for it. "The new poets took into their blood and tempers the Romantic increment, . . . their senses were trained to all the delicacy and alertness that Romantic experience made possible." But they "saw the evil trick of Romance" as well and set about in their various ways to remedy it. The second phase of Romanticism was characterized by a common purpose of "converting Romance into a vital transforming force that should actually recreate in terms of beauty that common life, a loyal sharing in which can alone enable the individual, be he dreamer or worker, to fulfill the whole scope of his nature and reach his utmost effectiveness."

Clearly this is Gates's own manifesto. He envisions an enhancement of the quality of life throughout society by the general diffusion of Romantic sensibility. His overtones are persistently religious. The precious "Romantic increment" which is to "recreate" the "unlovely and sordid" world of late-nineteenth-century Europe and America is suggestively analogous to the "new supernatural sense" which Gates's maternal ancestor Jonathan Edwards observed to be "given to those that are regenerated," a mysterious attribute "which is in its whole nature diverse from any former kinds of sensation of the mind" (*A Treatise Concerning Religious Affections*, 1746). Quite probably Gates has the analogy with this distinctive feature of his forebear's theology in mind when he observes that "the experience offered in art rivals religious experience in renovating and stimulating power." He is writing to vindicate the spiritual import of Romanticism much as Edwards championed the work of the spirit in the Great Awakening.

But, again like Edwards, Gates is concerned to distinguish between true spiritual renovation and effects which are often mistaken for it. The first difference Edwards speaks of is that truly "gracious affections" have their "objective ground" in the "nature of divine things, as they are in themselves." The joy of "hypocrites" is really "a joy in themselves, and not in God." Their "rejoicings and elevations" are only an egocentric and meretricious reflection of self; for "having received what they call spiritual discoveries or experiences, their minds are taken up about them, admiring their own experiences." Hardly less scathingly Gates observes that Romantic poets "give us a report, not of some actual region of fact, but of the mirage thereof cast against the heavens by the haze of intense emotion in the midst of which they are perpetually moving and breathing." The "region of fact" that Gates speaks of, however, is not located in the "nature of divine things, as they are in themselves," but in common life. It is "in the unwrought dross and tortured material of commonplace existence" that the true Romantic artists will find "God in the making." They will "reveal God in the passing hours."

Gates thus comes to be the advocate of a program of "renovating imaginative realism" which he attributes to the poets of the post-Romantic period, particularly Arthur Hugh Clough, Matthew Arnold, and Elizabeth Barrett Browning. Only Browning is credited with much success in putting this program into poetic practice, however, and Gates rates her very highly. She both defines and illustrates the post-Romantic requirement that the poet "should be able to find even in the most sordid aspects of life, and in the most seemingly vulgar characters, meaning and suggestiveness that shall redeem them and give them imaginative power." In prose fiction the program is illustrated by Charlotte Brontë, the one English novelist to whom Gates devotes an essay. He puts her "with Mrs. Browning among those who domicile Romance in the midst of the dull facts of daily life."

Such phrases strikingly resemble many of Frank Norris's pronouncements on his brand of naturalism. Norris's purpose of imbuing naturalism with the spirit of romance had been formed well before he knew Gates, however; and he already had a partly completed manuscript of *McTeague* in hand when he came to Harvard in 1894 and enrolled in Gates's course in composition. Gates's influence on Norris–apart from his skillful and painstaking technical instruction, which Norris appreciated warmly–would seem to have consisted of confirming and perhaps giving further definition to Norris's own literary convictions. Nonetheless, he must have recognized *McTeague* as exemplifying the kind of romantic realism he was calling for.

In the impressionist school of criticism Gates sees another manifestation of the same spiritual renovation. The impressionist critic, employing all his art to render the precise shade of each unique, transitory moment of his reading, is revitalizing the experience of literature much as Wordsworth did that of nature. "The popularity of impressionism is only one sign more that we are learning to prize, above most things else, richness of spiritual experience. The sincere and significant mood—this is what we have come to care for, whether the mood be suggested by life, by nature, or by art and literature," The great virtue of impressionist criticism is that it fully honors "the vitalizing power of literature, its fashion of putting into play the whole nature of each reader it addresses and its consequent, unlimited, *creative* energy." He subscribes emphatically to the principle of indeterminacy, that is, the possibility of finding ever new meaning in a literary text. In contrast to the "studiously unequivocal" nature of scientific discourse, literature is endlessly reinterpretable. "Every piece of literature is a mimic piece of life that tempts the reader to capture from it, with mind and heart and imagination, an individual bliss; he may, in some measure, shape it as he will—work out his own destiny with it."

The reader may accomplish this "in some measure," but not quite unreservedly—here again Gates discerns the besetting danger of solipsism. Indeterminacy is the corollary of the romantic preoccupation with inward experience, which has produced a radical change in the ontological status of a work of literature. A poem is no longer an "external object"; for modern readers it has become "a series of thought-waves and nerve-vibrations that run at a special moment through an active brain and a sensitive temperament." From such a presupposition it is difficult not to conclude that the critic's task is to give a sincere report of his fugitive experience of the poem. The result, Gates concedes, is often fascinating as a kind of literature in its own right; but "can *criticism* properly speaking confine itself to the record of a momentary shiver across a single set of possibly degenerate nerves?" Gates takes seriously the physician and cultural critic Max Nordau's diagnosis of the fin de siècle sensibility as neurotic degeneracy. It is not just an academic matter for Gates to define a critical discipline which will militate against the solipsism of impressionist criticism.

That means subjecting its "wilfulness and caprice" to an objective control of some sort. Just as he admonishes the romantic poet or novelist to remain "essentially loyal to fact," Gates insists that "there is something objective in a work of art" which the critic is called on to respect. Failure to do so will prevent his work from being "properly critical"; but more than that, it will impoverish it aesthetically. The true "appreciative critic," then, is an impressionist making use of whatever disciplines may help bring his personal experience of a work into valid relation with its objective reality—that is to say, its historical reality.

Gates combines impressionism with a historicism akin to that of the German philosopher Wilhelm Dilthey, whom he mentions appreciatively. The critic wishing to "make his impression of a work of art something more than a superficial momentary irritation of pleasure and pain" will make every effort to bridge the gap between his own historical moment and that of the original creation of the work under consideration. He will attempt, with the aid of psychology, to trace "the swift concurrence of many images in the poet's mind," and with the aid of history and biography he will try to understand how that process was conditioned by the particular culture of the artist's time and place, and by his particular mind and temperament. By these means he will "discover and recreate in his own soul" the original experience of the author and his contemporary audience. He will "discern and realize those actual moods, those swift counterchanges of feeling, which once, in a definite place and at a definite moment, within the consciousness of a single artist evoked images and guided them into union." The critic will replicate, "as far as he can," the original moment of creation.

But this "mimetic pleasure" is only the beginning of the critical procedure that Gates prescribes. For it is still his own experience of the work of art that the critic is dealing with, and that is necessarily "something far subtler than any mere repetition of the mood of the creative artist; it contains in itself a complexity and a richness of suggestion and *motifs* that correspond to all the gains the human spirit has made since the earlier age." Appreciation recapitulates *Geistesgeschichte*. Even as he attempts to "recover imaginatively" the moment of the work's creation, the critic inevitably finds himself evoking other moments in the cultural continuum between that time and his own. The critic, for example, attempting to "catch the very mood that underlies the tender mystic wistfulness of Lippo Lippi's Madonnas" will immediately find himself having recourse to "many nicely modulated contrasts" with Madonnas by later artists. Indeed, despite what Gates sometimes seems to be saying, such contrasts are not really subsequent to the imaginative recovery of the original mood of the work; they are integral to it: it is by them that the original mood "will define itself for the critic." But the most important contrast of all is that between the simple religious devotion informing Lippi's work and the "wise, pathetic insight" of the modern sophisticate. The poignancy which this contrast, especially, imparts to the critic's perception of the work is an essential ingredient of his enjoyment of it—even *the* essential ingredient, it would seem. By this historically oriented impressionism the whole past experience of the human spirit becomes *our* experience, since—as Gates puts it in a striking legal metaphor—"we have gathered into ourselves all the usufruct of it."

The appreciation of each work in itself involves the apprehension of the whole of the tradition in which both the work and its present interpreter stand. In the last analysis that principle is what must control the vagaries of impressionism. A little like T. S. Eliot insisting on the individual poet's responsibility to the "ideal order" of European literature, Gates calls the impressionist critic into communion with the past.

In his review of George Saintsbury's *History of Criticism* (1901) he throws out a formulation which might stand as a manifesto of this aspect of his critical program. "All the productions of art and of literature," he declares, "now fall for the critic into their relative places as partial revelations of beauty—as special incarnations of aesthetic pleasure, that depend for their degrees and kinds upon the peculiar spiritual energy that is characteristic of each artist and of his age and race." The tradition is the final object of the critic's contemplation.

Gates's amalgam of impressionism and historicism seems to anticipate Eliot's organic idea of tradition. It can also be seen to adumbrate some of the theoretical concerns of hermeneutics in recent years, such as indeterminacy, the ontology of the work of art, the nature of historical consciousness. However, it is not as an influence or a precursor that Gates deserves to be read today. His work, slight as it is in bulk, represents a significant cultural witness and a permanently valuable critical achievement.

Reference:

John S. Coolidge, "Lewis E. Gates: The Permutations of Romanticism in America," *New England Quarterly*, 30 (March 1957): 23-38.

Basil Gildersleeve
(23 October 1831-9 January 1924)

Rhonda Skillern
University of Texas

BOOKS: *A Latin Grammar* (New York: Richardson, 1867; revised edition, New York & Baltimore: University Publishing, 1872), revised and enlarged by Gildersleeve and Gonzalez Lodge as *Gildersleeve's Latin Grammar* (New York & Boston: University Publishing, 1894);

A Latin Exercise Book: With References to Gildersleeve's Latin Grammar (New York & Baltimore: University Publishing, 1871; revised, 1873);

A Latin Reader (New York & Baltimore: University Publishing, 1875);

A Latin Primer (New York & Baltimore: University Publishing, 1875); revised by Gildersleeve and Chapman Maupin (New York: University Publishing, 1882);

Essays and Studies, Educational and Literary (Baltimore: Murray, 1890);

Latin Composition, by Gildersleeve and Lodge (New York & Boston: University Publishing, 1899; revised, 1904);

Syntax of Classical Greek from Homer to Demosthenes, 2 volumes, by Gildersleeve and C. W. E. Miller (New York & Cincinnati: American Book Co., 1900, 1911);

Hellas and Hesperia, or The Vitality of Greek Studies in America (New York: Holt, 1909);

The Creed of the Old South, 1865-1915 (Baltimore: Johns Hopkins Press, 1915);

Selections from the Brief Mention of Basil Lanneau Gildersleeve, edited by Miller (Baltimore: Johns Hopkins Press, 1930).

OTHER: *The Satires of A. Persius Flaccus*, edited by Gildersleeve (New York & Cincinnati: Harper, 1875);

The Apologies of Justin Martyr, edited by Gildersleeve (New York: Harper, 1877);

Pindar: The Olympian and Pythian Odes, edited by Gildersleeve (New York: Harper, 1885; revised, 1890);

The Histories of Herodotus, edited by Gildersleeve (New York: Appleton, 1899).

Basil L. Gildersleeve

Basil Lanneau Gildersleeve, professor, editor, and philologist, was possibly the leading classical scholar in nineteenth-century America. While teaching Latin and Greek at the University of Virginia and later at Johns Hopkins University he wrote textbooks, edited classical works, and wrote essays for various journals. As influential as he was in establishing classical studies in the United States, however, Gildersleeve made his greatest contribution to American letters by founding in 1880 the *American Journal of Philology*, which he edited until 1920.

He was born in Charleston, South Carolina, to Benjamin Gildersleeve, a Presbyterian pastor, and Emma Louisa Lanneau Gildersleeve. Although the young Gildersleeve received no formal education until he reached thirteen, he was a precocious child who, under the tutelage of his parents, especially a stern father, learned to read the Bible "from cover to cover" by his fifth birthday. According to his own account his boyhood education in the classics began early: "Latin I learned at a tender age, and I 'got through' Caesar, Sallust, Cicero, Virgil, and Horace before the time when boys of today have fairly mastered the rudiments.... Of Greek I learned enough to make out the New Testament.... French I picked up after a fashion" (*Forum,* February 1891). After attending Charleston College in 1845 and Jefferson College in Pennsylvania in 1846 he enrolled at Princeton College, from which he graduated in 1849. Incidentally, this was the year in which he chanced to hear Edgar Allan Poe recite "The Raven" and some other poems before an audience in Richmond. In a letter written to James A. Harrison of the University of Virginia (and later quoted by Harrison in the *Independent,* 20 September 1900), Gildersleeve recalled that "I have retained the impression that he did not read very well. His voice was pleasant enough, but he emphasized the rhythm unduly–a failing common, I believe, to poets endowed with a keen sense of the music of their own verse." During the following year Gildersleeve became extremely enamored of German literature–especially Johann von Goethe–so after teaching for one year at a private school in Richmond he joined other young American men who were traveling to the land of German idealism. For three years he attended the Universities of Berlin, Bonn, and Göttingen, receiving the Ph.D. degree from Göttingen in 1853. He was just twenty-two. "To Germany and the Germans," he later wrote, "I am indebted for everything professionally in the way of apparatus and of method, and of much, very much, in the way of inspiration."

He studied on his own and even attempted to write a novel during his first three years back in America. Then in 1856 he was appointed professor of Greek at the University of Richmond; he also taught Latin for five of his twenty years of instruction there. While the Civil War was in progress he served in the Confederate Army during the summers, suffering a wound in 1864 that left him with a limp. Gildersleeve remained ever mindful of being a southerner, and his war experience not only inspired his writing *The Creed of the Old South, 1865-1915* (1915), but influenced his interpretations of ancient wars; for example, in defending Pindar from scholars who accused him of treasonous sympathy with Athens during the Persian War, Gildersleeve remarks that "a little experience of a losing side might aid historic vision." Referring to himself in the third person, Gildersleeve explains in his preface to *Essays and Studies, Educational and Literary* (1890) that "eight of the papers that go to make up this volume were written in the years 1867-1869, by a man of the Old South, and form a part of his life-long work for the furtherance of higher education and literary development among the Southern people, with whom he is identified by birth, by feeling and by fortune."

In 1866 he married Eliza Fisher Colston of Virginia. They had two children, a son, Raleigh Colston, and a daughter, Emma Louise, who later married Gardner M. Lane, the son of a professor of Latin at Harvard.

Gildersleeve did not publish until 1867 when he issued the first edition of *A Latin Grammar,* modeled on his Greek grammar already in progress. The Latin work underwent two revisions and is still consulted by classics students today. He developed a Gildersleeve Latin Series by adding *A Latin Exercise Book* in 1871 and *A Latin Reader* and *A Latin Primer* in 1875. He also edited *The Satires of A. Persius Flaccus* in 1875, appending 146 pages of philological notes to 67 pages of the poet's text. His candid introduction to Persius, who he admits "is one of those literary celebrities whose title to fame is not beyond dispute," remains readable and informative.

This scholarly assiduity prompted newly opened Johns Hopkins University to offer Gildersleeve the first chair in classics as professor of Greek in 1876, a position he would hold until his retirement from teaching in 1915. By most accounts he proved to be an exacting instructor. One of the first recipients of a Johns Hopkins fellowship, Walter Hines Page, studied under Gildersleeve for two years but complained that this "great teacher talked too much of Southern needs," adding that in teaching Page "scholarship" Gildersleeve had "also taught him to be dissatisfied with it as a life work."

Gildersleeve at the time he was offered the first chair in classics as professor of Greek at Johns Hopkins University

Indeed, other former students and literary critics have accused Gildersleeve of emphasizing too much the narrow philological aspects of classical language above broader Greco-Roman philosophical concepts, though Gildersleeve himself stressed that philology as "a great laboratory of systematic research" was "in the service of culture." What his students reacted to were the new "scientific methods" that he and others had imported to American graduate schools from German universities, and they sometimes failed to see that "minute grammatical study" could have an "aesthetic result." Ironically, Gildersleeve viewed his analytic philology as a defense against the more sweeping ravages of science and "depressing tendencies of modern . . . American civilization" (*Essays and Studies*). His essay entitled "Limits of Culture," originally in the 1 April 1867 edition of the *Southern Review* (and republished in *Essays and Studies),* denounced a Harvard professor's proposal to reduce the number of classics courses required of university students so that they could pursue more practical, scientific interests. Gildersleeve claimed that such mea-

sures would "break up the unity of life," explaining that "it is in this inseparable union of antiquity with modern life that classical philology bases its claim as a study of indispensable importance." Since he detested translations, viewing them as he did written histories (which were all partial) and centralized government (which was imposed), he argued that the truest path to the "high ideals of antiquity" consisted of linguistic inquiry. Revealingly, he interpreted the Harvard proposal as a Yankee attack on southern higher education—"an assault which is part of the grand attempt to crush all individuality of development into a homogeneous centralization" (*Essays and Studies*).

In 1877 his edition of *The Apologies of Justin Martyr* appeared, a work noted for being a treasury of Gildersleeve's syntactic formulae. Throughout the late 1870s he presented papers to the American Philological Association meetings (he was twice elected to the presidency of this organization); the first essay, entitled "On $\epsilon\grave{\imath}$ with the Future Indicative and $\grave{\epsilon}\acute{a}\nu$ with the Subjunctive," indicates his rather narrowing field of specialization. Still, it was his interest in the broadest aspects of philology that inspired his founding in 1880 of the *American Journal of Philology*. Devoted to "publication and research in the general field of philology and research," the quarterly also circulated much of Gildersleeve's best syntactical work. Its "Brief Mention" section, originally reserved for short book reviews, eventually evolved into an editor's corner in which Gildersleeve remarked on subjects ranging from the "Sexual System of Cases" to "Americanism": he also expediently responded to unfavorable reviews of his own work. His commentaries were so well received for their critical appraisals, "wit and genial humor," that his friend and colleague C. W. E. Miller compiled a volume entitled *Selections from the Brief Mention of Basil Lanneau Gildersleeve* (1930). This volume best conveys Gildersleeve's punctilious personality, but the highly allusive wit relished by his contemporaries strikes a modern reader as discreetly addressed to the polyglot.

His edition of *Pindar: The Olympian and Pythian Odes* appeared in 1885, offering copious grammatical notes and an introduction to the themes, dialects, syntax, and meters of that "thorough-paced aristocrat." Gildersleeve also brought out in 1890 a work of more general scope, *Essays and Studies,* which contained eight analytical literary essays on various classical figures and five on the importance of classical scholarship in America; he warned in the latter section that without classical and religious instruction the educational atmosphere of America would become an "experiment" conducted "in a vacuum." These and other writings demonstrated his reverently protective attitude toward his Western heritage.

In 1892, still attempting to articulate southern concerns, he contributed an essay titled "The Creed of the Old South" to the *Atlantic Monthly*. Gildersleeve's sympathetic portrayal of the Confederate soldier is partially obscured by muddled imagery (the Civil War is compared to an omelette, for instance); it was perhaps more difficult for Gildersleeve to interpret his own experience than to analyze the words of ancient Greeks and Romans. He visited Greece for the first and only time in 1896, and this tour inspired "A Southerner in the Peloponnesian War," a personal essay in which he revealed disturbing Civil War memories. The two papers about his southern background were published in book form in 1915 under the title *The Creed of the Old South, 1865-1915*.

Gildersleeve was known to many as a Greek syntactician, and he eventually produced a two-volume project on the *Syntax of Classical Greek from Homer to Demosthenes*. After collaborating for nine years with Miller, he and his coauthor presented part 1 in 1900; the second part appeared in 1911. Meanwhile he published as *Hellas and Hesperia, or The Vitality of Greek Studies in America* (1909) the lectures he had delivered at the University of Virginia in 1909.

Gildersleeve retired from academic work in 1915, having served as one of the founding faculty members of Johns Hopkins University. He had been professor of Greek there for thirty-nine years. His many honors had included membership in the American Academy of Arts and Letters and honorary doctor of letters degrees from both Oxford and Cambridge. After suffering a long illness he reluctantly resigned as editor of the *American Journal of Philology* in 1920. He died on 9 January 1924.

Letters:
The Letters of Basil Lanneau Gildersleeve, edited by Ward W. Briggs, Jr. (Baltimore & London: Johns Hopkins University Press, 1987).

References:
Ward W. Briggs, Jr., and Herbert W. Benario, eds., *Basil Lanneau Gildersleeve: An American Classicist* (Baltimore & London: Johns Hopkins University Press, 1986);

Oscar Cargill, *Intellectual America* (New York: Macmillan, 1941);

James A. Harrison, "New Glimpses of Poe," *Independent,* 52 (20 September 1900): 45-47;

Edd Winfield Parks, *Segments of Southern Thought* (Athens: University of Georgia Press, 1938).

Papers:
The major collection of Gildersleeve's papers is housed at Johns Hopkins University.

James Gibbons Huneker
(31 January 1857-9 February 1921)

Arnold T. Schwab
California State University, Long Beach

BOOKS: *Mezzotints in Modern Music* (New York: Scribners, 1899; London: Reeves, 1900);

Chopin: The Man and his Music (New York: Scribners, 1900; London: Reeves, 1901);

Melomaniacs (New York: Scribners, 1902; London: Laurie, 1906);

Overtones: A Book of Temperaments (New York: Scribners, 1904; London: Isbister, 1904);

Iconoclasts: A Book of Dramatists (New York: Scribners, 1905; London: Laurie, 1905);

Visionaries (New York: Scribners, 1905; London: Laurie, 1906);

Egoists: A Book of Supermen (New York: Scribners, 1909; London: Laurie, 1909);

Promenades of an Impressionist (New York: Scribners, 1910; London: Laurie, 1910);

Franz Liszt (New York: Scribners, 1911; London: Chapman & Hall, 1912);

The Pathos of Distance: A Book of a Thousand and One Moments (New York: Scribners, 1913; London: Laurie, 1913);

Old Fogy: His Musical Opinions and Grotesques (Philadelphia: Presser, 1913);

New Cosmopolis: A Book of Images (New York: Scribners, 1915; London: Laurie, 1915);

Ivory Apes and Peacocks (New York: Scribners, 1915; London: Laurie, 1915);

The Development of Piano Music from the Days of the Clavichord and Harpsichord to the Present Time (New York: Boston & Chicago, 1915-1916);

Unicorns (New York: Scribners, 1917; London: Laurie, 1918);

The Philharmonic Society of New York and its Seventy-Fifth Anniversary: A Retrospect (New York: 1917?);

The Steinway Collection of Paintings by American Artists, Together with Prose Portraits of the Great Composers (New York: Steinway, 1919);

Bedouins (New York: Scribners, 1920; London: Laurie, 1920);

Steeplejack, 2 volumes (New York: Scribners, 1920; London: Laurie, 1921);

Painted Veils (New York: Boni & Liveright, 1920; London: Laurie, 1930);

There are no "schools" in art or literature, only good amateurs and artists; there are no Types, only individuals.

As Ever James Huneker

Variations (New York: Scribners, 1921; London: Laurie, 1922);

Essays by James Huneker, edited by H. L. Mencken (New York: Scribners, 1929; London: Laurie, 1930);

Americans in the Arts: Critiques by James Gibbons Huneker, 1890-1920, edited by Arnold T. Schwab (New York: AMS Press, 1985).

The most versatile of American critics, James Gibbons Huneker wrote about music, drama, and art as well as literature. As the preeminent aesthetic journalist in America between 1890 and 1920, unlike typical academic critics of the period he was willing to commit himself on living artists; in fact, he sought them out. Henrik Ibsen, Bernard Shaw, August Strindberg, and James Joyce; Richard Strauss, Claude Debussy, and Arnold Schönberg; Paul Cézanne and Henri Matisse–these were only a few of his prize foreign catches. "Almost singlehanded," says Alfred Kazin in *On Native Grounds* (1942), "he brought the new currents of European art and thought to America and made them fashionable." He also encouraged the most daring and enduring *American* composers, playwrights, painters, sculptors, fictionists, and poets of his day, a contribution not fully revealed until the appearance, almost sixty-five years after his death, of *Americans in the Arts: Critiques by James Gibbons Huneker, 1890-1920* (1985).

Born on 31 January 1857 in Philadelphia to John Huneker, a middle-class convivial father who loved music, art, and the theater, and Mary Gibbons Huneker, a pious, intellectual mother, daughter of an Irish poet, Huneker grew up surrounded by arts, artists, and books. His formal education was limited to seven years at the Broad Street Academy, Philadelphia's best private school, where he excelled in French and acquired a taste for French literature which became his lifelong specialty as a literary critic. Urged by his mother to become a priest and by his father a lawyer, he himself was determined to become a concert pianist, and studied piano for years in Philadelphia. In May 1878 he married Elizabeth Holmes, the first of his three wives, from whom he was eventually divorced in 1891 after the birth of two daughters who died in infancy. (His second marriage, in 1892, to Clio Hinton, a well-known sculptress who became the mother of his only surviving child, Erik, ended in divorce in 1899, but his third, to Mrs. Josephine Ahrensdorf Laski in 1899, lasted the rest of his life.) In September 1878 he embarked on the first of his many visits to Europe, a nine-month stay in Paris, where he studied piano and reveled in the city's attractions. Here, too, he began to write, contributing letters to the *Philadelphia Evening Bulletin* about concerts, plays, and art salons.

Returning to Philadelphia, he studied and taught piano and finally, by 1885, drifted into music journalism, writing for the newly founded *Etude.* Moving in 1886 to New York, he joined the *Musical Courier* and for fifteen years, from 1887 to 1902, made his reputation as the magazine's "Raconteur," conducting a column of critiques, book reviews, short stories, parodies, fantasies, news items, anecdotes, and puns. He also served from 1891 to 1895 as music and (uncredited) drama critic of the *New York Recorder,* a new daily newspaper; drama and music critic of another New York daily, the *Morning Advertiser,* from 1895 through March 1897; music critic (using the signature "Melomaniac") of the weekly magazine *Town Topics* from October 1897 into 1902; music critic (1900-1902), drama critic (1902-1904), art critic (1906-1912), and general critic (1916-1917) of the *New York Sun;* drama critic of *Metropolitan Magazine* (1905-1906); foreign correspondent and feature writer for the *New York Times* (1912-1916); "The Seven Arts" columnist of the magazine *Puck* (1914-1916); and music critic of the *Philadelphia Press* (1917-1918), *New York Times* (1918-1919), and the *New York World* (1919 until his death).

The step from music criticism to literary criticism was inevitable for the "Raconteur," whom the personal need for variety and the necessity of filling a long, weekly column led from the musical associations of Charles Baudelaire, Théophile Gautier, Joris-Karl Huysmans, George Moore, and others to their nonmusical books. Reading French and German easily, by the mid 1890s Huneker knew the work of the leading modern novelists of France and Germany as well as England and America. Possessing the self-educated man's almost excessive respect for sources and authorities, he had something of the scholar's bent for accuracy and thoroughness which the exigencies of journalism often frustrated. He also brought to literary criticism a powerful curiosity about the writer as a unique individual and as the product of his age; a taste for both the poetically romantic and the psychologically realistic; an ear for musical verse and subtle prose rhythms; and a penchant for the serious and honest treatment of sex.

In the 1880s and 1890s the critic who probably influenced Huneker most was Huysmans. He was fond of repeating the Frenchman's claim that impartiality was impossible for a critic and that there were no such things as literary schools: "only the writer's temperament matters, only the working of the creator's brain." The other critics Huneker admired, emulated, and frequently quoted were Gautier, Georg Brandes, Remy de

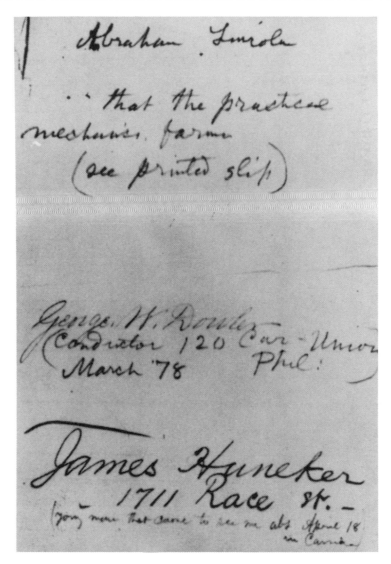

Page from Walt Whitman's notebook recording a visit from Huneker in April 1878 (courtesy of the Charles E. Feinberg Collection, Library of Congress)

Gourmont, and Arthur Symons. On the other hand, he disliked pedantic, dogmatic academicians such as Ferdinand Brunetière, the renowned critic and editor of the *Revue des Deux Mondes,* whom Huneker denounced in 1900 as the author, with Max Nordau–who in his sensational *Degeneration* had attacked later nineteenth-century literature as a product of degenerates–of the "most solemnly absurd criticism of the century." Academic criticism, he later quipped, "may be loosely defined as the expression of another's opinion. . . . [Impressionistic criticism] tells how much *you* enjoyed a work of art . . . [academic criticism] what some other fellow liked."

In the early 1890s Huneker was writing appreciatively about Ibsen and Maurice Maeterlinck and becoming increasingly familiar with the strong dramas of Strindberg, Gerhart Hauptmann, Hermann Sudermann, and Arthur Schnitzler, which he saw at the Irving Place Theater, New York's German-language playhouse. He condemned the British public's hysteria over the Oscar Wilde scandal and refused to join the bandwagon in the posthumous vogue of Robert Louis Stevenson: the latter, he eventually concluded, wrote "superlatively well" but had little to say. As for American writers, as early as 1889 he had published a spirited defense of Walt Whitman (which he later partly recanted). He never lost his early admiration for Edgar Allan Poe, who, he exulted in 1901, had become the best-known American writer in Europe. In 1895 he described Henry

Tintype of Huneker as a young man

James—whom he mentioned more than any other American author—as "our greatest artist." He was fond of quoting the anecdotes of Mark Twain, "one of the most original writers America has produced," he wrote in 1899, "and more of an artist than is generally believed. . . . For me [*The Adventures of Huckleberry Finn*] is the great American novel. . . ." Younger American writers did not escape his eye. He was impressed, for example, by Henry B. Fuller's first book, *The Chevalier of Pensieri-Vani* (1890), and became the Chicago novelist's most persistent supporter. In 1901 he warmly welcomed Frank Norris's *The Octopus,* which he called the "biggest novel of the purely American type since *Silas Lapham.*"

Huneker's fourth book, *Overtones: A Book of Temperaments* (1904), consisting, like most of his books, of articles first published in magazines or newspapers, contained his first literary essays in book form. But it was his next work, *Iconoclasts: A Book of Dramatists* (1905), made up of his most substantial drama critiques for the *New York Sun,*

that established his position as a literary (and drama) critic. With its studies of Ibsen, Strindberg, Shaw, Maeterlinck, and others, the book ran to more than 110,000 words, its length forcing Huneker to omit some studies as well as a thirty-page bibliography. One of the first books by an American on modern Continental dramatists, *Iconoclasts* was well received, and for many years it remained Huneker's best-seller.

As the art critic for the *New York Sun,* Huneker, free-lancing in other fields, turned increasingly to nondramatic literary criticism. From January 1906 until May 1907 he contributed to the *New York Times* monthly reviews of books, often about French writers. By the end of 1907 his unsigned book reviews and literary essays were also being printed on the editorial page of the *New York Sun,* which Remy de Gourmont commended in the *Mercure de France* for its services on behalf of French literature, describing Huneker as "one of the best informed" of foreign critics, "one of those who judge us with the most sympathy and also with the most freedom."

In 1909 Huneker's essays on Stendhal, Baudelaire, Gustave Flaubert, Ibsen, Friedrich Nietzsche, and others, which had first appeared in major American literary magazines, were reprinted in *Egoists: A Book of Supermen,* dedicated to Georg Brandes. Though these writers were strikingly different in most ways, Huneker believed that they had one important trait in common—a devotion to individualism, the one philosophical principle upon which his critical creed rested. Broad-minded, cosmopolitan critics admired *Egoists,* Huneker's own favorite among his books, but other reviewers quibbled with his lack of "general ideas" and his subjects, the critic for the *Outlook* (19 June 1909), for example, calling the latter a "singularly unpleasant group all touched with insanity," and wondering whether their contribution to literature was as important as Huneker thought. "The damn ignoramuses speak of me as digging up queer birds &c," Huneker wrote his brother John, "as if they had never followed the great intellectual currents of the 19th century. . . . In what back alleys of the brain live our provincial critics."

The Pathos of Distance: A Book of a Thousand and One Moments (1913), a collection of personal reminiscences and brief essays on music, drama, art, and literature, most reprinted from the *New York Sun,* was perhaps Huneker's most personal and representative book. Its literary subjects included George Moore, John M. Synge, William

Huneker's second wife, sculptress Clio Hinton, circa 1890

Butler Yeats, Gautier, Maeterlinck, Walter Pater, Thomas Holley Chivers, Alphonse Daudet, Gourmont, Chateaubriand, Nietzsche, Paul Verlaine, and Henri Bergson. The last chapter, "A Belated Preface to *Egoists*," was a reply to those who had decried Huneker's lack of general ideas or, more reprehensively, had questioned the importance of his "supermen" (resembling the preface to *La Culture des Idées* [1901], in which Gourmont admits that his book was not held together by any "common idea"). To Huneker the sweetest words about *Egoists* came from his friend Joseph Conrad, whom he had interviewed for the *New York Times* in 1912. "Apart from the temperamental sympathy I feel for your work," Conrad wrote him in 1913, "the lightness of your surface touch

playing over the deeper meaning of your criticism is very fascinating. One feels grateful to you for your pages of acute and sincere judgement familiarly expressed—as a friend talks."

Cropping up frequently in his column "The Seven Arts" were the names of Flaubert, Nietzsche, Anatole France, Ivan Turgenev, Leo Tolstoy, and Feodor Dostoyevski. But in 1915 Huneker also urged American writers to read the fiction of William Dean Howells to learn a "sense of proportion, continence of expression, the art of exquisitely simple prose, and vital characterization." At the same time he praised bold young writers such as Van Wyck Brooks, whose *America's Coming-of-Age* (1915), he maintained, had dethroned "our Yankee demigods of plaster and

Huneker, circa 1895 (photograph by Sargent)

plush" from their "musty, dusty pedestals."

In *Ivory Apes and Peacocks* (1915, the comma after the first word was inadvertently omitted from the title), with its important essays on Whitman, Conrad, Dostoyevski, and Tolstoy, and the then little-known Jules Laforgue, Huneker was once more in the role of aesthetic scout. His reminiscence and criticism of Whitman disturbed those who felt that he underestimated Whitman's poetry (which he did) and that it was bad taste, if not libel, to suggest openly that the bard of democracy was a homosexual. Huneker implied more about the poet's sexual activities than could be proved (though it should not be forgotten that he had visited Whitman at least once in Camden as a young man and used to talk with him in Philadelphia in the early 1880s); but he helped to focus attention on a matter that subsequent American critics, following the lead of Continental Whitman scholars, have not been able to ignore.

One of Huneker's most memorable scoops occurred in February 1917 when he reviewed for the *New York Sun* James Joyce's *A Portrait of the Artist as a Young Man,* published in New York the preceding December. "Indubitably a fresh talent," he wrote. Joyce reminded him of Anton Chekhov and Guy de Maupassant. *Unicorns* (1917), in which the review soon reappeared, was the first book by an American to contain more than a passing reference to Joyce. Though Huneker mentioned Gertrude Stein and André Gide, surprisingly, neither they nor D. H. Lawrence were among his subjects.

Unicorns, with its essays on Joyce, Gourmont, George Sand, Huysmans, Mikhail Artzybashev, W. H. Mallock, Wilde, George Moore, James, modern French literature, and style and rhythm in English prose, together with those on composers and painters from several countries, was one of Huneker's most varied, cosmopolitan collections. But too few readers were in the mood for aesthetics in 1917. Not many critics, however, were as condescending as the austere moralist Paul Elmer More, who complained in the *Nation* (11 October 1917) that Huneker's unicorn commonly turned out to be a "rhinoceros snouting in the mud." H. L. Mencken, now Huneker's loudest champion and a wartime battler against Anglo-Saxon professors, replied in the *Smart Set* (December 1917) that Huneker was worth "not only a whole herd of Harvard poets and essayists, but the whole of Harvard"—a claim which must have embarrassed as well as pleased Huneker.

In his last years he wrote relatively little about literature, mostly brief comments on books—often by Americans—for the Sunday *World.* Among the newer writers he praised were Carl Van Vechten and Christopher Morley. Yet, he did not neglect his old favorites, lauding Howells in 1919 and, in the most substantial literary essay of his last year, reviewing Henry James's recently published letters for the *Bookman* of May 1920. *Bedouins* (1920) contained essays on Poe and Anatole France, and Huneker's posthumous collection *Variations* (1921) included pieces on Moore, Baudelaire, and his beloved Flaubert.

Huneker was neither a systematic nor a voluminous theorist as a literary critic. Most of his ideas on his craft are scattered among the essays dealing with specific writers or in his letters. In no more than three books did he devote so much as an essay or a chapter to criticism as such: *Promenades of an Impressionist* (1910) contains a section entitled "Concerning Critics" in the chapter on "Literature and Art"; his autobiography, *Steeplejack* (1920), contains a chapter called "Criticism"; and *Bedouins* contains a rambling, whimsical one headed "Concerning Calico Cats." From these

Huneker's third wife, Josephine Ahrensdorf Laski, whom he married in 1899 (courtesy of Dartmouth College Library)

sources one can piece together something of a critical theory, though it is sketchy and inconsistent.

Huneker's attitude toward criticism, first of all, is easygoing, tolerant, almost flippant. Art, to him, is a mystery which no critic can fully penetrate. "In the realm of the blind," he writes, "the cock-eyed is king" (*Unicorns*). He proclaims no exalted position for the critic, announces no missionary work in the wilds of Philistinism. He repeats the idea that everyone is a critic. "The difference between your criticism and mine," he writes, "is that I am paid for mine–and you must pay for your privilege to criticize" (*Bedouins*). He stresses the absoluteness of the subjective. "We only formulate our preferences into laws," he says; to be honest and fair, "a critic should confess his limitations, draw up at the beginning of a book a formal scenario of his temperament, prejudices, his likes and dislikes" (*Steeplejack*).

The critic is of a lower species than the pure creative artist. "At best the critic sits down at a Barmecide's feast, to see, to smell, but not to taste the celestial manna vouchsafed by the gods. We are only contemporaries of genius" (*Bedouins*). The creator, nevertheless, is indebted to the critic, who is the "middleman, the interpreter, the vulgariser." Though his plane is truth, not beauty, the critic must have an artistic temperament and a credo. Yet, "as art is art and not nature, criticism is criticism and not art. . . . At best it mirrors [the artist's] art mingled with the personal temperament of the critic" (*Promenades of an Impressionist*).

Huneker's ideas about the effect of criticism shifted with his moods. In 1907, or earlier, he wrote: "Books breed books, ideas and moods beget moods and ideas" (*Egoists*). By 1913 he felt that "no critic has ever settled anything" (*The Pathos of Distance*). And in 1918 he noted: "There is a lot of nonsense written about the evil that a book may accomplish. Books never kill, even their vaunted influence is limited. . . . I confess I even doubt the value of so-called constructive criticism, . . . You tickle an artist in print and he flatters you in private. . . . Great artists are secretly contemptuous of what amateurs–meaning critics–may say of them, no matter the thickness of the butter they spread on the critic's bread" (*Steeplejack*).

Huneker's native bent inclined him toward art that dealt with the psychological aspects of the human condition, more than its economic or political ones. Sociology garbed as art bored him; this is why he was not admired by Marxist critics such as Bernard Smith. An intellectual aristocrat, he distrusted any form of explicit or implied collectivism. Though philosophically opposed to socialism he was not unaware of social ills in America; the truth-telling Gorky, he wrote ironically in *Iconoclasts*, would not be welcome in America, our "happy, sun-smitten land, where poverty and vice abound not, where the tramp is only a creation of the comic journals." But Huneker preferred not to hear the truth if it were conveyed in the inartistic preaching of the Muckrakers.

An heir to nineteenth-century romanticism, he espoused two primary creeds: the uniqueness of man and the relativism of values–creeds that form the basis of impressionism, which, as Norman Foerster pointed out in *Towards Standards* (1928), "is only a late form of the romantic theory of criticism." The dilemma of trying to steer between the dangers of the swashbuckling subjective–what if "yours is a mean little soul . . . and your pen a lean, dull one; would your critical adventures be worth relating?" (*Steeplejack*)–and the dullness of the academic objective (the value of which was impressed upon him by more systematic thinkers such as William C. Brownell,

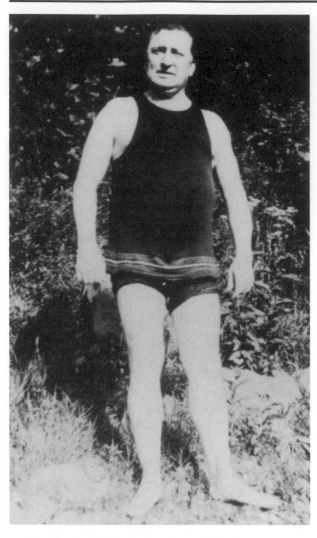

Huneker in 1899 (courtesy of Mrs. John J. Lonergan)

whom he admired) caused Huneker to resort to a kind of hybrid form of biographical-analytical-anecdotal aesthetic criticism. Fortunately, both his personality and his pen were rich and lively. Though he was sometimes inaccurate (as Bernard Shaw complained) and occasionally trivial, he was never dull.

What he mainly objected to, in the work of the academic critics of the 1890s and later, was their inflexible application of the moral yardstick to literature, their parochialism, their pompous tone, and their pedestrian style. His attacks on the narrowness, intolerance, and antisexuality of Puritanism are what particularly endeared him to Mencken, Edmund Wilson, and the younger critics. "Good art," he insisted, "is never obscene; the only obscene art is bad art" (*Steeplejack*). His attitude toward sex in literature is reflected in the words spoken by Ulick Invern, the hero of his

one novel, *Painted Veils* (1920): "Sex is as sane, as clean as any other physical function. . . . Fornication, conception, childbearing are natural. Treat them naturally. Don't slop over them."

The most obvious characteristics of Huneker's method and style are his use of comparisons, his multiple allusiveness, and his interpretation of one art in the terms and images of another. These reflect his wide reading, retentive memory, and his aim to stimulate by suggestion. He is fond of directly stated comparisons between writers in which he emphasizes a fact or condition by comparing it at the expense of a prime example of such fact or condition. "Compared to Gorky's rank, unsavoury, but sincere notation of life," he writes, "Thomas de Quincey's narrative of his youthful woes in Oxford Street . . . is an idyll" (*Iconoclasts*). Allusions and comparisons often flow one after another with little or no elaboration. His juxtapositions frequently produce comic effects based on incongruity. He calls Huysmans the "prose singer of neuresthenia, a Hamlet doubting his digestion, a Schopenhauer of the cook-shops" (*Egoists*). He likes to twist familiar phrases, often biblical or hymnal, with a facile jauntiness that sometimes seems too glib, too conspicuous. Honoré de Balzac, he writes, is one "from whom all blessings, all evils, flow in the domain of the novel" (*Ivory Apes and Peacocks*).

He constantly applies the terminology of one art to another. Music and painting, sound and color are his favorite sources for words and images with which to discuss literature. Ibsen's themes in *When We Dead Awake* (1899), are "developed at moments with contrapuntal mastery" (*Egoists*). Whitman's *Leaves of Grass* (1855) contains "rude red music" (*Ivory Apes and Peacocks*), Huneker apparently referring to the red-bloodedness of the sexual imagery in the poems and liking the alliteration of the "r" as well as the "u" sounds. (It is characteristic of his wit, sophistication, and sensitivity to language that, finding the real Whitman in the Calamus poems, he should slyly describe the poet's democratic philosophy as "inflated humbuggery.") In his rush to communicate the sense impressions of his polyphonic mind, Huneker sometimes blurs the effect on him of a work of art; at other times the device helps him to suggest nuances of response.

His style resembled his conversation, which was rapid, associative, witty, wide-ranging, and flamboyant. A master of the short, incisive statement—"far better an honest staccato phrase," he advised, "than a wilderness of sostenutos"

Huneker in Atlantic City, New Jersey, September 1915, about to make his first flight (courtesy of Dartmouth College Library)

(*Letters*)–he wrote many memorable descriptions bordering on the epigrammatic. Hedda Gabler goes through life, he observes, "with the chip of chastity on her shoulder" (*Iconoclasts*). George Sand was a "maternal nymphomaniac, a metaphysical Messalina" (*Unicorns*). George Eliot was the "great fossil dinosaur of mid-Victorian fiction" (*Bookman,* May 1920). Shaw he dubbed "St. Bernard" (*The Pathos of Distance*). Many of Huneker's picturesque phrases are printed in the revised edition of Frank J. Wilstach's *Dictionary of Similes* (1924).

The style, to be sure, contains more glitter than glue. It lacks cohesion of ideas, progression, direction, and logical development within the paragraph. Undoubtedly, he wrote too much and revised too little, largely because of the pressure of earning a living with his pen. He was concerned, above all, with infusing vitality, gusto, wit, and color into criticism in order to send the reader scurrying to the work that aroused such enthusiasm in the critic.

Yet, he did not confine himself to personal impression and arresting prose. Absorbed in personality, well posted, ordinarily, on biographical sources, he nevertheless criticized a novel or play

with some objectivity. He outlines plots, traces influences, quotes authorities, even those with whom he disagrees. His forte is appreciation, but he does not always praise; when he finds fault, it is usually on grounds of technique, preachiness, or prose style, as in his criticism of that worst of great writers, Theodore Dreiser. He can be highly factual, as his essays on Ibsen, Flaubert, and Baudelaire reveal, but he is not content to stop with the facts, using them instead to develop his appreciative analysis. And his objectivity is usually tempered with humility, knowledge of human nature, and a sense of humor.

The first effective opponent of the "genteel tradition," Huneker was the most venturesome literary critic of his generation. The leading critic of the next one, T. S. Eliot, recalled that as a Harvard undergraduate he had found Huneker's essays "highly stimulating because of the number of foreign authors, artists, and composers whom he was able to mention and whom I had then never heard of." Van Wyck Brooks observed that Huneker "shoveled into the minds of the young precisely what they did not learn in college." His essays, particularly those in *Egoists*, were eye openers to the youthful Ben Hecht, Floyd Dell,

Kenneth Burke, Malcolm Cowley, S. N. Behrman, and Edmund Wilson.

In *The New American Literature, 1890-1930* (1930), Fred Lewis Pattee described Huneker as the "most remarkable literary critic of the period" and in "certain areas of contemporary art and literature, the most erudite critic that America has yet produced." George E. DeMille devoted a forty-page essay to Huneker in *Literary Criticism in America* (1931) in which he associated him with the great French critics of the nineteenth century–Charles Augustin Sainte-Beuve, H. A. Taine, and Jules Lemaître–and placed him in the "very front rank" of American critics with James Russell Lowell, Poe, and James. Ludwig Lewisohn acknowledged in *Expression in America* (1932) that the entire modern period of American culture was "scarcely thinkable" without Huneker's efforts. Henceforth, no literary historian would ignore him–as evidenced, for example, by Oscar Cargill's *Intellectual America* (1941), Alfred Kazin's *On Native Grounds* (1942), Harry Levin's essay in *Literary History of the United States* (1948), and Van Wyck Brooks's *The Confident Years: 1885-1915* (1952).

Though the leftist critics of the 1930s thought Huneker's antipathy to socialism and his apolitical attitude indicated a shallow intellect, and the textual exegetes felt that he seldom came close enough to a work of art, he continues to be quoted. Of his nineteen major books all but four–*The Pathos of Distance, New Cosmopolis* (1915), *Steeplejack,* and *Variations*–are in print in 1988, partly, no doubt, because they are out of copyright. The recent publication of his long-buried critiques of Americans in literature as well as the other arts will surely strengthen his reputation as one of our most brilliant and prescient critics.

Letters:

Letters of James Gibbons Huneker, edited by Josephine Huneker (New York: Scribners, 1922);

Aubertine Woodward Moore, "Some Hitherto Unpublished Letters of James Gibbons Huneker," *Musical Leader,* 45 (7 June 1923): 533-534;

Intimate Letters of James Gibbons Huneker, edited by Josephine Huneker, with a foreword by Benjamin De Casseres (New York: Liveright, 1924).

Bibliography:

Joseph Lawren, in *James Gibbons Huneker,* by Benjamin De Casseres (New York: Joseph Lawren, 1925).

Biography:

Arnold T. Schwab, *James Gibbons Huneker: Critic of the Seven Arts* (Stanford: Stanford University Press, 1963).

References:

Van Wyck Brooks, "Huneker in Retrospect," *High Fidelity Magazine,* 10 (December 1960): 38-41, 123-125;

Norman T. Byrne, "James Gibbons Huneker," *Scribner's Magazine,* 71 (March 1922): 300-303;

Benjamin De Casseres, *James Gibbons Huneker* (New York: Joseph Lawren, 1925);

Eliot C. Fay, "Huneker's Criticism of French Literature," *French Review,* 14 (December 1940): 130-137;

Henry T. Finck, "James Huneker, Virtuoso of the Paragraph, Friend of the Arts," *New York Evening Post,* 19 February 1921, I: 12;

Lawrence Gilman, "The Playboy of Criticism," *North American Review,* 213 (April 1921): 556-560;

[Robert Cortes Holliday], "Murray Hill's Recollections of James Huneker," *Bookman,* 53 (April 1921): 124-127;

Harry Levin, "The Discovery of Bohemia," in *Literary History of the United States,* edited by Robert E. Spiller and others, 3 volumes (New York: Macmillan, 1948), II: 1065-1079;

Edward C. Marsh, "James Huneker: Individualist," *Forum,* 41 (June 1909): 600-605;

Jerome Mellquist, *The Emergence of an American Art* (New York: Scribners, 1942);

H. L. Mencken, Introduction to *Essays by James Huneker,* edited by Mencken (New York: Scribners, 1929);

Edward P. Mitchell, *Memoirs of an Editor* (New York: Scribners, 1924);

John Paul Pritchard and John M. Raines, "James Gibbons Huneker, Critic of the Seven Arts," *American Quarterly,* 2 (Spring 1950): 53-61;

Edgar Smith Rose, "James Gibbons Huneker: Critic of the Seven Arts," Ph.D. dissertation, Princeton University, 1955;

Charles J. Rosebault, "Huneker as his Friends Saw Him," *New York Times,* 20 February 1921, III: 14;

Arnold T. Schwab, "The Apprenticeship of a

Critic: James Gibbons Huneker (1857-1899)," Ph.D. dissertation, Harvard University, 1951;

Schwab, "Georg Brandes and James Huneker: A Cosmopolitan Friendship," *Modern Language Forum,* 38 (September-December 1953): 30-49;

Schwab, Introduction to *Americans in the Arts, 1890-1920: Critiques by James Gibbons Huneker* (New York: AMS Press, 1985);

Schwab, "Irish Author and American Critic: George Moore and James Huneker," *Nineteenth Century Fiction,* 8 (March 1954): 356-371; 9 (June 1954): 22-37;

Schwab, "James Huneker on Whitman: A Newly Discovered Essay," *American Literature,* 38 (May 1966): 208-218;

Schwab, "James Huneker's Criticism of American Literature," *American Literature,* 29 (March 1957): 64-78;

Schwab, "Joseph Conrad's American Friend: Correspondence with James Huneker," *Modern Philology,* 52 (May 1955): 222-232;

George Sylvester Viereck, "James Huneker: Super Critic," *Current Literature,* 47 (July 1909): 57-59.

Papers:
The major collection of James Gibbons Huneker's correspondence, manuscripts, and family papers is at Dartmouth College, most of it obtained from Huneker's widow. Other important collections are at Princeton University (the Charles Scribner's Sons Archives), New York Public Library (especially the John Quinn and the H. L. Mencken papers), the University of Virginia (the Clifton Waller Barrett Collection), Yale University, Stanford University (manuscripts), Library of Congress (Manuscript and Music Divisions), and the Enoch Pratt Free Library, Baltimore (H. L. Mencken Collection). Most of the books, pamphlets, and music from Huneker's library are in the New York Public Library; the rest are at Dartmouth.

Henry James

(15 April 1843-28 February 1916)

Sarah B. Daugherty
Wichita State University

See also the James entry in *DLB 12, American Realists and Naturalists.*

BOOKS: *A Passionate Pilgrim, and Other Tales* (Boston: Osgood, 1875);

Transatlantic Sketches (Boston: Osgood, 1875);

Roderick Hudson (Boston: Osgood, 1876; revised edition, 3 volumes, London: Macmillan, 1879; 1 volume, Boston & New York: Houghton, Mifflin, 1882);

The American (Boston: Osgood, 1877; London: Ward, Lock, 1877);

French Poets and Novelists (London: Macmillan, 1878);

Watch and Ward (Boston: Houghton, Osgood, 1878);

The Europeans (2 volumes, London: Macmillan, 1878; 1 volume, Boston: Houghton, Osgood, 1879);

Daisy Miller: A Study (New York: Harper, 1878);

An International Episode (New York: Harper, 1879);

Daisy Miller: A Study. An International Episode. Four Meetings, 2 volumes (London: Macmillan, 1879);

The Madonna of the Future and Other Tales, 2 volumes (London: Macmillan, 1879);

Hawthorne (London: Macmillan, 1879; New York: Harper, 1880);

Confidence (2 volumes, London: Chatto & Windus, 1880; 1 volume, Boston: Houghton, Osgood, 1880);

A Bundle of Letters (Boston: Loring, 1880);

The Diary of a Man of Fifty and A Bundle of Letters (New York: Harper, 1880);

Washington Square (New York: Harper, 1881);

Washington Square, The Pension Beaurepas, A Bundle of Letters, 2 volumes (London: Macmillan, 1881);

The Portrait of a Lady (3 volumes, London: Macmillan, 1881; 1 volume, Boston & New York: Houghton, Mifflin, 1882);

The Siege of London, The Pension Beaurepas, and The Point of View (Boston: Osgood, 1883);

Henry James (photograph by Katherine Elizabeth McClellan)

Daisy Miller: A Comedy in Three Acts (Boston: Osgood, 1883);

Portraits of Places (London: Macmillan, 1883; Boston: Osgood, 1884);

Tales of Three Cities (Boston: Osgood, 1884; London: Macmillan, 1884);

A Little Tour in France (Boston: Osgood, 1885; revised edition, Boston & New York: Houghton, Mifflin, 1900; London: Heinemann, 1900);

The Author of Beltraffio, Pandora, Georgina's Reasons, The Path of Duty, Four Meetings (Boston: Osgood, 1885);

The Art of Fiction (Boston: Cupples, Upham, 1885);

Stories Revived, 3 volumes (London: Macmillan, 1885);

The Bostonians: A Novel (3 volumes, London: Macmillan, 1886; 1 volume, London & New York: Macmillan, 1886);

The Princess Casamassima: A Novel (3 volumes, London: Macmillan, 1886; 1 volume, New York: Macmillan, 1886);

Partial Portraits (London & New York: Macmillan, 1888);

The Reverberator (2 volumes, London: Macmillan, 1888; 1 volume, New York: Macmillan, 1888);

The Aspern Papers, Louisa Pallant, The Modern Warning (2 volumes, London: Macmillan, 1888; 1 volume, New York: Macmillan, 1888);

A London Life, The Patagonia, The Liar, Mrs. Temperly (2 volumes, London: Macmillan, 1889; 1 volume, New York: Macmillan, 1889);

The Tragic Muse (2 volumes, Boston & New York: Houghton, Mifflin, 1890; 3 volumes, London: Macmillan, 1890);

The American: A Comedy in Four Acts (London: Heinemann, 1891);

The Lesson of the Master, The Marriages, The Pupil, Brooksmith, The Solution, Sir Edmund Orme (New York: Macmillan, 1892; London: Macmillan, 1892);

The Real Thing and Other Tales (New York: Macmillan, 1893; London: Macmillan, 1893);

Picture and Text (New York: Harper, 1893);

The Private Life, The Wheel of Time, Lord Beaupré, The Visits, Collaboration, Owen Wingrave (London: Osgood, McIlvaine, 1893);

Essays in London and Elsewhere (London: Osgood, McIlvaine, 1893; New York: Harper, 1893);

The Private Life, Lord Beaupré, The Visits (New York: Harper, 1893);

The Wheel of Time, Collaboration, Owen Wingrave (New York: Harper, 1893);

Theatricals, Two Comedies: Tenants, Disengaged (London: Osgood, McIlvaine, 1894; New York: Harper, 1894);

Theatricals, Second Series: The Album, The Reprobate (London: Osgood, McIlvaine, 1895; New York: Harper, 1895);

Terminations: The Death of the Lion, The Coxon Fund, The Middle Years, The Altar of the Dead (London: Heinemann, 1895; New York: Harper, 1895);

Embarrassments: The Figure in the Carpet, Glasses, The Next Time, The Way It Came (London: Heinemann, 1896; New York & London: Macmillan, 1896);

The Other House (2 volumes, London: Heinemann, 1896; 1 volume, New York & London: Macmillan, 1896);

The Spoils of Poynton (London: Heinemann, 1897; Boston & New York: Houghton, Mifflin, 1897);

What Maisie Knew (London: Heinemann, 1897; Chicago & New York: Stone, 1897);

In the Cage (London: Duckworth, 1898; Chicago & New York: Stone, 1898);

The Two Magics: The Turn of the Screw, Covering End (London: Heinemann, 1898; New York & London: Macmillan, 1898);

The Awkward Age (London: Heinemann, 1899; New York & London: Harper, 1899);

The Soft Side (London: Methuen, 1900; New York: Macmillan, 1900);

The Sacred Fount (New York: Scribners, 1901; London: Methuen, 1901);

The Wings of the Dove (2 volumes, New York: Scribners, 1902; 1 volume, Westminster, Constable, 1902);

The Better Sort (London: Methuen, 1903; New York: Scribners, 1903);

The Ambassadors (London: Methuen, 1903; New York & London: Harper, 1903);

William Wetmore Story and His Friends, 2 volumes (Edinburgh & London: Blackwood, 1903; Boston: Houghton, Mifflin, 1903);

The Golden Bowl (New York: Scribners, 1904; London: Methuen, 1905);

The Question of Our Speech, The Lesson of Balzac: Two Lectures (Boston & New York: Houghton, Mifflin, 1905);

English Hours (London: Heinemann, 1905; Boston & New York: Houghton, Mifflin, 1905);

The American Scene (London: Chapman & Hall, 1907; New York & London: Harper, 1907);

Views and Reviews (Boston: Ball, 1908);

Italian Hours (London: Heinemann, 1909; Boston & New York: Houghton Mifflin, 1909);

The Finer Grain (New York: Scribners, 1910; London: Methuen, 1910);

The Outcry (London: Methuen, 1911; New York: Scribners, 1911);

A Small Boy and Others (New York: Scribners, 1913; London: Macmillan, 1913);

Notes of a Son and Brother (New York: Scribners, 1914; London: Macmillan, 1914);

Notes on Novelists with Some Other Notes (London: Dent, 1914; New York: Scribners, 1914);

The Ivory Tower, edited by Percy Lubbock (London: Collins, 1917; New York: Scribners, 1917);

The Sense of the Past, edited by Lubbock (London: Collins, 1917; New York: Scribners, 1917);

The Middle Years, edited by Lubbock (London: Collins, 1917; New York: Scribners, 1917);

Gabrielle de Bergerac, edited by Albert Mordell (New York: Boni & Liveright, 1918);

Within the Rim and Other Essays, 1914-15 (London: Collins, 1918);

Travelling Companions, edited by Mordell (New York: Boni & Liveright, 1919);

A Landscape Painter, edited by Mordell (New York: Scott & Seltzer, 1919);

Master Eustace (New York: Seltzer, 1920);

Notes and Reviews (Cambridge, Mass.: Dunster House, 1921);

The Art of the Novel: Critical Prefaces, edited by Richard P. Blackmur (New York: Scribners, 1934);

The Notebooks of Henry James, edited by F. O. Matthiessen and Kenneth B. Murdoch (New York: Oxford University Press, 1947);

The Art of Fiction and Other Essays, edited by Morris Roberts (New York: Oxford University Press, 1948);

The Scenic Art: Notes on Acting & The Drama: 1872-1901, edited by Allan Wade (New Brunswick: Rutgers University Press, 1948; London: Hart-Davis, 1949);

The Complete Plays of Henry James, edited by Leon Edel (Philadelphia & New York: Lippincott, 1949; London: Hart-Davis, 1949);

Eight Uncollected Tales, edited by Edna Kenton (New Brunswick: Rutgers University Press, 1950);

The American Essays, edited by Edel (New York: Vintage, 1956);

The Future of the Novel: Essays on the Art of Fiction, edited by Edel (New York: Vintage, 1956);

The Painter's Eye: Notes and Essays on the Pictorial Arts, edited by John L. Sweeney (London: Hart-Davis, 1956; Cambridge: Harvard University Press, 1956);

Parisian Sketches: Letters to the New York Tribune, 1875-1876, edited by Edel and Ilse Dusoir Lind (New York: New York University Press, 1957);

The House of Fiction: Essays on the Novel, edited by Edel (London: Hart-Davis, 1957);

Literary Reviews and Essays, edited by Mordell (New York: Twayne, 1957);

French Writers and American Women, edited by Peter Buitenhuis (Branford, Conn.: Compass, 1960);

Selected Literary Criticism, edited by Morris Shapira (New York: McGraw-Hill, 1965);

Theory of Fiction: Henry James, edited by James E. Miller, Jr. (Lincoln: University of Nebraska Press, 1972);

Henry James: Literary Criticism, edited by Edel and Mark Wilson, 2 volumes (New York: Library of America, 1984);

The Complete Notebooks of Henry James, edited by Edel and Lyall H. Powers (New York: Oxford University Press, 1987).

Collections: *Novels and Tales of Henry James*, 14 volumes (London: Macmillan, 1883);

The Novels and Tales of Henry James, selected and revised by James, New York Edition, 26 volumes (New York: Scribners, 1907-1918);

The Novels and Stories of Henry James, edited by Lubbock, 35 volumes (London: Macmillan, 1921-1923);

The Complete Tales of Henry James, edited by Edel, 12 volumes (London: Hart-Davis, 1962-1964; Philadelphia & New York: Lippincott, 1962-1964);

The Bodley Head Henry James, edited by Edel (London: Bodley Head, 1967-);

The Tales of Henry James, edited by Maqbool Aziz (London: Oxford University Press, 1973-).

OTHER: Emile Zola, *Nana: A Realistic Novel*, prefatory note by James (London: Vizetelly, 1884);

Guy de Maupassant, *The Odd Number*, translated by Jonathan Sturges, introduction by James (New York: Harper, 1889);

Alphonse Daudet, *Port Tarascon*, translated by James (New York: Harper, 1891; London: Sampson, Low, Marston, Searle & Rivington, 1891);

Rudyard Kipling, *Mine Own People*, introduction by James (New York: United States Book Co., 1891); introduction republished in Kipling's *Soldiers Three* (Leipzig & London: Heinemann & Balestier, 1891);

Wolcott Balestier, *The Average Woman*, preface by James (London: Heinemann, 1892; New York: United States Book Co., 1892);

"Nathaniel Hawthorne," "James Russell Lowell," and "Ivan Turgenieff," in *Library of the World's Best Literature*, edited by Charles Dudley Warner, 30 volumes (New York: Peale & Hill, 1896-1897); volume 12, pp. 7053-7061; volume 16, pp. 9229-9237; volume 25, pp. 15057-15062;

Hubert Crackanthorpe, *Last Studies,* appreciation by James (London: Heinemann, 1897);

Pierre Loti, *Impressions,* introduction by James (Westminster: Archibald Constable, 1898; New York: Brentano's, 1900);

"The Future of the Novel," in *The International Library of Famous Literature,* edited by Richard Garnett in association with M. Leon Vallée, Alois Brandl, and Donald G. Mitchell, 20 volumes (London: Standard, 1899): volume 14, pp. xi-xxii; republished in *The Universal Anthology,* edited by Garnett, Vallée, and Brandl, 33 volumes (London: Clarke/New York: Merrill & Baker/Paris: Terquem/Berlin: Bibliothek Verlag, 1901): volume 28, pp. xiii-xxiv;

Oliver Goldsmith, *The Vicar of Wakefield,* introduction by James (New York: Century, 1900);

Honoré de Balzac, *The Two Young Brides,* translated, with an introduction, by James (London: Heinemann, 1902; New York: Appleton, 1902);

Gustave Flaubert, *Madame Bovary,* translated, with an introduction, by James (London: Heinemann, 1902; New York: Appleton, 1902);

"Sainte-Beuve," in *American Literary Criticism,* edited by William Norton Payne (New York, London & Bombay: Longmans, Green, 1904);

Letter by James to the Hon. Robert S. Rantoul in *The Proceedings in Commemoration of the One Hundredth Anniversary of the Birth of Nathaniel Hawthorne Held at Salem, Massachusetts, June 23, 1904* (Salem, Mass.: Essex Institute, 1905);

William Shakespeare, *The Tempest,* introduction by James, in *The Complete Works of William Shakespeare,* 40 volumes (New York: Sproul, 1907-1909): volume 16, pp. ix-xxxii;

Rupert Brooke, *Letters from America,* preface by James (New York: Scribners, 1916; London: Sedgwick & Jackson, 1916).

Henry James was a highly self-conscious author with a systematic interest in the techniques of novel writing—an interest that culminated in the landmark prefaces to the New York Edition of his own works. Remarkable for his cosmopolitan perspective, he could be snobbish in his re-

James, age seventeen, in Geneva

views of American writers, ignoring many of the authors championed by his friend William Dean Howells. But like Howells he urged his readers to appreciate foreign literature, writing witty, urbane essays that served as an antidote to his country's provincialism. Another of James's assets was his flexibility. To some extent he can be classified with Howells as a realist who mediated between the extremes of romanticism, with its emphasis on pure spirituality, and naturalism, with its focus on impersonal, deterministic forces. Increasingly, however, James insisted on the author's freedom to express his subjective vision, whether or not it coincided with commonly held views of "reality." James was therefore less dogmatic than Howells, and his freedom from "a priori restrictions" has enhanced his reputation among modern theorists.

James's decision to be a man of letters, not of business, resulted in large measure from the upbringing given him by his liberal parents. His father, Henry James, Sr., was a Swedenborgian philosopher who had rebelled against the Calvin-

James's sketch of his sister Alice included in a letter to his mother in 1872. Henry and Alice were on a European tour when James wrote this letter (courtesy of the Houghton Library, Harvard University).

ism of his own youth. When the young Henry, under pressure from his schoolmates, asked him to name his profession, he replied, "Say I'm a philosopher, say I'm a seeker for truth, say I'm a lover of my kind, say I'm an author of books if you like; or, best of all, just say I'm a student." Henry's mother, Mary Robertson Walsh James, was a serene, capable woman with a large tolerance for "father's *ideas*," as they were known in the family circle. Repeatedly, the elder Jameses moved from one city and country to another in quest of the ideal environment in which to rear their five children. the eldest son, William (1842-1910); Henry, who always regarded William as his senior rival; and the youngest siblings, Garth Wilkinson (1845-1883), Robertson (1846-1910), and Alice (1848-1892). For Henry, an observant and introspective child, these moves provided a rich fund of impressions. At the same time they sharpened his critical sense; for as Leon Edel has noted in *Henry James: The Untried Years, 1843-1870* (1953) he reacted to his excessive freedom by attempting to bring reason and order out of the world's chaos.

James's earliest recollections testify to his precocious sense of the picturesque, an important term in both his fiction and his criticism. According to his autobiography, *A Small Boy and Others* (1913), his first memory was of the Place Vendôme in Paris, where his family had sojourned less than two years after his birth in New York City; and he also remembered his grandmother's home in Albany, where he spent his third and fourth years in an environment that still bore traces of Dutch colonial life. In 1845 the Jameses moved to 58 West Fourteenth Street, New York, establishing a household with a distinctly literary atmosphere. Henry's aunt Kate Walsh, who lived with the family, shared accounts of her European travels, while a visiting cousin, reading aloud from *David Copperfield,* introduced the small boy to Charles Dickens. Ralph Waldo Emerson, who personified the "wonder of Boston," was another visitor; so, too, was William Makepeace Thackeray, who examined Henry's jacket and explained that if he were to go to England he would be addressed as "Buttons." And New York City, with its bookstores, theaters, and art galleries, also contributed to the development of his aesthetic sense. "My face was turned from the first," he wrote, "to the idea of representation—that of the gain of charm, interest, mystery, dignity, distinction, gain of importance in fine, on the part of the represented thing (over the thing

of accident, of mere actuality, still unappropriated). . . ." His facility in French, so crucial to his literary career, resulted from tutoring by a series of governesses chosen mainly for the purity of their accent and was reinforced by his subsequent visits to Europe.

From 1855 to 1859 the family made another extended pilgrimage abroad. During this visit James witnessed the scenes described in the novels he had read back home in the States: the castles and ruins of the French and Swiss romance writers, the London of Dickens, the Paris of Honoré du Balzac. If, as he was later to observe, "It takes certainly a great deal of life to make a little art," his sense of the importance of history and culture was forged by his own experience. He also acquired a lifelong interest in the diversity of national types. His father moved the family in an unsuccessful search for a school that would instill in his children his ideal of a denationalized humanity; but Henry, whose interest was literary, not philosophical, was fascinated by human variety, and especially by the polarity between America and Europe.

When the Jameses settled in Newport, Rhode Island, in 1858, the painter John La Farge became Henry's mentor. La Farge urged him to read the *Revue des Deux Mondes,* to translate Prosper Mérimée and Alfred de Musset, and to become a writer instead of following in the footsteps of William, who was studying art. Joining him in his literary efforts was Thomas Sergeant Perry, a close friend who was also to become a man of letters.

Before discovering his vocation, however, James made an abortive attempt to pursue more conventional academic studies. In 1859 his father uprooted the family once again and enrolled him at a scientific school in Geneva, Switzerland—his parents' complaint being, as he later said, that he "read too many novels, or at least read them too attentively." But he soon dropped the study of all subjects except languages, devoting his spare time to reading the issues of *Cornhill Magazine* and *Once a Week* that his father, despite his reservations, continued to send him. The failed experiment in Geneva was followed by a brief sojourn in Bonn, where he doggedly studied German history and philosophy. At this juncture he had a strong desire to return to the United States: as he wrote Perry, he distrusted the "estrangement of American youngsters from the land of our birth."

Courtesy of the Worcester Art Museum, Massachusetts   *Photograph by Gessford*

John Singer Sargent and Edith Wharton, two of James's closest friends

But following his return to Newport, circumstances conspired to make him a spectator and a critic of American life, not a participant therein. In October 1861 he suffered a back injury while attempting to extinguish a local fire–an "obscure hurt" that prevented him from fighting in the Civil War, as his younger brothers eventually did. In 1862-1863 he enrolled in the Harvard Law School but once again found himself bored with his formal studies; instead he cultivated his literary friendships with the Brahmins, including Charles Eliot Norton and Oliver Wendell Holmes, and spent winter afternoons listening to James Russell Lowell discoursing by lamplight on English and French literature.

His association with the Brahmins inspired his first ventures as a literary critic. On 30 July 1864 he offered his first essay to the *North American Review,* which published it the following October; and between that date and 1870, the year that marked the end of his youth, he wrote more than seventy articles and reviews for that journal

and for the *Atlantic Monthly,* the *Nation,* and the *Galaxy.* All these periodicals were edited by men of letters whose earnest desire–to quote Norton– was "to raise the standards of criticism and scholarship among us." And there is no doubt that James, who in *Notes on Novelists with Some Other Notes* (1914) described himself as "an extremely immature aspirant to the rare laurel of the critic," was flattered by the respect of his elders. He especially recalled the day when he traveled from Boston to Cambridge to visit Norton, a "representative of culture" with "a great and arduous mission": to bring "civilisation" to "a young roaring and money-getting democracy, inevitably but almost exclusively occupied with 'business success.' "

Quite naturally, then, James's early reviews reflect his adoption of Brahmin standards; though he was a young man when he wrote them, he attempted to sound much older, sometimes to the point of being pompous. His chosen models were Matthew Arnold, the advocate of "the best that is known and thought in the world," and Edmond Schérer, a French critic notable for his "moral consistency." And since popular literature failed to meet these ideals, most of James's opinions were negative. Justifiably, he waxed indignant over the poor quality of British and American best-sellers: entertaining novels designed for "those jolly barbarians of taste who read . . . only for what they call the 'story' "; sentimental novels whose youthful heroines uttered such inanities as "all sermons are nice" and "everything is pleasant"; and sensational novels whose characters were motivated by lust ("Beasts and idiots," he gravely observed, "act from their instincts; educated men and women . . . act from their reason, however perverted, and their affections, however misplaced.") Less justifiably, he could be condescending in his treatment of major authors. He condemned Walt Whitman's *Drum Taps* (1865) because the poet had failed to view the Civil War "from a height," as Matthew Arnold would have done; and he denounced Dickens–perhaps his own favorite novelist during his boyhood–because he was "nothing of a philosopher." He also dealt harshly with Anthony Trollope and George Eliot because, in their devotion to the commonplace as literary material, they lapsed into dullness and triviality. Thus, as a result of his Brahmin heritage, there was an elitist strain in much of James's criticism. Even after he relinquished his role as American cultural missionary, he continued to scorn most popular literature, to be impatient with bourgeois realism, and to prefer books that appealed to a sophisticated audience.

Nonetheless, James established his independence from his mentors, and one can see the justice of Henry Seidel Canby's remark that Boston proved "too professionally intellectual for his artist's mind." James's reviews testify both to the originality of his literary interests and to the imaginative freedom that led to his expatriation. Unlike the Brahmins he was primarily interested in fiction, not in poetry or philosophical prose; and he insisted from the first that a novel should be a presentation of human character, not a mere exposition of its author's philosophy. This concern for the psychology of the individual resulted in the earliest of his technical formulations: that the protagonist should be the thematic and structural "center" of the novel; that plots should be open-ended, allowing readers to infer the consequences of a character's "final state of mind"; and that narratives should be subtle, free

An 1886 drawing of James by Sargent used as the frontispiece for volume 1 of The Letters of Henry James *(1920)*

from needless intrusions and "trivial and shallow . . . moralizing." Forty years later he expounded these principles in the prefaces to the New York Edition.

Significantly, too, the type of character preferred by James was not the Arnoldian hero but the rebellious, suffering heroine of the Victorian novel–Eliot's Hetty Sorrel or Trollope's Glencora Palliser. Such women, in James's view, personified "the sentiment of freedom" that asserted itself against a dull, provincial society. If his cousin Minny Temple, who died in 1870, became the real-life model for his Isabel Archer and Milly Theale, these characters were their literary antecedents.

Finally, James's imaginative–even escapist–impulse was evidenced by his liking for the "irresponsible" romance. Despite his demand for high seriousness and his avowed preference for psychological as opposed to literal "adventure," he was beguiled by the plots of Sir Walter Scott and George Sand. The early James was embarrassed by his taste for pure fabulation, which seemed to have little relevance to contemporary culture. Ultimately, however, his love of "Story"–"the spoiled child of art," as he called it in his preface to the New York Edition of *The Ambassadors* (1903)—made him a more subtle, flexible critic than were the dogmatic realists. Not only did he come to appreciate the romance as a genre, but he eventually realized that the subjectivity of the writer's perspective is unavoidable.

The next phase of James's career, extending from the late 1860s to the mid 1870s, was marked by his growing restlessness and his increased attraction to Europe. Before expatriating himself permanently in 1875, he made two extended journeys abroad: the first from February 1869 to April 1870, the second from May 1872 to September 1874. His letters and travel essays express his fascination with Europe's history and picturesque charm, despite his occasional bouts of ill health. The intervals he spent in the United States, however, reinforced his sense that his native land afforded little inspiration to an aspiring author. Upon his return to New England in 1870 he complained of the parochialism of "our dear detestable common Cambridge"; even Emerson, whom he visited in Concord, struck him as one of the "exquisite provincials." Nor was he pleased with New York City, where he tried to establish himself as a writer during the winter of 1874-1875. In particular he noted the "extraordinary absence of a serious male interest": if downtown Manhattan was the realm of the businessmen, uptown, where he lived, was that of the ladies and children, the pastry cooks and music masters. And in the eyes of the passionate pilgrim to Europe the appearance of the city itself was "*hideous.*" ("If one could only get over the trick of judging things aesthetically!" he exclaimed in a letter to a friend.)

Not surprisingly, James's reviews of the 1870s reflect his isolation and malaise. Though he believed that the United States might "yield its secrets . . . to a really *grasping* imagination," he treated the local colorists with ironic humor and sarcasm. (As he observed in reviewing one mediocre novel, "If this is the most that local influences can do for the aspiring and confiding American artist, he will not be encouraged to appeal to them.") He ignored his greatest compatriot, Mark Twain, except for passing references to his "drollery." Indeed, among Americans, only Howells escaped his irony, his international novels and travel sketches being somewhat similar to James's own.

To develop his readers' aesthetic sense, James promoted French literature, especially the

Alice James (courtesy of the Houghton Library, Harvard University)

descriptive writings of Théophile Gautier and Hippolyte Taine. At the same time he suspected that too great a devotion to picturesque surfaces might result in a lack of moral substance. "The French," he wrote, "possess that lively aesthetic conscience which, on the whole, is such a simplifier." Despite his boredom with his homeland, James was to remain profoundly American in his emphasis on moral and spiritual values. His favorite authors, in fact, portrayed the conflict between an idealistic character and an aesthetically attractive but morally bankrupt society. He found this pattern in the fiction of the conservative French writers who published in the *Revue des Deux Mondes:* Alexandre Dumas fils, Octave Feuillet, Gustave Droz, and Victor Cherbuliez. And drawing on these works as sources he repeated the paradigm in his own novels and stories, including *Roderick Hudson* (1876), *The American* (1877), *Daisy Miller: A Study* (1878), and *The Portrait of a Lady* (1881).

A more enduring literary hero was Ivan Turgenev, whose self-imposed exile from provincial Russia foreshadowed James's from the United States. In his 1874 essay on the novelist (first published in the April issue of the *North American Review*), James emphasized Turgenev's use of character as compositional "center" and his belief in the "intrinsic value of 'subject,' " the best characters being those who furnished the greatest "information about the human mind." Significantly, too, he noted the polarity between Turgenev's male and female figures: the men were often flawed by a "fatal weakness of will," whereas the women represented "strength of will–the power to resist, to wait, to attain." Leon Edel has noted a similar pattern in James's fiction, attributing it to the cultural and family pressures that made him uncertain of his own masculinity. One might add that James's reading probably shaped his sense of his personal experience.

Another important model was Honoré de Balzac, the subject of an 1875 essay written near the end of James's residence in New York and published in the December issue of *Galaxy*. In contrast with Turgenev, Balzac seemed "superficial" because he stressed aesthetic values rather than moral ones. Yet James was fascinated by the intensity of his characterizations, by the richness of texture that made his novels "ideally real," and by the magnitude of his attempt to depict all of French society. James was to return to him repeatedly as a writer of epic proportions, a Colossus who towered over his successors.

In November 1875 James moved to Paris with the intention of making it his home for some years. This decision was strongly influenced by his literary tastes. Paris, after all, was the city described in the pages of Balzac and the *Revue des Deux Mondes,* the home of his hero Turgenev and also of Gustave Flaubert and his circle, whom James referred to as "the grandsons of Balzac." Edel has even suggested that James's move to Paris mirrored a typically Balzacian plot: he was indeed the young man from the provinces seeking his fortune in the great city.

On the whole, however, his experience was disappointing, though it contributed to his growth as a writer and critic. Turgenev, who was also an outsider, proved to be as charming as his novels had been: for James he would remain "the beautiful Russian genius." James also developed a certain sympathy for Flaubert, the leader of the Parisian *cénacle* and the host of its gatherings on Sunday afternoons. The young critic had been sickened by "the pettiness and ugliness" of *Madame Bovary* (1857), but he now saw something

"almost tragic" in the writer's difficult search for the *mot juste*–the right word–and in his "vainly colossal attempts to press out the least little drop of *passion*."

But the younger members of the circle– Edmond de Goncourt, Emile Zola, Alphonse Daudet, and Guy de Maupassant–provoked both anxiety and condescension on James's part: he pronounced them "a queer lot, and intellectually very remote from my own sympathies." They ridiculed James's favorite authors (Cherbuliez, Droz, and Feuillet, he said, were "not even conceivable" in Flaubert's salon); they told dirty jokes (including one concerning Algernon Charles Swinburne, two Englishmen, and a monkey that left James, even in later years, with a "lurid impression"); and they bragged about their researches into the seamier side of life (Goncourt announcing that his next subject would be "A whorehouse *de province*"). Their novels, too, could be unsavory. "I heard Emile Zola characterize [Droz's] manner . . . as *merde à la vanille* [manure with vanilla]," he wrote Perry. "I send you by post Zola's own last– *merde au naturel*. Simply hideous." There was, of course, an element of bravado in James's letters: he clearly enjoyed playing the sophisticate and shocking his friends back home. But it is also clear that James once more felt isolated, excluded by a group of authors who did not speak or read English and "couldn't really understand it if they did."

His published reviews also document his quarrel with the French. The pilgrim with a "lurking tenderness" for the old "picturesque Paris" did not like to see the legend debunked, and the critic who admired Turgenev's heroines did not enjoy novels featuring prostitutes and other loose women. Moreover, on philosophical grounds James objected to literary naturalism, the mode defined by Zola and embraced by most of the younger members of Flaubert's circle. Though James acknowledged the forces of heredity and environment, he believed in the possibility of spiritual struggle and even, at times, of victory. Consequently, he deplored the pessimism of the naturalists, most of whose characters were overwhelmed by outward circumstances.

Inevitably, then, James grew disenchanted with the grandsons of Balzac. "I have done with 'em, forever and am turning English all over. I desire only to feed on English life and the contact of English minds. . . ," he wrote his brother William in July 1876. And the following December he took up residence in London. Characteristi-

James in 1897 at Dunwich, England, photographed by his cousin, Miss Leslie Emmet

cally, however, he assumed the role of critic and outsider, expressing ambivalence toward the British as he earlier had toward the Americans and the French. He did find new values in the novels of the Victorians: though he had belittled Eliot and Trollope for their devotion to the commonplace, he now praised them for being "more at home in the moral world" than were their Gallic rivals. But his sojourn in Paris had made him acutely conscious of literary form and of the comparative formlessness of most English fiction. The difference between a British and a French novel, he wrote, was that "between a copious 'Irish stew,'. . . with its savory and nourishing chunks and lumps, and a scientific little *entrée,* compactly defined by the margin of its platter." Significantly, he chose to make his publishing debut in England with *French Poets and Novelists* (1878)–an anthology including his essay on Turgenev, the supreme practitioner of structural economy and narrative subtlety.

As for English culture, he realized that it, too, had its limitations. He led a more active social life than ever before, dining out frequently and meeting such literary figures as James Anthony Froude, Matthew Arnold, Leslie Stephen, Robert Browning, Alfred Tennyson, Holman Hunt, and James Bryce, as well as Trollope and Eliot. Yet he perceived that the London "social herd" was "potentially deadly provincial," and he was determined to avoid sinking into "dull British acceptance and conformity." As he wrote to Grace Norton, he thought of himself as a "cosmopolitan": "and to be–to have become by force of circumstances–a cosmopolitan, is of necessity to be a good deal alone."

When he published *Hawthorne* in 1879 he discovered just how lonely a cosmopolitan might be. He was commissioned to write this critical biography by John Morley, the editor of the English Men of Letters series published by Macmillan. The invitation itself was an honor and a tribute to his newfound fame as the author of *Daisy Miller:* as Hawthorne was the only American subject in the series, so he was the only American contributor. Nonetheless, he found the writing of the book to be a difficult task. Though as a youth he had revered Hawthorne and had bitterly mourned his death in 1864, he now complained of the "slenderness of the subject." His own experience made Hawthorne's life appear comparatively dull, while his acquaintance with foreign authors–particularly Balzac–made the writing of the American seem abstract and unrealistic. (As James had observed in reference to Hawthorne's travel sketches, his predecessor "was not a man of the world,–of this world which we after all love so much better than any other.") Then, too, James was annoyed by the American chauvinism of George Parsons Lathrop's biography of the author, a book that he was obliged to use as his principal source of factual information.

Unfortunately, his frustration with his subject was evident in his own study, which in turn offended its American readers. Repeatedly he expressed pity for "Poor Hawthorne," who lived in a country lacking in social complexity and picturesque interest. His catalogue of everything "absent from the texture of American life"–a list based on Hawthorne's preface to *The Marble Faun* (1860)–has often been quoted: "No sovereign, no court, no personal loyalty, no aristocracy, no church, no clergy, no army, no diplomatic service, no country gentlemen, no palaces, no castles, nor manors, nor old country-houses, nor parsonages, nor thatched cottages nor ivied ruins. . . ." Quite obviously, this passage reflects James's sense of his personal situation: whatever

Henry and William James, 1900 (courtesy of Houghton Library, Harvard University)

its faults, Britain was far more interesting than rural New England. Similarly, when he noted the intellectual isolation of the "young man of beautiful genius," he was commenting on his own experience even more than on that of Hawthorne. After all, one motive for his expatriation had been a desire to meet other novelists, to seek the literary society that was lacking in his native land. Little wonder, then, that he felt sorry for a writer confined to a "large dry village."

But James also criticized Hawthorne for failing to make the most of his limited opportunities. In particular he noted his deficiencies as a social observer and his tendency to resort to allegory, "one of the lighter exercises of the imagination." At this point, as Robert Emmet Long has argued, James aligned himself with the younger generation of realists against the older generation of romantics. The romantics, including Hawthorne, had attempted to symbolize a transcendent spiritual realm: for them, allegory was no mere exercise. But for James and the realists, spiritual truth was inseparable from ordinary experience: hence James's belief that the balloon of romance must be tethered to the ground of observable reality. At the same time he could not classify Hawthorne with Sir Walter Scott and George Sand, the British and European Romantics for whom transcendent experience took the form of passionate adventure. Indeed, another of James's charges was that Hawthorne's figures were too passionless, his plots too static. Hawthorne, then, was truly a frustrating figure: not enough of a realist to be taken altogether seriously, yet too much of a Puritan to exemplify the romantic freedom that James valued in Scott and Sand.

Underlying this frustration, however, was a deep respect for an author whose work had been a source of his own fiction and who would continue to influence him in future years. The most telling passage in *Hawthorne* praises the writer's power "to take a picturesque view of one's internal possibilities, and to find in the landscape of the soul all sorts of fine sunrise and moonlight effects." Through his focus on human psychology, Hawthorne, like James himself, achieved a synthesis of realism and romance. Though he was deficient as a social observer, he was keenly aware of the individual consciousness; and though his allegories were sometimes mechanical, he dramatized spiritual truths that were partially concealed by the surface of experience.

But James's audience was in no mood for subtleties. Predictably, the book was warmly received by the British but condemned by his compatriots, who read it when he committed the tactical error of allowing Harper to publish an American edition. Even Howells, who was usually an ally, chided him in the columns of the *Atlantic Monthly* for his devotion to ivied ruins and other "dreary and worn-out paraphernalia." James, however, was unrepentant. "It is on manners, customs, usages, habits, forms, upon all these things matured and established, that a novelist lives. . . ," he wrote Howells, adding that he would "feel refuted" only when America had produced a novelist "belonging to the company of Balzac and Thackeray." Each critic, of course, was defending his own art of fiction. To Howells, who hoped for a new American realism, the ivied ruins symbolized a threat, a regression to derivative, sentimental fiction; to James, they symbolized the history and culture that made it possible to write social novels rather than pure romances. James could respect Howells's point of view, but he scorned his less sophisticated detractors. "Whatever might have been my own evidence for calling American taste 'provincial,' my successors at least will have no excuse for not doing it," he wrote Perry. And he also declared, "I expect to be in London for the rest of my natural life. . . ." There is some justice, then, in Long's remark that *Hawthorne* completed James's conquest of London. "Conquest" should be understood in a figurative sense, for he would always remain an outsider. But he reconciled himself to his status as "cosmopolitan," declaring his independence from all critical movements–including the school of American realism whose tenets he partially supported.

The 1880s, when James came to regard London as his home, have often been called his "middle years." The decade began auspiciously with the success of *The Portrait of a Lady,* the novel which he hoped would be to his former work "as wine is unto water." Serialized in both *Macmillan's Magazine* and the *Atlantic Monthly,* it yielded him financial security–an income of five hundred dollars a month–as well as the recognition he had long craved.

Nonetheless, he suffered from fatigue and depression, and there was a resultant decline in his productivity as a writer. Peevish critics continued to attack his fiction, complaining that it contained too much character analysis and too little "story." In 1882 Howells unwittingly made matters worse by publishing an essay on James in the *Century Magazine,* a British literary journal. Referring to James's narrative technique he stated that the art of fiction had become "finer" than it had been in the days of Dickens and Thackeray: "We could not suffer the confidential attitude of the latter now, nor the mannerism of the former. . . ." This remark was quite accurate: whereas the Victorians had tended to moralize, the authors of the "new school"–including James, Turgenev, and himself–restricted the use of narrative commentary. But the offended British seized on the unflattering comparison, accusing James and Howells of forming an "American Mutual Admiration Society" and repeating the charge that the new novels were boring. ("Was ever any reader kept out of bed by his desire to finish the 'Portrait of a Lady' or [Howells's] 'A Modern Instance'?" asked one reviewer.) To James, this "idiotic commotion" proved that the British, too, could be blindly chauvinistic.

Yet he also knew that his exile was permanent. An extended visit to the United States in 1881-1882 had left him bored, restless, and "horribly homesick for the ancient world." Moreover,

he suffered bereavements that ended the early phase of his adult life. His mother died in January 1882, and his father, whose perpetual optimism had been a source of encouragement, died the following December. He also lost two of his literary mentors. In April 1882 he attended the funeral of Emerson, whose idealism he had embodied in some of his own fictional characters. As he wrote in his memorial essay, "no one has had so steady and constant, and above all so natural, a vision of what we require and what we are capable of in the way of aspiration and independence." And 1883 marked the death of Turgenev, who had so poignantly dramatized the tragic outcome of such aspirations. These losses intensified the mood of sadness that James often betrayed in reviewing lyric poetry, a genre expressing the nostalgia that critics and novelists tended to conceal.

Still, James was determined to build a career for himself. When he returned to London after settling his father's estate, he made a number of new social and literary acquaintances, including George du Maurier, the Edmund Gosses, and the Humphry Wards. In November 1883 Macmillan published the first collected edition of his novels and stories, a project in which he took considerable pride. And even during his bouts of depression he aspired to be a major novelist. "When I am really at work, I'm happy, I feel strong, I see many opportunities ahead," he wrote in his journal. "I shall have been a failure unless I do something *great*!" The next great project, it developed, was the writing of two lengthy social novels. Following a trip to Paris in February 1884, during which he revisited Flaubert and his circle, he decided to "do" Boston and London as Zola had "done" Paris. This goal he accomplished in *The Bostonians* and *The Princess Casamassima,* both of which were serialized in 1885-1886.

"The Art of Fiction," his critical manifesto of September 1884, reflects his experience as a reviewer and as a practicing novelist. Published in *Longman's Magazine,* the essay responded to Sir Walter Besant's "Fiction as One of the Fine Arts," a lecture given the previous April at the Royal Institution. Besant, a popular writer of entertaining romances and of sentimental fiction arousing sympathy for the poor, boasted that he had written eighteen novels in eighteen years. His talk was rambling and inconsistent; but his "first proposition"–that fiction was as much an art as painting, sculpture, music, or poetry–gave James the

James, 1901, in the garden at Lamb House, his home in the south of England from 1898 until his death in 1916 (courtesy of Lamb House, Rye)

opportunity to educate his own audience. In particular James satirized the popular demand for stories "full of incident and movement" and for happy endings featuring "a distribution . . . of prizes, pensions, husbands, wives, babies, millions, appended paragraphs, and cheerful remarks." No doubt he thought of the reviews of *The Portrait of a Lady.*

Ironically, however, the "general laws" laid down by Besant served only to reinforce these popular prejudices. For example, his statement that "the story is everything" was an obvious appeal to the jolly barbarians. James countered by defending psychological fiction and by asserting that plot should be the outgrowth of characterization: "What is character but the determination of incident? What is incident but the illustration of character? What is . . . a novel that is *not* of character?" One may object that this formula is too restrictive; it does not, for instance, apply to such narratives as *Treasure Island* (1883), a book James found "delightful" but difficult to analyze. But

given the bias of his readers, there was merit in his attempt to broaden their conception of "adventure." It was an adventure, he argued, "for a Bostonian nymph to reject an English duke"–the psychological drama portrayed in his own novella *An International Episode* (1879).

He also objected to Besant's belief in the "conscious moral purpose" of the novel. To James this phrase recalled the didactic and sentimental fiction that he had so often read and reviewed. As he had complained in a letter to Howells, he was disgusted with the "floods of tepid soap and water . . . vomited forth" by the English novelists. Indeed, at this point he had acquired a new respect for the French; they, at least, were "serious and honest." "The Art of Fiction," however, lectures both the sentimentalists, who embraced a "shallow optimism," and the naturalists (especially Zola), whose work was "vitiated by a spirit of pessimism on a narrow basis." For James the morality of fiction resulted not from some obvious message but from "the qual-

James, circa 1903

ity of the mind of the producer." Here again he asserted his independence, dissociating himself from both the French and the "Anglo-Saxon" schools of criticism.

Finally, he took exception to Besant's rule that "everything in Fiction which is invented and is not the result of personal experience and observation is worthless." James responded with a poetic defense of the creative imagination: "Experience is never limited, and it is never complete; it is an immense sensibility, a kind of huge spiderweb of the finest silken threads suspended in the chamber of consciousness, and catching every airborne particle in its tissue. It is the very atmosphere of the mind; and when the mind is imaginative . . . it takes to itself the faintest hints of life, it converts the very pulses of the air into revelations." This passage underscores James's freedom from the most restrictive dogmas of realism. Like the other realists of the nineteenth century he insisted on "the importance of exactness—of truth to detail"; indeed, he said that "the air of reality" was "the supreme virtue of a novel." These statements were probably influenced by his own plans for *The Bostonians* and *The Princess Casamassima,* novels that required the taking of copious notes. Yet, as Mark Spilka has ar-

gued, the essay also anticipates James's later fiction, which focuses not on external detail but on the subjective apprehension of experience. Thus, there are affinities between James and the modernists who followed him: like them, he recognized that a novel is an imaginative construct rather than a transcription of extraliterary "reality." And as a result of his belief in the writer's personal consciousness, he eventually accepted fiction quite different from his own, becoming a more sympathetic and flexible critic. In "A Humble Remonstrance" (*Longman's Magazine,* December 1884), Robert Louis Stevenson took him to task for slighting the romance in favor of the novel; but as James replied, he had no real quarrel with those who worked in other modes, his essay having been "simply a plea for liberty."

"The Art of Fiction," then, marks a transition in James's criticism. His early essays and reviews had tended to be negative, for he had defined his principles by engaging in arguments with his predecessors and peers. Later, however, he made a conscious effort to accept authors on their own terms, presenting them to his readers as individual "cases." His flexibility was increased by the hostile reception of both *The Bostonians* and *The Princess Casamassima.* As he said in his let-

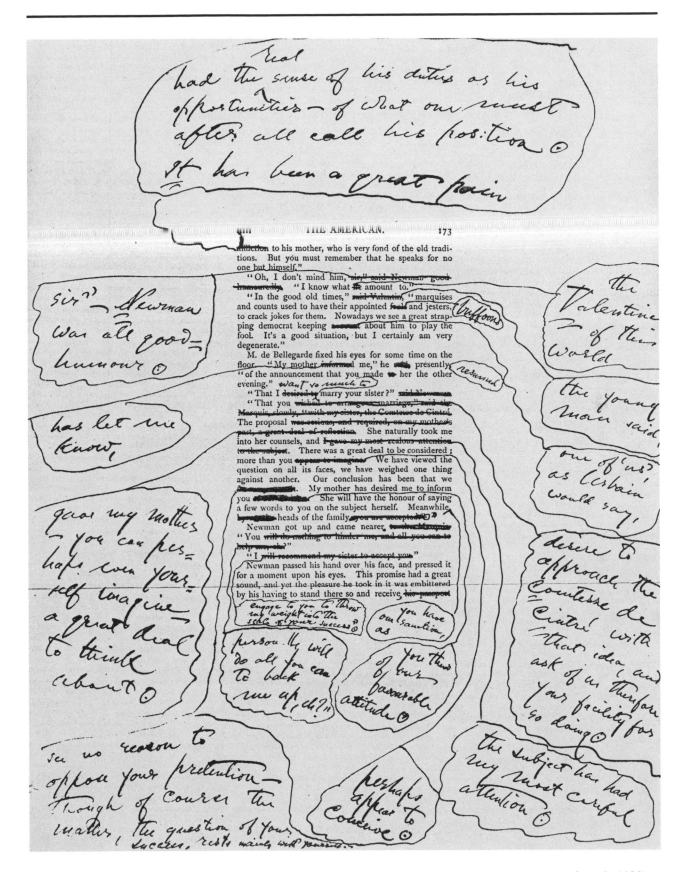

had the *real* sense of his duties as his opportunities — of what one must after all call his position. It has been a great pain

THE AMERICAN.   173

...tiction to his mother, who is very fond of the old traditions. But you must remember that he speaks for no one but himself."

"Oh, I don't mind him, ~~sir,~~ ~~said Newman~~ ~~good-humouredly,~~ "I know what ~~it~~ amount to."

"In the good old times," ~~said Valentin,~~ "marquises and counts used to have their appointed ~~fools~~ *buffoons* and jesters, to crack jokes for them. Nowadays we see a great strapping democrat keeping ~~account~~ about him to play the fool. It's a good situation, but I certainly am very degenerate."

M. de Bellegarde fixed his eyes for some time on the floor. "My mother ~~informed~~ *resumed* me," he ~~said,~~ presently "of the announcement that you made ~~to~~ her the other evening." *want so much to*

"That I ~~desired to~~ marry your sister?" ~~said Newman.~~

"That you ~~wished to arrange a marriage,~~" ~~said the Marquis,~~ slowly, ~~"with my sister, the Comtesse de Cintré.~~ The proposal ~~was serious, and required, on my mother's part, a great deal of reflection.~~ She naturally took me into her counsels, and ~~I gave my most zealous attention to the subject.~~ There was a great deal to be considered ; more than you ~~appear to imagine.~~ We have viewed the question on all its faces, we have weighed one thing against another. Our conclusion has been that we ~~~~. My mother has desired me to inform you ~~~~ She will have the honour of saying a few words to you on the subject herself. Meanwhile, ~~by us, the~~ heads of the family, ~~you are accepted.~~"

Newman got up and came nearer, ~~to the Marquis.~~ "You ~~will do nothing to hinder me, and all you can to help me, eh?~~"

"~~I will recommend my sister to accept you.~~"

Newman passed his hand over his face, and pressed it for a moment upon his eyes. This promise had a great sound, and yet the pleasure he took in it was embittered by his having to stand there so and receive ~~his passport~~

engage to you to throw my weight into the scale of your success

you have our sanction, as

personally will do all you can to back me up, eh?"

of your favourable attitude

---

sir," Newman was all good-humour

has let me know,

gave my mother — you can perhaps even yourself imagine — a great deal to think about

see no reason to oppose your pretension — though of course the matter, the question of your success, rests mainly with yourself.

perhaps appear to conceive

the Valentin of this world

the young man said,

one of us, as Lisbain would say,

desire to approach the Comtesse de Cintré with that idea — and ask of us therefore your facility for so doing

the subject has had my most careful attention

Page from James's revision of The American *for the New York Edition (* The Letters of Henry James, *volume 2, 1920)* ters, he was left with a contempt for the "critical world" and also with a sense of the vanity of negative criticism. Thus, he allied himself with the "producers" against the critics, sometimes referring wistfully to authors who were more popular than he or who maintained their productivity in the face of adverse circumstances. And when younger writers sought his counsel, he urged them to practice their art without worrying over categories or definitions. "Oh, do something from your point of view. . . ," he wrote in 1889 to a summer seminar on "The Novel" in Deerfield, Massachusetts. "An ounce of example is worth a ton of generalities. . . ."

Moreover, he had taken his own advice, for he devoted the later 1880s primarily to his creative work. During a sojourn in Italy from December 1886 to June 1887, he composed eight or ten short stories and a celebrated novella, *The Aspern Papers* (1888); and upon his return to London, he began work on *The Tragic Muse* (1890), the longest of his serialized novels.

Naturally, the busy author wrote less criticism than he had in his younger years, and the essays he did write reflect changes in his approach. Not only were they more positive but they were more truly cosmopolitan: his long residence abroad had lessened his interest in the polarity between "the English and American worlds." He also ceased to be a book reviewer, preferring to write lengthier, more personal essays. For one thing he was dismayed that the pay for an article was "pitiful as an equivalent of labour"; and for another he had grown impatient with the British and American periodicals, which he likened to regular trains that could not run unless all their seats were occupied, if only by stuffed mannikins.

Freed from the constraints of literary journalism, James could devote his attention to the authors he knew and liked. Indeed, the titles of his subsequent volumes of essays call attention to their subjective nature. That of *Partial Portraits* (1888) contains a pun: as he explained to Frederick Macmillan, it suggests "both that the picture is *not* down to the feet, as it were, and that the appreciation is favourable. . . ." The volume includes his memorial essays on Emerson, Trollope, Eliot, and Turgenev, and ends, appropriately, with "The Art of Fiction." Similarly, *Essays in London and Elsewhere* (1893) is a collection of miscellaneous pieces reflecting James's personal tastes: it includes his impressions of London, of the actress Fanny Kemble, and of Robert Browning's fu-

neral in Westminster Abbey. Not all of these essays, then, are critical in the strict sense of the word: the memorial pieces are mainly biographical, and the tributes to friends (including Constance Fenimore Woolson and Mrs. Humphry Ward) are social compliments rather than serious assessments of their fiction.

In several of his essays, however, he showed his appreciation of authors whom he had previously undervalued. He dealt with Stevenson, for example, not merely as a romancer who depicted a fanciful quest for buried treasure but as a serious writer with a talent for "reducing the extravagant to plausible detail." Such a synthesis of realism and romance would characterize James's own later fiction. Also noteworthy are his efforts to do justice to the French. A lengthy essay on Maupassant, written in 1888, acknowledges that despite his amorality the author was a "lion in the path," a brilliant stylist who conveyed sensory impressions with unparalleled power. James subsequently developed a new if grudging respect for Maupassant's master, Flaubert. In the 1870s he had treated him as something of a fanatic, a captive of his obsession with "the torment of style," but in 1893 he suggested that Flaubert's dedication might have its own rewards: "his life was that of a pearl-diver, breathless in the thick element while he groped for the priceless word, and condemned to plunge again and again." This comment, too, suggests the direction in which James himself would proceed, both in his art and in his life. Like Flaubert he would develop a personal style of speaking and writing and would choose a literary lifestyle, attracting a group of young disciples who would address him as *"cher maître."*

But these developments did not take place until the turn of the century. From 1890 to 1895 James was distracted, and his career disrupted, by his ill-starred ventures as a dramatist, first undertaken when the actor Edward Compton persuaded him to rewrite *The American* as a play. James was pleased with the prospect of earning more money and of gaining a popular audience. Moreover, he had always been fascinated by drama as a literary form. In an 1875 review of Alfred Tennyson's plays he had argued, indeed, that the drama was "the very noblest" of all genres, the one that most needed "a masterly structure." And he added that to "work successfully beneath a few grave, rigid laws, is always a strong man's highest ideal of success." In 1891 he even boasted to his brother William that he had found

James at Lamb House in 1906

his "*real* form," compared to which "the pale little art of fiction" had been, for him, "a limited and restricted substitute."

Unfortunately, James was not very reliable as a drama critic and even less so as a critic of his own plays. With some reluctance he did learn to appreciate Henrik Ibsen, whose symbolic, highly charged dramas in which "the Ego lunges against the Ego" probably influenced James's late fiction. His plays, however, were inspired by the inferior authors of the well-made dramas he had seen in his youth: "*À moi*, Scribe; *à moi*, Sardou, *à moi*, Dennery!" he exclaimed in his notebooks. And when he added his unique elliptical dialogue to his derivative, mechanical plots, he only made his plays more difficult to act—though he attributed the problem to the obtuseness of the actors. His career as a dramatist ended on the night of 5 January 1895, when he and his play *Guy Domville* were booed by a London audience. "I'm the *last*, my lord, of the Domvilles!" declaimed the actor playing the title role. Replied a voice from the gallery, "It's a bloody good thing y'are."

From 1895 to 1900 James lived through his "treacherous years," as Edel has called them. Determined once more to practice the art of fiction, he still suffered from an acute sense of being unwanted. Consequently, he turned inward, withdrawing from London and finally moving to Lamb House, Rye, in 1898. Most of his energies were devoted to his experimental works: *The Spoils of Poynton* (1897), *What Maisie Knew* (1897), *The Turn of the Screw* (1898), and *The Awkward Age* (1899). These novels and novellas deal with the irrational, phantasmagoric elements of experience—or as he later wrote in his preface to the New York Edition of *The American*, with "the things that can reach us only through the beautiful circuit and subterfuge of our thought and our desire."

The few critical essays of this period reflect James's feelings of isolation. In "The Future of the Novel," first published in *The International Library of Famous Literature* (1899), he expressed pleasure that fiction was widely read but feared that best-sellers would destroy serious literature: "The flood at present swells and swells, threatening the whole field of letters, as would often seem, with submersion." Nonetheless, he could be generous in his praise of authentic talent. Privately and publicly he encouraged Sarah Orne Jewett and Mary Wilkins Freeman to practice their art of American local-color fiction—a mode that belatedly won his approval. He also became a friend to Stephen Crane, whose "possibilities and powers" he recognized. But his practice as a writer had become increasingly remote from that of the American realists. "I have lost touch with my own people. . . ," he later confessed to Hamlin Garland.

James in Italy, 1907, visiting Howard Sturgis and Mr. and Mrs. Edward Boit (courtesy of the Houghton Library, Harvard University)

In Britain he was bemused by the popular success of George Du Maurier's *Trilby* (1894) and of Rudyard Kipling's violent fiction and jingoistic ballads. In "The Present Literary Situation in France," an 1899 essay, he could only compare the bleakness of the contemporary scene with the richness of the past: the great historians, critics, and dramatists were all dead, and of the novelists, only Zola still survived. At the turn of the century he read and subsequently wrote essays on two Italian novelists, Matilde Serao and Gabriele D'Annunzio, but he criticized both for their exclusive emphasis on sexual passion. "Shut out from the rest of life," he wrote, ". . . [passion] has no more dignity than . . . the boots and shoes that we see, in the corridors of promiscuous hotels, standing, often in double pairs, at the doors of rooms."

In 1900 James recovered from his depression, writing the novels that most critics judge to be his best: *The Wings of the Dove* (1902), *The Ambassadors* (1903), and *The Golden Bowl* (1904). At this point he became a "master" to young writers who–often to his chagrin–sent him their own novels for comment and criticism. The Master's response was to imagine how these books might be rewritten in a Jamesian fashion. As he explained to young Howard Sturgis, "I, as a battered producer and technician myself, . . . can only read critically, constructively, *re*constructively, writing the thing over (if I can swallow it at all) *my* way. . . ."

His published criticism was largely retrospective; instead of reviewing contemporary literature, he paid homage to his own masters.

Belatedly, he praised Hawthorne for grounding his romances in psychological realism–for seeing "the quaintness or the weirdness, the interest *behind* the interest, of things, as continuous with the very life we are leading." He also wrote new tributes to Flaubert and Zola: though he still criticized their limited treatment of "consciousness," he had found them, as artists, to be far more serious than their Anglo-Saxon peers. His greatest interest, however, was in two French novelists of the mid-nineteenth century, Balzac and Sand. These authors, who had shaped his youthful imagination, likewise dominated his last volume of criticism, *Notes on Novelists* (1914): the book contains two essays on Balzac (first published in 1902 and 1913) and three on Sand (1897, 1899, 1914).

Balzac was James's favorite writer, from whom, by his own account, he learned more about the art of fiction than from anyone else. As in the past, he praised Balzac's colossal attempt to depict all of French civilization, calling him a "Gulliver among the pigmies," a monument so massive that one could hardly walk around it. But whereas James had once criticized his superficiality, he now praised him for entering his characters' consciousnesses without making moral judgments. Moreover, as Peter Brooks has noted, James displayed a new taste for Balzacian melodrama–the intense representations of life that reveal the conflicts behind the facade of everyday manners, as his own novels so often do. To the later critic such elusive spiritual truths were far more significant than conventional moralizing. Finally, Balzac's greatness resulted from conscious artistry, and his example was therefore instructive to other novelists. In 1905, during a visit to the United States, James lectured a Philadelphia audience on "The Lesson of Balzac." In fact, he noted, Balzac had taught him many lessons: the rendering of characters "from their point of vision," the fusion of description with action, and the narration of the passage of time without reliance on "a blank space" or "a row of stars."

James's interest in Sand is more puzzling, for as a pure romancer she discouraged the criticism that Balzac, a Romantic realist, seemed to invite. In part James was intrigued by her personality, and especially by her lack of feminine modesty. But he also admired her literary style, which he likened to a citadel where, "in spite of all rash *sorties,* she continues to hold out." The same, of course, could be said of James's late style, which became so much an expression of the man that it characterized his speech as well as his writing. (Using an unkinder metaphor H. G. Wells compared it to that of a hippopotamus trying to pick up a pea.) James was equally impressed by Sand's imaginative ability, her power to transmute "the crude primary stuff " of her experience–including her many love affairs–into the material of her fiction. His essays on Sand thus reveal his continued fascination with the artist's creative genius.

James's rereading of his favorite authors helped to inspire his most sustained critical project, the prefaces to the New York Edition (1907-1918) of his novels and stories. As in his discussions of Sand, he tried to elucidate the mysterious connection between autobiography and art. He promised Scribners that his prefaces would be "colloquial," even "confidential"; and one motive for his journey to America in 1904-1905 may have been a desire to renew his acquaintance with the scenes of his earliest efforts. His prefaces, then, are not impersonal accounts of the art of fiction but narratives telling the "story of [his] story." Typically, James relates how a "germ"–perhaps an anecdote or "a mere floating particle in the stream of talk"–began to grow in his consciousness. He was a listener and observer but never, he insists, a mere imitator: like Sand, he found that "the minimum of valid suggestion" served him better than the maximum.

Balzac, too, was a figure behind the prefaces. Edel has suggested that the scheme of the New York Edition is itself Balzacian: like the edition of the *Comédie Humaine* that James had reviewed in 1875, it was originally planned to comprise twenty-three volumes (though it was expanded to twenty-six); and in Balzacian fashion it can be subdivided into "scenes of international life" and "scenes of English life." (The "scenes of American life," including *Washington Square* and *The Bostonians,* were omitted–perhaps because these novels, with their ironic tone, violated James's Balzacian doctrine that characters should be treated seriously.) Within the prefaces James invoked Balzac when he emphasized the importance of realistic texture and "the play of *representational* values." Clearly, he wanted to "do" his characters and settings in a manner reminiscent of his literary father.

More generally, the prefaces elaborate the ideas that James had developed during four decades as a critic. In his major phase he was so ashamed of his early reviews that he discouraged those who tried to unearth them; but in fact his

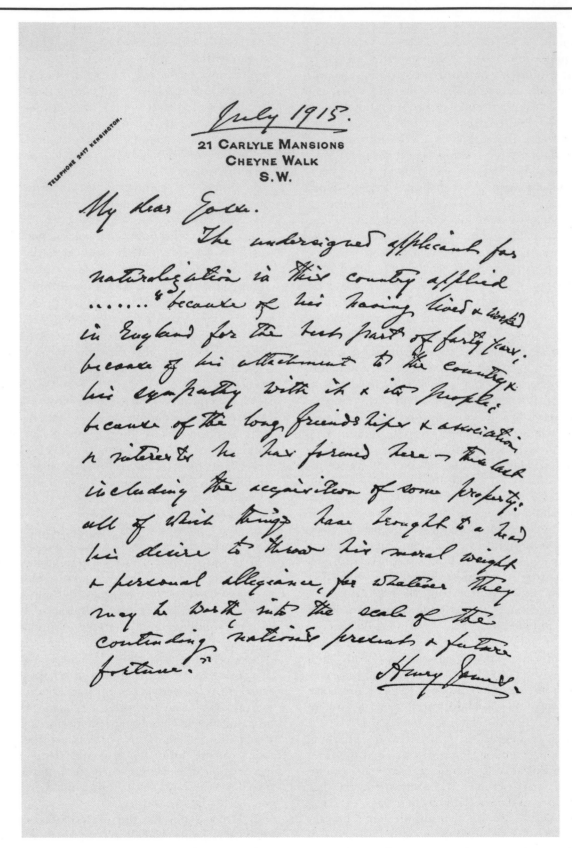

James's letter to Edmond Gosse quoting a portion of his application for British citizenship. Gosse, Prime Minister Herbert Henry Asquith, and others sponsored James's application (courtesy of Lamb House, Rye).

basic principles were remarkably consistent. As always, he stressed his concern for human psychology–his "interest in personal character and in the 'nature' of a mind." And once more, as in his defense of Turgenev against the naturalists, he contended that some subjects were superior to others: "I confess I never see the *leading* interest of any human hazard but in a consciousness . . . subject to fine intensification and wide enlargement." He further noted, as in his remarks on Hawthorne and Stevenson, that the psychological novel transcended the distinctions between realism and romance. A character with "an 'exciting' inward life" could transform even mundane incidents into an "adventure"; and conversely, an intelligent figure with a sense of the uncanny could make even "prodigies" seem part of ordinary existence.

His interest in psychology was also the basis of his principles of "composition": by conceiving of characters as "centres," he had been able to compose more tightly structured fiction than the works of the Victorians, which he referred to as "large loose baggy monsters." Moreover, the problem of characterization led him to consider that of narrative strategy and point of view. A character could be presented directly, through the rendering of his or her consciousness of events; or indirectly, through a single "reflector" or a series of successive "centres"; or dramatically, through a reliance on action and dialogue rather than narrative. Among James's critical writings these technical discussions are perhaps most valuable–not because his methods are an absolute standard but because the prefaces demonstrate that a novel, like a poem, is a literary form. As he had complained in "The Art of Fiction," too many readers–and writers–had assumed "that a novel is a novel, as a pudding is a pudding, and that our only business with it could be to swallow it."

From 1906 to 1909 James's work on the New York Edition consumed most of his time and energy. As he carefully revised his novels, so he labored to make his prefaces *"right"*–to present his own case as thoughtfully as possible. Unfortunately, the reaction of his readers was disappointing. Within the Master's circle the prefaces were acknowledged as an achievement: a review in the *Times Literary Supplement* by Percy Lubbock, one of his protégés, was especially pleasing to James. Elsewhere, however, the prefaces were largely ignored, and the edition was a financial failure both for Scribners and himself. Hence, James called the project "a monument

(like Ozymandias) which has never had the least intelligent critical justice done it." Only after his death were his prefaces recognized as landmarks in the aesthetic history of the novel.

After completing the prefaces, James was eager to return to his creative work. He was plagued, however, by recurrent bouts of depression and ill health, especially after the death of his brother William in 1910. His major literary project was his unfinished autobiography, which detailed his youthful memories of New York, Europe, and New England. As he wrote these reminiscences, he was supported by his coterie of loyal friends, including Lubbock, who was to write a book in praise of his artistry, and Edith Wharton, who in 1912 secretly diverted eight thousand dollars of her own royalties into his meager account at Scribners.

The tone of James's last essays, which he collected in *Notes on Novelists,* can best be described as magisterial. Despite his lack of popular acclaim, he was certain of the principles he had developed in his prefaces and expounded to the young writers who sought his advice. On 7 May 1912, the centenary of Browning's birth, he delivered a lecture entitled "The Novel in *The Ring and the Book*" to the Academic Committee of the Royal Society of Literature. He explained how Browning's poem might be rewritten as a Jamesian novel, with Caponsacchi serving as the central consciousness. The audience was spellbound by James's presence and manner: wrote one reporter, "One merely listened to the voice of this charming old artist as though in the enchantment of a dream."

Less favorably received was "The Younger Generation," an essay first published in 1914 in the *Times Literary Supplement.* Though James was inundated with novels from young writers hoping for a favorable notice of their work, they were, for the most part, disappointed. He was kind to his protégés Hugh Walpole and Compton Mackenzie, and also to his friend Edith Wharton; but he attacked the novelists of "saturation"–especially Arnold Bennett and H. G. Wells–for their excessive concern with sociology and for the absence of a psychological "centre" in their works. The chief metaphor he used to describe their art–or rather their artlessness–was that of the squeezing of an orange, an image suggesting both the richness of life and the crudity with which they treated it. Privately, he used metaphors that were even harsher: he told Max Beerbohm that one of Bennett's novels reminded him of "the slow squeezing-out of a big, dirty sponge," and he wrote H. G. Wells, "Your capacity for chewing up the thickness of the world . . . while you fairly slobber, so to speak, with the multitudinous taste—this constitutes for me a rare and wonderful exhibition." Wells retaliated with his famous parody in *Boon*, which likened a novel by James to a church with an altar displaying "a dead kitten, an egg-shell, a bit of string." Clearly, James was at odds with the new generation of social realists. To him their novels represented life without art; to them his novels epitomized art without life.

Though his writing was little read or appreciated, James did receive acclaim as an elder statesman of letters: honorary degrees from Harvard in 1911 and from Oxford in 1912; a golden bowl presented to him on his seventieth birthday by some 250 well-wishers; and the Order of Merit in 1916, shortly after he became a British subject. Following his death on 28 February 1916 his funeral was attended by most of literary London.

Nonetheless, in his final years he felt that he had outlived his time. "And the hungry generations tread me down!" he once exclaimed. Moreover, World War I not only put an end to the life he had known but also shook his deepest conviction, the one on which his art was founded: his faith in human character and the "cultivated consciousness." In 1915 he wrote "The Founding of the *Nation*," an article on one of the periodicals in which his earliest reviews had been published. Nostalgically, he looked back on the Brahmin idealism that had inspired him for the past fifty years— "the fond assurances . . . that were to keep on and on, seeing themselves not only so little menaced but so admirably crowned." But now, he added, those fifty years could only be called "the Age of the Mistake."

And, indeed, James was largely neglected during the two decades that followed his death. His reputation was kept alive by a small group of critics: Joseph Warren Beach, who explicated his methods and championed his conscious art against Victorian artlessness; Lubbock, who expounded the lessons of the master in *The Craft of Fiction* (1921); and R. P. Blackmur, who collected his prefaces in *The Art of the Novel* (1934), presenting them as "an essay in general criticism." Only in the 1940s, however, did James receive widespread recognition as a critic and novelist. The centenary of his birth in 1943 sparked new interest in his career; the publication of his notebooks in 1947 enhanced his image as a craftsman; and

the advent of the New Criticism led scholars to see him as a major artist, a theorist and practitioner of the novel as a literary form. So great was the critics' adulation that it provoked a reaction from Maxwell Geismar and others, who repeated the charges made by Wells.

More recently, a consensus has developed that James was a less dogmatic formalist than some of his admirers. His techniques were more varied than his prefaces, quoted out of context, might suggest; and when he wrote as a "producer," he assumed the problematic role of reader and critic of his own works, often acknowledging his uncertainties. Then, too, one should bear in mind James's statement that the house of fiction has many windows, each occupied by a different writer. His critical essays, which should be read along with the prefaces, are proof of his efforts to appreciate other authors, despite the limits of his taste and method.

Further evidence of his flexibility is that today's critics view him from different perspectives, using his writings to support their individual theories. Those who stress the referential value of language have praised him as a realist, a believer in "truth of detail" and "solidity of specification." Others, however, have seen him as a neoromantic or proto-modernist, citing his emphasis on the author's subjective vision and his faith in the power of art to create values despite "the fatal Futility of fact." Still others have used his writing to test the principles of deconstruction, showing how he frustrates the desire for unambiguous meaning even while appearing to satisfy it.

"Art lives upon discussion, upon experiment, upon curiosity, upon variety of attempt, upon the exchange of views and the comparison of standpoints," wrote James in "The Art of Fiction." Thanks to his curiosity and independence, he has furthered this discussion not only in his time but in ours.

Letters:

The Letters of Henry James, edited by Percy Lubbock, 2 volumes (London: Macmillan, 1920; New York: Scribners, 1920);

Henry James: Letters to A. C. Benson and Auguste Monod, edited by E. F. Benson (London: Mathews & Marrot/New York: Scribners, 1930);

Theatre and Friendship: Some Henry James Letters with a Commentary by Elizabeth Robins (London: Cape, 1932; New York: Putnam's, 1932);

Henry James and Robert Louis Stevenson: A Record of Friendship and Criticism, edited by Janet Adam Smith (London: Hart-Davis, 1948);

Virginia Harlow, *Thomas Sergeant Perry: A Biography and Letters to Perry from William, Henry, and Garth Wilkinson James* (Durham, N.C.: Duke University Press, 1950);

Selected Letters of Henry James, edited by Leon Edel (New York: Farrar, Straus, & Cudahy, 1955);

Henry James and H. G. Wells: A Record of Their Friendship, Their Debate on the Art of Fiction, and Their Quarrel, edited by Edel and Gordon N. Ray (London: Hart-Davis, 1958);

Edel and Lyall H. Powers, "Henry James and the *Bazar* Letters," *Bulletin of the New York Public Library*, 62 (February 1958): 75-103;

Henry James: Letters, edited by Edel, 4 volumes (Cambridge & London: Harvard University Press, 1974-1984).

Bibliographies:

Maurice Beebe and William T. Stafford, "Criticism of Henry James: A Selected Checklist," revised list, *Modern Fiction Studies*, 12 (Spring 1966): 117-177;

Robert L. Gale, "Henry James," in *Eight American Authors: A Review of Research and Criticism*, revised edition, edited by James Woodress (New York: Norton, 1971), pp. 321-375;

Mary Lee Field, "Henry James's Criticism of French Literature: A Bibliography and a Checklist," *American Literary Realism*, 7 (Autumn 1974): 379-394;

Beatrice Ricks, *Henry James: A Bibliography of Secondary Works* (Metuchen, N.J.: Scarecrow, 1975);

Kristin Pruitt McColgan, *Henry James 1917-1959: A Reference Guide* (Boston: G. K. Hall, 1979);

Dorothy McInnis Scura, *Henry James 1960-1974: A Reference Guide* (Boston: G. K. Hall, 1979);

Leon Edel and Dan H. Laurence, *A Bibliography of Henry James*, third edition, revised with the assistance of James Rambeau (Oxford: Clarendon Press, 1982);

Linda J. Taylor, *Henry James 1866-1916: A Reference Guide* (Boston: G. K. Hall, 1982);

John Budd, *Henry James: A Bibliography of Criticism, 1975-1981* (Westport, Conn.: Greenwood, 1983).

Biographies:

Theodora Bosanquet, *Henry James at Work* (London: Hogarth Press, 1924);

Pelham Edgar, *Henry James: Man and Author* (London: Richards, 1927);

Clinton Hartley Grattan, *The Three Jameses: A Family of Minds: Henry James, Sr., William James, Henry James* (New York: Longmans, Green, 1932);

Simon Nowell-Smith, *The Legend of the Master: Henry James* (New York: Scribners, 1948);

F. W. Dupee, *Henry James* (New York: Sloane, 1951; revised edition, Garden City: Doubleday, 1956);

Leon Edel, *Henry James: The Untried Years, 1843-1870* (Philadelphia & New York: Lippincott, 1953);

Robert Charles LeClair, *The Young Henry James, 1843-1870* (New York: Bookman, 1955);

Edel, *Henry James: The Conquest of London, 1870-1881* (Philadelphia & New York: Lippincott, 1962);

Edel, *Henry James: The Middle Years, 1882-1895* (Philadelphia & New York: Lippincott, 1962);

Edel, *Henry James: The Treacherous Years, 1895-1901* (Philadelphia & New York: Lippincott, 1969);

Edel, *Henry James: The Master, 1901-1916* (Philadelphia & New York: Lippincott, 1972);

Harry T. Moore, *Henry James and His World* (New York: Viking, 1974);

Norman Page, ed., *Henry James: Interviews and Recollections* (New York: St. Martin's Press, 1984).

References:

Charles R. Anderson, "James and Zola: The Question of Naturalism," *Revue de Littérature Comparée*, 57 (July-September 1983): 343-357;

Quentin Anderson, *The American Henry James* (New Brunswick: Rutgers University Press, 1957);

Paul Armstrong, *The Phenomenology of Henry James* (Chapel Hill: University of North Carolina Press, 1983);

Rama Kant Asthana, *Henry James: A Study in the Aesthetics of the Novel* (New Delhi: Associated Publishing House; Highlands, N.J.: Humanities Press, 1980);

Louis Auchincloss, *Reading Henry James* (Minneapolis: University of Minnesota Press, 1975);

Thaddeo K. Babiiha, *The James-Hawthorne Relation: Bibliographical Essays* (Boston: G. K. Hall, 1980);

Martha Banta, *Henry James and the Occult: The Great Extension* (Bloomington: Indiana University Press, 1972);

Laurence Barrett, "Young Henry James, Critic," *American Literature,* 20 (January 1949): 385-400;

Joseph Warren Beach, *The Method of Henry James* (New Haven: Yale University Press, 1918);

Millicent Bell, *Edith Wharton and Henry James: The Story of Their Friendship* (New York: Braziller, 1965);

Mutlu Konuk Blasing, "The Story of the Stories: Henry James's Prefaces as Autobiography," in *Approaches to Victorian Autobiography,* edited by George P. Landow (Athens: Ohio University Press, 1979);

Ralph F. Bogardus, *Pictures and Texts: Henry James, A. L. Coburn, and New Ways of Seeing in Literary Culture* (Ann Arbor: UMI Research Press, 1984);

Wayne C. Booth, *The Rhetoric of Fiction* (Chicago: University of Chicago Press, 1961);

Peter Brooks, *The Melodramatic Imagination: Balzac, Henry James, Melodrama, and the Mode of Excess* (New Haven & London: Yale University Press, 1976);

Peter Buitenhuis, *The Grasping Imagination: The American Writings of Henry James* (Toronto: University of Toronto Press, 1970);

Edwin Cady, *The Light of Common Day: Realism in American Fiction* (Bloomington: Indiana University Press, 1971);

Henry Seidel Canby, *Turn West, Turn East: Mark Twain and Henry James* (Boston: Houghton Mifflin, 1951);

Oscar Cargill, *The Novels of Henry James* (New York: Macmillan, 1961);

David A. Cook, "James and Flaubert: The Evolution of Perception," *Comparative Literature,* 25 (Fall 1973): 289-307;

Lauren T. Cowdery, "Henry James and the 'Transcendent Adventure': The Search for the Self in the Introduction to *The Tempest,*" *Henry James Review,* 3 (Winter 1983): 145-153;

Viris Cromer, "James and Ibsen," *Comparative Literature,* 25 (Spring 1973): 114-127;

Sarah B. Daugherty, "James, Renan, and the Religion of Consciousness," *Comparative Literature Studies,* 16 (December 1979): 318-331;

Daugherty, *The Literary Criticism of Henry James* (Athens: Ohio University Press, 1981);

Daugherty, "Taine, James, and Balzac: Toward an Aesthetic of Romantic Realism," *Henry James Review,* 2 (Fall 1980): 12-24;

Jeanne Delbaere-Garant, *Henry James: The Vision of France* (Paris: Belles-Lettres, 1970);

George E. DeMille, *Literary Criticism in America* (New York: Russell & Russell, 1967);

Stephen Donadio, *Nietzsche, Henry James, and the Artistic Will* (New York: Oxford University Press, 1978);

Leon Edel, *The Prefaces of Henry James* (Paris: Jouve, 1931);

Edel, ed., "Autobiography in Fiction: An Unpublished Review by Henry James," *Harvard Library Bulletin,* 11 (September 1957): 252-255;

Michael Egan, *Henry James: The Ibsen Years* (London: Vision Press, 1972);

Robert Falk, "The Literary Criticism of the Genteel Decades: 1870-1900," in *The Development of American Literary Criticism,* edited by Floyd Stovall (Chapel Hill: University of North Carolina Press, 1955), pp. 113-158;

Falk, *The Victorian Mode in American Fiction 1865-1885* (East Lansing: Michigan State University Press, 1964);

Mary Lee Field, " 'Nervous Anglo-Saxon Apprehensions': Henry James and the French," *The French-American Review,* 5 (Spring 1981): 1-13;

Rosemary F. Franklin, *An Index to Henry James's Prefaces to the New York Edition* (Charlottesville: Bibliographical Society of the University of Virginia, 1966);

Maxwell Geismar, *Henry James and the Jacobites* (Boston: Houghton Mifflin, 1963);

David Gervais, *Flaubert and Henry James: A Study in Contrasts* (New York: Barnes & Noble, 1978);

William R. Goetz, "Criticism and Autobiography in James's Prefaces," *American Literature,* 51 (November 1979): 333-348;

John Goode, "The Art of Fiction: Walter Besant and Henry James," in *Tradition and Tolerance in Nineteenth-Century Fiction: Critical Essays on Some English and American Novels,* edited by David Howard, John Lucas, and John Goode (London: Routledge & Kegan Paul, 1966), pp. 243-281;

Philip Grover, *Henry James and the French Novel: A Study in Inspiration* (New York: Barnes & Noble, 1973);

Richard A. Hocks, *Henry James and Pragmatistic Thought: A Study in the Relationship between the*

Philosophy of William James and the Literary Art of Henry James (Chapel Hill: University of North Carolina Press, 1974);

Laurence B. Holland, *The Expense of Vision: Essays on the Craft of Henry James* (Princeton: Princeton University Press, 1964);

Marcia Ann Jacobson, *Henry James and the Mass Market* (University: University of Alabama Press, 1983);

Vivien Jones, *James the Critic* (New York: St. Martin's, 1985);

Susanne Kappeler, *Writing and Reading in Henry James* (New York: Columbia University Press, 1980);

Cornelia Pulsifer Kelley, *The Early Development of Henry James* (Urbana: University of Illinois Press, 1930; revised, 1965);

James K. Kirschke, *Henry James and Impressionism* (Troy, N.Y.: Whitson, 1981);

James Kraft, "An Unpublished Review of Henry James," *Studies in Bibliography*, 20 (1967): 267-273;

David A. Leeming, "Henry James and George Sand," *Revue de Littérature Comparée*, 43 (January-March 1969): 47-55;

Thomas M. Leitch, "The Editor as Hero: Henry James and the New York Edition," *Henry James Review*, 3 (Fall 1981): 24-32;

Robert Emmet Long, *The Great Succession: Henry James and the Legacy of Hawthorne* (Pittsburgh: University of Pittsburgh Press, 1979);

Percy Lubbock, *The Craft of Fiction* (London: Jonathan Cape, 1921);

Paul Maixner, "James on D'Annunzio—'A High Example of Exclusive Estheticism,'" *Criticism*, 13 (Summer 1971): 291-311;

Anne T. Margolis, *Henry James and the Problem of Audience: An International Act* (Ann Arbor: UMI Research Press, 1985);

Timothy P. Martin, "Henry James and Percy Lubbock: From Mimesis to Formalism," *Novel*, 14 (Fall 1980): 20-29;

F. O. Matthiessen, *Henry James: The Major Phase* (New York: Oxford University Press, 1944);

Matthiessen, *The James Family: Including Selections from the Writings of Henry James, Senior, William, Henry & Alice James* (New York: Knopf, 1947);

Harold McCarthy, *Henry James: The Creative Process* (New York: Thomas Yoseloff, 1958);

Walter R. McDonald, "The Inconsistencies in Henry James's Aesthetics," *Texas Studies in Literature and Language*, 10 (Winter 1969): 585-597;

James E. Miller, Jr., "Henry James and the Language of Literature and Criticism," *Revue de Littérature Comparée*, 57 (July-September 1983): 303-313;

Miller, "Henry James in Reality," *Critical Inquiry*, 2 (Spring 1976): 585-604;

Elsa Nettels, *James & Conrad* (Athens: University of Georgia Press, 1977);

Sergio Perosa, *American Theories of the Novel, 1793-1903* (New York: New York University Press, 1983);

Perosa, "James, Tolstoy, and the Novel," *Revue de Littérature Comparée*, 57 (July-September 1983): 359-368;

Dale Peterson, *The Clement Vision: Poetic Realism in Turgenev and James* (Port Washington, N.Y.: Kennikat Press, 1975);

Ross Posnock, *Henry James and the Problem of Robert Browning* (Athens: University of Georgia Press, 1985);

Lyall H. Powers, *Henry James and the Naturalist Movement* (East Lansing: Michigan State University Press, 1971);

Strother B. Purdy, *The Hole in the Fabric: Science, Contemporary Literature, and Henry James* (Pittsburgh: University of Pittsburgh Press, 1977);

John W. Rathbun and Harry H. Clark, *American Literary Criticism, 1860-1905* (Boston: Twayne, 1979);

Morris Roberts, *Henry James's Criticism* (Cambridge: Harvard University Press, 1929);

John Carlos Rowe, *Henry Adams and Henry James: The Emergence of A Modern Consciousness* (Ithaca: Cornell University Press, 1976);

Rowe, *The Theoretical Dimensions of Henry James* (Madison: University of Wisconsin Press, 1984);

Richard Ruland, "Beyond Harsh Inquiry: The Hawthorne of Henry James," *ESQ*, 25 (Second Quarter 1979): 95-117;

Charles Schug, *The Romantic Genesis of the Modern Novel* (Pittsburgh: University of Pittsburgh Press, 1979);

D[avid] Seed, "Henry James's Reading of Flaubert," *Comparative Literature Studies*, 16 (December 1979): 307-317;

Seed, "The Narrator in Henry James's Criticism," *Philological Quarterly*, 60 (Fall 1981): 501-521;

Mark Spilka, "Henry James and Walter Besant: 'The Art of Fiction' Controversy," *Novel*, 6 (Winter 1973): 100-119;

William T. Stafford, *A Name, Title, and Place Index to the Critical Writings of Henry James* (Englewood, Colo.: Microcard Editions Books, 1975);

Donald David Stone, *Novelists in a Changing World: Meredith, James, and the Transformation of English Fiction in the 1880's* (Cambridge: Harvard University Press, 1972);

Edward Stone, *The Battle and the Books: Some Aspects of Henry James* (Athens: Ohio University Press, 1964);

H. Peter Stowell, *Literary Impressionism, James and Chekhov* (Athens: University of Georgia Press, 1979);

William Veeder, *Henry James—The Lessons of the Master: Popular Fiction and Personal Style in the Nineteenth Century* (Chicago: University of Chicago Press, 1975);

George Watson, *The Literary Critics: A Study of English Descriptive Criticism*, second edition (Totowa, N.J.: Rowland & Littlefield, 1973);

René Wellek, "Henry James's Literary Theory and Criticism," *American Literature*, 30 (November 1958): 293-321;

Wellek, *A History of Modern Criticism: 1750-1950* (New Haven & London: Yale University Press, 1965);

Viola Hopkins Winner, *Henry James and the Visual Arts* (Charlottesville: University of Virginia Press, 1970).

Papers:

Most of Henry James's letters and manuscripts are in the Houghton Library at Harvard University. Also of interest to students of James's criticism are the archives of the publisher of the New York Edition, Charles Scribner's Sons, at Princeton University. Other materials are at Yale University, the Library of Congress, the University of Leeds, Colby College, the University of Rochester, the University of Chicago, the University of California at Los Angeles, the British Museum, the Huntington Library, San Marino, California, the Pierpont Morgan Library, New York City, the New York Public Library, the Buffalo Public Library, and the Century Association in New York City.

George Parsons Lathrop

(25 August 1851-19 April 1898)

Theodore R. Hovet
University of Northern Iowa

BOOKS: *Rose and Roof-tree: Poems* (Boston: Osgood, 1875);

A Study of Hawthorne (Boston: Osgood, 1876);

Afterglow (Boston: Roberts, 1877);

Somebody Else (Boston: Roberts, 1878);

In the Distance (2 volumes, London: Sampson Low, Marston, Searle & Rivington, 1882; 1 volume, Boston: Osgood, 1882);

An Echo of Passion (Boston: Houghton, Mifflin, 1882; London: Hamilton, Adams, 1884);

Spanish Vistas, by Lathrop and Charles S. Reinhart (New York: Harper, 1883);

History of the Union League of Philadelphia (Philadelphia: Lippincott, 1884);

Newport (New York: Scribners, 1884; London: Sampson Low, 1884);

True and Other Stories (New York: Funk & Wagnalls, 1884);

"Behind Time" (New York: Cassell, 1886);

Gettysburg: A Battle Ode (New York: Scribners, 1888);

Two Sides of the Story: Oley Growe's Daughter–Captain Billy–Mrs. Winterrowd's Musicale–"Unfinished"–March and April–Raising Cain (New York: Cassell, 1889);

Would You Kill Him? (New York: Harper, 1890);

Nathaniel Hawthorne (Philadelphia: Lippincott, 1890);

The Letter of Credit, by Lathrop and William H. Rideing (New York: Collier, 1890);

Dreams and Days: Poems (New York: Scribners, 1892);

Gold of Pleasure (Philadelphia: Lippincott, 1892);

A Story of Courage, by Lathrop and Rose Hawthorne Lathrop (Boston & New York: Houghton, Mifflin, 1894);

The Scarlet Letter; Dramatic Poem, music by Walter Damrosch (Boston: Houghton, Mifflin, 1895).

PLAY PRODUCTION: *Elaine*, adapted by Lathrop and Harry Edwards from Alfred Tennyson's poem, New York, Madison-Square Theater, 28 April 1887.

OTHER: *Masque of Poets*, edited by Lathrop (Boston: Roberts, 1878);

The Complete Works of Nathaniel Hawthorne, edited, with introductory notes, by Lathrop (Boston & New York: Houghton, Mifflin, 1883);

Nathaniel Hawthorne, *Mosses from an Old Manse*, edited, with an introduction, by Lathrop (Boston & New York: Houghton, Mifflin, 1883);

Hawthorne, *Twice-Told Tales*, edited by Lathrop (Boston & New York: Houghton, Mifflin, 1883);

Hawthorne, *A Wonder-Book, Tanglewood Tales, and Grandfather's Chair*, edited by Lathrop (Boston & New York: Houghton, Mifflin, 1883);

"Nathaniel Hawthorne's College Days," in *Some Noted Princes, Authors, etc.*, edited by James Parton (New York: Crowell, 1885);

Representative Poems of Living Poets, American and English, Selected by the Poets Themselves, introduction by Lathrop (New York: Cassell, 1886);

"Ralph Waldo Emerson," in *Appleton's Cyclopedia of American Biography*, 6 volumes, edited by James Grant Wilson and John Fiske (New York: Appleton, 1887-1889), II: 343-348;

Walter Damrosch, *The Scarlet Letter*, libretto adapted by Lathrop from Nathaniel Hawthorne's novel (Leipzig: Breitkopf & Härtel, 1896).

PERIODICAL PUBLICATIONS: "Hawthorne's French and Italian Note-Books," *St. Paul's Magazine*, 9 (December 1871): 311-313;

Review of George L. Eastlake's *Hints on Household Taste in Furniture, Upholstery and Other Details*, edited by Charles C. Perkins, *Atlantic Monthly*, 30 (December 1872): 748-749;

"A Class Day at Harvard," *Appleton's Journal*, 10 (25 July 1873): 113-115;

"The Outside of a College Regatta," *Appleton's Journal*, 10 (16 August 1873): 201-204;

"Pebbles from Nahout," *Appleton's Journal*, 10 (6 September 1873): 294-297;

"A Great Man in a Green Hat," *Aldine*, 6 (September 1873): 172-173;

"Adrift on an Island," *Appleton's Journal*, 10 (11 October 1873): 459-461;

Review of Henry Blackburn's *Normandy Picturesque*, *Atlantic Monthly*, 33 (January 1874): 111-112;

Review of Blackburn's *Artists and Arabs; or, Sketching in Sunshine*, *Atlantic Monthly*, 33 (February 1874): 239;

"In a Market-Wagon," *Atlantic Monthly*, 33 (March 1874): 297-300;

"Tallyrand's Penknife," *Appleton's Journal*, 11 (30 May 1874): 673-676;

"Growth of the Novel," *Atlantic Monthly*, 33 (June 1874): 684-697;

"The Novel and Its Future," *Atlantic Monthly*, 33 (September 1874): 313-324;

"Early American Novelists," *Atlantic Monthly*, 37 (April 1876): 404-414;

"Poe, Irving, and Hawthorne," *Scribner's Magazine*, 11 (April 1876): 799-806;

Review of Ralph Waldo Emerson's *Letters and Social Aims*, *Atlantic Monthly*, 38 (August 1876): 240-241;

"Fitz-Greene Halleck," *Atlantic Monthly*, 39 (June 1877): 718-729;

"Some Aspects of DeQuincey," *Atlantic Monthly*, 40 (November 1877): 569-584;

"The Study of Art in Boston," *Harper's Monthly*, 58 (May 1879): 818-839;

"Coleridge as Poet and Man," *Atlantic Monthly*, 45 (April 1880): 483-498;

"The Sorcery of Madjoon," *Scribner's Monthly*, 20 (July 1880): 416-422;

"The Iron Gate and Other Poems," *Atlantic Monthly*, 46 (November 1880): 705;

"Literary and Social Boston," *Harper's Monthly*, 62 (February 1881): 381-398;

"A Nation in a Nutshell," *Harper's Monthly*, 62 (March 1881): 541-555;

"Keenan's Charge," *Scribner's Monthly*, 22 (June 1881): 257-258;

"A Clever Town Built by Quakers," *Harper's Monthly*, 64 (February 1882): 323-338;

"Hawthorne's Home and Study," *Our Continent*, 1 (15 March 1882): 76;

"The Ancestral Footstep," *Atlantic Monthly*, 50 (December 1882): 823-825;

"Quixote in America," *Life*, 1 (25 January 1883): 38-40;

"The Hawthorne Manuscripts," *Atlantic Monthly*, 50 (March 1883): 363-375;

"The Heart of the Alleghenies," *Harper's Monthly*, 67 (August 1883): 327-339;

"Combination Novels," *Atlantic Monthly*, 54 (December 1884): 796-805;

"All Round Spain," *Harper's Weekly*, 29 (15 August 1885): 535;

"A Model State Capital," *Harper's Monthly*, 71 (October 1885): 715-734;

"An American Lordship," *Century*, 9 (December 1885): 217-228;

"The Book Battalion," *Literary News*, 7 (February 1886): 60;

"The Prospect for American Dramatists," *Theatre Arts Monthly*, 1 (24 May 1886): 281-283;

"An Author Who Could Not Help It," *Lippincott's*, 38 (October 1886): 423-430;

"The Library Movement in New York," *Harper's Monthly*, 73 (November 1886): 813-833;

"The Book of American Figure Painters," *Lippincott's*, 38 (December 1886): 754-759;

"The Bailing of Jefferson Davis," *Century*, 11 (February 1887): 636-644;

"Literary Backbiting," *North American Review,* 144 (February 1887): 200-207;

"Some New England Authors," *Chautauquan,* 7 (March 1887): 360-362;

"Home Life of New York Authors," *Chautauquan,* 8 (December 1887): 132-136; (January 1888): 216-219;

"Anglo-American Copyright," *North American Review,* 146 (January 1888): 80;

"George Meredith," *Atlantic Monthly,* 61 (February 1888): 178-193;

"Authors at Home; George H. Boker in Walnut St. Philadelphia," *Critic,* 9 (14 April 1888): 175-176;

"The Dissenter," *Critic,* 13 (20 October 1888): 185-187;

"False Modesty in Readers," *North American Review,* 148 (February 1889): 180-183;

"The Public Library at New London," *Harper's Weekly,* 33 (27 July 1889): 507;

"Talks with Edison," *Harper's Monthly,* 80 (February 1890): 425-435;

"Audacity in Women Novelists," *North American Review,* 150 (May 1890): 609-617;

"Edison's Kinetograph," *Harper's Weekly,* 35 (13 June 1891): 446-447;

"Cooper's Novels," *Once a Week,* 8 (27 October 1891): 6;

"Defence of New York," *Harper's Weekly,* 35 (14 November 1891): 894-895;

"Justice According to Herbert Spencer," *Once a Week,* 8 (24 November-1 December 1891): 6;

"Cardinal Manning," *Harper's Weekly,* 36 (23 January 1892): 79;

"Was Tennyson Consistent," *American Catholic Quarterly Review,* 18 (January 1893): 101-121;

"Catholic Tendency in American Literature," *American Catholic Quarterly Review,* 18 (April 1893): 372-391;

"The Progress of Art in New York," *Harper's Monthly,* 86 (April 1893): 740-752;

"Eccentricity of Criticism," *Harper's Weekly,* 39 (30 March 1895): 302;

"Orestes Brownson," *Atlantic Monthly,* 77 (June 1896): 770-780;

Review of Samuel T. Pickard's *Hawthorne's First Diary; with an account of its discovery and loss, Book Buyer,* 16 (February 1898): 59-61;

Review of Katrina Trask's *John Leighton, Jr., Bookman,* 6 (February 1898): 557-558;

"Some Forgotten Hawthorne Verses, printed in 1845 in one of Griswold's books, and their

authenticity," *New York Times Saturday Review* (19 March 1898): 161-162;

"An American School of Dramatic Art"; "The Inside Working of the Theatre," *Century,* 34 (June 1898): 265-275.

During the last quarter of the nineteenth century George Parsons Lathrop was a major figure in American letters, helping to establish realism as the central mode of literary expression and identifying the novel as one of the major artistic forms of modern culture. He also was an astute student of earlier American literature and an influential spokesman for making women writers a part of the mainstream of American literature.

Lathrop was born in Hawaii in 1851 to Frances Maria Smith and George A. Lathrop, chief administrator of the U.S. marine hospital in Honolulu. In 1859 Lathrop came to New York where he attended private schools. From 1867 to 1870 he pursued his studies in Dresden, Germany, where he met Rose Hawthorne, daughter of Nathaniel Hawthorne. Upon his return to America he attended Columbia Law School for one term and then worked briefly in a law office in New York. He married Rose Hawthorne in 1871. A few years thereafter he left the practice and from 1875 to 1877 was assistant editor of the *Atlantic Monthly* under William Dean Howells. He then became editor of the *Boston Sunday Courier* from 1877 to 1879. After the death of their only child in 1881, the Lathrops traveled in Europe. Returning to New York in 1883, Lathrop engaged in various literary pursuits. He wrote novels, poems, critical reviews; and travel essays. In addition Lathrop and Harry Edwards dramatized Alfred Tennyson's "Elaine" at New York's Madison-Square Theater, which was successfully performed in 1887, and in 1896 he adapted Hawthorne's *The Scarlet Letter* for Walter Damrosch's acclaimed opera of the same name. He also edited, with an introduction and biographical sketch, the Riverside edition of Hawthorne's works in 1883. That same year Lathrop founded the American Copyright League, which was instrumental in enacting the international copyright law seven years later. In 1891 he and Rose entered the Catholic Church. In addition to founding the Catholic Summer School of America, Lathrop became an influential spokesman for the Church. He died in New York City, 19 April 1898.

Lathrop's major achievement as a literary critic is his theory of the novel. In two important

Nathaniel Hawthorne's daughter Rose, whom Lathrop married in 1871 (courtesy of Walter How)

articles published in the *Atlantic Monthly* in 1874 ("Growth of the Novel" and "The Novel and Its Future") he argued that traditionally in Western culture drama had been the most influential literary genre, followed by lyric poetry. As he rather colorfully stated, "dramas are the cathedrals of poetry; the lyric verse is their adornment" ("The Novel and Its Future"). However, he continues, modern societies no longer build "cathedrals nor write great dramas." Instead, "the novel ... attracts to itself our chief energies," and it serves as "a portable drama, requiring no stage, no actors, no lights or scenery, and no fixed time of enactment." Moreover, the novel is particularly "adapted to the various and complex inner life of the modern world." In short, the novel is the most "popular" and "powerful" form of modern literature.

Having established the novel as the central form of modern literature, Lathrop asserts in his *Atlantic Monthly* essays that realism is its most appropriate method. The novel has become popular because it deals with the inner life of the individual. The inner life, however, is to a great extent shaped by the details of daily life. Hence, the novel "deals perforce most prominently with the surface of life, the appearance of things"; it succeeds "in rescuing from nothingness these ephemeral appearances, the beautiful or amusing trivialities through which we daily take our way" ("Growth of the Novel"). However, in order to do this successfully, it must not merely record, for then it becomes what Lathrop calls "literalism." "Realism," as opposed to literalism, penetrates "beneath the deceptive cloak of outwardly uneventful days" and "endeavors to trace the outlines of the spirits that are hidden there.... " "In short," Lathrop concludes the later essay, "realism reveals. Where we thought nothing worthy of notice, it shows everything to be rife with significance."

Lathrop also has clearly defined opinions as to what techniques are required in order to enable the realistic perspective to reveal what is hidden. The most important of these is that the novelist "must seek always to lose *himself* . . . in giving life to his imaginary persons." He disappears, in other words, for the sake of "dramatic representation." To Lathrop, even some of the great nineteenth-century novelists err in this respect. Charles Dickens, for example, constantly intrudes into his works with his "antic" characterizations and "preposterous sense of the ridiculous." George Eliot intrudes with her frequent analyses of character and event. Goethe intrudes through his penchant for allegory. In other words, antic characterizations, analyses, and allegorical representations are examples of the ways that novelists mistakenly let nondramatic elements come between the reader and the portrayal of character and event. Of all the nineteenth-century novelists Lathrop believes that Ivan Turgenev, Honoré de Balzac, and Nathaniel Hawthorne are the most successful in allowing the drama to unfold directly before the eyes of the reader.

This belief that the novelist should be as invisible as possible leads to some significant consequences when Lathrop turns to the question of literature and morality. Invisibility, or at least impartiality, means that the novelist should not moralize upon events and characters: he must forget his personal likes and dislikes in his writings, even cultivating "a warm and sensitive charity" because a "profound moral influence is wholly indirect, in art."

Armed with this conclusion, Lathrop by the end of the 1880s became one of the most effective spokesmen in America against the stultifying effects of Victorian "good taste," thereby helping to clear the way for the full assault of naturalism. As he put it in the *Critic* in 1888, "American literature is in no danger from excess of virility, or of strong motives and powerful execution; but, on the contrary, is suffering from inordinate refinement, myopic vision, and all manner of artificial, enfeebling restraints" ("The Dissenter"). Elaborating on this argument in the *North American Review* ("False Modesty in Readers") a few months later, Lathrop points out that many American readers "are pleased with a work of fiction so long as it presents a certain artificial resemblance to life, but begin to clamor against it if they find that it is too nearly true to actual human existence. They do not want a novel to be too real. . . ." More specifically, they do not want realistic novels that deal with "sexual passion. . . . although this passion is the most potent of all in the world, is at the very basis of life." "Why," Lathrop asks, "should this chief element in the problem of human existence and society alone be ignored?"

Lathrop's belief that the function of the novelist is to dramatize the commonplace events of life also resulted in an impassioned defense of women writers. In an 1890 essay in the *North American Review* entitled "Audacity in Women Novelists" he attacks the belief that there are some subjects, primarily sexual in nature, with which women writers should not deal. The woman novelist, he asserts, "should be freed from the narrow bounds of that mere conventional identity to which we are all confined so long as we consent to regard ourselves simply as others regard us–as one of the crowd who must behave and think in a set manner. The author must rise out of this little individuality into the larger one of a free, observant, independent mind–quite untrammeled by personal considerations–before he or she can depict life well in novel or play. If this privilege is to be denied to women, it is clear that their function as authors must be seriously limited. But it is equally clear that they do not intend to submit to such denial." Lathrop then launched into an argument which sounds strikingly contemporary. The artist, more than any other human being, must have an element of both sexes. Therefore the male writer must have a strong feminine element in his sensibility, the woman writer a strong masculine one. To quote Lathrop, "every imaginative mind of the best and strongest sort must unite some of the elements of both sexes; as the perfect flower contains alike stamen and pistil." This kind of imaginative mind is capable of penetrating beyond the surface of reality. As he put it, "as we are all obliged to live under the shadow of the tree of the knowledge of good and evil, it will be wise to make the best of our lot, and to throw as much light as possible into the shadow. . . . Women can aid in doing this quite as well as men. . . . " After pointing out that George Eliot and Elizabeth Barrett Browning were prime examples of this kind of union of feminine and masculine, Lathrop lists Elizabeth Stoddard, Mrs. Humphry Ward, and Olive Schreiner as contemporary writers who also displayed it. Lathrop concludes his essay thus: "Shakespeare, with all his comprehensiveness, placed life before us mainly from the masculine point of view. Not until the view of women shall receive a similar illustration can the imaginative genius of humanity reach its greatest development. . . . The result may take for its fulfillment a thousand years. But we may

Lathrop, circa 1896

as well begin training the eyes of the race to see it. . . . "

Another great strength of Lathrop as a critic is his grasp of earlier American literature. In "Early American Novelists" (*Atlantic Monthly,* April 1876) he gives a perceptive analysis of Charles Brockden Brown, pointing out that he is one of the first novelists to create believable women characters and that he was instrumental in bringing into existence an American "man of letters." He also gives a highly appreciative account of James Fenimore Cooper and defines concisely the importance of the Leatherstocking tales to American mythology. Lathrop also pays tribute to Edgar Allan Poe's originality.

When it comes to the most well-known New England writers, Lathrop is as learned as he is enthusiastic. In *A Study of Hawthorne* (1876) he acknowledged that the "strictly New England atmosphere seems to chill and restrain his dramatic fervor. . . . " But, Lathrop continued, this atmosphere ultimately made the novelist a greater artist because "isolation and a certain degree of limitation . . . belong peculiarly to American originality." In Hawthorne's case isolation fed a "metaphysical instinct" while encouraging him to appreciate "all forms of human or other life." This conjunction of the metaphysical and the natural made Hawthorne the leader of "a wholly new order of novelists," and he must be placed "on a plane between Shakespeare and Goethe."

Lathrop's belief that provincial isolation stimulated American genius led him to criticize Henry James's *Hawthorne* (1879), a work that relies upon Lathrop's for its biographical information and for its argument that American provincialism and a lack of cultural traditions had irreparably damaged Hawthorne's art.

Lathrop also ably defended Ralph Waldo Emerson's place in world literature. In an excellent article for *Appleton's Cyclopedia of American Biography* (1887), he gives an unusually lucid account of transcendentalism, another target of James's thrusts against American provincialism, a concise summary of Emerson's literary career, and a highly appreciative account of Emerson's art. He argues that Emerson is essentially a prophet, "a John crying in the wilderness," who in an excessively materialistic society "came forward as the most idealistic writer of the age." As a consequence, "he is the most original writer as a poet, seer, and thinker that America possesses."

Lathrop is less effective in dealing with contemporary literature. Unlike William Dean Howells or Harry Thurston Peck, he does not provide his readers with valuable guides to recent European literature nor to the more important contemporary writers in America. For example, he never forgave Henry James for his study of Hawthorne, and as late as 1886 he dismissed him as a writer who "is growing diffuse and loose." Similarly, he barely acknowledges Howells, arguing that he scarcely touches "the larger traits of life, and the great events in a career" ("Some New England Authors," *Chautauquan*, March 1887). Nor does he have much sympathy for the "regional" fiction of the period.

Even less impressive is Lathrop's attempt to define what might be called a "Catholic aesthetic." After his conversion to Catholicism in 1891, he wrote a lengthy article for the *American Catholic Quarterly Review* (April 1893) in which he evaluates American writers according to the degree to which they expressed a "Catholic tendency." By this standard, Emerson, whom Lathrop had earlier praised is judged as "useless, being . . . utterly devoid of ground principles or coherent thought." Henry Wadsworth Longfellow, James Russell Lowell, and John Greenleaf Whittier, in contrast, are effusively praised. Not surprisingly, Hawthorne bears off the laurels, particularly for *The Marble Faun* (1860).

In spite of such aberrations as this, however, Lathrop's insistence upon a true realism which did not shun the shadows of life was an important contribution to literature and his defense of women writers was far advanced for his time. He was also instrumental in creating for his readers a sense of America's literary past.

Reference:

Sergio Perosa, *American Theories of the Novel: 1793-1903* (New York: New York University Press, 1983), pp. 92-99.

Papers:

George Parsons Lathrop's manuscripts, letters, and personal documents are scattered in libraries across the United States. Significant holdings are located at the Beinecke Rare Book and Manuscript Library, Yale University; Houghton Library, Harvard University; and the University of Notre Dame Archives.

Thomas R. Lounsbury
(1 January 1838-9 April 1915)

Myron Simon
University of California, Irvine

BOOKS: *History of the English Language* (New York: Holt, 1879; revised and enlarged, 1894);

James Fenimore Cooper (Boston & New York: Houghton, Mifflin, 1882);

Studies in Chaucer: His Life and Writings, 3 volumes (New York: Harper, 1892);

Shakespeare as a Dramatic Artist (New York: Scribners, 1901);

Shakespeare and Voltaire (New York: Scribners, 1902);

The Standard of Pronunciation in English (New York & London: Harper, 1904);

The Text of Shakespeare (New York: Scribners, 1906); republished as *The First Editors of Shakespeare* (London: Nutt, 1906);

The Standard of Usage in English (New York & London: Harper, 1908);

English Spelling and Spelling Reform (New York & London: Harper, 1909);

The Early Literary Career of Robert Browning (New York: Scribners, 1911; London: Unwin, 1912);

The Life and Times of Tennyson [From 1809 to 1850], edited by Wilbur L. Cross, with the assistance of Helen McAfee (New Haven: Yale University Press, 1915).

OTHER: Geoffrey Chaucer, *The Parlament of Foules,* edited, with an introduction, notes, and glossary, by Lounsbury (Boston: Ginn, Heath, 1883);

Edward Tomkins McLaughlin, *Studies in Medieval Life and Literature,* edited by Lounsbury (New York & London: Putnam's, 1894);

Chaucer, *The Complete Works of Geoffrey Chaucer,* introduction by Lounsbury (New York: Crowell, 1900);

Chaucer, *The Canterbury Tales,* introduction by Lounsbury (New York: Crowell, 1903);

Charles Dudley Warner, *The Complete Writings of Charles Dudley Warner,* 15 volumes, edited, with a biographical sketch, by Lounsbury

Thomas R. Lounsbury

(Hartford, Conn.: American Publishing Co., 1904);

Yale Book of American Verse, edited by Lounsbury (New Haven: Yale University Press, 1912).

Thomas Raynesford Lounsbury was one of the first American scholars to enter the field of literary history. His studies of Geoffrey Chaucer, William Shakespeare, Robert Browning, Alfred Tennyson, and James Fenimore Cooper were important advances in the knowledge of these writers and their times. His pioneering history of the English language was for many years the standard introduction to the subject, and he made valuable contributions to the swelling debate at the turn of the century over the vocabulary, pronunci-

136

ation, and spelling of the English language in America. And Lounsbury was unquestionably a major formative influence in the development of English as an independent academic discipline in American schools and colleges.

He was born in Ovid, New York, the son of the Reverend Thomas Lounsbury, a Presbyterian minister of strongly abolitionist sentiments who was the author of *Pro-Slavery Overthrown* (1847). His mother, Mary Janette Woodward Lounsbury, was the daughter of a major in the American Revolution. Lounsbury prepared for college at the Ovid Academy and entered Yale in 1855. He was an outstanding student, winning prizes in English composition, debate, and oratory and serving as one of the editors of the *Yale Literary Magazine.* Elected to Phi Beta Kappa, he received his bachelor of arts degree in 1859. Lounsbury spent the next three years in New York City as a member of the editorial staff preparing Appleton's *New American Cyclopedia.* In 1862 he enlisted in the Union army as a first lieutenant in the 126th New York Regiment and served throughout the Civil War. Captured at Harpers Ferry, he was exchanged and returned to active duty. At the battle of Gettysburg, in which his regiment suffered heavy losses, he was one of the few officers who survived without injury.

Discharged from military service in June 1865, Lounsbury did not return to editorial work in New York City. Instead, he turned to the teaching of Greek and Latin at Lespinasse's French Institute in New York and, subsequently, became the private tutor to a family in New Jersey. During these years immediately following the war Lounsbury undertook a strenuous program of self-education in Old and Middle English and made himself expert in the burgeoning field of English philology. In January 1870 he began his career of thirty-six years as a teacher of English and librarian in the Sheffield Scientific School at Yale. In 1871 he was advanced from the rank of instructor to professor of English, and in the same year he married Jane D. Folwell. The four decades that followed encompassed Lounsbury's achievement of wide recognition as a vanguard scholar in the new field of English.

The college curriculum by which Lounsbury had been educated was narrowly restricted to Greek and Latin, rhetoric, mathematics, logic, and ancient history. To be sure, there might be some small attention to the physical sciences and, increasingly after about 1840, instruction in the modern languages slowly became available. The overriding emphasis of the curriculum, however, was manifestly classical. There was no English faculty as such, although the rhetoric faculty provided some unsystematic and largely elocutionary instruction in English and American literature. Henry Seidel Canby described his Yale undergraduate education in the 1890s as an old curriculum "still tottering like a rotted house about to fall and in parts already fallen." In the decades following the Civil War the old curriculum became progressively less tolerable to undergraduates with scientific and utilitarian outlooks or to those who yearned for a more vitally contemporary education. Consequently, the classical curriculum began slowly and grudgingly to give way to demands for more varied and more general curricula preparatory to a wide range of vocations and to the new professional and graduate schools. Yale's Sheffield Scientific School, which evolved out of new programs in chemistry and engineering in the 1850s, was one of the earliest and boldest departures from the classical undergraduate curriculum, and it became a model for those eager to promote or vilify the emergence of scientific and liberal educational programs.

In the Sheffield Scientific School modern languages replaced Greek and Latin; and, accordingly, the great Sanskrit scholar and pioneer linguist William Dwight Whitney had moved from Yale College to the Scientific School to teach French and German a decade before Lounsbury was appointed to teach the English language and composition. But the growth of English quickly surpassed that of the other modern languages due to the strong Anglophilia of the period, the heightened interest in the history of the English language that resulted from the early nineteenth-century flowering of Germanic philology, and the obvious appeal to students of studying their own, as opposed to a foreign, language. Most important, the triumph of modern over classical languages and of English over the other modern languages was assured by the enactment in the 1870s and 1880s of the elective system in American colleges. Some limited instruction in modern languages, English literature, physical sciences, and social sciences had, of course, antedated the introduction of the elective system by President Charles W. Eliot of Harvard, but it was the elective system that freed these subjects for growth and expansion. And, in the ensuing competition for enrollments, English and the social sciences were notably successful. By the time of Lounsbury's death in 1915, the Scientific School was at the point of merging with Yale College, and Yale's English faculty had become a large and justly celebrated department of the university.

In this new era of gradual accommodation to broadened educational ends English emerged as a department with belles lettres as its central concern, although the method of literary study remained classical in its extrinsic focus upon linguistic and historical details. Similarly, the rhetoricians and philologists absorbed into these new English departments sought to preserve tradition in their heavily technique-oriented approach to composition and their highly prescriptive view of English usage. Situated from the beginning of his career in a scientific school meant to provide a modern, utilitarian alternative to the classical Yale College, Lounsbury was far less the captive of the classical tradition than contemporaries like Francis Andrew March of Lafayette College, who in 1857 became the first American to be given the title professor of the English language, and Francis James Child of Harvard, who in 1876 became the first holder of the title professor of English literature after having been initially appointed Boylston professor of rhetoric and oratory in 1851. In the course of his career from rhetorician to philologist to literary historian Child summarized the early history of English departments in their effort to achieve academic respect and autonomy. But Lounsbury had been offered his initial appointment in a school that had, in a sense, anticipated the elective system and was, therefore, eager to expand its curriculum. When he made acceptance of his appointment as instructor of English composition contingent upon his being allowed at once to give an extensive course in English literature beginning with Chaucer and continuing through Shakespeare to later writers like John Dryden and Alexander Pope, "the condition was immediately accepted," according to Wilbur L. Cross, "with particular enthusiasm."

A strong-minded, practical, and resourceful man whose vigorous manner and sturdy appearance might more readily have identified him as a soldier than a scholar, Lounsbury took full advantage of his special opportunities at the Scientific School to build an English program accountable not to venerable traditions but rather to the principle of rational inquiry and to the disinterested search for truth. His year-long course in English literature, first offered in 1870-1871 and thereafter expanded to two years, appears to have been unprecedented. Other schools listing a

course in English literature had, in the traditional fashion, based instruction upon the contents of historical manuals, but Lounsbury judged it essential to the understanding of his students that "either a whole work of an author should be studied, or a part forming by itself a complete whole." That is, unwilling to acquiesce in the extension of the mode of instruction in classics to instruction in "modern" English literature, he rejected the manuals with their scraps of reading and their accumulations of frequently irrelevant historical information as a substitute for close, appreciative readings of the texts themselves. He thereby anticipated the objections to potted literary history that were advanced by the New Critics of the 1940s and 1950s. Moreover, Lounsbury applied linguistic study to serviceable intellectual ends in pursuing instruction in the history of the English language "so far only as it contributes to the comprehension of the writer's meaning, and of the changes that have gradually taken place in the history of our speech." And unlike the rhetoricians at Harvard and elsewhere who focused narrowly upon the technical means of gaining facility in expression by separating thought from expression and consciously striving to produce a contentless rhetoric, Lounsbury drew composition topics from the literature under study. He encouraged his students to choose their own topics whenever possible, and he established the practice of meeting his students in private conference for further discussion once he had read and returned their essays.

Lounsbury's creation of a program that integrated the study of language, literature, and composition was from the start a success. Moreover, since he taught students preparing for careers in business, engineering, chemistry, and medicine, his English program was a vital part of the Scientific School's notable early effort to design undergraduate curricula that integrated the sciences and the humanities. Van Wyck Brooks has observed that Lounsbury exemplified a "noble Yankee humanism," and that humanism is evident in the course of scientific and literary studies that he helped importantly to shape as an alternative both to the genteel, functionless classicism still defended by Yale's president Noah Porter in the 1880s and the aggressive philistinism loudly advocated by Prof. William Graham Sumner. Within a year of receiving his instructorship, Lounsbury was appointed professor of English and a member of the Scientific School's governing board. For the next two decades professors from every

Photograph of Lounsbury which appeared in the March 1903 Critic *(photograph by Cox)*

part of the United States visited Lounsbury's classroom to witness his methods of teaching English. Lounsbury's influence was certainly felt in Yale College, despite the fact that the college's faculty and students generally regarded utilitarian "Sheff" with condescension. Henry A. Beers had been appointed English tutor at the college only a year after Lounsbury's arrival, and Cross noted that "Beers learned from Lounsbury." This influence proved to be most significant in that Beers became the teacher of Cross, Charlton Lewis, William Lyon Phelps, John Berdan, Henry Seidel Canby, Chauncey Brewster Tinker, and others whose distinction as teachers and literary historians brought increasing recognition of Yale's English department after the turn of the century. If Lounsbury is not as well known as he deserves for his role in the establishment of English as a major academic discipline it may be because the deep social chasm then existing between technical

and classical colleges had an isolating effect upon his reputation. And it is also the case that Lounsbury, an indefatigable researcher and writer, was little interested in assuming a position of professional leadership. Unlike his Yale colleague Albert S. Cook, he did not become active in the newly formed Modern Language Association. To the extent that he is remembered, then, it is chiefly for his widely adopted textbook on the English language, his landmark critical biography of Cooper, and his foundation studies of Chaucer and Shakespeare.

To a degree unmatched by any of his contemporaries Lounsbury produced definitive scholarship both in English linguistics and literary history. And just as his English curriculum-making was the most advanced of its time in the United States, his revisionist positions as a linguist and literary historian frequently broke precedents. When Lounsbury published his *History of the En-*

glish Language in 1879, orthodox philologists still regarded modern languages as "fallen" from the perfection of the classical languages, and they took the departures of American English from British English to be vulgar errors. They equated linguistic change with the corruption of good manners and, accordingly, understood the grammarian's function to be corrective. But far from embracing this neoclassical view of language with its moralistic defense of the "rules," Lounsbury boldly allied himself with such naturalistically oriented scientific linguists as his Sheffield colleague William Dwight Whitney in regarding languages as organic—and, hence, constantly changing—cultural phenomena to be studied descriptively rather than prescriptively.

In *Language and the Study of Language* (1867) and *The Life and Growth of Language* (1875), books originating as lectures to the students at the Scientific School, Whitney established himself as a genuine forerunner of modern linguistic science by his assertion that "all living language is in a condition of constant growth and change" and by his recognition that such an assertion transformed linguistics from a subject of theological and philosophical speculation into a natural or physical science. An enemy of mystification, of imprecise and erroneous ideas, Whitney was a trenchant and systematic critic who cleared the ground for the revolution in linguistic scholarship that lay just ahead in the new century. He had been a member of the Sheffield faculty for a decade before Lounsbury's appointment; and, although only by that much his senior, there is evidence that Lounsbury revered him. Whitney's name does not appear in *History of the English Language,* but any reader of Whitney will detect his presence there when Lounsbury says that "a scientific treatise has no business to set as a standard of authority the preference of particular persons" and that "the language can be safely trusted to take care of itself." From the outset of their collaboration of nearly twenty-five years in the modern language program of the Scientific School, Lounsbury's conception of language was deeply informed by Whitney's. Perceiving the intellectual and the practical value of Whitney's new perspective, Lounsbury did not hesitate, as the book evolved out of the requirements of his freshman English class, to base his *History of the English Language* upon what was plainly the most advanced general linguistics available during the 1870s.

The result was a textbook, many times republished, that became the standard introduction to the history of the English language in colleges throughout the nation for more than thirty years. Indeed, in the 1957 edition of Albert C. Baugh's *A History of the English Language* (1935), the author noted that, more than sixty years after the publication of its revised and enlarged edition of 1894, Lounsbury's *History of the English Language* remained one of "the better known histories of English." Given Lounsbury's conviction that linguistic training should be preparatory to literary study, his is unique among histories of the English language in its discussion of Old English poetry and prose, the rise of English medieval literature, and early Scottish literature.

Having taken language to be an entirely human institution, a living organism whose changing forms and functions are open to rational investigation, Lounsbury brought exactly the same assumptions to bear upon the study of literature. What joins Lounsbury the literary historian to Lounsbury the linguist is his predisposition to challenge conventional views. Like Whitney he had only contempt for the kind of quasi-religious scholarship that mystified the object of its study; and he had little respect for mere antiquarianism. Instead, his painstaking, exhaustive researches were characteristically directed toward the exposure of error and the fashioning of more credible explanations that rested securely upon careful examination of all the available facts. He typically worked against the grain in a revisionist spirit that bespoke the skeptical manner of a scientist; and he was at his best in the settling of disputed points. In fact, Canby observes, Lounsbury's "specialty was to expose the folly of scholars and critics of the past."

Personal accounts of Lounsbury mention his boldness, courage, and belligerence. Cross speaks of the "pugnacious" Lounsbury who "enjoyed verbal sparring." But Cross also recalls that when he and William Lyon Phelps were prevented from teaching novels "too outspoken on the facts of sex," it was Lounsbury alone who intervened with the Yale administration and gained the necessary permission. Lounsbury came honestly enough by his hatred of ignorance and parochialism, for his father had written polemics against slavery and Lounsbury's own courage had been tested in battle. Canby surmises plausibly that Lounsbury's wartime experiences had something to do with "his grudge against human stupidity." But his combative stance was also the consequence of a fervently rationalistic outlook that was doubtless reinforced by his long association with the Scientific School: what was not supported by the facts, what was untrue or misleading, he would oppose with his full force. Lounsbury was the kind of historical critic whose inferences derive from long and intimate acquaintance with texts and their settings. He was a fairminded but slashing critic of fanciful interpretations and uncorroborated opinions, however venerable and widely accepted they might be.

Published in 1882, Lounsbury's critical biography of James Fenimore Cooper was one of the first volumes in Charles Dudley Warner's American Men of Letters series. And that series, roughly coinciding with the publication in 1878 of Moses Coit Tyler's *History of American Literature, 1607-1765,* provided a major impetus to the scholarly study of American literature at a time when the mood of American literary scholarship was heavily Anglophile. From the vantage point of Lounsbury's academic contemporaries Cooper simply was not as appropriate a choice for scholarly investigation as the English popular ballad was; and a scholar less independent than Lounsbury would hardly have selected him as the subject of his first venture into the writing of literary history. Moreover, Lounsbury's task was further complicated by the unwillingness of Cooper's family to lend any assistance to his biographer. And the bitter controversies that had dogged Cooper's life at home and abroad made it certain that a balanced portrayal would be hard to achieve. Finally, Lounsbury himself had deep reservations about Cooper the man and the novelist. But he understood Cooper's importance as the first American writer to win fame both on the Continent and in Great Britain, and he recognized that the numerous disputes to which Cooper's life and art gave rise had produced seriously distorted accounts of both. Lounsbury's biography, coolly separating facts from legends and distinguishing the imaginative power that invented Leatherstocking from Cooper's deficiencies of style and narrative technique, was so scrupulously researched and precisely set forth that a century after its publication it has been supplemented but not superseded. He patiently explicated Cooper's grievances, supplied justifications for his behavior when the facts warranted them, and followed the course of his social thought without extenuating his mercurial shifts of position and his occasional bigotry. In 1949 James Grossman, the author of the Cooper volume in the new American Men of Letters series, referred to Lounsbury's work as "remarkably accurate in view of the fact that the biographer was not given access to the family papers." And Robert E. Spiller, the doyen of Cooper studies, in 1954 described Lounsbury's "classic" biography as the one to which we "still owe most of our fundamental concepts of the author of *The Last of the Mohicans.*"

Although the distance from the Cooper biography to the magisterial three-volume *Studies in Chaucer* published a decade later must appear great, these books are closer in spirit and method than may be supposed. Here again, as in his later books, Lounsbury emphasizes the reception of the author and his works in order to separate fact from legend. Here again, he is the scientific historian fiercely resolved to sort out truth from error by filtering all the biographical and textual records through the fine mesh of his extensive learning and skeptical intelligence. To his credit as a literary historian Lounsbury never views the artist and his works as mere functions of their environment. He does not acknowledge any power of absolute determination in the social conditions from which art arises, as so many other literary historians did and still do. However, while his literary studies do, indeed, take into account the work of art as well as its historical matrix, it cannot be said that Lounsbury escaped the prevailing tendency of literary historians to neglect analysis of the literary texts themselves.

Chaucer scholarship surged forward in England and Germany after the middle of the nineteenth century. And the major contributions of F. J. Child notwithstanding (Lounsbury's book is dedicated to him), *Studies in Chaucer* was welcomed by Brander Matthews as "the most important contribution yet made by an American scholar to the great unwritten history of English literature." In 1908 Eleanor P. Hammond, in her synoptic manual of Chaucer scholarship, judged Lounsbury's work to have "very great merits, and a few minor faults." She pronounced his work, especially the first two chapters ("The Life of Chaucer" and "The Chaucer Legend"), "an admirable survey of the progress from romance to fact in the biography of Chaucer." For example, it was Lounsbury who first demonstrated that John Leland's life of Chaucer–a principal source for Thomas Speght and other later biographers–was virtually worthless. He carefully reviews, and dismisses as lacking evidence, the most widespread and lasting of the traditions associated with Speght's life of Chaucer, the legend that his house was situated in Woodstock. And of William

Godwin's 1803 biography, he writes that Godwin was "always ready to tell what he did not know, to describe what he had not seen, and to explain what he did not understand." Lounsbury was remorseless in his efforts to purge the literary historian of his "besetting sin, the stating as true what he was anxious should be true." This dedication to setting the record straight is richly evident in all eight "chapters" of his *Studies in Chaucer,* each of which is more properly describable as a monograph. The combined length of the first two chapters is 224 pages, and each of the still exceedingly useful chapters on Chaucer's learning and his literary reputation is more than 250 pages. Lounsbury's extensive discussion of the *Romance of the Rose* is a particularly good instance of his boldness and independence, for he stood against George Lyman Kittredge and the rest of modern Chaucer scholarship in his assertion that Chaucer alone translated the *Roman de la Rose.* And there the matter rests, since F. N. Robinson, in his edition of Chaucer's works, has concluded that "if there is no definite evidence in favor of Chaucer's authorship, there is also no conclusive reason for rejecting it." Lounsbury's Chaucer is an intensely human, even racy, natural figure who more than any other English writer clung to "the language of common life." Indeed, Lounsbury may have gone too far in representing Chaucer as, like himself, an agnostic and irreverent skeptic.

Like *Studies in Chaucer* Lounsbury's next work was a massive project—issued in three volumes between 1901 and 1906—which he called the "Shakespearean Wars" series. This general title refers to the many controversies stimulated by Shakespeare's celebrity, and Lounsbury proposed to write a systematic history—from Shakespeare's own times to the end of the eighteenth century—of the disputes over, first, the nature of his genius as a dramatist and poet and, second, the establishment of the purest texts of his plays and poems. Although it was the dispute over Shakespeare's texts that initially interested Lounsbury, he perceived that the two controversies were "inextricably bound together" since the view taken of Shakespeare as a dramatist or poet would almost certainly affect the emendations made in his texts. Accordingly, the first volume of the "Shakespearean Wars" is *Shakespeare as a Dramatic Artist* (1901), where the central issue is the conflict that "raged with violence for fully three centuries" between defenders of the French and English neoclassical drama on the

one hand, and the proponents of what would later be called romantic drama on the other. In this volume and its successor, *Shakespeare and Voltaire* (1902), Lounsbury argued that it was upon Shakespeare, the "chief representative" of the romantic drama, that the brunt of the rules-oriented neoclassical attack fell. And it was Shakespeare's immense popularity that forestalled the complete triumph of neoclassical drama during the Restoration and eighteenth century and contributed importantly to its defeat by the end of that century. These two volumes move far beyond Shakespearean biography into a resonantly comparative brand of literary history that traces the powerful renewal of the classical tradition and the parallel effort of writers to moderate or escape its influence. Lounsbury demonstrates the formative role of Shakespeare's presumed indifference to the "rules" in the evolution of that conflict, and he points out that "it was under the banner of Shakespeare that Victor Hugo and his allies fought and won the battle of *Hernani,* and freed the French stage from the trammels which for centuries had cramped the freedom of its movements."

In his portrayal of the opprobrium with which classical critics responded to violations of the unities, the mixing of comic with tragic scenes, and the direct presentation of violence on stage, Lounsbury was as sharply disapproving of their authoritarian prescriptiveness as he had earlier been in his criticism of neoclassical philologists. He was contemptuous of rules vague in their origins, dubious in their authority, and questionable in their relevance; and he made no secret of his displeasure with such critics as Thomas Rymer and Voltaire. Of Rymer he says, "His methods of criticism were very much of the nature of those with which purists have made us all familiar in judging of the correctness of image." Whether the "dogmatically certain rules" that Rymer laid down "were right or wrong was a detail which did not engage his attention." As writers conformed or did not conform to these rules: "they were adjudged innocent or guilty."

The Text of Shakespeare (1906), the third volume of the "Shakespearean Wars," displays Lounsbury's investigative scholarship at its best. Recognizing that the history of Shakespeare's texts was largely unknown and much complicated by the fact that Shakespeare's eighteenth-century editors were often themselves authors mired in bitter controversy, Lounsbury undertook—by tireless reading of the primary sources—to search out and reconstruct that history from Shakespeare's times to the beginning of the nineteenth century when Shakespeare's texts were increasingly entrusted only to professional scholars. In fact, his account extends just to the editions of Alexander Pope and Lewis Theobald, whose conflict is the principal subject of Lounsbury's study. In his thorough examination of this dispute he became the first scholar to understand fully the meaning of the 1729 *Dunciad* as a part of the Shakespeare controversy. And he discovered how ill founded was the reputation for dullness that Theobald derived from the 1729 *Dunciad*. The Theobald unearthed by Lounsbury proved in fact to be an intelligent and reliable scholar whose merits entitle him to be regarded as the founder of genuine textual criticism in England. This striking revision of eighteenth-century literary history was the result of Lounsbury's inveterate inclination to question and to challenge received opinion that rested only upon tradition. But from his fastidious attention to evidence it is clear that he was no less inclined to make certain that such dramatic reversals of the facts were not achieved spuriously: "though the facts revealed in these investigations turn out distinctly favorable to Theobald, they have in no case been manipulated in order to produce whatever impression they convey. So far as one can be permitted to trust his own motives, I have not been conscious of the least inclination to give an account of any circumstances which is not in accordance with the precise truth; or to draw any inferences or to make any assertions which were not supported by reasonable and even convincing proofs. This has been particularly my aim in the case of those statements which conflict with views generally held or beliefs assumed as established in current literary history."

As Lounsbury acknowledged, the space allotted to his detailed analysis of Pope's role in the Shakespeare controversy obliged him to defer to a fourth volume his account of the controversy in the later eighteenth century. However, this volume was never written because by 1906 Lounsbury's poor health and failing vision had seriously curtailed his capacity for research. He was no longer able to undertake the sustained reading progress demanded by his rigorous conception of historical scholarship. Once able to work through two nights and the intervening day without sleep, Lounsbury now found that he could work only slowly and intermittently on his new project, the life and times of Tennyson. He turned increasingly after 1906, the year of his retirement from teaching, to the public debate over the changes occurring in the English language; and published books on pronunciation, usage, and spelling that he could assemble from information he had much earlier collected and from articles he had already printed. The incomplete Tennyson study—edited by Wilbur Cross and Helen McAfee and published posthumously, in 1915—was begun as early as 1897 but very little was added to the manuscript after 1906. And the four lectures on *The Early Literary Career of Robert Browning* that he gave for the Barbour-Page Foundation at the University of Virginia and published in 1911 were also drawn from research conducted a decade or more earlier.

Despite the adverse circumstances under which they were composed these last works possess Lounsbury's characteristic virtues. His description of the rise, fall, and revival of Browning's contemporary reputation has proven to be essentially accurate, although important details have been added by later scholars. The unfinished Tennyson biography, less a life than a survey of the state of reviewing and criticism during the first half of the nineteenth century, inaugurated the study of Tennyson's contemporary reputation. In a 1968 assessment of Tennyson scholarship Lounsbury's work is judged "still worth reading for the sensitivity of its criticism and for its veracious evocation of the critical climate conditioning Tennyson's early career." And Lounsbury's contribution to the debate over English usage places him in the vanguard of modern linguistic science. Even H. L. Mencken, whose claims for the increasing independence of American from British English placed him in opposition to Lounsbury's more cautious view, praised Lounsbury's "attacks on certain familiar follies of the grammarians," his "sound knowledge of the early history of the language," and his "admirable spirit of free inquiry." Far from denying the existence of American English, Lounsbury was concerned to point out that both the champions of "Americanisms" and those taking them to be corruptions of "good" English were ignorant of the fact that most such expressions could be shown to have originated in England. In defending usage as the only appropriate and reasonable standard of acceptability as set against the prescription by arbitrary rules of a fictitious standard, Lounsbury never lost sight either of the impossibility of defining widely acceptable linguistic standards or of the social appetite for such standards and their potential utility when meaningfully articulated. Hence, as one of the first American scholars to perceive the discrepancies between educated usage and the synthetic rules declared authoritative by amateur philologists, he attacked the purist argument against the split infinitive by noting precedents for it in the best English writers. But in proposing the written language in general and its use in particular by the best authors as the optimal basis of any practicable attempt to define standards of usage, Lounsbury took a position that modern linguists—who privilege spoken language and emphasize the broad social range of linguistic performance—have found too narrow. The issue is far from settled, however, in that recent discussions of the relation between orality and literacy have reopened the question of the status of written language.

In summarizing Lounsbury's distinction as a founder of English as an academic subject it can be said that he was by himself a veritable English faculty. In the newly born English department the faculty were either specialists in Germanic philology or rhetoricians or literary historians. Rarely were they, like Lounsbury, linguists, composition teachers, and historians of both English and American literature. The comprehensiveness and depth of his learning did much to make English a respectable discipline at Yale and else-where. It should also be remembered that as a linguist and literary historian he was a true pioneer, writing books of a kind that none in America had written before him. Lounsbury's prodigious learning was, moreover, conveyed to his readers in an orotund Johnsonian style justly celebrated for its wit and expressiveness. At its best his prose possesses genuine literary distinction. One of the original members of the American Academy of Arts and Sciences, Lounsbury was awarded honorary doctorates by Yale, Harvard, Princeton, Lafayette, and Aberdeen.

References:

Henry Seidel Canby, *Alma Mater* (New York: Farrar & Rinehart, 1936), pp. 11, 93-95, 213-217;

Russell H. Chittenden, *History of the Sheffield Scientific School of Yale University, 1846-1922*, volume one (New Haven: Yale University Press, 1928), pp. 156-160;

Wilbur L. Cross, *Connecticut Yankee: An Autobiography* (New Haven: Yale University Press, 1943), pp. 110-118, 130, 146-150;

Edward Finegan, *Attitudes toward English Usage* (New York: Teachers College Press, 1980), pp. 77-79;

Brander Matthews, "Thomas Raynesford Lounsbury: an American Scholar," *Century*, 55 (February 1898): 561-565.

Hamilton Wright Mabie

(13 December 1845-31 December 1916)

David J. Rife
Lycoming College

BOOKS: *Norse Stories Retold from the Eddas* (Boston: Roberts, 1882; London: Richards, 1902);

My Study Fire (New York: Dodd, Mead, 1890; London: Dent, 1893);

Under the Trees and Elsewhere (New York: Dodd, Mead, 1890; London: Dent, 1893);

Our New England (Boston: Roberts, 1890);

Short Studies in Literature (New York: Dodd, Mead, 1891);

Essays in Literary Interpretation (New York: Dodd, Mead, 1892; London: Dent, 1894);

An Undiscovered Island (New York: Dodd, Mead, 1893);

My Study Fire: Second Series (New York: Dodd, Mead, 1895);

Books and Culture (New York: Dodd, Mead, 1896; Edinburgh & London: Blackwood, 1898);

Essays on Nature and Culture (New York: Dodd, Mead, 1896; Edinburgh & London: Blackwood, 1898);

Essays on Work and Culture (New York: Dodd, Mead, 1898);

In the Forest of Arden (New York: Dodd, Mead, 1898);

The Life of the Spirit (New York: Dodd, Mead, 1899; Edinburgh & London: Blackwood, 1900);

William Shakespeare: Poet, Dramatist, and Man (New York: Macmillan, 1900; New York & London: Macmillan, 1901);

A Child of Nature (New York: Dodd, Mead, 1901);

Parables of Life (New York: Outlook, 1902; revised and enlarged edition, New York & London: Macmillan, 1904);

Works and Days (New York: Dodd, Mead, 1902);

Backgrounds of Literature (New York: Outlook, 1903; enlarged edition, New York & London: Macmillan, 1904);

In Arcady (New York: Dodd, Mead, 1903);

The Great Word (New York: Dodd, Mead, 1905);

Christmas To-Day (New York: Dodd, Mead, 1908);

The Writers of Knickerbocker New York (New York: Grolier Club, 1912);

American Ideals, Character and Life (New York: Macmillan, 1913);

Japan To-Day and To-Morrow (New York: Macmillan, 1914);

Fruits of the Spirit (New York: Dodd, Mead, 1917);

Essays in Lent (New York: Dutton, 1919).

OTHER: *The Portrait Gallery of Eminent Lawyers*, edited by Mabie (New York: Shea & Jenner, 1880);

Joseph Francois Michand, *The History of the Crusades*, edited, with an introductory essay and a supplementary chapter, by Mabie (New York: Armstrong, 1882);

The Memorial Story of America, edited by Mabie and Marshal Bright (Philadelphia & Chicago: Winston, 1893);

Fairy Tales That Every Child Should Know, edited by Mabie (New York: Doubleday, Page, 1905);

Myths That Every Child Should Know, edited by Mabie (New York: Doubleday, Page, 1905);

Legends That Every Child Should Know, edited, with an introductory essay, by Mabie (New York: Doubleday, Page, 1906);

Heroes Every Child Should Know, edited, with an introductory essay, by Mabie (New York: Doubleday, Page, 1906);

Famous Stories Every Child Should Know, edited, with an introductory essay, by Mabie (New York: Doubleday, Page, 1907);

Essays That Every Child Should Know, edited, with an introductory essay, by Mabie (New York: Doubleday, Page, 1908);

Fairy Tales From Grimm, edited, with an introductory essay, by Mabie (Philadelphia: Stern, 1909);

Folk Tales Every Child Should Know, edited, with an introductory essay, by Mabie (New York: Doubleday, Page, 1910);

The Blue Book of Fiction: A List of Novels Worth Reading Chosen From Many Literatures, edited by Mabie (Cincinnati: Globe-Wernicke, 1911).

PERIODICAL PUBLICATIONS: "A Typical Novel" [essay-review of William Dean Howells's *The Rise of Silas Lapham*], *Andover Review*, 4 (November 1885): 417-429;

"Pessimism in Literature," *Christian Union*, 32 (19 November 1885): 8;

"The Spiritual Element in Modern Literature," *Andover Review*, 6 (October 1886): 364-372;

"The Significance of Modern Criticism," *Andover Review*, 14 (June 1891): 583-598;

"A Year's Literary Production," *Forum*, 12 (February 1892): 797-806;

"The Two Eternal Types in Fiction," *Forum*, 19 (March 1895): 41-47;

"Literature as a Resource," *Chautauquan*, 22 (October 1895): 65-74;

"American Literature and American Nationality," *Forum*, 26 (January 1899): 633-640;

"The Poetry of the South," *International Monthly*, 5 (February 1902): 200-223;

"Ralph Waldo Emerson in 1903," *Harper's Monthly*, 106 (May 1903): 903-908;

"Nathaniel Hawthorne," *North American Review*, 179 (July 1904): 12-23;

"The American Woman in Literature," *Munsey's*, 36 (January 1907): 420-425;

"A Few Books of To-Day," *Outlook*, 102 (23 November 1912): 643-652.

When Hamilton Wright Mabie died, the man assigned to write his obituary for the *New York Globe* dawdled for several days before producing a single unpublishable sentence: "Hamilton Wright Mabie conducted young ladies into the suburbs of culture and left them there." As an oblique reference to a column Mabie had written for the *Ladies' Home Journal* (1902-1912), as well as to his long list of publications designed to provide spiritual uplift to the general public, this is a valid statement. But in its disregard for Mabie's vital involvement in the literary life of his period, it is fragmentary and unfair. Regrettably, this picture of Mabie as a dispenser of cultural and moralistic pap has persisted for nearly three quarters of a century, obscuring his minor but very real contribution to literary criticism. The books Mabie published on literary subjects, especially during the 1890s, offer a valuable index to the major concerns and strategies of the much maligned Genteel Tradition and provide an essential link between the idealism of Ralph Waldo Emerson's age and the harsher realism of William Dean Howells's. In this respect Mabie qualifies for a place in the cultural history of the United States by virtue of his representativeness. He also occasionally demonstrated an ability to go beyond the stringent patterns of conservative, genteel thought to display the intellectual independence of a first-rate critic. This happened so infrequently, however, that Mabie must be consigned to secondary status among critics of his generation. So apart from the historical centrality of his role as a leading cultural arbiter during one of the most volatile epochs in American letters, Mabie is chiefly interesting today for the way in which he and his colleagues effected a compromise between Emersonian idealism and the realistic tendencies of their own day, achieving what has variously been called practical or critical idealism—a posture that assumes spiritual resonance behind every action and event, no matter how seemingly anthropocentric or deterministic. In discussing Theodore Dreiser's *Sister Carrie* (1900) and *Jennie Gerhardt* (1911), for instance,

Mabie regarded exposure to the "disease of society" as a wholesome necessity ("A Few Books of To-Day," 1912). As a consequence of this philosophy, Mabie and other idealists were able to rationalize World War I as an occasion for moral enlightenment—a pathetic coda to an outmoded doctrine.

Hamilton Wright Mabie was born in Coldspring, New York, a picturesque village on the east bank of the Hudson River, the youngest child of Sarah Colwell Mabie, who descended from wealthy Scotch-English ancestry, and Levi Jeremiah Mabie, whose precursors were French political exiles (the family name had originally been Mabille). As Mabie approached school age, the family moved to Buffalo to take advantage of the business opportunities generated by the opening of the Erie Canal. Studious and alert in the classroom, Mabie once played hooky for an entire week—a minuscule blemish on an otherwise blameless life. In 1858 the Mabies moved to Brooklyn, where Levi Mabie's wholesale boot and shoe business prospered for a while, allowing Hamilton to intern under an excellent tutor. When he was sixteen, Mabie passed the college entrance examinations, but because of his relative youth he remained in Brooklyn for another year before enrolling at Williams College. He was fortunate there to come under the influence of Arthur Latham Perry (father of Bliss Perry) and of Mark Hopkins (then president of Williams College), and to make long-lasting friendships with such future men of prominence as Francis L. Stetson, G. Stanley Hall, and Sanford Dole. Mabie read omnivorously during these years and was active, as contributor and editor, with the college literary magazine, the *Williams Quarterly*. He was unquestionably grooming himself for a literary career. But because he had neither self-confidence nor parental sanction, he did what so many others were doing at the time and enrolled in law school after taking his degree.

Although Mabie completed the program at Columbia Law School, passed the bar exams in 1869, and went to work for an established firm, he disliked practicing law as much as he had hated studying it. To compensate, he read literature in his office instead of tending to his professional obligations, and he cultivated a busy social life. At one social gathering he met Jeannette Trivett, whom he married in 1876; at another he encountered the redoubtable Frances E. Willard, champion of the Women's Christian Temperance Union. Learning of Mabie's growing antagonism

toward his legal career and of his love for literature, Willard put him in touch with Edward Eggleston; through Eggleston Mabie gained an interview with Lyman Abbott, who hired him in the summer of 1879 to work for the popular, reputable weekly magazine the *Christian Union* (renamed the *Outlook* in 1893), an association that lasted until Mabie's death.

For several years Mabie must have questioned the wisdom of changing careers. He scarcely distinguished himself in his first five years with the *Christian Union*, an apprenticeship devoted to journalistic scrub work and an occasional book review. Although Mabie did edit a book, *The Portrait Gallery of Eminent Lawyers* (1880), shortly after joining the *Christian Union*, it doubtless served more to exorcise his legal demon than to insinuate him into a life of letters. Nor did his second work, *Norse Stories Retold from the Eddas* (1882), signify that its author was an embryonic litterateur of distinction. Nevertheless, over a long, productive career, Mabie seems never to have undertaken a project, gone on a vacation, or learned an interesting fact without putting it into print. To an unusual degree, the man and his work were indistinguishable.

In 1884 Mabie's fortunes improved, as he was first promoted to associate editor of the *Christian Union* and then unanimously (and surprisingly, given his modest literary accomplishments) elected to the Author's Club, whose members included such men of established reputation as Eggleston, Richard Watson Gilder, Brander Matthews, and Edmund Clarence Stedman—heady company indeed for a man who until recently had written a religious gossip column that hardly anyone read. With newly acquired prestige and confidence Mabie began to branch out in his literary activities, for the first time writing articles for journals other than the *Christian Union* and developing a critical stance while joining in the controversy over realism. In 1885 Mabie published in the respected *Andover Review* the most impressive essay of his career, a review of William Dean Howells's *The Rise of Silas Lapham*. One of the high points of the realism war, Mabie's essay ("A Typical Novel") takes Howells's novel and the new realism in general to task for falsifying reality and failing to regard man as a spiritual agent. As naturalism became increasingly prominent in American literature, however, Mabie radically restructured his views of realism and became one of Howells's most ardent supporters. Unfortunately, he was never again to exhibit the abun-

Mabie, circa 1900

dant critical acumen of the long, carefully reasoned, persuasive "A Typical Novel."

Mabie's reputation as one of America's most popular men of letters in the quarter-century before World War I began in 1890 with the publication of *My Study Fire*, a collection of previously published essays. Comprising thirty-two chapters, *My Study Fire* generally focuses on the permutations caused by the changing of the seasons on the relationship between the man of letters and his books. Mabie wishes in this work to express feeling and sentiment with respect to literary life but not to propound any definite or critical program. Filled with literary allusions, discussions of dead writers, and a seeming antipathy for the conditions and events of the external world, *My Study Fire* was an anachronism in its own day; today it often embarrasses the reader with its bookish sentimentality and cloying gentility. The same

holds true for *Under the Trees and Elsewhere* (1890), a companion piece and an outdoor version of *My Study Fire*. Whereas literary mawkishness imbues the earlier book, romantic bathos saturates *Under the Trees and Elsewhere*. It was enormously popular, as was *My Study Fire: Second Series* (1895), demonstrating once again the often inverse relationship between the intrinsic value of a work and its reception by the public.

Published in the same year as *Under the Trees and Elsewhere* and marking a welcome departure from its predecessors, *Short Studies in Literature* is Mabie's first book to deal exclusively with literary matters. Although rangy and suggestive, it is also sketchy and superficial—limitations acknowledged in the preface. After characteristically establishing a moral framework—"that there is an intelligence, an order and a purpose behind life"—Mabie, disclosing an unexpected indebtedness to Hippolyte Taine, goes on to discuss "the popular origin of the great literary forms, dramatic and epic, in which the larger movements of the race in history, and its larger movements in thought, are embodied and preserved." Though such an ambitious objective necessarily results in a befuddling variety of topics, Mabie nevertheless frequently manages to provide provocative insights; and while he is invariably optimistic–as indeed he was in everything he wrote–he is not brainlessly so. If Mabie might properly be labeled an aesthetic sentimentalist on the basis of his two earlier literary books, he emerges as a critical or practical idealist with *Short Studies in Literature*, as the following excerpt demonstrates: "To those who look deeply enough, the apparent chaos and disorder of this age are the signs of one of those building eras, which enrich and enlarge human life; its license and occasional lawlessness are the overflow of that energy which bursts forth whenever the spirit of man drinks again of the wine of new-truth and feels the thrill of a new impulse of life." Contrary to his posthumous reputation, Mabie brings similar reasonableness and moderation even to discussions of such usually inflammatory subjects as Emile Zola and other European naturalists, all of whom are worthy of study because of their earnestness "to represent the fact as they see it, ... the common purpose of all great writers of fiction." But if Mabie, here and elsewhere, echoes Taine, he also rejects that influential critic's reluctance or inability to penetrate beyond the surface–the factness–of things in order to acknowledge the sky as well as the earth, to use one of Mabie's more familiar leitmotivs.

The year after *Short Studies in Literature* Mabie published his most ambitious book to date, *Essays in Literary Interpretation*. Like the earlier volume, it is devoted exclusively to literary topics, but unlike *Short Studies in Literature*, which contains more than thirty short, generally superficial essays, *Essays in Literary Interpretation* comprises eight long articles, three of which are intellectually rigorous forays into theoretical criticism, marking a new–and more or less final–advance in Mabie's critical development. Half the chapters are synoptic, turgid, eminently forgettable considerations of individual writers (Dante Gabriel Rossetti, Robert Browning, John Keats, and Dante); the final chapter, "A Word About Humour," has nothing whatever to do with anything else in the book. It is possible that Mabie concluded *Essays in Literary Interpretation* thus in an effort to leave

the reader in a smiling mood after the preceding ponderosities.

The theoretical chapters of the work are a different matter. For instance, in the first essay, "Some Aspects of Modern Literature," Mabie seems to approve of realism when he says that it is proper that writers disclose "the unclean and loathsome as persistently as the pure and good" because "we are determined to know what is in man at all risks to our taste and our conventional standards." However, Mabie's willingness to accept the fullness of the human condition–in its darkness as well as its light does not exemplify the kind of rigorous respect for fact so characteristic of the criticism derived from either the New Critics or the humanist school of Irving Babbitt, Paul Elmer More, and Norman Foerster. If anything, this ostensibly liberal position grew from Mabie's conviction that even the darkest, most despicable of human tendencies are moving inexorably toward a higher, moral goal. Although this is faulty reasoning (what the philosopher G. E. Moore called the "naturalistic fallacy"), it nevertheless represents a broadening perspective over "A Typical Novel" and helps to clarify the particularity of Mabie's idealism. In one of the other two theoretical articles, "Personality in Literary Work," Mabie discusses the mystique of the artist, elaborates his concept of the ideal, and offers several very transparent observations about personality in literature. In the second, "The Significance of Modern Criticism," he discusses literary criticism as an original, creative endeavor, linking it at points with great imaginative literature. For Mabie, as for the age itself, belles lettres began to give way to criticism.

By the mid 1890s Mabie was an established professional man of letters who was much in demand on the lecture circuit. He was probably the most widely traveled commencement speaker of his day, and Mark Twain called him the best master of ceremonies he had ever seen. In his personal life, he had lost his father and, at great expense to his wife's health, gained two daughters. Mabie's life, like the lives of so many other Victorian Americans, was incredibly busy and impressively productive. Partly as a result of this activity, the books that Mabie published after *Essays in Literary Interpretation* neither deepened his critical method nor significantly extended his range of inquiry. In fact, most of the books Mabie published in the last two decades of his life fall within the category of spiritual and ethical self-improvement. A partial listing of the table of con-

Mabie's house in Summit, New Jersey

tents of *The Life of the Spirit* (1899) will go far to characterize that book as well as *A Child of Nature* (1901), *Works and Days* (1902), *In Arcady* (1903), *The Great Word* (1905), *Fruits of the Spirit* (1917), and *Essays in Lent* (1919): "The Religious Conception of Life," "The Consciousness of Sin," "Not Rejection, but Redemption," "In Troubled Times." Only slightly secularized sermons, the chapters of these books had for the most part appeared as unsigned editorials in the *Outlook*.

Mabie did not by any means forsake literature in these years, but the bulk of his criticism appeared in periodical publications. Three exceptions are *Books and Culture* (1896), *William Shakespeare: Poet, Dramatist, and Man* (1900), and *Backgrounds of Literature* (1903). The spirit of Matthew Arnold pervades the pages of the first of these books, in which Mabie sets out to assist his readers in achieving culture through a deeper appreciation and understanding of great works. It is a book for the enrichment of the self through the absorption of the classics, essentially the Bible and the works of Homer, Dante, Shakespeare, and Goethe. Mabie also seizes an opportunity to

set the record straight regarding idealism, acknowledging that it has "been associated in recent years with vagueness of thought, slovenly construction, and a weak sentimentalism" when in fact "The true Idealist has his feet firmly planted on reality, and his idealism discloses itself not in a disposition to dream dreams and see visions, but in the largeness of a vision which sees realities in the totality of their relations and not merely in their obvious and superficial relations." *Books and Culture* is aimed at the young–or at least the unlettered–who are interested in attaining culture; it deals only in the most general way with specific works, and though nothing Mabie says is fresh or new, with the possible exception of his discourse on idealism, it deserves credit for attempting to discover, as Howard Mumford Jones said in *The Theory of American Literature* (1948), "A working relationship among idealism, literature, and the liberal state."

Nor does Mabie's next literary text offer anything fresh or new. Stimulated by his joyous trips to England as well as by his lifelong devotion to great writers, the Shakespeare book amounts to an obligatory performance for a ranking man of letters; and as such, it qualifies as an old-fashioned, pedestrian effort in the genre of popular biography. Though it added nothing to Shakespeariana, it was, with a few exceptions by academics, received favorably by the reviewers and enthusiastically by the general public, creating a demand for several subsequent printings and updated, "corrected" editions. Largely because of this work, his delivery of the Thomas Lectures in 1900, and his appointment the following year to the Turnbull lectureship at Johns Hopkins University, the University Club of New York honored Mabie in 1901 with a ceremonial dinner at which more than a hundred worthies, including Twain, Gilder, Matthews, Howells, Nicholas Murray Butler, and Henry Van Dyke, paid their respects and delivered panegyrics to the man of the hour. Organized by Howells, the grand affair was reported in soporific detail by the *New York Times Book Review*.

In Mabie's next critical work, *Backgrounds of Literature*, his intention to illuminate "the artistic value of backgrounds" for William Wordsworth, Emerson, Washington Irving, Goethe, R. D. Blackmore, Sir Walter Scott, and Walt Whitman is often nicely though discursively realized. Although Mabie's critical method here, as in some earlier works, owes a debt of influence to Taine, the critical perceptions, several of which contain striking insights, belong to him alone. While *Backgrounds of Literature* marks Mabie's last full-scale work of criticism, he continued to work within this genre until the end of his life. The critical essays and reviews he placed in a variety of journals cluster around three broad, often interrelated subjects: individual writers, especially Howells; the realism-idealism question; and literary nationalism, which Mabie zealously promoted. But these essays are scattered beyond convenient recovery and overwhelmed by Mabie's incessant involvement in matters of education, self-improvement, and saccharine morality.

Mabie's congenital optimism was severely challenged by the death of his mother in 1905 and of his elder daughter, Lorraine, the following year; ironically, Mabie had tentatively agreed at this time to write a book on happiness—a project he soon abandoned. But that Mabie's idealism prevailed is indicated by his selection by the Carnegie Endowment for International Peace to a prestigious, unofficial ambassadorship to Japan in 1912-1913. As President Taft said, "No one could have been . . . a better embodiment of the spirit of international brotherhood." When World War I broke out a year after his return, Mabie redoubled his efforts to spread the gospel of light, increasing a pace that had been at full throttle throughout his professional life. His health, which had always been vigorous, began seriously to deteriorate during a lecture series at the University of Pennsylvania, and he died a year later on the last day of 1916 at the age of seventy-one.

Mabie's reputation began to suffer a cataclysmic reversal almost from the moment of his death. His considerable fame as a public figure had fed upon those transitory activities that hold little interest for the student of American literature in the second half of the twentieth century: farraginous journalism, platitudinous public performances, relentlessly moralistic books. Furthermore, Mabie failed to deepen his position as critical idealist after the 1890s. The spokesmen of the 1920s and 1930s seized upon these shortcomings to make of him and his genteel fellows—often including Howells—a compound symbol of everything the experience-oriented post-World War I generation was rebelling against: cultural desiccation, tender sensibility, and conventionality of every description. In the eyes of such writers as Ludwig Lewisohn, H. L. Mencken, George De Mille, and Van Wyck Brooks, Mabie came to represent an inhibitive, even a destructive force that had impeded American letters from achieving a virile maturity. They could not have been aware of Mabie's solid promotion of not only Howells but also of such writers as Elizabeth Stoddard, Frank Norris, Jack London, Harold Frederic, and Theodore Dreiser, nor of his vigorous, if infrequent, denunciations of the enervated state of American literature. In bits and pieces Mabie's critical fortunes began to improve after World War II as scholars made systematic attempts to come to grips with a period that had long resisted satisfactory definition. Now, Mabie's comments on such central questions as literary nationalism and on such figures as Arnold, Edgar Allan Poe, and Howells turn out to have been brilliant and, in a minor sense, prophetic in the way they anticipate the currently accepted wisdom of much later, more rigorously trained critics. But such favorable comments are neither concentrated nor extensive enough to resuscitate Mabie's enfeebled reputation. It is likely that he will continue to be remembered, when he is remembered at all, for his mild, idealistic criticism and his representativeness as a Victorian American man of letters.

Interviews:

John D. Barry, "A Talk with Hamilton W. Mabie," *Illustrated American*, 2 February 1895, p. 143;

James MacArthur, "Living Critics: Hamilton Wright Mabie," *Bookman*, 2 (December 1895): 298-305;

Cromwell Childe, "Authors at Home: Hamilton Wright Mabie in Summit, New Jersey," *New York Times Book Review*, 21 May 1898, p. 337.

Bibliography:

David J. Rife, "Hamilton Wright Mabie: An Annotated Bibliography of Primary and Secondary Materials," *American Literary Realism*, 9 (Autumn 1976): 315-380.

Biographies:

Edwin W. Morse, *The Life and Letters of Hamilton W. Mabie* (New York: Dodd, Mead, 1920);

David J. Rife, "Hamilton Wright Mabie: A Critical Biography," Ph.D. dissertation, Southern Illinois University, 1974.

References:

David J. Rife, "Hamilton Wright Mabie and W. D. Howells: A Literary Friendship," *American Literary Realism*, 19 (Winter 1987): 30-47;

Rife, "Hamilton Wright Mabie to R. W. Emerson: An Unpublished Letter and a Debt of Influence," *American Transcendental Quarterly*, no. 40 (Fall 1978): 323-327;

Henry Van Dyke, "Hamilton Wright Mabie," *Book Buyer*, 18 (May 1899): 279-281.

Papers:

The major collections of Hamilton Wright Mabie's correspondence are housed at the Library of Congress, Harvard University, the American Academy of Arts and Letters, the New York Public Library, Louisiana State University, Columbia University, Johns Hopkins University, Princeton University, Duke University, the Joint University Libraries (Nashville), the University of Virginia, and Yale University. Only the first three of these repositories contain more than one hundred items.

Brander Matthews
(21 February 1852-31 March 1929)

Nancy Warner Barrineau
University of Georgia

BOOKS: *Edged Tools. A Play in Four Acts* (New York: French, 1873);

Too Much Smith, Or, Heredity, A Physiological and Psychological Absurdity in One Act, as Arthur Penn, adapted from *La Postérité d'arun Bourgmestre* by Mario Uchard (New York: Werner, 1879);

The Theaters of Paris (London: Low, Marston, Searle & Rivington, 1880; New York: Scribners, 1880);

French Dramatists of the 19th Century (New York: Scribners, 1881; London: Remington/New York: Scribners, 1882; revised and enlarged, New York: Scribners, 1891; revised and enlarged again, 1901);

The Home Library, as Arthur Penn (New York: Appleton, 1883);

In Partnership; Studies in Story-telling, by Matthews and H. C. Bunner (New York: Scribners, 1884; Edinburgh: Douglas, 1885);

The Last Meeting; A Story (New York: Scribners, 1885; London: Unwin, 1885);

A Secret of the Sea (New York: Scribners, 1886; enlarged edition, London: Chatto & Windus, 1886);

Cheap Books and Good Books (New York: American Copyright League, 1888);

Check and Counter-Check, A Tale of Twenty-five Hours, by Matthews and George H. Jessop (Bristol: Arrowsmith, 1888); republished as *A Tale of Twenty-five Hours* (New York: Appleton, 1892);

Pen and Ink; Papers on Subjects of More or Less Importance (New York & London: Longmans, Green, 1888; revised and enlarged edition, New York: Scribners, 1902);

American Authors and British Pirates (New York: American Copyright League, 1889);

A Family Tree, and Other Stories (London & New York: Longmans, Green, 1889);

With My Friends; Tales Told in Partnership (New York: Longmans, Green, 1891);

Americanisms and Briticisms, with Other Essays on Other Isms (New York: Harper, 1892);

In the Vestibule Limited (New York: Harper, 1892);

Tom Paulding; The Story of a Search for Buried Treasure in the Streets of New York (New York: Century, 1892);

The Decision of the Court; A Comedy (New York: Harper, 1893);

The Story of a Story, and Other Stories (New York: Harper, 1893);

The Royal Marine; An Idyl of Narragansett Pier (New York: Harper, 1894);

Studies of the Stage (New York: Harper, 1894);

This Picture and That; A Comedy (New York: Harper, 1894);

Vignettes of Manhattan (New York: Harper, 1894; London: Harper, 1912);

Bookbindings Old and New; Notes of a Booklover, with an Account of the Grolier Club of New York (New York & London: Macmillan, 1895);

Books and Play-books; Essays on Literature and the Drama (London: Osgood, McIlvane, 1895);

His Father's Son; A Novel of New York (New York: Harper, 1895; London: Longmans, Green, 1895);

Aspects of Fiction and Other Ventures in Criticism (New York: Harper, 1896; New York & London: Harper, 1900; enlarged edition, New York: Scribners, 1902);

An Introduction to the Study of American Literature (New York & Cincinnati: American Book Co., 1896; enlarged, 1911);

Tales of Fantasy and Fact (New York: Harper, 1896);

Outlines in Local Color (New York & London: Harper, 1898);

The Action and the Word; A Novel of New York (New York & London: Harper, 1900);

A Confident Tomorrow; A Novel of New York (New York & London: Harper, 1900);

The Historical Novel, and Other Essays (New York: Scribners, 1901);

Notes on Speech-making (New York & London: Longmans, Green, 1901);

Parts of Speech; Essays on English (New York: Scribners, 1901);

Photograph by Histed

The Philosophy of the Short Story (New York & London: Longmans, Green, 1901);

Cuttyback's Thunder; Or, Frank Wylde. A Comedy in One Act, adapted from *Serment d'Horace,* by Henry Mürger (Boston: Baker, 1902);

The Development of the Drama (New York: Scribners, 1903);

Recreations of an Anthologist (New York: Dodd, Mead, 1904);

American Character (New York: Crowell, 1906);

The Spelling of Yesterday and the Spelling of Tomorrow, circular no. 4 (New York: Simplified Spelling Board, 1906);

Inquiries and Opinions (New York: Scribners, 1907);

A Gold Mine, A Play in Three Acts, by Matthews and Jessop (New York & London: French, 1908);

The Spelling of the Poets, circular no. 21 (New York: Simplified Spelling Board, 1908);

The American of the Future, and Other Essays (New York: Scribners, 1909);

Molière, His Life and His Works (New York: Scribners, 1910; London: Longmans, 1910);

A Study of the Drama (Boston & New York: Houghton Mifflin, 1910);

A Study of Versification (Boston & New York: Houghton Mifflin, 1911);

Fugitives from Justice (New York: Corlies, Macy, 1912);

Gateways to Literature, and Other Essays (New York: Scribners, 1912);

Vistas of New York (New York & London: Harper, 1912);

Shakspere As a Playwright (New York: Scribners, 1913; London: Longmans, Green, 1913);

On Acting (New York: Scribners, 1914);

A Book About the Theater (New York: Scribners, 1916);

These Many Years, Recollections of a New Yorker (New York: Scribners, 1917);

The Principles of Playmaking; and Other Discussions of the Drama (New York & London: Scribners, 1919);

The Englishing of French Words, published with *The Dialectal Words in Blunden's Poems* by Robert Bridges (Oxford: Clarendon, 1921);

Essays on English (New York: Scribners, 1921);

The Tocsin of Revolt, and Other Essays (New York & London: Scribners, 1922);

Playwrights on Playmaking, and Other Studies of the Stage (New York & London: Scribners, 1923);

The Clown: In History, Romance and Drama (Springfield, Ohio: Crowell, 1924);

Suggestions for Teachers of American Literature (New York: American Book Co., 1925);

Rip Van Winkle Goes to the Play, and Other Essays on Plays and Players (New York & London: Scribners, 1926);

Papers on Playmaking, edited, with a preface, by Henry W. Wells (New York: Hill & Wang, 1957);

Papers on Acting, edited, with a preface, by Wells (New York: Hill & Wang, 1958).

PLAY PRODUCTIONS: *Very Odd,* Indianapolis, Academy of Music, 13 October 1871;

Marjory's Lovers, London, Royal Court Theatre, 18 February 1884; New York, Madison Square Theatre, 11 January 1887;

A Gold Mine, by Matthews and George H. Jessop, Memphis, New Memphis Theatre, 1 April 1887;

This Picture and That, Denver, Lyceum Theatre, 15 April 1887;

On Probation, by Matthews and Jessop, Decatur, Illinois, 9 September 1889;

Decision of the Court, New York, Hermann's Theatre, 23 March 1893;

Frank Wylde, Denver, Lyceum Theatre, 30 December 1894;

Peter Stuyvesant, Governor of New Amsterdam, by Matthews and Bronson Howard, Providence, Rhode Island, 25 September 1899; New York, Wallack's, 2 October 1899.

OTHER: *Comedies for Amateur Acting,* edited, with a prefatory note, by Matthews (New York: Appleton, 1880);

Poems of American Patriotism, edited by Matthews (New York: Scribners, 1882; revised and enlarged, 1922);

Richard Sheridan, *Sheridan's Comedies: "The Rivals" and "The School for Scandal,"* edited, with an introduction, notes, and a biographical sketch, by Matthews (London: Osgood, 1885; New York: Crowell, 1904);

Actors and Actresses of Great Britain and the United States, from the Days of David Garrick to the Present Time, edited by Matthews and Laurence Hutton, 5 volumes: volume 1, *Garrick and*

His Contemporaries; volume 2, *The Kembles and Their Contemporaries;* volume 3, *Kean and Booth and Their Contemporaries;* volume 4, *Macready and Forrest and Their Contemporaries;* volume 5, *The Present Time* (New York: Cassell, 1886); volume 5 revised and republished as *The Life and Art of Edwin Booth and His Contemporaries* (Boston: Page, 1900);

William Dunlap, *André; A Tragedy in Five Acts,* introduction by Matthews (New York: Dunlap Society, 1887);

John Daly Burk, *Bunker Hill; or, The Death of General Warren,* introduction by Matthews (New York: Dunlap Society, 1891);

Charles Lamb, *The Dramatic Essays of Charles Lamb,* edited, with an introduction and notes, by Matthews (New York: Dodd, Mead, 1891);

Washington Irving, *Washington Irving's Tales of a Traveller,* edited, with an introduction, by Matthews (New York & London: Longmans, Green, 1895);

Great Plays (French and German) by Corneille, Molière, Racine, Lessing, Schiller, and Hugo, edited, with an introduction and notes, by Matthews (New York: Appleton, 1901);

American Familiar Verse, Vers de Société, edited, with an introduction, by Matthews (New York & London: Longmans, Green, 1904);

The Short Story; Specimens Illustrating Its Development, edited, with an introduction and notes, by Matthews (New York: American Book Co., 1907);

The Oxford Book of American Essays, edited by Matthews (New York: Oxford University Press, 1914);

The Chief European Dramatists; Twenty-one Plays from the Drama of Greece, Rome, Spain, France, Italy, Germany, Denmark, and Norway, from 500 B.C. to 1879 A.D., edited, with notes, biographies, and bibliographies, by Matthews (Boston & New York: Houghton Mifflin, 1916);

Henry Cuyler Bunner, *The Poems of H. C. Bunner,* edited by Matthews (New York: Scribners, 1917);

The Chief British Dramatists, Excluding Shakespeare; Twenty-five Plays from the Middle of the Fifteenth Century to the End of the Nineteenth, edited, with notes, bibliographies, and biographies, by Matthews and Paul Robert Lieder (Boston & New York: Houghton Mifflin, 1924).

PERIODICAL PUBLICATIONS: "Molière en Amérique," *Molièriste,* 3 (August 1881): 131-136;

"The Philosophy of the Short Story," *Lippincott's,* 36 (October 1885): 366-374;

"On Certain Recent Short Stories," *Cosmopolitan,* 11 (September 1891): 636-640;

"American Criticism To-Day," *Chap-Book,* 5 (October 1896): 474-479;

"New Trials for Old Favorites," *Forum,* 25 (August 1898): 749-760;

"Mr. Howells As a Critic," *Forum,* 32 (January 1902): 629-638;

"Criticism and Book-Reviewing," *Cosmopolitan,* 33 (May 1902): 89-95;

"Literature in the New Century," *North American Review,* 179 (October 1904): 513-525;

"An Apology for Technic," *North American Review,* 180 (June 1905): 868-879;

"The Modern Novel and the Modern Play," *North American Review,* 181 (November 1905): 699-711;

"Ibsen the Playwright," *Bookman,* 22 (February 1906): 568-575; 23 (March 1906): 18-27;

"The Story of the Short-Story from Esop to Kipling," *Munsey's,* 35 (August 1906): 539-547;

"Fenimore Cooper," *Atlantic Monthly,* 100 (September 1907): 329-341;

"Mark Twain and the Art of Writing," *Harper's,* 141 (October 1920): 635-643;

"The Modernity of Molière," *Outlook,* 131 (May 1922): 35-36, 39-40;

"Mark Twain As Speech Maker and Story Teller," *Mentor,* 12 (May 1924): 24-28.

James Brander Matthews, though almost unknown today, was one of the major critics of his generation. In December 1893, shortly before he turned forty-two, a number of the decade's most prominent literary figures–among them Charles Dudley Warner, Richard Watson Gilder, William Dean Howells, and Mark Twain–toasted his achievements at a dinner in his honor at Sherry's in New York City. Most of Twain's keynote address (called by Matthews "absolutely and without exception the funniest speech I ever heard in my life" and considered by Twain one of his own best efforts) capitalized on Matthews's rather formidable name: "BRAND-er MATH-thews! B-r-r-r-an-der Math-thews! makes you think of an imprisoned god of the Underworld muttering imprecations and maledictions." But in the end Twain says, "Let him have full credit. When he

got his name it was only good to curse with. Now it is good to conjure with."

Matthews's contemporaries acknowledged him as the prime authority in the United States on American, French, and British drama. His influential position led one critic to call him "the Father of Our Interest in Drama in this country" and a contemporary reviewer to complain that Matthews "monopolized the shelves of books about the theatre." He was also a prodigious reviewer, short-story writer, novelist, and dramatist of considerable popularity, some of whose early work appeared under the pseudonym Arthur Penn (as whom he once inscribed a book "To J. Brander Matthews, with the very best wishes of his very best friend"). With characteristic humor and humility, he once said, "I don't write much. Perhaps a hundred thousand words a year."

Matthews was also well known because of his involvement in the international copyright movement in the 1880s; the spelling reform movement (as first chairman of the Simplified Spelling Board) after the turn of the century; the Modern Language Association of America, which elected him president in 1910; and the National Institute of Arts and Letters, of which he was one of the first hundred members elected. He also helped found the American Copyright League, which pressed for the first American law governing international copyright. The law, on behalf of which he wrote a number of articles, was enacted in April 1883.

He was famous as well for his extensive book collection, mostly first editions, autographed and dedicated to him by his contemporaries. But he was best known as professor of literature at Columbia University, his alma mater, from 1891 until 1899 and then as professor of dramatic literature, the first position of its kind in the United States (created especially for him because of his practical experience as a dramatist), until he retired in 1924. Among his close friends were Twain, Howells, James Russell Lowell, Thomas Bailey Aldrich, Edwin Booth, Matthew Arnold, Thomas Hardy, Edmund Gosse, Henry Irving, Andrew Lang, Theodore Roosevelt, and Rudyard Kipling. When he died at the age of seventy-seven he was eulogized in the *New York Times* as "one of the last of the 'eminent Victorians' of American origin."

Matthews was born in New Orleans on 21 February 1852 to Virginia Brander Matthews, a southerner, and Edward Matthews, a wealthy New Englander. Because of his father's many busi-

Matthews, circa 1910

ness ventures Matthews spent his earliest years traveling through the United States and Europe. The family spent most of its summers in Europe—Paris, Basel, Naples, and Rome—and took extended tours there in 1857-1858 and 1866-1867 while his father added to his prestigious art collection. When Matthews was seven the family moved to a house on New York's Fifth Avenue, and he remained a staunch New Yorker for the next seventy years.

While he was young Matthews read widely, especially drama and criticism, starting with Arnold, whom he credited with opening his eyes "to the value of culture, to the purpose of criticism and to the duty of 'seeing the thing as it is.'" He also read Lowell and August Wilhelm Schlegel and began attending the theater in both Europe and New York, where he was known for years as a regular "first-nighter." He entered Columbia

College as a sophomore in 1868, and after graduation in 1871 he entered Columbia Law School, receiving an LL.B. degree in 1873. His education was meant to prepare him for managing the family millions, but during the panic of 1873 his father lost the bulk of his fortune in railroad speculation. Always the optimist, Matthews wrote later that this loss allowed him to pursue his real interests, writing plays and writing about them, which quickly opened up to him a host of other literary activities. In 1873 he married Ada Smith, a well-known English actress performing under the stage name Ada Harland, and they had one daughter, Edith Virginia Brander Matthews.

Several of Matthews's plays were produced successfully. The most popular was *A Gold Mine* (one of the plays that Theodore Dreiser's Sister Carrie sees in New York), which, beginning in 1887, ran for several years starring, among others, Nat C. Goodwin. Though writing plays was never his real career, in his autobiography, *These Many Years, Recollections of a New Yorker* (1917), he claimed that "the critic who has himself attempted the art is likely to be more competent, to have a keener insight into [drama's] principles and its practices, its traditions and its technic, than the critic who has never adventured himself into the studio and the stage."

Matthews's plays and criticism of the stage are governed by his appreciation of what the audience of a particular place and time demands. His goal as a critic was to show how drama of succeeding eras was different from, not necessarily superior or inferior to, what preceded it and to help the reader understand plays in their proper context. He thought that plays are written mainly to be performed, not simply read. He always claimed that "the greatest enemy of the drama is the highbrow," and he stood directly counter to academic critics who demanded that plays be first of all "literary." He saw his primary task as educating the American public about drama. As Jack E. Bender writes, "What made for success in the theatre? What was literature? How could the two be brought together? This was the search of Brander Matthews."

In the 1870s, while still a law student, Matthews began to write essays on various literary subjects which he sent "in turn to every one of the few American magazines then existing: the *Atlantic Monthly*, the *Galaxy, Harper's Monthly, Lippincott's Magazine*, and *Putnam's Monthly*." He published *Edged Tools*, his first play, in 1873, the same year he received his law degree. In May

1874 (not August 1873, as he wrote years later) "The Parody of the Period," his earliest piece of criticism and one of the first critical essays to quote a poem by George Washington Cable, appeared in *Galaxy. The Theaters of Paris,* Matthews's first critical book, appeared in 1880. Comprised mainly of essays published in periodicals in the 1870s, it reflected what he had learned during his many summers as a play watcher in Paris.

But his significant drama criticism began in 1881 with the publication of *French Dramatists of the 19th Century,* which twenty years later critic William Peterfield Trent called "the best single volume on its subject." It chronicles the history of contemporary romantic French drama, something no one else had yet attempted in French or English. The introductory chapter, "The Romantic Movement," is followed by essays on Victor Hugo ("the central individuality" of "the impatient romanticists"), Alexandre Dumas, Eugene Scribe, Emile Augier, Alexandre Dumas *fils,* Victorien Sardou, Octave Feuillet, Eugène Labiche, Henri Meilhac and Ludovic Halévy, and Emile Zola, as well as a concluding chapter on the "present tendencies" of French drama. Five editions of the book appeared before Matthews's death, the later ones adding two chapters and updating the study to the turn of the century. Based on two decades of serious playgoing in America, England, and France, the book argues that at this point French drama was "conspicuously and incomparably superior to the plays of any other country." Years later he wrote, rather proudly, that when Francisque Sarcey, one of his teachers in the art of drama, reviewed the book in *Temps,* his only complaint was that Matthews was "too Parisian" in his point of view. In 1881 Matthews also published his one essay written in French, "Molière en Amérique." In 1907, in recognition of his service to French literature, Matthews was awarded the Legion of Honor.

The 1880s was a decade of literary clubs, and Matthews was a member and often a founder of a number of them in England and the United States, including the Grolier Club, the Authors Club, the Kinsmen, the Nineteenth Century Club, the Savile Club, the Rabelais Club, and the Atheneum, to which he was nominated by Matthew Arnold. This was also his first decade of reviewing. When Walter Pollock became editor of the *Saturday Review* in 1883 Matthews became a regular contributor, first as an American visitor in England and later as a resident New York theater critic. He also began writing reviews for a score of other magazines, including the *New York Times Book Review,* where his articles appeared weekly for many years.

In 1881 and 1883 Matthews traveled to London to begin research for what he hoped would be a biography of Richard Sheridan, a dramatist who remained one of his lifelong interests. The result was *Sheridan's Comedies: "The Rivals" and "The School for Scandal,"* an edition with an introduction and notes by Matthews, published in 1885. That same year he and Laurence Hutton, a drama critic as prolific as Matthews himself was, founded the Dunlap Society. Later Matthews wrote introductions to the society's editions of William Dunlap's *André; A Tragedy in Five Acts* (1887) and John Daly Burk's *Bunker Hill; or, The Death of General Warren* (1891). In 1886 he and Hutton coedited the popular five-volume work entitled *Actors and Actresses of Great Britain and the United States, from the Days of David Garrick to the Present Time,* a collection of biographical essays about seventy-five leading actors and actresses from 1750-1886, for which Matthews also wrote several of the essays. The approach in this mammoth undertaking—the weaving together of biography, criticism, and anecdotes from contemporary periodicals, historical sources, and memoirs—was a new one at the time. The twofold aim of this work, and of Matthews's drama criticism for almost five decades, was to make the actor and the stage of his day accessible to the modern reader and to show that the drama of the United States and England belong to the same tradition.

Pen and Ink; Papers on Subjects of More or Less Importance (1888) was Matthews's next important critical venture. It includes "On the Antiquity of Jests," "The Ethics of Plagiarism," "The True Theory of the Preface," "The Philosophy of the Short Story," "A Note on the Essay," "Two Latter-Day Lyricists" (Frederick Locker and Austin Dobson), "The Songs of the Civil War," "On the French Spoken by Those Who Do Not Speak French," "The Dramatization of Novels," and "The Whole Duty of Critics." Its contents illustrate Matthews's increasing interest in poetry and fiction, subjects which would soon occupy him even more as he began to teach literature at Columbia. *Studies of the Stage* (1894) covers a variety of topics more central to his dramatic interests: "The Dramatization of Novels," "The Dramatic Outlook in America," "The Players," "Charles Lamb and the Theater," "Two French Theatrical Critics" (Francisque Sarcey and Jules Lemaître), "Shakspere, Molière and the Modern English

Comedy," "The Old Comedies," and "A Plea for Farce," all essays gathered from various periodicals.

During these years Matthews was working rather aimlessly in his father's law firm, going to court infrequently, and then only to defend his family's waning financial interests. But most of his time he spent writing articles, short stories (which he claimed were modeled after "the ingeniously invented tale of Thomas Bailey Aldrich, with an amusing twist of surprise at the end"), plays, anonymous reviews (for which he later developed an acute distaste) for magazines like the *Nation* and the *Critic*, and criticism of the theater—usually as Arthur Penn—for *New York Life*. *Books and Play-books; Essays on Literature and the Drama* (1895) is made up of previously collected essays as well as some which he had recently published in current periodicals. The latter include "The Evolution of Copyright," "On Certain Parallelisms between the Ancient and the Modern Drama," "The Whole Duty of Critics," "Two Scotsmen of Letters: Mr. Andrew Lang; Robert Louis Stevenson," "The Centenary of Fenimore Cooper," "Mark Twain's Best Story," "Of Cervantes, Zola, Kipling and Co.," and "Of Mr. Charles Dudley Warner As a Writer of Fiction."

An Introduction to the Study of American Literature (1896), one of Matthews's most popular books, sold 250,000 copies in its first twenty-five years. Its information is fundamental, aimed at high-school students, yet for the time its approach was novel. The first book to result directly from his teaching career, it applies Matthews's theories of drama to larger literary study. That is, he leaned heavily on biographical information and anecdotes, writing in a conversational style which he hoped would attract readers for those authors whose works made up the American literary canon: Benjamin Franklin, Washington Irving, James Fenimore Cooper, William Cullen Bryant, Edgar Allan Poe, Ralph Waldo Emerson, Nathaniel Hawthorne, Henry Wadsworth Longfellow, John Greenleaf Whittier, Oliver Wendell Holmes, Henry David Thoreau, James Russell Lowell, Francis Parkman, Daniel Webster, Abraham Lincoln, James Whitcomb Riley, and Mark Twain. Later he added a chapter about the beginning of the twentieth century, but like most of Matthews's criticism, the book's strength lies in its evaluation of the past, not the present.

Much of *Aspects of Fiction and Other Ventures in Criticism* (1896) is merely a republication of Mat-

Matthews in old age

thews's previously collected essays. One new essay, "American Literature" (originally a speech delivered to the National Educational Association), renews his plea for serious attention to American literature as one branch of English literature, the other to be more properly labeled British literature. In it, despite his defense of American writing, he continued to argue that the goal of literary study is "that American cosmopolitanism which is the antithesis of both provincialism and colonialism." The other significant new essay included is "Two Studies of the South," a review essay which asks the question, "Why was it that the Old South contributed so little to the literature of America?" Typically, Matthews concluded that the South's social and cultural character was the force which shaped antebellum literature.

The Historical Novel, and Other Essays (1901) is made up of pieces which were either new or collected for the first time from various periodicals. It includes several general studies—the title essay, "Romance against Romanticism" (a defense of the former and a clarification of the distinction between the two made in "Novel-Reading and Novel-Writing," a famous lecture which William Dean Howells had delivered on the lecture circuit in 1899), "The Study of Fiction," "Literature as a Profession," "The Conventions of the Drama," and "The Art and Mystery of Collaboration"—as well as essays on Alphonse Daudet, William Makepeace Thackeray, H. C. Bunner, and William Archer.

The Philosophy of the Short Story (1901), which began as an anonymous essay published in the 1880s in *Saturday Review,* collected and synthesized Matthews's theories about a genre which had only recently achieved critical status. In this essay Matthews had written, "The short story, properly and technically so called, is a work of art of a distinct kind, and the writing of short stories is a distinct department of literary art." He proposed the label "short story" to identify the genre. On the basis of this essay (perhaps, as one critic calls it, "Matthews' most important contribution to formal criticism"), which became "The Philosophy of the Short Story" (1885) and the book by the same name sixteen years later, Fred Lewis Pattee credits Matthews as the first critic to perceive that the short story was indeed a new genre and "to formulate those laws in a preliminary canon."

The Development of the Drama, which Matthews had been planning since 1873, followed in 1903. By then, firmly ensconced in his teaching career at Columbia, he was increasingly drawn to the construction of literary theory, not simply the study of individual plays and authors. This work traces the history of the drama from the Greeks and Romans to the nineteenth century and closes with a final chapter about the future of the drama. Typically for Matthews, this literary history is shaped by a recognition of "the threefold influence exerted on the form of the drama of every epoch by the demands of the actors, by the size and shape and circumstances of the theaters of that time, and by the changing prejudices of the contemporary audiences." Matthews claimed that the approach had never before been applied to drama history on this scale, and Bender called the book "the first attempt to consider the history of drama of the western world as an art of the theatre."

Inquiries and Opinions (1907) is a collection of essays about assorted literary topics, including literature in the twentieth century, Poe and the detective story, Twain, Guy de Maupassant, Henrik Ibsen, the art of the stage manager, and a de-

fense of authors "borrowing" from each other. Its scope illustrates the growing competition of fiction with drama, his first love, for Matthews's critical attention. This book prompted one reviewer, William Lyon Phelps, to call Matthews "a true cosmopolitan in scholarship" and "a quite different person from the modern Ph.D. product, 'made in Germany.'" After reading it Howells wrote to Matthews, "I agree with it so perfectly that I do not see why I did not write it, except that I could not."

In 1910 Matthews published *Molière, His Life and His Works,* the long, ambitious book which he had been planning to write since a trip to Paris in 1873. It is a critical biography devoted to Matthews's favorite playwright, and its method is the same as any other of his books on drama: it is centered on Molière the man and traces his development as a dramatist strongly tied to his era. It ends with a comparison of Molière and Shakespeare, a subject which would continue to fascinate Matthews.

A Study of the Drama, essays distilled from Matthews's pioneering drama course at Columbia, most of which had already been published in various periodicals, appeared that same year. It explores "the structural framework which the great dramatists of various epochs have given to their plays," and as a result "it discusses only incidentally the psychology, the philosophy, and the poetry" of specific plays. The following year he published *A Study of Versification,* which also resulted from a course he was teaching at Columbia. These books were essentially published versions of his class notes. In fact, Matthews later told students at the beginning of his courses, "you will do me the favor not to buy my books. . . . I have said in them what I shall say in these lectures." And, true to his promise, he would lecture directly from the books.

Gateways to Literature, and Other Essays (1912) is a typical Matthews collection of essays on various literary topics, among them the economic interpretation of literary history, as well as some of his old favorites: Anatole France, Poe, Cooper, and Bronson Howard. One reviewer lambasted the book for its distracting use of simplified spelling, the practice which prompted Rudyard Kipling to write to Matthews, "WHY do you spell after the manner of the Savage and the Insane? . . . If you want to be fonetik be fonetik al thru and dam the konsekwenzes but for pittee's sāk dont spangle yŭr bŭks with small attem's at Krim." Another reviewer praised the book as the best possible treatment in so short a space and then proceeded to sum up neatly the best and worst of Matthews's criticism: "One leaves the book with something between surprise and irritation that one who can be so shrewd and just a critic seems often contented merely to chatter."

Shakspere As a Playwright (1913) is a companion volume to Matthews's biography of Molière which uses the same methods without the benefit of as much biographical information. It seeks to remedy the fact that "the British had chosen to consider Shakspere chiefly as a poet, whereas the French had preferred to treat him rather as a psychologist and the Germans as a philosopher." Matthews, of course, examined Shakespeare (whose name he always "simplified") solely as a dramatist and related him "more intimately to the theater of his own time, to the actors of his own company, and to the contemporary spectators for whose pleasure he composed his plays."

A Book About the Theater (1916) includes nineteen mostly new essays about a wide variety of practical dramatic topics, such as the five-act structure of plays, collaboration, the dramatization of novels and novelization of plays, puppet plays, pantomimes, acrobatics, scene painting, and the history of minstrelsy. The same year Matthews edited *The Chief European Dramatists,* a collection ranging from Aeschylus's *Agamemnon* to Ibsen's *A Doll's House,* for which he also wrote the introduction and biographical and critical appendices.

The essays in *The Principles of Playmaking; and Other Discussions of the Drama* (1919) cover a wide variety of dramatic subjects, some–the simplification of scenery, writing a play, and musical drama conventions–very practical, others–like Irish drama, Shakespeare, and Matthew Arnold–more theoretical. By this point in his career Matthews's most valuable contribution lay in his extremely long association with the theater and his ability to remember minute details about what was by then drama history, so perhaps the most significant essay historically is "Memories of Edwin Booth," reminiscences of an actor whom Matthews had known on and off the stage since 1865.

Matthews's criticism, though still cogent, had by now lost its edge. In *The Tocsin of Revolt, and Other Essays* (1922) he returned to some favorite topics (Twain, Theodore Roosevelt, the definition and defense of American literature, Molière), his style becoming more tedious and sentimental, obviously belonging more to the nineteenth century than the third decade of the twentieth. Burton Rascoe called the volume's title piece, an essay about the conflict of youth and age, "the grumblings of a crusty old chap about nothing in particular, but just to be grumbling." Yet elsewhere he admitted that Matthews's "mind is crabbed but it is not confined." At seventy Matthews was the dean of American drama criticism, but increasingly he seemed to live and write out of the world of past interest and experience, partly because he preferred it, but partly because, like Jules Lemaître, he had always believed that "criticism of our contemporaries is not criticism, it is conversation." The negative result of this attitude, as Randolph Bourne, a particularly scathing reviewer of *These Many Years,* had written, was to make Matthews seem at this point in his life "the chief of the naiver specimens, a race to whom literature was a gesture of gentility and not a comprehension of life."

Playwrights on Playmaking, and Other Studies of the Stage (1923) is a collection of previously published essays on tragedy; Shakespeare; Thackeray, Twain, and James in the theater; as well as a few new pieces. Taken as a whole the collection exhibits a surprising range for a man in his seventies with failing health. The next year he and Paul Robert Lieder coedited *The Chief British Dramatists, Excluding Shakespeare,* a selection of plays introduced by a Matthews essay on the history of the English theater, beginning with medieval drama and ending with Oscar Wilde, Sir Arthur Wing Pinero, and Henry Arthur Jones. For Matthews, this is where modern drama ended, for he had little interest in the explosion taking place in the American theater after World War I. According to a contemporary he claimed that "he did not have time to read the younger men." As Bender wrote, Matthews was becoming "truly a symbol of gentility out of touch with modern thought in the theatre," increasingly obsessed, like his mentor Matthew Arnold, with "the cultural ideal and the codification of a doctrine of the theatre." And so he missed dramatists like Eugene O'Neill, as well as fiction writers of the new century such as Theodore Dreiser.

Matthews's last collection of essays, *Rip Van Winkle Goes to the Play, and Other Essays on Plays and Players* (1926), illustrates his tendency in his last years to write exclusively about drama, abandoning the many other interests which had claimed him for the past few decades. It includes "Uncle Sam, Exporter of Plays," "What is a 'Wellmade' Play?," "The Question of the Soliloquy," "On the Right of an Author to Repeat Himself," (a particularly apt defense of Matthews's own rather circular and repetitious writing career), "The Development of Scenic Devices," "Memories of Actresses," and "The Art of Acting." There are no problems with identifying the Matthews canon, for with this final volume, which appeared three years before his death, he had seen to it that nearly everything of value that he had published in magazines throughout a remarkably long and productive career, especially his many essays on drama, was collected and republished under his own supervision.

Brander Matthews is almost unknown, even to advanced students of American literature. In fact, his most enduring claim to fame is that he was one of three writers whom Twain attacked in "Fenimore Cooper's Literary Offenses" (1895). But Twain, after reading "New Trials for Old Favorites" (1898), Matthews's typically judicious and low-keyed response to the attack, acknowledged his mistake, though, unfortunately, his recantation was much more private than the attack had been. In a letter in 1898 to a friend who had mailed him Matthews's essay, Twain wrote, "I haven't any right to criticize books, and I don't do it except when I hate them." But of Matthews he wrote: "Brander knows literature, and loves it; he can talk about it and keep his temper; he can state his case so forcibly that you have to agree with him, even when you *don't* agree with him; and he can discover and praise such merits as a book has, even when they are half a dozen diamonds scattered through an acre of mud. And so he has a right to be a critic." Brander Matthews was a critic who outlived his times and most of his contemporaries. Much of what he wrote seems in retrospect quaint and outdated, but Twain's assessment still remains in large part true, and Matthews deserves critical reevaluation.

Interview:

"The Literary Spotlight, XX: Brander Matthews," *Bookman*, 57 (June 1923): 432-436.

References:

Jack E. Bender, "Brander Matthews: Critic of the Theatre," *Educational Theatre Journal*, 12 (October 1960): 169-176;

The Bookshelf of Brander Matthews (New York: Columbia University Press, 1931);

Randolph Bourne, "A Vanishing World of Gentility," *Dial*, 64 (March 1918): 235;

Nicholas Murray Butler, "Brander Matthews," in *Commemorative Tributes to Van Der Stacken and Chadwick; Woodbury and Cole; Hadley and Alderman; Matthews; Channing* (New York: American Academy of Arts and Letters, 1932);

Clayton Hamilton, "Brander," *Scribner's Magazine*, 88 (July 1929): 82-87;

H. L. Kleinfield, "The Tutelage of a Young American: Brander Matthews in Europe, 1866," *Columbia Library Columns*, 13 (February 1964): 35-42;

William Lyon Phelps, "A Cosmopolitan Critic," *Forum*, 39 (January 1908): 377;

Burton Rascoe, "Critics," *New York Tribune*, 8 October 1922, p. 8;

Rascoe, "Three American Critics," *Bookman*, 56 (October 1922): 222-224;

William Peterfield Trent, "Brander Matthews As a Dramatic Critic," *International Monthly*, 4 (August 1901): 289-293;

Trent, "Mr. Brander Matthews As a Critic," *Sewanee Review*, 3 (May 1895): 373-384;

Blanche Colton Williams, "Brander Matthews–A Reminiscence," *Ms.*, 1 (July 1929): 1, 9.

Papers:

Brander Matthews willed all his books, manuscripts, letters, and papers to Columbia University to add to the Brander Matthews Dramatic Museum, which he had established in 1911. After it was closed in 1971 these materials, along with other Matthews acquisitions made since 1929, were transferred to Columbia's Butler Library, where they are now located in the Rare Book and Manuscript Library collection.

James Herbert Morse

(8 August 1841-21 May 1923)

Michael Kreyling
Vanderbilt University

BOOK: *Summer Haven Songs* (New York & London: Putnam's, 1886).

PERIODICAL PUBLICATIONS: "Bret Harte's Prose and Poetry," *Critic*, 2 (22 April 1882): 109-110;

"The Native Element in American Fiction: Before the War," *Century*, 26 (June 1883): 288-298;

"The Native Element in American Fiction: Since the War," *Century*, 26 (July 1883): 362-375;

"Schools of Fiction," *Critic*, 8 (15 October 1887): 185-186;

"Richard Henry Dana, Sr.," *Critic*, 8 (12 November 1887): 239-240;

"John Greenleaf Whittier: 1807–December 17–1887," *Critic*, 8 (17 December 1887): 307-308;

"Every Man His Own Censor," *Critic*, 14 (16 February 1889): 78-79;

[A Tribute to Lowell at 70], *Critic*, 14 (23 February 1889): 88-89;

"Octavius Brooks Frothingham," *Critic*, 27 (7 December 1895): 379;

"Harriet Beecher Stowe," *Critic*, new series 26 (4 July 1896): 1-2;

"Francis James Child," *Critic*, new series 26 (26 September 1896): 181;

"Coventry Patmore," *Critic*, new series 26 (5 December 1896): 365-366;

"Thomas Bailey Aldrich," *Critic*, new series 28 (4 December 1897): 335-336;

"Mr. Frank R. Stockton at Convent Station, N. J.," *Critic*, new series 29 (6 April 1898): 259-261;

"The New Vocabulary," *Independent*, 65 (1 October 1908): 765-767;

"Hunting for the Wild," *Independent*, 71 (27 July 1911): 201-202;

"The Younger Choir," *Independent*, 71 (16 November 1911): 1083-1087;

"American Nature Poetry," *Independent*, 72 (20 June 1912): 1357-1361.

James Herbert Morse was born to Augustus and Lucinda Wright Morse at Hubbardston, Massachusetts, in 1841. He attended Harvard University and earned his A.B. degree in 1863 and his A.M. degree in 1866. In 1868 he became cofounder and head of the Morse and Rogers School, a private, classical institution for boys in New York City which operated until 1904. Morse married Lucy Gibbons in 1870, and the couple divided their time between residences in New York City and Cotuit, Massachusetts.

In literary taste, as in ancestry (the family founders settled in Massachusetts in 1635), Morse seems to have been the classic Puritan; his major forms of expression were the lyric and the review essay. He wrote and published hundreds of lyrics during his long career, most of which fall into the category of nature poetry. Morse, however, was known to crusade in verse–one poem, for instance, addresses the issue of international copyright legislation. Most of Morse's poems found publication as filler in the weeklies and monthlies of his day, but nearly 150 of them are collected in his only book, *Summer Haven Songs* (1886). In these poems George Parsons Lathrop, reviewing them in the *Critic*, found an affinity for Matthew Arnold and the milder passages of Arthur Hugh Clough. Morse, Lathrop decided, was not always musical–he sounded like a tuning fork rather than the artfully plucked lute– but deserved respectful attention as a poet of "thoughtful, refined and reflective verse." Thoughtfulness, refinement, reflection controlled by Arnoldian precepts of taste and judgment also identify Morse's literary criticism.

Some of Morse's earliest essays appeared in the New York weekly the *Critic*, one of several publications upholding genteel standards in the arts. Morse enjoyed a long and apparently mutually satisfying relationship with the editors and readers of the *Critic*, for his essays and poems appeared steadily from the early 1880s until the late 1890s. On later mastheads Morse is listed as "staff contributor."

The Critic

Published weekly, at 743 Broadway, New York, by

THE CRITIC COMPANY.

Entered at Second-Class Mail-Matter at the Post-Office at New York, N. Y.

NEW YORK, OCTOBER 15, 1887.

AMERICAN NEWS COMPANY *general agents. Single copies sold, and subscriptions taken, at The Critic office, No. 743 Broadway. Also, by Charles Scribner's Sons, G. P. Putnam's Sons, E. P. Dutton & Co., Brentano Bros., and the principal news-dealers in the city. Boston: Damrell & Upham (Old Corner Book-store). Philadelphia: John Wanamaker. Washington: Brentano Brothers. Chicago: Brentano Bros. New Orleans: George F. Wharton, 5 Carondelet Street. San Francisco: Strickland & Pierson. London: B. F. Stevens, 4 Trafalgar Square. Paris: Galignani's, 224 Rue de Rivoli. Rome: Office of the Nuova Antologia.*

Schools of Fiction.

IT IS quite probable that American Fiction will survive the discussion going on now for some time past between the advocates of realism and those of the older schools, just as many innocent children survive the noisy clatter of tongues about the cradle. Realism is a good-sized infant. It has been born a long time. Indeed, it has been born a good many times, first and last; and on each occasion has shown a little more vigor than on the last—the vigor depending on parentage and sustenance. We shall probably every year require more truth in fiction, because there is every year more known and usable truth at hand. But the effort at truth is a recognized feature of all growth in literary work; and the success of books and authors, one may venture to say, has always, in the long run, been proportioned to their truth to reality. The man is to be commiserated for lack of human experience who does not see the full proportions of truth—idealized, it may be, in the statement, but none the less truth to nature—in Homer's matchless picture of the quarrels in the Greek camp about Troy; in Dan Chaucer's company of Canterbury pilgrims, with their intensely human experiences; in the little family of the Vicar of Wakefield drinking their cup of wretchedness until it comes near to being a cup of the fatal hemlock. The truth is more or less dressed for company; and fashions of dress change, but unless truth were present men would not go with a thrill of pleasure into the company of Homer and Chaucer and Goldsmith.

In the criticism, by our friends the realists, on the old idols of fiction, we are often with the critics—always with them when, with Dr. Samuel Johnson, they strike at a false note. Few modern critics hold their authors to truth more than Dr. Johnson. Romance has its own way of displaying truth; but romance hardly wins attention unless it does somehow succeed in telling the truth. Walter Scott often failed, and the critics of his day were not silent; a any one may see who will take the trouble to read English magazines of the early part of the century. His success lay in his wonderful faculty of reaching deep-lying truth in human nature. His most romantic tales—those least in accord with our present methods—the tales dealing with the Crusaders—are truer to truth than they seem to the careless reader. They deal with an artificial life and distorted beliefs, and are valuable chiefly as they correctly represent that artificiality and distortion. The reality of character is everywhere visible, and charms us only as it is reality, under whatever pleasant disguise, or antique fashion of speech, it may be introduced. Hawthorne drew a picture of Puritanism in Hester Prynne and Dimmesdale, coloring it with the superstitions which made the atmosphere of the times. If he put in more of this witch-haunted atmosphere than the times warranted, or made it more an element in the formation of character than was warranted by the facts, the intelligent reader will stand by and let the realist have his whack. 'The Blithedale Romance' belongs to a new era and a new growth of superstition. The figures are set in a new atmosphere, and are to be censured only as they fail in interior correctness and conformity to their surroundings. The worm takes the hue of the leaf which is its habitual food. Balzac, in 'Van Claes' searching for the 'Absolute,' paints with great precision and power the alchemist of the Dark Ages set down in a modern laboratory. The atmosphere differs but slightly from that of the half-taught New England mechanic who shuts himself up in a back-shop to discover the principle of 'perpetual motion.' He is next door to a lunatic asylum, and the air screams with insanity. Balzac was searching after truth, in all probability, no more than was Hawthorne. The truth is that one man sees through wider spaces than another, gets more distant figures and a larger horizon. Great moral forces are at work on the inner thought of men in the mass, and the higher order of novelists see better than others the relation of those forces to individual character; and they are great only as they bear the searching eye of the expert. There are moral epidemics that remain local, others that spread over a nation. They can, in either case, be drawn falsely, or drawn correctly; and, in the long run, we are won only as we discover truthfulness in the delineation.

So the attack now making by the modern realist on old schools of fiction is justified just as far as recent acquisition of knowledge has made it possible to detect error in earlier attempts to state fact. The attack has many forms, and is often useful; but, in the judgment of many good critics, it is as often misdirected and narrow, based on an imperfect, or distorted, vision of social history. By one class of critics the best of the last half-century of novelists are charged with telling too little; by another, with describing more than was visible or tangible; by still another with being didactic; by a fourth class, with being too hopeful. The first set of critics point to a new French school of writers, and would have us round out truth by telling details which, in the judgment of society, are better not told. It is now some thousands of years since organized society began to settle for itself the boundaries between the too much and the too little, between a wise and an unwise reticence. The settlement is not always made by a majority vote; Matthew Arnold's 'remnant' has much to do with it. Nor is it unhappily a full and final settlement. Each generation has its own views and records a law for itself, and also records the protest of its recalcitrant members. To-day the protest seems more vigorous than the law. We want to go back to the Byronic verse, the Richardson frankness of fiction, the Elizabethan license of drama. Zola shall be our prophet and leader. There is a spasm for frankness. But organized society, which always favors reticence, has its own spasms of virtue, and holds together wisely only as it wisely adheres to a policy of reticence. It declares Emerson to have been in the right when he objected to having the natural decay of the physical form elucidated at the breakfast-table and in the parlor. Acquaintance with human infirmities makes neither good manners nor a good digestion, both of which are desirable ends in human life.

But the sensational and pest-house realist has less justification than the realist of the class most in vogue to-day in America. For while science is rightly engaged in measuring the duration of the electric flash, to the end of making a more commodious world, the novelist may justify himself for an equally minute investigation into the manners of the back-shop; since those, after all, like the electric spark, are cumulative as social forces. No intelligent man can rightly complain of accurate investigation into the trifles of motives and manners; but it is hardly to be expected that the light reader who reads for rest and relief should interest himself long in such an investigation. We turn the electric spark over to the electrician, the insect and his ways to the entomologist, the flecks on the human cuticle to the physician, and bid the investigators God-speed. Have we not often felt inclined to bestow a parting benediction on the minute

chronicler and the analytic novelist whose delicate and expressive workmanship we would compare only with the best of the scientific specialists in the laboratory?

It used to be very particularly charged against the American novel that it was over-didactic in moralizing too much. To-day it may justly be charged against the fashionable novel that it is over-instructive in itemizing too much; and we are inclined to believe that this form of didacticism is as wearing as the other. That it is in accord with the modern spirit of research, and must needs have its day and do its office, is not to be denied; but how long will it satisfy the higher inquisitiveness of man? The physician is surely right when he carries into the sick-room the medicine he has concocted, and not the full chemical laboratory where the parts were mixed. The student wants details, and can hardly have enough of them; but trustworthy results are all that the world in general has time to note. If the results are not correct, that is the condemnation of the manipulator. But even here a distinction is to be drawn; and this brings us to our fourth class of critics, who believe that the old form of novel was too genially hopeful. We would meet them by asserting, without much fear of general contradiction, that hopefulness, even a little in excess, is a good thing and brings a better thing. It is the condition on which depend youth and health, vigorous manhood and all successful leadership, serene old age and a cordial eulogy afterwards. In the sick-room the physician's drug is less potent than his smile. He wins the largest practice in the end who brings with his potion a cheerful countenance. It is sometimes necessary to re-break a limb in order to set it properly, and possibly that was the task of the realistic critic. But may there not be an intolerable perseverance in such preliminaries? 'Your limb is all right, it will get well,' says one surgeon, as he adjusts the splints. 'It is all wrong,' says another; 'I saw a man die the other day with such a leg.' One surgeon may be as expert as the other; but it is needless to ask any intelligent person which manipulator rescues the most limbs. We see the method of wise reticence and cheerfulness applied in every department of suffering—from the nursery to the rheumatic's torture-chamber; and who that has watched the application long will doubt the efficacy of the method? Who is there that loves a grumbling epicure? Who does not love a well-fed and hopeful undertaker? Who does not feel his own days lengthen when a friend's countenance brightens? The critic in the fourth form of the realistic school fails in this hopefulness of temperament. He sees that in human life virtue is generally joined with a base metal to toughen it; and employs his faculties in determining the weight of the base. It is his business to lay stress on the weaknesses of society, on its foibles. If he is without humor, he carries it grimly. A sense of humor is a high quality which lifts one's work into a delightful tea-table tattle. Wit is a delectable condiment, and, with subtlety of intelligence, may introduce one into cabinets. But the great multitude ask for more than wit, humor, and a subtlety of intelligence in alliance with cynicism. They want them in alliance with hopefulness; for the mass of mankind are eternally hopeful, and will walk over brimstone with a man like Thackeray, who is of a cheerful countenance.

Every long life divides itself into periods of success and periods of failure, and of these two, or a mingling of them, the novelist has his choice. Either period is competent to the realist, as it is to the romanticist. The one will be judged by his truth to detail, the other will be held to correctness in essentials, and the length and vigor of fame in each case will depend, at bottom, one imagines, on success in telling the truth attractively; for each school has it in its power to be both truthful and attractive. The pith of our criticism on the realistic critics of the fourth school then is, that they prefer the period of failure in life for their field of operations. If there is a bottomless pit, they want to find it; not in order to cross it, or to get away from it, but because it exercises a kind of fascination on them. Is there no reality in the Delectable Mountains beyond? There are misfortunes enough in life; but they have their alleviations and, at last, an end. In every family we know, the happy climax is quite as frequent as the hopeless fall. People are born and sport and love and marry and get rich, as often as they fail and toil and hate and unmarry and die. There is steadfastness and firm friendship and heroism; self-sacrifice, mixed and unmixed with selfishness. These surely, in their best estate, are worthy of contemplation. In youth we see nothing else for long. As we grow up, we value little else; and amid the ills of old age we need the sight of these beyond all else. Natural selection finds its best conditions for an eternal evolution in an atmosphere, natural to the race, of eternal hopefulness.

JAMES HERBERT MORSE.

Reviews

"The Ancient Cities of the New World."*

STUDENTS of American archæology owe to M. Désiré Charnay, for certain portions of his work, their very hearty thanks. He has visited many of the most interesting of the ruins of
Mexico
fine coll
tures w
Further,
cised st
copies w
as the o
siderabl
which r
students
for doin
The l
which h
in Frenc
in a ver
& Bros.
who is f
is the a
annoyin
more th
On page
fever is
Cruz usu
of the y
Puebla
Cruz rai
train ar
San Cos
All of t
hands of
to Irvls,
by Mexi
gating u
and the
of Mexi
the abol
that 'm
wives, a
M. Char
sweeping
church c
writes:
first aut
stake.'
celebrat
persons
forty-eig
the Inq

* The Anc
and Central
J. Gonino a

Essay by Morse

One of his earlier essays, "Bret Harte's Prose and Poetry" (22 April 1882), assesses the rise and fall of postbellum America's first literary star. Morse cautions his readers not to concentrate too much on Harte's "meteoric" rise and equally swift eclipse, for he did make a permanent contribution to American letters. True to his scholarly background, Morse points out similarities between Harte and Charles Dickens, but the ultimate aim of his essay is to argue that Harte's humor "was purely and savagely American"—American because it originated in the "grim, strong, deep" Puritan view, was rinsed in Kentucky bourbon, and finally was sun-cured on the golden slopes of California. The eye for the new detail craved by a curious and hungry East was, however, not mated with "a sustained power of imagination." Harte, Morse ultimately decides, could not carry out the plot and character obligations of the novel and therefore fell short of his aspirations as a writer.

In "Schools of Fiction" (15 October 1887) he echoes the genteel party line in a high-minded attack on realism. Realism, he argues, is no more revolutionary than truth in fiction, and Sir Walter Scott's tales—a favored target of the militant realists—are "truer to truth than they seem to the careless reader." The vogue for Zolaesque realism is, in Morse's Arnoldian view, no more than "a spasm for frankness" in literature, and "organized society"—which he happily upholds—has the resilience to manage the twitch. No one, for long, would willingly read about "the period of failure in life"; readers will call for hope, will turn away from the realists when they become frustrated in their search.

Other *Critic* essays by Morse review the lives and works of the elder New England authors. The death of Richard Henry Dana, Sr., in 1879 seems to Morse to have marked a significant change from a world in which the note of nature could be clearly heard to a new, but not so brave, world in which there was only the cacophony of "the machinery of factories, the scream of the locomotive." Furthermore, Morse laments, the new order has abolished neighborliness. There seemed to be in 1887 too many people, "known only to the tax-gatherer." The homogeneity of the old New England audience had been broken. Morse sensed the machine-in-the-garden anxiety that has become a standard interpretation of nineteenth-century American life and art.

Morse published additional essays on John Greenleaf Whittier, James Russell Lowell, Francis

James Child (one of his Harvard professors), Octavius Brooks Frothingham, Harriet Beecher Stowe, Thomas Bailey Aldrich, and others. A motif in all of these essays is the fate of the Puritan voice in the changing American chorus. The essay on Aldrich, for example, deals with the fading Boston milieu of the transcendentalist era at least as much as it focuses on Aldrich as poet. Harriet Beecher Stowe, representative of the finest New England culture, wins Morse's estimation as a major American writer. *Uncle Tom's Cabin* (1852), Morse writes, is the pinnacle of literary achievement for Stowe and for the New England culture and tradition she embodies. After this work, however, Morse notes a severe falling-off in Stowe's writing, noting that her later sketches of local life and character lack a compelling central force. Stowe was "not artist enough to be George Eliot," but before her decline she had struck her blow for New England art and morality .

Most of Morse's critical positions and precepts are advanced in a pair of long essays he contributed to the *Century* in June and July 1883. "The Native Element in American Fiction" is divided into two parts, covering the periods before and immediately following the Civil War. Taken together they provide one of the most thorough historical surveys of American fiction of the nineteenth century, in which the critic discusses themes that American literary criticism was to "rediscover" in the next century.

Morse's genteel and romantic critical bias informs "The Native Element in American Fiction." Early in the essay he observes that "the finest standard of emotion is hardly to be found actually embodied in any single person; it is a creation of the mind, an ideal, for which human life suggests the material,—a beautiful image to which we cling with all our secret forces,—not within the *actual,* nor yet wholly beyond the *possible.*" It is not difficult to predict, from this first principle, how Morse will subsequently judge American writers. But he still provides a few surprising perceptions.

Morse knew Charles Brockden Brown's novels and identified them as romances in terms similar to those used by Richard Chase in *The American Novel and Its Tradition* (1957). Brown's "constitutional melancholy" produced works too morbid and gloomy for Morse's favor, but he nevertheless credited Brown with easing the way for European literary influence upon American forms and materials.

Morse skirts Washington Irving, who had only a "coquettish" relationship to fiction, lauds James Kirke Paulding for sounding early notes of American humor, discusses the "frothy" works of little-known John Neal, and pauses for a discussion of James Fenimore Cooper, with whom "we begin to hold up our heads among the romancers of the world." Cooper had his flaws–his landscapes lacked the particularity of Irving and Paulding, and his portrayal of American social life was not up to Stowe's standard–but he provided romantic heroes of the right class and must therefore be admitted to the upper echelons of American fiction.

Catherine Sedgwick and Lydia Maria Child were "doing something to emancipate the American mind from foreign types" by writing novels with native heroes and action. They also maintained a high standard of behavior in their characters and in their authorial imaginations. In the South a trio of writers–John Pendleton Kennedy, William Gilmore Simms, and Edgar Allan Poe–"introduced the lurid element." Kennedy's *Quodlibet* (1840), *Rob of the Bowl* (1838), and *Swallow Barn* (1832) "are mostly trash"; *Horse-Shoe Robinson* (1835) is better but owes it all to Cooper. Simms descends to the depths of "cold horror" in *Mellichampe* (1836) and only barely rises in *The Partisan* (1835). For Morse, Poe is the opium-crazed misfit of the Griswold slanders, working in "that unsunned mind of his, producing shapes grotesque and horrible, in an atmosphere whose murkiness was only surpassed by its miasmatic vapors." Poe possessed a "marvelous ingenuity" but no human art.

However, Nathaniel Hawthorne rescued American writing. If the southerners had squandered their subject matter, Hawthorne increased the worth of his New England legacy a hundredfold. In Morse's appreciation Hawthorne became a tragic artist of the stature of Aeschylus. He cultivated the material of New England and saved it from the overliteral interpretations of such writers as Cotton Mather. Anticipating twentieth-century critics, Morse points out how Hawthorne's devil is not the tangible Satan of Mather but the "projection" of the characters' tortured minds. Morse's notice of light and dark motifs to underline psychological themes also anticipates twentieth-century critical studies of Hawthorne.

A curious note in the essay is the paradoxically vivid sense one gets of Herman Melville's obscurity. Morse mentions Melville in only one sentence and then only as the author of *Typee* (1846) and *Omoo* (1847), "sea-tales, in which, however, he fell short of Cooper." Melville's peers in Morse's assessment, Maria J. McIntosh, P. Hamilton Myers, and Emily Chubbuck, had already faded from the canon. Sylvester Judd and Harriet Beecher Stowe stand with Hawthorne as the significant American authors of midcentury.

Readers after the Civil War, according to Morse, succumbed to a "mania for facts," and a magazine industry sprang up to meet the demand. Bret Harte was one of the earliest suppliers of the new and exotic. Morse repeats in the second part of "The Native Element in American Fiction" most of his earlier essay on Harte, adding Ivan Turgenev to Dickens as a European writer with whom Harte warranted comparison.

Of the dozens of authors working local-color material, Morse singles out George Washington Cable as worthy of comparison with Harte. He devotes a lengthy discussion to Cable's art of fitting material to form. Even though Morse finds *The Grandissimes* (1880) a bit too unique, its failure to "cooperate with the other forces of civilization," by not portraying a more victorious resolution to the race problem in the novel and in American history, is not so flagrant to Morse that he refuses all praise to a novel so popular with readers in the three decades after its publication.

Morse reserves most of his thunder, however, for the realists Henry James and William Dean Howells and what he sees as their mistaken literary mission. "All true work every where," Morse insists, "should play into the hands of honor and morality" and thereby protect and promote the best in civilization. The new "research" style in fiction and criticism fails in this office, and Howells and James are the chief culprits in America: "Howells and James are alike in one respect. They both feel the effect of the scientific critical spirit. Both seem inclined to deny the existence of what cannot meet the five senses. They are capable of passions only in a restricted way–grown-up passions, modified by culture, or business, or the club gossip–not the romantic passion of youth, not the steady, powerful currents which to-day float the light gondolas of love, and to-morrow carry navies of ambitious hopes."

Howells had scuttled the literary convoy by failing to kindle real sympathy for his characters–in himself or in his readers. The characters of *A Modern Instance* (1882), for example, are "almost wholly creatures of his note-book." Bartley Hubbard "simply falls"; he is no villain to be reckoned with. Marcia Gaylord is likewise no exemplary heroine; she is too narrow, shallow, common. All realists fail, Morse argues, when they adopt the common for their subject matter, for no one wants to read about characters no better, and possibly worse, than oneself.

James, Morse writes, is a man "of passions refined away by the intellect." He creates too many characters who criticize other characters. They all know too much and say too much about one another, some law of good taste and manners seems to have been fractured. James, moreover, neglects the "native element" by setting his novels abroad. When he does set one at home, *The Europeans* (1878) for instance, he gets the New England social character wrong. Morse was a New Englander with two centuries of background, a man for whom Boston was the sanctuary of American civilization, and for James to point out New England small-town foibles is almost the unpardonable sin.

After the turn of the century Morse continued to contribute to the weeklies, chiefly to the *Independent*. He gradually lost his combative tone of the 1880s and 1890s; his essays assume a more nostalgic, sometimes bemused, sense of resignation. He writes on various topics—slang, the education of boys—but seems most earnestly devoted to poetry, particularly nature poetry. In "Hunting for the Wild," a 1911 essay based on a European rail trip, Morse finds fault with the various forests he had seen through his window. Domesticated groves—olives and mulberries, pollarded *allées*, commercial forests—all lack the American forest sublimity that inspired William Cullen Bryant and Cooper. As the forest vanishes so does the religious element that naturally dwelled there: "the groves were God's first temples, and yet not wholly built for the Sunday edition of the Gospel of Gain." To rekindle the divine in nature is one of Morse's touchstone concepts. That such a divine spark had glowed in the poets of his youth he accepts as fact. In his old age the spark seems to have been smothered.

The younger poets he reads and reviews seem chosen for their nature imagery, uplifting themes, traditional verse forms, though he does not champion their work. In a typical omnibus review for the *Independent* (16 November 1911), Morse reviews twenty-five poets; not even the recognizable names among the list (George Sterling, Sara Teasdale, Joyce Kilmer) are thought to be poets of innovation and lasting talent. Morse seems to prefer writers who resemble himself—"thoughtful, refined and reflective" poets of nature. In an essay of the following year, "American Nature Poetry" (20 June 1912), Morse laments the demise of the vast American nature of which Bryant wrote. Bryant, Morse reminisces at the age of seventy, was the first American singer to get "the forest-pitch." True, it was toned down with the bass of the "Puritan-Pilgrim pulpit," but it was an American voice to meet the voices of the English Lake School. "When we had large forests, unchecked rivers, untrenched mountains, the imagination reveled in long winters, in shadows that traversed the wide openings, in waters darkling under still pines." Now, Morse laments, there is none of that except in minor voices. Ralph Waldo Emerson, Whittier, and Lowell were the last great voices of American nature poetry. Walt Whitman, a fellow contributor to the *Critic* in the 1880s, wrote his best nature poetry in prose: in verse "his wooing became too indiscriminate." The affair between Henry David Thoreau and Nature was stilted: "she was demure enough, talked botany. . . . She never let him get even a platonic kiss."

After 1915 James Herbert Morse ceased to publish and passed into obscurity. He died in New York City in 1923. His criticism is easy to characterize—perhaps deceptively easy. His sole published book contains minor lyrics celebrating nature and upholding noble thoughts and sentiments expressed in forms that do not disturb tradition. His periodical criticism is consistent with his poetry. It is scholarly, proper, temperate, and traditional. He espouses the genteel position of such contemporaries as J. G. Holland, Richard Watson Gilder, and Charles Dudley Warner. His criticism is strengthened and deepened by a thorough and lucid familiarity with the history of American fiction from Charles Brockden Brown onward. His prejudice for the New England current—over the southern or frontier—is understandable and not obtrusive. His work is useful now as an example of antirealist criticism and as an early and quite thoroughly historically informed reading of American fiction, complete with blind spots and prejudices that are perhaps not fully appreciated now that the canon is set.

Frank Norris
(5 March 1870-25 October 1902)

Joseph R. McElrath, Jr.
Florida State University

See also the Norris entry in *DLB 12, American Realists and Naturalists.*

BOOKS: *Yvernelle: A Legend of Feudal France* (Philadelphia: Lippincott, 1892);

Moran of the Lady Letty: A Story of Adventure off the California Coast (New York: Doubleday & McClure, 1898); republished as *Shanghaied* (London: Richards, 1899);

McTeague: A Story of San Francisco (New York: Doubleday & McClure, 1899; London: Richards, 1899);

Blix (New York: Doubleday & McClure, 1899; London: Richards, 1900);

A Man's Woman (New York: Doubleday & McClure, 1900; London: Richards, 1900);

The Octopus: A Story of California (New York: Doubleday, Page, 1901; London: Richards, 1901);

The Pit: A Story of Chicago (New York: Doubleday, Page, 1903; London: Richards, 1903);

A Deal in Wheat and Other Stories of the New and Old West (New York: Doubleday, Page, 1903; London: Richards, 1903);

The Responsibilities of the Novelist and Other Literary Essays (New York: Doubleday, Page, 1903; London: Richards, 1903);

The Joyous Miracle (New York: Doubleday, Page, 1906; London: Harper, 1906);

The Third Circle (New York & London: John Lane, 1909);

Vandover and the Brute (Garden City: Doubleday, Page, 1914; London: Heinemann, 1914);

Collected Writings Hitherto Unpublished in Book Form, volume 10 of *Complete Edition of Frank Norris* (Garden City: Doubleday, Doran, 1928);

Frank Norris of "The Wave": Stories and Sketches from the San Francisco Weekly, 1893 to 1897, edited by Oscar Lewis (San Francisco: Westgate Press, 1931);

The Literary Criticism of Frank Norris, edited by Donald Pizer (Austin: University of Texas Press, 1964);

Frank Norris (photograph by Arnold Genthe)

A Novelist in the Making: A Collection of Student Themes and the Novels Blix *and* Vandover and the Brute, edited by James D. Hart (Cambridge: Harvard University Press, 1970).

Collection: *Complete Edition of Frank Norris*, 10 volumes (Garden City: Doubleday, Doran, 1928).

PERIODICAL PUBLICATIONS: "A Delayed Masterpiece," *Wave*, 15 (25 April 1896): 8;

"Fiction in Review," *Wave*, 15 (18 July 1896): 12;

"A Summer in Arcady," *Wave*, 15 (25 July 1896): 9;

"What Is Our Greatest Piece of Fiction[?]," *San Francisco Examiner*, 17 January 1897, p. 30;

168

"The Newest Books," *Wave*, 16 (31 July 1897): 13;

"The Frivolous Gyp," *Wave*, 16 (18 September 1897): 12;

"Happiness by Conquest," *Wave*, 16 (11 December 1897): 2;

"Holiday Literature," *Wave*, 16 (11 December 1897): 8;

"Reviews in Brief," *Wave*, 16 (25 December 1897): 12;

"A Miraculous Critic," *San Francisco Sunday Examiner Magazine*, 25 June 1899, p. 30;

"Frank Norris' Weekly Letter," *Chicago American Art and Literary Review*, 25 May 1901, p. 8; 1 June 1901, p. 5; 15 June 1901, p. 5; 29 June 1901, p. 8; 6 July 1901, p. 8; 10 August 1901, p. 8; 31 August 1901, p. 8;

"Told by Frank Norris," *Brooklyn Daily Eagle*, 18 January 1902, p. 8;

"It Was a Close Call," *Brooklyn Daily Eagle*, 25 January 1902, p. 8;

"What Frank Norris Has to Say About the Unknown Writers [*sic*] Chances," *Brooklyn Daily Eagle*, 1 March 1902, p. 10.

Frank Norris has been viewed as a significant literary critic in one major way. His principal and quite specific image for most has been that of a spokesman for the literary movement which first developed in France in the wake of Balzacian and Flaubertian realism and was then brought to 1890s America: literary naturalism, or Zolaism, as it was sometimes called. Norris is seen as its premier American apologist, offering a positive and even celebrative description of the qualities of naturalism which distinguished it from romanticism and realism. Thus, typical is C. Hugh Holman's picture of him as a touchstone figure in *A Handbook to Literature* (1980): he was the movement's "most vocal expounder as the century ended." To that cameo was added this enhancement: "Frank Norris . . . wrote naturalistic novels in conscious imitation of Zola and made a critical defense of the school, *The Responsibilities of the Novelist*, in which he saw its real enemy was Realism and not Romanticism." One does not, then, offer an explanation of the naturalistic tradition in America without making reference to Norris as both a practitioner and a theorist. At a time when naturalism was being angrily dismissed as merely "dirty" or reviled as "ultraRealism" in an unnaturally gruesome and salacious vein, he saw something else, and a good deal more, in the new tradition.

Norris was uniquely suited for the main role he has been assigned in histories of American letters, for his literary experience and temperament—his personality as a litterateur, in short—had developed in such a way by the mid 1890s as to position him for a remarkably sensitive insight into the workings of the naturalistic sensibility. As Holman suggests, on occasion Norris could sound both the strident note and the doctrinaire tone. But his enthusiastically positive outlook was dominant when writing in his idiosyncratic way about naturalism, and that was largely the result of an orientation remarkably pluralistic and tolerant of diversity. He was born in Chicago to Benjamin Franklin and Gertrude Doggett Norris in 1870, moving to the San Francisco area in 1884; and he came of age during the heyday of progressive realism when William Dean Howells and others were nearing the end of the uphill trek begun by Honoré de Balzac a generation earlier. Studying at Berkeley (1890-1894) and then Harvard (1894-1895), Norris clearly had realist sympathies by the time he finished his preparation for a career as a professional writer in 1895. This showed in the several critical pieces he wrote in 1896; and in early 1897 he even proclaimed in the *San Francisco Examiner* (17 January) that Howells's *A Modern Instance* (1882) was "among the masterpieces of fiction" because it is "relentlessly" and "remorselessly" true to American life—that is, because of its realism. It was *the* novel that "most aptly interprets the phases of American life." Although he would also chide rather than praise Howells for his kind of realism more than once, Norris was unquestionably a member of the "club" and loyal to its ideals. At the same time, though, the imaginative Victorian boy reared by a *bas bleu* mother attracted to Walter Scott, Robert Browning, Charles Dickens, and Alfred Tennyson never overcame his allegiance to the romantic—or even wanted to sever his roots in such a medium. Like Henry James, who praised Robert Louis Stevenson's *Treasure Island* (1883) in *The Art of Fiction* (1884), and Howells, who admitted breathlessness when reading Norris's first novel, the adventure tale *Moran of the Lady Letty* (1898), Norris appreciated romance when it was well executed. Victor Hugo, for example, never received anything but respectful mention from him.

Literary historians have tended to oversimplify the relationship between the realists and romantics in post-Civil War America, clarifying the real tension between the two schools by render-

Norris, circa 1885 (courtesy of the Bancroft Library, University of California, Berkeley)

sternation of some who would rather that Norris had been either realist or romantic, and thereby simplified matters, he was eclectic in taste. He could celebrate Howells for having written one kind of "Great American Novel" and in the very same essay opine that Lew Wallace had produced another in his historical romance *Ben Hur* (1880).

Norris clearly saw the difference between the two. In his 1897 *Examiner* piece on Howells and Wallace he noted that the two types of novels they had written were composed "according to such opposing theories of literary art" that they cannot be compared but only contrasted. And yet, to him, there was no paradox in appreciating each. The realistic had its place; and so did its unalike and distant relative.

As to the third category—into which his own major works fall—Norris had much to say as critic about what had been achieved and what was possible via such hybridization. He was most receptive when he encountered romantically heightened realism, or realistically informed romanticism; indeed, the works of his mature phase, *The Octopus: A Story of California* (1901) and *The Pit: A Story of Chicago* (1903), were such syntheses. By 1901 his orientation to this type of fiction was as self-conscious as it was fixed. And, when one eventually wonders where naturalism finds a place amidst realism and romanticism, he needs pause here. For it is the third category that is naturalism's frame of reference and it is therein that Norris describes it. To him, the two older and larger movements were streams feeding into what he preferred to see as the main current of modern literature, producing something as new as it was stimulating: the naturalistic.

Norris's first reflections on the subject were articulated following his 1894-1895 sojourn at Harvard, where he went after four years at Berkeley, to study French literature and to receive instruction in fictional composition under the direction of Prof. Lewis E. Gates. Initiating a two-year stint as a writer for the San Francisco weekly the *Wave*, he served as a book reviewer and essayist, as well as in many other capacities through 1897. Immediately the characteristic pattern of his thought began to assume definition. On 2 May 1896, in a review entitled "Theory and Reality," he easily employed realistic criteria for evaluation: "the novel . . . should tell a real story, of real people and real places." In light of this principle, he lauded Howells's handling of the "ultimate physical relation of man and woman" in *A Parting and A Meeting*, contrasting it with Mrs.

ing a black-versus-white polarity. In some situations, such as Norris's (and even James's and Howells's at times), the either/or opposition was not so clear-cut. In fact, when Norris pictured radical extremes, his examples were those of meretricious romanticism ("sentimentalism," he termed it in 1901) and an equally valueless kind of realism which was too literal or superficial. As reader, he saw a large middle ground between the two negative poles and, in effect, had three categories with which to classify the varieties of fine prose fiction that he found: first, praiseworthy realism like that of *A Modern Instance* which displayed "a consistency and a plausibleness that are convincing beyond any possibility of doubt" as well as "a thorough technical knowledge of the novelist's trade"; second, imaginatively invigorating romanticism characterized by its vivid, grand, dramatically significant action; and, last, an especially noteworthy type of art combining the best qualities of those two traditions. Thus, to the con-

The Imperial.

The main entrance was by the cigar stand in the vestibule. It opened directly into the bar-room paved with marble flags. To the left was the bar, the counter of which was a single slab of polished Cherry ~~redwood~~. Behind it was a large plate mirror, on one side of this was the cash register, on the other a parian marble statue of the diving girl. The glasses and and bottles were arranged in pyramids here and there. The three silent bar-tenders in clean linen coats and white aprons moved about deftly opening bottles and mixing drinks with extraordinary dexterity and occasionally turning to punch the indicator of the cash register. On the other side of the room hung a large copy of a French picture representing a Sabbath, Witches, goats and naked girls whirling through the air. Underneath it was the lunch counter where clam-fritters, the specialty of the house could be had three afternoons in the week. Near by was a racing chart, where the day's entries, pools, and weights, and mounts were set forth. By the side of the lunch-counter stood two nickel-in-the-slot machines.

One of Norris's themes written for Prof. Lewis E. Gates's composition course at Harvard in 1895 (courtesy of the Bancroft Library, University of California, Berkeley)

J. R. Jarboe's lamentably inept treatment of the same topic in *Robert Atterbury*. Next in 1896, Norris revealed as well his loyalty to and appreciation of romanticism: Emile Zola's *Rome* had appeared and he reviewed it. "Zola's *Rome*" (6 June 1896) expressed Norris's virtually unbridled enthusiasm for Zola's grand style; the novel was "crammed with tremendous and terrible pictures, hurled off, as it were, upon the canvas, by giant hands wielding enormous brushes." He laid down the book, "breathless," declaring it "almost impossible to criticize such a literary achievement." Finally, though, definition occurred. After noting Zola's power in rendering visible the "exterior aspects" of the Roman setting and the analytic skill with which he produced an unflinching exposé of the inner workings of the papacy, he qualified the point regarding Zola's realism by observing that "*Rome* is not all mere description and ecclesiastical intrigue"–not merely surface, detail, and political analysis. Rather, he observed, a "real thread of passion runs through the story. The critic who can see no romance in naturalism may reflect upon [the] story of Benedetta and Davio": thwarted love, stabbings at night, a poisoning, and the death of the heroine upon the corpse of her lover. Norris thus argued for the first time a point that was of enormous importance to him as a budding naturalist, that Zola was both realistic *and* romantic. In fact, that appeared to be of much greater significance to Norris than variant traits observed by others defining naturalism in his time and subsequently in the twentieth century. For example, other critics have much more emphatically stressed philosophical determinism as the most salient feature of naturalism. Norris did heed that. The point does appear in the review when he finds *Rome* especially "faithful to the gospel of Naturalism" in its attention to the influence of heredity in the heroine's experience. But Norris did not present that datum as critics do now when they view hereditary and environmental determinisms as the essence of naturalistic fiction. Norris, instead, was more interested in the literary qualities of Zola's work–the nature of the story-telling itself and the genre of which it was characteristic. And he was annoyed by the fact that the romantic content of Zola's fiction had been neglected by those who saw only the realistic method at work.

Consequently, it was not surprising that the stylistic and generic qualities of Zolaism, and not the deterministic ideology of naturalism, comprised the core subject of Norris's first formal essay (versus review) to appear in the *Wave*–a piece entitled "Zola as a Romantic Writer" (27 June 1896). One sees a straight line of development from the *Rome* review to the more expansive apologia for Zola presented in this central essay of the Norris canon. That Zola's naturalism has been misunderstood is the keynote: they are wrong who believe that naturalism is "a sort of inner circle of realism–a kind of diametric opposite of romanticism." Norris's corrective thesis closes the first paragraph: "Naturalism, as understood by Zola, is but a form of Romanticism after all." Once committed to the sensational strategy of overturning a status quo notion so as to put in place his definition of naturalism, Norris clearly followed the logic of his argument, qualifying his earlier (and later) expressed admiration for Howells for the sake of dramatically separating Zola from that "inner circle of realism" in which he had been wrongly placed. Zola as realist was too limited a conception for Norris to countenance; and he responded in kind by first swinging to the opposite extreme, making a wholly adversarial response to the notion of Zola-as-realist as he defined realism in strictly Howellsian terms. Thus, realism was pictured as dealing only with the commonplace in life: the ordinary, the typical, and the normative in everyday experience. Howells, who championed the "poetry" of the commonplace, was lampooned by Norris, as were the sometimes tame and trivial materials with which Howells worked. That finished and the contrast point clearly made, Norris retracted slightly and acted in a more conciliatory manner toward Howells. He was trying to be fair, but he did want to make it clear how absurd it was to put Zola in the same category with Howells. Thus, he wrote that the Howellsian novel "is interesting–which is after all the main point–but it is the commonplace tale of commonplace people made into a novel of far more than commonplace charm. Mr. Howells is not uninteresting; he is simply not romantic"; and, since he confines himself to the ordinary and "there is no romance," Howells is not at all like Zola. That Zola should be cited "as a realist, and a realist of realists, is a strange perversion." Norris then turned to *Nana* (1880), *Le Rêve* (1888), *Lourdes* (1894), *Rome* (1896), and other manifestations of Zola's "love of the extraordinary, the vast, the monstrous, and the tragic" to illustrate what it was that never appeared in a Howellsian novel.

With the contrast between Zola and writers flourishing in the realist tradition of Jane Austen

Norris, circa 1900 (courtesy of the Bancroft Library, University of California, Berkeley)

made as clearly and simply as was necessary for the *Wave* readership to understand his working terminology, Norris then took the next step, which was to qualify his extreme position on realism so as to insure that Zola and naturalism were not simply transferred from the realistic category into that of an "inner circle" of romanticism. Norris did not want that either, and thus the clarification found in the finale of the piece.

Norris repeats that naturalism is "a form of romanticism after all." But its form should not be confused with the pure romanticism that flourished in the early nineteenth century. The difference lies chiefly in Zola's "choice of Milieu." The novels of the *Rougon-Maquart* (1871-1893) series are set not among "the personnel of a feudal and Renaissance nobility," the old romantic milieu, but "among the lower—almost the lowest—classes" in mid-nineteenth-century France. "This is not romanticism" in the old sense, then. Zola's "drama of the people, working itself out in blood and ordure" in a way true to the contemporary scene, represents a modern innovation, a new development in an old tradition. Likewise, as has been explained, it "is not realism" of the commonplace

variety; it is more true to human nature because it goes beyond the restrictive bounds set by the quotidian realists. Zola transcends both categories, producing a new type of fiction: naturalism "is a school by itself, unique, sombre, powerful beyond words" as it imaginatively addresses the real without the severe limitations imposed by the Howellsian school.

Norris thus closed via negations: naturalism is neither one nor the other, but unique. And yet it *is* historically tied to aspects of both traditions. It is a "form" of romanticism: into a new school is extended particular romantic traits, such as the "love of the extraordinary." While it is not Howellsian, Norris's emphasis on choice of a "Milieu" true to the modern order does tie naturalism to another dimension of nineteenth-century realism exemplified by Balzac, whose fictional world anticipated Zola's. Having set up a dialectic between realism and romanticism, Norris pictured Zola as effecting a synthesis of the two.

Norris returned to this line of reasoning later, in 1901. But during the remainder of his *Wave* tenure he apparently felt that he had had his say on misapprehensions of Zola's place in

Norris's home in San Francisco

nineteenth-century art, and he went on to other matters, applying rather than elaborating his concept of naturalism. And, to the surprise of students of naturalism who do not include James Lane Allen in the ranks, Norris focused enthusiastically on Allen's now forgotten work entitled *Summer in Arcady: A Tale of Nature* (1896). It is a light novel like Norris's own *Blix* (1899), a romantic love idyll. But Norris found it "vitally" and "relentlessly true." *Summer in Arcady* interposed no screen between the reader and the two lovers, "that bit of human life [Allen] is studying." That Allen's frank depictions of sexual stirrings in the young hero and heroine appeared in an American book appears to have impressed Norris (for, by French standards, nothing remarkable occurs in the novel). Allen's "manner of treatment" of sexuality was what led Norris to cite "the naturalistic point of view assumed by Mr. Allen." After quoting examples of Allen's depiction of excitation and increasingly conscious sexuality in Daphne and Hillary, Norris offered his appreciative interpretation: these characters "are little better than natural, wholesome brutes, drawn to each other by the force of nature, . . . irresistibly, blindly, moved only by an unreasoned animal instinct." This is, almost verbatim, the language Norris used to describe his Trina and McTeague in

his first full-scale naturalistic novel, *McTeague: A Story of San Francisco* (1899). In 1896 Norris had found an American precedent for what he was then developing in his own manuscript which would define the essence of naturalism for a good many reviewers.

After the appearance of the *Summer in Arcady* review in July 1896, Norris continued to write short stories, articles on local events, paragraphs on topical matters, interviews, reviews, and literary essays for the *Wave*–through the beginning of 1898 when he moved to New York City to work for S. S. McClure and Doubleday and McClure, and to begin his career as a novelist in earnest. (Six novels appeared between late 1898 and early 1903, Norris dying at thirty-two of peritonitis following an appendectomy in October 1902.) But while he remained one of several literary commentators for the *Wave*, it was the practicing naturalist rather than the critic who became dominant as Norris developed his novels of degeneration, *McTeague* and *Vandover and the Brute* (1914), the latter having the Balzacian-Zolaesque subtitle "A Study of Life and Manners in an American City at the End of the Nineteenth Century" in manuscript. In fact, it was not until the publication of *The Octopus* in April 1901 that Norris held forth as a critic again, after a three-year hiatus. For the literary supplement to the *Chicago American* newspaper he produced a series of "Weekly Letters" (25 May-31 August 1901). With subjects such as how genuine originality can be extinguished in the cant-ridden literary world and why it is better to find an unintrusive narrator like Zola, as opposed to William Makepeace Thackeray, Norris's pieces ranged in quality from perceptive statements on literary technique to what Donald Pizer has identified in *The Literary Criticism of Frank Norris* (1964) as "personal gossip"—Pizer using the descriptive term Norris himself employed in a 10 September 1901 letter to Isaac F. Marcosson. On 3 August, though, Norris picked up the thread he had dropped in June 1896, addressing Chicago on the topic he had earlier explained to a San Francisco readership.

While his conclusion was virtually identical, Norris's proffered reason for writing about naturalism was new. The "Weekly Letter" pieces in the *Chicago American Art and Literary Review* were not produced by an aspiring young author of 1896; in the spring of 1901 Norris's persona was that of an author who had arrived. He was an insider to the literary establishment who had not only published five novels but had also been a manuscript reader for Doubleday in New York. What had annoyed Norris at Doubleday was the boast of would-be novelists claiming that their fictions were better because they had been based on real-life events. In the 31 August 1901 "Weekly Letter" Norris reduced the true-to-life epithet to nothing more than mere accuracy, observing that it does not necessarily make a novel better. Like Zola (see the preface to *L'Assommoir*, 1877), Norris was by 1901 fixated on Truth as the ultimate revelation of fine art, and his retort was that the true-to-life, the accurate, did not automatically insure such a revelation, even though details may be provided "with the meticulous science of the phonograph or pictured with the incontestable precision of the photograph." To be a documentary realist—or to employ the then widely lambasted methods of "ultraRealism" just described—was not enough. To pile up facts was insufficient, as Howells too had earlier observed in chapter 2 of *Criticism and Fiction* (1891). Illustrating what he meant, Norris speculated on how an accurate description of a black sheep may be correct but it would not be a true description of a sheep since it pictured an exception, a peculiar variant finally giving a false impression as to what sheep are like. Accuracy in that case would not

count for much. Indeed, some stories "can be accurate and yet lamentably—even wickedly—untrue."

In a different way, then, Norris once again began his approach to Zola by diminishing the idea that realism was innately valuable. But then he qualified his point by replacing his would-be novelist of the true-to-life manuscript with Leo Tolstoy, elevating the level of discussion and modifying the definition of realism considerably. For, to Norris's mind, Tolstoy was a realist who did provide something of the "true metal" (as he later made clear when discussing *Anna Karenina* [1875-1877] in "The National Spirit as It Relates to the 'Great American Novel,'" *Boston Evening Transcript*, 5 February 1902). Having redeemed realism as capable of revealing Truth, he next brought forward a romantic example in art, citing Victor Hugo's *Hernani* (1830). Then with both authors acknowledged as truth-tellers in place, he proceeded dialectically once again, noting the limitations of the realistic and romantic traditions which his touchstone figures represented. Tolstoy's shortcoming was that he would typically confine his fiction to "probabilities only," limiting his imagination as he remained "accurate." (Norris further described Tolstoy's imaginative limitations in "Story-Tellers Vs. Novelists," *World's Work*, 3 [March 1902], 1894-1897.) Hugo would go to the opposite extreme, "confined by nothing save the limitations of his own imagination" as he aimed for "the broad truth of the thing." The "purely" romantic Hugo, as he was described in "Zola as a Romantic Writer," demonstrates his shortcoming when he "puts into his people's mouths the words they would have spoken if only they could have given expression to his [Hugo's] thoughts." That is, the consideration of how the real-life counterparts of his characters would normally think and speak would not significantly govern Hugo's characterizations.

Thus, Norris allows that the realism of Tolstoy may transcend mere accuracy, and he admits that romanticism may imaginatively "elevate" scenes too far above the probable, as when Hugo strives "to create the impression of Truth." The question of what the ideal balance is thus emerges. "To what, then," Norris asks, "should the truth of the novel be referred—to what standard? By what touchstone may we recognize the true metal?" Realistic accuracy and the romantic thirst for the "broad truth" are both needed; but, since the two schools are so far apart, can that be found? A resounding yes is the answer to the question Norris phrases thus: "Does Truth lie 'in the

Norris (resting his foot on his dog, Monk) and fraternity brothers at the University of California, 1893 (courtesy of the Bancroft Library, University of California, Berkeley)

middle'?" He, of course, has his answer ready: "Is it not the school of Naturalism, which strives hard for accuracy and truth?" Taking "the best from each" tradition, Zola stands "in the middle," and *La Débâcle* (1892) especially exemplifies the ideal.

During the autumn of 1901, while Norris was composing *The Pit* as well as producing short stories, he next began to write essays for *World's Work*, the *Boston Evening Transcript*, the *Critic*, and an as yet unidentified newspaper syndicate. This body of work was the source from which the posthumously published collection *The Responsibilities of the Novelist and Other Literary Essays* was created in 1903. Until Donald Pizer published *The Literary Criticism of Frank Norris* in 1964, *The Responsibilities of the Novelist* was a main determinant of

Norris's image as a critic. That was unfortunate, for none of the essays on naturalism discussed thus far was included. Moreover, as Pizer has observed, much of the 1901-1902 work that was collected lacked the "dash, the excitement, and convincingness" of earlier pieces such as "Zola as a Romantic Writer." Instead, the gaseousness of pop-journalism rhetoric, a tone of moral exhortation which too easily led to pomposity, and an overuse of the authoritative "insider" point of view turn up too often. It is not surprising that reviews of *The Responsibilities of the Novelist*, a volume Norris did not himself prepare, were not enthusiastic. But that was not because Norris was a naturalist, or a Zolaist under attack. In fact, as one reads essays such as "The Great American Novel," "Why Women Should Write the Best Nov-

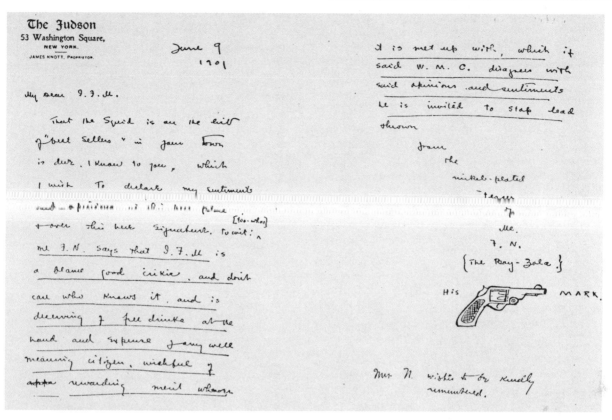

Letter from Norris that journalist Isaac F. Marcosson included in his Adventures in Interviewing, *1919*

els: And Why They Don't," "Simplicity in Art," and "The Mechanics of Fiction," he will look in vain for what C. Hugh Holman describes as a "critical defense of the school" of naturalism. It is not that *The Responsibilities of the Novelist* contradicts Norris's naturalistic point of view; but it is simply not a defense of the movement. One of the essays, "A Problem in Fiction: Truth Versus Accuracy," for example, is about the same topic presented in the 31 August 1901 "Weekly Letter" described above. In the earlier essay Norris did defend naturalism. But in this variation on the "mere accuracy" theme Norris developed his point without reference to Zola or naturalism. On the contrary, he employed Scott's *Ivanhoe* (1819) to make his point. The only essay offering anything like a "critical defense" of a school is "A Plea for Romantic Fiction," and the school was not naturalism.

A 1903 reader first encountering Norris via *The Responsibilities of the Novelist* would have had no reason to think of Norris as "the most vocal expounder" of naturalism at the turn of the century; and a good deal of confusion appears to have resulted as students of Norris the naturalistic novelist have turned to this collection for his

theory. Those searching for Norris's critical standpoint are limited to two sentences in "A Plea for Romantic Fiction": "Romance may even treat of the sordid, the unlovely—as for instance, the novels of M. Zola. (Zola has been dubbed a Realist, but he is, on the contrary, the very head of the Romanticists.)" But that is merely an illustration of the variety to be found within romanticism, together with an aside on Zola which is potentially misleading for those not familiar with Norris's earlier development of the idea. Romanticism, not the previously defined "form of romanticism" that is naturalism, is the topic here.

Norris begins this essay by differentiating between three types of fiction: romance at its dynamic best; what is often termed romanticism but is really "sentimentalism" ("cloaks and daggers or moonlight and golden hair" pictured in the Middle Ages); and that "harsh, loveless, colorless, blunt tool called Realism." He celebrates romance which has been given a bad name but *can* address the dynamic realities of the present once removed from antiquarian settings and their trappings. He celebrates the romantic sensibility as capable of going farther and deeper than others into human experience. It has "the wide world for range." It dives deep into the "unplumbed depths of the human heart, and the mystery of sex, and the problems of life, and the black, unsearched penetralia of the soul of man." Norris could have gone on to focus on how naturalism grew out of such a sensibility, but he did not this time. Rather, he chose to wax moralistically, to speak as the earnest Victorian American who articulated his fervid idealism in the first two essays presented in *The Responsibilities of the Novelist*, the title piece and "The True Reward of the Novelist." Romance is not the same as fantastic "sentimentalism," and it is not inferior to realism; once properly understood, it is clearly a type of art which has a "mission of teaching"; romance should "by right divine" be recognized as "a teacher sent from God," and not treated as a pariah. Thus the essay is a somewhat emotional bit of special pleading and equally a polemic directed against a literary establishment which had developed the habit of condescending toward a tradition Norris still admired. "A Plea for Romantic Fiction" is designed to restore romanticism at its best to a condition of respectability in the eyes of serious, moral, truth-seeking American readers. Again, it is not an essay on naturalism, just as *The Responsibilities of the Novelist* is not a book on naturalism.

To see Norris as naturalistic critic, and to see also why one would describe the Hawthornesque defender of the romantic pictured above as a naturalist as well, it is essential to turn from *The Responsibilities of the Novelist* to view the entirety of his canon of essays and reviews. For the fullest possible picture of the critical ideas he developed during his brief career, however, one should also turn to his short fiction featuring literary shoptalk (such as "His Sister" in *Frank Norris of "The Wave"* [1931] and "Dying Fires" in *The Third Circle* [1909]), the interviews with performing artists he conducted for the *Wave*, and especially his novels. *Vandover and the Brute*, *McTeague*, *The Octopus*, and *The Pit* are all experiments in naturalism complementing his critical statements. Moreover, they also reveal other critical preoccupations which Norris harbored, such as his hostility toward academic art with its encouragement of imitation and discouragement of "working from nature"; his dislike of preciosity of any kind and loathing of the decadent mode; and his admiration for realism, like Rudyard Kipling's, which does not stand in high relief in his essays.

It is his definition of naturalism, however, that has earned Norris a place in the history of American literary criticism. It is a peculiar one since it is broad enough to include almost anything so long as it does not restrict the pursuit of truth, limit one to the commonplace, or allow one to drift off into the realm of the wholly imaginary (the "purely" romantic). His broad synthetic definition differs from others which have been provided since and which are now dominant. It was not so narrow as that presented by Vernon L. Parrington in *Main Currents in American Thought* (1930), not so reductively philosophical as the majority of those presently enjoying popularity, and it did *not* posit romanticism or realism as "the enemy." His naturalism was a positive movement, turning away from what was meretricious in previous developments in the western literary tradition, combining and advancing what was the best that had been developed through the end of the nineteenth century. It was that forward movement for which Norris was the "most vocal expounder as the century ended."

Letters:

Frank Norris: Collected Letters, edited by Jesse S. Crisler (San Francisco: Book Club of California, 1986).

Bibliographies:

Kenneth A. Lohf and Eugene P. Sheehy, *Frank Norris: A Bibliography* (Los Gatos, Cal.: Talisman Press, 1959);

Joseph Katz, "The Shorter Publications of Frank Norris: A Checklist," *Proof*, 3 (1973): 155-220;

Jesse S. Crisler and Joseph R. McElrath, Jr., *Frank Norris: A Reference Guide* (Boston: G. K. Hall, 1975);

William B. Dillingham, "Frank Norris," in *Fifteen American Authors Before 1900*, revised edition, edited by Earl N. Harbert and Robert E. Rees (Madison: University of Wisconsin Press, 1984), pp. 402-438;

McElrath, *Frank Norris and "The Wave": A Bibliography* (New York: Garland, 1988).

Biography:

Franklin Walker, *Frank Norris: A Biography* (Garden City: Doubleday, Doran, 1932).

References:

Lars Ahnebrink, *The Influence of Emile Zola on Frank Norris* (Uppsala, Sweden: A. B. Lundequistska Bokhandeln, 1947);

George Becker, "Realism: An Essay in Definition," *Modern Language Quarterly*, 10 (June 1949): 184-197;

Malcolm Cowley, " 'Not Men:' A Natural History of American Naturalism," *Kenyon Review*, 9 (Winter 1947): 414-435;

Richard Allan Davison, "The Remaining Seven of Frank Norris' 'Weekly Letters,' " *American Literary Realism*, 1 (Summer 1968): 47-65;

William B. Dillingham, *Frank Norris: Instinct and Art* (Lincoln: University of Nebraska Press, 1969);

Warren French, *Frank Norris* (New York: Twayne, 1962);

Don Graham, *The Fiction of Frank Norris: The Aesthetic Context* (Columbia: University of Missouri Press, 1978);

James D. Hart, *A Novelist in the Making* (Cambridge: Harvard University Press, 1970);

Charles G. Hoffman, "Norris and the Responsibility of the Novelist," *South Atlantic Quarterly*, 54 (October 1955): 508-515;

C. Hugh Holman, *A Handbook to Literature*, fourth edition (Indianapolis: Bobbs-Merrill, 1980), pp. 113, 286;

Joseph Katz, "The Elusive Criticisms Syndicated by Frank Norris," in *Proof*, edited by Katz (Columbia: University of South Carolina Press, 1973), III: 221-251;

Joseph Kwiat, "Frank Norris: The Novelist as Social Critic and Literary Theorist," *Arizona Quarterly*, 18 (Winter 1962): 319-328;

Rodrique E. Labrie, "The Howells-Norris Relationship and the Growth of Naturalism," *Discourse*, 16 (Summer 1968): 363-370;

Robert C. Leitz III, "The *Moran* Controversy: Norris's Defense of His 'Nautical Absurdities,' " *American Literary Realism*, 15 (Spring 1982): 119-124;

Ernest Marchand, *Frank Norris: A Study* (Stanford: Stanford University Press, 1942);

John E. McCluskey, "Frank Norris' Literary Terminology: A Note on the Historical Context," *Western American Literature*, 7 (Summer 1972): 148-150;

Robert A. Morace, "Frank Norris' Letter to F. B. Millard," *Quarterly News-Letter* (Book Club of California), 51 (Fall 1976): 90-92;

Wayne Morgan, "Frank Norris: The Romantic as Naturalist," in *American Writers in Rebellion from Twain to Dreiser* (New York: Hill & Wang, 1965), pp. 104-145;

Grant Overton, Foreword to *Complete Edition of Frank Norris*, volume 7 (Garden City: Doubleday, Doran, 1928), pp. xxxiii-lll;

Vernon L. Parrington, *Main Currents in American Thought*, volume 3 (New York: Harcourt, Brace, 1930), pp. 329-334;

Donald Pizer, *The Literary Criticism of Frank Norris* (Austin: University of Texas Press, 1964);

Pizer, *Realism and Naturalism in Nineteenth-Century American Literature* (Carbondale: Southern Illinois University Press, 1966);

H. Willard Reninger, "Norris Explains *The Octopus*: A Correlation of His Theory and Practice," *American Literature*, 12 (May 1940): 218-227;

Reviews of *The Responsibilities of the Novelist and Other Literary Essays*, in *Frank Norris: The Critical Reception*, edited by Joseph R. McElrath, Jr., and Katherine Knight (New York: Franklin, 1981), pp. 309-321;

Charles C. Walcutt, "Frank Norris on Realism and Naturalism," *American Literature*, 13 (March 1941): 61-63.

Papers:

The largest and most significant collection of Frank Norris's books and manuscripts is at the Bancroft Library, University of California, Berkeley. Other noteworthy collections are at the Alderman Library, University of Virginia, and the Newberry Library, Chicago.

Walter Hines Page

(15 August 1855-21 December 1918)

Ann Massa
University of Leeds

BOOKS: *The Rebuilding of Old Commonwealths: Being Essays towards the Training of the Forgotten Man in the Southern States* (New York: Doubleday, Page, 1902); republished as *The School That Built a Town* (New York: Harper, 1952);

A Publisher's Confession, anonymous (New York: Doubleday, Page, 1905; London: Gay & Bird, 1905); enlarged edition, credited to Page (New York: Doubleday, Page, 1923; London: Heinemann, 1924);

The Southerner: A Novel, as Nicholas Worth (New York: Doubleday, Page, 1909; London: Heinemann, 1910).

PERIODICAL PUBLICATIONS: "The Southern Educational Problem," *International Review,* 11 (October 1881): 309-320;

"The 'New' Southern Problem: From a Southern Point of View," *Independent,* 37 (4 June 1885): 712-713;

"The Negro on the Negro," *Independent,* 39 (6 January 1887): 7-8; (13 January 1887): 43-44; (20 January 1887): 74; (27 January 1887): 107; (3 February 1887): 137-138; (17 February 1887): 202-203; (24 February 1887): 235;

"The End of the War, and After," *Atlantic Monthly,* 82 (September 1898): 430-432;

"The Making of Literature," *State Normal Magazine,* 3 (1899): 461-471;

"A Wholesome Stimulus to Higher Politics," *Atlantic Monthly,* 83 (March 1899): 289-292;

"The Pan-American Exposition," *World's Work,* 2 (August 1901): 1015-1048;

"A Closer Relation between Librarians and Publishers," *Library Journal,* 27 (March 1902): 166-170;

"The Rebuilding of Old Commonwealths," *Atlantic Monthly,* 89 (May 1902): 651-661;

"Four Agencies for Southern Education" *Independent,* 54 (15 May 1902): 1156-1158;

"An Intimate View of Publishing," *World's Work,* 4 (September 1902): 2561-2565;

"The Cultivated Man in an Industrial Era," *World's Work,* 8 (July 1904): 4980-4985;

"The People as an Exhibit," *World's Work,* 8 (August 1904): 5110-5113;

"A Glance at the Ending Year," *World's Work*, 11 (December 1905): 7003-7008;

"The Autobiography of a Southerner Since the Civil War," as Nicholas Worth, *Atlantic Monthly*, 98 (July 1906): 1-12; (August 1906): 157-176; (September 1906): 311-325; (October 1906): 474-488;

"A Comprehensive View of Colleges," *World's Work*, 12 (July 1906): 7789-7794;

"Charles D. McIver," *South Atlantic Quarterly*, 5 (October 1906): 389-392;

"McIver, a Leader of the People," *World's Work*, 13 (December 1906): 8565-8567;

"A Journey through the Southern States," *World's Work*, 14 (June 1907): 9003-9042;

"The Writer and the University," *Atlantic Monthly*, 100 (November 1907): 685-695;

"Gifford Pinchot, the Awakener of the Nation," *World's Work*, 19 (March 1910): 12662-12668;

"Teaching Morals by Photographs," *World's Work*, 19 (March 1910): 12715-12725;

"The Hookworm and Civilization," *World's Work*, 24 (September 1912): 504-518;

"What the *World's Work* is Trying to Do," *World's Work*, 25 (January 1913): 265-268.

Ellen Glasgow, one of many southern writers whose talent Walter Hines Page was quick to perceive and encourage (he published her early work *The Voice of the People* in 1900), wrote to him in 1902: "When I hear . . . of the many forms your amazing energies acquire, I begin, indeed, to regard you as a kind of animated Colossus, or a second Theodore Roosevelt." Roosevelt, along with Woodrow Wilson, William Graham Sumner, and Frederic Harrison, was one of the many nonfiction writers whom Page considered "literary" and was enthusiastic about publishing.

Page's career was indeed multifaceted. He was one of the first fellows of the Johns Hopkins University (1876-1878) and a teacher of English literature and rhetoric in Louisville, Missouri (1878-1880). After marrying Willa Alice Wilson in August 1880 (three children would be born of the union), Page became an investigative journalist for the *Missouri St. Joseph Gazette* and subsequently a writer for the *New York World* (1881-1883), the *North Carolina State Chronicle* (1883-1885), the *Brooklyn Union* (1885), and the *New York Evening Post* (1887). Page's career picked up in 1887 with his appointment to the *Forum*, a leading current affairs magazine: first as its business manager and then in 1891 as its editor. A

move to Boston came in 1895 when he accepted a position at Houghton, Mifflin, becoming in 1898 editor of its journal, the *Atlantic Monthly*. With Frank Doubleday he founded Doubleday, Page and Company in 1900. Page remained with the firm until 1913; however, in 1900 he had launched his own magazine, the *World's Work*, a nonfiction illustrated monthly chiefly devoted to social issues. Concomitantly his interest in literary matters waned. He served on presidential commissions for educational and agricultural reform and was Woodrow Wilson's ambassador to England from 1913 until ill health forced him to resign in August 1918. As an editor, a critic, and a literary theorist he was progressive and wide-ranging, though his sense of what constituted "literature" was a paradoxical mixture of conservatism and radicalism.

Page was born in Cary, North Carolina, to Catherine Frances Roboteau and Allison Francis Page, a slaveholder who nevertheless held liberal tendencies and northern sympathies. His native state was the last to secede from the Union, and his family were reluctant Confederates. Page himself made good in Boston, New York, and finally in England; yet he was above all a southerner, interested in southern regional culture and anxious, as the first southern editor of the *Atlantic Monthly*, to break New England's cultural monopoly. He was fascinated by and nostalgic for the southern past and attracted to those who had written about it: Sidney Lanier and Henry Timrod, for instance. At the same time he was committed to discovering and helping contemporary southern writers of promise–Charles Waddell Chesnutt and Mary Johnston were his protégés. His sense that economic reform was vital to a new South and his perception that the economic basis of the old South had been disastrous led this young man with a literary bent to a preoccupation with the progressive commercial and industrial basis which he felt was vital to a continuous and developing culture. This mixture of interests was reflected in his sometimes contradictory attempts to make publishing pay by the ingenious marketing of best-sellers and to promote an American, particularly a southern, literature of distinction.

Eclecticism in his career and independence in his tastes can in part be traced to an influential teacher whom he encountered while a student at Randolph-Macon College (1873-1876): Thomas Randolph Price, professor of Greek and English, who was as enthusiastic for English litera-

Page (far right) with Wilbur F. Tillet and John Banks Wardlaw, two of his classmates at Randolph-Macon College

ture as for the classics, and who taught Page to love Alfred Tennyson and William Shakespeare. At Johns Hopkins (1876-1878) Page responded to another man with a foot in two worlds: Basil Gildersleeve, a classicist of international reputation who cared deeply for Sir Walter Scott and Robert Burns. Page was able to mix admiration of Rudyard Kipling's idiomatic art with dislike of British imperialism and politics (a dislike he suspended when World War I forced the declaration of loyalties). He opposed William Jennings Bryan's politics, but by his own definition—"the sheer force of words, artistically aimed"—he thought the "Cross of Gold" speech first-rate literature. He disliked Walt Whitman's celebration of the body, but in his own novel, *The Southerner* (1909), offered a treatment of the problem of interracial sexual attraction which was preceded

only by Mark Twain's *The Tragedy of Pudd'nhead Wilson* (1894) and Kate Chopin's "Desirée's Baby." However, the central paradox in Page's career was that in spite of the primary significance he attached to literature he remained, in effect, on the fringes of literature. His best-remembered writings are such sociopolitical essays on southern problems as "The Forgotten Man" (1897); his best writing, his letters. His literary criticism, widely scattered in letters and editorials, remains uncollected. It is, however, part of the canon of realistic criticism. Whether Page's ideas were formative for any writer is unclear. But he represents importantly the incidence of realistic and naturalistic literary theory in late-nineteenth- and early-twentieth-century America. And he was, of course, in his various positions of power, able to encourage and publish the writers he admired.

Self-caricature by Page (by permission of the Houghton Library, Harvard University)

ward literature from which he never deviated throughout his career. He believed that literary criticism should be more a guide to what is worthwhile than patrician and elitist in its taste, and he employed his editorial positions to solicit the kinds of manuscripts that he wanted. His interest in social issues led him to value writing that had a social purpose and that would be salutary for the democratic masses. He was thus uneasy with the sort of interiorism he encountered in Henry James and the stylistic self-consciousness of Stephen Crane. Enough of a businessman to yield to the public taste for well constructed romances with good narrative pacing, his own predilection was for realist works sharply situated in regional settings and expressive of the promise that a democratic policy can help to alleviate established social abuses. In this sense literature could be the highest expression of the human spirit. He thus laid much emphasis on the relationship between literature and the democratic order and argued that America must eventually produce the greatest of all literatures because it was the most democratic of societies. As literature was the reflection of life, and as "life" was available to every human being, every man was a potential writer who only needed encouragement. Indeed, unless literature concerned itself with the everyday activities and struggles of human beings it was worthless. "A man who would make American literature must feel . . . a keen common interest in all kinds of men, and a kinship with them, and he must know and feel the strong positive forces of life."

It was a point of view which lay close to that of both William Dean Howells and Frank Norris. But Howells was too sanguine and too genteel for Page (though this was a misreading of Howells), who found Howells's writing "high and clear and clear and graceful," but "not exciting." Page preferred the roughness, the earthiness, the common touch of Norris, who seemed to him to have a genuine and moving originality, a "sensationalism." Page called himself a "sensational editor": "every piece of literature (I mean the real thing) is sensational." He felt that Norris covered the panorama of American life more fully and more accurately than anyone else and that, importantly, Norris gave due weight to economic matters.

Storytelling, documentary literature, interpretations of American life, local color: these were the kinds of literature that were grist to Page's mill. He liked Hamlin Garland and Booth Tarkington for their sense of the Middle West;

Frank Norris was employed as a manuscript reader for Doubleday, Page, which published *The Octopus* (1901) and most of Norris's subsequent works. Page, on Norris's urgings, contracted to publish Theodore Dreiser's *Sister Carrie* (1900), but the matter is not altogether to his credit. Doubleday and his wife so opposed the book that Page temporized until he realized that the firm could be sued for contract violation. Upton Sinclair's *The Jungle* (1906) also appeared under Page's aegis.

Once Page gained control of the *Forum* in 1891 he was in a position to advance an attitude to-that at least one editor of the magazine shall visit every section of the country at least once a year, & *at times* of course other countries also ~ The real work of making a "live" magazine cannot be done in an office.

There is, therefore, no mystery about the work: the main thing to be said about it is that it is work, unceasing, hard work; but do not forget that it is interesting work. If an article does not [

Manuscript page from "What the World's Work *is Trying to Do." Page founded the journal* World's Work *and edited it from 1900 to 1913 (Walter Hines Page,* A Publisher's Confession, *enlarged edition, 1923).*

Theodore Roosevelt speaking at the laying of the cornerstone for Country Life Press in September 1910. Page is standing behind him; F. N. Doubleday is seated at left (by permission of the Houghton Library, Harvard University).

Sarah Orne Jewett and Mary Freeman Wilkins for their pictures of New England. He felt that Joel Chandler Harris's *Uncle Remus* (1880) outranked Harriet Beecher Stowe's *Uncle Tom's Cabin* (1852)–which, for its pathos rather than its propaganda, he nevertheless thought one of the great books of American literature. *Uncle Remus* was one of those rare works in which every touch was true, which caught background and created foreground. "The old cabin is there . . . filled with the film of old cobwebs and recollections; and, in the back-ground, the whole structure of Southern life is painted." Not surprisingly, Page was worried when Frederick Jackson Turner's thesis "The Significance of the Frontier in American History" appeared in 1893; for if Turner were right in predicting a homogeneous society and one American type, what would happen to the richness of regional literature? Would American literature become altogether elegiac? And, not surprisingly, Page, like Howells, wondered if the logic of realism did not tend toward nonfiction as the ultimate literary form. After all, Page argued, books are not literature. Literature existed

before books. Literature is not learning; "it is Thought." Long before Edmund Wilson did so, Page rated Abraham Lincoln's speeches as part of the best American literature. Lincoln's prose had proportion, structure, a suffusive political imagination, and, above all, "a severe plainness." Lincoln's writings met Page's criteria: terseness, directness, simplicity–that is, thought artistically expressed. Manner, then, did matter, though Page was consistently hostile to "literary" speech. "There is no vehicle . . . that can carry great literature except those plain words that roll out of our mouths when we suffer great emotion, when we weep, when we pray, when we laugh. Those words we speak in the earnest moments of our life, those idioms that we use then–they are the clothing that takes the common thought and in the hand of a great master immortalizes it. Keep close, close, close to the idiom."

For fiction Page advocated common language and homely subject matter. Perhaps because of his concern for the democratic, common, and universal aspects of literature his views might have been seen to militate against art. Page's collection of essays, *A Publisher's Confession* (1905), contained a piece entitled "Why Bad Novels Succeed and Good Ones Fail"; and it was, he said, simplicity of form which made the difference. In this curious essay Page made some uneasy distinctions between "Literary" quality, which bad novels lacked, and a "Genuine" quality, which they had. The commercial publisher in Page clashed with the critic. "I cannot weep because Mr. James and Mr. Howells do not find many readers." Their language was too literary, their subject matter insufficiently everyday. On the contrary, Winston Churchill deserved to succeed because his books "have a quality that is very rare in this world. . . . They have construction. They have action. They have substance. A series of events come to pass in a certain order, by a well-laid plan. Each book makes its appeal as a thing built, finished, shaped, if not well-proportioned, substantial. It is a real structure– not a mere pile of brick and lumber. The bricks and lumber that went into them are not as fine nor as good as somebody else may have in his brickyard and his lumberpile. But they are put together. A well shaped house of bad bricks is a more pleasing thing than any mere brick pile whatever."

All of Page's limitations as a critic are evident here. What he was arguing for as a priority for good fiction was accessibility to a general readership. He denied the merits of literary criticism and asserted those of public taste. What failed to sell was in all senses a failure. If for his time Page was in the forefront of realistic and naturalistic theory, he seemed to have an inflexible sense of what a novel should do, and to deny any scope to innovative and experimental fiction. One wonders what he made of James's 1908 preface to the New York Edition of *The Portrait of a Lady*, which used Page's architectural metaphor to such different, and more compelling, effect.

But Page was often sure and liberal in his responses. His assessment of Edgar Allan Poe was sensitive: the acutest critic America had known and the writer of many of the world's best short stories and a little of the most delicious verse in the language. He was alert to the surge of progressivist and populist sentiment in the 1890s and responded favorably to its expression in such writers as Hamlin Garland and Frank Norris. He aspired to an American democratic literature as an amalgam of regional voices and local-color emphasis. He was a proponent of nonfiction literature, persuading Booker T. Washington, for example, to write *Up From Slavery* (1901) and counseling W. E. B. Du Bois to avoid the trite fictionalization of what it was to be black. His activities as political activist and diplomat have been amply documented by scholars. His work as literary critic, editor, and publisher in the cause of American literature warrants much more detailed study than it has so far been given.

References:

John Milton Cooper, Jr., *Walter Hines Page: The Southerner as American, 1855-1918* (Chapel Hill: University of North Carolina Press, 1977);

C. Hartley Grattan, "The Walter Hines Page Legend," *American Mercury,* 6 (September 1925): 39-51;

Grattan, "Walter Hines Page–Patriot or Traitor," *Nation,* 121 (4 November 1925): 512;

Ross Gregory, *Walter Hines Page: Ambassador to the Court of Saint James* (Lexington: University of Kentucky Press, 1970);

Burton J. Hendrick, *The Earlier Life and Letters of Walter H. Page* (London: Heinemann, 1928);

Hendrick, *The Life and Letters of Walter H. Page,* 3 volumes (London: Heinemann, 1924; Garden City: Doubleday, Page, 1925);

Edwin Mims, "Walter Hines Page: Friend of the South," *South Atlantic Quarterly,* 18 (April 1919): 97-115;

Robert J. Rusnak, *Walter Hines Page and The World's Work 1900-1913* (Washington: University Press of America, 1982);

Ellery Sedgwick, "Walter Hines Page," *World's Work,* 37 (February 1919): 375-378;

Charles G. Sellers, Jr., "Walter Hines Page and the Spirit of the New South," *North Carolina Historical Review,* 29 (October 1952): 481-497;

Frederick B. Weaver, "Walter Hines Page and the Progressive Mood," Ph.D. dissertation, University of North Carolina, 1956.

Papers:

The main collections of Walter Hines Page papers are at Duke University Library, the Houghton Library of Harvard University, the Library of Congress, North Carolina State Department of Archives and History, and Randolph-Macon College.

Fred Lewis Pattee

(22 March 1863-6 May 1950)

William Lomax
University of California, Los Angeles

BOOKS: *Literature in the Public Schools* (Cincinnati: Teachers Co-operative, 1891);

The Wine of May, and Other Lyrics (Concord, N.H.: Republican Press Association, 1893);

Pasquaney: A Study (Bristol, N.H.: F. L. Pattee, 1893; revised, 1929);

A History of American Literature, with a View to the Fundamental Principles Underlying Its Development; A Textbook for Schools and Colleges (Boston, New York & London: Silver, Burdett, 1896; revised and enlarged, New York & Boston: Silver, Burdett, 1903);

Reading Courses in American Literature (New York & Boston: Silver, Burdett, 1897);

The Foundations of English Literature; A Study of the Development of English Thought and Expression from Beowulf to Milton (Boston & New York: Silver, Burdett, 1899; London: Silver, Burdett, 1900);

Mary Garvin; The Story of a New Hampshire Summer (New York & London: Crowell, 1902);

The House of the Black Ring (New York: Holt, 1905);

Elements of Religious Pedagogy; A Course in Sunday School Teacher-Training (New York: Eaton & Mains/Cincinnati: Jennings & Graham, 1909);

The Breaking-Point; A Novel (Boston: Small, Maynard, 1912);

Compelled Men (New York: Association Press, 1913);

A History of American Literature Since 1870 (New York: Century, 1915);

Side-Lights on American Literature (New York: Century, 1922);

The Development of the American Short Story; An Historical Survey (New York & London: Harper, 1923);

Tradition and Jazz (New York & London: Century, 1925);

The New American Literature, 1890-1930 (New York & London: Century, 1930);

Beyond the Sunset (Bristol, N.H.: Musgrove, 1934);

Fred Lewis Pattee (courtesy of Pennsylvania State University Libraries)

The First Century of American Literature, 1770-1870 (New York & London: Appleton-Century, 1935);

The Feminine Fifties (New York & London: Appleton-Century, 1940);

187

Penn State Yankee; The Autobiography of Fred Lewis Pattee (State College: Pennsylvania State College, 1953).

OTHER: *Shakespeare's Tragedy of Macbeth*, edited by Pattee (Boston & New York: Silver, Burdett, 1897);

"American Literature," in *New American Supplement to Encyclopaedia Britannica*, 5 volumes (New York: Werner, 1897), I: 158-165;

"Canadian Literature," in *New American Supplement to Encyclopaedia Britannica*, 5 volumes (New York: Werner, 1897), II: 675-677;

James Russell Lowell, *Conversations on Some of the Old Poets*, introduction by Pattee (New York: Crowell, 1901);

Booklovers Reading Club Hand-Book: course 4, *American Vacations in Europe;* course 5, *Six New England Classics;* course 19, *Out-of-Door Americans;* course 22, *Studies in American Literary Life*, editorial notes by Pattee (Philadelphia: Booklovers Library, 1901);

The Poems of Philip Freneau, Poet of the American Revolution, 3 volumes, edited, with an introduction, by Pattee (Princeton: Princeton University Library, 1902-1907);

Benjamin Gill, *Sermons and Addresses*, edited, with an introduction, by Pattee (State College: Pennsylvania State College, 1913);

"The Short Story," in *The Cambridge History of American Literature*, 4 volumes (New York: Putnam's/Cambridge: Cambridge University Press, 1917-1921), II: 367-395;

Century Readings for a Course in American Literature, edited by Pattee (New York: Century, 1919; revised and enlarged, 1922; revised and enlarged again, 1926); revised and enlarged as *Century Readings in American Literature* (New York & London: Century, 1932);

Mary Wilkins Freeman, *A New England Nun and Other Stories*, introduction by Pattee (New York: Harper, 1920);

American Short Stories, edited, with an introduction, by Pattee (New York: Duffield, 1925);

Charles Brockden Brown, *Wieland; Or, The Transformation, together with Memoirs of Carwin the Biloquist, a Fragment*, edited, with an introduction, by Pattee (New York: Harcourt, Brace, 1926);

James Fenimore Cooper, *The Last of the Mohicans; Or, A Narrative of 1757*, introduction by Pattee (New York: Macmillan, 1927);

Century Readings in the American Short Story, edited by Pattee (New York & London: Century, 1927);

Entry on George Washington Atherton, in *Dictionary of American Biography*, 22 volumes (New York: Scribners, 1928-1944), I: 404-405;

Entry on Frances Eliza Hodgson Burnett, in *Dictionary of American Biography*, 22 volumes (New York: Scribners, 1928-1944), III: 297-298;

Entry on George Washington Cable, in *Dictionary of American Biography*, 22 volumes (New York: Scribners, 1928-1944), III: 392-393;

Entry on Francis Marion Crawford, in *Dictionary of American Biography*, 22 volumes (New York: Scribners, 1928-1944), IV: 519-520;

Entry on Rebecca Blaine Harding Davis, in *Dictionary of American Biography*, 22 volumes (New York: Scribners, 1928-1944), V: 143-144;

Entry on Richard Harding Davis, in *Dictionary of American Biography*, 22 volumes (New York: Scribners, 1928-1944), V: 144-145;

Entry on Philip Morin Freneau, in *Dictionary of American Biography*, 22 volumes (New York: Scribners, 1928-1944), VII: 27-28;

Entry on Evan Pugh, in *Dictionary of American Biography*, 22 volumes (New York: Scribners, 1928-1944), XV: 257-258;

"The Short Story, The United States," in *Encyclopaedia Britannica*, 14th edition (Chicago: Encyclopaedia Britannica, Inc., 1929), XX: 581-583;

Rowland Evans Robinson, *Uncle Lisha's Shop and A Danvis Pioneer*, foreword by Pattee (Rutland, Vt.: Tuttle, 1933);

Mark Twain; Representative Selections, edited, with an introduction, by Pattee (New York: American Book Co., 1935);

John Neal, *American Writers; A Series of Papers Contributed to Blackwood's Magazine (1824-1825)*, edited by Pattee (Durham: Duke University Press/Cambridge: Cambridge University Press, 1937);

"The Nobel Lewis," in *Essays in Honor of A. Howry Espenshade* (New York: Nelson, 1937), pp. 7-20;

"The Biglow Papers," in *Dictionary of American History*, 6 volumes (New York: Scribners, 1940), I: 184.

PERIODICAL PUBLICATIONS: "Is There an American Literature?," *Dial*, 21 (1 November 1896): 243-245;

"Fear in Macbeth," *Poet Lore*, 10 (January-March 1898): 92-95;

Pattee (far right) with (left to right) fellow Dartmouth students Christian P. Anderson, Benjamin S. Simonds, and Walter S. Sullivan. The four climbed Mt. Cardigan in 1888 (courtesy of Pennsylvania State University Libraries).

"Critical Studies in American Literature, No. 1. An Epic: Longfellow's 'Evangeline,'" *Chautauquan,* 30 (January 1900): 415-420;

"Critical Studies in American Literature, No. 3. An Essay: Emerson's 'Self Reliance,'" *Chautauquan,* 30 (March 1900): 628-633;

"Critical Studies in American Literature, No. 5. A Lyric Poem: Poe's 'Ulalume,'" *Chautauquan,* 31 (May 1900): 182-186;

"Critical Studies in American Literature, No. 6. The Historical Romance: Cooper's *Last of the Mohicans,*" *Chautauquan,* 31 (June 1900): 287-292;

"Philip Freneau," *Chautauquan,* 31 (August 1900): 467-475;

"Bibliography of Philip Freneau," *Bibliographer,* 1 (March 1902): 97-106;

"Longfellow and German Romance," *Poet Lore,* 17 (Spring 1906): 59-77;

"The Mettle of New Hampshire," *Granite Monthly,* 48 (January 1916): 15-23;

"The Journalization of American Literature," *Unpopular Review,* 7 (April-June 1917): 374-394;

"Americanism thru American Literature," *Educational Review,* 57 (April 1919): 271-276;

"Thaddeus Stevens," *Dartmouth Alumni Magazine,* 13 (December 1920): 78-85;

"The 'Log' Unseats 'Mark Hopkins,'" *Nation,* 117 (18 July 1923): 55-57;

"The Present Stage of the Short Story," *English Journal,* 12 (September 1923): 439-449;

"The Shot of Acestes," *New York Evening Post Literary Review,* 4 (1 December 1923): 299-300;

"Those Fiery Radicals of Yesteryear," *New York Times Book Review*, 24 February 1924, pp. 2, 23, 26;

"American Literature in the College Curriculum," *Educational Review*, 67 (May 1924): 266-272;

"Call for a Literary Historian," *American Mercury*, 2 (June 1924): 134-140;

"Recent Poetry and the Ars Poetica," *Southwest Review*, 10 (January 1925): 16-32;

"James Fenimore Cooper," *American Mercury*, 4 (March 1925): 289-297;

"Herman Melville," *American Mercury*, 10 (January 1927): 33-43;

"When Shall We Three Meet Again?," *Dartmouth Alumni Magazine*, 19 (January 1927): 238-247;

"The Mission of the Christian College," *Mount Union College Bulletin*, 28 (April 1927): 3-11;

"The Contemporary Prize Novel; Analysis of Mazo de la Roche's *Jalna;* Discussion of J. Brooks Atkinson's *Henry Thoreau: the Cosmic Yankee*," *Creative Reading, a Course in Current Literature* (1 March 1928): 3-30;

"On the Rating of Mark Twain," *American Mercury*, 14 (June 1928): 183-191;

"Short Story Influence in the Novel; Analysis of Morley Callaghan's 'Strange Fugitive'; Discussion of Hendrik W. Van Loon's 'Life and Times of Pieter Stuyvesant,' " *Creative Reading, a Course in Current Literature* (November 1928): 3-30;

"Cooper the Critic," *Saturday Review of Literature*, 5 (15 June 1929): 1107-1108;

"Life Story Novel; Analysis of Dorothy Canfield's *The Deepening Stream;* Discussion of Will James' *Lone Cowboy: My Life Story*," *Creative Reading, the Medium of Critical Analysis*, 5 (15 October 1930): 573-602;

"Anthologies of American Literature before 1861," *Colophon*, 4 (March 1934): n. pag.;

"The British Theater in Philadelphia in 1778," *American Literature*, 6 (January 1935): 381-388;

"Gentian, Not Rose: The Real Emily Dickinson," *Sewanee Review*, 45 (April-June 1937): 180-197;

"Constance Fenimore Woolson and the South," *South Atlantic Quarterly*, 38 (April 1939): 130-141;

"The Soul of Florida," *South Atlantic Quarterly*, 43 (October 1944): 338-348;

"Fishing in Florida," *South Atlantic Quarterly*, 47 (July 1948): 375-386.

A widely respected educator, editor, critic, and scholar in his day, Fred Lewis Pattee, writes a reviewer in *Choice* (December 1973), "is today remembered (if at all) as one of the first professors of American literature and one of the first writers to attempt a comprehensive examination of our literary heritage. Hence, he occupies a small place in the literary histories for having been a 'pioneer.' " The published author of well over a hundred poems, a handful of short stories, and three novels–all of which have been forgotten–Pattee's literary reputation must rest solely on critical and scholarly work which has largely been superseded by later work. Yet he was one of the most influential figures in the decline of English literary colonialism and the subsequent declaration of American literary independence in the early years of the twentieth century. Without the foundations laid by Pattee the history of American literary education might have been far different.

Fred Lewis Pattee was born on 22 March 1863 in Bristol, New Hampshire, the oldest of three children born to Lewis Franklin and Mary Philbrick Ingalls Pattee. The Pattee family, which traced its descent from William Patee, who arrived in Boston during Revolutionary times and later settled in New Hampshire, was deeply rooted in the rocky New England soil, and "Yankee" values permeated Fred Lewis Pattee's life and thought. From the land Pattee absorbed a love of nature and rural life which he never lost. From his mother, a fond singer of sentimental songs, he inherited his pervasive romanticism. And from his devout Methodist upbringing, a childhood "saturated with the Bible," he developed a disciplined, moral life-style.

From an early age, too, Pattee established a dual career as writer and teacher. As a Bristol teenager he worked for three years as a printer's apprentice and there began to write, anticipating a journalistic career. Later, at the New Hampton Institute, he edited the school paper. In 1884 Pattee entered Dartmouth College, where he wrote poetry, fiction, and criticism, though little of it was ever published. At Dartmouth Pattee was chosen class poet and, as a senior, edited and wrote a regular column for the *Dartmouth Literary Monthly*. More important, Pattee read Hippolyte Taine's *History of English Literature* (1864; translated, 1873) and listened to Charles F. Richardson, Winkley Professor of English at Dartmouth, lecture from the proof sheets of his two-volume history of American literature entitled *American Literature, 1607-1885* (1887-1889). Taine and Rich-

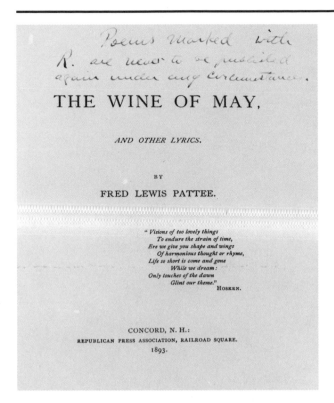

Title page, with Pattee's inscription, for his privately printed collection of poetry (courtesy of Pennsylvania State University Libraries)

ardson provided the models for Pattee's later efforts to write his own literature text. Unable to support himself by writing, Pattee turned to teaching and, beginning in 1886, held teaching posts in Candia, New Hampshire, and Bowdoinham, Maine, and then, after graduation from Dartmouth in 1888, in Eatontown, New Jersey, Mendon, Massachusetts, and finally, in 1890, at Coe's Northwood Academy in Northwood Centre, New Hampshire, where he served as principal for four years. During these full years of writing and teaching while pursuing his formal education Pattee worked at various odd jobs, including one summer as a reporter for the *Boston Herald* and another as a census enumerator; was seriously weakened by a lung disease which affected him his entire life; and, on 9 March 1889, married Anna L. Plumer, a childhood friend from Bristol.

In 1891 Pattee received an M.A. degree from Dartmouth and published his first book, *Literature in the Public Schools*, a fifty-two-page pamphlet which advocated greater emphasis on literature in the classroom. Two years later Pattee privately published three hundred copies of a collection of his own poetry, *The Wine of May, and Other Lyrics*. He was a prolific but untalented

poet, and critical reception of the book was so disappointing that Pattee attempted to gather and destroy extant copies. The same year saw *Pasquaney: A Study*, an eighty-three-page potpourri of pictures, poems, history, and a personal essay about Pattee's childhood around Lake Pasquaney near Bristol. The book reflected that nostalgic feeling of belonging to an older, slower, and more romantic world which was a persistent undercurrent in Pattee's later writing.

When, in 1894, a former Dartmouth classmate resigned as head (and only member) of the English department at Pennsylvania State College, Pattee applied for the position, sending copies of his first two books with the application. He was accepted and appointed assistant professor of English and rhetoric—the beginning of a thirty-four-year tenure at Penn State, during which most of his major critical and historical work was done.

In 1895 Pattee was promoted to full professor, and his daughter, Sarah Lewis Pattee, was born. The Pattees were happy in the isolated rural setting below Mount Nittany, but, as a technical school, Penn State drew only students Pattee called "ludicrously unprepared in English." He needed a specialized text for them if he was to develop the literature program he wished. Finally, in early 1896, Silver, Burdett published his oft-revised *A History of American Literature, with a View to the Fundamental Principles Underlying its Development; A Textbook for Schools and Colleges*. It was soon being used in nearly three dozen schools and colleges and in six editions between 1896 and 1909 sold nearly a quarter-million copies. His purpose, adapted from Taine, who was a major influence on Pattee, was to "follow the development of the American spirit and of American thought under the agencies of race, environment, epoch, and personality." Pattee theorized, first, that literature cannot be taught outside the context of history and, second, that American literature must be taught as an autonomous discipline because of the uniqueness of American conditions of history, race, environment, and language. These were relatively disturbing ideas in the 1890s, for the prevailing attitude was that American literature was merely a subsidiary of English literature. Later in 1896 Pattee clarified his theory with a brief article in the *Dial* entitled "Is There an American Literature?" which argued persuasively for the independence of American literature. The response to the article, Pattee wrote, was "instant and devastating"–a

Pattee, circa 1894, the year he began his career at Penn State (courtesy of Pennsylvania State University Libraries)

clear sign that Pattee was questioning sacred writ. The *Dial* article and the textbook were major milestones in the growth of American literary autonomy.

Pattee's early years at Penn State were among the busiest of his long literary career. The success of his textbook led directly to several other works, including *Reading Courses in American Literature* (1897), a short guide to literary study; a school edition of *Macbeth* (1897); a companion volume to his American literature text, *The Foundations of English Literature; A Study of the Development of English Thought and Expression from Beowulf to Milton* (1899), research for which took Pattee on a bicycle tour of Britain in 1897; four outline courses for the Booklovers Reading Club series (1901); an edition of James Russell Lowell's *Conversations on Some of the Old Poets* (1901); and articles on American and Canadian literature for the *Encyclopaedia Britannica*. While maintaining his prolific literary productivity, Pattee also entered fully into the social and intellectual life of the campus. Soon after arriving, he organized a drama club and a faculty literary club, both of which still exist, and in 1901 he wrote the school's alma mater. A licensed Methodist

preacher, Pattee also served, for twenty years beginning in 1905, as superintendent of the college Methodist Sunday school and, for sixteen years beginning in 1912, as campus chaplain. Dissatisfaction with the materials he was given for Sunday school led Pattee to publish *Elements of Religious Pedagogy; A Course in Sunday School Teacher-Training* in 1909. *Compelled Men* (1913) is an eighty-three-page collection of his chapel talks.

The Lowell and *Macbeth* editions also signaled the start of a forty-year career as an editor, which produced works by Philip Freneau, Benjamin Gill, Mary Wilkins Freeman, Charles Brockden Brown, James Fenimore Cooper, Mark Twain, and John Neal, an anthology of short stories, and two Century readers. The most significant of these were his three-volume edition of Freneau's poems (1902-1907) and the first Century reader. Pattee's Freneau has been supplanted by more recent scholarship, but he is cited by most Freneau scholars, and his edition remains a basic source for Freneau students. *Century Readings for a Course in American Literature* (1919), one of the first comprehensive college readers in American literature, became a basic text in numerous colleges and was revised or re-

Pattee (standing left) with his class in bibliography at Penn State (courtesy of Pennsylvania State University Libraries)

printed eight times between 1919 and 1932.

Pattee wrote little poetry after 1900 and almost no short fiction, but books, reviews, and essays on American authors and history appeared regularly until the last decade of his life. He became an authority on the American short story, edited *American Short Stories* (1925) and *Century Readings in the American Short Story* (1927), and wrote *The Development of the American Short Story; An Historical Survey* (1923), a work still useful today. His chapter on the short story for *The Cam-*

bridge History of American Literature in 1918, distorted by his propensity to emphasize minor writers, was less successful.

As a critical essayist Pattee was addicted to easy catch phrases and absolute, peremptory judgments; his criticism bristles with the "To understand, one must . . ." formula. But he also wrote as a teacher, and even his most scholarly work is presented in a relaxed and readable style. Thus, his two essay collections from these years, *Side-Lights on American Literature* (1922) and *Tradition*

THE PENNSYLVANIA STATE COLLEGE
STATE COLLEGE, PA.

DEPARTMENT OF ENGLISH

State College, Pa.
December 26, 1914.

The Neale Publishing Co.

New York City

Dear Sirs:

I am writing a history of American literature since 1870 which the Century Company is to bring out this autumn and parts of which will appear in the Century Magazine if not crowded out by the war material. I am perplexed at one point: is Ambrose Bierce an important figure? If you so consider him, why do you do so? I confess I have conflicting ideas about him. Sometimes I am inclined to take him at his own estimate and again I consider him a bluff and "wind-bag". Which is he? Why is he not given more attention in the histories and the critical estimates of American Literature? I am seeking the light. Just at present I am inclined not to mention him at all in the record. How did the collected edition, I have not seen it, - sell? Did its reception make you believe he is a writer with a real place in our literature?

Hoping to hear from you , I am

Very sincerely yours,

Fred Lewis Pattee
Professor of English.

Letter from Pattee to Ambrose Bierce's publisher (Walter Neale, Life of Ambrose Bierce, *1929)*

464

completest expression of our civilization; if its influence were not

greater than all the pulpits, than all the newspapers between the

oceans, it would not be so important that its message should be true."

They would ~~bring~~ *produce* a new American literature, one stripped of prudish-

ness and convention; they would go down among the People and tell them

the plain God's Truth *as Zola defined Truth,* for the People were hungry for ~~them~~ *it:* "In the

larger view, in the last analysis, the People pronounce the final

judgment. The People, despised of the artist, hooted, caricatured,

and vilified, are, after all, and in the main, the real seekers after

Truth." ~~The group was a~~ *The group was a* ~~passing~~

passing phenominon. Many of ~~them~~ *its members* were dead before they had fairly

begun their work: Walcott Balestier and Stephen Crane at thirty, Frank

Norris at thirty-two, Henry Harland and Harold Frederic *in the early*

~~early~~ forties, *and the others, like R.H. Davis for instance, turned*

at length to historical romance & other conventional fields.

The impetus undoubtedly came from the enormous and sud-

den vogue of Kipling. Balestier was his brother-in-law and had col-

laborated with him *in writing* ~~on~~ The Naulaka, *when he had written the* ~~story~~ *novel Benefits.* The vigor and directness and pic-

turing power of the new *Kipling were* ~~qualities~~ qualities that ap-

pealled strongly to young men of journalistic training. *like him* They were

cosmopolitans *and had seen unusual areas of life* Crane had represented his paper in the Grecian-Turkish

war and in the Cuban campaign, Norris had been in the South African

war, Richard Harding Davis ~~who crossed on to Europe~~ had been at all

the storm centres of his time, Frederic was the European correspon-

dent of the New York Times, and Harland *became editor at length* ~~was the man~~ of the

London Yellow Book.

The genius of the group undoubtedly was *Stephen* Crane *(1871-1900).* He was

frail of physique, neurotic, intense, full of a vibrant energy that

drove him too fiercely. ~~Examti~~ He was naturally lyrical, romantic,

impulsively creative, but his training made him , as it made most of

the group, a realist- a depressed realist after Zola. His earliest

work *was* ~~is~~ his best, Maggie, a Girl of the Streets, a grim and ~~impressxxxx~~

forgot a work of remarkable promise, but remarkable only for its promise.

Page from the revised typescript for Pattee's A History of American Literature Since 1870 *(courtesy of Pennsylvania State University Libraries)*

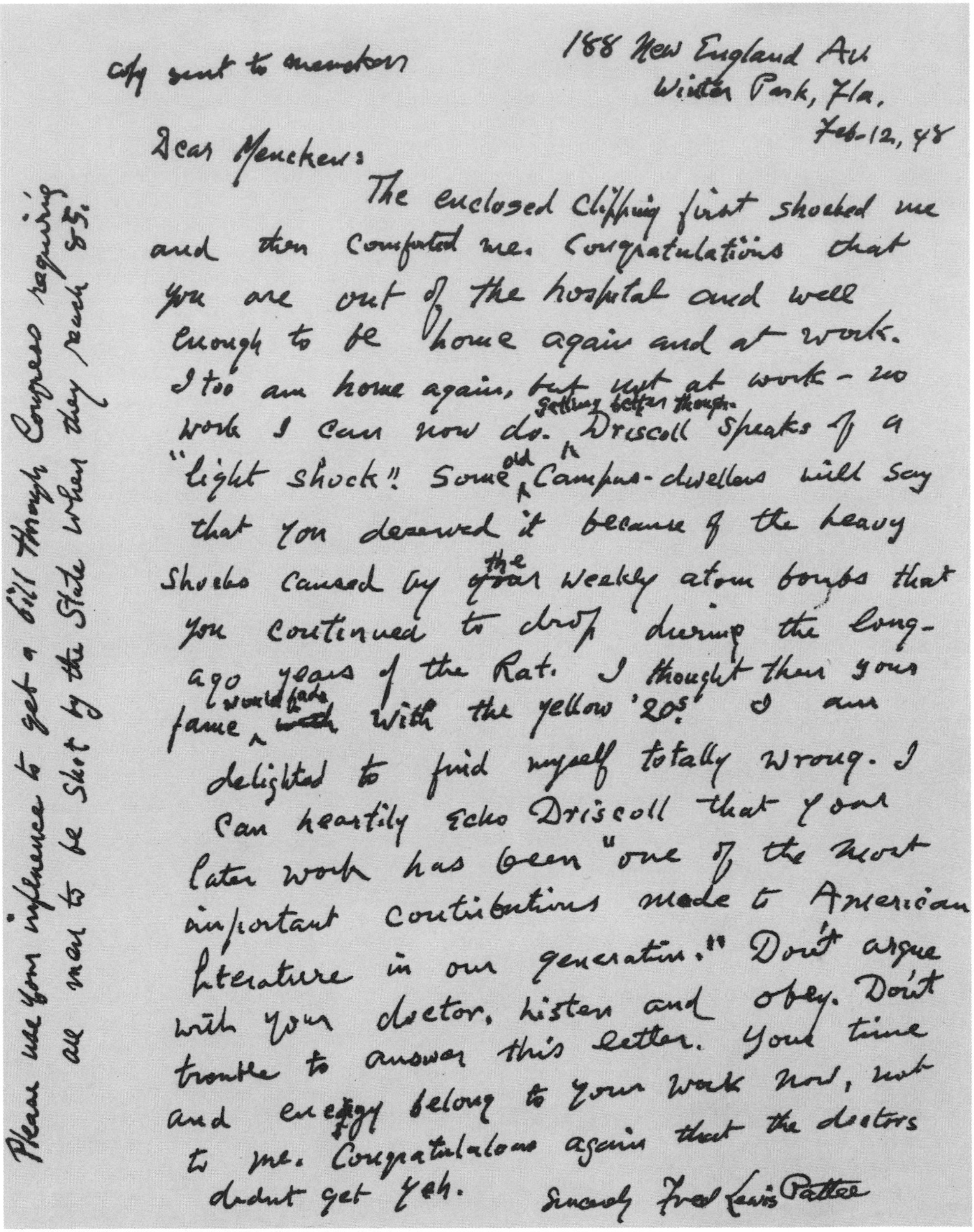

[handwritten letter]

copy sent to mencken

188 New England Av
Winter Park, Fla.
Feb-12, 48

Dear Mencken:

The enclosed clipping first shocked me and then comforted me. Congratulations that you are out of the hospital and well enough to be home again and at work. I too am home again, but not at work — no work I can now do. *getting better though.* Driscoll speaks of a "light shock". Some old Campus-dwellers will say that you deserved it because of the heavy shocks caused by *the* your weekly atom bombs that you continued to drop during the long-ago years of the Rat. I thought then your fame *would fade* with the yellow '20s. I am delighted to find myself totally wrong. I can heartily echo Driscoll that your later work has been "one of the most important contributions made to American literature in our generation." Don't argue with your doctor, listen and obey. Don't trouble to answer this letter. Your time and energy belong to your work now, not to me. Congratulations again that the doctors didn't get you.

Sincerely Fred Lewis Pattee

[left margin, vertical]
Please use your influence to get a bill through Congress requiring all men to be shot by the State when they reach 65.

Letter from Pattee to H. L. Mencken (courtesy of Pennsylvania State University Libraries) and Jazz (1925), are still entertaining today, even though their value as criticism has faded.

Of all the works which he produced during the Penn State years, however, those which are most significant for an understanding of Pattee himself and his critical philosophy are the novels and his important three-volume history of American literature. By any standards Pattee's novels are poor stuff, but when *Mary Garvin; The Story of a New Hampshire Summer* (1902), his first novel, sold thirty-five hundred copies–a best-seller in his eyes–he was convinced his literary future lay in fiction. That future ended in 1912 after only three undistinguished novels, but two of them provide important insights into the critical stance of his histories. In *Mary Garvin,* notable for its evocation of New England rural life and its thickly accented Yankee dialect, Pattee opposes two worlds, the sophisticated artificiality of Boston and the "little paradise" of rural Danville, New Hampshire. Luke Farnum rejects the love of Mary Garvin, a "wild and artless" country maid, for a beguiling Bostonian, Alice Bradley. For Luke, a country boy, this is a false, unnatural act, and Alice's influence makes him insincere and dissimulative, though she herself is honest and attractive. Luke, realizing that he cannot leave his natural country environment, returns to Mary. *The Breaking-Point* (1912) chronicles the martyrdom of a modern "Christ" by the Pharisees of a New England congregation. John Galt, a country minister new to city life, saves a prostitute, Isobel Carniston, from suicide, then continues, as a shepherd's duty, to help her. His congregation and fellow ministers, however, drive him from his pastorate for associating with her: "Bostonitis," or false piety, triumphs over the "romance" of Good Samaritanism. The fundamental conflicts in these two novels–between country and city, romantic and classic, natural and artificial–are the dichotomies which structure the critical world of Pattee's essays and of his most important work, his ambitious three-volume history of American literature, begun in 1915 with *A History of American Literature Since 1870,* continued in 1930 with *The New American Literature, 1890-1930,* and concluded in 1935 with *The First Century of American Literature, 1770-1870.*

Pattee saw the Civil War as a turning point in American literary history, for, after a century of English literary dominance, post-Civil War trends seemed to signal imminent literary emancipation. In Bret Harte, Mark Twain, Jack London, and numerous regionalists Pattee saw the open-

ing of a new literary frontier which would finally free America from European dominance. Boston, for Pattee, had become a symbol of the elitist view that Brahmin art epitomized "American" values and creative power. In his autobiography, *Penn State Yankee* (1953), Pattee contrasts the simple, rural farm life of his own family with the urban, patrician life of the Boston Adamses. Both, he implies, are equally venerable in American history. For Pattee, the real New England was not the polished, civilized artificiality of Boston life, but the rough, natural "out back" of rural life, and the real America was not restricted to the urban Northeast, but included *all* of America. The "flowering of New England" was literary oppression. Thus, *A History of American Literature Since 1870* caused a furor, writes William L. Werner ("Fred Lewis Pattee: Author, Scholar, Teacher"), because, for the first time, it was history of "contemporary writing that had *not* flowered in New England."

Pattee also championed the "people" over the literati. "Dozens of histories of American literature," he lamented, "but as yet no literary history of the American *people.*" Thus, Pattee chronicled popular literature generally ignored by traditional historians–magazines, best-sellers, gift books, and annuals. A historian, he argued, must account for high sales and popularity. Walt Whitman may be great, but only the elite read him; Louisa May Alcott's *Little Women* is read by everyone.

Finally, Pattee canonized countless minor writers, and his histories are storehouses of data on lesser-known figures who have dropped out of modern texts. He compared Mary Wilkins Freeman favorably with Nathaniel Hawthorne, for example, and his discussion of her, wrote Brent L. Kendrick in 1985, "was then–and remains today–one of the most sensitive in Freeman literary criticism."

This was history of movements and ideas rather than of genres or individuals, of society rather than of works, and of American literature rather than of "English literature in America." It was a manifesto, not only of independence, but of a new historicism which forever changed the study of American literature. The moment of triumph for Pattee came with a paper read before the Modern Language Association at Ann Arbor in 1923 and subsequently published in the *American Mercury* for June 1924 as "Call for a Literary Historian." In this seminal paper Pattee argued that literary history till then had been mostly biographical, often more myth than fact. In his own library of over a hundred volumes of American literary history he could not find one which was truly an *American* history. Therefore, Pattee issued "ten commandments" for literary historians. The two most important were that the literary historian must place literature against the background of history while remaining unprovincial, and he must also deal with subliterary and popular literature such as magazines, which are the literature of democracy. The paper had wide-ranging effects and, republished as the lead essay in Norman Foerster's *The Reinterpretation of American Literature* in 1928, served as a rallying point for men, like Foerster and Robert Spiller, who forged the new American literature.

Pattee's historical role in the "reinterpretation" of American literature was thus a significant one. Time, however, has revealed his critical role to have been an ephemeral one. His threefold strategy for historical revolution was influential, but his critical stance was too idiosyncratic to survive.

Romanticism was the touchstone of Pattee's critical ideology, and "romantic" became his highest critical accolade. "The great ages of the human spirit and the great periods in the history of literature," wrote Pattee, "have been always the romantic ages." America after 1815 was such an age, and Pattee's own age was another: "I confidently believe that we are on the threshold of the greatest literary era American has ever known. A new and glorious romantic period is upon us that will glorify our civilization. . . ." Pattee's romanticism was never a rigorously defined concept, but a visceral, organic conviction of feeling. "Poetic," "living," "heart," "natural," "soul," "life," "spirit," "truth"—these words formed the core of Pattee's critical vocabulary, and his criticism therefore is often vigorously personal, subjective, impressionistic, often more poetry than criticism, more literary reverie than scholarly monograph, itself more romantic than objective. "Criticism," wrote Pattee, "should be rulings of a supreme court of literature. Whatever else is extreme and impassioned, criticism should be serene; whatever else is distorted, criticism should be the truth."

The enemies of Pattee's romanticism were classicism and realism. That which is "classical and finished and beautiful" lacks life and "perishes at last of its own refinement." Art and beauty are but the sterile surface, not the soul, of literature. The highly cultured but artificial life of Boston, far from being the pinnacle of American creative power, was in fact mere surface, provincial, soulless. Other lands may be classic, said Pattee, but America is romantic.

Although he called himself a twentieth-century realist, Pattee was dismayed by the post-Civil War trend toward literary realism, which he viewed as ruinous literary decline: "The transcendentalists as they wrote were concerned with the *unseen;* in a later period came the realists who dealt with the *seen;* now come the ultra-naturalists who deal with the *obscene.*" He was even more disturbed by the propensity of many American writers who began as romantics to turn in later life to realistic modes, to pessimism, bitterness, "art," and satire. Cooper, William Dean Howells and Twain all succumbed to this peculiar "American evolution." Similarly, Pattee decried the commercialization of art–"this dragging of our fiction in the mud of ignorance and cheap slap-stick sensation!" Charlie Chaplin, he lamented, has become the degraded essence of modern drama.

For Pattee, all of this represented a rejection of truth and poetry for mere science and journalism. In "The Shot of Acestes" (1923), his most widely reprinted essay and an important statement of his literary philosophy, Pattee vigorously condemns modern realism. Modern writers are "self-hypnotized in umbilical contemplation." Modern fiction has become diseased, fatal to "truth," and modern poetry has "touched the fatal pitch of realism and has befouled its wings." Such literature prefers manner to matter, brilliancy of style and effect to truth and moral philosophy–and so is ephemeral. Henry James was brilliant, but cold and clinical–"human life from the standpoint of the laboratory and the test tube"–and he falls, therefore, "inevitably into second place as an interpreter of human life." Jack London, lacking "poise and moral background and beauty of style," must be considered an "ephemeral sensation." James Branch Cabell, Sherwood Anderson, Theodore Dreiser, H. L. Mencken–all have fallen short. Because the human soul is "incurably romantic and idealistic," realism can never speak for the soul.

The irony of Pattee's critical philosophy was that, in condemning the ephemerality of realism, Pattee condemned himself to ephemerality. By focusing so powerfully on history and ideas, and by locating literary greatness in external verities, he failed to recognize the role of change and development and could not accept or understand new

*Pattee lecturing at Rollins College, where he taught from
1928 to 1941 (courtesy of Pennsylvania State
University Libraries)*

modes of art. Thus, the young Twain was a "glorious romanticist," but the aging Twain was inferior, a mere "artist." The young Howells was a "poet, a romancer, a dreamer," but the work of the mature Howells was "an artificial acquirement like the taste for olives." Emma Lazarus had passion, emotion, and lyric power, and Rose Terry Cooke treated New England with sympathy and comprehension and delicacy. But Emily Dickinson wrote only "eccentric fragments . . . mere conceits, vague jottings of a brooding mind. . . . They should have been allowed to perish as their author intended"—a notorious judgment which Pattee moderated in a 1937 essay, "Gentian, Not Rose: The Real Emily Dickinson," but which he never totally relinquished. Pattee's attack on eastern writers led Ernest Leisy to accuse Pattee of "frontieritis"—the antithesis of Bostonitis—and to remark of Pattee's third volume of history: "There is not another handbook that admits into its pages so much doggerel" (*American Literature* [January 1936]). Pattee's criticism was doomed

therefore to fade with the passing of his school of romantic philosophy, and it was soon overwhelmed by the New Criticism. But his historical work has assumed lasting significance in the evolution of American literature and has established what reputation he retains today.

While pursuing these battles in print, Pattee continued, as he had from the beginning of his career, quietly and steadily to build a reputation as a popular and effective teacher. From his earliest teaching assignments in small New England schools Pattee had organized American literature courses, a revolutionary activity for the time, and many of his published writings were efforts to create material to be used by students. He has therefore been honored by many as the first "Professor of American Literature," a title bestowed on him formally by Penn State in 1920. James J. Martine has shown that the title itself was actually a compromise to resolve an internal administrative squabble at the college, but, as a symbolic title, it does reflect legitimate accomplishment. Toward the end of his Penn State career Pattee accepted a succession of summer teaching posts and visiting professorships–at Penn State, Dartmouth, Columbia University, the University of Illinois (which tried unsuccessfully to lure him away from Penn State), and, from 1924 to 1936, at Vermont's Bread Loaf School of English. Pattee also lectured widely, served as chairman of the American literature group for MLA in the mid 1920s, and was one of the original editors of the journal *American Literature*, founded in 1929, in part as a result of Pattee's work. It is interesting that Pattee accomplished all of this without the now-revered Ph.D. degree. On a sabbatical tour of Europe in 1902 Pattee studied at Göttingen, ostensibly for the purpose of earning a Ph.D., but, considering his success as writer and teacher, he saw no point to making the necessary sacrifices, and he never did earn the degree. He later received honorary Litt.D. degrees from Lebanon Valley College in 1915 and Dartmouth in 1923. Pattee retired from Penn State in 1928 as emeritus professor of American literature, the only man in the school's history to be honored by three separate classes (1899, 1924, 1930) as "the most influential man associated with the students." Today the Penn State University library bears Pattee's name.

Pattee spent his last year at Penn State without his wife, who had died on 13 September 1927. After leaving Penn State he moved to Florida, where he married Grace Garee on 25 November 1928, and joined the faculty of Rollins College in Winter Park, where he taught for thirteen years. There he completed the second and third volumes of his history of American literature; contributed regularly to *American Literature;* published a last book of poetry, *Beyond the Sunset* (1934), and his third collection of essays, *The Feminine Fifties* (1940); and contributed articles to the *Dictionary of American History* and the *Dictionary of American Biography*. Grace Pattee died 30 April 1946, and Pattee, after spending his last two years mostly in hospitals, died 6 May 1950. He was returned home to be buried in Bristol, New Hampshire.

Although his major works were reprinted in the 1960s, little, aside from Martine's 1973 study, has been published on Pattee since his death. However, Pattee remains an influential figure in the establishment of American literature as an autonomous discipline, free of English domination and sectionalism. He was also important for his scholarly spadework on American writers, including Freneau and a host of lesser writers who "deserve passing mention," and for his books and essays which relate literary history to social history, thus helping to establish the new historicism of American literature. Finally, Pattee established American literature as an important part of modern liberal education, and his accomplishments as a teacher played a small but significant role in building the foundations on which modern American literary education and research rest.

Interview:
"Stay in Your Own Backyard," *Old Main Bell,* 7 (May 1931): 13, 17.

Bibliographies:
Philip Allison Shelley, "A Token of the Season," *Headlight,* 14 (December 1944): 4-36;

William L. Werner, "The Pattee Collection: Library of American Literature," *Headlight,* 17 (June 1948): 4-15;

Werner, "Manuscripts in the Pattee Collection" and "Writings of Fred Lewis Pattee," *Headlight,* new series 3 (May 1956): 11-32.

References:
S. Bradley, "American Lit's Pa," *Saturday Review,* 37 (20 February 1954): 22-23;

William Chislett, " 'Tradition and Jazz,' " in his *Moderns and Near-Moderns* (New York: Grafton, 1928), pp. 220-222;

Irving Garwood, *Questions and Problems in American Literature, Based Upon the Text of Pattee's Century Readings in American Literature* (New York & London: Century, 1927);

William S. Harris, "Fred Lewis Pattee," *Granite Monthly,* 24 (February 1898): 80-83;

Jay B. Hubbell, *Who Are the Major American Writers?* (Durham: Duke University Press, 1972), pp. 244-248;

Brent L. Kendrick, ed., *The Infant Sphinx: Collected Letters of Mary E. Wilkins Freeman* (Metuchen, N.J.: Scarecrow Press, 1985), pp. 381-386;

Klaus Lubbers, *Emily Dickinson: The Critical Revolution* (Ann Arbor: University of Michigan Press, 1968), pp. 137-138, 169-171;

James J. Martine, *Fred Lewis Pattee & American Literature* (University Park & London: Pennsylvania State University Press, 1973);

Ferner Nuhn, "Teaching American Literature in American Colleges," *American Mercury,* 13 (March 1928): 328-331;

Erwin W. Runkle, "Professor Pattee and Penn State," *Old Main Bell,* 5 (April 1929): 3-5;

William L. Werner, "Fred Lewis Pattee: Author, Scholar, Teacher," *Headlight,* 17 (June 1948): 1-3;

Werner, "In Memoriam: Fred Lewis Pattee, 1863-1950," *American Literature,* 22 (January 1951): 573-574;

Werner, "The Writing Career of Fred Lewis Pattee," *Headlight,* new series 3 (May 1956): 5-7.

Papers:
The great bulk of Fred Lewis Pattee's papers and manuscripts is in the Pattee Library at Pennsylvania State University. A smaller collection of papers is located at Rollins College in Florida.

Harry Thurston Peck

(24 November 1856-23 March 1914)

Theodore R. Hovet
University of Northern Iowa

BOOKS: *The Semitic Theory of Creation: A Study of Language* (Chicago: Barclay, White, 1886);

The Adventures of Mabel, as Rafford Pyke (New York: Dodd, Mead, 1897);

The Personal Equation (New York: Harper, 1898);

Greystone and Prophyry (New York: Dodd, Mead, 1899);

What is Good English? and Other Essays (New York: Dodd, Mead, 1899);

William Hickling Prescott (New York: Macmillan, 1905);

Twenty Years of the Republic (New York: Dodd, Mead, 1906);

Hilda and the Wishes (New York: Dodd, Mead, 1907);

Literature (New York: Columbia University Press, 1908);

Studies in Several Literatures (New York: Dodd, Mead, 1909);

The New Baedeker (New York: Dodd, Mead, 1910);

A History of Classical Philology from the Seventh Century, B.C., to the Twentieth Century, A.D. (New York: Macmillan, 1911).

OTHER: *Harper's Dictionary of Classical Literature and Antiquities,* edited by Peck (New York: American Book Co., 1896);

Masterpieces of the World's Literature, Ancient and Modern, 20 volumes, edited by Peck, Frank R. Stockton, and Julian Hawthorne (New York: American Library Society, 1898-1899); revised and enlarged as *The World's Great Masterpieces; History, Biography, Science, Philosophy, Poetry, the Drama, Travel, Adventure, Fiction, etc.,* 30 volumes, edited by Peck, Stockton, Nathan Haskell Dole, Hawthorne, and Caroline Ticknor (New York: American Literary Society, 1901);

The New International Encyclopædia, edited by Peck, Daniel Coit Gilman, and Frank Moore Colby (17 volumes, New York: Dodd, Mead, 1902-1904; 20 volumes, 1904);

Harry Thurston Peck

The Standard Illustrated Book of Facts, edited by Peck and Robert Campbell Auld (New York: Syndicate Publishing Company, 1912).

PERIODICAL PUBLICATIONS: "My Literary Passions," *Bookman,* 1 (July 1895): 400-402;

"The First of the Realists," *Bookman,* 2 (October 1895): 130-133;

"The Question of the Laureate," *Bookman,* 2 (December 1895): 292-297;

"*Jude the Obscure,*" *Bookman,* 2 (January 1896): 427-429;

"William Dean Howells," *Bookman*, 4 (February 1897): 529-541;

"Richard Harding Davis," *Bookman*, 5 (August 1897): 462-468;

"The Cook-Stove in Poetry," *Bookman*, 8 (September 1898): 50-53;

"The New American Aristocracy," *Cosmopolitan*, 25 (October 1898): 701-708;

"Stéphane Mallarmé," *Bookman*, 8 (November 1898): 227-229;

"A New Writer Who Counts," *Bookman*, 9 (June 1899): 344-346;

"Balzac and His Work," *Cosmopolitan*, 27 (July 1899): 238-245;

"Anthony Trollope," *Bookman*, 37 (April 1901): 114-125;

"A Chat About Sherlock Holmes," *Independent*, 53 (21 November 1901): 2757-2760;

"Émile Zola," *Bookman*, 16 (November 1902): 233-240;

"Our American Laureate," *Munsey's Magazine*, 36 (February 1907): 531-536;

"Intimate Talks About Books That Are Worthwhile," *Munsey's Magazine*, 37 (August 1907); (September 1907); (October 1907); (November 1907); (December 1907); 38 (January 1908); (February 1908); (March 1908);

"One of the Parnassiens," *Bookman*, 29 (April 1909): 174-178;

"Swinburne and the Swinburnians," *Bookman*, 29 (June 1909): 374-384;

"Then and Now," *Bookman*, 30 (February 1910): 589-602;

"Mark Twain a Century Hence," *Bookman*, 31 (June 1910): 382-393.

Through his reviews and articles in the *Bookman*, *Munsey's Magazine*, and *Cosmopolitan*, as well as his several collections of essays, Harry Thurston Peck instructed a great number of American readers at the turn of the century on the importance of the realistic and naturalistic movements and kept them abreast of the latest developments in Continental literature. When he addressed the American literary tradition, he was less successful.

Peck was born on 24 November 1856 in Stamford, Connecticut, the son of Harry and Harriet Elizabeth Thurston Peck. After his graduation in 1881 from Columbia College, where he edited the college paper, *Acta Columbiana*, he studied classical philology in Paris, Berlin, and Rome, returning to the United States to receive a Ph.D.

in 1883 from Cumberland University and in 1884 a L.H.D. from Columbia. In 1882 he married Cornelia M. Dawbarn, by whom he had two daughters. That same year he was appointed a tutor at Columbia, advancing to become professor of Latin language and literature from 1886 to 1910. He was also editor of *Harper's Dictionary of Classical Literature and Antiquities* (1896) and a co-editor of *The New International Encyclopædia* (1902-1904). In addition, he was literary editor of the *New York Commercial Advertiser* (1897-1901) and a staff member of *Munsey's Magazine* (1907-1911). His chief editorial position, however, was with the *Bookman* from 1895 to 1907, during which time he not only wrote much of each issue but also the responses for the famous "Bookman's Letter-Box." In addition to his academic and editorial work he wrote a number of books on subjects other than literary criticism: history (*Twenty Years of the Republic*, 1906), poetry (*Greystone and Prophyry*, 1899), children's literature (*The Adventures of Mabel*, 1897, and *Hilda and the Wishes*, 1907), and travel sketches (*The New Baedeker*, 1910). He was divorced from his first wife in 1906 and the following year married Elizabeth Hickman Du Bois. Peck's career came to a tragic end when he was sued in 1910 for breach of promise by a former stenographer and was soon thereafter fired from his academic and editorial positions. In 1913 he was forced to declare bankruptcy, and on 23 March 1914 he committed suicide.

A close observer of the literary scene both at home and abroad, Peck became a witty and informative guide to the realistic and naturalistic movements. Beginning in July and October 1895 in reviews in the *Bookman* of the literary criticism of William Dean Howells and of Charles Tarver's *Gustave Flaubert*, he established his central thesis that realism was the authentic voice of modern literature, but that its integrity was constantly being threatened by the "trivialism" one finds in some of the fiction of Howells, or by the "excesses" of recent naturalistic novels such as Thomas Hardy's *Jude the Obscure*.

While his characterization of Howells and Hardy might irritate today's readers, he was able to focus the attention of his audience on what he considered the great accomplishment of the modern tradition, the development of realistic and naturalistic fiction. In his opinion the titan of modern literature was Honoré de Balzac. As he put it in a lively article in *Cosmopolitan* in July 1899, it is only in Balzac that the reader will find "the life and character of an entire nation drawn . . . in their true relations and with the multitudinous completeness of reality." He concludes his essay by stating that "my own belief is that at the last his name will be placed higher still than Shakespeare's at the very apex of the pyramid of literary fame." William Makepeace Thackeray and Anthony Trollope were the other two unquestionable masters of realism, according to Peck. As he explained in an essay in the *Bookman* in April 1901, in contrast to "the cult of the Unmentionable" perpetuated by such neonaturalists as Guy de Maupassant, Catulle Mendes, and Joris-Karl Huysmans in France or George Moore, George Gissing, and Frank Norris in Great Britain and America, of the "truer realism there have been just three great masters, and these are Balzac, Thackeray, and Trollope. All three of them are free alike from any taint of Naturalism and from the paltriness of Trivialism." Interestingly, Peck rated Trollope right behind Balzac and ahead of Thackeray, primarily because "he reveals to us a larger world than Thackeray's, and always with a perfect comprehension of it. It is a Briton's world, as Balzac's is a Frenchman's. . . . "

Despite his frequent denunciations of the corruptions of naturalism, Peck was not so much a genteel opponent of the movement as a critical uncle. His admiration for Emile Zola, for example, was unbounded. Writing in the *Bookman* in November 1902 on the occasion of Zola's death, he pointed out that like "rationalism in theology" and "materialism in philosophy" the French author's belief "that the novelist is a demonstrator" and "his study is a laboratory" in which to "arrive at new and unsuspected truths" was "consistent with the whole tone of modern thought" and "nothing new can now be said" of them. American readers must recognize that despite subject matter distasteful to most of them "his work speaks for itself" and that *L'Assommoir* (1877), *Nana* (1880), and *La Débâcle* (1892) must rank as "colossal masterpieces."

His admiration for writers who could create fictional worlds which seemed to capture the essence of a national culture, as did Balzac, Zola, and Trollope, gave him a highly individualized view of contemporary American writers. He argued in his February 1897 review of Howells that in *A Modern Instance* (1882) and *The Rise of Silas Lapham* (1885) he came close to achieving greatness and to writing "*The* American Novel." However, he felt that Howells's career in Boston did irreparable damage to his artistic vision, for that

city's provincialism "narrowed his marvellous gifts of delineation to a single sphere and made him the novelist of a section, when his genius might otherwise have become broadly national." Also, Peck was highly critical of Henry James because he had abandoned American culture for a marginal British society that had no roots in political or social reality. Its province was the drawing room rather than the great stage of history which Balzac and Zola had depicted. As he put it, James's "little corner of observation is so very little, his lenses are so carefully adjusted to one particular focus, and his instrument is so obviously an opera-glass and not a telescope, as to make his books the impressions of a first-nighter rather than the accurate cosmic view of a sociological astronomer."

While this assessment of James was grossly unfair, it reflected a perspective which allowed Peck to see other aspects of the contemporary literary scene with admirable clarity. To cite the most striking instance, Peck rated Edith Wharton as one of the major contemporary writers, insisting that she was no mere feminine imitator of James, but "a new writer who counts," as he titled his review of *The Greater Inclination* in the June 1899 *Bookman*. Peck also had great skill in describing in a short essay written for an American audience the origin and significance of current literary movements overseas. In a November 1898 *Bookman* essay on Stéphane Mallarmé he gave his readers a lucid account of literary impressionism in France. Eleven years later he gave them a reliable account of the French "Parnassiens" (*Bookman*, April 1909) and a remarkably vivid account of the Pre-Raphaelites in "Swinburne and the Swinburnians" (*Bookman*, June 1909). Nor did he fail to notice developments in the more popular literary forms. In two 1907 essays in his series for *Munsey's Magazine* titled "Intimate Talks About Books That Are Worthwhile" he delivered a learned assessment of Edgar Allan Poe's and Emile Gaboriau's contributions to the detective story. In keeping with his interest in this genre, he argued in the *Independent* (21 November 1901) that Arthur Conan Doyle must be considered a major writer. Finally, Peck was not oblivious of how contemporary literature reflected current social developments. In a remarkable essay on Richard Harding Davis (*Bookman*, August 1897) he argued that this author's popularity could be accounted for by the fact that he had learned his style on the modern newspaper and that he was "writing for the still nebulous and in-

Peck (far right) with James MacArthur and an unidentified woman

choate, but gradually uniting fragments of what will at some time crystallise into a well-defined social caste" which Peck frankly titled "the American aristocracy," a group he had brilliantly analyzed in *Cosmopolitan* in October 1898.

As a historian of American literature Peck is much less interesting. He was, of course, hampered by his age's unawareness of Herman Melville and Emily Dickinson. But even when this is taken into account his description of America's literary past is threadbare. He demonstrates little more than commonplace appreciation of the achievements of Walt Whitman, Henry David Thoreau, Ralph Waldo Emerson, and Nathaniel Hawthorne. Instead he devotes his most thorough analyses to writers whom he himself judges as minor: Bayard Taylor, Nathaniel Willis, Thomas Bailey Aldrich, and Edmund Clarence Stedman.

His essay in *Munsey's Magazine* titled "Our American Laureate" (February 1907) explains much about Peck's inability to come to terms with the great American writers of the mid nineteenth century. He begins the essay by pointing out the European stereotype of the American as "a loud-mouthed braggart, worshipping bigness, glorifying materialism, and caring nothing for what

belongs to the spirit and the soul." Peck argues that in actuality, however, Americans are marked by "innate gentility" which reveres the ideal, particularly in women and children. This is the reason that Henry Wadsworth Longfellow is America's most popular poet and must be considered its laureate. While Peck acknowledges that Whitman is undoubtedly a poet of great power, his is the voice that has given credence to the European stereotype of the American. Quoting Sidney Lanier, he characterizes Whitman as " 'poetry's butcher,' offering as food 'huge raw collops cut from the rump of poetry,' arguing that because a Western prairie is wide, therefore debauchery is admirable, and because the Mississippi is long, therefore every American is god." Longfellow's poetry, in contrast, not only has "the power to stir the blood" but also points "always upward to a noble and inspiring ideal of human life—of a life that is more than the life of the flesh, since it means strenuous effort and high endeavor toward truth and righteousness and justice." In other words, Peck applies a standard of gentility to American literature which he would have condemned in discussions of European writers. Perhaps it is this standard which also let him publish a ridiculous essay on how England must soon select its poet laureate in order to be ready to stem the yellow peril evident in Japan's new military might (*Bookman*, December 1895), or to write an equally foolish review of Charlotte Perkins Stetson ("The Cook-Stove in Poetry," *Bookman*, September 1898) in which he condemns the poet's feminism, arguing that being a good housewife is more valuable than "gadding around the town to visit Browning clubs and University Extension lectures, or . . . yawping at a woman's suffrage meeting."

However, it must be noted that Peck had a strikingly comprehensive view of more recent American literature. Not only did he follow the careers of Howells, James, Wharton, Stephen Crane, and Norris closely, but he seemed to have been familiar with almost every writer who is studied today in courses on American realism and naturalism. Thus, in a retrospective essay on the past fifteen years of the *Bookman* ("Then and Now," February 1910), he discussed not only the importance of American regionalism but also provided a literary map of the United States that included writers like Kate Chopin, Sarah Orne Jewett, and Edward Eggleston. In this essay and others he also discussed such writers as Jack London, Hamlin Garland, Booker T. Washington, Paul Laurence Dunbar, and Harold Frederic, whose *The Damnation of Theron Ware* (1896) he admired immensely. In addition, in the June 1910 *Bookman* he wrote a sensitive and appreciative essay, "Mark Twain a Century Hence," in which he predicted that a significant number of Twain's works would endure as classics of American literature.

As a brief survey of Peck's critical writings would indicate, he played an important role in America's cultural history. During a time of intense materialism he taught Americans to appreciate the importance of contemporary literature; during a time of extreme nationalism he taught them to look beyond their own borders for significant cultural developments. Most important, he was one of a handful of critics who articulated clearly the means and ends of literary realism and naturalism, thereby making coherent the vast cultural shift which carried the Western world from romanticism to modernism.

References:
Thomas Beer, *The Mauve Decade: American Life at the End of the Nineteenth Century* (New York: Knopf, 1937), pp. 185-199;

George S. Hellman, "Men of Letters at Columbia," *Critic*, 43 (October 1903): 316-327;

Walter Guest Kellog, "Harry Thurston Peck," *American Mercury*, 30 (September 1933): 83-88.

Papers:
The most extensive collection of Harry Thurston Peck's letters, manuscripts, and miscellaneous documents is located at the Butler Library, Columbia University.

Bliss Perry

(25 November 1860-13 February 1954)

Myron Simon
University of California, Irvine

BOOKS: *The Broughton House* (New York: Scribners, 1890);

Salem Kittredge and Other Stories (New York: Scribners, 1894);

The Plated City (New York: Scribners, 1895);

The Powers at Play (New York: Scribners, 1899);

A Study of Prose Fiction (Boston: Houghton, Mifflin, 1902);

The Amateur Spirit (Boston & New York: Houghton, Mifflin, 1904);

Walt Whitman: His Life and Work (Boston & New York: Houghton, Mifflin, 1906; London: Constable, 1906);

John Greenleaf Whittier: A Sketch of His Life (Boston & New York: Houghton, Mifflin, 1907);

Park-Street Papers (Boston & New York: Houghton Mifflin, 1908);

The American Mind (Boston & New York: Houghton Mifflin, 1912; London: Constable, 1913);

Thomas Carlyle: How to Know Him (Indianapolis: Bobbs-Merrill, 1915);

Fishing with a Worm (Boston & New York: Houghton Mifflin, 1916);

The American Spirit in Literature (New Haven: Yale University Press, 1918);

A Study of Poetry (Boston & New York: Houghton Mifflin, 1920; London: Constable, 1921);

Life and Letters of Henry Lee Higginson (Boston: Atlantic Monthly Press, 1921);

The Praise of Folly and Other Papers (Boston & New York: Houghton Mifflin, 1923);

Pools and Ripples: Fishing Essays (Boston: Little, Brown, 1927);

Emerson Today (Princeton: Princeton University Press, 1931);

Richard Henry Dana, 1851-1931 (Boston & New York: Houghton Mifflin, 1933);

And Gladly Teach: Reminiscences (Boston & New York: Houghton Mifflin, 1935).

OTHER: *Sir Walter Scott's Woodstock*, edited, with an introduction and notes, by Perry (New York & London: Longmans, Green, 1895);

Selections from Edmund Burke, edited, with an introduction and notes, by Perry (New York: Holt, 1896);

Scott's Ivanhoe, edited, with an introduction and notes, by Perry (New York: Longmans, Green, 1897);

Daniel Webster, *Representative Speeches*, edited by Perry (New York: Doubleday & McClure, 1898);

The Heart of Emerson's Journals, edited by Perry (Boston & New York: Houghton Mifflin, 1926);

Selections from the Prose Works of Ralph Waldo Emerson, edited, with an introduction and notes, by Perry (Boston & New York: Houghton Mifflin, 1926);

John Galsworthy, *The Patrician*, edited, with an introduction, by Perry (New York: Scribners, 1926);

Izaak Walton, *The Complete Angler; Or, The Contemplative Man's Recreation*, introduction by Perry (Boston: Goodspeed, 1928);

Edwin Arlington Robinson, *Poems*, edited, with a preface, by Perry (New York: Macmillan, 1931);

The Heart of Emerson's Essays, edited, with an introduction and notes, by Perry (Boston & New York: Houghton Mifflin, 1933).

Bliss Perry was a much admired teacher of oratory and composition at Williams College and of literature at Princeton and Harvard Universities. In his thirties he also gained some renown as a writer of fiction. During the next decade he gained further recognition and substantial influence as editor of the *Atlantic Monthly* and principal literary adviser to the Houghton, Mifflin publishing house. He was a polite critic whose graceful essays on literature and nature were gathered into several volumes, and most of his decorously composed books, both fiction and nonfiction, reached a wide audience. Throughout his career he was in demand as a public lecturer. Together with Henry Van Dyke and Hamilton Wright Mabie, Perry represented the last glow of New England's Indian summer, the continuance into the early twentieth century of what George Santayana disapprovingly termed the Genteel Tradition. At a time when many new American writers had become alienated from New England's literary and moral legacy, Perry warmly affirmed it.

He was born on 25 November 1860 in Williamstown, Massachusetts, the seat of Williams College. His paternal forebears were artisans who had emigrated from London in 1666. By the early eighteenth century the Perrys had turned to farming; and by the first half of the next century the family had produced several Harvard graduates and a college professor. Perry's father, Arthur Latham Perry, was raised in rural poverty owing to the premature death of his father, a Congregational minister. Yet, by doing farm work, he managed to pay for his academy education; and, attracted by Mark Hopkins's reputation as a teacher, he journeyed from New Hampshire to Williams. There he so favorably impressed Hopkins that a year after his graduation he was in-

vited to return to Williams as professor of history and economics. Three years later, in 1856, he married Mary Smedley, whose ancestors had been among the first settlers of Williamstown and whose father was both a physician and a farmer. It was not unusual at the time that a scholar should farm or that a farmer should be learned. As Van Wyck Brooks notes in *New England; Indian Summer, 1865-1915* (1940), the pursuit of culture by rustic as well as urban Yankees was deeply rooted in the New England past and persisted into the last half of the nineteenth century: "The day had not yet passed when country parsons tutored bright farmers' boys in Greek, while the neophyte paid for his tutoring by doing the chores. . . . No doubt, there were other boys like Bliss Perry's father, who left his Latin grammar at the end of a furrow, after glancing at the declensions and conjugations, repeating them aloud as he ploughed the furrow down and back, then turning the page and ploughing with another lesson." Situated "in a quiet country lane with no shops and only a dozen very simple houses," the house in which Bliss Perry was reared nevertheless had lots of books. Although he was assigned the customary chores of a country boy and participated fully in outdoor recreations, Perry read widely and studied assiduously. Since his family and regional traditions linked farming and learning, practical matters and high thinking, the active life and the reflective life, Perry seems never to have felt any need during his long academic and intellectual career to distance himself from his rural origins. Throughout the years of his membership in the lofty cultural circles of Princeton, Boston, and Cambridge, he remained faithful to the pristine virtues and decent manners of the older New England villages.

Surrounded by the natural beauty of the northern Berkshires, Williamstown afforded Perry a youth rich in opportunities for camping, hunting, fishing, bird-watching, and butterfly collecting. And, given the solidly Congregational convictions of his own and most of the other faculty families, he "never saw wine served at table, nor entered a theatre nor heard a symphony concert" until he was past twenty-one. After preparing for college at the Greylock Institute in South Williamstown, Perry emulated his father by attending Williams and becoming a member of its faculty. Until he left Williamstown in 1886 for two years of graduate study in Germany, Perry lived an essentially Arcadian life in which honesty, fair-mindedness, and decency were the rules of behavior; and he continued to observe those rules in the far more sophisticated circles within which he moved after departing from Williamstown. Consequently, his moral and literary values remained firmly retrospective. He much preferred Ralph Waldo Emerson and Nathaniel Hawthorne to the newer American writers as he preferred the older New England towns to those altered by industrialization and immigration. So Perry manifestly belongs with the line of genteel authors and critics–from Bayard Taylor, Edmund Clarence Stedman, and Thomas Bailey Aldrich to Richard Watson Gilder, Mabie, and Van Dyke–who stood for ethical ideals, refined manners, and traditional literary forms. Like them, Perry perceived his role to be–in historian Henry F. May's phrase–that of a "custodian of culture." It must be added, however, that Perry's tolerance and objectivity combined to make him perhaps the most liberal voice of the Genteel Tradition.

Since the classical curriculum was still in force during Perry's undergraduate days at Williams, he was well drilled in Latin, Greek, and mathematics; but he received little education in English other than what was to be found in the superficial manuals of the period. He was, however, well trained in rhetoric and oratory and became a skillful writer and deliverer of speeches and a successful debater. He worked with his customary seriousness at the vocal exercises and the skills of breathing and intonation that enabled him to become an exceptionally proficient speaker. This attainment proved to be a decisive influence upon the course of Perry's life, for by winning the prizes in elocution and extemporaneous speech at his graduation in 1881 he became an obvious choice for the instructorship in rhetoric and public speaking that had fortuitously opened at the end of that academic year. Thus began a brilliant teaching career that, with interruptions for study and lecturing abroad and for editing the *Atlantic Monthly,* extended to his retirement from Harvard in 1930.

That first year of teaching at Williams allowed Perry four months of advanced study in elocution under Prof. J. W. Churchill of Andover Seminary, then famous throughout New England for his public readings of Charles Dickens and Mark Twain. For the next four years Perry energetically taught composition and coached oratory and debate; but he devoted his nights to the study of French and German, to reading his way through Chaucer, Shakespeare and other Elizabethan dramatists, and to beginning the study of

Perry in 1899, the year he became editor of the Atlantic Monthly *(photograph by Bachrach)*

Anglo-Saxon from the few texts then available. Although there was no one at Williams who could help him to acquire an education in early English literature and the history of the English language, Perry independently set his course toward a career in English philological scholarship. His arduous program of self-study was rewarded when, in the spring of 1886, he was promoted to a professorship and given two years' leave of absence for graduate study. Since Germany was then the center of advanced scholarship in English, Perry enrolled at the University of Berlin–where he studied Germanic linguistics under Julius Zupitza–and, subsequently, at the University of Strasbourg–where he studied *Beowulf,* the Middle English romances, English prosody, Chaucer, and Shakespeare with Bernhard ten Brink.

Perry performed his philological labors diligently, but he decided against writing the dissertation (on the textual origins of *The Taming of the Shrew*) and taking the oral examination that would have earned him Strasbourg's Ph.D. degree. The obvious explanation of Perry's decision is that the doctorate was not yet a requirement for promotion in American colleges; and, in any event, Perry had already been promoted to a professorship at the college where he expected to remain. Moreover, two years of linguistic investigation and textual criticism had persuaded him that his more genuine interest lay in the aesthetic part of literary study. And, relatedly, the impulse to become a writer of fiction had quickened during his European *Wanderjahre*. He had published a few stories before going abroad, but in the decade following his return he produced two novels and two collections of short stories.

Married upon his return in the summer of 1888 to Annie L. Bliss, daughter of the old friends of his parents after whom he had been named, Perry resumed his teaching duties at Williams. It was soon apparent, however, that he was no longer content to confine his teaching to composition and public speaking. Over the objections of his classical colleagues, he introduced a required course in Anglo-Saxon prose and Chaucer; and he thereby became one of the pioneers in the establishment of English as a discipline. And, stirred increasingly by his own experience as a writer, he made his old course in descriptive writing more imaginative by building into it the realistic methods of contemporary writers like Gustave Flaubert, Rudyard Kipling, and Robert Louis Stevenson. After his stories and essays began to find their way into print in such magazines as *Scribner's* and the *Atlantic Monthly*, Perry decided to try his hand at a novel. In 1890 Scribners published *The Broughton House*, by the standards of its time an honest account of marital conflict that wavers in confronting the possibility of an adulterous relationship and offers instead the pointless sentimentality of an abandoned wife's suicide. By the age of thirty the obscure Williams elocution coach had acquired a professorship, a European education, and the beginnings of a literary reputation. In the spring of 1893 Perry accepted the chair of "oratory and aesthetic criticism" at Princeton, and in that more cosmopolitan setting he soon found wider opportunities than had been afforded in backwater Williamstown.

At Princeton, Perry offered freshmen a survey of English literature, lectured to seniors on both poetics and prose fiction, and provided graduate seminars on Robert Browning and on the influence of the French Revolution upon English poetry. Perry noted in his autobiography, *And Gladly Teach: Reminiscences* (1935), that under the broad rubric of "aesthetic criticism" he was free to teach virtually any literary topic in which he was interested. Although his New England conscience kept him fully involved in his professorial duties, his desire to write fiction was no less imperative throughout the 1890s. His first volume of stories, *Salem Kittredge and Other Stories*, was published by Scribners in 1894, and the next year Scribners published his second novel, *The Plated City*. Like Perry's first novel, *The Plated City* dealt with a controversial subject, the color line in the North. Despite the distastefulness of this subject to the conventional audience for fiction in 1895, he managed to achieve a good reception for the novel by his characteristic "mingling of romance and realism, of sentiment and irony." In his fiction as in his criticism Perry displayed a blend of open-mindedness and reticence, of honesty and decorum, so that if he never broke free of the old dispensations, neither was he ever an entrenched, illiberal enemy of new ideas. Clearly at home in the Genteel Tradition, his modesty, vigor, and reasonableness made him an attractive figure to both unbending reactionaries like Owen Wister and Henry Van Dyke and the more democratic upholders of cultural uplift like William Dean Howells and Woodrow Wilson. Van Dyke and Wilson were his colleagues at Princeton, and with Philadelphia and New York close at hand Perry greatly enlarged his contact with authors and editors. He made the acquaintance of Mark Twain, George Washington Cable, Frank R. Stockton, Weir Mitchell, Richard Henry Stoddard, and Edmund Clarence Stedman. He came to know the gray eminences of the powerful monthly magazines: E. L. Burlingame of *Scribner's*, Richard Watson Gilder of the *Century*, and Henry M. Alden of *Harper's*. As Perry recalled, "The contact with authors and publishers during those years at Princeton was stimulating to a young fellow after the relative isolation of Williamstown."

The publication in 1899 of Perry's second collection of stories, *The Powers at Play*, represented the high-water mark as well as the conclusion of his career as a writer of fiction, for the stories that comprised this volume had appeared earlier in the most widely read and prestigious monthlies of this time: *Scribner's*, *Harper's*, the *Century*, and *McClure's*. The volume's principal theme, as in Perry's other works of fiction, was the contrast between the older rural New England with its predominantly Yankee stock and the region's increasingly industrialized, ethnically mixed population centers. Written very near the time that May has

Perry in 1933

identified as marking the "end of American innocence," Perry's stories both eulogized and elegized the Yankee virtues of conscience, candor, and duty. As he wrote, the village culture that had long housed and transmitted these virtues was vanishing. It is not clear why the flow of Perry's fiction stopped so abruptly in 1899, but from this time editing and critical writing–rather than fiction–filled the hours he could spare from his primary commitment to teaching. Beginning with schoolroom editions of Sir Walter Scott and

Edmund Burke, Perry had by 1897 undertaken the editing of an eighteen-volume set of *Little Masterpieces* for the house of Doubleday and McClure. This series, designed to provide selections from canonical English and American writers in an inexpensive format, was not a profit-making venture, despite the fact that nearly a million copies were sold within the first few years. It represented instead Perry's desire to improve "the standard of literary taste in the United States by placing some of the best work of the greatest writers within reach of everybody."

Loyal to New England's literary and cultural heritage and eager to bring that heritage to a rapidly expanding, increasingly heterogeneous nation, Perry was a suitable choice when the editorship of the *Atlantic Monthly* fell vacant in the summer of 1899. Despite the steady conviction that teaching was his primary vocation, he accepted the offer to succeed Walter Hines Page, who had suddenly resigned. By that time Perry had been elevated to the Holmes Professorship of English and Belles Lettres and had become the director of graduate studies in English at Princeton. Reluctant to cut his academic ties, he continued to teach during the first year of his editorship and commuted weekly between Princeton and Boston. But by the autumn of 1900 he had fully committed himself to the *Atlantic Monthly* and taken up residence in what he significantly referred to as "old" Cambridge, a place where "business" was not yet the ruling passion, where there still existed "among its old American families the sense of continuity," a place "like an island in the stream of new and alien races swarming into Greater Boston." His acceptance in 1903 into Boston's Saturday Club (the famous Brahmin society founded in 1856 whose members included Ralph Waldo Emerson, Henry Wadsworth Longfellow, James Russell Lowell, Oliver Wendell Holmes, Nathaniel Hawthorne, and John Greenleaf Whittier) was the indubitable sign that he had been received into Boston's highest cultural circle.

Lowell, the founding editor of the *Atlantic Monthly*, had given the magazine a decidedly social and political orientation; but his successor, James T. Fields, narrowed its scope by making it into an organ of the Boston area's literati. Turning a magazine of New England literature into one that was more comprehensively American was the achievement of the next editor, William Dean Howells. Thomas Bailey Aldrich and Horace Scudder sought to preserve the reputation of the *Atlantic* as the nation's premier literary monthly; but, as its reputation flourished, its circulation dropped to the alarmingly low figure of seven thousand. Like such other "quality" monthlies as the *Century* and *Scribner's*, the *Atlantic* was challenged in the 1890s by a flood of new, highly successful "ten-cent" magazines like *McClure's*, which placed their chief emphasis upon timely and controversial articles on government, public affairs, and commerce. The *Century* and *Scribner's* had maintained circulation by broadening their scope accordingly, but it was not until Page be-

came Scudder's assistant in 1896 and succeeded him in 1898 that the *Atlantic* followed suit. Under Page, the *Atlantic* shocked its small but faithful readership by turning to political controversy, social reforms, and the exposure of corruption in government. Page had been hired to revive the *Atlantic,* and he surely did so; but only a year into the new editorial policy, he had accepted a loftier position in the publishing world and returned to New York. It was at this critical juncture in the history of the *Atlantic* that Perry became its seventh editor.

An admirer of the magazine's literary ancestry but also genuinely concerned about social issues and essentially liberal in his individualism, pacifism, and antibusiness outlook, Perry possessed the necessary balance to move the magazine firmly along its new course while yet sustaining its dedication to traditional forms of literary excellence. His modesty and tact, practicality, and keen awareness of audience also helped to ensure his moderately successful middle course between the policies of Scudder and Page. Conscious of having undertaken an important responsibility, he was determined to see it through; and—despite the offer of an attractive Harvard professorship in 1905—he served the *Atlantic* for a full decade, until the summer of 1909. The title of Perry's *Park-Street Papers* (1908) refers to the address of the *Atlantic* from the date of its acquisition by the Houghton, Mifflin Company in 1880 to the last year of his editorial tenure when its owner—and, subsequently, its editor—had become Ellery Sedgwick, who more single-mindedly than Perry moved the *Atlantic* into modern times. *Park-Street Papers* accurately captures the spirit of Perry's editorship in its selection from the annual "Toastmaster" essays he composed for subscribers and included in each January number, together with his commemorative essays on Hawthorne, Longfellow, Aldrich, Whittier, and the almost forgotten "originator" of the *Atlantic,* Francis H. Underwood, who, as literary advisor to the magazine's founder, Moses Dresser Phillips, had developed the initial idea for the journal. Perry's deepest editorial loyalty was to the magazine's identification with moral idealism and high literary distinction, and he endeavored to be worthy of that inheritance as he tried to stay abreast of contemporary values and new writing. In commemorating literary figures of New England's flowering and Indian summer, Perry was aware that he was presenting their achievements to modern readers "who could not be expected to share fully" his own respect and enthusiasm for them. Nevertheless, he persisted in the tasks of preserving and transmitting what he knew to be of value in the past.

Perry's editorial influence expanded in 1902 when, after the death of Horace Scudder, he became the senior literary adviser at Houghton, Mifflin. What Scudder had impressed upon him was "the opportunity for public service afforded by the combined offices of editor of the *Atlantic* and literary adviser to a publishing house which was then specializing in American literature and educational textbooks." He assumed the general editorship of both the Cambridge Poets editions (for which he promptly commissioned the William Allan Neilson *Shakespeare* and the F. N. Robinson *Chaucer*) and the Riverside Literature series. Given his literary orientation, he immediately undertook the considerable task of persuading the firm to issue an edited but arguably complete fourteen-volume text of Henry David Thoreau's journals as well as the ten volumes of Emerson's journals. Perry's selections from this edition, *The Heart of Emerson's Journals* (1926), and his two volumes of selections from Emerson's essays (1926, 1933) did much to keep Emerson in public view during the 1920s and 1930s. Perry's *John Greenleaf Whittier* (1907), a brief life with selections from the poems, was similarly useful. Predictably, Perry was not rigidly conservative in his recommendations, for if he urged the inclusion of Richard Watson Gilder's genteel verses in the prestigious Fireside Poets series, he also finally voted in favor of the Houghton, Mifflin publication of Edwin Arlington Robinson's *Captain Craig* (1902) despite his reservations about the obscurity and eccentricity of Robinson's poetry.

During his decade with the *Atlantic* and period of closest association with Houghton, Mifflin, Perry transformed himself from a fiction writer into a literary critic. It must be added, however, that in the graceful, well-paced, eminently readable style of the critic may be found the residual skills of the public speaker and the novelist. It is also noteworthy that, as a critic, Perry often displays the merits of his wide reading, tolerance, and objectivity–qualities that elevate the worth of his books well above that of works by Mabie and Van Dyke, the genteel critics with whom he is commonly grouped. The outgrowth of his lectures, Perry's first critical book, *A Study of Prose Fiction*, was published in 1902 and many times reprinted. It did much to establish his reputation as a critic because it was perhaps the most widely consulted

study of the novel before Percy Lubbock's *The Craft of Fiction* (1921). Beyond its beginnings in Princeton lecture rooms, *A Study of Prose Fiction* derives much of its alertness to the emerging forms of narrative art from Perry's experience as both a fiction writer and magazine editor of fiction. Although he judges no American writer the equal of James Fenimore Cooper, Hawthorne, and Edgar Allan Poe and places Mark Twain and Henry James in the second rank with Bret Harte and Frank R. Stockton, he also makes distinctions that indicate the intelligence of his fundamentally conservative position: "There are sensitive, highly cultivated people who cannot read books like *Anna Karenina* or *Madame Bovary*, but it is idle to deny that these great books are realistic in method and that they are masterpieces of art." By the same token, although Perry continued to defend the doctrine of poetic justice as practiced by the "greatest masters" of the art of fiction, he could find Thomas Hardy's *Tess of the d'Urbervilles* (1891) "an admirable expression of a poignant, thoughtful, yet thoroughly pagan interpretation of life."

Perry faithfully discharged what he understood to be the critic's role as custodian of the moral standards to which society in its own interests holds the artist accountable. However, he also demonstrated the critical capacity to perceive in the artist's personal vision his justification for experiment and innovation; and he was, accordingly, able to write the first really penetrating study of Walt Whitman. When Whitman's old friend John Burroughs abandoned the biography he had long promised to write for Houghton, Mifflin, Perry was asked to undertake it. Since Burroughs turned over to him the Whitman materials he had collected, as did many others who had been associated with Whitman, Perry was able to make use of many firsthand impressions and much previously untouched manuscript material. He helped to establish the facts of Whitman's ancestry and early life, and he did so objectively without resorting to fanciful speculations. He neither attacked nor defended Whitman but confined himself to the evidence and such conclusions as could be reasonably inferred. It is, indeed, a measure of the book's balance and objectivity that when *Walt Whitman: His Life and Work* was published in 1906 genteel readers were offended by Perry's positive estimate of Whitman while Horace Traubel and other Whitman enthusiasts thought Perry too critical. Forty years later Gay Wilson Allen called the book the first scholarly bi-

Portrait of Perry by Charles Hopkinson

ography of Whitman and "still one of the best." Allen observes that "Perry helped greatly to bring about a more intelligent attitude toward both the man and his work." He sympathetically separated the legendary Whitman from the actuality, on the one hand, and was among the first to note the significance of parallelism in Whitman's style, on the other. Perry contributed to the acceptance of *Leaves of Grass* by comparing it to the experiments of such international figures as Claude Monet, Auguste Rodin, and Richard Strauss; and he made it seem a less shocking work by noting its correspondences with Oriental poetry and the Bible.

In 1903 the *Atlantic* editor and recent author of *A Study of Prose Fiction* met President Charles W. Eliot of Harvard at the Saturday Club and began a friendship with this liberal champion of educational reform. By 1904 Eliot had persuaded Perry to teach Barrett Wendell's course in the English neoclassical writers while Wendell was abroad. A year later Eliot offered a professorship that Perry felt obliged to decline because of his commitments to the *Atlantic* and his Whitman biography. But in the spring of 1906 Perry accepted a professorship of English lit-

erature, effective the following February, with the understanding that he would teach only half-time until he concluded his editorship in the summer of 1909. He spent that first year of full-time teaching since the 1898-1899 year at Princeton not in Cambridge, however, but in France as the Harvard exchange professor at the Sorbonne and other universities. The function of the exchange lectureship was to explain American civilization to a wide range of French audiences. These lectures were the first expression of Perry's desire—unfulfilled, as it turned out—to write a comprehensive history of American literature. Reworked upon his return to Cambridge in the summer of 1910, the lectures were subsequently repeated in Berkeley, Boston, and elsewhere and published as *The American Mind* in 1912.

In 1915 Perry published *Thomas Carlyle: How to Know Him*, a simply written introduction for the general reader, which—like Perry's later *Emerson Today* (1931)—reflected both a strong affinity for his subject and the desire to demonstrate its lasting relevance. But Perry's most ambitious project during the first half of his Harvard career was the study of American literature in its cultural setting that began with the lectures collected in *The American Mind* and continued for several years beyond the 1918 publication of *The American Spirit in Literature*. Owing possibly to the origins of the former in lectures to foreign audiences and to the composition of the latter during wartime, both books are uncritically optimistic in their view of the American achievement. In *The American Mind,* for example, Perry suggests that the prevailing sentimentality and avoidance of sexuality in American literature represent an ingrained national idealism more valuable "than a few masterpieces more or less." Although he judiciously eschewed the blatantly moralistic and patriotic style of orthodox critics like Henry Van Dyke and Stuart P. Sherman, both books fell safely within the Genteel Tradition.

It is true that, while stressing the importance of English influence upon the American colonies and nation, Perry recognized that a distinctively American point of view had existed since colonial times. Acknowledging the richness of Anglo-American literary relations, he perceived as well the sheer Americanness of Emerson, Hawthorne, Poe, and Whitman. But in *The American Spirit in Literature,* published three years after Van Wyck Brooks's *America's Coming-of-Age* (1915) had announced the death of the Genteel Tradition and the release of powerful new creative energies, Perry was silent about the literary revolt that was already under way. He ignored Theodore Dreiser and Stephen Crane, dismissed Jack London and Frank Norris as inferior to John Muir in their accounts of the American West, and asserted that American fiction seemed only "to be marking time and not to be getting noticeably forward." He praised the poetry of Gilder, Aldrich, and Stedman; but he failed to notice Robinson, Carl Sandburg, and the launching of *Poetry: A Magazine of Verse*. It is clear that as the elements of experiment and social protest in the new literature become more prominent Perry's conservatism hardened. He responded with frequent displeasure to the increasingly negative and despairing orientation of the modern writers. Or, more accurately, he turned away from them–since he was not inclined to take adversarial positions–toward the older writers who seemed to him worth preserving. As might have been expected, *The American Spirit in Literature* was savagely attacked by antigenteel critics like H. L. Mencken (*Smart Set*) and Lawrence Gilman (*North American Review*) who had little respect for either professors or custodians of American idealism.

Nevertheless, for the next three or four years Perry remained dedicated to writing what he hoped would be his magnum opus, a two-volume history of American literature for which he regarded as preparatory efforts the lectures published in 1912 and the concise *American Spirit in Literature* volume of 1918 that he contributed to the Yale Chronicles of America series. Indeed, Perry had contracted to finish the history by 1920, and he was just the sort of disciplined writer who had invariably adhered to schedule. But the deadline passed and the history was finally abandoned because he found the research for the earlier periods more difficult than he had anticipated, because he lost confidence in some of the generalizations so glibly fashioned for the lectures in France and the Yale Chronicles, and because he doubtless felt too much out of sympathy with his own times and with newly acclaimed writers like Sherwood Anderson and Ernest Hemingway to write the kind of history likely to be approved. In 1923 Perry addressed the New England Watch and Ward Society, Boston's Comstockian society for the suppression of "impure" literature, on the subject of "Pernicious Books," something the liberal young Princeton professor and *Atlantic* editor would have been less inclined to do.

In place of the history Perry published in 1920 for his students of poetry at Harvard a textbook whose title, *A Study of Poetry*, suggests that it was conceived as a companion volume to his highly successful study of the novel. Interestingly enough, as he turned away from the socially and ethically charged issues confronting the historian of American literature and focused more narrowly upon poetry itself, Perry's tolerance and objectivity were once again evident. While arguing the general superiority of traditional poetic themes and forms, Perry here understands the case for free verse and other types of experiment. He speaks of pitying the traditionalist unable to appreciate Robert Frost, Robinson, Edgar Lee Masters, and Sandburg, although he characteristically adds that he feels still more pity for the young rebel unable to enjoy "Lycidas" and the "Ode to Dejection." *A Study of Poetry* is a far more academic treatise than Perry's study of the novel, and it was less successful in both sales and influence. But, again, it reveals him at his best to be a conservative critic whose honesty and good sense keep him from the embittered resistance to modern writing that typified most of the critics assignable to the Genteel Tradition.

As his reluctance to leave Princeton and phased acceptance of the Harvard appointment both indicate, Perry seems always to have found his truest vocation in teaching. So it was undoubtedly a source of profound satisfaction to him that the twenty years at Harvard which brought his career to its close were the time of his greatest fame as a teacher. He often lectured to classes of six hundred or more students drawn by the extraordinary feeling for literature and elocutionary skill of this engagingly modest Yankee. In the Harvard English graduate program where philology would remain the dominant emphasis until the 1940s, Perry–like Irving Babbitt–offered a stimulating alternative for students whose interests were literary and humanistic. Not long after joining the Harvard faculty he introduced the first course in Emerson to be offered in an American college, and there was no writer he taught with greater pleasure and authority. Perry had discovered Emerson's essays when he was sixteen, and he remained a devout admirer of the man and his works for the rest of his life. It was, therefore, fitting that upon his retirement as Higginson Professor of English Literature in 1930 he was invited to deliver a series of lectures on Emerson. These lectures, published in 1931 as *Emerson Today*, stand as the climax of Perry's effort to resolidify Emerson's reputation–at a time when both popular and intellectual interest in him had waned–by confronting and countering the charges brought against him and by underscoring the bases of his enduring value as a moralist.

In retirement Perry quietly distanced himself from what he termed "the hurry and confusion of this twentieth century," its "sleek materialism," and its pessimism. The product, as M. A. DeWolfe Howe noted, of a "simple old New England," Perry had loved nature from his boyhood and his values were those of a Yankee stoic: honesty, self-discipline, and fortitude in the service of a common-sense idealism. From 1897 Perry had spent his summers in Greensboro, a village in the Green Mountains that he described as "the unspoiled essence of primitive Vermont." And upon retirement he made his permanent residence in the similarly unspoiled village of Exeter, New Hampshire, thereby returning to a rural society essentially unchanged from the one in which his father had been born. Estranged from his native Massachusetts by its industrial development, ethnic transformations, and venal politics and largely unresponsive to the national crises of the 1930s and 1940s, Perry deliberately chose to be obsolete and passed the remainder of his long life tranquilly in Exeter where he died, nearly forgotten, in 1954. To the end he preferred the old books–Emerson's *Essays, Walden, The Scarlet Letter, Moby-Dick,* and *Leaves of Grass*–to any of the new ones. And his fondness for older forms of behavior may be seen in the affectionate memoirs he wrote of fellow members of the Saturday Club and the American Academy of Arts and Letters like Henry James, John Burroughs, William Crary Brownell, Woodrow Wilson, Thomas Wentworth Higginson, Julia Ward Howe, William Vaughn Moody, Henry Lee Higginson, Henry P. Walcott, Moorfield Storey, and Richard Henry Dana III. In a sense Perry anticipated Van Wyck Brooks as the empathic chronicler of New England's flowering and Indian summer. But in Perry's case there had been no dramatic turnabout from censure to celebration of the American past. Unlike Brooks, Perry never deviated from the tradition.

Reference:

M. A. DeWolfe Howe, "Bliss Perry," in *The Saturday Club: A Century Completed, 1920-1956,* edited by Edward W. Forbes and John H. Finley, Jr. (Boston: Houghton Mifflin, 1958), pp. 131-136.

Papers:

The bulk of Perry's papers may be found in the Houghton Library of Harvard University. In the Bliss Perry file "Papers, 1892-1942," there are about six hundred items. Other Perry papers may be found in the file containing "Papers of Robert Grant," in the file containing "Unbound Correspondence of Houghton Mifflin Company, about 1850-1958," and in the file containing "Papers of M. A. Dewolfe Howe, 1876-1959." Other Bliss Perry papers may be found among the "Papers of William S. B. Braithwaite" in the University of Virginia Library.

Percival Pollard
(29 January 1869-17 December 1911)

University of Hamburg, Germany

BOOKS: *Cape of Storms: A Novel* (Chicago: Echo, 1895);

Dreams of To-Day (Chicago: Way & Williams, 1897);

The Kiss That Killed (New York: Town Topics, 1898);

The Imitator (St. Louis: Reedy, 1901);

Lingo Dan (Washington, D.C.: Neale, 1903);

Their Day in Court (New York & Washington, D.C.: Neale, 1909);

Masks and Minstrels of New Germany (Boston: Luce, 1911; London: Heinemann, 1911);

Vagabond Journeys: The Human Comedy At Home and Abroad (New York: Neale, 1911).

OTHER: *Figaro Fiction,* includes stories by Pollard (Chicago: Dailey, 1892);

Posters in Miniature, foreword by Pollard (New York: Russell, 1896; London: Lane, 1896);

In Memoriam, Oscar Wilde, essays by Ernest La Jeunesse, André Gide, and Franz Blei, translated, with an introduction, by Pollard (Greenwich, Conn.: Literary Collector Press, 1905); republished as *Recollections of Oscar Wilde* (Boston & London: Luce, 1906);

Oscar Wilde, *Intentions,* introduction by Pollard (New York: Brentano's, 1905).

Percival Pollard

Percival Pollard, associated with several turn-of-the-century periodicals, should be chiefly remembered as a literary critic of the aesthetic-impressionist school. In introducing foreign literature and art, especially the European fin de siècle and avant-garde, Pollard is second only to James Gibbons Huneker. He denounced commercial timidity in publishing and criticism, "discovered" and boosted Ambrose Bierce, and influenced H. L. Mencken. As a writer of short stories and a novel, Pollard gained little renown. With even less success, he tried play writing. He mainly contributed to little magazines; occasionally he was also an editor.

His father, Joseph Pollard, was British and his mother, Marie Pollard, German; he was born in Greifswald, in the Prussian province of Pomerania, and spent his early years in Newcastle, England, where his grandfather was a rich coal merchant. After his parents divorced, his father, a grain merchant, married another German, a former language teacher who saw to it that the eight-year-old boy intensified his German and learned French. Thus Pollard became fluent in three languages. He entered Eastbourne College in Sussex in September 1880.

In 1885, at sixteen, Pollard moved with his parents to the United States into the area of Austin, Texas, where the second Mrs. Pollard had relatives. Two years later the family settled in the small community of Washington, Iowa. This town was the model for the village of Lincolnville in Pollard's novel *Cape of Storms* (1895). After three years young Pollard moved to St. Joseph, Missouri, where he first worked as a railroad employee and then as a reporter for the *Saint Joseph Daily News.* After one year of service with that newspaper, in the spring of 1891 he left for Chicago, where he worked for several little magazines. He also placed his productions in better-known periodicals such as *Harper's Weekly, New England Magazine,* and *Reedy's Mirror.* In January 1893 he became the main literary critic for *Belford's Monthly Magazine,* writing under the impressionistic headings of "Glimpses" and (later) "Ramblings." At about this time he married Sarah Lindsey Myers. He also began a lifelong literary relationship with Ambrose Bierce. Earlier Walter Blackburn Harte, Pollard's friend, had started praising Bierce in *New England Magazine,* which he subedited, but it was Pollard who became Bierce's devoted champion.

In the spring of 1894 a new little magazine appeared, the *Chap-Book,* reminiscent in its title and content of the *Yellow Book.* Avant-garde in its first year, the *Chap-Book* quickly aged, but it gave rise to other modern little magazines, to which Pollard contributed as well. Generally, their idol was the dandy, their ideology art for art's sake, their tone decadent. After an abortive attempt to found a journal of literature and the arts, in May 1895 Pollard began the *Echo,* intending it as a vehicle for poster publication. Feeling the *Echo* might also fail, he moved it to New York early in 1896, only to relocate it quickly in Chicago, where it ultimately folded the next year.

An inheritance from his paternal grandmother gave Pollard financial independence. He became a press agent for the actor Richard Mansfield in the fall season of 1896. By December Pollard was in New York, where he contributed to *Town Topics* and the *Criterion.* His colleagues at the *Criterion* included Vance Thompson, James Huneker, and C. F. Nirdlinger. In March 1897 he officially joined the staff of *Town Topics,* which proved a lifelong association.

Pollard was divorced in the spring of 1899, and at the same time his relationship with the *Criterion* was terminated. As a consequence he lost many of his friends and colleagues. Walter Blackburn Harte died in 1899 as well. Pollard withdrew with his second wife to Saybrook, Connecticut. In March 1902 his father died, and

Caricature of Pollard

Pollard went abroad, first to England and then to Germany. He returned to the United States late in 1902 and bought a summer cottage in Saybrook in 1903 and a house in Milford, Connecticut, two years later. His life there was interrupted by longer journeys to Europe, which are reflected in his subsequent writings. One trip to Berlin in 1905 prompted Pollard, among other things, to translate three essays on Oscar Wilde from French and German and edit them as a small commemorative volume.

He began creative writing in the short-story genre and published more than fifty specimens in *Figaro* (of which he was, for a time, part owner) between 25 June 1891 and 21 December 1893. They border on literary hackwork but foreshadow his more uniform collection *Dreams of To-Day* (1897). He started writing a novel in 1894, *Cape of Storms,* but did not find a publisher and had it privately printed under the Echo imprint in 1895. Its main theme is the "new woman," although the male character's forgiveness of the young lady's relationship with another man introduces a new element to the social behavior of the time. Pollard's critical preoccupations, such as cosmopolitanism, elitism, and the realism vs. romance issue, accentuate this fiction. The name of one minor character, the novelist Wreath, contains an overt allusion to Hamlin Garland. The male protagonist, a draftsman named Richard Lancaster, condemns Wreath outright, calling him "a charlatan" and "a trumpeter of theories," and laughingly satirizes his muckraking. The novel's immediate reception was lukewarm, and this failure probably heightened Pollard's contempt for the novel as an art form. In particular he attacked "the so-called novel with a purpose." "The purpose," he reasoned, "so seldom permits of art!"

Pollard next edited a book of posters from France, England, Germany, and America, including specimens from the *Echo* and the *Chap-Book* drawn by Will H. Bradley. Other artists represented were Jules Chéret, C. D. Gibson, Eugene Grasset, T. T. Heine, Phil May, Edward Penfield (who also provided an introduction), and Henri de Toulouse-Lautrec.

Pollard's three critical books are the sum of his journalistic writings, the reworking of older articles and new material gleaned from his travels. *Their Day in Court* (1909) is Pollard's main critical work and consists of three parts: "Women, Womanists and Manners"; "Men and Manners"; and "Criticism." The basic structure of this book might be called a rearranged dialectic, the antithesis coming first, then the thesis, and lastly the synthesis; however, the chain of argumentation is not logical but associative.

Pollard describes his approach as a "critical excursion" and his observations as "my personal impressions." He disapproves of the "impersonal attitude" and opts instead for an all-embracing individualism. The central theme of *Their Day in Court* is "the Case of American Letters and its Causes," that is, the supposedly poor state of American literature and criticism. Pollard's methods of impressionism and subjectivism seem insufficient to his purpose; a proper diagnosis of the problem and more effective remedy would demand a more precise investigation than he is prepared to undertake. Pollard affirms aestheticism and condemns materialism: "Art for art's sake may be an absurd shibboleth; yet it is not so damnable as art for dollar's sake." Pollard proclaimed a declaration of independence from the dollar. Principally, for him the end of criticism was tri-

une: selection, protection, and correction. Pollard advocated literary Darwinism: "It is not the survival of the fittest, but the survival of the average that we should dread."

The main thrust of part 1 is directed against the mincing style of female writers and male feminists. Pollard's enemies are "the ladies and the ladies-men" alike; he mocks: "American art is essentially feminine." As for style, it is notable in its absence.

Part 2 is the "male" counterpart of part 1; the "Men-and-Manners" topic harks back to the gentlemanly ideal which Pollard first encountered during his British college education. Part 2 considers a wider range of literature than part 1. A host of American writers are compared to English authors and briefly contrasted with French, German, and other European men of letters. Pollard generally classifies English literature one category higher: "The average second-rate novelist in England is about as good a workman as our American first-raters." Chapter 7 in part 2 consists of Pollard's exaggerated praise of Ambrose Bierce. Pollard clearly overdrew his critical account when he said of Bierce's story collection *In the Midst of Life* (1892): "No other American book written in the last fifty years will survive so long. Upon that I stake my own critical reputation."

In part 1 Pollard had deplored the lack of good critics in America. In part 3 he redefines criticism as a subjective act of appreciation according to standards of personal judgment and genuine understanding: "Criticism at its best, I will ever maintain, is nothing but the honest expression of personal impressions; it can have worth only when the personality behind it has the taste, the artistic instinct and the stern righteousness which separate wheat from tares; can feel the spirit in other artists, and spot the shoddy and the mountebank." He claimed authority in dramatic criticism because of his personal involvement in the independent theater movement of the late 1890s. But *Their Day in Court* contains only sporadic references to drama and hardly any general dramatic principles. Pollard seems to be better informed on modern German drama than on the American stage, an impression confirmed by his next book, *Masks and Minstrels of New Germany* (1911). Of American theater critics only Huneker and Nirdlinger are acknowledged.

Ambrose Bierce called *Their Day in Court* "amusing, clever–and more." But Pollard's philippic against the stylistic deficiencies of others

Caricature by de Fornaro autographed by Pollard

came close to throwing stones from a glass house, and Van Wyck Brooks, in *The Confident Years: 1885-1915,* states that "Pollard, in *Their Day in Court,* wrote without any distinction himself."

Pollard's life ended suddenly. H. L. Mencken, who took part in his funeral, provides an authentic report on Pollard's death in a letter dated 20 December 1911 to Pollard's successor at *Town Topics.* After a wrong diagnosis, a brain abscess was finally discovered and operated upon by a leading American specialist. The help came much too late. Pollard died in Baltimore without ever regaining consciousness. The funeral was attended only by the second Mrs. Pollard, two of

her female friends, Mencken, Bierce, and Walter Neale, the publisher.

Vagabond Journeys: The Human Comedy At Home and Abroad appeared 19 December 1911, the day of Pollard's cremation, and Neale carried three copies to the funeral. The book was a timely summation of Pollard's career, the preface concluding with the invitation: "I would ask the reader to explore—myself." In *Vagabond Journeys* Pollard is at his best. He goes beyond literature and becomes a critic of culture and civilization. The reading public he had in mind was the "intelligent minority." His approach was again very personal and impressionistic.

Pollard's development is typical of a critic's growth. He began as a journalist and ventured into neighboring fields, but literary criticism came to constitute the essence of his work. Pollard's books mature. The comparatively heterogeneous *Their Day in Court* shows his stance and struggle as a literary critic in America. The highly diversified *Masks and Minstrels of New Germany* provides information on the actual situation of drama and poetry in that country. The balanced and well-structured *Vagabond Journeys* presents the complexity of his aesthetic world view. The judicial examination in the first book occasionally borders on pathos. The factual orientation of the second sometimes loses its focus to its variety. But the humanistic exploration of the third paints a sharper panorama with a rather harmonious succession of personal impressions. Throughout his career Pollard's observations grew wider in scope and deeper in subject matter, while his outlook and aspirations always remained cosmopolitan.

Pollard's relative importance can best be ascertained by a comparison with similar critics. He had an impact on Mencken, who acknowledged: "Next to Carter, I learned most from Percival Pollard—particularly the value, to a critic, of concentrating on a few men." Mencken was certainly fascinated by Pollard's aggressive manner. In his elitist assertions Pollard showed an affinity to Friedrich Nietzsche, though in comparing their treatment of Nietzsche, Mencken's critical superiority becomes obvious.

Thirty years after Pollard's death Henry Steele Commager dismissed him entirely with "nor is it clear that fourth-raters like Edgar Saltus and Percival Pollard deserve any attention whatever" ("Mind of an American Generation," *New York Herald Tribune Books,* 30 November 1941). However, Ambrose Bierce had previously

Pollard (far right), Ambrose Bierce (center), Herman Scheffauer (left), and others, probably at Pollard's summer home in Saybrook, Connecticut (courtesy of Stanford University Libraries)

applauded his promoter Pollard with satirical exuberance in a welter of forceful imaginative epithets: "that hardy and ingenious explorer, that sun-eyed searcher of the intense inane, that robber-baron invader of literature's loud oblivion, that painstaking chiffonnier of fame's eternal dumping ground, Mr. Percival Pollard of the *Echo*" (*San Francisco Examiner*, 20 July 1896).

As a mediator between Europe and America in the arts, Pollard ranks behind James Gibbons Huneker, whose scope is broader, insight deeper, and judgment better grounded. Huneker is less repetitive, more stringent and thorough. However, Pollard outdid Huneker in strongly rejecting the effeminate and the sentimental, which

his own creative writing nevertheless sometimes betrays. In addition, Pollard's struggle for an independent criticism, free from the pressure of the advertisers, deserves respect. Pollard was eventually accused of the same charge he had lodged against Huneker, namely a neglect of Americans. Louis Filler, in *Crusaders for American Liberalism* (1950), was angered by Pollard's disregard of the social muckrakers in American literature. On the other hand, Pollard's book *Their Day in Court* has been characterized by Douglas C. Stenerson as "the first in twentieth-century America devoted primarily to literary muckraking." In his autobiography, *Steeplejack* (1920), Huneker labeled Pollard "a capital critic"—an ambiguity. Huneker intended it ironically, as Pollard was not principal in his field. He played on Pollard's alliterative style and jabbed at Pollard's deadly critical assaults. With this tag Huneker also alluded to Pollard's condemnation of the pernicious role of capital in criticism and poked at Pollard's aspiration to be *the* cultural critic of the European and American capitals.

Percival Pollard is rarely read today, though there is a confident assertiveness in his criticism which is attractive. He resolutely promoted the new, especially as it originated in the cosmopolitan centers of Europe and paved the way for the American reception of the budding modernist movement. Pollard called for critics who had taste and good instinct and who could spot and condemn the phony, but he never defined what constituted good taste. In 1969 the Johnson Reprint Company honored Pollard's historical role with an edition of *Their Day in Court,* his most representative book. But any current interest in Pollard is merely academic. Some of his critical views are simply outdated (for example, his aristocratic and manly pretensions) as they are based on passé social and moral conditions. *Masks and Minstrels of New Germany* had no lasting positive reception, partly because its pro-German attitude was ill timed in relation to World War I. Pollard's best book, *Vagabond Journeys,* mirrors his life as a cosmopolitan litterateur and benefits from an observant eye as well as an analytical and reflective mind combined with a charming sense of humor. Many of his views have largely lost their relevancy, but in some of his cultural sketches (for example, in "Paris As It Passes," "Berlin: Art Appetite Compared With Boston," or "London: A Prizefight by Whitechapel Rules") he captured the spirit and atmosphere of his age.

References:

"A Critic Too Far Ahead of His Time," *Current Literature,* 52 (March 1912): 339-340;

James Gibbons Huneker, *Letters of James Gibbons Huneker,* edited by Josephine Huneker (New York: Scribners, 1922), pp. 209-213;

George N. Kummer, "Percival Pollard: Precursor of the 'Twenties,'" Ph.D. dissertation, New York University, 1946;

Andy Logan, "That Was New York: Town Topics I & II," *New Yorker,* 41 (14 August 1965): 37-91; (21 August 1965): 41-98;

Henry F. May, *The End of American Innocence; A Study of the First Years of Our Own Time 1912-1917* (New York: Knopf, 1959), pp. 193-216;

H. L. Mencken, *Letters of H. L. Mencken,* selected and annotated by Guy J. Forgue, with a personal note by Hamilton Owens and a new foreword by Daniel Aaron (Boston: Northeastern University Press, 1981);

Mencken, *Prejudices: First Series* (New York: Knopf, 1923), pp. 129-134;

Walter Neale, *Life of Ambrose Bierce* (New York: Neale, 1929);

Max Putzel, *The Man in the Mirror: William Marion Reedy and His Magazine* (Cambridge, Mass.: Harvard University Press, 1963);

Arnold T. Schwab, *James Gibbons Huneker: Critic of the Seven Arts* (Stanford, Cal.: Stanford University Press, 1963);

Douglas C. Stenerson, Introduction to Pollard's *Their Day in Court* (New York & London: Johnson Reprint Co., 1969), pp. v-xxvii.

Charles F. Richardson

(29 May 1851-8 October 1913)

Kermit Vanderbilt
San Diego State University

BOOKS: *A Primer of American Literature* (Boston: Houghton, Osgood, 1878; revised edition, Boston: Houghton, Mifflin, 1883);

The Cross (Philadelphia: Lippincott, 1879);

The Choice of Books (London: Low, Marston, Searle & Rivington, 1881; New York: Useful Knowledge Publishing Co., 1882; revised edition, New York & London: Putnam's, 1905);

American Literature, 1607-1885, 2 volumes (New York & London: Putnam's, 1887, 1889);

The End of the Beginning, anonymous (Boston: Little, Brown, 1896);

A Study of English Rhyme (Hanover, N.H.: Printed for classroom use, 1909).

OTHER: *The College Book*, edited by Richardson and Henry A. Clark (Boston: Houghton, Osgood, 1878);

James Fenimore Cooper's The Last of the Mohicans, edited by Richardson (New York: Longmans, Green, 1897);

The Complete Works of Edgar Allan Poe, edited, with an introduction, by Richardson (New York & London: Putnam's, 1902);

Daniel Webster for Young Americans, edited, with an introduction and notes, by Richardson (Boston: Little, Brown, 1903).

Charles Francis Richardson (courtesy of Dartmouth College Library)

One of the healing outcomes of the American Civil War was a renewed and deepening interest in the nation's literature. That interest, quickened by the centennial enthusiasm that was building toward 1876, was also being felt for the first time within the academy. Moses Coit Tyler, at the University of Michigan, found himself writing against the centennial deadline to finish the first scholarly history of American literature. He realized, however, that his scope was too ambitious, and (missing the deadline by two years) contented himself with a two-volume history of the colonial writers. Several years passed before Charles Francis Richardson of Dartmouth College, emboldened by Tyler's pioneering work, set out to write that first large-scale literary history of America. Richardson's treatment within and beyond Tyler's colonial period was different in conception and, by comparison with Tyler, notably drab in spirit and style. Even so, it is indispensable to any appreciation of American literary historiography. Richardson grappled with the vexing issues of historical evolution and literary nationalism and also revealed how an American professor was responding to the aesthetic ideas of the time, including the controversy generated outside the academy by such realists as William Dean Howells and Henry James.

Richardson was born in Hallowell, Maine, to Moses Charles Richardson, a physician, and Mary Savory Wingate Richardson. He graduated from Dartmouth, his father's alma mater, in 1871. After a decade in journalism, during which time he served as literary editor of the *New York Independent* and editor of the *Philadelphia Sunday School Times* and *Good Literature* in New York, he joined the faculty of Dartmouth in 1882, assuming the Winckley Chair of Anglo-Saxon and English Language and Literature vacated by Edwin D. Sanborn. He was married to Elizabeth Miner Thomas on 12 April 1878. Upon his arrival at Dartmouth Richardson immediately introduced a three-hour course in American literature for seniors. During the next three decades he lectured to the men of Dartmouth, including future scholars like Fred Lewis Pattee, on the riches of their native literature. Outside the classroom, his tall, lean figure was exaggerated by the tiny dog he was fond of walking about campus. Intimidating to students at first, he was, nevertheless, known affectionately among them as "Clothespins" and was the inevitable subject of their humorous cartoons. On his death two years after retirement in 1911, he was eulogized in the *Boston Post* by President Nichols: "The college has never had a more inspiring teacher. No one has ever given to more men a love of the best things in literature and an appreciation of its deep messages." To the present day, in the Class of 1902 Room of Baker Library, hangs the large portrait of "The Immortal Clothespins," preserving the figure of one of the best-loved men ever to teach American literature at Dartmouth.

Richardson's early claims as a scholar, before he joined the Dartmouth faculty, lay in *A Primer of American Literature* (1878), a miniature volume of 117 pages with equally miniature commentaries on some one hundred writers. To mark literary periods, Richardson had appropriated pivotal war years—1775, 1812, and 1861—without arguing their significance in literary history. Perhaps intended as a handbook for students and a pocket-sized digest for travelers, the volume must have had little scholarly value to the classroom professor or even to its author, though it probably convinced Dartmouth authorities that Richardson might become a devoted teacher of literature. If so, he more than satisfied their hopes. No doubt wisely, Richardson ignored much of his primer when a decade later he produced the admirable, two-volume *American Literature, 1607-1885* (1887, 1889). This was to be his foremost achievement as a scholar and critic. Indeed, it is his only work that commands attention a century later.

In the introduction to volume 1 of his history, Richardson established a polemical, transoceanic perspective of American literature. He charged that European and English critics had recently praised American fiction as irresponsibly as they had earlier denounced it. The time had come, Richardson suggested, to subject American writers to the same questions and unrelenting standards applied to literature in any age and country. The evenhanded literary historian should pose eight internal and external considerations as he approached the writers: to inquire into the author's aim, method, relation to other native writers, influence on them, debt to English literature, "intrinsic success," probable future rank, and the general effects of tides in literary taste. Richardson did not promise that he would absolutely pursue these problems. In fact, he did not consistently do so.

Richardson separated his two volumes into examinations of the American mind and belles lettres, subtitled *The Development of American Thought* (1887) and *American Poetry and Fiction* (1889). Richardson thus assumed the robes of an intellectual historian for an entire volume. But he implied that he would submit ideas to aesthetic evaluation, for in chapter 1 of *The Development of American Thought*, "The Race-Elements in American Literature," he defined literature as "the written record of valuable thought, having other than merely practical purpose." Though Richardson minimized environmental considerations for the literary historian, he suggested a quasi-Tainean causality for the evolution of literature: "Behind literature is race; behind race, climate and environment." Richardson defined the problem of nationalism environmentally as well and plainly entered a pervasive Anglo-Saxon bias: "The history of American literature is the history of the literature of the part of the English people, under new geographical and political conditions, within the present limits of the United States."

Richardson now tried to explain the slow progress of colonial literature, but his presuppositions served him quite haphazardly. He wavered in the treatment of the American environment as a decisive influence on the early literary product. At times he viewed the colonists as men of intrinsically stalwart character who brought with them from the old world the moral virtues favorable to the development of a distinguished native literature. The Dutch, Swedes, and Quakers possessed the character, thrift, "rectitude of purpose," and political goals on which the foundations of literature could be built. The Massachusetts colonists influenced literary development even more powerfully than the Quakers, however, because of more favorably inborn, racial characteristics; the

Quakers lacked the assertive "Saxon" moral attributes of the New England Puritan. In general, Richardson credited the colonial immigrant with a penchant for living in peace, and this character trait encouraged a respect for the life of the mind, which in turn encouraged the growth of literature. When the impulse to war had arisen in the land, the genuine American spirit had been subverted and literary expression suffered.

Early in his second chapter, "The New Environment of the Saxon Mind," Richardson reiterated the autonomy of colonial imagination, selfhood, and race; and he now emphatically ruled out geographical determinism: "Climate does not make character; still less does it produce literature." Richardson asked, then, how a distinctly national American literature had come into being. He could not deny the earlier historical assumptions about certain environmental influences in colonial America. The imperatives of economic and political survival in the new-world wilderness began to create a new man, a national type, an emerging national unity, and thus the possibilities for an American literature. But the going was slow, since the colonists lived in a land barren of historical and aesthetic associations. Literature "suffers in an environment which is crude and raw." Out of these largely adverse conditions, Richardson did not quite know how to explain the rise of a postcolonial literature. Indeed, after 177 pages of his literary history, he announced, "Thus far we have found not one American book of the first literary rank"; and some 150 pages later, "We had scarcely any literature at all when Emerson began to write."

In all of volume 1, only the essays of Washington Irving and Oliver Wendell Holmes unequivocally satisfied what Richardson now and again fashioned as workable criteria of aesthetic value. Often enough his pages repay rereading because they reveal the foundations of what Richardson assumed to be aesthetic judgments, such as the idea that English literature was the touchstone of American writing. Such comparisons could, but did not, tempt Richardson to ask further questions of literary-historical influence. Instead, he invoked the English author seemingly to humble American readers and particularly the literary nationalists, whose "fulsome puffery" of inferior colonial literature had been especially misguided. When Richardson sent down his aesthetic verdicts apart from the contrast or corroboration of English literary example, he became the distinctly old-fashioned critic who es-

Richardson in 1911 (courtesy of Dartmouth College Library)

chewed any argued analysis of whatever evidence he deigned to submit. He states, for example, that John Smith belonged neither to America nor literature. Richardson then provides two and one-half pages of uninterrupted quotation—a "fair example of Smith's method and style"—with all of his literary characteristics and deficiencies supposedly self-evident. William Bradford's was a "better English style," though the "literary merit" of his and John Winthrop's histories was "inferior" somehow. In John Woolman's journal one sensed a "purer literary style" than in David Brainerd's diary (did Richardson recall the Englishman Charles Lamb's praise of Woolman?), and the reader was then assigned the labor of discovering that purity within an extended quotation from Woolman. Henry David Thoreau was inferior to Ralph Waldo Emerson, though he described the heart of nature "in simple, true, poetic, eloquent words"; but there was more "largeness and light" in Walt Whitman. Finally, Mark Twain, who rated no mention in the fiction chapters of volume 2, here was lumped with other would-be humorists whose works were dismissed by Richardson as inadequate to their literary mode: "Humor . . . must coexist with literary qualities, and must usually be joined with such pathos as one finds in Lamb, Hood, Irving, or Holmes."

The second volume of Richardson's history consists of seven chapters on American poetry and five on fiction. Viewing Richardson first as a historian and critic of American poetry, one is not surprised, after volume 1, that he invoked the English example, or that he failed to enunciate or clearly imply the definition and evolution of periods, genres, modes, and metrics, or to argue the aesthetic principles with which he judged literary excellence. His criteria were at times, once more, vaguely Saxon and universal. Henry Wadsworth Longfellow had been recognized in America and "other great Teutonic countries" as the national poet, and his work as possessing "universal interest which is a mark of true literary achievement." At other times Richardson seemed closer to Henry James's impressionist dictum that the writer receive and register an immediate response to the vivid "color of life." Here Richardson administered the obscure test of "spontaneity" and "vividness," noting their absence in Whitman, Sidney Lanier, and many Civil War poets, though not in Paul Hamilton Hayne, Henry Timrod, and Edmund Clarence Stedman.

The most important critical principle that Richardson seemed at first to adopt for his literary evaluations was that of organic expression, what Emerson had demanded as a "metre-making argument" for a new American poetry that would successfully wed new form with new experience. On his opening page Richardson just barely implied the Emersonian formula in a definition of poetry more clearly indebted to Edgar Allan Poe: "Poetry is the rhythmical expression of beauty or imagination," he wrote (substituting "expression" for Poe's "creation"), and in significant apposition, Richardson added that such expression is "the verbal utterance of the ideal." He linked the poetic idea more emphatically to its necessary form later when he wrote that in Poe "the artistic act fitly follows the artistic thought." But the organic principle served Richardson unevenly as an instrument of aesthetic evaluation. He stumbled over his nineteenth-century moralistic demand for "valuable thought," now become the poetic expression of the "ideal," and so he abandoned the functional principle of aesthetic "fitness" of technique to content that he so plainly had stated in the case of Poe.

Even in Poe, expectably, Richardson ignored literary form when he disapproved of content. Or he criticized the "unduly physical and material" in Whitman and also complained that Whitman's technique failed to express ethereal and "rhythmical beauty." At other times Richardson endorsed the vision of Longfellow ("tender, sweet, and human") and then lapsed into idle and separate enjoyment of the poet's "best hexameters," which had a "genuine musical beauty of their own." Emerson's unorthodox thought in his essays, scorned by Richardson in volume 1, was even less acceptable in the poetry, and his unorthodox metrics, rather than giving appropriate expression to the thought, were merely unpolished and inferior art. The unruly Emerson's unruly "form and finish" reached a point where he "almost defies the laws of poetics."

For Richardson, poetry morally and artistically remained "the highest and most permanent form of literature." He observed this hierarchy of literary forms after his seven chapters on poetry when he required but five more to survey the supposedly inferior art of American fiction. He now singled out the few worthy practitioners of fictional genres. As before, he praised Saxon characteristics and relied on a quasi-organic formula of artistic expression. He reemphasized, however, the Victorian imperative that writers' ideas should be suitably elevated. In fact, Richardson shifted the internal emphasis to moral substance more strongly than in the poetry chapters, since fiction, for him, did not rival the "higher art" of poetry. He rephrased for fiction the requisite of ideal and valuable thought: like poetry, the best fiction must be "complete" as it delineated "life . . . [to] include the body, mind, and soul of man, in his journey from the infinite to the infinite." With this preliminary ruling Richardson could dispatch the architects of realism whose finite vision and moral content were limited in range and less than wholesome. He posed the Jamesian question, "Which is the more important, the thing told or the way of telling it?" Predictably, Richardson replied, "The former; because all art is grounded on the necessity that the subject should have some reason for existence or delineation." The worthy subject embraced the immortal soul of man, and presumably this moral content made American literature properly Saxon and universal. James Fenimore Cooper's was an "honest Saxon soul," Nathaniel Hawthorne's art expressed his region's Anglo-Saxon ethics, which, to Richardson, elevated it into the company of universal literature. Richardson discovered the same "universal interest" in the salutary pages of even local colorists Bret Harte, Mary Noailles Murfree, and George Washington Cable. The narrow subject matter of the realists, by contrast, had rightly given them "a somewhat limited minority" of American and English, that is, Anglo-Saxon, readers.

Richardson had trouble identifying indigenous influences, historical continuity or change, and clues to aesthetic power in American fiction as well as in American poetry. Viewed a century later, Richardson's groping for historical principles, cultural definitions, and aesthetic judgments elicits sympathy, just as his daring to comprehend the entire American literary history merits respect and gratitude. The wide range of problems he addressed (and others that he ignored) have never been adequately solved by literary historians and critics who have come after him. Not until the 1920s did members of the profession begin to reinterpret American literature in a fashion that would define, with any sophistication, the history of American genres and modes. Richardson's inarticulate commentary on the literary text represented the state of literary analysis and judgment in the American academy well into the 1940s, and not until the heirs of F. O. Matthiessen in the 1950s did aesthetic considerations properly intersect the historical in literary scholarship. As to the influence Richardson could claim among his contemporaries, he lived to see his *American Literature* through various republications, including "popular" and "student" editions. The effects of his work elsewhere in the academy may also be gauged by observing the activity of many professors who soon embarked on their own American literary histories, encouraged no doubt by the ambitious example and, it may be, by some of the instructive weaknesses of Dartmouth's worthy trailblazer.

References:

Howard Mumford Jones, *The Theory of American Literature* (Ithaca: Cornell University Press, 1948), pp. 99-100;

Fred Lewis Pattee, Preface to *The First Century of American Literature, 1770-1870* (New York: Appleton-Century, 1935), p. v;

Kermit Vanderbilt, *American Literature and the Academy: The Roots, Growth, and Maturity of a Profession* (Philadelphia: University of Pennsylvania Press, 1986), pp. 104-122.

Papers:

The archives of the Baker Library at Dartmouth College contain Richardson papers and memorabilia consisting of correspondence, photographs, and miscellaneous writings.

George Santayana

(16 December 1863-26 September 1952)

Paul C. Wermuth
Northeastern University

See also the Santayana entry in *DLB 54, American Poets, 1880-1945, Third Series*.

BOOKS: *Sonnets and Other Verses* (Cambridge, Mass. & Chicago: Stone & Kimball, 1894; revised and enlarged edition, New York: Stone & Kimball, 1896);

The Sense of Beauty: Being the Outlines of Aesthetic Theory (New York: Scribners, 1896; London: A. & C. Black, 1896);

Lucifer: A Theological Tragedy (Chicago & New York: H. S. Stone, 1899); revised as *Lucifer; Or, The Heavenly Truce: A Theological Tragedy* (Cambridge, Mass.: Dunster House, 1924);

Interpretations of Poetry and Religion (New York: Scribners, 1900; London: A. & C. Black, 1900);

A Hermit of Carmel And Other Poems (New York: Scribners, 1901; London: Johnson, 1902);

The Life of Reason; Or, The Phases of Human Progress: Introduction and Reason in Common Sense (New York: Scribners, 1905; London: Constable, 1905);

The Life of Reason; Or, The Phases of Human Progress: Reason in Society (New York: Scribners, 1905; London: Constable, 1905);

The Life of Reason; Or, The Phases of Human Progress: Reason in Religion (New York: Scribners, 1905: London: Constable, 1905);

The Life of Reason; Or, The Phases of Human Progress: Reason in Art (New York: Scribners, 1905; London: Constable, 1905);

The Life of Reason; Or, The Phases of Human Progress: Reason in Science (New York: Scribners, 1906; London: Constable, 1906);

Three Philosophical Poets: Lucretius, Dante, and Goethe (Cambridge: Harvard University, 1910; London: Oxford University Press, 1910);

Winds of Doctrine: Studies in Contemporary Opinion (London: Dent/New York: Scribners, 1913);

Egotism in German Philosophy (New York: Scribners, 1915; London & Toronto: Dent/New York: Scribners, 1916); republished as *The*

George Santayana

German Mind: A Philosophical Diagnosis (New York: Crowell, 1968);

Character and Opinion in the United States: With Reminiscences of William James and Josiah Royce and Academic Life in America (London: Constable, 1920; New York: Scribners, 1920);

Soliloquies in England, and Later Soliloquies (London: Constable, 1922; New York: Scribners, 1922);

Poems, Selected by the Author and Revised (London: Constable, 1922; New York: Scribners, 1923);

Scepticism and Animal Faith: Introduction to a System of Philosophy (London: Constable, 1923; New York: Scribners, 1923);

Dialogues in Limbo (London: Constable, 1925; New York: Scribners, 1926; enlarged edition, New York: Scribners, 1948);

Platonism and the Spiritual Life (London: Constable, 1927; New York: Scribners, 1927);

The Realm of Essence: Book First of Realms of Being (London: Constable, 1927; New York: Scribners, 1927);

The Realm of Matter: Book Second of Realms of Being (London: Constable, 1930; New York: Scribners, 1930);

The Genteel Tradition at Bay (New York: Scribners, 1931);

Some Turns of Thought in Modern Philosophy, Five Essays (Cambridge: Cambridge University Press, 1933; New York: Scribners, 1933);

The Last Puritan: A Memoir in the Form of a Novel (London: Constable, 1935; New York: Scribners, 1936);

Obiter Scripta: Lectures, Essays and Reviews, edited by Justus Buchler and Benjamin Schwartz (London: Constable, 1936; New York: Scribners, 1936);

The Realm of Truth: Book Third of Realms of Being (London: Constable, 1937; New York: Scribners, 1938);

The Realm of Spirit: Book Fourth of Realms of Being (London: Constable, 1940; New York: Scribners, 1940);

The Background of My Life, volume 1 of *Persons and Places* (New York: Scribners, 1944; London: Constable, 1944);

The Middle Span, volume 2 of *Persons and Places* (New York: Scribners, 1945; London: Constable, 1947);

The Idea of Christ in the Gospels; Or, God in Man, A Critical Essay (New York: Scribners, 1946);

Dominations and Powers: Reflections on Liberty, Society, and Government (London: Constable, 1951; New York: Scribners, 1951);

My Host the World, volume 3 of *Persons and Places* (New York: Scribners, 1953; London: Cresset, 1953);

The Poet's Testament: Poems and Two Plays, edited by John Hall Wheelock and Daniel Cory (New York: Scribners, 1953);

The Idler and His Works, and Other Essays, edited by Cory (New York: Braziller, 1957);

George Santayana's America: Essays on Literature and Culture, edited by James Ballowe (Urbana: University of Illinois Press, 1967);

The Genteel Tradition: Nine Essays by George Santayana, edited by Douglas C. Wilson (Cambridge: Harvard University Press, 1967);

Santayana on America: Essays, Notes, and Letters on American Life, Literature, and Philosophy, edited by Richard C. Lyon (New York: Harcourt, Brace & World, 1968);

Physical Order and Moral Liberty: Previously Unpublished Essays of George Santayana, edited by John and Shirley Lachs (Nashville: Vanderbilt University Press, 1969);

Poems of George Santayana, selected by Robert Hutchinson (New York: Dover, 1970);

Lotze's System of Philosophy, edited by Paul Grimley Kuntz (Bloomington: Indiana University Press, 1971);

The Complete Poems of George Santayana: A Critical Edition, edited by William G. Holzberger (Lewisburg: Bucknell University Press/ London: Associated University Presses, 1979).

Editions and Collections: *The Works of George Santayana,* Triton Edition, 15 volumes (New York: Scribners, 1936-1940);

The Works of George Santayana, one volume to date: *Persons and Places: Fragments of Autobiography,* edited by William G. Holzberger and Herman J. Saatkamp, Jr., volume 1 of *The Works of George Santayana* (Cambridge: MIT Press, 1986).

OTHER: "Cervantes (1547-1616)," in *A Library of the World's Best Literature, Ancient and Modern,* edited by Charles Dudley Warner, 30 volumes (New York: Peale & Hill, 1896-1897), volume 8: pp. 3451-3457;

Introduction to *Hamlet,* in *The Complete Works of William Shakespeare,* edited by Sidney Lee, 40 volumes (New York: Sproul, 1907-1909), volume 30: ix-xxxiii;

Iris Origo, *Leopardi: A Biography,* foreword by Santayana (Oxford: Oxford University Press, 1935), pp. v-vi;

"My Poetry," in *The Philosophy of George Santayana,* edited by Paul A. Schilpp (Evanston & Chicago: Northwestern University, 1940; revised, 1951), pp. 598-600.

PERIODICAL PUBLICATIONS: "Walt Whitman: A Dialogue," *Harvard Monthly,* 10 (May 1890): 85-92;

"Emerson's Poems Proclaim the Divinity of Nature, with Freedom as His Profoundest Ideal," *Boston Daily Advertiser,* 23 May 1903, Special Emerson Supplement, p. 16;

"Shakespeare: Made in America," *New Republic,* 2 (27 February 1915): 96-98;

"Genteel American Poetry," *New Republic,* 3 (29 May 1915): 94-95;

"Dickens," *Dial,* 71 (November 1921): 537-549;

"Marginal Notes on Civilization in the United States," *Dial,* 72 (June 1922): 553-568;

"Proust on Essences," *Life and Letters,* 2 (1929): 455-459;

"Tragic Philosophy," *Scrutiny,* 4 (March 1936): 365-376;

"Tom Sawyer and Don Quixote," *Mark Twain Quarterly,* 9 (Winter 1952): 1-3.

George Santayana is one of the most notable, and paradoxical, figures in American intellectual life. He is, for example, a philosopher whose work combines naturalism and platonism; whose philosophy is highly literary, while his literary works are highly philosophical. He was an academician who hated the academy; a Catholic who didn't believe Catholic dogma; and an American by residence, education, and profession, who maintained his Spanish citizenship, although as an adult he never lived in Spain.

Perhaps this paradoxical quality was partly a result of a life divided between not only two cultures but also between two centuries. Consequently, his work, which is in many ways modern and advanced, is in other ways old-fashioned. Early in his career he thought of himself as a poet, and he continued to write verse at least occasionally throughout his life. Yet it was always traditional, formal, and severely classical. His literary criticism rarely essays a modern figure, concentrating instead on established authors of earlier periods. He lived through the great intellectual changes of the late nineteenth and the first half of the twentieth centuries, yet he cultivated a calm, detached independence as he surveyed the world about him.

He was born in Madrid on 16 December 1863. His mother, Josefina Borrás de Santayana, though Spanish, was born in Scotland and lived most of her life in Virginia, the Philippines, and Boston. Her first husband, George Sturgis, was an American businessman who met her in the Philippines. They were married in 1849. After his death in 1857 she carried out his wishes to rear their children in Boston. On a later visit to Spain she renewed an earlier acquaintance with Augustín Ruiz de Santayana, a civil servant she had known in the Philippines. They were married shortly thereafter. George Santayana was their only child.

In 1866 Santayana's parents separated, his mother taking the three surviving children from her first marriage (two had died in infancy) with

her to Boston. When Santayana was nine, his father sent him to live with his mother; both parents thought his opportunities would be better there. He attended the Brimmer School, Boston Latin, and Harvard University. This was obviously a superior American education at the time; but Santayana claims a lonely and unhappy youth. He was not close to his Sturgis relatives, except for a half sister, Susanna; he suffered, he said, from being a foreigner in a strange land: a Latin in an Anglo-Saxon country, a Catholic in Protestant Boston, and a "sensitive youth" in a driving business environment. He also suggests that his family existed in a sort of genteel poverty, although they lived on affluent Beacon Street.

At Harvard, Santayana was active in its intellectual circles; he wrote for the *Harvard Monthly* and the *Harvard Crimson,* drew cartoons for the *Harvard Lampoon,* and acted in Hasty Pudding theatricals. Despite all this, however, he retained the feeling of isolation from mainstream culture and was unsympathetic with many common American values–an attitude which helped develop his own independence. He graduated in 1886 with Honors in Philosophy and Honorable Mention in English Composition.

Despite his alienation, however, he must have been highly regarded by his teachers. He was given the Walker Fellowship for graduate study in Germany and held it for two years. After returning and finishing his thesis on the philosophy of Hermann Lotze, he was awarded the Ph.D. (1889) by Harvard and was promptly hired, at twenty-six, as an instructor in the philosophy department. His former teachers were now his colleagues, and they were an illustrious group: William James, Josiah Royce, George Herbert Palmer, and Hugo Münsterberg among them.

He was not overfond of his colleagues; his essays on James and Royce in *Character and Opinion in the United States* (1920) convey a subtle tone of condescension. He disliked the company of professors ("I never had a real friend who was a professor," he once said), finding them conventional and intellectually timid; he preferred the company of students. Besides, he thought that Charles W. Eliot, then president of Harvard, did not like him, probably because he "wrote verses, was discernibly a Catholic, and disliked Browning." One result was that he waited nine years to be promoted to assistant professor and another nine years before he became a full professor.

The Three Philosophers *by Winifred Rieber; Harvard professors Josiah Royce, George Palmer, and William James (courtesy of Harvard University Portrait Collection, Gift Harvard Alumni and Friends of Professors James, Royce, and Palmer, 1920)*

To an outsider Santayana appears to have had a splendid and reasonably productive career at Harvard. Though teaching was not his favorite activity, he once referred to it as a "delightful paternal art," and he had several famous pupils, including Wallace Stevens, T. S. Eliot, and Conrad Aiken. But the sense of not quite belonging was pervasive, as well as the need to give his time more completely to writing. Thus when his mother died and left him a small legacy in 1912, he promptly resigned and left not only Harvard and the academic life, but America as well. During the subsequent forty years of his life (he was at this time already forty-nine) he never returned to America, not even for a visit.

"I have no American or English blood," he once said; "I was not born in the United States; I have never become an American citizen; as soon as I was my own master I spent every free winter and almost every summer in Europe; I never married or kept house or expected to end my days in America." Yet he retained a queer sort of affec-

tion for America, one that was probably enhanced by distance. He was able to assess its importance to him, and, while always sharply critical of what he conceived to be its failures, he also found virtues that were important and admirable. Indeed, when asked by *The Dial* in 1922 to comment on a book of essays by American intellectuals entitled *Civilization in the United States,* (edited by Harold Stearns) which was largely contemptuous of American life, Santayana was virtually the only defender of America.

The rest of his life was spent in various places in Europe. After a few summers with his father in Spain he moved to England where he lived for five years, including the duration of World War I, at which time he sympathized with the British. He later established Rome as his base, and though he often resided elsewhere for brief periods, he always returned there, living mostly in hotels. During World War II he moved into a nursing home operated by a religious order, the convent of the Blue Nuns, and remained there after the war until his death in

1952, turning out a steady stream of books and articles on a wide range of subjects.

Santayana's primarily literary works are confined largely to his years at Harvard. Of the seven titles he published during this time, three are volumes of verse, two are works of literary criticism, and only two are philosophy (although one of these was a multivolume work.) He taught at Harvard for five years before his first book, *Sonnets and Other Verses* (1894), was published. His second book, *The Sense of Beauty: Being the Outlines of Aesthetic Theory* (1896), was in aesthetics; it is significant that this book was followed by his first promotion. Then followed three literary volumes in quick succession: a verse drama, *Lucifer: A Theological Tragedy* (1899), *Interpretations of Poetry and Religion* (1900)—his first work in literary criticism—and another volume of verse, *A Hermit of Carmel And Other Poems* (1901).

By 1904 he had been on the Harvard faculty for fifteen years and had produced only one slender book that was in his discipline—and that was in the fringe area of aesthetics. However, in 1905-1906, *The Life of Reason* appeared in five volumes, a substantial work of philosophy that greatly enhanced his professional reputation. Indeed, Santayana was promoted to professor in 1907.

Santayana published only one more book during his American years, a collection of literary criticism entitled *Three Philosophical Poets: Lucretius, Dante, and Goethe* (1910). All his subsequent work—and it was not only primarily philosophical but was also quite extensive—was published after he left the United States in 1912.

As a literary critic Santayana presents the reader with some unusual difficulties. First, of course, is the fact that his literary criticism as such is not very extensive; he published only the two volumes mentioned above. But while he did not produce any further separate volumes of criticism, he nonetheless continued to write essays occasionally throughout his life on authors he liked or had occasion to examine; and some of his best pieces are found in his philosophical texts or in periodicals. All these gathered together would result in at least a third volume of considerable interest. In addition, his work on aesthetics is closely related to his criticism, and such books as *The Sense of Beauty* and *Reason in Art* (1905; volume four of *The Life of Reason*) are important to an understanding of his literary attitudes. Furthermore, he wrote a number of essays on movements such as transcendentalism, pragmatism, and the Genteel Tradition which are closely related to literature.

Such a variety presents, however, a second problem, and that is the seamless way such matters overlap in Santayana's work. Often, it is difficult to describe a given piece as philosophy or criticism. Even his major critical works, *Interpretations of Poetry and Religion* and *Three Philosophical Poets*, are essentially philosophical. He is more of a critic of culture than a literary critic in the narrow sense. He is interested in how literature interprets a culture, how it reflects human concerns rather than how it is constructed or reflects contemporary interests. Most of the time he does not analyze a text closely but operates at the highest level. The most abstract concerns, the largest implications, the longest view—these constitute his approach.

His method of development can pose a problem in that he tends to work by analogy, aphorism, wit, irony, and understatement, rather than by analysis and illustrative examples. This method, however attractive, sometimes results in a lack of clarity and precision of statement; and he often uses abstract terms as if there were agreement on their meaning. For example, he defined the Genteel Tradition (a term that he coined) as a combination of transcendentalism and Calvinism. Though fascinating in its suggestiveness, it is not easy to see the relationship of this definition to what most readers understand as its most evident characteristics—its squeamishness and evasiveness.

Many of Santayana's critical principles are given their first expression in his work in aesthetics, especially in *The Sense of Beauty*, which grew out of what he called his "sham course" in the subject at Harvard: "I was a kind of poet, I was alive to architecture and the other arts, I was at home in several languages: 'aesthetics' might be regarded as my specialty. Very well: although I didn't have, and haven't now, a clear notion of what 'aesthetics' may be, I undertook to give a course in that subject. It would help define my status. I gave it for one or two years and then I wrote out the substance of it in a little book: *The Sense of Beauty*." His "little book" quickly became a standard work, and, as he remarked later, it was always his best seller.

The book was important because it took a psychological approach to beauty. This was new in that the author approached the question of beauty not in order to decide what one ought to like, but rather to analyze the "nature and elements of our aesthetic judgment." A second interesting point in the volume was the definition of beauty: "Beauty is pleasure regarded as the quality of a thing." Beauty is a value, he says; this value is positive; it is an ultimate good, and therefore its value is intrinsic; and finally these elements become objectified into the qualities of things. Beauty exists, in other words, only in the mind of the beholder. This view now seems to be accepted as a genuine contribution to aesthetics.

Santayana's explanation of the psychological basis of aesthetic judgments has been described as a form of naturalism, and in the book he deals with feeling as it is rooted in the natural and physical. He distinguishes three types of beauty: the first is beauty of materials, that is, the sense organs themselves which become the avenues of aesthetic perception. A second, and higher, type of beauty consists of form, "where sensible elements by themselves indifferent, are so united as to please in combination"; and the greatest of this type is that which brings about some recognition of the unity of things. (Here can be seen an important point of his later criticism: the best art expresses the ideal unity of life and aspirations.) Yet a third type is beauty of expression, that is, the aesthetic values that the associations of an object may hold for us: "Expressiveness is thus the power given by experience to any image to call up others in the mind."

In this book several other themes appear which will be more fully developed in Santayana's critical work. One of these is an attack on romantic art. Speaking of it as "indeterminateness of organization," he says that it is "disorganized, sporadic, whimsical, and experimental. The crudity we are too distracted to refine, we accept as originality, and the vagueness we are too pretentious to make accurate, we pass off as sublimity." He continues, "a work of art or an act of observation which remains indeterminate is, therefore, a failure, however much it may stir our emotions"; he adds that "sentimentalism in the observer and romanticism in the artist are examples of this aesthetic incapacity."

A second theme lies in the opinion that the ultimate function of art is to express the ideal: "No atheism is so terrible as the absence of an ultimate ideal, nor could any failure of power be more contrary to human nature than the failure of moral imagination. . . . " The Platonism expressed here reaches its ultimate expression in Santayana's later doctrine of essences.

Santayana (left) with a friend during one of his trips to Europe (courtesy of José-Maria Alonso Gamo)

Finally, suggestions of a moral criterion in judging literature are evident in this work, though this point will also be more thoroughly developed later. In *The Sense of Beauty* Santayana's task, according to George Howgate, was "to account for beauty on the ground of psychological determinism, and at the same time to justify its manifestations on moral and ideal grounds. His naturalism will explain beauty as a peculiarly subjective phenomenon, while his platonism will insist upon its absolute validity in the world of moral values."

Some years later in an essay entitled "What is Aesthetics?" published in *Philosophical Review* in 1904, Santayana argued that there was no separate science of aesthetics. The activity suggested by the word is a matter of values and is more the realm of the moral philosopher than the scientist. What does exist is an art of criticism, which he defines as "a reasoned appreciation of human works by a mind not wholly ignorant of their subject or occasion, their school, and their process of manufacture." His definition of good criticism is significant; it requires "a variety of considerations, more numerous in proportion to the critic's competence and maturity. Nothing relevant to the object's efficacy should be ignored, and an intelligent critic must look impartially to beauty, propriety, difficulty, originality, truth, and moral significance in the work he judges."

The "swallowing up" of aesthetic good in the rational life as a whole is the theme of *Reason in Art*. Santayana here asserts that all art springs first out of utility, after which it is developed into an expression of ideal aspirations. The moral function of criticism is also reiterated: "Any rational judgment on the beautiful must be a moral and political judgment, enveloping chance aesthetic feelings and determining their value. . . . All criticism is therefore moral, since it deals with benefits and their relative weight." The artist's job is to point to the highest possible good.

In this early work in aesthetics Santayana states the main themes which will dominate his literary criticism. First, art has an integral relation to life as a whole and does not exist alone. Second, the function of art is an idealizing one; it must not merely amuse but must contribute to man's understanding of life and its ideal ends. Third, the purpose of criticism is moral, inasmuch as the critic must choose between relative goods and make judgments of value. Finally, art must be comprehensive; the greatest artists are those who have achieved the most complete vision of the whole of life. One might also note that his taste in art is classical, with a strong emphasis on form and discipline, and that he had little patience for the diffuseness he associated with romanticism.

An understanding of Santayana's criticism should include knowledge of his religious theories, since they are integral to his philosophy. In 1930, on this subject, he said: "Like my parents, I have always set myself down officially as a Catholic; but this is a matter of sympathy and traditional allegiance, not of philosophy. In my adolescence, religion on its doctrinal and emotional side occupied me much more than it does now. I was more unhappy and unsettled; but I have never had any unquestioning faith in any dogma, and have never been what is called a practicing Catholic." Put briefly, he considered religion a form of poetry; but although he repudiated it as an account of matters of fact, he clung to it as an expression of the ideals of mankind, a supreme expression of human desires. "Religions are the great fairy-tales of the conscience," he said.

These views are developed most fully in *Interpretations of Poetry and Religion* and in *Reason in Religion* (1905), volume three of *The Life of Reason*. It is in the preface to the former work that he said: "Religion and poetry are identical in essence, and differ merely in the way in which they are attached to practical affairs. Poetry is called religion when it intervenes in life, and religion, when it merely supervenes upon life, is seen to be nothing but poetry." Therefore, he argues, "religious doctrines would do well to withdraw their pretension to be dealing with matters of fact. That pretension is not only the source of the conflicts of religion with science and of the vain and bitter controversies of sects; it is also the cause of the impurity and incoherence of religion in the soul, when it seeks its sanctions in the sphere of reality, and forgets that its proper concern is to express the ideal."

He does not, he says, expect his views to appeal to either the orthodox or to religious liberals. His system would reduce the former's "artful cosmos to an allegory," while the latter is simply vulgarizing religion by minimizing its expression. He reminds liberals that "mythology cannot become science by being reduced in bulk, but it may cease, as a mythology, to be worth having."

Reason in Religion reviews the history of western religion, explains the developmental process through which it evolved, and attempts to relate it to the life of reason. The conflict between reason and religion is caused by the claims of the latter to a literal truth which it does not in fact possess. Santayana seems to attribute this partially to the Jewish people, who introduced the concept of the one true god who excluded all others. On the other hand, the Greeks were "enlightened and ingenuous"; to them monotheism and polytheism seemed perfectly compatible and were an "intelligent variation of phrase to indicate various aspects or functions in physical and moral things." He goes on here to explain how religions grew out of primitive practices, suggesting that he was well acquainted with current anthropological knowledge.

Santayana's opinion of Protestantism is important to note. Naturally, he preferred the religions of ancient Greece, with their broad tolerance and frank mythology; yet he praises Christianity as an instrument for expressing the ideals of humanity. However, Protestantism he thought was really a new religion, hardly Christian at all, but really the religion of the Germanic peoples in Christian guise: "a religion of pure spontaneity, of emotional freedom, deeply respecting itself but scarcely deciphering its purposes. It is the self-consciousness of a spirit in process of incubation, jealous of its potentialities, averse to definitions and finalities of any kind because it can itself discern nothing fixed or final."

His attitude toward Protestantism colored Santayana's philosophy and is related to his lifelong antipathy toward anything German. Protestantism, he thought, developed into German philosophy (which he called Absolute Egotism, or Subjectivism), which in turn is the source of many modern speculative ills. Indeed, Santayana attributed a number of ills to Germany, including Romanticism. Here, though, is another note sounded frequently through his work: the division of western man into Teutons and Latins. Of course he preferred the Latin temperament—warm, aesthetic, religious, tradition-loving, and disillusioned—to the Teutonic temperament—cold, practical, egotistic, leveling, and pitifully eager and naive. This category included not only Germany but also England and the United States. Less valid than it was thought to be years ago, the view is part of Santayana's personal mythology and must be reckoned with.

Santayana's first volume of literary criticism, *Interpretations of Poetry and Religion,* is in many ways his finest achievement in the field. It contains his most detailed exposition of the view that poetry and religion are in their highest development synonymous as expressions of the highest rational ideals. The theme of the volume is the "moral function of the imagination, and the poetic nature of religion." It contains ten essays in a sequence that points up this thesis. The first, "Understanding, Imagination, and Mysticism," is an attack on mysticism and a justification of the moral function of the imagination when used with rational restraint to make up the shortcomings of the understanding.

The limitation of man's senses leads him to resort to imagination; the more profound minds are most swayed by emotion to find a noble answer to all questions, to pass beyond understanding to intuition. Yet this process involves dangers. As an a priori principle, imagination is irresponsible and may interfere with knowledge of the real world of facts and rational duty. It may even become dishonest by defending its view at all costs, thus forfeiting the symbolic truth which gave it a moral value in the first place. The result is mysticism, "the surrender of a category of thought on account of the discovery of its relativity." One can only seek expansion of the mind in the imagination applied to the world of knowledge: "Behind the discovered there is the discoverable, beyond the actual, the possible. Science and history are not exhausted. In their determinate directions they are as infinite as fancy in its indetermination." If mysticism is renounced, he says, and imagination retained, a rational world closer to the facts, to the ideal of the moral imagination, and more satisfying to the understanding can be built.

The next four essays, "The Homeric Hymns," "The Dissolution of Paganism," "The Poetry of Christian Dogma," and "Platonic Love in Some Italian Poets," show a development of the moral function of the imagination. In the first Santayana demonstrates the practical application of religion through history. Greek religion, for example, while it may appear to be "mere" poetry, actually directly influenced life and was a factor in conduct. Besides the gods who represented natural forces there were spirits of ancestors, gods of the hearth, and patrons of war and the arts. "This . . . is not mere poetry, but religion; it is a poetry in which men believe . . . , that beautifies and justifies to their minds the positive facts of their ancestral worship, their social unity, and their personal conscience." He interprets allegories of several Homeric hymns, showing that the Greeks grasped "that high essence of religion which makes religion rational."

"The Dissolution of Paganism" traces polytheistic theology in Greece down to the triumph of Christianity. In this mythology many gods had practical characteristics as well as specific activities in the physical sphere. But as man's knowledge of nature grew mythology faced a dilemma: it "must either be impoverished to remain sincere, or become artificial to remain adequate." In the decay, however, the gods could still survive as moral ideals; and it was thus that Plato conceived them. Aristotle, building on Plato, was the first to reach the conception of what may be called God. His conception, though, was too austere, and the inheritance of paganism fell to Christianity, which tried to unite ethical and naturalistic elements in a new way.

"The Poetry of Christian Dogma" tries to explain the constitution of this new union and the source of its success. Santayana questions why Christianity was successful when Neo-Platonism offered nearly as much and had the added advantage of being native. "Shall we say that the triumph of Christianity was a miracle? Is it not a doubtful encomium on a religion to say that only by miracle could it come to be believed?" Of course there was more; because of the decay of classic civilization religion had to preach redemption. Christianity did, and besides, was supernatural and furnished a relevance to human life.

The great innovation of Christianity was that its scheme was historical. The hero was man himself, something which no pagan religion had: Christianity taught that the world was made for man. This was not true, Santayana remarked, "if we are thinking of a scientific, not of a poetical explanation. As a matter of fact, man is a product of laws which must also destroy him, and which, as Spinoza would say, infinitely exceed him in their scope and power. His welfare is indifferent to the stars, but dependent on them.... [But] what is false in the science of facts may be true in the science of values." If we regard Christian legends as facts they lose their significance, for it is only as symbols that they become meaningful. Take, for example, the doctrine of eternal rewards and punishments; it symbolizes the "awful solemnity" of death, and the fact that in life one does not have infinite opportunities to reform and advance. It represents the finality of our activity in this world, together with the ideal meaning of that activity. It also expresses the truth that moral distinctions are absolute. Thus do religions express moral ideals; and moral significance is the criterion by which they should be judged.

In "Platonic Love in Some Italian Poets" Santayana tries to shed light on the concept of Platonic love, which he thinks is widely misunderstood. He defines it as "the transformation of the appreciation of beautiful things into the worship of an ideal beauty and the transformation of the love of particular persons into the love of God."

This conception was particularly characteristic of certain Italian poets of the thirteenth to sixteenth centuries, although their Platonism did not necessarily derive from Plato; it was Christian, medieval, and chivalrous. Among them are Dante, Cavalcanti, Michael Angelo, and Lorenzo De' Medici—but not Petrarch, whose mind was

Portrait of Santayana by Denman W. Ross

"not truly distinguished." All fall in love with a person who suggests ideal beauty yet who eventually disappoints them by in the end not fulfilling it, thereby suggesting that, in comparison with the ideal, every human perfection becomes a shadow and a deceit. Dante's love for Beatrice, for example, represents the unattainable and transmuted ideal. "Having recognized that she was to his childish fancy what the ideals of religion were to his mature imagination, Dante intentionally fused the two, as every poet intentionally fuses the general and the particular, the universal and the personal. Beatrice thenceforth appeared, as Plato wished that our loves should, as a manifestation of absolute beauty and as an avenue of divine grace." Such a Platonic feeling, according to Santayana, is "nothing else than the application to passion of that pursuit of something permanent in a world of change, or something absolute in a world of relativity, which was the essence of the Platonic philosophy." The virtue of this philosophy is that it reveals some glimpses of the ideal.

Having thus outlined his conception of religious development from paganism through Christianity to Platonic idealism (which is, of course, an ascending order), Santayana now turns to some "modern" writers and tries to assess them in light of these criteria. William Shakespeare, Robert Browning, Walt Whitman, and Ralph Waldo Emerson, however, do not compare well; all fall short, to some degree, of being ideal poets. In large part due to the chaos of modern life and the loss of religion, they seem unable to grasp the whole of reality, to give a complete picture of human existence, or to offer the mind an ideal worthy of contemplation.

Of the four, Shakespeare comes closest to fulfilling Santayana's ideal. No other poet has expressed such a wide variety of human life, but he has no religion; the world of his works is only the world of men; "the cosmos eludes him." For Santayana, Shakespeare "depicts human life in all its richness and variety, but leaves that life without a setting, and consequently without a meaning." According to Santayana, "In Shakespeare's time and country, to be religious already began to mean to be Puritanical; and in the divorce between the fullness of life on the one hand and the depth and unity of faith on the other, there could be no doubt to which side a man of imaginative instincts would attach himself." Shakespeare thus cannot be the highest type of poet, "for what is required for theoretic wholeness is not this or that system but some system. Its value is not the value of truth, but that of victorious imagination," he says.

Browning and Whitman, on the other hand, were barbarians; that is, they were concerned exclusively with presenting sensations, experiences, feelings, passions. The barbarian is "the man who regards his passions as their own excuse for being; who does not domesticate them either by understanding their cause or by conceiving their ideal goal." Such poetry has pleasing qualities; its emphasis on spontaneity, sensuousness, and irrationality fits certain moods of all men. But here such things are presented as ends in themselves. Whitman is, of course, of a lower order than Browning, being concerned almost exclusively with a mere succession of images and sensations. For him, the surface of life is absolutely all there is.

In Browning, the barbarian is more subtle. His success is more obvious than his failure; yet failure there is, "failure to achieve any finality, or

to achieve a recognition even of the traditional ideals of poetry and religion." Experience is all he offers, energy and action are his goals, and he never rises to a contemplation of life or its ends; he never sees life steadily or whole. Lovers in his poems, for example, never rise to the level of those in Dante or Cavalcanti; they remain always on the level of mere passion. Browning was "a lover of experience; the ideal did not exist for him."

Transcendentalism as Emerson practiced it was an inspirational rather than a systematic philosophy; he simply ignored problems that did not interest him. According to Santayana, the trouble with Emerson was that he was a mystic, or had strong tendencies in that direction. He had no consistent philosophical system and never bothered with disciplining his mind enough to develop one. He used the intuitive method of reaching truth, and while he sometimes came up with rare beauties and insights, he frequently came up with nonsense. Preferring "a fresh statement on a fresh subject" to any laborious formulation, he used the transcendental method to its greatest advantage. But Emerson is an example of the thinker whose imagination has invaded the sphere of understanding and discredited the work of reason. He was thus simply "a Puritan mystic with a poetic fancy and a gift for observation and epigram."

These four writers failed in varying degrees to meet the highest demands of art and poetry, a fact related to the "moral crisis and imaginative disintegration" of our time, caused in large part by the fact that the imagination has never successfully united the two diverse currents of our civilization, which derives its culture from Greece and its religion from Christianity. "A man cannot serve two masters," said Santayana sadly. One unfortunate result is a new belief in man's absolute power, which in turn has made men indifferent to the traditional disciplines, or in fact to any discipline at all. Ignorance of the past and contempt for tradition are the characteristic attitudes of a time whose dominant note is one of disintegration. These writers, especially Whitman and Browning, are representatives of and contributors to that general chaos.

The penultimate essay in *Interpretation of Poetry and Religion* is its weakest, though Santayana thought he had found suggestions of a possible philosophic reconstruction in *La Gloire du néant* by French author Jean Lahor (real name: Henri Cazalis), which tried to combine the pantheism of the Hindus with contemporary natural science and the ideals of ancient Greece. Santayana thought this attempt at reconciliation between practical optimism and speculative pessimism was better than current philosophies, because—as he often pointed out—the first need is to recognize the materialistic basis of existence upon which can be constructed some Platonic system of ideals; because the only immortality life offers is that of the highest ideals.

In the final essay, "The Elements and Function of Poetry," Santayana recapitulates some of the views earlier expressed and summarizes his main principles. He first distinguishes three types of poetry. The first is sensuous poetry, concerned chiefly with meter, sound, and virtuosity in general. The second is poetry of fancy; that is, the first type with emotion and perception added. The third presents a unity and is the best type, poetry of the creative reason. He also examines some other phases of the higher function of poetry: the creation of characters, for example, and backgrounds—not mere landscape, but the cosmic landscape—and dramatic situations. The poet should offer experience, but the experience must furnish enlightenment, defined as some comprehension of the greater unity of the whole: "Poetry is not at its best when it depicts a further possible experience, but when it initiates us, by feigning something which as an experience is impossible, into the meaning of the experience which we have actually had." As he concludes: "Poetry raised to its highest power is then identical with religion grasped in its inmost truth; at their point of union both reach their utmost purity and beneficence, for then poetry loses its frivolity and ceases to demoralize, while religion surrenders its illusions and ceases to deceive."

Santayana's other work of literary criticism is *Three Philosophical Poets*, published ten years after *Interpretations of Poetry and Religion*. In discussing Lucretius, Dante, and Goethe, Santayana's objective is to define the perfect poet, according to the standards described in the earlier volume. These standards, however, are little changed.

He begins with the relationship between poetry and philosophy, asserting that the greatest poetry is philosophical because it has the largest grasp of existence: "the vision of philosophy is sublime. The order it reveals in the world is something beautiful, tragic, sympathetic to the mind, and just what every poet, on a small or on a large scale, is always trying to catch." The objective of philosophy is insight, the "steady contem-

Santayana in 1946 (courtesy of James Turnure)

plation of all things in their order and worth"; a philosopher who attains this insight is a poet. On the other hand, a poet who "turns his practiced and passionate imagination on the order of all things, or on anything in the light of the whole, is for that moment a philosopher." Thus the notion that poets are poor philosophers is not true. Neither is it true that a long poem is a contradiction in terms; long philosophical poetry is the most supreme kind.

This suggests another of Santayana's repeated views; that the subject matter of a poem is more important than its form. A poet should have a classical appreciation of form, but it is essential that he have a comprehensive understanding of his subject. (Once, when his own poem *Lucifer* was criticized, Santayana retorted that its real poetry lay in its subject matter. "Of course," he said, "if you don't feel the poetry of things, you will not feel it in some verbal reflection of it caught by a poet; but I am a true poet in feeling that poetry, and the critics are not good critics if they fail to perceive it.")

Three Philosophical Poets, then, is more a consideration of the philosophic visions of the three poets than a comparison of their verse—though

Santayana would perhaps not admit such a distinction. He sees Lucretius as representative of naturalism and materialism, a poet who sees the world as a great machine; and *De Rerum Natura* describes "the nature, that is, the birth and composition of all things." Dante, on the other hand, is the poet of supernaturalism, the sources of which are in "the solitude of the spirit and in the disparity, or opposition, between what the spirit feels it is fitted to do, and what, in this world, it is condemned to waste itself upon." Finally, Goethe represents romanticism and incidentally the Teutonic and Protestant "races." (Since Protestantism was basically Teutonic in origin, it was therefore also racial.) Romanticism "expresses the self-trust of world-building youth, and mystical faith in will and action." The greatest monument to this attitude is *Faust*. "Goethe," Santayana says, "is the poet of life; Lucretius the poet of Nature; Dante the poet of salvation." Goethe deals "with human life in its immediacy, treated romantically; Lucretius with a vision of Nature and of the limits of human life; Dante with spiritual mastery of that life, and a perfect knowledge of good and evil."

Unfortunately, to have a perfect poet it would be necessary to combine the best elements of all three, since none by himself is quite adequate. Each lacks vital elements that one or both of the others have. It is necessary for the artist to combine all of these great qualities to realize that ideal analyzed in *Interpretations of Poetry and Religion* and achieve the highest degree of completeness. However, such a poet has never existed, but "he is needed nevertheless. . . . It is time some genius should appear to reconstitute the shattered picture of the world. He should live in the continual presence of all experience, and respect it; he should at the same time understand nature, the ground of that experience; and he should also have a delicate sense for the ideal echoes of his own passions, and for all the colours of his possible happiness. All that can inspire a poet is contained in this task, and nothing less than this task would exhaust a poet's inspiration."

Santayana's views here do not differ significantly from those of the earlier volume. He insists on the ideal function of the poet and the necessity for art to be comprehensive, integrative, and ideal. This account of the book, however, cannot do justice to the intricacy, insights, and interest of it. *Three Philosophical Poets* soars far above the usual work of literary criticism. Santayana's style by this time had developed into

an instrument of great flexibility, imaginativeness, and beauty, and it carries the reader along in a kind of fascinated absorption.

The remainder of Santayana's literary criticism is scattered through his subsequent books and periodical contributions. Though it is clear from many references that he read widely, he did not choose to do more on other authors, probably because he had established his principles and saw no further need to reiterate them. He did other pieces of less importance on Emerson and Whitman; in 1903 he gave a lecture on Emerson's poetry which was reprinted in the *Boston Daily Advertiser*, and an undergraduate essay on Emerson's optimism was printed in 1964 for the first time in *Emerson Society Quarterly* (collected in *George Santayana's America*, 1967). Similarly, he wrote a piece on Whitman for the *Harvard Monthly* in 1890 and in 1915 published a brief essay in the *New Republic* entitled "Genteel American Poetry," largely on Whitman. There are frequent references to both authors in his other works; but the formal pieces on them in *Interpretations of Poetry and Religion* constitute his considered judgment and contain essentially all that he had or wanted to say about them.

Other comments on American authors are scattered and thin, usually as incidental parts of philosophical essays on American culture. He did write a short article at the request of Cyril Clemens about *The Adventures of Huckleberry Finn;* but he seemed uncomfortable dealing with novels and seldom criticized one. This piece is curious because it is Tom Sawyer who catches his interest, rather than Huck Finn; but it is not one of his better pieces. His essays on William James and Josiah Royce, from *Character and Opinion in the United States,* are fine pieces of prose and might be included here, though their subjects were not literary men. Brief allusions to Henry James, to Oliver Wendell Holmes, Henry Adams, and other writers appear; and he discusses on a personal level the young poets he knew at Harvard—Franklin Sanborn, Trumbull Stickney, and Howard Sturgis. Finally, in an essay "Tragic Philosophy" he takes issue with a remark made by his former pupil T. S. Eliot, but the piece contains no critique of Eliot's work.

Shakespeare was the subject of several other pieces; in 1908 Santayana wrote an introduction to *Hamlet;* and in 1915 he wrote an article for the *New Republic* on "Shakespeare: Made in America"—an amusing attempt to translate one of Shakespeare's sonnets into modern American English. Again, however, his essential statement on Shakespeare is embodied in the essay in *Interpretations of Poetry and Religion*. The same is true for Browning; he never did another analysis of Browning, but references to him appear frequently, all underlining the attitude expressed in "The Poetry of Barbarism."

There are two other important critical essays, however; one is "Shelley: or the Poetic Value of Revolutionary Principles," originally part of *Winds of Doctrine: Studies in Contemporary Opinion* (1913); the other is an essay on Charles Dickens, published in *Soliloquies in England, and Later Soliloquies* (1922).

The essay on Shelley is one of his best pieces, and this is probably due to the fact that he was quite sympathetic to a poet of the ideal who, repelled by the world, created his own under strong Platonic influence. Of course, Santayana says, many of Shelley's beliefs were childish and cruel; and he did not understand the constitution of nature. Furthermore, revolutionary people are disinherited, have a strange poverty of mind, and are humorless: "They wish to be the leaders of mankind, but they are wretched representatives of humanity." Yet they are also men of insight and hope. Shelley was an idealist in almost every sense of the word, deeply and constantly, like Plato. He had also an extraordinary moral fervor, and his genius combined a vivid love of ideal good on one hand, and on the other, much suffering and horror at the touch of actual evils in his life. Shelley, who created what he called "beautiful idealisms of moral excellence," had "the purest, tenderest, richest, most rational nature ever poured forth in verse." He thus fulfilled to a great degree one of the chief requirements for a poet: the creation of an ideal world, the depiction of life as it should be rather than as it actually is.

Santayana's fondness for Dickens is evident in his piece on that author, and it seems to have surprised many commentators. Some have even proposed that the essay hints at a relaxation of his high standards. He wrote the essay during World War I while living in England; when he was not able to fix his thoughts on abstract matters, he began to read Dickens, he said, and thus learned to love "that humbler side of English sentiment and virtue." What he liked in Dickens was his genuine and enormous human sympathy, his love of detail, his harsh and uncompromising comic spirit, his humility, and his positive and clear distinction between good and evil as he saw it.

Of course Dickens had shortcomings. He was almost wholly insensitive to religion, science, politics, art, and other great themes of the human imagination. He had no ideas on anything, but he did have "a vast sympathetic participation in the daily life of mankind." He had "more genius than taste, a warm fancy not aided by a thorough understanding of complex characters." What is left is still a great deal—almost everything that counts, says Santayana: his love for simple things and simple people, for example, and a true vision of human existence and joy; the gift of humor, of mimicry, and of unrestrained farce. When people say he exaggerates, they are not speaking the truth. The world is in truth a caricature of itself, and true humor is the perception of this. Such people as Dickens depicts, said Santayana, actually exist: "We are such people ourselves in our true moments, in our veritable impulses; but we are careful to stifle and to hide those moments from ourselves and from the world; to purse and pucker ourselves into the mask of our conventional personality; and so simpering, we profess that it is very coarse and inartistic of Dickens to undo our life's work for us in an instant, and remind us of what we are."

Dickens did not by any means appreciate all the values of life, and yet his was the "perfection of comedy, [and] of morals" for two reasons: "He put the distinction between good and evil in the right place, and . . . he felt this distinction intensely."

His Dickens essay points up an important fact about Santayana's criticism, and that is its essential balance and sympathy. The reader concentrates on his large philosophical assertions and grapples with his lofty standards of expectation but often misses the pleasure and enjoyment Santayana displays with the work of the author under discussion. He is able to appreciate and point out the virtues of the author, even though his final estimate may be, on balance, unfavorable. Even Browning and Whitman are handled with a good deal of understanding and sympathy for their very real virtues.

His remaining work in English literature is not significant, consisting of incidental remarks about Matthew Arnold, Aldous Huxley, and others, as well as personal comment on Robert Bridges and Lionel Johnson, whom he knew. Thus, Shakespeare, Browning, Shelley, and Dickens constitute the body of his important work in this area.

Santayana at the Clinic of the Blue Nuns

This is one chief way he differs from the ordinary literary critic.

No account of Santayana's criticism would be complete without some description of his views on the Genteel Tradition. This complex of attitudes and feelings was a cultural matter in America, though it is probably most familiar to students of literature. For most literary people, however, it involved a set of taboos about what writers could and could not deal with, especially in fiction. William Dean Howells, in *Criticism and Fiction* (1891), detailed something of this in his account of "a tradition of decency" in the American novel, caused partly by the fact that the audience for novels was mostly female.

For Santayana, however, the set of taboos posed a much more complex, philosophical problem. He saw it as one of the major reasons American writers were unable to produce a genuinely original literature. He traces it back to Calvinism during the Puritan period which left, after its own demise, a residue of guilt (the "agonized conscience") in subsequent intellectual activity from which American writers were unable wholly to escape. This sense of guilt was later to combine with transcendentalism to create an even more separated sense, in intellectual life, from the mainstream of American life.

He sees this combination as having created a deep division in the American psyche between the everyday life of the country—which consists of feverish activity, business enterprise, invention—and the intellectual life, which consists of values emphasizing faith to outworn creeds and a heavy sense of duty. He epitomized this division with a famous image of the skyscraper (representing the vigorous main thrust of American material life) standing beside a reproduction of a colonial mansion (representing the intellectual and cultural life—the feeble and bloodless Genteel Tradition.) The latter was also the realm of the female, while the former was the male sphere.

His first comment on this matter occurred in a lecture in California in 1911, subsequently published in *Winds of Doctrine* (1913) as "The Genteel Tradition in American Philosophy." In this essay he professed to see some hopeful signs in the works of American humorists (briefly alluded to), and in Walt Whitman, who had given a rude shock to the tradition. Unfortunately, Whitman's revolt had had little result, since he offered nothing to put in the place of the Genteel Tradition. A more significant change, however, was William James's pragmatism, which offered a new way of

In European literature, after the three philosophical poets, there is even less. He did a short essay on Marcel Proust related to his own doctrine of essences; he wrote an introduction to excerpts from *Don Quixote* in the *Library of the World's Best Literature* (1897); and a foreword to a book on Leopardi by Iris Origo, a relative. None of these is a major piece, though all contain some interesting insights. Finally, Santayana wrote nothing on any German authors except Goethe, and the essay in *Three Philosophical Poets* might be supplemented with "Some Hints of Egotism in Goethe," part of *Egotism in German Philosophy* (1915). He did virtually nothing on French literature, either, nor even on Spanish literature. All this means, though, is that his literary criticism, which we tend to think of as a separable activity, was for him simply a part of his total overall philosophy. He was not seeking to offer his opinions of literary figures in themselves, but he used literary figures to explain and illustrate his philosophy.

thinking about reality and seemed to offer an alternative to the Genteel Tradition; thus the essay closed on a hopeful note.

However, twenty years later Santayana returned to the subject in *The Genteel Tradition at Bay* (1931), an attack on the New Humanism of Irving Babbitt and Paul Elmer More. In their notions of humanism he found merely a new absolutism which was not humanistic at all. Outlining the history of humanism, he concludes that the New Humanism is nothing more than an attempt to resuscitate the Genteel Tradition and impose narrow, rigid conceptions of moral values on others.

In a sense, Santayana's best study of the Genteel Tradition is his novel, *The Last Puritan* (1935), a witty account of the struggle of a New Englander named Oliver Alden to find a way to enjoy the possibilities of life even though he is hopelessly inhibited, even paralyzed, by the inherited sense of duty and conscience that most sensitive Americans carry around as part of their intellectual baggage. The novel was astonishingly successful, even being distributed by the Book-of-the-Month club; and it remains a fine example of the philosophical novel.

Santayana's writing on the Genteel Tradition is among his best: witty, lively, and accessible to most readers. His account of its philosophical backgrounds—Calvinism and transcendentalism—may puzzle some readers; but his approach to such subjects was always historical, seeking in the past for an understanding of the present. And with the passage of time his interpretation of the Genteel Tradition has taken on greater significance and meaning for students of that attitude.

Santayana produced some of the best literary criticism of his age despite the fact that it was only a part of his total philosophy. He not only had the advantage of a wide background in philosophy, history, and languages, as well as considerable knowledge of the other arts, but he was also a novelist and a practitioner of the art of poetry himself. He presents, therefore, a sophisticated and broad view that few of his contemporaries can approach, and his cosmopolitanism at least matches that of Henry James. In addition, his detachment gave him a degree of objectivity that was unusual. Not that he was completely impartial—"a man cannot sit above the clouds and have no prejudices," he once said—but he had the ability to consider all possible facets of a matter and to choose the view most congenial. His detachment also gave him some sense of the relative im-

portance of things, seen in the long view, so he was less subject to temporary enthusiasms like those that can sometimes afflict literary critics.

His literary values were essentially those of the nineteenth century. He never took to the kind of changes wrought by Whitman and later moderns; in fact, he was temperamentally opposed to the modern world itself, or rather the values it proposed. He saw modern man as a victim of the four "R's" as he called them—Renaissance, Reformation, Revolution, and Romanticism—which had brought about the chaos of modern life. Personally he preferred an older world, one of settled traditions, of discipline and order; but as he often pointed out, he was quite able to adapt to the world as he found it.

One finds in his work some important features of the nineteenth-century idea of poetry. For example, the notion that poetry should present an idealized view of life was a quite common conception in nineteenth-century American poetry. This is, in turn, related to the belief that there is such a thing as a poetic subject matter, and that some subjects are not fit for poetry—an opinion that prompted much of his opposition to Walt Whitman when he first began to publish. Such views may well be part of the extravagant admiration for Shelley who was one of the most influential poets of that age.

Santayana's heavy historical emphasis was also characteristic of that age. Nearly all his critical pieces devote ample space to the historical setting of an author and his work; the past offers a large part of the explanation of what they are and why. Santayana's evaluation of nearly all writers is set into the context of the age as well as against the background of how their age developed.

Santayana's aesthetic interests were a part of the turn-of-the-century literary world, too; and his beginning as a poet and aesthete was very much consistent with that time. So too was his early work in aesthetics itself, a rather trendy subject then. His emphasis on morality in literature was also common to that age. Finally, his prose style itself is much more reminiscent of the great nineteenth-century writers than it is of modern work, which tends to emphasize simplicity, directness, and bluntness.

In some respects, however, his work is strikingly modern. Certainly his emphasis on the naturalistic basis of thought and action is modern, as is his full acceptance of science and scientific discoveries. His interest in anthropology and mythology seems modern, too and consistent with attitudes of poets like Eliot and Yeats, who found mythology a critical need for their work. Finally, Santayana's sense of tolerance and acceptance seems much more consistent with our time than the rigidities of, say, Babbitt and More.

Letters:

The Letters of George Santayana, edited by Daniel Cory (New York: Scribners, 1955; London: Constable, 1955).

Bibliography:

Herman J. Saatkamp, Jr., and John Jones, *George Santayana: A Bibliographical Checklist, 1880-1980* (Bowling Green, Ohio: Philosophy Documentation Center, Bowling Green University, 1982).

Biographies:

George W. Howgate, *George Santayana* (Philadelphia: University of Pennsylvania Press/London: Oxford University Press, 1938);

Richard Butler, *The Life and World of George Santayana* (Chicago: Regnery, 1960);

M. M. Kirkwood, *Santayana: Saint of the Imagination* (Toronto: University of Toronto Press, 1961);

Daniel Cory, *Santayana: The Later Years: A Portrait with Letters* (New York: Braziller, 1963);

Willard E. Arnett, *George Santayana* (New York: Washington Square Press, 1968);

Newton P. Stallknecht, *George Santayana* (Minneapolis: University of Minnesota Press, 1971);

John McCormick, *George Santayana: A Biography* (New York: Knopf, 1987).

References:

Van Meter Ames, *Proust and Santayana: The Aesthetic Way of Life* (Chicago: Willet, Clark, 1937);

Willard E. Arnett, "Santayana and the Fine Arts," *Journal of Aesthetics and Art Criticism,* 16 (1957): 84-95;

Arnett, *Santayana and the Sense of Beauty* (Bloomington: Indiana University Press, 1955);

Maurice Cohen, "Santayana on Romanticism and Egotism," *Journal of Religion,* 66 (1966): 264-281;

Joe Lee Davis, "Santayana as a Critic of Transcendentalism," in *Transcendentalism and Its Legacy,* edited by Myron Simon and Thornton H. Parsons (Ann Arbor: University of Michigan, 1966): 150-184;

Norman Henfrey, ed., *Selected Critical Writings of George Santayana,* 2 volumes (Cambridge: Cambridge University Press, 1968);

Q. D. Leavis, "Critical Writings of George Santayana, An Introductory Note," *Scrutiny,* 3 (December 1935): 278-295;

Kenneth Lynn, "Santayana and the Genteel Tradition," *Commentary,* 73 (May 1982): 81-84;

John M. Major, "Santayana on Shakespeare," *Shakespeare Quarterly,* 10 (1959): 469-479;

Wilfred M. McClay, "Two Versions of the Genteel Tradition: Santayana and Brooks," *New England Quarterly,* 55 (September 1982): 368-391;

Edgar L. McCormick, "Walt Whitman, Santayana's Poet of Barbarism, *Serif,* 5, no. 15 (1968): 24-28;

John W. Rathbun and Harry Hayden Clark, *American Literary Criticism 1860-1905* (Boston: G. K. Hall, 1979);

Paul A. Schilpp, ed., *The Philosophy of Santayana,* (Chicago: Northwestern University, 1940);

Irving Singer, ed., *Essays in Literary Criticism of George Santayana* (New York: Scribners, 1956);

Newton P. Stallknecht, "George Santayana and the Uses of Literature," *Yearbook of Comparative and General Literature,* 15 (1966): 5-18;

William Walsh, "Santayana as a Critic," *Review of English Literature* (Leeds), 5, no. 1 (1964) 69-77;

Paul C. Wermuth, *George Santayana as a Literary Critic,* Ph.D. dissertation, Pennsylvania State University, 1955;

Wermuth, "Santayana and Emerson," *Emerson Society Quarterly,* 31 (1963): 36-40;

Wermuth and J. F. S. Smeall, "Santayana and the Language of Shakespeare," *North Dakota Quarterly,* 30 (1962): 1-7;

Elkin C. Wilson, *Shakespeare, Santayana and the Comic,* (University: University of Alabama Press, 1973).

Papers:

The largest collection of Santayana papers is at Columbia University's Butler Library in New York. There are also collections at Harvard's Houghton Library; at the Humanities Research Center, University of Texas; and at the University of Virginia.

Horace Elisha Scudder

(16 October 1838-11 January 1902)

Peter A. Brier
California State University, Los Angeles

See also the Scudder entry in *DLB 42, American Writers for Children Before 1900.*

BOOKS: *Seven Little People and Their Friends* (New York: Randolf, 1862);

Life and Letters of David Coit Scudder (New York: Hurd & Houghton, 1864);

Dream Children (Cambridge, Mass.: Sever & Francis, 1864);

Stories from My Attic (New York: Hurd & Houghton, 1869);

Doings of the Bodley Family in Town and Country (New York: Hurd & Houghton, 1875);

The Dwellers in Five-Sisters' Court (New York: Hurd & Houghton, 1876);

The Bodleys Telling Stories (New York: Hurd & Houghton, 1878);

The Bodleys on Wheels (Boston: Houghton, Osgood, 1879);

The Bodleys Afoot (Boston: Houghton, Osgood, 1880);

Mr. Bodley Abroad (Boston: Houghton, Mifflin, 1880);

Stories and Romances (Boston: Houghton, Mifflin, 1880);

Boston Town (Boston: Houghton, Mifflin, 1881);

The Bodley Grandchildren and Their Journey in Holland (Boston: Houghton, Mifflin, 1882);

Noah Webster (Boston: Houghton, Mifflin, 1882);

The English Bodley Family (Boston: Houghton, Mifflin, 1884);

Life and Letters of Bayard Taylor, by Scudder and Marie Hansen-Taylor (Boston & New York: Houghton, Mifflin, 1884);

A History of the United States of America, Preceded by a Narrative of the Discovery and Settlement of North America and of the Events Which Led to the Independence of the Thirteen English Colonies, for the Use of Schools and Academies (Philadelphia: Butler/Boston: Ware, 1884);

The Viking Bodleys (Boston: Houghton, Mifflin, 1885);

Men and Letters: Essays in Characterization and Criticism (Boston & New York: Houghton, Mifflin, 1887);

Portraits and Biographical Sketches of Twenty American Authors (Boston & New York: Houghton, Mifflin, 1887);

Literature in School: An Address and Two Essays (Boston & New York: Houghton, Mifflin, 1888);

George Washington: An Historical Biography (Boston & New York: Houghton, Mifflin, 1889);

Fables and Folk Stories (Boston: Houghton, Mifflin, 1890); republished as *The Book of Fables and Folk Stories* (Boston: Houghton, Mifflin, 1906);

A Short History of the United States of America, for the Use of Beginners (New York: Taintor/Boston: Ware, 1890);

The Riverside Primer and Reader, by Scudder, J. F. Hall, and C. F. Newkink (Boston: Houghton, Mifflin, 1893);

Childhood in Literature and Art (Boston & New York: Houghton, Mifflin, 1894);

Henry Oscar Houghton: A Biographical Outline (Cambridge, Mass.: Houghton, Mifflin, 1897);

A History of the United States of America, With an Introduction Narrating the Discovery and Settlement of North America (New York & Chicago: Sheldon, 1897);

James Russell Lowell: A Biography, 2 volumes (Boston & New York: Houghton, Mifflin, 1901).

OTHER: *Men and Manners in America One Hundred Years Ago,* edited by Scudder (New York: Scribner, Armstrong, 1876);

Recollections of Samuel Beck, With Passages from His Notebooks, edited by Scudder (London: Low, Marston, Searle & Rivington, 1877);

American Poems: Longfellow, Whittier, Bryant, Holmes, Lowell, Emerson, edited, with biographical sketches and notes, by Scudder (Boston: Houghton, Osgood, 1879; revised edition, Boston & New York: Houghton, Mifflin, 1892);

American Prose: Hawthorne, Irving, Longfellow, Whittier, Holmes, Lowell, Thoreau, Emerson, edited, with an introduction and notes, by Scudder (Boston: Houghton, Osgood, 1880; revised

243

Horace Elisha Scudder (photograph by Smith, Boston)

and enlarged edition, Boston & New York: Houghton, Mifflin, 1892);

The Children's Book: A Collection of the Best and Most Famous Stories and Poems in the English Language, edited by Scudder (Boston: Houghton, Mifflin, 1881);

The Book of Fables, Chiefly from Aesop, edited by Scudder (Boston: Houghton, Mifflin, 1882);

The Book of Folk Stories, retold by Scudder (Boston: Houghton, Mifflin, 1887);

Masterpieces of American Literature, edited by Scudder (Boston: Houghton, Mifflin, 1891);

Verse and Prose for Beginners in Reading, compiled by Scudder (Boston & New York: Houghton, Mifflin, 1893);

The Writings of Henry David Thoreau, 10 volumes, edited by Scudder (Boston & New York: Houghton, Mifflin, 1894-1895);

Masterpieces of British Literature, edited by Scudder (Boston: Houghton, Mifflin, 1895);

The Complete Poetical Works of John Greenleaf Whittier, edited by Scudder (Boston & New York: Houghton, Mifflin, 1895);

The Complete Poetical Works of James Russell Lowell, edited by Scudder (Boston & New York: Houghton, Mifflin, 1897);

The Book of Legends Told Over Again, retold by Scudder (Boston: Houghton, Mifflin, 1899);

Fables, Folk Stories and Legends, edited by Scudder (Boston: Houghton, Mifflin, 1899);

The Complete Works of Nathaniel Hawthorne, 22 volumes, edited by Scudder (Boston & New York: Houghton, Mifflin, 1900-1901).

PERIODICAL PUBLICATIONS: "The Life of William Blake," *North American Review,* 99 (October 1864): 465-482;

Review of *Irene, the Missionary* by J. W. DeForest, *Atlantic Monthly,* 45 (May 1880): 680-681;

Review of *Old Friends and New* by Sarah Orne Jewett, *Atlantic Monthly,* 45 (May 1880): 685-686;

Review of *Democracy* by Henry Adams, *Atlantic Monthly,* 46 (September 1880): 421-422;

Review of *Dr. Heidenhoff's Process* by Edward Bellamy, *Atlantic Monthly,* 46 (December 1880): 824-826;

Review of *The Grandissimes* by George Washington Cable, *Atlantic Monthly,* 46 (December 1880): 829-831;

Review of *Washington Square* by Henry James, *Atlantic Monthly,* 47 (May 1881): 709-710;

Review of *The Trumpet Major* by Thomas Hardy, *Atlantic Monthly,* 47 (May 1881): 712-713;

Review of *The Portrait of a Lady* by Henry James, *Atlantic Monthly,* 49 (January 1882): 126-128;

Review of *Dr. Breen's Practice* by William Dean Howells, *Atlantic Monthly,* 49 (January 1882): 128-130;

Review of *A Modern Instance* by William Dean Howells, *Atlantic Monthly,* 50 (November 1882): 709-713;

"Two Women of Letters (Maria Edgeworth, Mary Russell Mitford)," *Atlantic Monthly,* 51 (March 1883): 413-416;

Review of *An Autobiography* by Anthony Trollope, *Atlantic Monthly,* 53 (February 1884): 267-271;

Review of *A Roman Singer* by Francis Marion Crawford, *Atlantic Monthly,* 54 (September 1884): 421-422;

Review of *Ramona* by Helen Hunt Jackson, *Atlantic Monthly,* 55 (January 1885): 127-130;

Review of *Marius the Epicurean* by Walter Pater, *Atlantic Monthly,* 56 (August 1885): 273-277;

Review of *The Rise of Silas Lapham* by William Dean Howells, *Atlantic Monthly,* 56 (October 1885): 554-556;

Review of *The Bostonians* by Henry James, *Atlantic Monthly,* 57 (June 1886): 850-853;

Review of *The Late Mrs. Null* by Frank Stockton, *Atlantic Monthly,* 58 (July 1886): 133-134;

Review of *The Yoke of the Torah* by Sidney Luska, *Atlantic Monthly,* 60 (August 1887): 415-416;

Review of *Looking Backward* by Edward Bellamy, *Atlantic Monthly,* 61 (June 1888): 845-846;

Review of *Robert Elsmere* by Mrs. Humphry Ward, *Atlantic Monthly,* 62 (November 1888): 700-704;

Review of *A Hazard of New Fortunes* by William Dean Howells, *Atlantic Monthly,* 65 (April 1890): 563-566;

Review of *The Tragic Muse* by Henry James, *Atlantic Monthly,* 66 (September 1890): 419-422;

Review of *A New England Nun* by Mary E. Wilkins and *Strangers and Wayfarers* by Sarah Orne Jewett, *Atlantic Monthly,* 67 (June 1891): 845-850;

Review of *Criticism and Fiction* by William Dean Howells, *Atlantic Monthly,* 68 (October 1891): 566-569;

Review of "The Real Thing" by Henry James, *Atlantic Monthly,* 72 (November 1893):695-696;

Review of *The Cliff Dwellers* by Henry B. Fuller, *Atlantic Monthly,* 73 (April 1894): 555-557;

Review of *Bayou Folk* by Kate Chopin, *Atlantic Monthly,* 73 (April 1894): 558-559;

Review of *Pembroke* by Mary E. Wilkins, *Atlantic Monthly,* 74 (August 1894): 272-274;

"Richard Harding Davis," *Atlantic Monthly,* 75 (May 1895): 654-658;

Review of *My Literary Passions* by William Dean Howells, *Atlantic Monthly,* 76 (November 1895): 701-703;

Review of *Red Man and White* by Owen Wister, *Atlantic Monthly,* 77 (February 1896): 264-265;

Review of *The Damnation of Theron Ware* by Harold Frederic, *Atlantic Monthly,* 78 (August 1896): 270-272;

Review of *Novels, Tales, Sketches* by Sir James Barrie, *Atlantic Monthly,* 79 (May 1897): 705-707;

Review of *The Choir Invisible* by James Lane Allen, *Atlantic Monthly,* 80 (July 1897): 143-144.

Shy and somewhat reserved, largely because of intermittent deafness, a gracious, bearded, and rotund self-styled "literary workman" who resembled the prototype of the old New England authors he championed, Horace Elisha Scudder not only edited the *Riverside Magazine for Young People* but also founded the Riverside Literature series of texts for schools and colleges. Henry Wadsworth Longfellow, Ralph Waldo Emerson, John Greenleaf Whittier, and James Russell Lowell entered the American curriculum through his efforts. He created the Cambridge Poets series, consisting of one-volume editions on major American and British poets. According to Howard Mumford Jones, through this series Scudder "performed one of the most amazing feats in the history of American books." As editor of the *Atlantic Monthly* from 1890 to 1898, Scudder advised, guided, corrected, and cajoled Sarah Orne Jewett, Theodore Roosevelt, Woodrow Wilson, and Henry James. He began as a promoter of juvenile literature; he emerged a prominent biographer and editor who, as reviewer and occasional essayist, did significant critical work on contemporary writers.

Scudder's father, Charles Scudder, was a successful hardware merchant and a devout but genial Congregationalist. His mother, Sarah Lathrop Coit, came from a family of educators, founders of the St. Paul School in New Hampshire. One of Horace's brothers (the father of Vida Dutton Scudder) died in a drowning accident while serving as a missionary in India; another brother became an important entomologist. It remained for Scudder, the youngest child, to bring together this rich legacy of entrepreneurial acumen, dedicated service, and reverence for intellect in a life of letters. After graduating in 1858 from Williams College–where he had studied philosophy, made first contact with his future patron, Henry Oscar Houghton, and edited the *Williams Quarterly*–Scudder tutored, considered the ministry, and wrote his first children's stories. His mysterious hearing problem dissuaded him from a public career as teacher or churchman. At his father's request, he wrote a biography of his dead brother, the missionary David Coit. During this period he tried his hand at reviewing and in 1864 placed an important essay on William Blake in Charles Eliot Norton's *North American Review.*

In this essay, essentially a review of Alexander Gilchrist's monumental illustrated Blake, Scudder established the centrality of biography to his critical method. No one could sketch a life more neatly than Horace Scudder; he brought this talent to perfection in his introductory essays to the Cambridge Poets editions. From early versions of Lowell "essays" and "notes" in the Riverside Literature series to the two-volume life of the poet, one can trace Scudder's gradual development of the biographical "introduction" into the full sweep of magisterial biography, from the "sketch" to the "life." In *James Russell Lowell: A Biography* (1901), a project Scudder kept postponing because of his many editorial duties, he finally achieved a work as great as any by the Victorian masters. Martin Duberman, in his 1966 biography of Lowell, acknowledges that although Scudder's biography "suffers fatally from being a tribute . . . and is superseded by new materials, it must be remembered that Scudder was the first to research Lowell's life in depth and his considerable efforts turned up basic data on which scholars have ever since relied." So thorough is Scudder's documentation and so lively his historical grasp that *James Russell Lowell* has been called a history of American literature in the nineteenth century.

The Blake essay of 1864 foreshadows Scudder's talent for research and accuracy; it also stresses his belief in "imagination," the power of literature to illuminate reality, not merely to transcribe it. Blake's identification of his own imagination with the "highest expression of his soul" gives readers "sudden vistas of immortality" that they might otherwise never attain. Scudder praises what he calls Blake's blending of "objective" and "subjective" imagination. The influence of Emerson is apparent, but Scudder must be given credit for the originality of his insistence on the power of imagination to render the factual in its fullest sense. He applied this insight with growing subtlety in the editorial years, and when he finally had the editorship of the *Atlantic Monthly* he was able to challenge openly the assumptions of William Dean Howells's literary realism that had become heavily identified with the magazine's point of view.

In the same year that he published the Blake essay, Scudder produced *Dream Children.* Its title recalls Charles Lamb's familiar essay, and, indeed, Scudder hoped to rediscover Lamb's evocation of innocent imagination. "The beauty we dream about may be the most real after all," announces Scudder in his preface. Whatever the mystical direction of these sentiments, they struck Henry Oscar Houghton as proof that Scudder understood what children thought and would therefore be the right man to head up a juvenile periodical. (Scudder, who had been writing children's stories since the late 1850s, had already acquired the sobriquet of "the American Hans Christian Andersen.") By searching for the most honest juvenile fiction, the most sensitive illustrators, and by reaching for the most attractive design and publication values, Scudder made the *Riverside Magazine for Young People* a classic of its kind. Although the magazine was not a commercial success, it secured for Houghton such important authors as the "real" Hans Christian Andersen and Frank Stockton. By 1872 Houghton was sufficiently impressed with his "workman" to offer him a partnership. Professionally secure, Scudder married Grace Owen the following year, and they settled in Cambridge, Massachusetts. The couple later had twin daughters.

When Hurd and Houghton lost money in 1874, Scudder backed out of the partnership. Houghton never permitted him to wander far, but Scudder did use the relative independence of the next ten years to pursue his greatest interests, all of which were intertwined: American literature, history, and education. He felt it essential for the nation to embrace its own literature and history to balance the heavy influence of British and other European traditions. Scudder believed that not merely national pride but rather na-

Scudder at work

tional survival and moral character were at stake. His ideas on the role literature and history should play in education earned him a position on the Massachusetts Board of Education, an offer of a professorship at Williams College, and the chance to name his own salary as James Pulitzer's literary editor for the *New York World*. A devoted Bostonian, Scudder turned down his alma mater and New York, but he did overcome his reserve and traveled to San Francisco in 1888 to address the National Teachers' Association with the following challenge: "Unless the definite end of ennobling the mind through familiarity with literature of the spirit is recognized in our school curriculum, the finest results of education will be lost." Scudder foresaw that American society would make increasing demands on education as parental and religious authority weakened. His faith in the ability of American litera-

ture to instill national identity and morality in America's schoolchildren, without encouraging uncritical or reactionary political views, was a disinterested conviction in the Arnoldian sense. His shrewd patron did not question Scudder's philosophy; Houghton was confident it could make Houghton, Mifflin rich. In addition to the Riverside Literature series, which consisted of inexpensive texts of American and British classics, Houghton, Mifflin eventually launched three major book series that capitalized on Scudder's editorial ideas: American Men of Letters, edited by James T. Fields and Charles Dudley Warner; American Statesmen, edited by John T. Morse; and American Commonwealths, edited by Scudder.

In 1887 Scudder published a collection of literary lectures, *Men and Letters: Essays in Characterization and Criticism*. Most striking is their constant reiteration of the principle of cultural nationalism. Scudder is here more "objective" than "subjective." His concern is now to locate the "spiritual" in historical and social forces. He still has praise for Emerson's "great gift to his countrymen" of the "serenity of his life and thought," but Emerson's basic indifference to the "nation" is a weakness. "It is precisely this passion of nationality which differentiates seers and poets. Milton had it. Carlyle had it. Tennyson had it. Victor Hugo had it. Goethe did not have it. The absence of this passion is indeed the sign of an inferior ethical apprehension." Nevertheless, William Shakespeare's transcendent realism is acknowledged as superior to Anthony Trollope's faithfulness to "external reality." However, only the truly educated mind will be able to respond to Shakespeare in the future because of the absence of the "democratic" in his plays—a crack in the Bard's armor. In another essay Scudder discusses the American theater and argues that, with the exception of the Civil War, America has had no subject "dramatic" enough to provide a significant historical drama. Throughout these essays, one has the impression that Scudder's ancestral Puritan individualism has yielded important ground to institutionalism and statism; that Scudder's hopes for literature are increasingly identified with the educational and social realities of his time; that in a democracy with universal education and a yellow press, literature must preserve the "spirit" of the "nation," not only of the person. And yet several essays cannot be categorized in this way. "The Shaping of Excelsior" is a brilliant comparison of variants of Longfellow's poem. In "Landor as a Classic" Scudder argues convincingly that Walter Savage Landor's famous "conversations" do not merely recreate the minds and voices of the principles involved; they go further and underscore the "style" the speakers *sought* to embody.

When Scudder returned to Houghton, Mifflin's full-time employ in 1890, it was to take the reins of the *Atlantic Monthly*, which H. O. Houghton and Company had acquired in 1874. For almost ten years Scudder not only edited the magazine but also contributed a large number of reviews and essays. Admirers of Scudder's "skillful literary workmanship," wrote an anonymous eulogist in March 1902, "are unaware that he has contributed more pages to the *Atlantic* than any other writer." Scudder began his editorship by translating his sense of the "nation" into an increase of the magazine's coverage of politics and education—or of anything having "a direct bearing upon the public life of the country." He solicited a paper from Theodore Roosevelt on civil-service reform and got Alfred T. Mahan to contribute his prophetic "The Isthmus and Sea Power." In literary matters he wanted to encourage an early version of modern formalism, criticism that would focus analytically on texts. He brought to the *Atlantic Monthly* George Pierce Baker, Gamaliel Bradford, John Jay Chapman, George Lyman Kittredge, and George Santayana. Perhaps his greatest achievement was his loyalty to Henry James, whose reputation Scudder championed in spite of objections from the magazine's staff and readership to the seventeen installments of *The Tragic Muse*. Scudder wrote a memorable defense of the novel in September 1890. The essay, wrote James to Scudder, "brought tears to my eyes—giving me a luxurious sense of being understood, perceived, felt."

Scudder's sensitivity to James's purposes came from a revived sense of the interrelationship between "subjective" and "objective," between the poet and the moralist, the individual spirit and the national soul. Scudder's grasp of cultural and aesthetic ambiguities seems stronger than it had been in the *Men and Letters* collection of 1887. In reviewing James's "The Real Thing" in November 1893, Scudder praises the Master for providing "a most ingenious satire on realism in fiction." Scudder's moral standards often tempted him to lean toward Howells's "realism," but an innate distaste of cant, tract, and all forms of sentimentality always brought him back to his awe of the "spiritual" power of the greatest literature. He could praise the national thrust of literary regionalism and local color in George Washington Cable and Bret Harte, but his love of style, imagination, and aesthetic nuance usually prevailed. Ten years before taking over the *Atlantic Monthly*, he had faulted the historical novelist William Waldorf Astor for permitting historical accuracy to get the better of his art as a novelist. Realism cannot be its own rationale. In November 1888, in an important review of Mrs. Humphry Ward's *Robert Elsmere*, Scudder insisted that "Permanence is one of the attributes of a work of literary art. . . . When an author deliberately uses fiction to accomplish certain results, it is clear that when the occasion passes the use of the book has departed."

Scudder's diabetes aged him prematurely, and an attack of bronchopneumonia in January 1901 drove him into a long convalescence that he used to go over the draft of his life of Lowell—the last of a series of biographies that includes studies on Bayard Taylor and Noah Webster. A "literary workman" to the end, he died shortly after seeing the two volumes to press.

Letters:

The Andersen-Scudder Letters: Hans Christian Andersen's Correspondence with Horace Elisha Scudder, edited and translated, with notes, by Waldemar Westergaard (Berkeley: University of California Press, 1949).

References:

Ellen B. Ballou, *The Building of the House: Houghton Mifflin's Formative Years* (Boston: Houghton Mifflin, 1970);

Martin Duberman, *James Russell Lowell* (Boston: Houghton Mifflin, 1966);

M. A. De Wolfe Howe, *The Atlantic Monthly And Its Makers* (Boston: Atlantic Monthly Press, 1919);

Howard Mumford Jones, *The Age of Energy, Varieties of American Experience 1865-1915* (New York: Viking, 1971);

Jones, "Massachusetts, There She Is," *Violence and Reason* (New York: Atheneum, 1969);

Helen McMahon, *Criticism of Fiction: A Study of Trends in the Atlantic Monthly 1857-1898* (New York: Bookman Associates, 1952).

Papers:

Horace Elisha Scudder's correspondence and diaries, including his papers relating to the Lowell biography, are at the Houghton Library at Harvard. There are Scudder letters in the Stedman Collection of the Butler Library at Columbia University and at the Huntington Library in San Marino.

Vida Dutton Scudder

(15 December 1861-9 October 1954)

Carey Wall
San Diego State University

BOOKS: *How the Rain Sprites Were Freed,* as Davida Coit (Boston: Lothrop, 1885);

The Grotesque in Gothic Art (N.p., 1887);

Mitsu-Yu Nissi; or the Japanese Wedding, by Scudder, as V.D.S., and Frona M. Brooks, as F.M.B. (Boston: Young, 1888);

The Life of the Spirit in the Modern English Poets (Boston: Houghton, Mifflin, 1895);

The Witness of Denial (New York: Dutton, 1895);

Social Ideals in English Letters (Boston: Houghton, Mifflin, 1898; revised and enlarged, 1923);

Introduction to the Study of English Literature (New York: Globe School Book Co., 1901; revised edition, New York: World Book Co., 1914);

A Listener in Babel: Being a Series of Imaginary Conversations Held at the Close of the Last Century and Reported by Vida D. Scudder (Boston & New York: Houghton, Mifflin, 1903);

The Disciple of a Saint: Being the Imaginary Biography of Raniero di Landoccio dei Pagliaresi (New York: Dutton, 1907; London: Dent, 1907);

Socialism and Character (Boston & New York: Houghton Mifflin, 1912; London: Dent, 1912);

Le Morte d'Arthur of Sir Thomas Malory and Its Sources (New York: Dutton, 1917; London: Dent, 1917);

The Church and the Hour: Reflections of a Socialist Churchwoman (New York: Dutton, 1917);

Social Teachings of the Christian Year: Lectures Delivered at the Cambridge Conference, 1918 (New York: Dutton, 1921);

Brother John: A Tale of the First Franciscans (Boston: Little, Brown, 1927; London: Dent, 1927);

The Franciscan Adventure: A Study of the First Hundred Years of the Order of St. Francis of Assisi (London & Toronto: Dent/New York: Dutton, 1931);

On Journey (New York: Dutton, 1937; London: Dent, 1937);

The Privilege of Age: Essays Secular and Spiritual (New York: Dutton, 1939; London: Dent, 1939);

Vida Dutton Scudder

Father Huntington: Founder of the Order of the Holy Cross (New York: Dutton, 1940);

My Quest for Reality (Wellesley, Mass., 1952).

OTHER: George MacDonald, *Poems,* edited, with an introduction, by Scudder and Clara French, as C.F. (New York: Dutton, 1887);

Macaulay's Essay on Lord Clive, edited, with an introduction, by Scudder (Boston & New York: Leach, Shewell & Sanborn, 1889);

An Introduction to the Writings of John Ruskin, edited, with an introduction, by Scudder (Boston & New York: Leach, Shewell & Sanborn, 1890; revised edition, Boston & Chicago: Sibley, 1901);

Percy Bysshe Shelley, *Prometheus Unbound*, edited, with an introduction, by Scudder (Boston: Heath, 1892);

Saint Catherine of Siena as Seen in Her Letters, translated and edited by Scudder (London: Dent/ New York: Dutton, 1905);

The Venerable Bede, *The Ecclesiastical History of the English Nation*, edited, with an introduction, by Scudder (London & Toronto: Dent, 1910; New York: Dutton, n.d.);

The Journal, with Other Writings of John Woolman, edited, with an introduction, by Scudder (London: Dent, 1910; New York: Dutton, n.d.);

Shorter English Poems, edited, with an introduction, by Scudder (Chicago & New York: Scott, Foresman, 1912).

PERIODICAL PUBLICATIONS: "The Poetic Element in Medieval Drama," *Atlantic Monthly*, 56 (September 1885): 407-415;

"The Educated Woman as a Social Factor: III," *Christian Union*, 35 (21 April 1887): 12-13;

"The Effect of the Scientific Temper on Modern Poetry," *Andover Review*, 8 (September 1887): 225-246; (October 1887): 351-366;

"The Poetry of Matthew Arnold," *Andover Review*, 10 (September 1888): 232-249;

"Womanhood in Modern Poetry," *Poet Lore*, 1 (15 October 1889): 449-465;

"A Comparative Study of Wordsworth's 'Michael,' Tennyson's 'Enoch Arden,' Browning's 'Andrea del Sarto,'" *Poet Lore*, 3 (16 February 1891): 87-93;

"Alfred de Vigny," *Wellesley Magazine*, 4 (16 May 1896): 421-428;

"Recollections of Ruskin," *Atlantic Monthly*, 85 (April 1900): 568-571;

"The Educational Element in Dante's Divine Comedy, I," *Kindergarten Review*, 13 (November 1902): 127-135;

"The Educational Element in Dante's Divine Comedy, II," *Kindergarten Review*, 13 (December 1902): 194-199;

"The Irish Literary Drama," *Poet Lore*, 16 (March 1905): 40-53;

"Religion and Socialism," *Harvard Theological Review*, 3 (April 1910): 230-247;

"The Forerunners," *Atlantic Monthly*, 107 (August 1911): 231-242;

"Masefield and Gibson: A Renaissance in Social Poetry," *Survey*, 31 (7 March 1914): 707-709;

"Woman and Socialism," *Yale Review*, new series 3 (April 1914): 454-470;

"Plato as a Novelist," *Yale Review*, new series 4 (July 1915): 788-804;

"John Woolman Today," *Friend*, 93 (March 1920): 434-437.

As a literary critic Vida Dutton Scudder was of her times, an idealist, but with strong leanings both toward the world and its politics and the church and its organizations. Her life was integrated by her attempts to unite literature, socialism, and Christianity. She was a member of the Wellesley College Department of English for forty-one years (1887-1928) but achieved her fame as an activist Christian socialist. She helped to found college settlements on the East Coast, working at Denison House; she worked to expand higher education for women; she propelled and initiated church organizations; she took part in public debate of the issues of her times (workers' rights, democracy, social community); she wrote many books, including *Socialism and Character* (1912), her own favorite, about the conjunction between the Christian message of brotherhood and the realities of the economic world. She was forceful in her own character more than in her ideas, the character interpreting the ideas, and today Scudder is probably of greatest scholarly and analytical interest as a professional woman of her period. She describes her full life in her autobiography, *On Journey* (1937).

Scudder was born in Madura, India, on 15 December 1861 to David Coit Scudder, a missionary, and Harriet Louisa Dutton Scudder. She was a niece of both E. P. Dutton, the publisher, and Horace Scudder, of the *Atlantic Monthly* and Houghton, Mifflin. Literature and literary criticism came into her life early and served to press her toward her lifelong endeavors to change society. Believing that literature arises out of social realities and that "the spiritual ideals of an age are to be read best through its imaginative art," she found that her early analyses of the works she loved as the glory of the English "race" held firm throughout the many decades of her life.

For Scudder the material and spiritual worlds interpenetrated one another. The truth to be derived from literature, then, even idealist truth, necessitated social action. Scudder's teaching career was one part of that action, for, with care not to slip into propaganda, she used the classroom to awaken her privileged students to a sense of the economic and spiritual deprivations suffered by centuries of the world's workers, including those of the nineteenth and twentieth centuries. In her first two critical books, which together constitute the major part of her contribution to American literary criticism, Scudder deals first with English Romantic and Victorian poetry and then with English Victorian prose, primarily the nonfiction. The important works of these periods represented to her the full emergence of an impulse that the canon of masterworks in English literature reveals to have been building for centuries: the impulse toward recognition of the value of every man's life.

The Life of the Spirit in the Modern English Poets (1895) grew out of the thesis she wrote for her master's degree from Smith College. Several stages in her education prepared Scudder to write from the beginning with a peculiar kind of confidence. (At the time of her retirement an article on her in the *Wellesley Alumnae Magazine* by a woman who had graduated in 1920 comments, "her books, read in a listening mood, will always reverberate with her unique liturgical utterance.") As the only child of a mother early widowed (Scudder's father accidentally drowned in 1862) and in possession of sufficient means, Scudder spent her girlhood traveling among and staying in beautiful European places. Then, when it was first established, she became a student of the Boston Girls' Latin School. Next, just when the first class had been graduated, Scudder entered Smith College, from which she graduated in 1884. She and a classmate spent the next academic year at Oxford University; they were among the first American women to be accepted as special students there. That year steadied Scudder's life. She had for many years been beset by a sense of the unreality of her life, but now she heard John Ruskin present the last set of lectures he gave before he retired. Ruskin showed her a way to link literature to social reality and social purpose. She returned to Smith to obtain her master's.

By the time she had taught the material of her thesis for several years and developed her analysis of nineteenth-century English poetry, Scudder produced a book with chapters entitled "Science and the Modern Poets," "Wordsworth and the New Democracy," "Ideals of Redemption, Medieval and Modern," "The New Renaissance," "Browning as a Humorist," "The Poetry of Search," and "The Triumph of the Spirit." While Scudder's activities were multifaceted (so that she never wrote most of the further literary

Portrait of Scudder by Charles Hopkinson (courtesy of Wellesley College Archives)

criticism she early assumed she would write), they were also coherently integrated by the single idea that every human being has a right to a life that allows him or her to develop "the life of the spirit." Introducing her argument, she wrote: "It is of course the wide vision of evolution that chiefly kindles [the modern English poets'] spirits. Nor need we wonder if some of the noblest songs of triumph were chanted before science had uttered her knowledge aloud. For the imagination is ever prophetic; and if science opens the road to the poet, it is no less true that the poet again and again opens the road to science. It seems as if every new thought stirred long in the unconscious soul of the race, and it were a matter of indifference whether poetry or science first found the spoken word." Evolution also brought recognition of the unity of life, a vision in earlier periods of only the greatest literature. The harmony of the universe was a "primary intuition" of the human heart, recently excitingly upheld by science: "Deeper than scientific ideas lies the scientific temper: reverence for Law, passion for Fact. . . . These are the principles which working inwardly and silently have renewed our poetry." So Scudder goes on before the winds of her idealism. Her genuine intellectuality disciplines her enthusiasm, but the doctrines of her period shape her view of the literature of earlier centuries.

Social Ideals in English Letters (1898) mines the same vein of analysis. This book is perhaps the more important of the two in that it is associated with a Wellesley course popular among students for decades; alumnae told her that it became even more important to them with the passage of years. The course had the same title as the book. In it Scudder used literature to guide Wellesley's young women to affirm the social responsibility arising from unfair advantage in a society that simply used up the lives of the multitude. In the book, speaking again of the poets, she said, "From Wordsworth to Byron, the poets were shaken and shaped by the political revolution. Yet the aim of all their passion was social. . . . their political opinions were simply means to an end; and that end was the opportunity for a full life, spiritual and natural, thrown open to every son of man." As for English prose between 1830 and 1860, fiction and nonfiction alike revealed "the growth of a new factor in consciousness: the awakening and gradual self-assertion of social conscience." Furthermore, this development projected both past and future: "A mighty struggle for social salvation, not yet fully in evidence, but inexorably preparing, lies behind all incidents of modern life and art. The great social literature before 1880 reveals that gathering of the forces. To discover the issue was the work of that period. To face it," Scudder wrote in the midst of the problems generated by the flood of immigration, "is the work of our own." Scudder's assessments of individual writers emerge from this perspective; chief among those she discusses are William Langland, Sir Thomas More, Jonathan Swift, Thomas Carlyle, Ruskin, and Matthew Arnold. The earlier sections of the book and the limited treatments of Charles Dickens, William Makepeace Thackeray, and George Eliot all serve as preliminaries to Scudder's major analysis of the separable strands of thought found in Carlyle's, Ruskin's, and Arnold's ideas of "what to do."

The problem and the glory in the course lay in Scudder's meaning what she said. Many a critic can write with logic and passion of truths (not merely arguments) that literature delivers,

but Scudder meant that one should act on these truths, and she showed the way herself. She debated the politics of chosen poverty but kept the money and position that gave her power. She questioned publicly the wisdom of needy Wellesley College in accepting money from robber barons. She spoke at Lawrence, Massachusetts, during the textile strike of 1912, tainting her Wellesley image just by being there even though her speech pleaded for obedience to law. When the *Boston Transcript* called for her resignation, the college authorities stood by her, but her department asked her to suspend her course on social ideals for a time.

Instead of writing the literary criticism that would have given her more prestige among professors, she wrote books designed to convince church members that their beliefs committed them to "social reconstruction." Idealism per se faded for Scudder. Socialism took form for her as the genuinely effective force that would hammer the world into the proper mold for the spiritual force of brotherhood, the real message in Christianity. In 1911, in an *Atlantic Monthly* essay called "The Forerunners," she divided disappointing theoretical idealism, with its negations emerging from its reliance on changing morality, from active socialism, with its power in social facts and economics. In *On Journey* she lists names that "suggest not only my social but my religious preoccupations," "fine figures from the early Labor Movement, usually pretty far to the Left—Paul Sabatier, Walter Rauschenbusch, Ernesto Buonaiuti." After she built and occupied a house in Wellesley, she conducted classes in her home, which was also living quarters and meeting place for friends involved in her social causes. The course on social ideals was clearly infected, from colleagues' cautious points of view, with Scudder's activism. After the suspension in 1912 Scudder brought the course back and taught it as an elective, which could not satisfy a major requirement. When Scudder retired, despite her protests, the course disappeared. "Adventures in Pedagogy," in *On Journey,* speaks of these things.

Possibly colleagues and administrators uneasily tolerated Scudder's "radical" presence not only because she was well connected and popular with students but also because she was so firm and convincing an advocate of the cause that was theirs: women's higher education. In 1936 she wrote, "I must regard the success of colleges for women as one of the few triumphs of idealism, in an age when the shipwreck of former standards and the disintegration of older cultures have precipitated society into a chaos before which men are helpless. I do not know for what reason this throng of educated women has been released into the larger life, just in the period when an old order of civilization is passing away, and the new order emerges in confusion. . . . In general [the women's colleges] mean for civilization the introduction of a new element; and for women, a change not only of social opportunity but of psychological makeup, resulting from a transformation of status, actual and prospective, which is not less than epoch-making." In the second edition of *Social Ideals in English Letters* Scudder commented, "All these social idealists envisage life from the man's point of view, and when they write about women not one of them escapes an overstress on sex. Sex is important but it does not constitute any larger element in life for the woman than for the man. And some women are not meant for firesides."

Poetry, as Scudder read it, validated her stance on women. In "Womanhood in Modern Poetry" (1889) she argued that "In three significant points, then, it would seem that our modern poetry assumes toward woman a novel attitude. It gives to the love between man and woman a slighter proportion among life's interests, it emphasizes physical charm less than moral and spiritual loveliness as the essential attraction of womanhood, and it endeavors to depict women as they are in themselves, rather than as they appear to the observation of the lover or the student." Robert Browning is the hero of this new depiction of women; Scudder compared and contrasted his presentation of women with William Shakespeare's. In Browning, "Women are no longer, as in the days of chivalry, placed upon remote heights, there to be adored from afar; they are brought face to face with the very turmoil of existence, in the world and in their own hearts. Fellow-workers, they stand by the side of men. They are called out from their seclusion, from the privacy of the hearth, to meet life's deepest and most tragic issues; and by virtue of the strength gained in that conflict, to join in the broader and more public struggle by which the great organism of society is working its way into freer, fuller life." Scudder found continuity, however, as well as change within the English tradition: "At the very bottom, the ideal of the sixteenth century and of the nineteenth meet. Our conception is freed from old limits, is involved with new forces; but to Browning, as to

Shakespeare, woman knows a moral pre-eminence, and her office in life is at once to inspire and to serve." For Scudder that service was enlargement, not submission. She continued, "It is in the world, and not without it, that women are henceforth to live." The love to which women were to devote themselves was for humankind, not for individual men.

Despite chivalry's old, ignorant misunderstanding of women, Scudder early added its highest literary expression, Sir Thomas Malory's *Morte d'Arthur,* to her teaching repertoire. She loved and honored Malory's presentation of chivalry as the best of the life of the spirit before the Renaissance. After fifteen years of teaching the Arthurian legend she wrote *Le Morte d'Arthur of Sir Thomas Malory and Its Sources* (1917), disclaiming any originality in her analysis; the book "makes no claim to explore any new territory, but it hopes to fill the modest function of a guide to a lovely country which is too rarely visited except by pioneers."

Scudder's *Introduction to the Study of English Literature* (1901) is also intended for students. Its informing idea is that "Literature bears only indirect relation . . . to dynasties and wars, while it bears direct relation to that life of the whole people whence it proceeds. This life, in its varying manifestations and its onward movement, the book tries constantly to suggest to the student's consciousness." Scudder's prose suits her goals; that of this "introduction" has the disciplined simplicity that Willa Cather also achieved.

Among today's critical tendencies Scudder's work has most affinity with feminist criticism. Its blend of idealism with attention to social realities and her commitment to "the cause of the future" make a direct link to the Utopian vein in contemporary feminist fiction and criticism. Scudder's literary critical impact was on her students rather than on professional literary critics. While she was very much a thinker of her time, she lived a mental and practical life of Emersonian self-reliance, which she balanced with a multilayered commitment to the values of community. Her work argues still for an understanding that literature belongs to everyone, not to elites; it contributes to the still-controversial argument that literature's power and meaning derive from its deep connection with social life.

References:
Jessie Bernard, *Academic Women* (University Park: Pennsylvania State University Press, 1964);

Van Wyck Brooks, "Art Bolshevism," *Sketches in Criticism* (New York: Dutton, 1932), pp. 135-141;

Theresa Corcoran, S.C., *Vida Dutton Scudder* (Boston: Twayne, 1982);

Allen Davis, *Spearheads for Reform: The Social Settlements and the Progressive Movement, 1890-1914* (New York: Oxford, 1967);

Peter J. Frederick, "Vida Dutton Scudder: The Professor as Social Activist," *New England Quarterly*, 43 (September 1970): 407-433;

Gerald Graff, "The Generalist Opposition," in his *Professing Literature* (Chicago: University of Chicago Press, 1987);

T. J. Jackson Lears, "The Religion of Beauty: Catholic Forms and American Consciousness," in his *No Place of Grace: Antimodernism and the Transformation of American Culture, 1880-1920* (New York: Pantheon, 1981), pp. 183-215;

Nan Bauer Maglin, "Vida to Florence: 'Comrade and Companion,'" *Frontiers*, 4 (Fall 1979): 13-20;

Arthur Mann, *Yankee Reformers in an Urban Age* (Cambridge: Harvard University Press, 1954);

William L. O'Neill, *Everyone Was Brave* (Chicago: Quadrangle, 1969);

Mercedes Randall, *Improper Bostonian: Emily Green Balch* (New York: Twayne, 1964);

Walter B. Rideout, *The Radical Novel in the United States, 1900-1954* (Cambridge: Harvard University Press, 1956).

Papers:

There is no major collection of Vida Dutton Scudder's literary papers. Minor collections of notebooks, journals, and correspondence are held by Wellesley College Archives and the Smith College Library. The archives of the Society of the Companions of the Holy Cross, Adelynrood, South Byfield, Massachusetts, contain material on her social reform activities, as do the records of the College Settlements Association in the Smith College Library and the Denison House records in the Schlesinger Library, Radcliffe College.

Maurice Thompson
(9 September 1844-15 February 1901)

Anne Bail Howard
University of Nevada at Reno

BOOKS: *Hoosier Mosaics* (New York: Hale, 1875);

The Witchery of Archery: A Complete Manual of Archery (New York: Scribners, 1879);

How to Train in Archery, by Thompson and Will H. Thompson (New York: Horsman, 1880);

A Tallahassee Girl (Boston: Osgood, 1882);

Songs of Fair Weather (Boston: Osgood, 1883);

His Second Campaign (Boston: Osgood, 1883);

By-Ways and Bird Notes (New York: Alden, 1885);

At Love's Extremes (New York: Cassell, 1885); republished as *Milly: At Love's Extremes* (New York: New Amsterdam Book Co., 1901);

A Banker of Bankersville (New York: Cassell, 1886);

Sylvan Secrets, in Bird-songs and Books (New York: Alden, 1887);

The Story of Louisiana (Boston: Lothrop, 1888);

A Fortnight of Folly (New York: Alden, 1888; New York & London: Street & Smith, 1902);

Poems (Boston & New York: Houghton, Mifflin, 1892);

The King of Honey Island (New York: Bonner, 1893);

The Ethics of Literary Art: The Carew Lectures for 1893, Hartford Theological Seminary (Hartford: Hartford Seminary Press, 1893);

The Ocala Boy, A Story of Florida Town and Forest (Boston: Lothrop, 1895);

How To Study History, Literature, The Fine Arts, by Thompson, Albert Bushnell Hart, and Charles Mason Fairbanks (Meadville, Penn.: Flood & Vincent, 1895);

Stories of Indiana (New York & Cincinnati: American Book Co., 1898);

Stories of the Cherokee Hills (Boston & New York: Houghton, Mifflin, 1898);

Alice of Old Vincennes (Indianapolis: Bobbs-Merrill, 1900);

My Winter Garden (New York: Century, 1900);

Rosalynde's Lovers (Indianapolis: Bowen-Merrill, 1901);

Sweetheart Manette (Philadelphia & London: Lippincott, 1901).

PERIODICAL PUBLICATIONS: "Longfellow—Flower de Luce," *Scott's Monthly Magazine,* 4 (July 1867): 491;

"The Pockets of North Georgia," *Appleton's Journal,* 7 (10 February 1872);

"The Long Bow," *Appleton's Journal,* 9 (19 April 1873): 525-526;

"Tallulah Falls," *Appleton's Journal*, 10 (20 September 1873): 372-373;

"Three Weeks of Savage Life," *Appleton's Journal*, 14 (4 September 1875): 303-305;

"Bow Shooting," *Scribner's Monthly*, 14 (July 1877): 273-287;

"The Battle of the Birds," *Appleton's Journal*, 4 (February 1878): 159-164;

"The Haunts of the Grayling," *Lippincott's Monthly Magazine*, 28 (September 1881): 268-272;

"Grand Traverse Bay," *Lippincott's Monthly Magazine*, 28 (October 1881): 321-333;

"A Prelude," *Atlantic Monthly*, 52 (July 1883): 23-24;

"Plantation Music," *Critic*, 4 (12 January 1884): 20;

"Sketching for Literary Purposes," *Critic*, 4 (26 January 1884): 37;

"The Limit of Expression," *Critic*, 5 (6 September 1884): 109-110;

"Novels and Novels," *Current Weekly*, 2 (18 October 1884): 244;

"In the Haunts of the Mocking-Bird," *Atlantic Monthly*, 54 (November 1884): 620-627;

"A Plea for the Present," *Critic*, 6 (27 June 1885): 311;

"The Forest Beauty," *Lippincott's Monthly Magazine*, 36 (August 1885): 200-206;

"The Genesis of Birdsong," *Atlantic Monthly*, 57 (May 1886): 613-619;

"Ceryle Alcyon," *Southern Bivouac*, 2 (October 1886): 293-297;

"The Eastern Literary Outlook," *Chatauquan*, 7 (February 1887): 277-279;

"The Motif of Birdsong," *Scribner's Monthly*, 2 (September 1887): 379-384;

"Studies of Prominent Novelists: Count Tolstoi, Alphonse Daudet, William Dean Howells, Thomas Hardy, Nathaniel Hawthorne," *Book News Monthly*, 6 (September 1887): 9-11; (October 1887): 53-54; (November 1887): 93-94; (December 1887): 223-224; (January 1888): 262-263;

"Paul Hayne and His Poetry," *America*, 1 (November 1887): 18;

"The Literary Lesson of Anarchy," *Book News Monthly*, 6 (February 1888): 265;

"Will the Reader Weep if the Writer Did Not?" *Book News Monthly*, 6 (May 1888): 400;

"Foreign Influences on American Fiction," *North American Review*, 149 (July 1889): 118-120;

"Ben and Judas," *Century Magazine*, 37 (October 1889): 893-902;

"The Domain of Romance," *Forum*, 8 (November 1889): 326-336;

"The Poetry of the Civil War," *Chatauquan*, 10 (February 1890): 567-571;

"A Pair of Old Boys," *Century Magazine*, 41 (December 1890): 246-249;

"The Theory of Fiction Making," *Chatauquan*, 14 (October 1891): 46-50;

"Love's Horizon," *Century Magazine*, 44 (May 1892): 34;

"A Woodland Mood," *Cosmopolitan*, 13 (June 1892): 185;

"The Romance and the Novel, *Chatauquan*, 16 (October 1892): 42-46;

"Where the Mocking Bird Sings," *Cosmopolitan*, 14 (December 1892): 193-199;

"An Impossibility," *Century Magazine*, 46 (June 1893): 320;

"The Melic Charm," *Independent*, 46 (4 January 1894): 3-4;

"A Beautiful Assassin," *Independent*, 46 (18 January 1894): 67;

"An Early Bluebird," *Independent*, 46 (22 February 1894): 227-228;

"The Sapphic Secret," *Atlantic Monthly*, 73 (March 1894): 365-372;

"Literature and Ignorance," *Independent*, 46 (29 March 1894): 391;

"Beside Running Water," *Independent*, 46 (19 April 1894): 485;

"Booming the Britons," *Independent*, 46 (31 May 1894): 678-679;

"Fiction and Moral Lessons," *Independent*, 46 (30 August 1894): 1112-1113;

"Verbal Adumbrations," *Independent*, 46 (20 September 1894): 1207;

"An Original Grotesque," *Independent*, 46 (11 October 1894): 1301-1302;

"The Ethical Discrimination," *Independent*, 46 (1 November 1894): 1399;

"Two Lyrics in One," *Independent*, 46 (15 November 1894): 1461-1462;

"On Being Independent," *Independent*, 46 (27 December 1894): 1680;

"A Halcyon Note," *Independent*, 47 (10 January 1895): 39-40;

"Budding Poets," *Independent*, 47 (24 January 1895): 104-105;

"Gryllus Grilled," *Independent*, 47 (28 March 1895): 397-398;

"A Leaf From a Fly-Book," *Independent*, 47 (18 April 1895): 509;

"Nuts from Perigord," *Chap-Book*, 2 (1 May 1895): 473-478;

"A Stroll in Indiana with a British Critic," *Independent*, 47 (9 May 1895): 616-617;

"A Man and a Bird," *Independent*, 47 (23 May 1895): 682;

"Bragget and Bird-Bolts," *Independent*, 47 (30 May 1895): 720-721;

"By a Woodland Spring," *Independent*, 47 (13 June 1895): 798-799;

"Toxophilus on the Kankakee," *Independent*, 47 (11 July 1895): 923-924;

"The Fletcher's Art," *Independent*, 47 (25 July 1895): 986;

"Is the New Woman New?" *Chap-Book*, 3 (1 October 1895): 380-389;

"Speaking of the Weather," *Independent*, 47 (17 October 1895): 1385;

"Balzac's Romances," *Independent*, 47 (21 November 1895): 1565-1566;

"Alexander Dumas, the Younger," *Independent*, 47 (12 December 1895): 1675-1676;

Review of *The Works of Edgar Allan Poe*, edited by Edmund Clarence Stedman and George Woodberry, *Independent*, 48 (13 February 1896): 220;

"The Turning of the Tide," *Independent*, 48 (20 February 1896): 238;

"The Return of the Girl," *Chap-Book*, 4 (15 March 1896): 401-410;

"Mullet, Mockingbirds and Montaigne," *Independent*, 48 (19 March 1896): 374-375;

"Some Faded Notes," *Independent*, 48 (16 April 1896): 511-512;

"Contemporary American Authors," *Chatauquan*, 23 (June 1896): 283-287;

"An Instance of Bird Study," *Independent*, 48 (23 July 1896): 989;

"Cacoethes Scribendi," *Independent*, 48 (24 September 1896): 1286-1287;

"Handmade Literature," *Independent*, 48 (10 December 1896): 1673-1674;

"A Winter Atom," *Independent*, 49 (28 January 1897): 108;

"A Leaf from an Old Book," *Independent*, 49 (11 February 1897): 171;

"From the Critic's Point of View [Rudyard Kipling]," *Chap-Book*, 6 (15 February 1897): 1189-1190;

"Foot-Notes for an Old Time Southern Book," *Independent*, 49 (15 July 1897): 897-898;

[Walt Whitman], *Chap-Book*, 7 (1 August 1897): 194-195;

"A Contribution to Pure Ignorance," *Independent*, 49 (21 October 1897): 1360;

"Novels and Morals," *Independent*, 49 (18 November 1897): 1485;

"Montaigne's Literary Recipe," *Independent*, 49 (9 December 1897): 1604-1605;

"The Bird in Literature," *Critic*, 29 (1 January 1898): 1-2;

"Montaigne's Materials," *Independent*, 50 (10 February 1898): 196-197;

"Montaigne's Philosophy," *Independent*, 50 (10 March 1898): 310-311;

"Vigorous Men; A Vigorous Nation," *Independent*, 50 (1 September 1898): 609-611;

"An Old Southern Humorist [William Tappan Thompson]," *Independent*, 50 (20 October 1898): 1103-1105;

"The Touch of Magic," *Independent*, 50 (3 November 1898): 1259-1260;

"A Southern Pioneer Poet [Albert Pike]," *Independent*, 50 (17 November 1898): 1396-1398;

"The Poetry of James Whitcomb Riley," *Critic*, 33 (December 1898): 460-464;

"The Return of Romance," *Independent*, 50 (15 December 1898): 1735-1736;

"The Source of Originality," *Independent*, 51 (2 February 1899): 351;

"The New Poetry," *Independent*, 51 (2 March 1899): 608-610;

"The Court of Judge Lynch," *Lippincott's Monthly Magazine*, 64 (August 1899): 254-262;

"The Literary Market," *Independent*, 51 (14 September 1899): 2485-2487;

"Bewildered Critics," *Independent*, 51 (9 November 1899): 3009-3111;

"Art and Money," *Independent*, 51 (14 December 1899): 3345-3347;

"The Magnetic Story," *Independent*, 52 (25 January 1900): 241-243;

"Writing the Record," *Independent*, 52 (15 April 1900): 930-933;

"Breezy Books for Summer," *Independent*, 52 (7 June 1900): 1387-1388;

"Critics and Romancers," *Independent*, 52 (9 August 1900): 1919-1921;

"A Literary Journey," *Independent*, 52 (22 November 1900): 2794-2796.

Poet and soldier, lawyer and politician, novelist and sportsman, Maurice Thompson stirred American interest in archery, but he hoped to be remembered for his poetry or at least for his most popular romance, *Alice of Old Vincennes* (1900). It is rather as a Don Quixote of romance, "tilting at windmills of literary pessimism" and other devilish companions of realism, as Robert

First page of the manuscript for Thompson's most popular novel, Alice of Old Vincennes *(Bookman, March 1901)*

Falk puts it, that Thompson claims attention here. The arch archer critic—who, one obituary claimed, would "sooner aim his barbed arrow at an adulterous novel than at a shrike"—kept his targets of Zolaism, debauchery, illicit love, Henry James, and Thomas Hardy steadily in sight over a career of a quarter century of defending romance, defying what he saw as creeping lewdness. A champion of the Genteel Tradition, a defender of romance like the critical idealists as described by John Rathbun and Harry H. Clark, he preferred the masters of the past, idolized Sir Walter Scott, and was uncomfortable with contemporary literature.

To twentieth-century eyes his own life reads like the romantic tales he wrote in the early years of his career. Born James Maurice Thompson on 9 September 1844 in Fairfield, Indiana, to the Reverend Matthew Grigg and Diantha Jaeger Thompson, he grew up on a remote plantation in north Georgia, far from conventional schooling. Encouraged by his educated mother and directed by tutors, he studied both nature and books, dividing his study time between the classics and the out-of-doors, acquiring both knowledge and skill in geology and ornithology, Greek and Latin, and archery and modern languages. When the Civil War came, the seventeen-year-old Thompson volunteered and served three years before returning to his impoverished family where for another three years he worked as a field laborer by day, trapping squirrels to buy books for his law and engineering studies. Although he considered himself a Southerner all of his life, he moved his ambitions to Crawfordsville, Indiana, where he started as a laborer and rose to chief engineer of a railroad before he entered law practice. During the 1870s and 1880s he managed a law practice with his brother, Will Henry Thompson, served in the state legislature, and continued the literary efforts he had begun in the South with contributions of verses, essays, and articles in the *Atlantic Monthly*, *Lippincott's Magazine*, and various newspapers. Drawing on his many interests and wide knowledge, he published articles in various fields. One series about archery, later published as *The Witchery of Archery* (1879), was credited with arousing popular interest in the sport throughout the country during the 1880s. Thompson was less successful with his historical romances—"popular, formulaic potboilers," according to Merrill Skaggs. But he became acquainted with literary men, like William Dean Howells, who respected Thompson's poetry and visited him to gain background for *A Modern Instance* (1882), and Charleston poet Paul Hamilton Hayne, whom he criticized for "sectionalism": "A poet must have wider visions," Thompson insisted. Thompson, as critic, did not take his own advice: his critical barbs from the beginning were aimed at realism, a foreign intruder that would corrupt American life and art. Beginning with reviews in various magazines and newspapers, Thompson maintained his opposition when he became nonresident literary editor of the *Independent* in 1889, a position that allowed him to keep his home in Crawfordsville, Indiana, and to continue to indulge his naturalist instincts from a winter residence on the Gulf of Mexico.

Realism, Thompson steadily maintained, was a foreign influence which pushed American writers to spice their works with "alien condiments" to compete with these "bad books, alien books, books inimical to republican life and deadly to the social simplicity and moral purity of a democratic people" (*North American Review*, July 1889). *The Ethics of Literary Art* (1893), delivered as the Carew lectures at Hartford Theological Seminary and later published as his only book of criticism, offers similar ideas that he was to repeat with little variation for the rest of his career.

Thompson argues in his preface that "life and literature cannot be separated so as to say what is vicious in life is harmlessly delectable in literature." Indeed, it is because art is so powerful a means of teaching that the responsible writer must understand that "the man or woman we meet in a book walks into our sanctuary of character and writes maxims on its walls." Modern realists, a long cry from Homer, Aeschylus, Shakespeare, and Scott, utter the lowest note of their civilization. While "obscenities" of the old writers could be excused as a taste of the period, as could the nakedness in Greek art, Thompson's time demanded a purer form.

Not photography but art, not science but romance exercise the literary imagination, and, more than that, "True art is necessarily optimistic," and "pure romance demands faith in the largest possibilities." A novel by Henry James or a poem by Walt Whitman, Thompson insists, does not "express any of the deep character of our civilization as a whole." Thus realism becomes not only un-American, but ungodly, unrepresentative as well. The reader wants to wash his hands after reading Emile Zola, preferring to have near him "large, strong, safe, steadfast" Scott.

Photograph of Thompson which appeared in the Bookman *soon after his death*

The particular targets in Thomas's *The Ethics of Literary Art* are James, Thomas Hardy, Zola, Whitman, Gustave Flaubert, Henrik Ibsen, Leo Tolstoy, and Guy de Maupassant, and these writers continued to attract Thompson's barbs. And the antidote for such poison remained the same: a return to healthful, virtuous romance.

Within months of the publication of *The Ethics of Literary Art*, Thompson was back on the same soap box in the *Independent*, repeating his edicts that "conscience must not be one thing in life and another thing in art." Indeed, critics' decisions should embody "holy truth," for it was wrong to praise any man or woman "for doing an evil thing with consummate art" (*Independent*, 1 November 1894). There had been a moment of proper realism, he claimed, for "the much-boasted faithfulness to life of our Whitmans, our

Ibsens, and our Tolstoys is a dirty wash of imitation" of the true Greek article as practiced by his admired Sappho (*Atlantic Monthly*, March 1894). Time did not change this stand: six years later Thompson found new occasion to condemn *Madame Bovary* for parading "shame in a splendid literary garb" (*Independent*, 25 January 1900).

Whitman particularly annoyed Thompson, a proper poet outraged at the idea of "poets in their shirt sleeves . . . accompanying their clever illiteracies with a rattling ragtime clickety clack of the end man's bones and the jigdancer's double shuffle" (*Independent*, 9 November 1899). That Whitman was not a poet was self-evident; rather than cosmic, he was "magmic . . . a disorderly mass" spurting from his pen, with "unbearable coarseness, ignorance, and egotism" (*Chap-Book*, 1 August 1897).

Romance writer Thompson, finally successful with his own work in *Alice of Old Vincennes*, believed that a revival of romances of the sort that he, Lew Wallace, and the idolized Scott wrote, would return American letters to virile health: "virility seeks a large canvas and long perspectives. . . . Large men instinctively do the 'big bow-wow,' as Scott phrased it" (*Independent*, 9 August 1900). The return to romance, following upon the fading end of realism, would indicate, Thompson believed, "a young, strong, virile generation pushing aside a flabby one."

When Thompson died in February 1901, at the height of the success of his most popular romance, writers of his obituaries expected his name to live not for his criticism but for his poetry. Now, the criticism, poetry, and romances are interesting primarily as historical curiosities—lively at the time, the vigorous response of a talented man longing for the past.

Bibliography:

Dorothy R. Russo and Thelma L. Sullivan, *Bibliographical Studies of Seven Authors of Crawfordsville, Indiana* (Indianapolis: Indiana Historical Society, 1952).

References:

William Malone Baskervill, *Southern Writers: Biographical and Critical Studies* (Nashville, Tenn.: M. E. Church, South, 1897);

Robert Falk, "The Genteel Decades, 1870-1900," in *The Development of American Literary Criticism*, edited by Floyd Stovall (Chapel Hill: University of North Carolina Press, 1955), pp. 113-157;

Rayburn S. Moore, *A Man of Letters in the Nineteenth Century South: Selected Letters of Paul Hamilton Hayne* (Baton Rouge: Louisiana State University Press, 1982);

Moore, "The Old South and the New: Paul Hamilton Hayne and Maurice Thompson," *Southern Literary Journal*, 5 (Fall 1972): 108-122;

Moore, *Paul Hamilton Hayne* (New York: Twayne, 1972);

John Rathbun and Harry H. Clark, *American Literary Criticism, 1860-1905* (Boston: Twayne, 1979);

Merrill Maguire Skaggs, "Varieties of Local Color," in *The History of Southern Literature*, edited by Louis D. Rubin (Baton Rouge: Louisiana State University Press, 1985);

Otis B. Wheeler, *The Literary Career of Maurice Thompson* (Baton Rouge: Louisiana State University Press, 1965).

William Peterfield Trent

(10 November 1862-6 December 1939)

Priscilla Wald
Columbia University

See also the Trent entry in *DLB 47, American Historians, 1866-1912.*

BOOKS: *English Culture in Virginia: A Study of the Gilmer Letters and an Account of the English Professors Obtained by Jefferson for the University of Virginia* (Baltimore: N. Murray, Publication Agent, Johns Hopkins University, 1889);

William Gilmore Simms (Boston & New York: Houghton, Mifflin, 1892; London, 1892);

Southern Statesmen of the Old Régime: Washington, Jefferson, Randolph, Calhoun, Stephens, Toombs, and Jefferson Davis (New York: Crowell, 1897);

The Authority of Criticism, and Other Essays (New York: Scribners, 1899; London, 1899);

John Milton: A Short Study of His Life and Works (New York & London: Macmillan, 1899);

Robert E. Lee (Boston: Small, Maynard, 1899; London: Kegan Paul, Trench, Trübner, 1899);

Verses (Philadelphia: Slocum, 1899);

Progress of the United States of America in the Century (London & Philadelphia: Linscott, 1901; London: Chambers, 1903);

War and Civilization (New York: Crowell, 1901);

A History of the United States, by Trent and Charles Kendall Adams (Boston: Allyn & Bacon, 1903; revised, 1909; revised again, 1922);

A History of American Literature, 1607-1865 (New York: Appleton, 1903; London: Heinemann, 1903);

A Brief History of American Literature (New York: Appleton, 1904);

Greatness in Literature and Other Papers (New York: Crowell, 1905; London: Harrap, 1905);

The Relations of History and Literature: An Address Delivered Before the Annual Meeting of the Virginia Historical Society (Richmond, 1906);

Longfellow and Other Essays (New York: Crowell, 1910);

An Introduction to the English Classics, by Trent, Charles L. Hanson, and William T. Brewster (Boston: Ginn, 1911; revised, 1916);

Great American Writers, by Trent and John Erskine (New York: Holt, 1912); also published as *Great Writers of America* (London: Williams & Norgate, 1912);

Daniel Defoe, How to Know Him (Indianapolis: Bobbs-Merrill, 1916);

Verse-jottings (New York, 1924).

OTHER: *John Milton's L'allegro, Il penseroso, Comus, and Lycidas,* edited, with notes and introductions, by Trent (New York & London: Longmans, Green, 1895);

Colonial Prose and Poetry, 3 volumes, edited by Trent and Benjamin W. Wells (New York: Crowell, 1901);

Poems for Young Folks (New York: Collier, 1903);

Southern Writers; Selections in Prose and Verse (New York: Macmillan, 1905);

The Cambridge History of American Literature, 4 volumes, edited by Trent, John Erskine, Stuart P. Sherman, and Carl Van Doren (New York: Putnam's, 1917-1921); condensed as *A History of American Literature* (New York: Putnam's, 1922; student's edition, 1923; republished in three volumes, 1943).

PERIODICAL PUBLICATIONS: "Greece and Modern Civilization," by Trent and H. B. Adams, *Chautauquan,* 9 (October 1888): 3-5;

"The Period of Constitution-Making in the American Churches," in *Essays in the Constitutional History of the United States in the Formative Period,* edited by John Franklin Jameson (Boston & New York: Houghton, Mifflin, 1889);

"The Position of Women in Ancient Greece," *Chautauquan,* 9 (June 1889): 505-507;

"The Novels of Thomas Hardy," *Sewanee Review,* 1 (November 1892): 1-25;

"The Old South," *Sewanee Review,* 1 (November 1892): 90-96;

"Reverend Charles Wolfe," *Sewanee Review,* 1 (February 1893): 129-152;

"The Teaching of English Literature," *Sewanee Review,* 1 (May 1893): 257-272;

William Peterfield Trent (photograph by Davis, Richmond, Virginia)

"Elegiac Poetry," *Sewanee Review*, 1 (August 1893): 410-418;

"Mr. Goldwin Smith on the United States," *Sewanee Review*, 2 (November 1893): 1-16;

"Francis Marion Crawford," *Sewanee Review*, 2 (February 1894): 239-256;

"Some Translations from Horace," *Sewanee Review*, 3 (November 1894): 111-128;

"Bartlett's Concordance of Shakespeare," *Sewanee Review*, 3 (February 1895): 249-256;

"Brander Matthews as a Critic," *Sewanee Review*, 3 (May 1895): 373-384;

"Mr. Thomas Hardy," *Citizen*, 1 (February 1896): 284-286;

"The Case of Josiah Philips," *American Historical Review*, 1 (April 1896): 444-454;

"Samuel L. Clemens as an Historical Novelist," *Bookman*, 3 (May 1896): 207-210;

"Theodore Roosevelt as a Historian," *Forum*, 21 (July 1896): 566-576;

"Anthony Trollope," *Citizen*, 2 (November 1896): 297-298;

"The Makers of the Union: Benjamin Franklin," *McClure's*, 8 (January 1897): 273-277;

"John Milton," *Sewanee Review*, 5 (January 1897): 1-16;

"Dominant Forces in Southern Life," *Atlantic Monthly*, 79 (January 1897): 42-53;

"Makers of the Union: George Washington," *McClure's*, 8 (February 1897): 309-313;

"Tendencies of Higher Life in the South," *Atlantic Monthly*, 79 (June 1897): 766-778;

"The Greek Elegy," *Sewanee Review*, 6 (January 1898): 1-28;

"Brander Matthews's New Stories," *Sewanee Review*, 6 (January 1898): 106-109;

"The Nature of Literature and Science," *Sewanee Review*, 6 (April 1898): 214-238;

"Recent Histories of Literature and Science," *Forum*, 25 (April 1898): 246-256;

"Tennyson and Musset Once More," *Bookman*, 7 (April 1898): 108-114;

"The Roman Elegy," *Sewanee Review*, 6 (July 1898): 257-275;

"In Re Imperialism: Some Phases of the Situation," *Sewanee Review*, 6 (October 1898): 479-499;

"Revival of Interest in Lord Byron," *Forum*, 26 (October 1898): 242-256;

"The Poetry of the American Plantations," *Sewanee Review*, 7 (October 1899): 481-492;

"Mr. McCarthy's Reminiscences," *Forum*, 28 (November 1899): 374-384;

"The Poetry of the American Plantations, Part II," *Sewanee Review*, 8 (January 1900): 73-88;

"Some Recent Balzac Literature," *International Monthly*, 1 (March 1900): 309-322;

"Mr. Stephen Phillips's Play," *Forum*, 29 (March 1900): 116-128;

"Gleanings from an Old Southern Newspaper," *Atlantic Monthly*, 86 (September 1900): 356-364;

"American Literature, 1880-1900," *Dial*, 28 (October 1900): 334-340;

"Mr. Frederic Harrison's New Essays," *Forum*, 30 (October 1900): 119-128;

"A New South View of Reconstruction," *Sewanee Review*, 9 (January 1901): 13-29;

"Brander Matthews as a Dramatic Critic," *International Monthly*, 4 (August 1901): 289-293;

"Moses Coit Tyler," *Forum*, 31 (August 1901): 750-758;

"A Retrospect of American Humor," *Century*, 41 (November 1901): 45-64;

"Sir Walter Besant," *Forum*, 34 (July 1902): 150-160;

"A New Book on Matthew Arnold," *Forum*, 34 (October 1902): 310-320;

"Lee's Life of Queen Victoria," *Forum*, 34 (April 1903): 547-560;

"Ralph Waldo Emerson," *Bookman*, 17 (June 1903): 421-425;

"A History of English Literature," *International Quarterly*, 8 (September-December 1903): 190-198;

"Two Estimates of Robert Browning," *Forum*, 35 (October 1903): 294-303;

"A New Edition of Defoe," *Forum*, 36 (April 1905): 625-634;

"Southern Writers," *Reader*, 6 (July 1905): 236-238;

"New Editions of Benjamin Franklin," *Forum*, 37 (January 1906): 398-410;

"Mr. Birkbeck Hill and His Edition of Johnson's 'Lives of the Poets,' " *Forum*, 37 (April 1906): 540-551;

"Thomas Hardy's Dynasts," *Forum*, 38 (July 1906): 86-94;

"A Talk to Librarians," *Sewanee Review*, 15 (July 1907): 297-315;

"New Light on Defoe's Life," *Nation*, 87 (September 1908): 259-291;

"Thoughts Occasioned by the Bi-Centenary of Dr. Johnson," *Nation*, 89 (September 1909): 249-251;

"Old Fashioned Remarks on Educational Topics," *Nation*, 91 (September 1910): 207-210;

"Colonel Roosevelt's Autobiography," *Independent*, 76 (November 1913): 341;

"Free Discourse Wherein the Doctrines Which Make for Tyranny are Displayed," *Nation*, 98 (February 1914): 207;

"William Pittis; the Difficulties of a Pamphleteer and Biographer," *Nation*, 98 (June 1914): 692-694, 722-724.

Although William Peterfield Trent is best known as a teacher and literary scholar, he received a law degree prior to his academic career. This combination served him well, and his scholarship reflects his political as well as aesthetic concerns as he strives to recast what had been thought of as academic debates in a moral context. As he asserts in "Literature and Morals" (*The Authority of Criticism, and Other Essays*, 1899), "all truly classic literature has a moral basis," and he goes on to assure his turn-of-the-century audience of a correlation between reading classics and preserving morality. It is, then, not surprising that he considered teaching literature more a calling than an occupation. In his vocation he campaigned particularly for increased attention to education, of women as well as men, and a more just treatment and evaluation of the South. Growing up in the Reconstruction South, Trent lamented the lack of attention granted to southern writers. He therefore devoted a substantial portion of his career to rectifying the situation. While teaching at the University of the South, Trent helped found the *Sewanee Review* in November 1892, the first issue of which opens with his essay on Thomas Hardy's novels. In November 1893 he assumed editorship of the journal, which he did not relinquish until July 1900 when he moved north to teach at Columbia University. Ironically, it was his work on William Gilmore Simms, part of his campaign for national recognition of southern literature, that precipitated this move. Theodore Roosevelt, impressed with the Simms book, passed it along to his friend Seth Low, president of Columbia University, who proceeded to offer Trent a job in the Barnard College department of English and comparative literature, where he taught until his retirement in 1929.

Trent, who was born 10 November 1862 to Peterfield and Lucy Carter Burwell Trent, was the only surviving son (his older brother died in infancy) of a southern aristocratic family destroyed by the Civil War. His father, a physician in the Confederate army, died in 1875. Trent's legacy was, therefore, a tempered pride in his heritage. A student once described him as having "a twinkle in his eye that went queerly with his dignified bearing." And his work, alternately somber, passionate, and playful, reflects that odd mixture. Trent approached his work as though he had a mission. Throughout his career he wrote tracts on teaching, stressing not only the moral importance of literature but also the teacher's role in making that available to students. He urged reevaluation of the canon, advocating especially the importance of neglected southern literature, but never at the expense of quality and, most of all, never urging its inclusion in a course or volume where it would be out of context. His lifelong devotion to the South, although tempered by ambivalence, took the form of several volumes of works on southern writers and political figures as well as the *Sewanee Review*. In addition to his legal expertise, his background in history and political science–garnered from a year at Johns Hopkins University (1887-1888) under the tutelage of Herbert B. Adams, John Franklin Jameson, Richard T. Ely, and Woodrow Wilson–provided the perspective on literature to which he continually adhered: literature provided a spiritual signpost, maintaining eternal values in a modernizing world. Nowhere is this spirit more apparent than in the three-thousand-page manuscript on Daniel Defoe, the result of several decades of obsessive research despite the paralytic effects of a stroke suffered in 1927, and a Defoe collection, left at Trent's death in 1939, which was subsequently obtained by the Boston Public Library.

Trent was teaching at the University of the South in Sewanee, Tennessee, and, perhaps inspired by his subject, about to embark on the founding of the *Sewanee Review,* when he completed his biography of William Gilmore Simms for the American Men of Letters series edited by Charles D. Warner. Trent argues in this volume, on which he began working in 1890, that the history and the literature of the South have not been fully appreciated; he presents Simms as a kind of hero, dedicated to the promotion of southern literature, like Trent himself, both through his writings and through a journal that he founded to that end. While Trent is temperate in his praise of his subject, he does assert in *Great American Writers* (1912) that "the work of Simms, for extent and contemporary importance, is far more worthy of attention than all of Melville's writing, with the one exception of *Moby Dick;* and the character of Simms was most engaging."

William Gilmore Simms (1892) is anecdotal, focusing more on Simms's life and career than on an in-depth critical appraisal of his work, which reflected Trent's historical training. In fact, in 1892, the year of its publication, William A. Dunning wrote to offer Trent a position teaching history and political science "at a woman's college in New York" (Barnard, ironically, where Trent would eventually come to teach English). Dunning writes that he would like to see Trent specialize in that discipline "rather than running off after strange gods in the literary line." Indeed, Trent describes himself as a "Professor of History" on the title page of the volume, and as a history professor he had particular reason to want to leave the University of the South because, as he complained to his former professor Herbert Adams in a letter in 1890, he could not concentrate on his historical pursuits when he was forced to teach English.

The major works that immediately precede and follow the Simms biography further attest to his intentions to pursue historical studies, especially concerning his regional background. His first long work, *English Culture in Virginia* (1889), which grew out of work he was doing for Adams on the history of the University of Virginia, recounts the devotion of Virginia statesmen in endeavoring, through education, to provide the proper soil in which a native culture could take root. He followed the Simms biography with *Southern Statesmen of the Old Régime* (1897), comprised of lectures delivered on the general history of the South at the University of Wisconsin at Madison in February and March 1896. In the preface to the latter text Trent calls himself "an American who is at the same time a Southerner, proud enough of his section to admit its faults, and yet to proclaim its essential greatness."

Still, the Simms biography carries undeniable evidence of Trent's ambivalence toward his own southern background. He locates the cause of the South's defeat in the Civil War in the evil effects that slavery had on the master and indicts that southern gentleman who "strove to resist the course of development his country was taking, and was crushed in the attempt." And he blames "the fact that [Simms] never rose to the front rank, even of his own country's writers . . . [on] the limitations imposed upon him by his Southern birth." But Trent's worst offense, from the southern point of view, is his suggestion "that the war was fought over Slavery (not States' Rights)." The book inspired a professor from the University of Virginia, Trent's alma mater, to write a letter to a Richmond newspaper urging the young professor's "instant dismissal from Sewanee." While this recommendation was not heeded, Trent suffered for his convictions. He reports, in a 1932 letter to a student writing a dissertation on academic freedom, that old friends of his mother's cut her on the street, and he complains in a letter to Adams in 1898 that some of the faculty, albeit a minority, considered him heretical and dangerous. A letter from good friend and future Columbia colleague Brander Matthews in August 1893 concerns Matthews's efforts to secure Trent an appointment at Yale, a task he did not relinquish until Columbia offered Trent a position in 1900. In addition, his marriage to Alice Lyman, a northerner, in 1896 could both suggest his ambivalence toward the South and compound his motivation to move north. In any case, although he pleads for the reader's clemency in evaluating Simms as an artist and a southerner, and although he declares that "out of the ashes of the old South, a new and better South has arisen," his sentiments were evidently not calculated to please his southern constituency. The ensuing controversy found him much censured in the South and apparently precipitated his permanent relocation to the North.

Trent was never willing to compromise his principles and beliefs, even in the service of a cause he embraced. *The Authority of Criticism, and Other Essays*, published just prior to Trent's northern migration, provides evidence of his sense of responsibility in his vocation; he strives to define his role as a teacher and a critic, a role, as he acknowledges in the title essay (first published in the April 1899 *Forum*), that is often contradictory. Articulating the dilemma as one that pits the "teacher" against the "reporter," a term he as-

signs to "all writers who minister to public curiosity," Trent argues for the necessity of both. While Trent the teacher advocates the need for authority, the need, that is, to guard and bequeath a canon of great art, Trent the critic/reporter acknowledges the importance of individual evaluation and a more impressionistic response. Thus he simultaneously celebrates the "broad and general enlightenment [that] will begin to draw upon us the moment we are brought in contact with great literature and art; provided always that our tendency to excessive individualism is checked by proper training" and applauds "the impressionist . . . [who], unfettered by rules and traditions, is likely to be sympathetic with the fresh tentatives which creative genius is continually making in what we may call the 'unclosed genres.' " He does, however, ultimately assert certain "universal principles, . . . such as the superiority of poetry to prose, of one genre to another, of form to formlessness." Trent's concern in this essay is to caution the critics against ignoring their duty to the public, which is to steer them through the morass of reading material with which they are confronted and make choices that will elevate them. Left to their own, he argues, they cannot be held entirely accountable for their failure to recognize great literature.

Trent proceeds in the volume to enact his claims; as critic, as spiritual guide, he leads the pilgrim/reader through a discussion of literature that, for him, is unarguably great. True to his understanding of his vocation, moreover, he considers not only the literary but the moral implications of his subject. The force of Percy Bysshe Shelley's art, for example, lies in its spiritual aspirations, his valiant efforts to triumph over his regrettably immoral early environment. His art becomes the evidence of his at least partial transcendence of the life which he had previously lived. Trent concludes his essay on Shelley, placed strategically between "The Authority of Criticism" and "Literature and Morals" to illustrate the methodology he embraces, by labeling the poet "the most aspiring spirit that ever succeeded in saving itself by means of its sylph-like wings from the ever greedy and onward rolling waves of the oblivious ocean." To Trent, the "oblivious ocean" of time will cleanse the shore of immoral refuse. The best of Shelley's art "saves" him from oblivion as it redeems his spirit from its sinful life.

Although in "Literature and Morals" Trent qualifies his spiritual message, he inevitably follows any qualification with another moral injunction; for example, he notes, "the idea that the novel must be made suitable to a school-girl is too ludicrous to warrant discussion, but the idea that the novel must answer the requirements of pure-minded men and women is one that should be present to every writer of fiction.... It is incumbent upon him to view life as a pure-minded, cleanhearted man of genius." He does not, however, exempt the reader from all responsibility but argues that he should "meet the author half way," paring down his "idiosyncracies" so as to form judgments that allow for an acceptance of new possibilities without abandoning the standards of common sense and human decency.

In the pieces on works and artists that follow Trent strives to maintain the balance he advocates in "The Authority of Criticism": to be at once the guardian of the canon and the impressionistic critic who asks the reader to respond openly to the work. He insists upon the virtual impossibility of translating Horace, advocates a middle ground between Matthew Arnold's apparent reverence and A. C. Swinburne's and George Saintsbury's curt dismissals of Lord Byron, and takes William Dean Howells to task for debunking romantic fiction in general by reviling its cheap imitations. In the other two methodological studies in the volume, he pushes his demands of criticism still further.

"Teaching the Spirit of Literature" (first published in the September 1896 *Atlantic Monthly*) contains an impassioned plea for teachers to "be brave enough to let the machinery go," that is, to bring the students into contact with the emotion of literature, with what is gripping and eternal. Exams, philology, and even for the most part, literary history, are distractions. Parents and teachers are too enchanted with "utility." Students are musical instruments, he claims, and during the course of the essay he sings out "the supremacy of literature as a study over all others that now occupy the world's attention." Unfortunately, he carries the message to the point of literary imperialism. In "The Nature of Literature," he writes, "by making free use of our elastic tests we shall not only be better able to sympathize with the literary tastes of people of inferior culture, and so be able to help them to rise in the scale of taste and intelligence, but also be more certain to comprehend and supply the literary needs of children, whether they are our own or else are confided to our guidance." Nevertheless, the spirit of the volume, charged with Trent's energy, enthusiasm

for and commitment to his subject, attests to his devotion to the study and teaching of literature in an age in which science, in the service of technology and cultural expansion, dominated both education and the popular imagination.

In 1899 Trent published *John Milton: A Short Study of His Life and Works*, which grew out of an article that appeared in the January 1897 *Sewanee Review*. The book, he claims, resulted from his conviction that the public had devalued Milton, and indeed, he strives systematically to exonerate both the poet and his works from, or at least to mitigate, the charges leveled against him by unsympathetic critics. He defends Milton passionately as a man whose uncompromising idealism might underlie his personal difficulties, especially with his first wife, as well as some of the harshness of his critical reception. Something of an idealist himself, Trent lauded Milton's ability to press "home the splendid truth that purity of mind and soul and body is to be aimed at and attained in our daily life below." Trent's own poetry, a collection of which came out in the same year, shows his marked tendency to idealization (Honoré de Balzac is a "mighty master of the heart of man"; Edward Gibbon, a "Matchless historian whose undazzled eye/Swept o'er the centuries as some mighty star/Traces wide Space"; William Gladstone, one of the "crowned heads that rule today"), to the point of lauding "Nature" as "Fairer than Venus of old,... the only, the true/Daughter of God." His line of defense for Milton is, then, hardly surprising, nor is his central praise of the poet, which revolves around what Trent calls Milton's "masculine vigor" and his "virility" as a poet and prose stylist; he concedes that Milton lacks the humor and human intimacy of other great poets but views his limitations in the context of the nobility and purity of his subject, again a "fault" of his idealism. Indeed, regarding Milton's art as "the noblest and most virile English in our literature," he blames his lack of popularity on women, whom he sees as constituting the majority of contemporary readership but lacking sufficient "sublimity of character" to appreciate a poet in whose work "woman ... plays no exalted part" and in which the sublime constitutes the chief theme. Nevertheless, Trent boldly declares Milton to be the complement of Shakespeare, "the stately, pure, noble lily of human genius on its spiritual and ideal side."

Trent shows the same unmitigated enthusiasm in his biography of Robert E. Lee, published, like the study of Milton, in 1899. In his preface to the biography, he remarks, "For my enthusiasm I do not ask to be forgiven, although I know that that is a serious fault in these critical days." Although Matthews deemed the volume "excessive," Trent remained undaunted. The ideals that inspired his adulation of Lee (Trent ranks himself among Lee's "lovers") provided the basis for his polemical *War and Civilization* (1901), comprised of two addresses: "War and Civilization," delivered at the annual meeting and banquet of the Alumni Association of the University of the South just after his appointment at Columbia in August 1900, and "Cosmopolitanism and Partisanship," delivered before the Literary Societies of Wake Forest College in July 1899. Both articles, which subsequently appeared in the *Sewanee Review* (October 1900 and July 1899 respectively), resemble Miltonian tracts in their unabashedly ideological treatment of contemporary political themes. Trent laments the prevalence of the war spirit (he vehemently opposed the Spanish-American War and the annexation of the Philippines) and the political corruption of the current system and counsels both private and public individuals to cultivate "cosmopolitanism," by which he means the same combination of traditionalism and impressionistic response that he lauds in the literary critic.

In December 1898 Edmund Gosse, general editor of an American history series, informed Trent that Moses Coit Tyler, because of illness, would be unable to write the history of American literature on which he was at work and requested that Trent complete the task. Trent finished the work, *A History of American Literature, 1607-1865*, in early 1903 while at Columbia. Shortly before its completion he complained to Gosse of the difficulty in reconciling his patriotism with his critical task, and indeed he begins the volume with the admission that "it would be hard to imagine a more hopeless literature, from the point of view of intrinsic aesthetic value, or, in other words, a literature less rich in striking works of imagination and fancy, than the body of writings produced in the American colonies before the Revolution." His subsequent contention that puritanism is not conducive to great art simultaneously highlights Milton's exceptional greatness and excuses early American literature. The issue apparently continued to bother him, however, for he remarks later in the volume that "Prof. S. L. Whitcomb, who cannot well be accused of lack of patriotism, manages to find but ten entries to chronicle for the year 1789," and he qualifies his own censure of

the earliest Americans with praise for "their piety, their learning, their courageous optimism, their general intellectual sanity, their attractive quaintness, and their essential manliness," giving vent, it seems, to the patriotism he had been suppressing.

Trent frames the volume around brief biographical sketches of the leading literary names of the period, perhaps in response to Gosse's request that he "find room for a little more biography, and a little less position criticism." There are no real surprises in the volume, which recognizes the literary merits of Benjamin Franklin's autobiography, celebrates the beginning of American literature in Washington Irving, and applauds the greatness of Nathaniel Hawthorne and Edgar Allan Poe. Shortly after the publication of the volume, Thomas Wentworth Higginson wrote to congratulate Trent on the breadth of his treatment but also to regret the omission of Helen Hunt Jackson and Emily Dickinson, a criticism which time would in part vindicate.

Observing again that "as a representative Southerner," Simms was "embarrassed by the lack of a proper environment for literary work," and concluding the work with Abraham Lincoln, "a fitting and auspicious name with which to close an account of the development of American literature," Trent was once again clearly not calculating to please his southern colleagues. Evidently, however, he did please publisher Henry Holt, who, in September following the publication of the volume, wrote to ask Trent to edit a "World Series," on the order of the "American Series." Trent became the general editor of the new series, thus establishing a lifelong friendship with Holt.

While at work on his literary history Trent also edited, with Benjamin W. Wells, a three-volume series that they called *Colonial Prose and Poetry* (1901). The volumes, *Pioneer Literature*, *Colonial Literature*, and *Revolutionary Literature*, had as much a historical as a literary purpose; the editors sought to trace the nation's early development through its poetry, theological writings, and annals. They acknowledge the lack of literary inspiration but present the documents for their historic interest and importance.

Meanwhile, however, Trent had not surrendered his straight historical work entirely to his more literary pursuits. In 1897 Charles Kendall Adams, then president of the University of Wisconsin, proposed *A History of the United States* (1903), a historical work designed to correct the deficiencies in United States history books in use at the time. Specifically, Adams wanted a book that would treat the southern point of view of the Civil War and the British side of the Revolutionary War more fairly and that would assign more importance to the role of the West in the growth and development of the nation. Finally, he felt that a United States history book should pay more attention to the development of government and industry, usually omitted presumably because it made for less interesting reading than heroes and wars. Trent edited the volume with Adams, but he had to complete the work alone because of Adams's death in 1902 prior to its publication.

Trent was simultaneously engaged in writing a volume for the Nineteenth Century series on the political development of the nation. This work allowed him to focus on some of the issues of the history book and to emphasize, as he notes in the preface of *Progress of the United States of America in the Century* (1901), the "prime importance [that] attaches to the history of the great experiment in self-government made by the American democracy . . . [without which] the world would have been left without some of the most important of all the political lessons it has ever been taught." The work was probably completed well in advance of its publication in 1903, since Trent signs the preface with his University of the South affiliation.

Another literary collection he was editing may also have been inspired by Adams's proposal for a more balanced portrayal of American history. In *Southern Writers; Selections in Prose and Verse* (1905) Trent intended to supplement the dearth of southern writers in American textbooks. Steering a middle course once again, Trent does not suggest that the writers included in this volume be universally canonized; instead he proposes the work "primarily for use in school and college classes in the South" while still advocating their importance to the Union as a whole. The motivating claim of this work is that "while the South has never been prolific of books and writers, its people have contributed a larger and a better share to the literature of the Republic than is generally admitted." Although *Southern Writers* attests to his continuing concern with the South, Trent's pressing concerns at this period seem to be more theoretical than regional.

Greatness in Literature and Other Papers (1905) charted the progress Trent had been making in his theorizing since *The Authority of Criticism, and Other Essays*. The essays collected therein grew out of talks and, in some cases, articles published previously, as in the earlier collection. Whereas *The Authority of Criticism* suggests a certain amount of struggle over self-definition, *Greatness in Literature* presents a carefully defined self with something of a mission to convert. The subtle distinction in tone provides evidence of Trent's growth, perhaps a result of his reception at Columbia, where he seems to have resolved some of the conflict he experienced at the University of the South. His tone is more that of a mentor seeking to help others formulate their own identities through answers to questions over which he had long been ruminating. Perhaps this is because he delivered most of the essays initially as talks, designed to engage the audience in more direct ways than a written piece. Trent prepared the first paper, "The Question of Greatness in Literature," in response to questions commonly asked by Columbia University summer students in 1901; the following December he delivered it as a lecture in Cincinnati and published it in *International Monthly* in May. In this essay Trent argues in favor of canon formation, that is, the need to distinguish levels of greatness in literature. He no longer qualifies this argument as he did in "The Authority of Criticism" but maintains wholeheartedly that "it is a law of the human mind and heart to seek the best and to pay it due homage when found."

The political implications of his argument stand out in his initial assertion that it is democracy that makes books prevalent and available and provides the public with the money to buy and the leisure to read them but also an overabundance of literature from which to choose and, perhaps, over which to stumble. Here he seems to allude to a favorite metaphor of his, the republican spirit in literature, that is, the need for mentors to guide and train the willing but ignorant populace. As in his earlier work he willingly dons the role of spiritual guide and proceeds to delineate the classifications of writers (from "world-writers" to "versifiers and scribblers") on the basis of categories that he defines. Even here, however, he does not fail to include the opinions of both contemporary and future readers, considering the extent of contemporary recognition and duration of fame important standards of evaluation.

Furthermore, as he maintains in the next essay, "A Word for Smaller Authors and for Popular Judgement," based on two short papers he had written for the *Churchman* in December 1897, literature that is not great has an important place in letters. And, conversely, despite critical opinion, if a writer has continued to lack popularity he must be missing a necessary qualification of greatness. Such qualifications can, however, be waived; for example, consistent with an almost messianic passion for Milton that persists throughout his work and that occasionally troubled some of his colleagues, he explains Milton's lack of popularity as the result of his having chosen "a form of expression that [has become] repellent to the masses."

Citing, among other evidence, the burgeoning number of literary groups, he deems his a critical rather than a creative age in "The Aims and Methods of Literary Study" (originally a lecture given in November and December 1901 and turned into an article for *Sewanee Review* in January 1904). Literature, he maintains, provides the "easiest access to the ideal," so literature teachers should focus on communicating the spirit of literature. To this end he addresses a later essay, "Teaching Literature" (originally a public lecture at Columbia University, July 1902; published in *Sewanee Review* in October 1904), in which he picks up on arguments laid out previously in "Teaching the Spirit of Literature": young students of literature should be encouraged to read literature rather than to study literary history and philology; teachers should focus on aesthetic appreciation, reading aloud to students, offering literature to which they will respond, emphasizing the merits rather than the defects of the texts. Once again he challenges many of the contemporary ideas about teaching literature, arguing that the study of literature need not conform to the manner in which other disciplines are studied; essays, for example, while good for compositional skills, should not focus on literature. Instead, students should be encouraged to enjoy and experience literature, that is, the spirit of literature. He sums up with the rallying cry: "Let us have fewer new bad essays written and more good old books read."

This method, he insists, will encourage cosmopolitanism because it will guide the young readers toward the ideals that make for great literature. And he holds this view to be particularly important for current and aspiring literature teachers, as he explains in "Some Remarks on Modern Book-Burning," part of which he read before the Amherst College English Club in April 1905. He defines "the man who cares only for

the books that expound and defend the causes he espouses [as] really a foe, and a very dangerous one, to literature." And he continues in "Literature and Science" (read to the Phi Beta Kappa of Lehigh University, June 1904) to explain that the spirit of literature fosters rather than opposes scientific exploration; the disciplines should be complementary rather than, as many of his contemporaries had suggested, competitive studies. Nevertheless, he insisted, in a talk delivered to the Men's English Graduate Club of Columbia University in December 1904 (collected in *Greatness in Literature* as "The Love of Poetry") that literature in its highest form, usually poetry, captures the reader's spirit through rapture: "It is great poetry–not the rapid transit inventions of modern science, wonderful as these are–that comes nearest in our mortal life to discharging the functions of those bearing the hero and heroine to some far-off land where the streams run felicity and the winds breathe joy."

Perhaps it was Trent's evident penchant for romance, as well as his scholarly vocation, that inspired him at this time to embark on the study of Defoe that would obsess him until the end of his life. And, in 1908, he would begin to satisfy another of his passions when he proposed to Columbia President Nicholas Butler that the university undertake the first complete edition of Milton's works, of which Trent was the general editor until ill health forced him to resign in 1926.

In 1910 Trent published his last volume of collected essays, *Longfellow and Other Essays*. By this time he had stopped writing articles at the prolific rate at which he had began and was engaged instead in more long-term editorial projects. Like its predecessor, this volume was comprised mainly of lectures, but Trent also included his introductions to volumes of Edmund Spenser and William Makepeace Thackeray. The essays are mostly shorter and less comprehensive than those in the two previous volumes of collected pieces. Practicing what he has been preaching, Trent argues warmly in favor of an avid appreciation of writers from Henry Wadsworth Longfellow, Sir Walter Scott, Alphonse Daudet, Thackeray, and Poe to Samuel Johnson, Spenser, and, of course, Milton. The remaining two essays in the volume, "The Relations of History and Literature" (a talk delivered to the Virginia Historical Society in January 1906 and later published as a pamphlet) and "A Talk to Would-Be Teachers" (delivered before the Men's English Graduate Club of Columbia University in March 1906 and published in the

July *Sewanee Review* as "An Academic Sermon") reveal his continuing concern with pedagogy. In the former Trent argues the advantages of scholars' crossing over disciplines and in particular he laments the scientific investigator who wants to limit history to papers and monographs at the expense of the historian who strives after the literary execution of an encompassing volume of history.

In the latter essay Trent addresses a slightly newer theme; the essay reads almost as a how-to manual or survival kit for an aspiring professor. He discusses the work load, inadequate facilities, and "cramping environment," especially of small colleges, and prescribes the importance of variety: the good teacher is always writing something, reads whenever he/she has the chance, and reserves one line of reading for recreational rather than academic purposes. Here Trent draws on his experience at the University of the South where, he tells the reader, he managed to teach eighteen hours of courses in several disciplines and subjects and serve as academic dean while editing and writing. But most important, he cautions, is for the teacher to remember to allow students the independence to think and not just to process the teacher's thoughts. From testimonies of his students over the years, from the warmth of their regard and the tenor of their reminiscences, Trent evidently counseled from experience.

Throughout his life he wrote essays and lectures while engaging in more long-term literary projects. His correspondence with Holt is filled with plans for series and a high-quality literary magazine that Holt eventually published as the *Unpopular Review*. During this correspondence, however, Trent seems to have functioned as the voice of reason, expressing the reservations that Holt, in his exuberance, neglected. In fact, consistent with his pedagogical character, Trent apparently enjoyed rethinking and revising old material. Certain themes and messages continually reappear but always with a slightly different slant. Nine years after the publication of his American literary history, and amidst the frustration with his work on Defoe that prompted Holt to write "Damn Defoe, or at least his demoralizing influence on you!," Trent and Columbia colleague John Erskine refined the former work and produced *Great American Writers* (1912), which quickly became an international classic and was even translated into Czech. The work, which begins with Franklin, focuses in on, and enlarges,

Trent's previous discussion of particular authors. The book is somewhat more anecdotal than its predecessor, and it largely follows the format of a basic critical biography for most of the writers treated. But the authors seem also to be expanding the scope of their speculations, adding some of the more critical evaluations that had troubled Gosse as well as a few generalizations about the character of America. Discussing William Cullen Bryant, for example, they write: "This is not the poetry of sophistication; it is rather the poetry of a simple age and people not yet intoxicated with their own material power and cut off by an ocean from the complex emotional and intellectual life of the old world."

During this period Trent also collaborated on literary projects with many of his Columbia colleagues. Along with Charles L. Hanson and William T. Brewster, he authored *An Introduction to the English Classics,* first published in 1911. The work, which is geared to students and teachers of English literature, shows evidence of the pedagogical themes that preoccupied Trent. The first part reads as a kind of tract, familiar to students of Trent's work, on the importance of teaching and studying literature. The authors delineate and examine the six categories of classics: novels and romances, narrative poems, dramatic poetry, nonnovel narrative and descriptive prose, descriptive and lyric poetry, and expository and argumentative prose. And they caution teachers that although they may want to focus on the ethical value of the literature they teach, they must remember the importance of literature that interests and delights, and they must not draw unnecessary distinctions among those functions. The second part of the work outlines major literary works and raises questions that are likely to arise or may be profitably raised in the classroom. The task required that its executors combine the skills of dedicated teachers, experienced editors (and indeed Trent edited a wide variety of works throughout his career), and wideranging literary historians.

Trent was making further use of the expertise gained in his American literary history in the massive edition of *The Cambridge History of American Literature* (1917-1921) on which he collaborated with Erskine, Stuart P. Sherman, and Carl Van Doren. According to the editors, the Cambridge history was to be larger than its predecessors, a collaborative effort of scholars throughout the United States and Canada. Including a voluminous bibliography treating all subjects and periods, it was intended to provide an extensive "survey of the life of the American people," an impressionistic sense of who they were and are through their writings and not just a history of those writings. It was through its comprehensiveness that the editors sought to make this literary history unique. Beginning with travelers and explorers and ending with the transcendentalists, the first volume includes not just poetry and fiction, but political writing, drama, essays, history, and theology. The subsequent four volumes incorporate such diverse categories as dialect writings, humorists, publicists, orators, newspapers, philosophy, economic treatises, popular bibles, patriotic songs and hymns, publishing, and non-English writings (German, French, and Yiddish).

But by this time Trent's real passion, and his albatross, was his work on Defoe. In December 1911, at the first dinner of the Hobby Club, founded to "promote social and literary intercourse among its members and discussion and consideration of various literary and economic subjects," Trent read a paper on his ongoing work on Defoe. His interest had begun seven years earlier, while preparing a biography and bibliography on Defoe for a couple of lectures in a course he was giving. His subsequent discovery of the chaos that characterized the extant Defoe biographies and studies, and the partisan nature of these works that was so inconsistent with Defoe's reputation among his contemporaries, led Trent to pursue research that was to culminate in the legacy of a three-thousand-page unfinished bibliographic manuscript. That night Trent tried to explain his obsession to the members of his club: "Curiosity, doggedness, and a certain sense of responsibility as a teacher continually occupied in emphasizing the need of minute, accurate research led me on, and I have kept going these seven years. Perhaps like Jacob I am doomed to serve seven years more, with no Leah in the meanwhile, and what a Rachel at the end!" Having discovered the verity in the charges leveled against Defoe by his contemporaries, Trent had to acknowledge that Defoe was "probably the most mendacious journalist and voluminous scribbler in the world's annals," but he refused to regret his preoccupation with his "sordid life." Instead, Trent revels in the pleasures of the literary detective's foiling the plots of an allusive master and of the student's rescuing from the "oceans of oblivion," a metaphor of which he appears to have been especially fond, "even a foot of the solid land of fact." But most of all Trent expresses

boundless joy at salvaging a reputation that was sullied by implications that overtly partisan biographies could do nothing to defend. Trent celebrates in his talk not the admittedly "unprincipled mercenary," but the man who, despite that, "was a most interesting and likable person, as well as an extraordinary genius of what I may call the plebeian variety." That Defoe became something of a cause célèbre and even a tragic hero to Trent is evident in his conviction that he was a man "more sinned against than sinning."

While he never published his magnum opus Trent did turn out what he calls "a small book" of about three hundred pages. The title of his work, *Daniel Defoe, How to Know Him*, published as part of the "How to Know the Authors" series in 1916, reveals his real motive: the literary detective, student of literature, and avidly compassionate biographer all wanted the public to know Defoe, the real Defoe, not just the great Defoe of *Robinson Crusoe* fame or the much aligned mercenary journalist, but "the greatest of plebeian geniuses." Given the stipulations of the series, and probably in conformity with what Trent would have wanted from his pre-opus introduction, little-known texts, stories, articles, and tracts comprise a substantial portion of the volume. But Trent makes his case with the zeal he had shown in the biographies of and articles on his previous concerns, the avidity of one telling a story he has long wanted to tell.

Perhaps that is the secret of a great critic and teacher: to have many stories that one wants to tell. Trent's early career was not easy. In addition to his mixed experiences at the University of the South, his critical reception was not always what he would have liked it to be. In a letter to his wife in 1897 he wrote, "I'm 35 years old and I've had to fight hard to get myself a small place in literature and even now I don't make enough by my pen alone to support me. I still get things returned–vide the *Authority* paper, and I dare say I shall for some time to come." But Trent had the tenacity and enthusiasm for his profession to persist. And he worked until his death, despite the paralytic stroke that restricted him to the home of his son and daughter-in-law in Beacon, New York. Even there, however, Trent persisted, surprising everyone one day by lifting himself out of the morris chair to which he had been confined and appending the moral: "Do not say can't to a paralytic who some years ago made up his mind to fight for health."

Trent is remembered for different things in different circles. His *New York Times* obituary stresses his work on Defoe, Milton, and Simms. Critics and literary historians might best remember him for his role in *The Cambridge History of American Literature* or perhaps in the founding of the *Sewanee Review,* neither of which the *Times* obituary even mentions. But those who knew him remember him best as an educator, the identity with which he would probably have been happiest. As he wrote to Minnie C. Yarborough of Hunter College in 1933: "I have as you know, written and edited many books myself, but I think I can truly say that I always looked on myself primarily as a teacher, not as a man of letters. I suspect that even if I live to be a hundred, I shall be found cherishing in my heart the profound conviction that there is no nobler profession than that of teacher. How could there be, when after all the son of God was Himself the greatest of all teachers? We speak of the Sermon on the Mount, but it would [be] as true to say The Teaching on the Mount." It is, then, appropriate that, besides his unfinished memoirs and the Defoe bibliographical study, the work he left when he died was "Thoughts on Teaching," a combination memoir and pedagogical tract that combines theory with delightfully touching and witty anecdotes about his own and his friends' experiences as teachers. The work resounds with the celebration of humanity and with the importance of humble introspection in one's life as in one's work that he believed great art promotes; it is the legacy he left to his children, Lucia, a poet, and William Peterfield, Jr., a cartoonist, as well as to his students, his colleagues, and his readers. And it is what he believed would keep mankind human in an age of technological advances. As he wrote in "Aviation Fancies" (*Verse-jottings,* 1924):

> If we go on progressing so,
> We soon shall cease ourselves to know,
> And, catching up with God too fast,
> Must come a cropper at the last.

References:

Jacques Barzun, ed., *A History of the Faculty of Philosophy, Columbia University* (New York: Columbia University Press, 1957);

George S. Hellman, "Men of Letters at Columbia," *Critic,* 43 (October 1903): 316-327;

W. H. Stephenson, "William Peterfield Trent as a Historian of the South," *Journal of Southern History,* 15 (May 1949): 151-177;

Franklin Trenaby Walker, "William Peterfield Trent: A Critical Biography," Ph.D. dissertation, George Peabody College for Teachers, 1943.

Papers:

The most substantial collection of William Peterfield Trent's papers is housed in the Butler Library, Columbia University.

Henry Van Dyke

(10 November 1852-10 April 1933)

Janice L. Edens
Macon College

BOOKS: *The Reality of Religion* (New York: Scribners, 1884; London: Unwin, 1885);

The Story of the Psalms (New York: Scribners, 1887);

The National Sin of Literary Piracy (New York: Scribners, 1888);

The Poetry of Tennyson (New York: Scribners, 1889; London: Mathews, 1890; revised and enlarged, New York: Scribners, 1891; revised and enlarged again, 1898);

God and Little Children (New York: Randolph, 1890);

Man Better than a Sheep (Princeton: Princeton Press, 1891);

A Brief for Foreign Missions (New York: Woman's Board of Foreign Missions of the Presbyterian Church, 1891);

Historic Presbyterianism (New York: Randolph, 1893);

Straight Sermons to Young Men and Other Human Beings (New York: Scribners, 1893); revised and enlarged as *Sermons to Young Men* (New York: Scribners, 1898; London: Dickinson, 1901); revised and enlarged again as *Manhood, Faith and Courage* (London: Hodder & Stoughton, 1906);

The True Presbyterian Doctrine of the Church (New York: Wm. C. Martin, 1893);

An Historic Church (New York: Wm. C. Martin, 1893);

The Bible As It Is (New York: Wm. C. Martin, 1893);

Is This Calvinism or Christianity? (Privately printed, 1893);

The Christ-Child in Art (New York: Harper, 1894);

Little Rivers (New York: Scribners, 1895; London: Nutt, 1895);

The People Responsible for the Character of Their Rulers (New York: Society of Sons of the Revolution, 1895);

The Story of the Other Wise Man (New York: Harper, 1896; New York & London: Harper, 1898);

Henry Van Dyke

The Gospel for An Age of Doubt (New York: Macmillan, 1896; London: Hodder, 1899);

Ships and Havens (New York: Crowell, 1897);

The Builders and Other Poems (New York: Scribners, 1897);

The First Christmas Tree (New York: Scribners, 1897);

The Lost Word (New York: Scribners, 1898; London: Clarke, 1899);

The Toiling of Felix (New York: Scribners, 1898);

The Cross of War (Privately printed, 1898);

The American Birthright and the Philippine Pottage (New York: Scribners, 1898);

Fisherman's Luck and Some Other Uncertain Things (New York: Scribners, 1899; London: Low, 1899);

The Gospel for a World of Sin (New York & London: Macmillan, 1899);

The Message of Christ to Mankind (Boston & New York: Houghton, Mifflin, 1899);

The Toiling of Felix and Other Poems (New York: Scribners, 1900; London: Hodder & Stoughton, 1911);

The Poetry of the Psalms (New York: Crowell, 1900);

The Friendly Year, edited by George Sidney Webster (New York: Scribners, 1900; revised, 1909; revised again, 1917, 1926);

Books, Literature and the People (New York: Cadmus Press, 1900);

The Ruling Passion (New York: Scribners, 1901);

The Blue Flower (New York: Scribners, 1902);

Joy and Power: Three Messages with One Meaning (New York: Crowell, 1903);

The Open Door (Philadelphia: Presbyterian Board, 1903);

Music, and Other Poems (New York: Scribners, 1904);

The Childhood of Jesus Christ (New York: Stokes, 1905);

Essays in Application (New York: Scribners, 1905); republished as *Ideals and Applications* (London: Hodder & Stoughton, 1906);

The School of Life (New York: Scribners, 1905);

The Spirit of Christmas (New York: Scribners, 1905);

The Van Dyke Book, edited by Edwin Mims (New York: Scribners, 1905; revised, 1921);

The Americanism of Washington (New York & London: Harper, 1906);

The Battle of Life (New York: Crowell, 1907);

The Good Old Way (New York: Crowell, 1907);

The Music-Lover (New York: Moffatt, Yard, 1907);

Days Off, and Other Digressions (New York: Scribners, 1907; London: Hodder & Stoughton, 1907);

Counsels by the Way (New York: Crowell, 1908);

The House of Rimmon (New York: Scribners, 1908);

Out of Doors in the Holy Land: Impressions of Travel in Body and Spirit (New York: Scribners, 1908; London: Hodder & Stoughton, 1908);

The White Bees, and Other Poems (New York: Scribners, 1909);

The Spirit of America (New York: Macmillan, 1910; London: Macmillan, 1912);

The Mansion (New York & London: Harper, 1911);

The Sad Shepherd (New York: Scribners, 1911; London: Harper, 1912);

Poems of Henry Van Dyke (New York: Scribners, 1911; London: Bird, 1913; revised and enlarged edition, New York: Scribners, 1920);

Who Follow the Flag (New York: Scribners, 1911);

The Unknown Quantity: A Book of Romance and Some Half-Told Tales (New York: Scribners, 1912; London: Harper, 1913);

Ars Argricolaris (New York: Privately printed, 1913);

The Angel of God's Face (Philadelphia: Westminster Press, 1913);

The Grand Canyon, and Other Poems (New York: Scribners, 1914);

The Lost Boy (New York & London: Harper, 1914);

Prayer for Christmas Morning (New York: Dutton, 1915);

The Red Flower (New York: Scribners, 1917; London: Hodder & Stoughton, 1918);

Fighting for Peace (New York: Scribners, 1917; London: Hodder & Stoughton, 1918);

The Valley of Vision: A Book of Romance and Some Half-Told Tales (New York: Scribners, 1919; London: Hodder & Stoughton, 1919);

The Broken Soldier and the Maid of France (New York & London: Harper, 1919);

The Golden Stars and Other Verses (New York: Scribners, 1919; London: Hodder & Stoughton, 1919);

What Peace Means (New York: Revell, 1919);

The Works of Henry Van Dyke, 18 volumes (New York: Scribners, 1920-1927);

Camp Fires and Guide Posts: A Book of Essays and Excursions (New York: Scribners, 1921; London: Hodder & Stoughton, 1921);

Companionable Books (New York: Scribners, 1922; London: Hodder & Stoughton, 1923);

Songs out of Doors (New York: Scribners, 1922);

Thy Sea is Great, Our Boats are Small (New York: Revell, 1922; London: Hodder & Stoughton, 1922);

Six Days of the Week: A Book of Thoughts About Life and Religion (New York: Scribners, 1924; London: Hodder & Stoughton, 1925);

Half Told Tales (New York: Scribners, 1925);

The King's Jewel (Chicago: Printing Arts Department of the School of the Art Institute of Chicago, 1925);

The Golden Key: Stories of Deliverance (New York: Scribners, 1926); enlarged as *The Golden Key: Stories of Deliverance, and Some Half-Told Tales* (New York: Scribners, 1927);

Light My Candle: A Book of Reflections, by Van Dyke and Tertius Van Dyke (New York: Revell, 1926; London: Oliphant, 1927);

Chosen Poems (New York: Scribners, 1927; London: Bird, 1928);

An Old Game (New York: Dingbat Press, 1927);

"Even Unto Bethlehem": The Story of Christmas (New York: Scribners, 1928);

The Man Behind the Book: Essays in Understanding (New York: Scribners, 1929);

The Travel Diary of an Angler (New York: Derrydale, 1929);

Gratitude (New York: Dutton, 1930).

Collection: *Avalon Edition*, 18 volumes (New York: Scribners, 1920-1927).

OTHER: *Henry Jackson Van Dyke*, edited by Henry Van Dyke and Paul Van Dyke (New York: Randolph, 1892);

Paul Van Dyke, *The Age of the Renascence*, introduction by Henry Van Dyke (New York: Christian Literature Co., 1897);

Henry Morse Stephens, *Counsel upon the Reading of Books*, introduction by Van Dyke (Boston: Houghton, Mifflin, 1900);

Historic Scenes in Fiction, edited by Van Dyke (Boston: Hall & Locke, 1902);

Poems of Tennyson, edited, with an introduction, by Van Dyke (Boston: Ginn, 1903);

Ora Fletcher Gardner and Frank L. Janeway, *Not in the Curriculum: A Book of Friendly Counsel to Students by Two Recent College Graduates*, introduction by Van Dyke (New York & Chicago: Revell, 1903);

Little Masterpieces of English Poetry, 6 volumes, edited by Van Dyke and Hardin Craig (New York: Doubleday, Doran, 1905); revised and republished as *Poetry*, 6 volumes, edited by Van Dyke, Craig, and Asa Don Dickenson (Garden City: Doubleday, Page, 1922);

Robert Haven Schauffler, *Where Speech Ends: A Music Maker's Romance*, prelude by Van Dyke (New York: Moffatt, Yard, 1906);

The Book of Common Worship, prepared by a committee chaired by Van Dyke (Philadelphia: Presbyterian Board, 1906; revised and enlarged, 1932);

The Whole Family: A Novel by Twelve Authors, by William Dean Howells, Mary E. Wilkins Freeman, Mary Heaton Vorse, Mary Stuart Cutting, Elizabeth Jordan, John Kendrick Bangs, Henry James, Elizabeth Stuart Phelps, Edith Wyatt, Mary R. Shipman Andrews, Alice Brown, and Van Dyke (New York: Harper, 1908);

The Poetry of Nature, edited by Van Dyke (London: Heinemann, 1909; New York: Doubleday, Page, 1911);

Mary Stewart, *Once Upon a Time Tales*, introduction by Van Dyke (New York: Revell, 1912);

Odes and Sonnets and Epigrams, edited by Van Dyke (Garden City: 1912);

"American Rights Imperilled," in *The World Peril: America's Interest in the War*, by members of the Princeton University faculty (Princeton: Princeton University Press, 1917);

Maurice Barrès, *The Faith of France: Studies in Spiritual Differences & Unity*, foreword by Van Dyke (Boston: Houghton Mifflin, 1918);

John B. Frazier, *The Navy Chaplain's Manual*, introduction by Van Dyke (New York: Federal Council of the Churches of Christ in America, 1918);

A Book of Princeton Verse 1916-1919, 2 volumes, edited by Alfred Noyes, Van Dyke, M. W. Croll, M. S. Burt, and James Creese, Jr. (Princeton: Princeton University Press, 1919);

Otto A. Rothert, *The Story of a Poet: Madison Cawein*, reminiscences by Van Dyke and others (Louisville, Ky.: Morton, 1921);

Austen Fox Riggs, *Just Nerves*, foreword by Van Dyke (Boston & New York: Houghton Mifflin, 1922);

Maurice Francis Egan, *Recollections of a Happy Life*, introduction by Van Dyke (New York: Doran, 1924);

"The Birth and Childhood of Jesus," in *An Outline of Christianity*, edited by Ernest F. Scott and Burton S. Easton (New York: Bethlehem, 1926);

The Poetic and Dramatic Works of Alfred Lord Tennyson, 7 volumes, introduction by Van Dyke (Boston: Houghton Mifflin, 1929);

"De Maximus," in *The Book of the Fly-Rod*, edited by Hugh T. Sheringham and John Moore (Boston: Houghton Mifflin, 1931; London: Eyre & Spottiswoode, 1931);

A Creelful of Fishing Stories, edited by Van Dyke (New York: Scribners, 1932).

Writer, minister, critic, professor, outdoorsman–Henry Van Dyke was a man of multiple talents and great energy. As a literary critic he sup-

Van Dyke (in front of tent) and an unidentified companion

ported the basic tenets of the Genteel Tradition well into the twentieth century, castigating the modern trend toward realism. His philosophy of art is best summed up in this statement: "The highest element in the best art is always moral, and fitted to make men and women better as well as happier. . . . Immoral art is one of the most evil influences in the world." For Van Dyke the aesthetic and the moral were intimately intertwined. Always the artist's duty was to elevate humanity, a belief reflected in his writing and his criticism.

Henry Jackson Van Dyke was born on 10 November 1852 in Germantown, Pennsylvania, to Henrietta Ashmead and Henry Jackson Van Dyke, a respected Presbyterian clergyman. The son was influenced by his father's role as minister, though the boy was not necessarily a model child. As his father said of his two sons, "Paul was born good, but Henry was saved by grace." In 1868 Van Dyke met Robert E. Lee, who gave him a ride on his horse, Traveller. Later in life he said the three men who had most influenced him were his father, General Lee, and Alfred Tennyson, and from that comment can be seen the keynotes of his life: the dedication to honor and beauty and the willingness to fight for a cause. He studied at the Brooklyn Polytechnic Institute

and received an M.A. from Princeton University in 1876. He was an ideal student, active in a myriad of extracurricular activities as well as his classes. Yet, not wishing to be considered a bookworm, Van Dyke often disguised how much he studied and was willing to involve himself in some youthful pranks. He included in his college scrapbook a poster offering a fifty-dollar "reward for the apprehension and conviction of the person or persons who took the gate and damaged the fences on the Seminary and Library grounds." In the margin is the note: "They didn't catch us. H.v.D."

When he entered Princeton Theological Seminary in September 1874 it was with the understanding that he might not become a minister, since his real dream was to be a writer. However, in 1879 he entered the Presbyterian ministry and four years later became the pastor of the famous Brick Presbyterian Church in New York City, where he gained a national reputation for his preaching. He had preached his first sermon on 21 October 1875 at Bryn Mawr, Pennsylvania, on "The Voice of God," about hearing God in nature, a theme that would resurface in much of his later writing. In fact, his love of the outdoors was a crucial part of his Christianity, and in the

early twentieth century he became a conservation-
ist speaking out for the preservation of Yellow-
stone. This dual belief in nature and religion
colored his literary criticism as well as his other
writing throughout his life.

As he was beginning his career as a minister, Van Dyke was also launching his career as a
writer. In September 1879 he went with his
friend the artist W. S. Macy to the Red River Valley wheat farms where he saw the problems with
large agricultural systems that were depleting the
land and exploiting migrant labor. With Macy he
did an illustrated article for *Harper's Monthly Magazine*; it was the lead article for the May 1880
issue.

His first books, *The Reality of Religion* (1884)
and *The Story of the Psalms* (1887) grew directly
out of his role as minister and would be followed
by many similar productions. By 1888, however,
he was already very much involved in the literary
scene, publishing a sermon he had preached on
the "National Sin of Literary Piracy," which attacked the American habit of printing pirated copies of foreign books.

Ironically, Van Dyke's first copy of a book
by Tennyson, *Enoch Arden, ect.* (1864), was a pirated edition, which he had bought for fifty cents
when he was fourteen. His love for Tennyson,
whom he ranked third among the English poets
after William Shakespeare and John Milton, remained a guiding factor during his life. In 1889
his first book of criticism, *The Poetry of Tennyson*,
was published. Before this collection of critical articles on Tennyson appeared, Van Dyke sent some
of them to the eighty-year-old poet, who responded with a letter of thanks, some autobiographical notes, and corrections in the
chronology for the second edition. The book,
which is based on the premise that poetry should
ennoble life, was well received by the public. On
18 August 1892 Van Dyke visited Tennyson at
the older man's invitation. Tennyson said he had
liked Van Dyke's book about him, with the exception of the criticism of *Maud* (1855). While the
poet took his afternoon nap, Van Dyke listened
to recordings of Tennyson reading his own poetry, and afterwards Tennyson personally read
Maud to him. As a result Van Dyke changed his
opinion of the poem in the third edition of his
book.

The Poetry of Tennyson remained Van Dyke's
principal volume of literary criticism, though he
wrote much about literature throughout his life,
blending it with religion and nature. His next sig-

Photograph used as frontispiece for Camp-fires and Guide-
posts, *Van Dyke's 1921 collection of essays and reminiscences*

nificant work was *Little Rivers* (1895), a collection
of essays about the value of the outdoors in the tradition of Henry David Thoreau, John Burroughs, and John Muir. *Fisherman's Luck and Some
Other Uncertain Things* (1899) was similar.

Van Dyke's short stories usually grew out of
his pastoral calling and often resembled parables.
Such is the case of his immensely popular *The
Story of the Other Wise Man* (1896). Originally read
as a Christmas sermon in his church and published in *Harper's Monthly* Christmas issue of
1892, it is the story of Artaban, a fourth Magus
who sells all he owns to bring three precious jewels to the newly born Christ child. During his journey, however, he is detained by various
individuals who need his aid and thus finally
uses up all his jewels without ever seeing Christ.
In the end at Golgotha he has a vision of Christ
telling him that in helping others, Artaban has actually seen and helped Christ himself. This story,
which has been published in at least eighteen editions in the United States and England and translated into many languages, fulfilled Van Dyke's
criteria for a good short story: intentional brevity; singleness of theme; an atmosphere which en-
hances the value of the theme; and a symbolic
meaning. It also reflects the limitations that mod-

ern critics have seen in both his writing and his Christianity–gaining grace is all too easy, too comfortable, too certain. As Bernard Baum has pointed out in his article "God of Hosts and Hostesses," Artaban doesn't really have to suffer or even encounter genuine suffering for the sake of his religion. Nor must he renounce tangibles since it is the very jewels he possesses that permit him to help others. This comfortable belief in Christian capitalism was reflected in an early sermon Van Dyke preached against communism and socialism: "For of two things you may be sure: first, if God has given you possessions in this world they are your own: second, He will certainly hold you to account for what you do with them."

After an illustrious career as a minister, Van Dyke agreed to accept a chair as Murray Professor of English Literature at Princeton in 1900. (He would retire from that position in 1923.) He had already been elected in 1898 by the Academy of Social Science Association to a group of literary men who helped create the National Institute of Arts and Letters. Yet, just as he had incorporated literature into his preaching, now he incorporated his preaching into his literature. His next book of literary criticism was a small volume entitled *The Poetry of the Psalms* (1900), which was later collected into books of essays such as *Counsels by the Way* (1908) and *Companionable Books* (1922). In it he discussed the Bible as literature, "a noble and impassioned interpretation of nature and life, uttered in language of beauty and sublimity, touched with the vivid colours of human personality, and embodied in forms of enduring literary art." He discussed the difficulties of reading the Psalms as poetry in English rather than the original Hebrew because of what is lost in the translation, both metrical verse and subtleties of language. Yet he went on to point out the value that is left and recommended the psalms as poetry to his readers.

Books, Literature and the People (1900), later collected into *Essays in Application* (1905), dealt with the difference between good literature and best-sellers and once again extolled the value of literature to "refresh the weary, to console the sad, to hearten up the dull and downcast, to increase man's interest in the world, his joy of living, and his sympathy with all sorts and conditions of men."

In 1913 Van Dyke was appointed by friend and former classmate Woodrow Wilson as ambassador to the Netherlands and Luxembourg, but he resigned in 1916 because of those countries' neutrality during World War I and became lieutenant commander for the Chaplain Corps of the U.S. Navy instead. Strongly anti-German, he saw no conflict between "deep faith and good fighting." During this time he turned increasingly to patriotic themes, publishing his well-known *Fighting for Peace* in 1917 and *What Peace Means* in 1919. Two of his talks, "In Defense of Religious Liberty," and "For Freedom of Conscience," a radio address of 3 October 1928, were distributed by the Democratic National Committee in 1928.

Companionable Books, a collection of appreciative essays about Van Dyke's favorite books and authors, was published in 1922. In addition to two chapters about the Bible, it contained discussions of Charles Dickens, William Makepeace Thackeray, George Eliot, John Keats, William Wordsworth, Robert Browning, Izaak Walton, Samuel Johnson, Ralph Waldo Emerson, and Robert Louis Stevenson, combining biographical comments with literary evaluation.

The Man Behind the Book: Essays in Understanding (1929) followed a similar format but attacked as well as praised. It began by considering Geoffrey Chaucer as English poetry's first luminary, Edgar Allan Poe as a minor but talented American poet, and Walt Whitman as a misunderstood poet-preacher whom Van Dyke deemed a far better writer than Poe. The next chapter attacked Edgar Lee Masters's *Spoon River Anthology* (1915), both for its view of life and for its free verse, which Van Dyke called "chop-stick prose–knock-kneed, splay-footed, St. Vitus prose." His essay did not mention Masters by name but called him "Spoon Riverman" and "the necrologist." Under the heading "Problematic Natures in English Literature" Van Dyke considered Lord Byron, William Hazlitt, Percy Bysshe Shelley, and Thomas Carlyle. The last section of the book dealt with four novels, George Meredith's *The Ordeal of Richard Feveral* (1859), Thomas Hardy's *Tess of the d'Urbervilles* (1891), Thornton Wilder's *The Bridge of San Luis Rey* (1927), and Willa Cather's *Death Comes for the Archbishop* (1927). He discussed each work favorably, first giving a biographical sketch of the author (though he admitted he knew little about Wilder other than what the book jacket provided), followed by a summary of the plot with comments along the way explaining what he found of value in the work.

Much of Van Dyke's later significant literary criticism came in the form of speeches and letters to friends, in which he attacked the new literary

Van Dyke in old age

movements he saw around him. He opposed art for art's sake because he felt all art should serve man and make him a better, happier person. Of free verse he was a little more tolerant, though he disliked most of it because he felt it lacked substance as well as form. Yet, he acknowledged that some had substance and some had both "and may be taken as an indication of the possibility of developing new metrical arrangements in English verse, which will have a measured and perceptible rhythm of their own." However, he found much free verse too strong and unconventional. He wrote to Edwin Mims at Vanderbilt University: "Must real poetry go off with a bang and fizz like soda water? or claim attention by its strong smell like Limburger cheese?"

He railed against what he called the "new fireworks school of criticism" and at seventy-five attacked the "Smart Aleck School" of writers who "demand too much from life and don't give enough." At a Germantown Business Man's Luncheon Club meeting on 28 March 1930, he publicly criticized the awarding of the Nobel Prize in literature to Sinclair Lewis because he felt Lewis's work presented too negative a view of America and its people. "It isn't the darkness of his views I object to," said Van Dyke, "it's the meanness of them." He felt that William Dean

Howells's *The Rise of Silas Lapham* (1885) gave a truer picture of America. He himself had seen many main streets in America and had met good people as well as base ones like those portrayed in Lewis's novel. He thought writers such as Willa Cather, Booth Tarkington, Hamlin Garland, Struthers Burt, and James Boyd were more deserving of the honor. In his speech accepting the prize in Stockholm, Lewis referred specifically to Van Dyke's criticism, calling him "the fishing Academician," and to the American Academy of Arts and Letters, to which Van Dyke was elected president in 1912. Lewis said that the academy did not "represent literary America today; it represents only Henry Wadsworth Longfellow."

Lewis reflected here the consensus of the literati of his times. In spite of the collected edition of Van Dyke's works which began appearing in the 1920s, he was already considered an outdated relic. Yet, until he died on 10 April 1933 at his home in Princeton, Avalon, he continued to comment on the world around him and "never missed a chance for a scrap–ecclesiastical, political, or literary."

Henry Van Dyke's stature as a literary critic, though solid throughout the late nineteenth and early twentieth centuries, has consistently dwindled since the 1920s. Though some of his work has remained popular with the general public–an edition of *The Story of the Other Wise Man* appeared in 1959–most critics today view him as a man of Victorian taste whose attitude toward the function of literature was too narrow and whose Christianity sat perhaps too easily on his shoulders. Yet, the man Helen Keller called "an architect of happiness" accomplished much; he was an influential and powerful speaker and writer who tried to bridge the gap created by World War I and contend positively with a world of growing skepticism and despair.

Biography:

Tertius Van Dyke, *Henry Van Dyke: A Biography* (New York: Harper, 1935).

References:

Bernard Baum, "God of Hosts and Hostesses," *Southern Humanities Review*, 3 (1969): 126-137;

William Herman Bos, "A Study of the Preaching of Henry Van Dyke," Ph.D. dissertation, University of Michigan, 1955.

Papers:

Though his correspondence is scattered around the country, a significant number of Henry Van Dyke's letters are housed in the Van Dyke Collection in the library archives at Princeton University. Manuscripts of his sermons reside in the Van Dyke Collection of the Presbyterian Historical Society in Philadelphia. The American Academy of Arts and Letters Library in New York has manuscripts of poems, letters, and addresses. Other manuscripts can be found at the University of Virginia, the Pennsylvania Historical and Museum Commission, New York University's Tamiment Library, the University of Southern California, the Henry E. Huntington Library and Museum in San Marino, California, Yale University, Columbia University, and the University of Texas.

Barrett Wendell
(23 August 1855-8 February 1921)

Fritz Fleischmann
Babson College

BOOKS: *The Duchess Emilia* (Boston: Osgood, 1885);

Rankell's Remains (Boston: Ticknor, 1887);

Cotton Mather, The Puritan Priest (New York: Dodd, Mead, 1891);

English Composition: Eight Lectures Given at the Lowell Institute (New York: Scribners, 1891);

Stelligeri, and Other Essays Concerning America (New York: Scribners, 1893);

William Shakspere: A Study in Elizabethan Literature (New York: Scribners, 1894);

A Literary History of America (New York: Scribners, 1900); school edition by Wendell and Chester Noyes Greenough published as *A History of Literature in America* (New York: Scribners, 1904);

Ralegh in Guiana, Rosamond and A Christmas Masque (New York: Scribners, 1902);

The Temper of the Seventeenth Century in English Literature (New York: Scribners, 1904);

Liberty, Union, and Democracy, the National Ideals of America (New York: Scribners, 1906);

The France of Today (New York: Scribners, 1907; London: Archibald & Constable, 1907);

The Privileged Classes (New York: Scribners, 1908);

The Mystery of Education, and Other Academic Performances (New York: Scribners, 1909);

The Traditions of European Literature from Homer to Dante (New York: Scribners, 1920);

Literature, Society, and Politics: Selected Essays, edited by Robert T. Self (St. Paul, Minn.: The John Colet Press, 1977).

OTHER: "A Review of American Literary Phases," in *Studies in American Literature*, edited by Frederick Spiers (Philadelphia: Booklover's Library Press, 1901);

"The American Intellect," in *The Cambridge Modern History*, volume 7, edited by A. W. Ward and others (New York: Cambridge University Press, 1903);

John A. Lomax, *Cowboy Songs and Other Frontier Ballads*, introduction by Wendell (New York: Sturgis & Walton, 1910).

Barrett Wendell

PERIODICAL PUBLICATIONS: "Francis Parkman," *Proceedings of the American Academy of Arts and Sciences*, 29 (May 1894): 435-447;

"Composition in the Elementary Schools," *New York Teachers' Monographs*, 1 (November 1898): 68-76;

"Samuel Eliot," *Proceedings of the American Academy of Arts and Sciences*, 34 (May 1899): 646-651;

"The Relations of Radcliffe College with Harvard," *Harvard Monthly*, 14 (October 1899): 3-11;

"Memoir of William Whitwell Greenough," *Proceedings of the Massachusetts Historical Society*, 34 (February 1901): 1-17;

Review of *The Transit of Civilization from England to America in the Seventeenth Century* by

Edward Eggleston, *American Historical Review*, 6 (July 1901): 802-805;

"Le President Roosevelt," *Revue Politique et Parlementaire*, 10 (February 1905): 7-15;

"Charles Eliot Norton," *Atlantic Monthly*, 103 (January 1909): 82-88;

"Abbott Lawrence Lowell, Twenty-Fourth President of Harvard College," *Harvard Graduates' Magazine*, 17 (March 1909): 397-403;

"A New England Puritan," *The Quarterly Review*, 218 (January 1913): 32-48;

"The Ideals of Empire," *Harvard Graduates' Magazine*, 25 (June 1917): 458-474;

"The Conflict of Idolatries," *Harvard Graduates' Magazine*, 27 (September 1918): 1-16;

"A Gentlewoman of Boston, 1742-1805," *Proceedings of the American Antiquarian Society*, 29 (October 1919): 242-293.

Barrett Wendell's importance was long obscured by the charge that he was nothing more than the last of the "Boston Brahmins," an eccentric Tory representative of the fading Genteel Tradition. A "master of paradox," as one early reviewer called him, Wendell would have been the first to agree with his critics that he was among the last scions of a dying age. But, despite his habitual self-deprecation, he was a pioneering and influential critic and educator. His advocacy of general education, his "invention" of English composition and creative writing as they are taught today, his path-breaking courses in American literature, his creation of the history and literature honors program at Harvard University, his insistence on "thinking things together" mark him as a forward-looking and, in many ways, a "modern" scholar.

Handicapped by lifelong feelings of inadequacy, he was only too aware of his lack of boldness to rebel and change the times he deplored. The man who once wrote, "my most poignant regrets have always been for the discretions of youth," encouraged young men (and a few women) to be bold, to think for themselves, and to take such risks as he had been unable to face. A conservative idealist, he emphasized merit and individuality as the highest democratic values. Looking into the history of his region, his country and its mother country (and later of other cultures as well), he hoped to find a past that would be useful for the challenges of the future.

Barrett Wendell was born in Boston on 23 August 1855, the descendant of seventeenth-century New York Dutch merchants (with a

Wendell in 1863

proudly preserved coat of arms) and a distinguished line of New England settlers; his ancestral relatives included New England governors, Puritan divines, and a Harvard president. His father, Jacob Wendell, nevertheless was a self-made man who rose from an impoverished childhood to the ownership of a successful textile company which bore his name.

Barrett (so named after the family of his mother, Mary Bertodi Barrett) was a "fairly conscientious" child but also "morbidly self-conscious and pettily ill-tempered." His health was never robust. In addition to a congenital nervous weakness, attributed to a genetic defect on his father's side, a teenage back injury made walking painful and led Wendell to adopt his later famous cane. Somewhat of a literary prodigy, he was educated mostly in private schools, developing great fondness for the Roman classics but also for contemporary English literature, as well as for music and the visual arts. He spent much of his time writing plays but had no interest in either physical or "religious exercises" (reared an Anglican, by age twenty-five he developed "tolerantly agnostic" religious views, "with sympathy for any honest faith, and an intellectual admiration for the logic of the Catholic Church").

In 1863 the Wendell family moved to New York, a city which the boy found "interesting but disconcerting," and came to dislike all his life as a place of "incessant change." In 1868 he fell in love with "Longfellow's Europe" on a three-month vacation with his parents, a passion reignited during another trip in the summer of 1871. His third visit occurred just two years later. After withdrawing from Harvard in April of his freshman year because of what he later called a "probably hysterical paralysis," Wendell took off in October of 1873 for a year of travel that took him to Brazil, Europe, North Africa, and parts of Asia. In 1874 he returned to Harvard for a successful (he did well in his classes and cofounded the *Harvard Lampoon*), though not brilliant, undergraduate career, graduating with the Class of 1877. The teacher who influenced him most was James Russell Lowell, in some of whose mental habits–his "whimsical instability of temper" and his "deep seriousness strangely at odds with his obvious mannerisms"–Wendell later recognized himself.

A year at Harvard Law School was followed by two years of reading law in New York and Boston firms, but in 1880, just before his scheduled marriage to Edith Greenough, the daughter of a prominent Boston family, Wendell failed the Massachusetts bar exam. In this situation he was unexpectedly offered a job as a theme reader by his former English professor, Adams Sherman Hill. Thus accidentally, as a stopgap affair, began his academic career. It was jeopardized more than once, and it was not until 1898 that he was promoted to full professor, but at his retirement in 1917 Wendell was one of the most honored academicians of his generation.

As a teacher Wendell became a legend at Harvard. While he was never comfortable on the faculty (he opposed the new Ph.D. orientation and Charles W. Eliot's elective system), he was popular with the students, who liked his wit and mimicked his eccentricities of dress, speech, and behavior. His courses covered a wide range of literature in English, but he was most notable as a pioneer of teaching writing and of introducing American literature into the curriculum.

His own writing courses, English 12 (elective composition, soon the best-enrolled course at Har-

Wendell in 1872

vard) and English 5 (advanced composition), made Harvard a mecca for aspiring writers, many of whom acknowledged his lasting influence. He also had a hand in starting the new *Harvard Monthly* and served for some time as its chief adviser.

In 1897 Wendell began to teach a course in American literary history and to prepare the ground for his future *A Literary History of America* (1900), which, despite its later notoriety, did much to establish its subject in American colleges. Wendell's interest in American literature and culture also made him a pioneer for American Studies. He championed interdisciplinary study as an antidote to the perceived fragmentation of the new Harvard curriculum, and he cofounded and served as the first chairman of the honors program in history and literature, now the oldest honors program at Harvard.

Wendell was a prolific writer whose oeuvre includes two novels, poetry and drama, as well as evolutionary studies of William Shakespeare (which brought him high praise from Sir Arthur Quiller-Couch). He wrote *The Temper of the Seven-*

teenth Century in English Literature (1904, based on his Clark Lectures at Trinity College in Cambridge) and *The Traditions of European Literature from Homer to Dante* (1920), as well as political essays on contemporary America and a widely acclaimed study of contemporary French culture and society. His later writings grew increasingly political and often controversial. Overall, his most influential and durable works were *Cotton Mather, The Puritan Priest* (1891), *English Composition: Eight Lectures Given at the Lowell Institute* (1891), and *A Literary History of America* (1900).

Politically, Wendell started out as a mugwump and potential Tammany man. But his sense of his own insecurity, augmented by his view of the alarmingly changing times, stifled the seeds of rebellion and led him to assume the role of a conservative enfant terrible (H. L. Mencken noted his "endless flounderings between orthodoxy and heresy"), whose wit did not spare his own weaknesses. He always admired the economic prowess of his loving and generous father, who supported him for many years. After 1893 Wendell grew increasingly conservative (he developed great pride in his aristocratic lineage and cherished all inherited tokens of his status), but he criticized inherited privilege along with, in his opinion, undeserved claims for equality and emphasized opportunity as the basis for American democracy. Soon, he even saw his friend and hero Theodore Roosevelt drifting "toward radical extreme." Wendell's political views took over much of his writing after 1900; *The Privileged Classes* (1908), an attack on the perceived insolence of the working classes, made him notorious and tinged later views of his entire work. But he remained looking forward as much as backward, an ambivalent iconoclast. His own failed rebellion against his age, as his biographer Robert T. Self has pointed out, helped to inspire such students as Van Wyck Brooks, who later became his critics (or rather critics of the image they perceived): "Wendell opened important trails even if he could not travel them." This is also true for his encouragement of such writers as Amy Lowell (with whom he had a long correspondence), Edwin Arlington Robinson, and his former student Robert Herrick.

Contradictions remain. While Wendell praised Amy Lowell, he opposed coeducation at Harvard because he wanted to preserve "masculine" competition in the classroom. While he encouraged his student W. E. B. Du Bois (who gratefully acknowledged him in his autobiogra-

phy), he rejected the idea of ever having a black person as a dinner guest. But while he also considered Jews his social inferiors and opposed further immigration of any ethnic group, he was a "mentor and friend to young Horace Kallen" (in 1924, Kallen's progressive *Culture and Democracy in the United States* was dedicated to "the memory of Barrett Wendell, Deep Seeing Interpreter of America and the American Mind") and a "gracious patron to Mary Antin," author of *The Promised Land* (1912). Clearly, the man was far more complex than the image that has survived him.

English Composition was an innovative and liberating book which remained in print until 1942 and greatly changed the teaching of college composition in the United States. Instead of admonishing students to memorize hundreds of rules, Wendell encouraged them to look at the composition ("theme") as a whole, not to become obsessed with "matters of detail" and to unlearn the assumption "that any given case must be either right or wrong." Experienced writers have only "a very few simple, elastic general principles," but they need "discretion"–that is, the power to make choices: "The question is not whether a given word or sentence is eternally right or wrong; but rather how accurately it expresses what the writer has to say." Working from the *end* of writing to the *means* of accomplishing it, Wendell's "general principles" addressed chiefly style and organization.

Sound organization requires the observance of three principles: Unity (each composition should be grouped around "one central idea"), Mass (each part should "readily ... catch the eye"), and Coherence (the relation between the parts "should be unmistakable"). Style is defined as "simply the expression of thought or emotion in written words; it applies equally to an epic, a sermon, a love-letter, an invitation to an evening party." Since the individual's grasp of the material world is limited by his or her capacity and perception, "the final reality of life is the thought, which, with the endless surge of emotion ... makes up conscious existence." Writing thus becomes a process of discovery, helping the writer to "find the thought and the emotion that together make that fresh marvel–himself." Each person's thought and emotion form a distinctly individual "immaterial reality"–"the reality that style must express."

Three qualities of style can be distinguished by their impact on the reader: "intellectual, emotional, and aesthetic." Following A. S. Hill's termi-

The Harvard Lampoon *editorial board, 1877. Standing (left to right): Barrett Wendell, F. J. Stimson, Robert Grant, W. S. Otis. Seated (left to right): C. A. Coolidge, J. T. Bowen, J. T. Wheelwright, J. T. Coolidge, Jr., F. G. Attwood, Francis McLennan.*

nology in his *Principles of Rhetoric and Their Applications* (1876), Wendell identifies these qualities as "Clearness," "Force," and "Elegance." The basis of style, however, is "good use, and good use alone." In a living language dictionaries and grammars can never totally codify good use; it is "not a system of rules, but a constantly shifting state of fact" determined by the agreement of competent users. To reach the widest possible audience, good use must be "Reputable as distinguished from vulgar, slangy, eccentric; National as distinguished from local or technical; Present as distinguished from obsolete or transient."

Wendell was distinctly modern in his insistence on the "purely symbolic" character of language and in his descriptive approach to teaching it. Inspiring confidence in students and encouraging them to find their own voice, *English Composition* "proved a landmark," as Wendell himself admitted: "It has stood the test of time."

Cotton Mather was Wendell's first major study of the American character: "To understand the America of today," he wrote in his conclu-

sion, "we must know the New England of the fathers; to know the first New England of the fathers, there is no better way than to study this man–its last, its most typical incarnation." Published in 1891, the same year as *English Composition*, the second centennial of the Salem witchcraft hysteria, Wendell's book proposed a revision not only of Mather's image but of the purposes of the first Puritan settlers. As Alan Heimert has formulated it, Wendell challenged the mythology "that New England had been settled out of a desire for political and economic liberty," insisting instead that "the fervent spirit of their faith" brought the settlers to America and stressing the force of ideas in American history. In 1963 Heimert thought *Cotton Mather* still "the best single-volume study" of its subject.

At a time when Mather's name represented medieval superstition and intellectual despotism to all but a few orthodox theologians, Wendell portrayed the "Puritan Priest" as "a good man" with admirable "depth of human nature" who "never ceased striving, amid endless stumblings and errors, to do his duty," conceived as "God's own

Wendell in costume for the March 1897 Harvard College stage production of his dramatic poem "Ralegh in Guiana"

work." Wendell acknowledged posterity's judgment of Mather as a "self-seeking" and "subtle priest . . . even if honest, dreadfully deluded and grotesquely lacking in judgment" as supported by the public records; his own study, however, was to let Mather "tell his story in his own words."

Wendell was the first to gather and examine systematically Mather's journals, a feat of scholarship that belies Wendell's lifelong assertion that he was not a scholar but a "mere man of letters" and which, despite such limitations of the work as Heimert has pointed out, makes *Cotton Mather*

a lasting contribution. The diaries, focusing on their author's inner life to the neglect of external events, reveal him as a man of passionate enthusiasm: "Pure in motive, noble in purpose, his whole life was one unending effort to strengthen in himself that phase of human nature whose inner token is a riot of mystical emotion, whose outward signs are unwitting manifestations of unfettered credulity and fraud." Mather's role in the Salem witchcraft trials manifested this dilemma most clearly. Unlike most contemporary writers (with the earlier exception of John Neal in *Rachel Dyer*, 1828), Wendell took the Puritans' belief in witchcraft seriously (to Mather, witch-craft was "the most terrible of realities"), going so far as to "heartily sympathize with those who in 1692 did their utmost to suppress it." (In his 1892 paper, "Were the Salem Witches Guiltless?"—collected in *Stelligeri, and Other Essays Concerning America* in 1893–Wendell recounts his own experiences with fraudulent occultism; he diagnoses a dangerous "evil" abroad in 1692 and wonders "whether some of the witches, in spite of the weakness and falsity of the evidence that hanged them, may not after all have deserved their hanging.") But, despite his sympathy for Mather, he blames him for his share in raising the panic and for not comprehending "the full strength of the case against him."

The price of ecstatic faith was self-delusion, and Mather's involvement in the Salem trials made the rest of his life a "constant, crescent failure." He failed especially at his chief goal, "the preservation, the restoration, of the pure polity of the fathers" (a cause he shared with his own father, "with an affection as brotherly as it was filial"). Posterity's conception of Cotton Mather also tainted its view of such works as his *Magnalia*, one of "the great works of English literature in the Seventeenth Century," and obscured Mather's civic and scientific merits (such as his advocacy of smallpox inoculation). Wendell's Mather emerges in the end as a tragic, transitional figure, caught between two ages and belonging fully to none–a position with which Wendell could easily identify.

A Literary History of America is Wendell's most characteristic work, both for his critical method of "thinking things together" and his struggle between his acknowledged prejudices and his professional judgment. Some of its major points first occur in *Stelligeri*, a collection of essays on American history and literature.

A socio-historical essay on the conditions of literature in Anglo-Saxon North America, *A Literary History of America* asks "what contributions America has made . . . to the literature of the English language." Defined as the "lasting expression in words of the meaning of life," literature is "the most ineradicably national of the fine arts" and therefore the most revealing document of a nation's experience and identity. Like *Cotton Mather*, Wendell's history is from the outset an inquiry into the American national character, leading from an examination of its historical roots to a prognosis for the future. Although Wendell always put his own sentiments up front (the possibil-

Wendell with his first grandchild

ity that one could deal "objectively" with the past would have seemed absurd to the man who wrote about his literary history to William James, "In sentiment it is Tory, pro-slavery, and imperialistic; all of which I fear I am myself"), the book is also a critical analysis of Wendell's own place in the history of his own class, region, and culture, a search for himself; as he knew, the book's paradoxes and contradictions are evidence of his own struggle.

Wendell arranged his study chronologically by century; in each, outlines of English and American history are followed by narrower categories. The whole work is broken down into six "books" in a fashion that is highly revealing. Books 1 and 2 cover the seventeenth and eighteenth centuries. Book 3 surveys history and literature in the nineteenth century; book 4 covers "Literature in the Middle States from 1798 to 1857," with chapters on Charles Brockden Brown, Washington Irving, James Fenimore Cooper, William Cullen Bryant, Edgar Allan Poe, and the "Knickerbocker

School." Book 5, over two hundred pages long, is entitled "The Renaissance of New England" and contains fifteen chapters in a mixed sequence of categories: individual authors (Ralph Waldo Emerson, John Greenleaf Whittier, Henry Wadsworth Longfellow, James Russell Lowell, Oliver Wendell Holmes, Nathaniel Hawthorne), groups by genre or location (orators, scholars and historians, "lesser men of Concord"), movements (Unitarianism, Transcendentalism, Antislavery), one chapter on the *Atlantic Monthly*, as well as a beginning ("Some General Characteristics of New England") and a concluding chapter ("The Decline of New England"). Book 6, "The Rest of the Story," consists of five chapters ("New York since 1857"; "Walt Whitman"; "Literature in the South"; "The West"; "The Present Time"), followed by an interpretive conclusion. As this blueprint reveals, Fred Lewis Pattee's facetious proposal for a substitute title, "A Literary History of Harvard University, with Incidental Glimpses of the Minor Writers of America," is not without its justification.

The chief idea governing the book is Wendell's famous thesis of "national inexperience." The early settlers, he says, shared three distinctive characteristics with their Elizabethan countrymen: "spontaneity, enthusiasm, and versatility." These traits were preserved in provincial America long after they had succumbed to political and social changes in England; until the nineteenth century, American culture grew out of "unique national inexperience." This had several consequences:

1. Until "national experience" began to accumulate, literature was caught in phases of development already overcome in England.
2. In a world "so relieved from the pressure of external fact that people generally behaved much better than is usual in earthly history," Calvinist thought with its premise of human depravity began to lose touch with politics and life. And the Unitarians and Transcendentalists who arrived at "fervid faith in the excellence of human nature," went astray in the opposite direction for the same reason, national inexperience: it "permitted almost unrestrained the development" of exemplars of a "moral purity" that made Calvinist damnation "seem an ill-conceived nursery tale."
3. The American Revolution was inevitable; in fact, it had its origin in inherited temper (it was fought not over the "glittering generalities" of radical thought which ruined the French Revolution but out of a deeply English desire to defend "true human rights . . . which experience has proved beneficial," an impulse "that the rights for which men should die are not abstract but legal"). The "original American temper" of its Elizabethan immigrants had remained "singularly unaltered" due to national inexperience (the Revolution relied on leaders who had "preserved the spontaneity and enthusiasm of earlier days"), while "the temper of the native English" had changed so much that "they honestly could not understand each other."

Wendell's general thesis produces valuable insights but also a number of distortions and misunderstandings. Not only does it reinforce the book's New England bias, but it assumes that all immigrants are assimilated into a largely homogeneous population ("our native type still absorbs the foreign"), an effort at wishful thinking which Wendell could not always sustain in real life. His thesis also contributes to his failure to come to terms with various individual writers, but this is even more a function of his political prejudices.

A writer's social status interests him greatly: Irving was the first of a long line who "proved . . . the social dignity of American letters": Cooper came from a family "of almost feudal superiority," while Poe was not of "the better sort." Not surprisingly, Wendell does best with writers who fit his general scheme as well as his social preferences. Among these, only Emerson and Hawthorne have "considerably . . . enriched the literature of our language." They represent the swan song of a New England whose highest intellectual production coincided with its highest political and economic prosperity: "Artistic expression is apt to be the final fruit of a society about to wither."

Wendell's omissions, as glaringly wrong as many of his inclusions, justify some of the book's later reputation. He has no black writers, few women; and the observation that Herman Melville's promise as a writer of "maritime adventure" "never came to fruition." More interesting than these obvious flaws, however, are those cases where Wendell's literary conscience struggled with his prejudices, for instance in his discussions of Poe, Harriet Beecher Stowe, and Walt Whitman.

In *Stelligeri* Poe appeared as "freakish," even though he "added a new note to literature." Now, Wendell grants him "swiftness of perception and fineness of taste"; a "melodramatic creature of genius" with the temper of an actor, Poe had an "artistic conscience" that was markedly American. His work differs from the decadent literature of Europe in that, "for all the decadent quality of his temper, there is a singular cleanness, something which for all the thousand errors of his personal life seems like the instinctive purity of a child." Despite his great power, "his chief merits prove merits of refinement." In later publications and speeches Wendell expands this assessment into a more and more unqualified endorsement.

His discussion of Stowe in *A Literary History of America* is almost uniformly favorable, a surprising result in view of his dislike for the antislavery movement (he blames it for, among other things, having caused the "dominance of the less educated classes" in his home state). He praises Stowe for knowing her subject matter from experience and for the high verisimilitude of *Uncle Tom's Cabin* (1852). *Old Town Folks* (1869), which he considers her best work, proves that she had "a spark of genius": "Had this genius pervaded her work, she might have been a figure of lasting literary importance."

Wendell had more trouble with Whitman. An earlier positive assessment in *Stelligeri* is followed here by scornful praise (which raised public outcries); but in his lectures at the Sorbonne, where he was a visiting professor, and in his later Harvard classes Wendell managed to present Whitman as the prophet of a new occidental literature.

To appreciate the poet Wendell had to overcome his distaste for Whitman's humble origins and "erratic habits," and he had to set aside his profound disagreement with Whitman's brand of egalitarian democracy, in his opinion a dangerous sham: "His creed seems to have been that, as God made everything, one thing is just as good as another"—"a complete confusion of values." In this respect Whitman is less American than European: "The saving grace of American democracy has been a tacit recognition that excellence is admirable." But in other respects the poet is "very American indeed": "the substance of which his poems are made . . . comes wholly from our native country." Like Hawthorne, Whitman possessed "true artistic temperament"; despite his faults (some stanzas of "Crossing Brooklyn Ferry" sound "as if hexameters were trying to bubble through sewage"), he has breathed "ennobling imaginative fervour" into the apparently base and sordid.

In the 1904 school edition of the volume Wendell further revised his statements on Poe and Whitman and commented on additional writers, including ones still living, whom he had excluded from the 1900 edition. Emily Dickinson is briefly mentioned; William Dean Howells, Henry James, Edith Wharton, and Frank Norris are critically appraised; Joel Chandler Harris in the South and Bret Harte in the West are singled out for praise. Most importantly, a whole chapter is now devoted to Mark Twain, who had been mentioned briefly but admiringly in the earlier book. *The Adventures of Huckleberry Finn* (1884) is "nothing short of a masterpiece" and ranks "among the few books in any literature which preserve something like a comprehensive picture of an entire state of society." Twain's work is an example of the most "characteristically American" literature.

At the end of *A Literary History of America* Wendell looks forward to the American literature of the future, which "can probably be expressed only in some broadly popular form" (he mentions newspaper humor, short magazine fiction, and the popular stage as the most likely candidates). How distinctive this will be is a question: "America seems more and more growing to be just another part of the world." (Again, this was not the final word. In 1910 Wendell commended the cowboy ballads collected by his former student John Lomax as part of the "native poetry of America.")

The book's conclusion sums up what has become Wendell's chief concern—the nature of American democracy: "The national ideal of America has never yet denied or even repressed the countless variety of human worth and power. It has urged only that men should enjoy liberty within the range of law. It has resisted both lingering and innovative tyranny," adhering to the principle that "each of us has an inalienable right to strive for excellence." And while the future is "that of a growing world-democracy" of possible conflict and darkness, the "simple, hopeful literature of inexperienced, renascent New England" can provide a kind of usable past: "There, for a while, the warring ideals of democracy and of excellence were once reconciled, dwelling confidently together in some earthly semblance of peace."

Barrett Wendell received acclaim throughout his career and was honored nationally and internationally in his later years. In 1868 he was elected to Phi Beta Kappa, elected fellow of the American Academy of Arts and Sciences in 1889, and Trustee of the Boston Athenaeum in 1890, when he also delivered the Lowell Institute lectures on "English Composition." (He lectured twice more under these prestigious auspices, in 1905 on "National Ideals of America" and in 1906 on "Impressions of Contemporary France.") From 1896 to 1901 he served as chair of the Harvard English Department. In 1902-1903 he was the Clark Lecturer at Cambridge's Trinity College, and he was chosen to represent Harvard at the Tercentenary of Oxford's Bodleian Library. In 1904-1905, as the first exchange professor to France, he gave the Hyde Foundation lectures at the Sorbonne (he later received an honorary doctorate from the University of Strasbourg and became, after his death, the first foreigner after whom a lecture room at the Sorbonne was named). Columbia and Harvard also awarded him honorary doctorates, and the University of Berlin offered him a visiting lectureship in 1914. In 1916 he was elected to the American Academy of Arts and Letters; at his retirement in 1917 Harvard and Boston honored him with a surprise dinner party; in 1920 he was elected to Harvard's board of overseers. Although Wen-

dell's name was already slipping into obscurity at the time of his death in 1921, these honors did reflect real merit. Wendell himself always remained diffident about his achievements ("my whole life seems to have been a bewildered effort to get ready," he wrote in 1916), and posterity took him—too much—at his word. But, as his friend Abbott Lawrence Lowell put it, "There was the real man, and what he thought himself to be; and the former was the larger of the two."

References:

Paul E. Cohen, "Barrett Wendell and the Harvard Literary Revival," *The New England Quarterly*, 52 (1979): 483-499;

Alan Heimert, Introduction to *Cotton Mather, The Puritan Priest* by Wendell (New York: Harcourt, Brace, World, 1963): vii-xxxix;

Mark A. DeWolfe Howe, *Barrett Wendell and His Letters* (Boston: Atlantic Monthly Press, 1924);

Robert T. Self, *Barrett Wendell* (Boston: G. K. Hall, 1975);

Barbara Miller Solomon, *Ancestors and Immigrants: A Changing New England Tradition* (Chicago & London: University of Chicago Press, 1956).

Papers:

Collections of Barrett Wendell's papers are located at the Houghton Library, Harvard University; Butler Library, Columbia University; and the New York Public Library.

William Cleaver Wilkinson

(19 October 1833-27 April 1920)

Jeffrey Steele

University of Wisconsin

BOOKS: *The Dance of Modern Society* (New York: Oakley, Mason, 1869);

A Free Lunch in the Field of Life and Letters (New York: Mason, 1874);

The Baptist Principle in its Application to Baptism and the Lord's Supper (Philadelphia: American Baptist Publication Society, 1881);

Webster, An Ode (New York: Scribners, 1882);

Preparatory Greek Course in English (New York: Phillips & Hunt/Cincinnati: Walden & Stowe, 1883);

Preparatory Latin Course in English (New York: Phillips & Hunt/Cincinnati: Walden & Stowe, 1883);

Poems (New York: Scribners, 1883);

College Greek Course in English (New York: Phillips & Hunt, 1884; revised edition, New York: Chautauqua Press, 1888);

Edwin Arnold as Poetizer and Paganizer: Containing an Examination of the "Light of Asia," for its Literature and for its Buddhism (New York & London: Funk & Wagnalls, 1884);

College Latin Course in English (New York: Chautauqua Press, 1885);

Classic French Course in English (New York: Chautauqua Press, 1886);

Classic German Course in English (New York: Chautauqua Press, 1887);

The Baptist Denomination (Boston, 1888);

The Epic of Saul (New York: Funk & Wagnalls, 1890; New York & London: Funk & Wagnalls, 1898);

The Epic of Paul (New York: Funk & Wagnalls, 1897; New York & London: Funk & Wagnalls, 1910);

The Epic of Moses: A Poem in Two Parts (Chicago: Scott, 1905; New York & London: Funk & Wagnalls, 1910);

Poetical Works, Uniform Edition, 5 volumes (Chicago: Scott, 1905);

Modern Masters of Pulpit Discourse (New York & London: Funk & Wagnalls, 1905);

Some New Literary Valuations (New York & London: Funk & Wagnalls, 1909);

The Good of Life, and Other Little Essays (New York & London: Funk & Wagnalls, 1910);

Daniel Webster; A Vindication, with Other Historical Essays (New York & London: Funk & Wagnalls, 1911);

Paul and the Revolt Against Him (Philadelphia & Boston: Griffith & Rowland Press, 1914);

Concerning Jesus Christ, The Son of God (Philadelphia & Boston: Griffith & Rowland Press, 1916);

Concerning Jesus Christ, The Son of Man (Philadelphia & Boston: Griffith & Rowland Press, 1918).

By the time William Cleaver Wilkinson was selected in 1892 as one of the founding members of the new University of Chicago faculty, he had already risen to prominence as an American educator. Serving as counselor of the Chautauqua Literary and Scientific Circle, he had published six popular volumes of Greek, Latin, French, and German literature in translation. These books, republished by the Chautauqua Press as The After-School series, were widely acclaimed by leading scholars as effective introductions to classic and foreign literature. Selling over 500,000 copies, Wilkinson's foreign classics furthered the aim of the Chautauqua movement: "to increase popular culture, both by broadening it in its base, and by building it higher." "It is not extravagant," Wilkinson added, "to expect that the ultimate influence of this movement for extending popular culture will report itself in augmented numbers of applicants for admission to college. . . . " In addition to his important role as a popularizer of foreign classics, Wilkinson published five volumes of poetry, a variety of works on religious topics, and three books of literary criticism. The latter have earned him a permanent, albeit narrow, niche in literary history. His evaluations of George Eliot, James Russell Lowell, William Cullen Bryant, William Dean Howells, Matthew Arnold, and others provide a lively example of Christian academic scholarship during a period in which many university presidents were ordained ministers.

Born in Westford, Vermont, to Dr. Thomas and Sarah Cleaver Wilkinson, his early career alternated between the competing claims of academic life and the ministry. After graduating from the University of Rochester (A.B., 1857), he attended Rochester Theological Seminary where he was ordained a Baptist minister in 1859. In 1863 he married Harriet Richardson, daughter of Prof. J. F. Richardson of the University of Rochester. During this period ministerial appointments at New Haven and Cincinnati bracketed an ad interim teaching position as professor of modern languages at Rochester. Finally, Wilkinson was forced to resign pastoral work because of ill health; and in 1872 he accepted a full-time teaching appointment at the Rochester Theological Seminary, where he served as professor of homiletics and pastoral theology until 1881. In 1881 he retired from Rochester to Tarreytown and devoted himself to literary work, until he accepted a professorship at the new University of Chicago in 1892.

Reading Wilkinson's criticism, one rarely forgets that behind the academic mask lies a minister; for his writing exhibits a passion for correctness, both literary and moral, that leads him to measure his subjects against high standards. Although generous at times in their praise, most of his essays end by finding fault with their subjects. Viewing literary production as an index of character, of the condition of the writer's soul, Wilkinson has a keen eye for moral and semantic declension. The writers that fare best at his hands are those who have avoided the taint of modern religious freethinking and whose works embody an essential moral vision and a purity of style. For these reasons he prefers Bryant to Lowell or Arnold; Howells to George Eliot.

"The Literary and Ethical Quality of George Eliot's Novels" (*A Free Lance in the Field of Life and Letters*, 1874) displays both the strength and weakness of Wilkinson's dual critical concern with good writing and moral correctness. Beginning with the observation that Eliot is a "prime elemental living power," a "moral living force," Wilkinson praises her profound psychological insight, precise dramatization of everyday life, vital and concise style, breadth of learning, humor, and pure moral spirit. If he had stopped there his essay would provide an excellent survey of Eliot's strengths as a writer. But Wilkinson goes on to conclude that, despite such literary merits, Eliot's fiction "unconsciously hinders the nobleness that she inculcates"; for it is flawed by a positivism and a note of despair that obfuscate Christian salvation, offering in its place only a stern stoicism. Although Eliot accurately depicts the "persistent immorality" of sin, she impedes others in "their struggles against sin" by presenting only "a world of pure naturalism." Shifting from literary to ethical evaluation, Wilkinson finally ceases to speak as a literary critic and begins to sermonize, fervently praying that Eliot's "heart will yet conquer and lead that great intellect captive to the foot of the Cross."

Most of the remainder of *A Free Lance in the Field of Life and Letters* consists of an important, 130-page analysis of James Russell Lowell's poetry and critical prose. Wilkinson's Lowell is a poetic genius, born too late to benefit from the "bracing moral atmosphere" of Puritanism. Trapped in the degenerate culture of Boston, "out of which the positive kernel of gospel has gone," he is doomed to proliferate isolated flashes of brilliance without the "impelling and steadying force" supplied by "a high conscious and determinate moral purpose." Infected by a spirit of religious liberalism that leads ultimately into "the boundless country of the unconditioned," Lowell's writing demonstrates wit at the expense of consistency, syntactic and semantic contortion instead of a straightforward earnestness born out of "tense moral conviction." Through extensive and, at times, insightful stylistic analyses, Wilkinson builds his portrait of Lowell as a brilliant, but undisciplined, writer who betrayed his finest inspiration by listening too long to the malignant influence of Goethe. The best literature and criticism, he concludes, needs "the vivific contact and virtue of supreme moral convictions"—a need that Wilkinson attempts to fill by the example of his own critical practice.

Among American writers, at this point in Wilkinson's career, only William Cullen Bryant meets his twin criteria of moral and literary purity. Wilkinson is struck by Bryant's "easy majesty of self possession," a contemplative calm that manifests itself through an "absolute perfection of finish." He finds Bryant's thoughts, like Horace's, to be "elaborately polished and clear, like cut diamonds." Neither ostentatious nor impulsive, Bryant's poetry exhibits passion that has been "taken up into the intellect and the imagination and sublimated there, but not extinguished." In contrast to the "heathenism" of Wilkinson's poetic contemporaries, Bryant's writing continues to live because of its fine style and moral poise.

Ten years later, in *Edwin Arnold as Poetizer and Paganizer* (1884), Wilkinson more explicitly connects perfection of style with perfection of character. A work of art, he argues, must be a "sincere and genuine" expression of "some real thought, sentiment, conviction, fancy, existing in [an author's] mind." While the presence of sincere conviction reveals itself in artistic unity and directness, a "lack of genuineness" results in artistic confusion and discord. Given his faith that literary practice directly signifies the condition of a writer's spirit, Wilkinson is able to assert that "Any single characteristic sentence" of a writer's "production enables the thoughtful judge of style to determine his true rank and worth in literature, with as much certainty as Cuvier felt in classifying an extinct animal on the basis of a single fossil bone."

The work under consideration, Edwin Arnold's *The Light of Asia* (1879), consists of a long narrative poem, presented as the meditation of an "imaginary Buddhist votary" who recounts the history of Guatama Buddha. Survey-

ing Arnold's versification, diction, syntax, and sources, Wilkinson challenges the positive reception of this work by asserting that it is bad poetry and worse religious doctrine. Not only does it distort the history and tenets of Buddhism, it establishes a pernicious moral influence by blurring the distinction between Christianity and Buddhism, which is "in part a Satanic travesty of Christianity." Finding Buddhism "devilish" in its beliefs and Hinduism brutal in its ethical practice, Wilkinson contends that "the attempt to domesticate Hindu speculation" is "premature," if not evil." Since Oliver Wendell Holmes, among others, commended Arnold's poem for its beauty and elevated morality, Wilkinson's arguments measure the mixed reception of Oriental thought during this period. In contrast to Ralph Waldo Emerson, Henry David Thoreau, and Holmes, he interprets the dissemination of Oriental philosophy as a sign of moral corruption. An expression of conservative religious sensibility, such a view indicates the growing influence of Oriental thought through the sheer vehemence of its reaction.

Twenty-five years later at the University of Chicago, after seven years' labor preparing his foreign classics in translation and after four volumes of didactic religious poetry, Wilkinson's criticism displays a poise and a judiciousness that had been missing at times in his earlier writing. The note of moral righteousness has not entirely disappeared, but it is balanced by a less grudging expression of admiration and a more reasoned explanation of dislikes. The opening essay of *Some New Literary Valuations* (1909), "William Dean Howells as a Man of Letters," stands out as a significant presentation of the thesis that Howells has not been "recognized as the great master of English style that he is." As in the case of Lowell, he sees in Howells a writer whose achievement would have been greater if he had embodied a deeper "moral earnestness." But by this point in his career Wilkinson is able to reflect self-consciously upon his religious biases. Howells's *Literary Friends and Acquaintances* (1900), he confesses, "has some things in it that I am Puritan enough—in taste—to regret seeing there." But the occasional breach of "esthetic, if not of ethical, propriety" troubles Wilkinson much less than it had earlier. In contrast to the sermonizing of his essays on George Eliot and Edwin Arnold, he is able to isolate his moral response to a relatively small portion of his critical evaluation. As a result he spends more of his time providing valuable analyses of Howells's style, humor, pathos, and dramatic qualities. Comparing Howells's writing favorably to that of both Leo Tolstoy and Henry James, Wilkinson finds in it a profound "realism," "absolute creative truth to life."

Yet at other moments in *Some New Literary Valuations* Wilkinson's tendency toward moralistic judgment blinds him. While his great admiration of Howells has been validated by later readers, his charge that Matthew Arnold's criticism displays both mental and moral deficiency seems bizarre. Equating authorial character and literary worth, Wilkinson eventually bases his assertion that there is a "flaw in the sanity and justness of Arnold's criticism" upon the latter's "mistaken" religious views. Failing to accept that the Bible teaches "the being of a personal God" and hence morally uninformed in many of his judgments, Arnold was "unconstitutionally fitted" to be a critic. Wilkinson's discussion in "Matthew Arnold as Poet" shifts the attack to Arnold's language, which he finds to be imprecise and unimaginative. In "John Morley as Critic of Voltaire and Diderot" Wilkinson even more vehemently lambastes the writing of a critic holding "incorrect" religious views. The most important aspect of Morley's writing, from his viewpoint, is its author's "character as atheist"–a fact that leads him to question Morley's "competence as a thinker." Morley's "antichristian purpose," he concludes, "insidiously bribed . . . his power to see the truth." Unable to recognize the evil tendencies found in Voltaire's and Diderot's religious heterodoxy and questionable manners, Morley displays a sad but "inevitable moral degeneration"–the fate suffered by all atheists.

In contrast Wilkinson finds much to praise in his essays on Alfred Tennyson, Edmund Clarence Stedman, and Tolstoy, all of whom display moral and literary correctness. While the discussion of Stedman maintains its interest primarily for the specialist interested in its moments of personal reminiscence, Wilkinson's essay on Tennyson (like his treatment of Howells) is noteworthy for its lengthy textual analyses, especially of the poet's "violence of expression." His judgment that Tennyson is the greatest lyric poet ever to have written is matched by his awe at the imaginative grandeur and power of Tolstoy's novels. Even though some readers have questioned the "ethical quality" of Tolstoy's fiction, Wilkinson is quick to assert that it is not "morally dangerous." Indeed, he goes out of his way to subsume all moral judgment beneath his aesthetic admiration.

Although erratic in his judgment, especially on religious topics, Wilkinson's writing during its best moments turns close scrutiny of semantic and syntactic detail into an inchoate stylistic analysis. At times Wilkinson rises above his prejudices to achieve memorable moments of critical observation, such as his declaration that Howells's writing captures the most evanescent thoughts and feelings "in the very act . . . of volatilizing themselves . . . with an effect like that of instantaneous photography seizing and picturing the posture of a body in motion." But probably more important than any of Wilkinson's critical pronouncements were his translations of classic and foreign literature. Through his work with the Chautauqua Literary and Scientific Circle he can be credited with introducing hundreds of thousands of Americans to the major works of Greek, Latin, French, and German writers. At times pedantic in his critical practice, often highly judgmental and exclusive, he contributed to a publishing venture with the broadest popular appeal–one that ironically may have helped to erode the high and precise standards that he labored to maintain.

Papers:
Correspondence relating to William Cleaver Wilkinson is included in the Presidents' papers, the William Rainey Harper papers, and the English Department records at the University of Chicago Library. The Department of Rare Books and Special Collections, University of Rochester Library, Rochester, New York, holds documentary records of Wilkinson's study and teaching at Rochester, alumni questionnaires filled out by Wilkinson, as well as five letters from him to the first two university presidents.

George Edward Woodberry

(12 May 1855-2 January 1930)

Michael L. Burduck
Tennessee Technological University

BOOKS: *A History of Wood Engraving* (New York: Harper, 1883; London: Sampson, Low, Marston, Searle & Rivington, 1883);

Edgar Allan Poe (Boston: Houghton, Mifflin, 1885); revised and enlarged as *The Life of Edgar Allan Poe*, 2 volumes (Boston & New York: Houghton Mifflin, 1909);

The North Shore Watch and Other Poems (Boston & New York: Houghton, Mifflin, 1890);

Studies in Letters and Life (Boston & New York: Houghton, Mifflin, 1890); republished as *Makers of Literature* (New York: Macmillan, 1900);

Wild Eden (New York & London: Macmillan, 1899);

Heart of Man (New York & London: Macmillan, 1899); republished as *The Heart of Man and Other Papers* (New York: Harcourt, Brace & Howe, 1920);

Nathaniel Hawthorne (Boston & New York: Houghton, Mifflin, 1902);

Poems (New York & London: Macmillan, 1903);

America in Literature (New York & London: Harper, 1903);

The Torch: Eight Lectures on Race Power in Literature (New York: McClure, Phillips, 1905);

Swinburne (New York: McClure, Phillips, 1905; London: Heinemann, 1905);

Ralph Waldo Emerson (New York: Macmillan, 1907);

The Appreciation of Literature (New York: Baker & Taylor, 1907);

Great Writers: Cervantes, Scott, Milton, Virgil, Montaigne, Shakspere (New York: McClure, 1907);

The Inspiration of Poetry (New York: Macmillan, 1910);

Wendell Phillips: The Faith of an American (Boston: Woodberry Society, 1912);

A Day at Castrogiovanni (Boston: Woodberry Society, 1912);

The Kingdom of All-Souls, and Two Other Poems for Christmas (Boston: Woodberry Society, 1912);

George Edward Woodberry

The Flight, and Other Poems (New York: Macmillan, 1914);

North Africa and the Desert: Scenes and Moods (New York: Scribners, 1914);

Two Phases of Criticism: Historical and Aesthetic (Boston: Woodberry Society, 1914);

Shakespeare: An Address (Boston: Woodberry Society, 1916);

Ideal Passion: Sonnets (Boston: Woodberry Society, 1917);

Nathaniel Hawthorne: How to Know Him (Indianapolis: Bobbs-Merrill, 1918);

Literary Essays (New York: Harcourt, Brace & Howe, 1920);

The Roamer and Other Poems (New York: Harcourt, Brace & Howe, 1920);

The Torch, and Other Lectures and Addresses (New York: Harcourt, Brace & Howe, 1920);

Literary Memoirs of the Nineteenth Century (New York: Harcourt, Brace, 1921);

Studies of a Littérateur (New York: Harcourt, Brace, 1921).

OTHER: Percy Bysshe Shelley, *The Complete Poetical Works*, 8 volumes, edited by Woodberry (Boston: Houghton, Mifflin, 1892; revised, 1901);

Charles Lamb, *The Essays of Elia*, edited, with an introduction, by Woodberry (Boston: Little, Brown, 1892);

The English Drama: Its Rise and Development to 1640, compiled by Woodberry, T. R. Price, and A. V. W. Jackson (Albany, N.Y.: Regents University Extension Department, 1893);

The Works of Edgar Allan Poe, 10 volumes, edited by Woodberry and E. C. Stedman (Chicago: Stone & Kimball, 1894-1895);

Selections from the Poems of Aubrey De Vere, edited, with a preface, by Woodberry (New York & London: Macmillan, 1894);

Tennyson's The Princess, edited, with an introduction and notes, by Woodberry (New York: Longmans, Green, 1896);

The Essays of Francis Bacon, edited, with an introduction, by Woodberry (New York: Century, 1900);

One Hundred Books Famous in English Literature, with Facsimiles of the Title Pages, introduction by Woodberry (New York: The Grolier Club of the City of New York, 1902);

Samuel Taylor Coleridge, *The Rime of the Ancient Mariner*, edited, with an introduction, by Woodberry (New York: American Book Co., 1904);

Introduction to *A Midsummer Night's Dream*, volume 6 of *The Complete Works of William Shakespeare*, 40 volumes, edited by Sidney Lee (New York: Sproul, 1907-1909);

Select Poems of Percy Bysshe Shelley, edited, with an introduction and notes, by Woodberry (Boston & London: Heath, 1908);

Sir Philip Sidney, *The Defense of Poesie; A Letter to Q. Elizabeth; A Defense of Leicester*, edited by Woodberry (Boston: Merrymount, 1908);

Percy Bysshe Shelley, *The Cenci*, edited, with an introduction and notes, by Woodberry (Boston & London: Heath, 1909);

Hermann Jackson Warner, *European Years: Letters of an Idle Man*, edited, with an introduction, by Woodberry (Boston & New York: Houghton Mifflin, 1911);

Warner, *New Letters of an Idle Man*, edited by Woodberry (London: Constable, 1913);

The Collected Poems of Rupert Brooke, edited, with an introduction, by Woodberry (New York: Lane, 1915).

Combining a native New England idealism with an ardent reverence for the classical Greek and Roman writers, George Edward Woodberry, teacher, poet, and scholar, produced a fairly large body of poetry and literary criticism. As a young man he heard Emerson's last lecture and helped catalog the library of James Russell Lowell, his mentor at Harvard who no doubt helped kindle his love of the classics and spark his ideality. Joel E. Spingarn, one of Woodberry's students, characterized his former professor in the *Dictionary of American Biography* as a thinker who attempted to mingle the individualism of the transcendentalist with the European Platonic and Roman Catholic tradition. This curious mixture of conflicting forces reveals itself in Woodberry's critical canon. Expressed with a refinement which one might not expect to see in the works of a man once described as "rebellious," his opinions brought the idealistic tenets of Lowell into the twentieth century. Woodberry's studies widened his students' knowledge of the literary past and instructed his disciples on how to analyze critically and venerate great literature. Agreeing with Aristotle, he believed that "art is nature regenerate, made perfect, suffering the new birth into what ought to be. . . ." In Woodberry, then, the old tradition lays the foundation for the new. His zealous love of literature led to his writing or editing more than forty book-length projects, including a biography of Edgar Allan Poe still recommended by many scholars. With the exception of his work on Poe, current students of American literature have virtually forgotten Woodberry's literary efforts. His criticism remains valuable, however, because it reflects Woodberry's belief that the critic should not stress the technical side of his craft but emphasize the importance of literary appreciation. He focuses on those universal elements of literature which help make it enjoyable for all readers.

Woodberry's New England heritage no doubt helped shape his subsequent literary views. The son of Henry Elliott and Sarah Dane Tuck Woodberry, he was born on 12 May 1855 in Beverly, Massachusetts, in the family's seaside home. Many of his ancestors were sea captains, sailors, or deacons of churches. His forebears' propensities toward individuality, adventure, and seriousness, as well as their awareness of spiritual and moral values, would eventually manifest themselves in Woodberry's personal and professional life. As a young man Woodberry attended Phillips Exeter Academy in New Hampshire, and he made various contributions to a weekly Exeter newspaper, the *Voice*. During adolescence, then, Woodberry committed himself to the literary life. After leaving Exeter, he entered Harvard with the class of 1876 but because of poverty and illness did not graduate until 1877. Two of his professors, Henry Adams and Charles Eliot Norton, influenced him strongly; Adams appealed to Woodberry's intellectual side by teaching him to develop an individual attitude toward history, while Norton's sense of aesthetics helped arouse Woodberry's lifelong devotion to Mediterranean culture. Woodberry edited the *Harvard Advocate*, publishing poetry, reviews, and editorials. President Charles W. Eliot of Harvard applauded Woodberry's moral character but expressed reservations concerning the aggressive manner in which Woodberry voiced his opinions. Upon graduating, he taught at the University of Nebraska, traveled in southern Europe, and contributed various pieces to such journals as the *Atlantic Monthly* and the *Nation*.

In 1885 Woodberry published his first substantial scholarly work, the biography of Poe. The book presents a distinctly two-sided view of its subject. Woodberry disapproved of Poe's personal life. Echoing Rufus W. Griswold (on whose writings Woodberry based his account), he depicts Poe as a habitual drunkard, an opium eater, and a friendless man incapable of noble affection or generous sacrifice. Regarding Poe the man of letters, however, he could bring himself to admire the author of "The Fall of the House of Usher." He praised Poe's artistic power and his ability to create "startling imaginative effects and to select the right means to bring them about directly, forcibly. . . ." Poe's theory of effect helped make his best tales immortal. In addition, Poe's aesthetic creed resembled the ideas which Woodberry himself would later espouse in his own criticism. Poe believed that beauty elevates the soul by appealing to man's sense of harmony; it belongs to the immortal part of man and makes him aware of eternity. This concept proved attractive to Woodberry. Yet this genteel New Englander remained haunted by the specter of Poe the man, and he continued to ponder how such a solitary, proud, and selfish human being as Poe could instill his works with a vital interest in humanity. Granted, Poe possessed talent, but his life and genius ran remote from mankind. The Poe myth perpetuated by Griswold remained firmly embedded in Woodberry's mind.

His condemnation of Poe's private life and his guarded praise for Poe's literary efforts make Woodberry's biography a curiously balanced portrait. Despite his reservations Woodberry tried to remain fair and did manage to assemble a great deal of material for the study of Poe. Still valuable scholarship, Woodberry's treatment of Poe served as a noteworthy literary debut.

In 1888 Woodberry became literary editor of the *Boston Post*. Two years later he completed his first important critical work, *Studies in Letters and Life*, which was reissued in 1900 as *Makers of Literature*. This book, a collection of essays originally appearing in the *Atlantic Monthly* and the *Nation* between 1878 and 1890, established his reputation as a critic.

Although an essay on the classically oriented poet Walter Savage Landor clearly demonstrates Woodberry's admiration for the ancient virtues of the Greeks and Romans—love of freedom, aspiration for wisdom, reverence for heroism, and delight in beauty for its own sake—the most important piece in the book remains "Illustrations of Idealism." In this selection Woodberry sets forth the doctrine he would preach most of his literary career: idealism generates an immortal spark in art whereas realism destroys. Woodberry begins by comparing the heroic, idyllic sculptures of Athens with the more fierce and ugly statuary of Pergamon. Having provided a historical framework for his argument, he then focuses on contemporary intellectual life. Woodberry detests realism because it fails to concentrate on the beautiful in life. It portrays sordidness and stresses the shocking aspects of existence. The resulting sense of uncertainty ruins man's faith in the ideal by stifling his spiritual insight. He holds that the history of art reveals that periods of idealism are eras of power, while those of realism are eras of decline. He goes on to state that "idealism, when it is living, cannot be otherwise than essentially religious." A knowledge of

Woodberry at about the time he became professor of literature at Columbia University

the past, as well as the moral principles derived from a representation of the ideal, will benefit the artist concerned with elevating man spiritually. Woodberry would do his best to remain true to this creed throughout his life.

On the recommendation of Lowell, Columbia University appointed Woodberry professor of English literature in 1891. Later his title became professor of comparative literature. Woodberry served as a brilliant and successful teacher. His devotion to young people helped him attract both future scholars and less committed pupils, and his unique influence inspired many a student, including Spingarn and John Erskine. In 1911, seven years after his departure from Columbia, his grateful former students established the Woodberry So-

ciety to foster his ideals in American life. His wide knowledge, passionate pursuit of truth, and genial, warmhearted sympathy with youth made lasting impressions on his students.

During the 1890s Woodberry continued to write articles and reviews. One of his most important collections, *Heart of Man,* was published in 1899. The book discusses those imaginative elements common to poetry, religion, and politics which stem from the same basic source, namely the universal leaning of mankind toward wisdom and virtue. Woodberry feels that human beings yearn for knowledge, and to help satisfy this need each age has its spokesman, a great writer who expresses not only the ideals of his own race but those of the entire human race as well.

In the initial essay, "Taormina," Woodberry presents his view that the artistic treasures of the past should serve as motivation for modern thinkers. The book's pivotal chapter, "A New Defense of Poetry," then presents an idealistic doctrine to which Woodberry would continue to adhere and later attempt to adapt to changing currents in American thought. He opens the essay by offering to renew the recurrent discussion of the nature of idealism. Throughout history men have questioned the validity of the ideal. In opposition Woodberry confidently states that those ideas which convinced the master minds of antiquity remain convincing. The sensible man must recognize "the eternal ground of reason on which idealism rests." Any individual concerned with spirituality allows idealism to play a prominent role in his life and consequently becomes immersed in universal, not merely individual, affairs.

Imaginative literature relies on an inward, spiritual order. Human life is best represented in literature through the use of ideal character types and ideal actions. For Woodberry the physical types imply spiritual qualities. Transcendental thought remains a potent influence during this stage of Woodberry's career. Literature's goal is for man to know himself so well that he can look into the hearts of others.

As "A New Defense of Poetry" continues, Woodberry once again chains realism to the whipping post. Realists want men to see things without really thinking about them. Overly concerned with minute fidelity to external detail, realism concentrates solely on men in specific temporal settings and fails in the larger vision. This "tendency to detail, which is the hallmark of realism," Woodberry remarks, "constitutes decline." Although often arising in periods of expanding knowledge, it caters to the lower and baser forms of life and reveals little more than savagery. Idealism maintains superiority over its rival by possessing universal appeal; it pursues wisdom and beauty, the ultimate goals of any nation. In addition, idealism emphasizes "race-ideas," those thoughts present in all human societies which focus on the valued life, moral choices, and aspirations and hopes. Six years after *Heart of Man* Woodberry would elaborate his position on race in *The Torch*.

Woodberry's stand on realism seems marred by a slight inconsistency. He states that realism fosters decay and decline but later goes on to admit that it often flourishes in periods of widening knowledge. Perhaps this apparent contradiction sows the seeds for the increased toleration of realism evidenced in his later work. In *Heart of Man*, however, he views the realist as a figure who deals with unassimilated raw material; the idealist alone produces a finely finished result.

Heart of Man concludes with an impassioned plea to youth. Always fond of his young students, the admired professor begs them to resist the demon of realism and act as their ideals command. Courage and perseverance must remain the watchwords. The reward will be a glimpse of a more perfect world.

Considered his finest biography, Woodberry's *Nathaniel Hawthorne* appeared in 1902. His sympathetic treatment of Hawthorne results in part from the heritage common to both men. Growing up in Beverly, Woodberry was familiar with the neighboring town of Salem. He also sprang from the same Puritan tradition and viewed Hawthorne as a kindred spirit.

Placing Hawthorne's works in an environmental and Calvinist context, Woodberry views the romancer's tales as idealized but true transcripts of a mode of life that had since succumbed to modernity. History stimulates Hawthorne's imagination by furnishing a certain authentic distinctness which helps to actuate the author's moral thought. Though Hawthorne relies on a strong sense of place, he escapes provinciality through his faithful response to the spiritual "race element" (a spiritual quality intrinsic in the group mind) which makes the works universal. *The Scarlet Letter* (1850), for example, attains the level of great romance because of its charm as a work of art as well as its moral universality. Yet certain aspects of the novel troubled Woodberry. For the most part the tale remains harsh and rigid and lacks a sense of true love. Woodberry suggests that at times Hawthorne seems unsympathetic toward his characters and steeps his work in overpowering gloom. In general, though, Woodberry praises such devices as Hawthorne's use of concrete symbols and various pictorial techniques and sees him as one of America's finest authors.

The following year Woodberry published *America in Literature*, which exhibits a somewhat detached insight and reflects its author's inability to sympathize with the bulk of his country's literary endeavors. His comments on American literature illustrate Woodberry's limitations as a critic. Clinging to the remnants of the Genteel Tradition, he fails to offer any real suggestions for transforming the United States into a realm of ideality. Always concentrating on the past, Woodberry neglects the American present.

Beginning with the Puritans, *America in Literature* emphasizes the idea that spiritual matters constituted the ultimate reality for early thinkers, so that these men did not attempt to create a unique form of literary expression. As time passed the colonists became increasingly interested in secular goals. Commenting as much on his own time as he is on the shifting emphasis in colonial America, Woodberry states that true literature seldom flourishes in a materialistically oriented society. After the Revolutionary War, however, the growing popularity of newspapers, periodicals, and public libraries attests to the development of a literary consciousness. Washington Irving and James Fenimore Cooper mark the true beginnings of American literature by helping to create a native folklore, while William Cullen Bryant voices the nation's fundamental religious feelings. These writers, unfortunately, serve as the exceptions, not the rules. For the most part American literature lacks thought, reflection, and meditation; it fails to brood significantly over life and experience.

This situation changes with the emergence of the great New England writers. Perhaps Woodberry's sense of local pride influences the opinions voiced in this chapter. Ralph Waldo Emerson emerges as the perfect example of radical spirituality, a writer whose works burst with a sense of man's inward life. A true intellectual, Henry Wadsworth Longfellow put America in touch with the literary past of northern and southern Europe, while Hawthorne, taking an original view of his world, allowed his imagination to ponder the realities of the young nation. Woodberry laments that writers have drifted away from the conditions that produced these great littérateurs.

With the exception of Poe, who went north to present his works to a more receptive audience, Woodberry has little use for Southern literature. He believes that this region prohibits the individual from expressing any opinion differing from that of the community. Consequently the South lacks true ideas or standards of taste and art. Regarding the West, Woodberry points to the absence of any truly imaginative spirit capable of remaking the world. He does acknowledge the importance of humor to the Western writers but fails to demonstrate a thorough familiarity with these figures. With the exception of Bret Harte, who is described as portraying the courage and

love present in man, few of these writers are discussed in detail. He glosses over Mark Twain (as elsewhere he does Henry David Thoreau, Herman Melville, and Walt Whitman), whom he views essentially as a mere clown.

Woodberry concludes that due to America's lust for material comfort, its first century of literary expression lags far behind Europe. The United States is void of true culture and its literature "lacks inspiration, passion, that deep stirring of the spirit of man. . . ." Most American writers appear too "sectional." The country needs a literary genius who will rely on universal human values and the academic tradition which fosters true knowledge of the past. *America in Literature* leaves the reader sensing that Woodberry sees little hope for future American letters; America has become barbarous and unable to pursue any idealistic dreams.

Despite Woodberry's reputation as a splendid professor and active scholar, his tenure at Columbia was about to end. For reasons still obscure, he resigned his chair in 1904. After leaving Columbia he spent part of his life as an itinerant teacher, lecturing at Amherst, Cornell, Wisconsin, and California and retreating on occasion to the Mediterranean countries. He believed that Columbia had wronged him, and his thoughts grew increasingly pessimistic. Yet he devoted a great deal of time to authorship and continued to hope that his idealism might revive the flagging American spirit.

In 1905 Woodberry published his fullest expression of his literary creed, *The Torch: Eight Lectures on Race Power in Literature.* The book conveys a deep sense of race and tradition, fundamental concepts in his philosophy. He believed one generation must "pass the torch" of ideas to future generations, for the entire race benefits from such transmission. Woodberry viewed "race" not as an ethnic entity but a spiritual quality of mind composed of imaginative memories and experience residual in the mind of man. (In this sense Woodberry's "race mind" is analogous to Carl Jung's racial subconscious.) Literature belongs to the entire world, and he looks forward to a future in which literary works will be not regional or national but an amalgamation of the imaginative energies of all lands and men.

Woodberry opens by reflecting on how great cultures die to enrich the souls of new nations. This sacrifice helps to preserve civilization's highest ideals. Although countries may disappear, the "race mind" continues to grow. Litera-

*Photograph of Woodberry used as the frontispiece for his
selected letters*

ture strives to free the individual soul and unify
mankind. We better appreciate this progress
when we employ history to evoke the great
power of authority and tradition. History becomes a process in which man progressively comprehends the universe, evaluates his humanity,
and passes on to future generations the fruits of
human achievement. History proves mortal and
dies, but literature imaginatively spiritualizes it.
Mythology, chivalry, and scripture, "the tongues
of imagination," preserve things of lasting significance. Literature, however, does not attempt to
build the ideal life wholly on the past; it rests
upon the future as well. As Woodberry remarks,
"so arises in race-life the creed of what man
wishes to believe and the dream of the life he desires to live." Reemphasizing the importance of history, he comments that great poets must be
scholars in order to appreciate fully the gifts of
preceding cultures.

In 1907, a productive year for Woodberry,
he published three books: a biography of
Emerson, *The Appreciation of Literature*, and *Great
Writers: Cervantes, Scott, Milton, Virgil, Montaigne,
Shakspere*. These works indicate that although
Woodberry was no longer an active academic he
continued to fan the critical spark within him.

Originally published in 1907 and reissued
in 1926 as a volume in the English Men of Letters series, *Ralph Waldo Emerson* explains to Englishmen the ways in which Emerson exemplifies
the American spirit. Woodberry admits to having
loved Emerson's works since childhood, but he
avoids treating his subject with too partisan a
spirit. The biography represents a fresh inquiry
into Emerson's transcendentalist ideas and gives
a balanced view of a man concerned with the primacy of the soul.

In the work Emerson emerges as a self-
reliant man concerned with the moral order.
This extreme individualist, however, failed to acknowledge the importance of history in the development of new ideas; he only saw the present
and overlooked how his thoughts and ideas were
fragments of concepts long present in the world.
In Woodberry's eyes Emerson elaborated a religious doctrine linked to Platonism. Unfortunately, Emerson seemed blind "to the life of
humanity in the race." Expressing the notion of individuality so zealously, he denied the importance of institutional life and rejected the
evolutionary spiritual conception of mankind.
"He isolated the soul and deprived it of all ancestral benefit," states Woodberry, who felt the life
of the race must take precedence over individual
life. Emerson's strengths lie in his assertion that
mystical moments visit the soul and divinely
guide it, and in the vigor with which he stood for
individual expression. Not genuinely intellectual,
Emerson's genius radiates an immense moral
strength.

Near the conclusion Woodberry utters a curious remark regarding Emerson's status. He
writes, "it is plain that no modern mind can
abide in his ideas." In addition, Emerson's total rejection of the past troubles Woodberry. Perhaps
Woodberry's idealism, tempered somewhat by the
realities of American life and culture, is gradually succumbing to the gloom that will darken his
later years.

Woodberry's attitude toward realism softens
slightly in *The Appreciation of Literature*. Realistic fiction, influenced by the extension of democracy,
presents a fuller portrait of life and allows all
members of society to exercise their intellects.
Yet Woodberry, not completely comfortable with
an art concerned with minute fidelity to detail, insists on the superiority of idealism.

To Woodberry, literature, which like all art
has pleasure as its direct aim, is not really known
but lived. In order to value literature a reader

must possess a curiosity and interest in life. An author demonstrates his originality by improving on his predecessors and incorporating ideal characters, actions, and plots into his literary efforts. Character, which contains the effect of the past and the promise of future acts, must occupy a higher position than action. Woodberry recognizes three types of experience which produce literature: personal, national, and universal. All three contribute to a work of art, but the last remains most important. He also lists three modes of criticism. Psychological theories focus on a writer's temperament and personality; the historical view studies environment, race, country, and epoch; aesthetic critics use formal standards to study a work. All three help a reader grasp a great work's meaning, but Woodberry cautions that too much biography and social detail become fatal diversions: "the prime consideration in the whole field of literary appreciation is to avoid making literary study a study of something else." Living in the mind and not in the senses, a reader must respond in a way that expands his consciousness of life and stimulates his soul. Principles, not mere facts, help man create an ideal reality.

Great Writers, Woodberry's third book of 1907, discusses Virgil, Cervantes, Scott, Milton, Montaigne, and Shakespeare. Each essay gives a condensed study of the life and work of its subject. In essence Woodberry felt that all six writers were knowledgeable scholars who emphasized ideal, universal values. Virgil, for example, relied on a broad base of scholarship and his uniquely Roman personality to idealize and enrich his nation's consciousness of the emotions possessed by all men. Cervantes, the author of *Don Quixote*, aware that reality often shatters such dreams, hoped to reform the world by stressing the value of high aims, heroism, and virtue. Imaginatively interpreting the human past, Scott created an impression of nobility within the reach of all mankind. Milton's *Paradise Lost*, a work of universal significance because it arises in the human soul, reflects the ideas of a poet who freely used the traditions of Athens, Rome, and Italy to look ahead to the future. Montaigne, a herald of the modern age, was a man of action not afraid to voice his convictions. Finally, Woodberry praises Shakespeare for advocating the active life, individuality, and the dominance of the personal will, energies which arise naturally in the souls of men and help them strive for achievement, enjoyment, and experience.

Woodberry would publish two additional important critical discussions. The first of these works, *The Inspiration of Poetry*, appeared in 1910. It attempts to reconcile traditional theories of the poetic impulse with the author's idealistic system. The divinely inspired poet must rely on emotion, which serves "as an evolutionary element in disengaging and establishing the intellectual powers of the race." Defining poetic energy as shared, social, controlled emotion, Woodberry states that rhythm provides the discipline through which the true poet transforms primitive passion into carefully regulated artistry. Although Woodberry's Platonism remains intact, he makes room for the nonrational in his philosophy by stating that the unconscious and passion help establish the eternal realm of the ideal. In the hands of true poets emotion can create new worlds of greater joy because it arises from the wellspring of the "race-soul."

Two Phases of Criticism: Historical and Aesthetic (1914) challenges the ideas of "New Critics" who want to free the critic from passing moral and intellectual judgment and discard the tenets of historical criticism, and who assert that the reviewer must re-create the work of art as it was in the mind of its original maker. Woodberry questions the efficacy of a purely aesthetic view of literary study. Criticism must be historical and judicial. Any attempt to echo the intention of an author must of necessity rely on history. Historical criticism remains essential for the critic hoping to become one with an author's soul. Since certain rules bind the artist a critic must evaluate the methods employed to convey a message and judge the wisdom of a writer's statements. Whereas aesthetic critics view the past as dead, the true scholar knows that "in realizing the dead selves of mankind, the soul accumulates power, breadth of outlook, tolerance and especially . . . faith and hope." As he concludes his study Woodberry regrets that Americans seem adverse to exploring the past for universal ideas. He implores young thinkers to search for the ideal world yet seems to believe America remains incapable of such a noble journey.

World War I shattered Woodberry's faith in man's ability to attain the Platonic ideal. As he states in a letter written in 1918, "I begin to realize now what a scene of blood and tragedy all human history is." Referring to himself as an intellectual wandering through a world of common laborers, he becomes a cultural exile. He continued to produce volumes such as *Literary Essays*

(1920) and *Studies of a Littérateur* (1921), but these were merely compilations of essays written earlier in life. His torch virtually extinguished, Woodberry retired to his ancestral home and sought refuge in his ancient love, Plato. Despite a few fairly recent reprints of his works, most of Woodberry's scholarship remains out of print. Unfortunately, few students today study this man who, insisting on the presence of independence, hope, and background knowledge in the critical process, contributed substantially to American literature. He died on 2 January 1930 in his home in Beverly.

Letters:

Selected Letters of George Edward Woodberry, edited, with an introduction, by Walter de la Mare (Boston & New York: Houghton Mifflin, 1933).

Bibliography:

R. R. Hawkins, "A List of Writings by and about George Edward Woodberry," *Bulletin of the New York Public Library*, 34 (May 1930): 279-296.

References:

John Erskine, "George Edward Woodberry," *Bulletin of the New York Public Library*, 34 (May 1930): 275-279;

Charles Glicksberg, "George Edward Woodberry," in his *American Literary Criticism: 1900-1950* (New York: Hendricks House, 1952), pp. 91-108;

R. B. Hovey, "George Edward Woodberry: Genteel Exile," *New England Quarterly*, 23 (December 1950): 504-526;

John Paul Pritchard, "George Edward Woodberry," in his *Criticism in America* (Norman: University of Oklahoma Press, 1956), pp. 156-162;

Pritchard, "George Edward Woodberry," in his *Return to the Fountains: Some Classical Sources of American Criticism* (Durham: Duke University Press, 1942), pp. 148-158;

Martha Hale Shackford, "George Edward Woodberry as Critic," *New England Quarterly*, 24 (December 1951): 510-527;

C. F. Thwing, "George Edward Woodberry," *Harvard Graduate Magazine*, 38 (June 1930): 433-443.

Papers:

The Butler Library of Columbia University contains the most extensive collection of Woodberry's correspondence and manuscripts. Harvard University's Houghton Library houses many letters written by and to Woodberry.

Checklist of Further Readings

Ahnebrink, Lars. *Beginnings of Naturalism in American Fiction*. Uppsala, Sweden: University of Uppsala, 1950; Cambridge, Mass.: Harvard University Press, 1950.

Aspiniog, Mark Louis. "Criticism in the Balance: The Literary Anthologist as Literary Critic and Promoter in Nineteenth-Century America," Ph.D. dissertation, Brown University, 1978.

Ballou, Ellen B. *The Building of the House: Houghton Mifflin's Formative Years*. Boston: Houghton Mifflin, 1970.

Becker, George. "Realism: An Essay in Definition," *Modern Language Quarterly*, 10 (June 1949): 184-197.

Bernard, Jessie. *Academic Women*. University Park: Pennsylvania State University Press, 1964.

Brawley, Agnes Bonner. "Attitudes Toward Realism and Science in the *Atlantic Monthly* from 1880 to 1900," Ph.D. dissertation, University of Wisconsin, 1956.

Brooks, Van Wyck. *New England: Indian Summer, 1865-1915*. New York: Dutton, 1940.

Brooks. *Sketches in Criticism*. New York: Dutton, 1932.

Brown, Clarence. *The Achievement of American Criticism*. New York: Norton, 1954.

Cady, Edwin H. *The Light of Common Day: Realism in American Fiction*. Bloomington: Indiana University Press, 1971.

Cady. *The Road to Realism*. Syracuse: Syracuse University Press, 1956.

Cady, and David L. Frazier, eds. *The War of the Critics Over William Dean Howells*. Evanston, Ill.: Row, Peterson, 1962.

Canby, Henry Siedel. *Alma Mater: The Gothic Age of the American College*. New York: Farrar & Rinehart, 1936.

Cargill, Oscar. *Intellectual America*. New York: Macmillan, 1941.

Carter, Everett. *Howells and the Age of Realism*. Philadelphia: Lippincott, 1954.

Cary, Richard. *The Genteel Circle: Bayard Taylor and His New York Friends*. Ithaca: Cornell University Press, 1952.

Chielens, Edward E. *American Literary Magazines: The Eighteenth and Nineteenth Centuries*. Westport, Conn.: Greenwood, 1986.

Clark, Harry Hayden. "The Influence of Science on American Literary Criticism, 1860-1910, Including the Vogue of Taine," *Transactions* (Wisconsin Academy of Sciences, Arts, and Letters), 44 (1955): 109-164.

Clark, ed. *Transitions in American Literary History*. Durham: Duke University Press, 1953.

Cowley, Malcolm. " 'Not Men:' A Natural History of Naturalism," *Kenyon Review*, 9 (Summer 1947): 414-435.

Cutting, Rose M. "America Discovers Its Literary Past: The Anthology as Literary History in the Nineteenth Century," Ph.D. dissertation, University of Minnesota, 1973.

DeMille, George E. *Literary Criticism in America*. New York: Russell & Russell, 1967.

Edwards, Herbert. "Zola and the American Critics," *American Literature*, 4 (March 1932): 114-129.

Falk, Robert. *The Victorian Mode in American Fiction 1865-1885*. East Lansing: Michigan State University Press, 1964.

Foerster, Norman. *American Criticism*. Boston & New York: Houghton Mifflin, 1928.

Frierson, W. G., and Edwards. "Impact of French Naturalism on American Critical Opinion, 1877-1892," *PMLA*, 63 (September 1948): 1007-1016.

Howe, Mark A. De Wolfe. *The Atlantic Monthly and Its Makers*. Boston: Atlantic Monthly Press, 1919.

Hubbell, Jay B. *The South in American Literature, 1607-1900*. Durham: Duke University Press, 1954.

Jones, Howard Mumford. *The Age of Energy, Varieties of American Experience 1865-1915*. New York: Viking, 1971.

Jones. *America and French Culture, 1750-1848*. Chapel Hill: University of North Carolina Press, 1927; London: Oxford University Press, 1927.

Jones. *The Theory of American Literature*. Ithaca: Cornell University Press, 1948.

Kindilien, Carlin T. *American Poetry in the Eighteen-Nineties*. Providence: Brown University Press, 1956.

Kolb, H. H., Jr. *The Illusion of Life: American Realism as a Literary Form*. Charlottesville: University Press of Virginia, 1969.

Kolb. "In Search of a Definition: American Literary Realism and the Cliches," *American Literary Realism*, 2 (Summer 1961): 165-173.

Lutwack, Leonard. "The Iron Madonna and American Criticism in the Genteel Era," *Modern Language Quarterly*, 15 (December 1954): 343-348.

Martin, Jay. *Harvests of Change: American Literature 1865-1914*. Englewood Cliffs, N.J.: Prentice-Hall, 1967.

Martin, Samuel. "*The Critic: A Critical Study*," Ph. D. dissertation, Columbia University, 1974

McMahon, Helen. *Criticism and Fiction: A Study of Trends in . . . The Atlantic Monthly 1857-1898*. New York: Bookman Associates, 1952.

Morgan, H. Wayne. *American Writers in Rebellion: From Mark Twain to Dreiser*. New York: Hill & Wang, 1965.

Morison, Samuel Eliot. *The Development of Harvard University since the Inauguration of President Eliot 1869-1929*. Cambridge, Mass.: Harvard University Press, 1930.

Mott, Frank Luther. *A History of American Magazines*, 5 volumes. Cambridge, Mass.: Harvard University Press, 1930-1968.

Parks, Edd Winfield. *Segments of Southern Thought*. Athens: University of Georgia Press, 1938.

Parrington, Vernon Louis. *The Beginnings of Critical Realism in America, 1860-1920*. New York: Harcourt, Brace, 1930.

Perosa, Sergio. *American Theories of the Novel 1793-1903*. New York: New York University Press, 1983.

Pierson, George Wilson. *Yale College: An Educational History 1871-1921*. New Haven: Yale University Press, 1952.

Pizer, Donald. *Realism and Naturalism in Nineteenth-Century American Literature*. Carbondale: Southern Illinois University Press, 1966.

Pochmann, Henry. *German Culture in America: Philosophical and Literary Influences, 1600-1900*. Madison: University of Wisconsin Press, 1957.

Pollak, Gustave. *Fifty Years of American Idealism: The New York Nation 1865-1915*. Boston: Houghton Mifflin, 1915.

Pritchard, John Paul. *Criticism in America*. Norman: University of Oklahoma Press, 1956.

Pritchard. *Return to the Fountains: Some Classical Sources of American Criticism*. Durham: Duke University Press, 1942.

Rathbun, John W., and Harry Hayden Clark. *American Literary Criticism 1860-1905*. Boston: G. K. Hall, 1979.

Rubin, Louis D., et. al., eds. *The History of Southern Literature*. Baton Rouge: Louisiana State University Press, 1985.

Salvan, Albert J. *Zola aux Etats-Unis*. Providence: Brown University Press, 1943.

Schug, Charles. *The Romantic Genesis of the Modern Novel*. Pittsburgh: University of Pittsburgh Press, 1979.

Spencer, Benjamin. *The Quest for Nationality: An American Literary Campaign*. Syracuse: Syracuse University Press, 1957.

Spiller, Robert, et. al., eds. *Literary History of the United States*, 3 volumes. New York: Macmillan, 1948.

Stovall, Floyd, ed. *The Development of American Literary Criticism*. Chapel Hill: University of North Carolina Press, 1955.

Tomsich, John. *A Genteel Endeavor: American Culture and Politics in the Gilded Age*. Palo Alto: Stanford University Press, 1971.

Vanderbilt, Kermit. *American Literature and the Academy: The Roots, Growth, and Maturity of a Profession*. Philadelphia: University of Pennsylvania Press, 1986.

Walcutt, Charles Child. *American Literary Naturalism, a Divided Stream*. Minneapolis: University of Minnesota Press, 1956.

Walker, Franklin. *San Francisco's Literary Frontier*. New York: Knopf, 1934.

Wellek, René. *A History of Modern Criticism 1750-1950*, 6 volumes. New Haven: Yale University Press, 1955-1986.

Contributors

Nancy Warner Barrineau ....*University of Georgia*

Peter A. Brier ....*California State University, Los Angeles*

Michael L. Burduck ....*Tennessee Technological University*

Robert E. Burkholder ....*Pennsylvania State University, University Park*

John S. Coolidge ....*University of California, Berkeley*

Sarah B. Daugherty ....*Wichita State University*

Janice L. Edens ....*Macon College*

Philip B. Eppard ....*State University of New York at Albany*

Fritz Fleischmann ....*Babson College*

M. E. Grenander ....*State University of New York at Albany*

Peter Groth ....*University of Hamburg, Germany*

Thomas Haeussler ....*University of California, Los Angeles*

Theodore R. Hovet ....*University of Northern Iowa*

Anne Bail Howard ....*University of Nevada at Reno*

Michael Kreyling ....*Vanderbilt University*

William Lomax ....*University of California, Los Angeles*

Ann Massa ....*University of Leeds*

Joseph R. McElrath, Jr. ....*Florida State University*

Thomas R. Nevin ....*John Carroll University*

John Pilkington, Jr. ....*University of Mississippi*

Kenneth M. Price ....*Texas A&M University*

Marc L. Ratner ....*California State University, Hayward*

David J. Rife...*Lycoming College*

Arnold T. Schwab ....*California State University, Long Beach*

Charles L. P. Silet ....*Iowa State University*

Myron Simon ....*University of California, Irvine*

Rhonda Skillern ....*University of Texas*

Jeffrey Steele ....*University of Wisconsin*

Paula M. Uruburu ....*Hofstra University*

Kermit Vanderbilt ....*San Diego State University*

Priscilla Wald ....*Columbia University*

Carey Wall ....*San Diego State University*

Paul C. Wermuth ....*Northeastern University*

Cumulative Index

Dictionary of Literary Biography, Volumes 1-71
Dictionary of Literary Biography Yearbook, 1980-1987
Dictionary of Literary Biography Documentary Series, Volumes 1-4

Cumulative Index

DLB before number: *Dictionary of Literary Biography*, Volumes 1-71
Y before number: *Dictionary of Literary Biography Yearbook*, 1980-1987
DS before number: *Dictionary of Literary Biography Documentary Series*, Volumes 1-4

A

B

Cumulative Index *(side tab)*

D

E

H

I

J

M

O

P

S

T

U

V

Y

Z